THE STATE OF NATIVE AMERICA

The State of Native America

Genocide, Colonization, and Resistance

edited by
M. Annette Jaimes

Race and Resistance Series

South End Press
Boston, Massachusetts

Design and typesetting by Sheila Walsh and the South End Press collective
Cover by Katherine Berney
Printed on acid-free paper
Manufactured in the United States

Library of Congress Cataloging-in-Publication Data
The State of Native America: genocide, colonization, and resistance/
edited by M. Annette Jaimes.
p.cm.
Includes bibliographical references and index.
ISBN 0-89608-425-6 (cloth): $40.00 — ISBN 0-89608-424-8 (pbk): $16.00
1. Indians of North America—Government relations—1934-
2. Indians of North America—Legal status, laws, etc. I. Jaimes, M. Annette
E93.S77 1992 Pʔr
323.1'197—dc20   91-37260
                            CIP

South End Press, 116 St. Botolph Street, Boston, MA 02115

For my parents,
Rudolph Jaimes
Maria Theresa Jaimes

Acknowledgments

A ny book of this sort requires the support, suggestions, and assistance of more people than can be named here. Each of them knows who she or he is, and to each of them, many thanks. Special notes of gratitude are of course due to each of the contributors, and to Cynthia Peters of the South End Press collective for her unstinting editorial guidance. Another goes to the Fourth World Center for Study of Indigenous Law and Politics at the University of Colorado at Denver for use of the title of its 1988 conference on native rights. Then there are the Institute for Natural Progress and Colorado AIM, members of which read and offered useful commentary on various of the essays included. Appreciation is also expressed to *Socialist Review, Journal of Ethnic Studies,* and *Insurgent Sociologist,* which published earlier versions of the essay on "Radioactive Colonization" by Ward Churchill and Winona LaDuke; to *Policy Perspectives,* which published an earlier draft of my own essay on identity; to *The Third Text,* which published the first version of Jimmie Durham's "Cowboys and—"; and to *Native Nations,* in which John Mohawk's epilogue initially appeared.

Contents

Wind River

The fact that we were
unconsciously part of a plan
to weaken and cross out the
Indianness in you
to pattern your land with our grain and beets
and corn and alfalfa
now clearly hits me.

It is like a blow to the gut
to learn that the years spent
on the reservation, the times
wading in the Wind River
were not the free years of childhood
but the manipulations of a power
hungry to exonerate itself, to
free itself, to purge the treaties
of any real meaning or responsibility.

They stole from me my innocence, leaving me
a co-conspirator, an enemy to the children
I grew with on the prairie, drove us apart
when we could have and should have
forged an alliance for our own survival.

The force of this unremitting design
has killed many of my friends and acquaintances
and left me forever with a feeling of unintentional
complicity and sadness.

There we were digging in the dirt
riding in the wind that blew away the
sound of the machinations; it was the
the blindness of the poor and
manipulated. Grandparents and parents
hungry, alone, driven by the Depression
and the desire to own "their own land"
so as not to be subject to the will of the other.
It was the desire
to free themselves from subordination.

To view this as accomplishment is now all mockery.
What was perceived as independence was nothing
but a molding into the design of the government
at the expense of you, the Indian, and of ourselves, the poor
white, destitute and
willing to participate in this unrevealed
plan.

No wonder the years of uneasiness have
resided within me; why would I feel
the beat of the drums and want to be
either more part of that life or
so far away as not to hear them anymore?
It was a subconscious realization of the true
depths of my "outsideness"
of my trespassing on territory that I
was not a part of.

> *DeLinda Wunder*
> an ally

Preface

The State of Native North America

Now, in 1992, the debate heats up regarding the significance of the Columbus voyages. In this country, powerful forces have been promoting the Quincentenary as the ideal occasion for a national and, indeed, international celebration of Western triumphalism in the "discovery and conquest" of the New World, which in turn has produced Western Civilization's highest expression of Freedom and Democracy. This official view of history would have prevailed were it not for a rising crescendo of voices—uninvited but insistent upon being heard—out of Native North America to challenge its authenticity. Recently, the conflict over Columbus has been joined with the debate on multiculturalism on U.S. campuses, which comes down to an ideological struggle, embodied primarily in the college curriculum, between a Eurocentric claim to universal truth and a more pluralistic view of the American experience. There will be no resolution unless, frankly, Eurocentric parochialism yields to the more inclusive pluralistic project.

As Director of the Center for Studies of Ethnicity and Race in America at the University of Colorado at Boulder, my responsibility is to develop credible academic programs in four Ethnic Studies fields: Afroamerican Studies, American Indian Studies, Asian American Studies and Chicano Studies. Afroamerican and Chicano Studies have twenty or more years of history behind them. During the past decade, Asian American Studies has received critical support from the demographically booming and economically significant Asian American communities on both coasts. American Indian Studies lingers far behind, with few established programs, hampered by an extreme shortage of Native American scholars able to find a place in academe. In short, the state of American Indian Studies reflects the state of Native North America, its poverty, marginalization, and continuously colonized condition.

For those of us in the academy and in the publishing world who subscribe to the multicultural project, our responsibility is to find ample space beyond tokenism for Native American scholarship and discourse. For both our program in American Indian Studies and South End Press, this book is a giant step in filling and, in turn, widening that space. Editor M. Annette Jaimes has gathered fifteen original essays focusing upon issues affecting Native North America today. These do not exhaust the long list of concerns held by Indian people, but they do address some key ones.

Many of the contributors to this volume are prominent American Indian scholars who have found their way into academic positions where they teach, write, and participate in campus discussions on a wide range of topics and influence curriculum in every way possible. I can personally attest to the charged atmosphere and frequent sparks generated by my colleagues in the American Indian Studies Program: M. Annette Jaimes, Ward Churchill, Vine Deloria, Jr., and Glenn T. Morris, the latter on our Denver campus. To my knowledge, most of the other contributors fulfill similar roles in the lives of their respective campuses. In addition, most of the contributors are activists, energetically seeking to realize their perspectives in "real world" contexts.

If one theme runs explicitly or implicitly through each of the contributions, it is that of indigenous demands for sovereignty, self-determination, and self-sufficiency. Non-Indian and even Indian readers not familiar with the state of Native North America may find some, if not most, of these essays morally disturbing and intellectually disruptive, as they are intended to be. They are designed to yank us out of our normal complacency so that we may begin to confront and question the all too many assumptions we have simply accepted about the original peoples of this continent. Whether we agree or disagree with, accept or reject, their premises and conclusions, we have nevertheless embarked on a long voyage to rethink old ideas about Native Americans and their contemporary and historical relationship with the dominant, Euroamerican society. Most of all, reading these essays will allow many of us to learn for the first time about the critical issues facing Native North America.

For those who wish to understand the anguish of native peoples as the country and the world prepare to celebrate the arrival of Columbus and the Europeans, and for those who wish to know the merits of expanding our basically Eurocentric curriculum to a more pluralistic, inclusive one, this book is a good place to start.

Evelyn Hu-DeHart
University of Colorado at Boulder, September 1991

Introduction

Sand Creek
The Morning After

M. Annette Jaimes

November 29, 1864: On that cold dawn, about 600 Southern Cheyenne and Arapaho People, two-thirds of them women and children, were camped on a bend of Sand Creek in southeastern Colorado. The People were at peace. This was expressed two months earlier by Black Kettle, one of the principal chiefs of the Cheyennes, in Denver to Governor John Evans and Colonel John M. Chivington, head of the Colorado Volunteers. "I want you to give all these chiefs of the soldiers here to understand that we are at peace, and that we have made peace, that we may not be mistaken for enemies." The Reverend Colonel Chivington and his Volunteers and Fort Lyons troops, numbering more than 700 heavily armed men, slaughtered 105 women and children and 28 men...A U.S. flag presented by President Lincoln in 1863 to Black Kettle in Washington, D.C. flew from a pole above the elder's lodge on that grey dawn. The People had been assured they would be protected by the flag. By mid-1865, the Cheyenne and Arapaho People had been driven out of Colorado.

Simon J. Ortiz
From Sand Creek

October 6, 1989: A dedication ceremony was held on the University of Colorado's Boulder campus. The American Indian community of the Boulder-Denver area, led by native students at the university, was celebrating the renaming of the former Nichols Hall. A delegation had been sent to the event by the Southern Utes who, along with their Ute Mountain cousins, are by now the only land-based Indians remaining in the state of Colorado. The Southern Cheyennes, direct descendants of the victims despite having been forced into Oklahoma, were represented by a female chief. Sage was burned and honoring songs sung for the women, children, and men who had been slaughtered at Sand Creek. A deep sigh as well as cheers escaped the crowd, numbering perhaps 400, when the plaque designating the building as "Cheyenne-Arapaho Hall" was finally unveiled. For at least that brief moment, the light of truth shone upon a fragment of the real history of the conquest of Native America.[1]

This dramatic event was the culmination of a twenty-year struggle to remove Nichols' name from a dormitory on the Boulder campus. Who was the individual constituting the locus of such conflict? David Nichols was by all accounts a successful businessman, proponent of statehood, and all-around pillar of the "original" Euroamerican community that settled what became a small city at the eastern base of the Rocky Mountains. Local legend has it that he was also something of a Paul Revere, making a grueling fifty-mile round-trip ride in 1873, racing on horseback from Boulder to Denver to secure the financial commitments necessary to keep the state's university from being built to the south, in Cañon City. Mission accomplished, he then mounted his trusty steed and galloped back to Boulder in time to ensure that the institution which was to power Boulder's growth would indeed be located there. Rather than garnering the "Harvard of the Rockies," Cañon City was left to become a backwater, the site of Colorado's first maximum-security prison. For his part, Nichols became the new university's first regent, a figure associated in his later years not only with wealth, but with the exercise of civic responsibility and cultural attainment.[2]

Yet there was always another aspect, much less remarked upon or analyzed, of the character of this superficially genteel figure. He was, to put the matter squarely, one of Chivington's right-hand men not only at Sand Creek itself, but throughout the 1864 Colorado Indian Campaign that led up to it. As Captain Nichols, commander of the Boulder Company (Company D) of the 3rd Colorado Volunteer Cavalry Regiment, Nichols had drawn first blood against the Cheyennes, butchering a small group under Big Bear at Buffalo Springs during October.[3] He then went on to Sand Creek, according to Western historian Patricia Nelson Limerick, who extensively researched his personal conduct at the request of the University's Board of Regents in 1987, where he "enthusiastically took part in a massacre in which Indians' brains were knocked out, children's ears were cut off, and men's and women's privates were cut out and used as tobacco pouches or saddle ornaments."[4] Nichols and his unit are singled out for praise in Chivington's after-action report as having been especially effective Indian-killers during the massacre.[5] Mustered out of service, the future regent participated fully in a systematic effort to falsify the circumstances that prevailed at Sand Creek: claiming huge numbers of warriors had been present when in fact there were almost none, denying that the victims were almost exclusively women, children, and old men (as the record so clearly demonstrated they were), insisting that wanton mutilation of the corpses had not occurred despite overwhelming evidence to the contrary. He sought thereby not only to justify his deeds, but to glorify them in the context of a "battle."[6] To the end, he remained unrepentant, subscribing even on his deathbed to Chivington's misbegotten sentiment: "I stand by Sand Creek."[7]

The Holocaust in North America

This America has been a burden of steel and mad death...

Simon J. Ortiz
From Sand Creek

Although contemporary history holds no shortage of genocidal examples to which the U.S. destruction of its indigenous population might be in some ways compared—Turkey's 1915 slaughter of over a million Armenians comes readily to mind, as does Paraguay's systematic murder of the Aché, Indonesia's butchery of at least a half-million East Timorese during the 1960s, the "auto-genocides" of as many as three million Bangladeshis and a million Khmers in Kampuchea (Cambodia) during the 1970s, and Brazil's ongoing eradication of the Amazon Basin peoples—the closest parallel is that of the campaigns of nazi Germany against the Slavic peoples to its east, and against the Jews and Gypsies, during the 1940s.[8] This is true for reasons of political philosophy and policy rather than some exceptionally lethal quality in either the nazi or Euroamerican performances. It is not just that they did what they did to targeted populations—the Turks, Paraguayans, Indonesians, Bangladeshis, Kampucheans, and Brazilians have done much the same—but that the Third Reich and the United States did what they did for virtually identical reasons. The others, with the possible exception of Brazil, deviate significantly in motivation, if not in method.

Both Chivington and Nichols embodied, as Creek/Cherokee Métis scholar Ward Churchill put it in a report prepared several years earlier than Limerick's,

> ...the behavior and the logic that have come to be associated with Hitler's SS. They defined their enemy in purely racial terms, they understood war only in terms of the sheer annihilation of the racial enemy, and they engaged in war because of a combination of abstract conceptions of "progress" on the one hand, and a related desire for pure material gain on the other. Both the SS and the Colorado Volunteers thought themselves to be superior beings and thus found themselves to be entitled to that which their racial enemies possessed. For the SS it was the myth of the superman and pursuit of *lebensraum* ("living room") in Poland and the Ukraine. For the Colorado Volunteers it was "manifest destiny" and Colorado statehood. In both examples, the policy pursued was extermination of the indigenous population and its replacement by the "racially superior stock" of the invaders. Sand Creek was, in a literal sense, the Cheyennes' Babi Yar. If the SS is to be comprehended as a criminal organization, formed solely for criminal purposes and composed of criminal individuals, so too must be our assessment of the 3rd Colorado Volunteers and its membership.[9]

In another passage, Churchill continued:

> It has been said that David Nichols in particular was, despite his active participation in the Buffalo Springs and Sand Creek atrocities, and his avid defense of these actions for the balance of his life, a "good man" who accomplished much of "socially redeeming value." The latter may be conceded without argument. He did. And he is hardly unique in this regard. Adolph

Hitler, after all, was instrumental in the creation of the *autobahn* and the Volkswagon, modern rocketry and the jet aircraft. He subsidized museums and the opera as no German leader before or since. Heinrich Himmler poured money into universities. Alfried Krupp was a virtually unrivaled industrialist in his day. Albert Speer was something of a genius as an architect. The list could certainly be continued at great length. Were the arguments now being mounted to "defend the honor" of David Nichols applied equally to Hitler, Himmler, Krupp and Speer, we could only conclude that they too are deserving of remembrance as good and worthy individuals, men whose crimes against humanity were mere "blemishes" on otherwise commendable records. Had Germany won the Second World War, they would surely be thus memorialized, the history of their conquest of the *Ostland* [land to the east] and the genocide which accompanied it constructed in such fashion as to emphasize their achievements while rationalizing or obscuring their "excesses." But Germany lost, the crimes of its leaders—both military and civilian—brought out for what they were. Their names are now all but universally reviled; no buildings named to commemorate their positive contributions to civilization stand on German campuses. The difference here is that, unlike Germany, the United States won its war of conquest and extermination. If you were ever inclined to wonder what it would be like to live in the Ukraine 50 or a hundred years after a nazi victory, all you need do is look around. You are living it right here, right now. That is why Nichols' name is affixed to a building at the University of Colorado, and the names of men like him are affixed to buildings, streets and parks in thousands of other places around this country today. [10]

What is so striking about cases like that of Nichols is precisely that the evil of which they stand accused is bound up, part and parcel, in the good which is attributed to them. The two aspects are quite inseparable, and this remains the case whether we refer specifically to Germany or the United States, or to some greater cultural totality binding the two together in terms of worldview. Neither the nazis nor the Euroamerican pioneers could accomplish what were being promulgated as positive achievements within their social orders other than by engaging first in the most horribly negative sorts of activity. To put it in more concrete terms, for the German settlement of the Ukraine to occur—establishing, from the nazi perspective, a culturally refined agrarian society—the indigenous Slavic population had first to be dramatically reduced in numbers (the Jews and Gypsies were exterminated for other reasons), and the survivors forcibly pushed from their homeland to some point beyond the new frontier of "Greater Germany." By the same token, creation of the State of Colorado, and the subsequent establishment of the University of Colorado, were utterly predicated upon the physical destruction of most Cheyennes and Arapahoes and the forced relocation of the remainder into Oklahoma. Hence, to condemn a Nichols for his responsibility at Sand Creek is simultaneously to condemn him for creating the very conditions necessary to render his other achievements; the two fit hand-in-glove; his good deeds would not have been possible without his evil actions. In this sense, he is fully emblematic of the society of which he was a part, the same society in which we now find ourselves. This is what, finally, must be understood and, once understood, acted upon.

There are those who say that Sand Creek was unfortunate, that it is to be regretted. I would argue that the only appropriate expression of regret in this regard is to do what is necessary to insure that it can never happen again. This means, more than anything, bringing about a fundamental alteration in the consciousness—a "denazification"—of this country. The people of the United States must finally stop denying Sand Creek its real significance. They must be educated to view the massacre, not as some isolated and tragic event, but as an apt symbol of the entire process by which this continent was "settled." They must be taught to look at individual perpetrators such as Nichols and see, not aberrations or monsters, but people who fit into their society rather well, typifying rather than deviating from the outlooks, attitudes and demands of their culture. Euroamerica as a whole must at last begin the painful process of true self-recognition, coming to grips with the realities rather than the myths of its heritage, staring these truths in the face and calling things by their right names for the first time. Ultimately, Sand Creek must be understood, not as an embarrassment which can be glossed over and avoided, but as the normative expression of what has come to be the dominant society in North America. Only through the engendering of such a perspective among the American "main-stream" can there be hope of a reforging of human relations which averts future Sand Creeks and indeed suspends continuation of the myriad Sand Creeks which swirl around us in this country each and every day. The removal of David Nichols' name from a building at the University of Colorado, and a renaming of that same building in honor of his victims at the institution he was so instrumental in founding, would be one small but mightily important step in the right direction. There must be many, many more such steps taken, here and everywhere.[11]

Of course, there were many who, even in the process of agreeing that the renaming was necessary, argued that such analyses "wont too far" or were "too extreme." Were they? Was what happened at Sand Creek somehow anomalous within the historical flow of the "Invasion of America"?[12] Comparable massacres of American Indians at the Washita River, Blue River, Sappa Creek, Bear River, and elsewhere in the Great Plains and Basin areas clearly suggest otherwise.[13] Similar examples might be readily drawn from each of the other geographic regions during the periods in which they were conquered.[14] And these were only the major slaughters. Murder on a lesser scale, such as that which occurred at Buffalo Springs, has usually gone unrecorded or at least unremarked in standard histories. If Sand Creek was an anomaly, then the "Settlement of the West" was composed of little other than anomalies, and so too the rest of the country. Wherein lies the norm required by historiography for proper understandings of the past? Perhaps in the "rhetoric of extermination" deployed during the mid-19th century by elected officials such as Colorado Governor John Evans, or military commanders like Chivington and General Philip Sheridan?[15] Or perhaps it rests in the enthusiastic endorsement of such rhetoric, and the policies and actions that accompanied them, by such reflectors of the popular sentiment as the *Rocky Mountain News*.[16] Wherever we turn, there is ample evidence to support the thesis that Sand Creek was indicative of the whole rather than a deviation from it.

Inevitably, such insights draw us toward the conclusion that there are distinct and pronounced commonalities between the attitudes and practices that obtained during the "Winning of the West" in the United States during the 19th century, and the nazi outlooks and policies evidenced within Germany's "War in the East" during the 20th century. The conventional response is that the comparison is strained or metaphorical at best, wildly inaccurate or deliberately deceptive at worst. But is it really? It is true that the nazis managed to kill truly vast numbers of people—perhaps 21 million in the USSR alone—in an incredibly short period of time.[17] There is no direct counterpart in terms of the sheer density of death in U.S. history; correspondingly, it is argued that the nazis were both quantitatively and qualitatively different from anything which emerged from Euroamerica. What goes unmentioned in such reasoning is that much, even most, of the imagined differentiation can be accounted for on the basis of the technological advances that had occurred between the period of the "Indian Wars" and World War II. The machinery of death available to the Chivingtons, Sheridans, and Custers on North America's Great Plains simply left them incapable of engaging in slaughter at the same pace as the nazis, no matter how hard they tried.

Still, there remains at issue the scale of human destruction involved. It may be, as Euroamerican apologists are prone to claim, that the nazis attained a higher body count during the early 1940s than did their Euroamerican cousins during the preceding four centuries. Yet the imagined distinction in this regard, if it exists at all, relates more to the fact that the nazis encountered more people available for the killing in eastern Europe than was the case in all of North America from 1500 to 1900. Should we compare the two processes from the perspective of relative rates of population attrition rather than by simply counting numbers of corpses, a far different picture emerges. It is generally agreed that the two identifiable ethnic populations most severely impacted—on a proportional basis—by nazi extermination campaigns were European Jews and Gypsies, liquidated at the rates of approximately 75 percent and 65 percent respectively.[18] Until very recently, it has been conventional anthropological wisdom in the United States that there were about one million indigenous people living north of the Río Grande in the year 1500. If this is juxtaposed to U.S. census data reporting in 1890 that fewer than 250,000 American Indians remained alive in that year, it is evident that the rate of annihilation of Indians was exactly equivalent to that suffered by the Jews.[19]

Even this fudges things to a considerable extent, however. As is well demonstrated by Lenore Stiffarm and Phil Lane in their contribution to this volume, estimates of precontact North American populations promoted by anthropologists such as Alfred Kroeber were deliberately fabricated—primarily for ideological reasons—to show a radically lesser number than were actually present. Instead of one million native people living north of the Río Grande at the point of first contact, more recent and honest studies have established that there were somewhere between nine and eighteen million.[20] These data reveal the actual rate of extermination pertaining to Native North America during the period of conquest as having been 98 to 99 percent overall. It is plain that the killing stopped only when there was quite literally no one in the target population left to kill, and that the killing process leading to this result was sustained without interruption, generation after generation, with a stamina even the nazis cannot be said to have mustered. Not only does the rate of extermination suffered by the indigenous people of North America vastly exceed that experienced by the Jews of Europe under the nazis, it represents a scale and scope of genocide without parallel in recorded human history.

Of course, as the scoffers point out, regardless of the true number of indigenous inhabitants in North America at the point of contact with Europeans, the great bulk of them died, not as the result of direct military action, or at the hands of some Euroamerican equivalent of the nazis' *einsatzgruppen* (killing squads), but as the result of famine and disease. This is said as if such a type of death were a purely natural phenomenon, a matter absolving the invader of responsibility for such an outcome. Far from naturally, however, the mass starvation at issue was largely induced through the deliberate dislocation of indigenous nations from their traditional homelands, the impounding of their resources, and destruction of their economies through military or paramilitary action. The situation is compounded by such apparently willful early experiments in biological warfare as Lord Jeffrey Amherst's inculcation of smallpox among the Ottawas in present-day Pennsylvania during the late 18th century and the U.S. Army's introduction of blankets laden with the same disease among the Missouri River Mandans during the 1830s. [21]

The meaning of such information may be apprehended only in the context of certain questions. For instance, how many of the millions of World War II Soviet dead resulted, not from guns and bombs, but from the hunger and disease attending Germany's overrunning of vast portions of the western USSR? For that matter, what proportion of those who died in the nazi camps expired as the result of starvation or typhus rather than shootings, hangings, and gassings? The percentages in each case are quite high, certainly well over half. If the nazis can be held accountable for such deaths, why not those in the Western hemisphere who earlier obtained, proportionately, even greater results through utilization of comparable methods? In each case, the human costs (to the invaded) associated with the pursuit of certain goals and policies was known—at least roughly—and were accepted (by the invaders) as being necessary and acceptable, even desirable.[22]

A Key to Liberation

I have always loved America; it is something precious in the memory in blood and cells which insists on story, poetry, song, life, life.

Simon J. Ortiz
From Sand Creek

George Santayana's dictum that those who do not learn from history will be fated to repeat it has never seemed more apt than in connection with U.S.-Indian relations. This is all the more true insofar as the real history of these relations is presently all but obscured by the distortions and self-serving apologetics of the conquerors' descendants. The matter is of vital importance, not merely as some abstract exercise in the seeking of "Truth," but because the nature of the past interactions between Euroamericans and American Indians within what is now the United States serves to define the facts of their present relationship. This direct extension of the conquest is, as even the federal government has officially acknowledged, a relationship between a colonizer and the colonized.[23] For those in governmental and corporate power in the U.S., this is a very convenient and profitable situation; to paraphrase Eduardo Galeano's description of a somewhat different setting, "Their wealth is our poverty."[24] This is, for what should be obvious reasons, a circumstance the U.S. elite very much wishes to continue.

For American Indians, any such continuation of business as usual represents nothing so much as the prolonging of mortal agony. Already the process in question has resulted—as Ward Churchill, Winona LaDuke, and the Institute for Natural Progress demonstrate in their essays herein—not only in expropriation of more than 95 percent of our original land base, but a complete loss of control over the resources within and upon our residual territory. Consequently, Native Americans as a group experience the most extreme poverty of any sector in the present North American population. Correlated to this impoverishment are other facts: Contemporary Indians experience, among many other blights, far and away the greatest rates of malnutrition, plague disease, death by exposure, infant mortality, and teen suicide of any group on the continent. Our average life span is now approximately thirty years less than that of a Euroamerican of either gender.[25] And our ability to favorably alter these conditions is drastically curtailed by the imposition of a federal order—described by Glenn T. Morris, Rebecca L. Robbins, Vine Deloria, Jr., Jorge Noriega, Tom Holm, Jim Vander Wall, Wendy Rose, Jimmie Durham, Theresa Halsey, and me in the material that follows—that has "legally" supplanted our traditional forms of governance, outlawed our languages and spirituality, manipulated our numbers and identity, usurped our cultural integrity, viciously repressed the leaders of our efforts to regain self-determination, and systematically miseducated the bulk of our youth to believe that all this is, if not just, at least inevitable.

For the great mass of non-Indian Americans, those who wish not to be nazis or the heirs to nazism, and whose collective conscience might bestir itself to compel some positive alteration in the colonial relationship were the facts known to them, our present realities largely remain as far from sight and mind as the history upon which they are predicated. Only in bringing about a fundamental change in their (lack of) consciousness concerning the American Indian experience can we hope to gain the allies necessary to effect the genuine decolonization of Native North America. Only in attaining such understanding can they, in turn, be afforded the ability and opportunity to take the positions and undertake the activities of allies, distanced through their thinking and their deeds from the status quo. Alternatively, we are mutually confronted with the specter not of simply a present determined by the unrelenting horror of America's past, but a future dictated by the never-quite-acknowledged ugliness of America's present. In a word, we face the consummation of American nazism, with all that implies in terms of racism, sexism, militarism, environmental devastation through rampant industrialism, and the final consolidation of the U.S. police state. To a very real extent, the key to reversing this process may be found in achieving the liberation of Native North America, the empire's first victim and in whose ongoing victimization the empire finds the cornerstone upon which the whole of its continued existence ultimately rests.

The State of Native North America

That dream
shall have a name
after all,
and it will not be vengeful
but wealthy with love
and compassion
and knowledge.
And it will rise
in this heart
which is our America.

Simon J. Ortiz
From Sand Creek

The purpose of this book is to make a contribution to the emergence of the consciousness necessary to realize the liberation of North America from the grip of its nazi heritage. It has been written primarily for consumption by a non-Indian readership. Secondarily, it is extended to those American Indians who have, because of the long-term colonization of their own nations and the systematic indoctrination by their conquerors that accompanies such phenomena, lost all sense of themselves, the nature of their oppressor, and the source of the problems afflicting their people. The logic guiding the collection assembled herein is that in knowledge there is power, and only through power can there be social transformation.

It seems a truism that no single volume can accomplish what is needed. Neither the editor nor the contributors pretend otherwise. The scope of what has happened to so many peoples, across such vast space and through five centuries, cannot possibly be encompassed between a set of book covers, perhaps not within any number of sets of book covers. Similarly, the breadth of what is now occurring within the complexity that is Native North America cannot be accommodated herein. Hence, it may be expected that much detail in each area of consideration will be absent, both topically and historically. Whole areas of concern will be omitted. The intended function of *The State of Native America* is not so much to attempt an exhaustive rendering of the available data as to create a valid framework for understanding the meaning of related information as it is encountered. It is urged, even expected, that readers will go on to absorb selections from among the materials cited by the various contributors, thereby expanding upon the inherently limited exposition we are able to provide in this volume.

The method used in putting the book together has been straightforward. A range of the major issues marking the contemporary colonization of Native North America was selected. These were matched with authors who had already exhibited expertise in the particular subject matter. Each author was then solicited to prepare an essay on his/her topic, anchoring it in its historical context while exploring its impact on present-day American Indians (and, as appropriate, non-Indians as well). The instructions on style were quite simple: stay within a reasonable page length, say what's really on your mind, and don't bother being polite. This last injunction was designed to encourage things being called by their right names rather than becoming bogged down in the euphemistic academic sterility that has plagued so much literature about the native people of this hemisphere. What was sought was a book that speaks clearly and directly to the points raised, and that is thus of actual utility in changing popular consciousness. We believe we have accomplished this result.

As with any volume including material garnered from the work of multiple authors, there are marked contrasts in the approaches taken to exposition. This is as it should be, because only in the harnessing of a great many voices and nuances in perspective to a common goal may we find the unity that will ultimately be our power. A preview of this may be discerned in the fact that, while most of the contributors to this book are themselves Native American—and thus can be said to speak with an "Indian voice"—others are not. The latter number among those who have already opened their eyes to the lessons of their history, do not wish to see it continue to be repeated and have therefore joined hands with their indigenous relatives. They have realized that the potential for their own liberation—and that of their children and their children's children—is inextricably joined to ours. Despite the fact of our coming from different traditions, we are now singing to the same drum, locked together in our common humanity and our common destiny.

In the end, this is the hope underlying *The State of Native America:* to play some part in the forging of such linkages between many, many more people. Ultimately, we must all go forward together or we are lost to the evil which has engulfed the land we mutually inhabit. There is no one else to save us. We must do it ourselves. It is our responsibility, collectively, to move beyond that which is, and that which has been, to achieve that which America can be. At that point, on the morning after, we can at last join with Simon Ortiz when he calls upon us to "look now, there are flowers and new grass and a spring wind rising from Sand Creek."[26]

M. Annette Jaimes
Boulder, Colorado
January 1992

Notes

1. See Maas, Carolyn, "Native American history celebrated: Blessing marks end of an era," *Campus Press*, University of Colorado at Boulder, October 9, 1989.

2. See Anonymous, *History of Clear Creek and Boulder Valleys*, Colorado, Baskin and Co., Chicago, 1880, pp. 668-9. Also see Anonymous, *Portrait and Biographical Record of Denver and Vicinity*, Chapman Publishing Co., Chicago, 1889, pp. 785-6. About Nichols' alleged ride, see Davis, William E., *Glory Colorado! A History of the University of Colorado, 1858-1963*, Pruett Press, Boulder, CO, 1965.

3. Nichols drew the first serious blood in behalf of the 3rd Colorado Volunteers on October 11, 1864, when he led a detachment of forty troops that surrounded a small encampment of Cheyennes at Buffalo Springs, near Valley Station in the northeastern part of the territory. By his own account, provided to Colonel Chivington in an after-action report on the same date, Nichols claimed to have slaughtered every Indian present: Big Wolf (a Cheyenne leader), five other men of fighting age, a fifteen-year-old boy, three women, and two infants. The good captain notes the killing was done despite the Indians having raised a white flag of truce. The report is reproduced *in toto* in United States War Department, *The War of Rebellion: A Compilation of the Official Records of the Union and Confederate Armies* (4 Series, 128 Volumes, U.S. Government Printing Office, Washington, D.C., 1880-1901), Series I, Vol. XLI, Part III, pp. 798-9.

4. Limerick, Patricia Nelson, "What's in a Name? Nichols Hall: A Report," unpublished study commissioned by the University of Colorado, 1987.

5. Nichols' Company D is the only unit specifically brought out by Chivington for special mention as having provided an extraordinary performance during the massacre. This occurs in the colonel's after-action report to his own commander, General S.R. Curtis, on November 29, 1864. See *The War of Rebellion*, Series I, Vol. XLI, Part I, p. 949.

6. On this subject, see the series of interviews with Nichols commissioned by the historian Hubert Howe Bancroft. Complete transcripts are housed in the Western History Collection, Norlin Library, University of Colorado at Boulder.

7. Chivington is quoted to this effect in numerous places, notably in Reginald S. Craig's apologetic biography, *The Fighting Parson: The Biography of Colonel John M. Chivington*, Westernlore Press, Los Angeles, 1959. The statement has come to be a virtual slogan for those who seek to advance rationalizations for the conduct of the 3rd Colorado and its commander. See Dunn, Lt. Col. William R., *"I Stand By Sand Creek:" A Defense of Colonel John M. Chivington and the Third Colorado Cavalry*, The Old Army Press, Fort Collins, CO, 1985.

8. On Turkey and Bangladesh, see Kuper, Leo, *Genocide: Its Political Use in the Twentieth Century*, Yale University Press, New Haven, 1981. On the Aché, see Arens, Richard, ed., *Genocide in Paraguay*, Temple University Press, Philadelphia, 1976. On East Timor and Kampuchea, see Chomsky, Noam, and Edward S. Herman, *The Political Economy of Human Rights*, Vol. 1: *The Washington Connection and Third World Fascism*, South End Press, Boston, 1979. On the Amazon Basin, see John Hemming, *Red Gold: The Conquest of the Brazilian Indians*, Macmillan, New York, 1978.

9. Churchill's study was prepared at a time when the university's housing office was recommending that a second dormitory on the Boulder campus be named in honor of a Sand Creek commander *cum* early regent. See Churchill, Ward, "A Summary of Arguments Against the Naming of a University Residence Hall After Clinton M. Tyler," unpublished report prepared at the request of the assistant vice chancellor for academic services, University of Colorado at Boulder, July 1981, p. 7. During the summer and fall of 1864, Captain Tyler formed and led an "independent company"—dubbed "Tyler's Rangers," operating separately from the 3rd Colorado—composed primarily of miners from Blackhawk, Colorado.

10. Ibid., pp. 7-8.

11. Ibid., p. 15.

12. The term is drawn from Francis Jennings in his *The Invasion of America: Indians, Colonialism, and the Cant of Conquest*, W.W. Norton and Co., New York, 1976.

13. The best overall treatment of Sand Creek, making the details accessible for ready comparison with other atrocities during the period, is Hoig, Stan, *The Sand Creek Massacre*, University of Oklahoma Press, Norman, 1961. On the massacre that occurred along the Washita River in western Oklahoma on November 28, 1868, see Hoig, Stan, *The Battle of the Washita: The Sheridan-Custer Indian Campaign of 1867-69*, University of Nebraska Press, Lincoln, 1976.

The massacre along the Blue River in western Nebraska that occurred on September 3, 1855 is depicted in Sandoz, Mari, *Crazy Horse: The Strange Man of the Oglalas,* University of Nebraska Press, Lincoln, 1961, pp. 63-85. Concerning the butchery at the Middle Sappa Creek in western Kansas on April 23, 1875, see Sandoz, Mari, *Cheyenne Autumn,* Avon Books, New York, 1964, pp. 120-6. For an excellent overview of the sort of warfare waged against the indigenous people of the plains region, see Andrist, Ralph, *The Long Death: The Last Days of the Plains Indians,* Collier Books, New York, 1964.

14. Examples are plentiful. For instance, Jennings (op. cit., pp. 15-32) extends a useful analysis of the reduction of indigenous national populations within what is now the northeastern United States. Moving to the Pacific Coast, Lynwood Carranco and Estle Beard offer an instructive case study in their *Genocide and Vendetta: The Round Valley Wars of Northern California,* University of Oklahoma Press, Norman, 1981.

15. The term is borrowed from Svaldi, David, *Sand Creek and the Rhetoric of Extermination: A Case-Study in Indian-White Relations,* University Press of America, Lanham, MD, 1989.

16. Hoig assembles an interesting selection from *Rocky Mountain News* reportage and commentary during the 1864-65 period in *The Sand Creek Massacre,* op. cit., pp. 163-76. A nearly complete microfilm collection of the *News* for these years is also housed in the Colorado Historical Association Library in Denver.

17. This is the official Soviet estimate of the USSR's war dead.

18. These are generally accepted percentages, as indicated by Irving Louis Horowitz in his *Genocide: State Power and Mass Murder,* Transaction Books, New Brunswick, NJ, 1982.

19. U.S. Bureau of the Census, *Abstract of the Eleventh Census: 1890,* U.S. Government Printing Office, Washington, D.C., 1896.

20. The smaller number is the maximum population estimate advanced by Cherokee scholar Russell Thornton in his *American Indian Holocaust and Survival: A Population History Since 1492,* University of Oklahoma Press, Norman, 1987. The larger figure is that extended by Henry F. Dobyns in his more speculative *Their Numbers Become Thinned: Native American Population Dynamics in Eastern North America,* University of Tennessee Press, Knoxville, 1983.

21. Even the arch-reactionary Smithsonian Institution has acknowledged the truth of Amherst's conscious utilization of biological warfare: "During the bitter fighting in 1763-1764 Gen. Jeffrey Amherst actually ordered that the Indians around Fort Pitt be infected with gifts of smallpox [laden] blankets. The Indian uprising failed, and Fort Pitt was easily relieved after a smallpox epidemic broke out among the warriors besieging the fort" (Jacobs, Wilbur R., "British Indian Policies to 1783," in *Handbook of North American Indians,* Vol. 4: *History of Indian-White Relations,* Smithsonian Institution, Washington, D.C., 1988, p. 10). As regards inculcation of smallpox among the Mandans in 1837, see Connell, Evan S., *Son of the Morning Star: Custer and the Little Big Horn,* North Point Press, San Francisco, 1984, pp. 15-6.

22. It should be borne in mind when considering these points that many of the nazi leaders sentenced to prison (e.g., Alfried Krupp von Bohlen und Hallbach) or death (e.g., Hans Frank) at Nuremburg for crimes against humanity were not accused of directly killing anyone, nor even of ordering their gassing, shooting, etc. Rather, they were shown to have implemented policies that led to mass death through disease, starvation, and so on. See Manchester, William, *The Arms of Krupp, 1587-1968,* Bantam Books, New York, 1968.

23. See, for an example of such official word usage, U.S. Commission on Civil Rights, *The Navajo Nation: An American Colony,* Washington, D.C., September 1975.

24. The equation is taken from Galeano, Eduardo, *The Open Veins of Latin America: Five Centuries of the Pillage of a Continent,* Monthly Review Press, New York, 1973.

25. These are the federal government's own data. See U.S. Bureau of the Census, Population Division, Racial Statistics Branch, *A Statistical Profile of the American Indian Population,* Washington, D.C., October 1984. Also see U.S. Department of Health and Human Services, Chart Series Book, Public Health Service, Washington, D.C., 1988 (HE20.9409.988).

26. Ortiz, Simon J., *From Sand Creek,* Thunder's Mouth Press, New York, 1981.

Table

Key Indian Laws and Cases

Ward Churchill and Glenn T. Morris

T he following is an annotated listing of the various statutes and cases that are key to understanding the federal-Indian relationship and that are therefore frequently referred to by the contributors to this book. The table is provided both to serve as a handy reference guide for readers and to prevent cumbersome formal citations from cluttering up the main texts. These should be considered in the context of Article IX of the Articles of Confederation (1781), which vested the Continental Congress with "the sole and exclusive right and power" of regulating the trade and managing all affairs with "Indians not members of the states," and of the so-called Commerce Clause of the Constitution, which stipulated that the federal government alone would be responsible for regulating trade with "Indian Tribes" in the same fashion it does so with foreign nations and between "the various states" of the union. Also at issue is Article I, Section 2 of the Constitution, which defines "Indians not taxed" as comprising a polity (or polities) separate from that of the United States, and Article I, Section 10, which precludes the federal government from entering into treaty agreements with any entity other than another fully sovereign national entity.

Laws

- *The Northwest Ordinance* (1789): The Ordinance (1 *Stat.* 50), promulgated in the context of the threat of Tecumseh's incipient confederation, essentially disavowed U.S. intent to exercise the doctrine of "Rights of Conquest" in its affairs with Indians, pledging the nation instead to conduct its Indian affairs on the basis "of utmost good faith." The U.S., of course, was comporting itself otherwise, even as the Ordinance went into effect.

- *Trade and Intercourse Acts* (1790-1834): This series of statutes, beginning with ch. 33, 1 *Stat.* 137 (now codified at 25 U.S.C. 177), served to codify the constitutional Commerce Clause, providing the federal government with tools to enforce its regulatory authority over its citizens in their interactions with native peoples. The 1790 Act was succeeded by other statutes in 1793, 1796, 1799, 1802, and 1834. Supplemental legislation, elaborating federal authority to punish U.S. citizens guilty of non-commercial crimes "in Indian Country," was enacted in 1802 and 1834. Over time, interpretation of these laws by federal courts came to be seen as binding upon the conduct of Indians as well as U.S. nationals. No basis in juridical logic for this latter interpretation exists.

- *The Indian Removal Act* (1830): This Act (ch. 148, 4 *Stat.* 411), passed on May 28,

1830, provided for "an exchange of lands with any of the Indians residing in any of the states and territories, and for their removal west of the river Mississippi." It was used as a basis by Andrew Jackson, in defiance of a Supreme Court opinion that the U.S. had no legal basis to do so, to set in motion the mass forced relocations of the Creek, Cherokee, Choctaw, Chickasaw, Seminole and scores of other American Indian nations located east of the Mississippi during the 1830s. The idea was to "clear" the native population from the entire region east of the Mississippi, opening it up for the exclusive use and occupancy of Euroamericans and their Black slaves. By and large, the survivors of these forced relocations were dumped in the "Permanent Indian Territory" of Oklahoma, an area belonging to other indigenous nations.

- *Suspension of Treaty-Making* (1871): The suspension was a rider attached to the annual Indian Appropriations Act—by which Congress purported to meet its existing treaty obligations and other responsibilities to the indigenous nations whose land it was occupying—for 1871 (ch. 120, 16 *Stat.* 544, 566, now codified at 25 U.S.C. 71): "[N]o Indian nation or tribe within the territory of the United States shall [henceforth] be recognized as an independent nation, tribe, or power with whom the United States may contract by treaty: *Provided further,* That nothing herein contained shall be construed to invalidate or impair the obligation of any treaty heretofore lawfully made with any such Indian nation or tribe." The recognition at issue, of course, had already occurred in at least 371 instances in which treaties had been ratified, and could thus not be invalidated or impaired by provision of the rider. Further, the law notwithstanding, the United States continued to mount treaty commissions to negotiate with native nations until at least 1905.

- *The Major Crimes Act* (1885): Under this statute (ch. 341, 24 *Stat.* 362, 385, now codified at 18 U.S.C. 1153), enacted on March 3, 1885, the United States unilaterally extended its jurisdiction for "the first time over American Indian national territories falling within its own claimed boundaries. Prior to the Act, exercise of their own jurisdiction within their borders was an expression of the sovereignty of indigenous nations understood and accepted by both the United States and American Indian peoples.

- *The General Allotment Act* (1887): By this measure (ch. 119, 24 *Stat.* 388, now codified as amended at 25 U.S.C. 331 *et seq.;* also known as the "Dawes Act" or "Dawes Severalty Act"), the U.S. intervened unilaterally in the internal affairs of native nations to break up their traditional systems of collective land tenure. In order to retain any land at all, native people—legally defined for the first time on the basis of a racist "blood quantum" code employed for identification purposes by the federal government—were compelled to accept individually deeded land parcels. "Full Blood Indians" were deeded with "trust patents," over which the government exercised complete control for a minimum of twenty-five years; "Mixed Blood Indians" were deeded with "patents in fee simple," over which they exercised rights, but were forced to accept U.S. citizenship in the process. Once each "federally recognized Indian" had received his or her allotment of land, the balance of reserved Indian land was opened up to non-Indian homesteading, corporate utilization, or incorporation into national parks and forests. Between 1887 and 1934, approximately two-thirds (100 million acres) of all Indian-reserved land was appropriated by the government through this mechanism.

- *The Indian Citizenship Act* (1924): Passed as a "clean-up measure," picking up all those missed or excluded by the General Allotment Act, the law (ch. 233, 43 *Stat.* 25), unilaterally conferred U.S. citizenship on "all non-citizen Indians born within the territorial limits of the United States." A number of indigenous nations, notably the Hopi and Onondaga, have refused to acknowledge that the Citizenship Act is in any way binding upon them, and continue to engage in such expressions of sovereignty as issuing their own passports.

- *The Indian Reorganization Act* (1934): The IRA (ch. 576, 48 *Stat.* 948, now codified at 25 U.S.C. 461-279; also known as the "Wheeler-Howard Act") was imposed by the United States to supplant traditional forms of indigenous governance in favor of a tribal council structure modeled after corporate boards. In order to put a "democratic face" on the maneuver, it was stipulated that each native nation to be reorganized agree to the process by referendum. The referenda were then systematically rigged by Commissioner of Indian Affairs John Collier. One result has been a deep division between "traditionals" and "progressives" (who endorse the IRA form of government) on many reservations to this day.

- *The Indian Claims Commission Act* (1946): The Claims Commission was established under the provision of a law (60 *Stat.* 1049) ostensibly designed to insure that indigenous nations which historically suffered illegal expropriation of their lands at the hands of the United States "receive justice." The gesture was probably provoked in large part by the fact that the U.S. was preparing to hang nazis at Nuremberg for having engaged, among other things, in "wars of aggression and conquest." In actuality, the Commission was not empowered to return land to any Indian nation, no matter how illegally it was adjudged to have been taken. To the contrary, it was required to assign an award of monetary compensation to such Indians—whether or not the Indians wished to sell their homelands—in each instance where an illegal taking was determined to have occurred. Awards were usually established on the basis of the estimated "price per acre" of the land *at the time it was taken* (often a century or more earlier), a practice which minimized the amounts of awards paid. The whole exercise was said to "quiet title" to all illegally taken Indian lands in favor of the United States. In sum, the U.S. was busily casting a veneer—but not the reality—of legitimacy over many of its land acquisitions in North America.

- *The Termination Act* (1953): The "Act" is actually House Concurrent Resolution 108, pronounced on August 1, 1953, which articulated a federal policy of unilaterally dissolving specific native nations. What followed was the "termination"—suspension of federal services to and recognition of the existence of the Menominee on June 17, 1954 (ch. 303, 68 *Stat.* 250); the Klamath on August 13, 1954 (ch. 732, 68 *Stat.* 718, codified at 25 U.S.C. 564 *et seq.*); the "Tribes of Western Oregon" on August 13, 1954 (ch. 733, 68 *Stat.* 724, codified at 25 U.S.C. 691 *et seq.*); and so on. In all, 109 native nations, or elements of native nations, were terminated by congressional action during the late 1950s. A handful were "restored" to federal recognition during the 1970s.

- *Public Law 280* (1954): Enacted on August 14, 1954, P.L. 280 (ch. 505, 67 *Stat.* 588, codified in part at 18 U.S.C. 1162 and 28 U.S.C. 1360), reduced the number of unterminated indigenous nations in California, Minnesota, Nebraska, Oregon, Washington, and Alaska by placing them under varying degrees of state jurisdictional authority. Partial reductions, embedded in attendant legislation, also affected the sovereignty of all other native nations within the U.S. The law was amended in 1968, after it had seen broad application, to require native consent prior to its being expanded further.

- *The Relocation Act* (1956): P.L. 959 provided funding to establish "job training centers" for American Indians in various urban centers, and to finance the relocation of individual Indians and Indian families to these locales. It was coupled to a denial of funds for similar programs and economic development on the reservations themselves. Those who availed themselves of the "opportunity" for jobs, etc., represented by the federal relocation programs were usually required to sign agreements that they would not return to their respective reservations to live. The result, by 1980, was a diaspora of Native Americans, with more than half of the 1.6 million Indians in the U.S. having been scattered to cities across the country.

- *The Indian Civil Rights Act* (1968): While it negated many of the worst potentialities of termination policy, the Indian Civil Rights Act (P.L. 90-284; 82 *Stat.* 77, codified in part at 25 U.S.C. 1301 *et seq.*) served to bind the forms assumed by indigenous governments even more tightly to federal preferences than had the IRA. In effect, it made native governments a functional part of the federal system itself. Such incorporation, however, afforded Indian people only constraints upon their sovereignty rather than any of the constitutional protections of basic rights and other benefits supposedly accruing to members of the U.S. polity. In 1978, in *Santa Clara Pueblo v. Martinez* (436 U.S. 49), the Act was interpreted to provide relief in federal court against tribal government actions only in matters pertaining to *habeas corpus*. The Act was then amended in 1986, under provision of the federal Anti-Drug Abuse Act (P.L. 99-570, 100 *Stat.* 3207) to allow tribal courts greater powers of penalization—up to one year imprisonment and $5,000 in fines—on certain types of criminal offenses.

- *The Alaska Native Claims Settlement Act* (1971): ANSCA (P.L. 92-203; 85 *Stat.* 688, codified at 43 U.S.C. 1601 *et seq.*), as the Act is known, converted the native nations of Alaska into thirteen regional and an assortment of individuated village corporations, all accommodated under Alaskan rather than federal charters, "without establishing any racially defined institutions, rights, privileges, or obligations, without creating a reservation system or lengthy wardship or trusteeship, and without adding to the categories of property and institutions engaging in tax privileges." In other words, Alaska's native nations were dissolved by congressional fiat, incorporated into the U.S. polity, and their approximately 44 million acres of property (as well as the timber on it and massive amounts of oil beneath it) were turned into U.S. "domestic assets." This has remained the case despite partial amendment of ANSCA in the Alaska National Interest Conservation Act (16 U.S.C. 3102) and the ANSCA Amendments of 1987 (P.L. 100-241; 101 *Stat.* 1788, codified at 43 U.S.C. 1601)

- *The Indian Self-Determination and Educational Assistance Act* (1975): This oddly titled statute (P.L. 93-638; 88 *Stat.* 2203, codified at 25 U.S.C. 450a and elsewhere in titles 25, 42 and 50, U.S.C.A.) does nothing at all to afford American Indians the internationally recognized right to determine for themselves their social, political, and economic relationships to the U.S. and other foreign powers. Rather, it requires that they be included more fully in staffing the various programs aimed at them by federal policymakers, who—the Act makes clear—continue to hold preeminent authority over Indian affairs. The statute would thus have been more accurately titled the "Indian

Self-*Administration* Act." This is particularly true of "education," which the government has always viewed as the ideal vehicle by which to condition Native Americans to accept the values, and thus the domination, of Euroamerica.

- *The Indian Child Welfare Act* (1978): Through this law (P.L. 95-608; 92 *Stat.* 3069, codified at 25 U.S.C. 1901 *et seq.*) the federal government finally renounced its century-old policy of forcibly and systematically transferring the care of native children to non-Indians through maintenance of a compulsory boarding school system and wholesale adoptions. The Act established for the first time specific procedures for the adoptive or foster-care placement of native children. In some part this was probably because there was increasing discussion of ratifying the 1948 Convention of Punishment and Prevention of the Crime of Genocide (such child transfer policies are a patent violation of Article IIe of the Convention). Also, it is probable that the government felt its child transfer policies had already accomplished their assimilative objectives and could thus be replaced by more sophisticated mechanisms such as the Indian Self-Determination and Educational Assistance Act. At present, application and interpretation of the Act remain unclear.

- *The American Indian Religious Freedom Act* (1978): It may seem curious that American Indians, who had mandatorily become U.S. citizens by 1924, should "need" a special statute passed in the late 1970s (P.L. 95-341; 92 *Stat.* 469, codified at 42 U.S.C. 1996) to be able to utilize the Free Exercise Clause of the First Amendment to the Constitution. A number of statutes and regulations promulgated during the late 19th and early 20th centuries, however, effectively criminalized a range of indigenous spiritual practices extending from the Lakota Sun Dance to the Potlatch ceremonies of the nations of the Pacific Northwest. Further, given that many native traditions embody a concept of sacred geography, loss of lands had by the late 20th century seriously curtailed site-specific practices of Indian spirituality. The 1978 Act pronounced that "it shall be the policy of the United States to protect and preserve [the] inherent right of the freedom to believe, express, and exercise the traditional religions" of American Indians, Alaskan Natives, and Native Hawaiians. It lacks any sort of enforcement provisions, however, and should therefore be viewed as a gesture (or perhaps a "policy aspiration") rather than as a law, per se. In addition, the federal courts have ruled in ten consecutive cases during the 1980s and early '90s denying any practical content to indigenous spiritual rights.

- *The Indian Mineral Development Act* (1982): At the outset of the Reagan administration's concerted "cost cutting" with regard to meeting its obligations to Indians, the Congress passed this Act (P.L. 97-382; codified at 25 U.S.C. 2101-2108) to "encourage" native nations to engage in wholesale mining of their residual land base—often with waivers of environmental protection safeguards and in arid or semi-arid locales that are not subject to reclamation once mined—in order to become "economically self-sufficient." The fact that such endeavors are both transient and capital intensive, thus requiring "participation" by major non-Indian corporations, which carry away most of the profits while leaving the ecological consequences behind, seems to have been precisely the point.

Cases

- *Fletcher v. Peck* (1810): In *Fletcher* (10 U.S. 87), Chief Justice of the U.S. Supreme Court John Marshall held that states claiming lands west of a line of demarcation declared by King George III in 1763 along the Alleghany and Appalachian mountain chains "owned" these areas even though Indian consent to cede them had never been obtained. Marshall for the first time referred to Indian lands as being "vacant."

- *Johnson v. McIntosh* (1823): In this case (21 U.S. 98 Wheat. 543), Chief Justice Marshall opined that the United States enjoyed preeminent sovereignty over its claimed territoriality by virtue of the "Doctrine of Discovery" and its subset, the "Rights of Conquest." In actuality, the Doctrine conveyed rights only to the various Crowns of Europe, not to outlaw republics that had violated the existing Laws of Nations by breaking away from their Crowns. Moreover, it acknowledged preeminent sovereignty as resting with indigenous nations rather than "discovering powers." What the latter legally obtained by virtue of "discovery" was a monopolistic right vis-à-vis other European states—a "sphere of influence," as it were—to go about acquiring (through purchase or agreement) territory within the discovered area from its rightful native owners. Rights of Conquest applied only in instances when it was necessary to fight a "Just War." Circumstances for the latter existed only when a) the natives engaged in unprovoked attacks upon discoverers, b) the natives refused to trade with the discoverers, or c) the natives refused to allow Christian missionaries to travel among them. None of these conditions were ever met within the context of U.S.-Indian relations.

- *The Cherokee Cases* (1831-1832): In *Cherokee Nation v. Georgia* (30 U.S. (5 Pet.) 1 (1831)) and *Worcester v. Georgia* (31 U.S. (6 Pet.) 551 (1832)), Chief Justice Marshall proceeded on the basis of his unfounded conclusions in *Fletcher* and *McIntosh* to argue that American Indian peoples comprised nations domestic to and dependent upon the United States. They occupied a status of "quasi-sovereignty," he asserted, being sovereign enough to engage in treaty-making with the U.S. (for purposes of conveying legal title to their lands), but not sovereign enough to manage their other affairs as fully independent political entities. The construction of this blatantly opportunistic monstrosity—which has been called "the equivalent of a woman's being part-pregnant"—laid the groundwork for the "Plenary Power Doctrine," holding that the federal government holds full and inherent power over Indian affairs and a concomitant "trust responsibility" over all Indian assets.

- *Ex Parte Crow Dog* (1883): The decision rendered in this case (109 U.S. 556) was that the U.S. had no jurisdictional authority to prosecute one Indian for killing another on an Indian reservation. The court's (correct) determination in this instance led to the extension of federal jurisdiction over Indian Country via the 1885 Major Crimes Act.

- *United States v. Kagama* (1886): Justice Samuel F. Miller rendered an opinion in this case (118 U.S. 375) which consolidated and extended Marshall's earlier assertion of federal plenary power over Indians. The Congress, Miller stated, had an "incontrovertible right" to exercise its authority over Indians as it saw fit—for "their own well-being," of course—and Indians lacked any legal recourse in the matter. This cleared the way for Congress to pass some 5,000 laws pertaining to the regulation of American Indians without the consent of, and often without so much as consulting with, the Indians themselves.

- *Lonewolf v. Hitchcock* (1903): In this case (187 U.S. 553), Justice Edward D. White reached the novel conclusion that the United States, as part of its plenary power over Indian affairs, could abrogate inconvenient sections of treaties with Indians at any time it chose, with or without Indian consent, and without disturbing the force of the treaty itself. In other words, the aspects of the treaties that vested land title in the U.S. would remain inviolate, while inconvenient obligations to pay for the land ceded—or preserve reservation areas—could be dispensed with at will. As always, this was couched in terms of its being "for the Indians' own good."

- *The Reserved Rights Cases* (1905-1908): In *United States v. Winans* (198 U.S. 371 (1905)) and *Winters v. United States* (207 U.S. 564 (1908)), the Supreme Court ruled that indigenous nations continued to enjoy the full range "of sovereign rights and prerogatives characterizing any other nation, not expressly removed from them by Act of Congress." Hence, the aboriginal and/or treaty rights of Indians outweighed the claims of the various states and individual citizens in such matters as off-reservation fishing and water usage. In adopting this posture, the court provided Congress with a perfect tool for centralized developmental planning in the West: Indian rights could be used as a "higher principle" with which to fend off unwanted initiatives by states, and then simply canceled by Congress at any moment it was deemed appropriate for federal purposes.

- *Tee-Hit-Ton v. United States* (1955): Extending the rationalizations offered in *Johnson v. McIntosh*, Justice Reed delivered the opinion in this case (348 U.S. 272) that the Tee-Hit-Ton band of the Tlingit Nation (in Alaska) could not establish aboriginal title to some 350,000 acres of territory the court acknowledged they had used and occupied since "time immemorial," there being no treaty by which Congress recognized their title. Hence, in the court's view, the Tee-Hit-Tons were not entitled to the land nor the resources upon it. The decision neatly finished the U.S. reversal of the "Discovery Doctrine" principle concerning who conveys title to whom in North America and effectively gutted whatever was left of aboriginal rights in U.S. jurisprudence.

- *McClanahan v. Arizona Tax Commission* (1973): In *McClanahan* (411 U.S. 104), the Supreme Court articulated for the first time the notion that Indian sovereignty was a mere "legal fiction" conveying no real legal entitlements, but which might serve instead as a convenient "backdrop" against which the meaning of treaties and other agreements might be read. This argument was used as a mainstay by attorney Allan van Gestel in his unsuccessful assertion of non-Indian interests in *County of Oneida v. Oneida Indian Nation* (470 U.S. 226 (1985)) and has subsequently attracted increasing interest on the part of anti-Indian litigators.

- *Oliphant v. Suquamish Tribe* (1978): In this case (435 U.S. 191), marked by wildly inaccurate revisions of the historical record, Justice William Rehnquist opined that indigenous nations held no jurisdictional prerogatives whatsoever—whether criminal or civil—over non-Indians living on their reservations. Rehnquist's thinking should not be construed to mean that residual Indian jurisdiction is restricted on a nation-by-nation basis to cover only their respective members. In the original formulation, non-member Indians living on reservations (a Crow, say, living on the Northern Cheyenne Reservation) were left subject to each nation's residual jurisdiction. The opinion was thus profoundly and objectively racist and drastically undercut what few jurisdictional prerogatives remained available to native nations. In the 1990 case *Duro v. Reina* (110 S.Ct. 2053), however, it was ruled that tribal jurisdiction pertained only to member Indians on each reservation. Hence, while certain of the most racist implications of the initial *Oliphant* opinion were negated, native national sovereignty was even further eroded.

- *Badoni v. Higginson* (1980): In what is usually known as the "Rainbow Bridge Case" (638 F.2d 172 (10th Cir. 1980), *cert. denied*, 452 U.S. 954 (1981)), the Supreme Court let stand a lower court decision that a joint Navajo-Hopi effort under the American Indian Religious Freedom Act to preserve a site of particular spiritual significance at the Rainbow Bridge geological formation was outweighed by the government's interest in flooding the area by building the Glen Canyon Dam. The high court's decision not to review the case effectively gutted whatever utility the 1978 congressional Indian religious freedom guidelines might have offered.

- *Montana v. United States* (1981): In this case (450 U.S. 544), the Supreme Court held—despite a ratified 1868 treaty by which the Crow Nation permanently reserved a portion of its original territory for its own "absolute and undisturbed use and occupancy"—that non-Indians who subsequently purchased land on the Crow Reservation were not subject to Crow hunting and fishing regulations on or near the Big Horn River, which runs through the reserved area. The ability of native nations to control the behavior of those residing within their boundaries was thus further diminished, even beyond the level imposed by *Oliphant*.

- *Merrion v. Jicarilla Apache Tribe* (1982): Heralded as a "major gain in the reassertion of tribal sovereignty" because it acknowledged native rights to levy severance taxes upon minerals extracted from their reserved lands, *Merrion* (102 S.Ct. 894) actually fit within the Reagan administration's campaign to diminish federal funding to Indians, "privatize" former areas of governmental operation, and "encourage economic development of federal trust lands." Key to understanding the meaning of the case is the court's language concerning the taxes at issue being used to defray the costs of "tribal self-government...and other programs." In effect, the decision provided an incentive for Indians to "cooperate" with transient extractive industries doing (or wishing to do) business on their land.

- *United States v. Dann* (1985): Justice William J. Brennan stated in this case (470 U.S. 39) that payment of federal monies into a U.S. Treasury account, over which Indians had no control, constituted "compensation" for "lost lands" even though the Indians—in this instance, two Western Shoshone sisters named Mary and Carrie Dann—were still living on it. The decision cleared the way for eviction of Indians from family plots even though they had never received a cent for their property.

- *Lyng v. Northwest Indian Cemetery Protective Association* (1988): Otherwise known as "The G-O Road Decision," this case (485 U.S. 439) resulted in an opinion, drafted by Justice Sandra Day O'Connor, that Indian religious rights were outweighed by society's "broader interest" in destroying their sacred sites for economic reasons, even if such interests were merely speculative, and even if such "development" had the effect of destroying the native spiritual tradition(s) at issue altogether.

- *Brendale v. Confederated Tribes and Bands of the Yakima Nation* (1989): The *Brendale* decision (109 S.Ct. 2994) limits the inherent sovereign ability of indigenous nations to control the use to which particular portions of their territory may be put. The question raised was whether the Yakima Tribal Government possessed a right to create zoning ordinances that would restrict land use by non-Indians living within reservation boundaries. The high court opined that it did not. Such control is thus restricted to the activities of member Indians residing on each reservation.

• *Employment Division, Department of Human Resources of Oregon v. Smith* (1990): In *Smith* (110 S.Ct. 1595), usually referred to as "The Peyote Case," Justice Antonin Scalia argued for the Supreme Court that ingestion of the mild hallucinogenic substance, peyote, by members of the Native American Church is not an activity deserving of protection under the Free Exercise Clause of the First Amendment of the Constitution, thus upending earlier precedents established in *People v. Woody* (61 Cal. 2d 716, 394 P.2d 813, 40 Cal Rptr. 69 (1969)), *Native American Church of New York v. United States* (468 F. Supp. 1247 (S.D.N.Y. 1979), and elsewhere. Rather than outlawing the practice, however, the high court simply passed the buck, opining that indigenous spiritual practices would henceforth be subject to supervision under the legal codes of individual states.

Chapter I

The Demography of Native North America
A Question of American Indian Survival

Lenore A. Stiffarm with Phil Lane, Jr.

The colony of a civilized nation which takes possession, either of waste country, or of one so thinly inhabited, that the natives easily give place to the new settlers, advances more rapidly to wealth and greatness than any other human society.

Adam Smith
An Inquiry into the Nature and Causes of the Wealth of Nations

The idea that social scientists have of the size of the aboriginal population of the Americas directly affects their interpretation of New World civilizations and cultures.

Henry F. Dobyns
Current Anthropology

The number of indigenous people inhabiting the North American continent at the point of first contact with Europeans has always been a highly political issue in the United States. For a number of reasons, all of them associated with the advancement of *post hoc* justifications for Euroamerican hegemony over the continent today, it has been expedient for non-Indian "experts" to minimize the size of aboriginal Indian populations, while denigrating the level of socio-economic attainment that presumably resulted in such sparseness of human presence. For all practical intents and purposes, the area north of the Río Grande has been conventionally depicted as being quite uninhabited at the time the major European influx began. In reality, however, things were altogether different. As the non-Indian scholar Francis Jennings has observed:

> European explorers and invaders discovered an inhabited land. Had it been a pristine wilderness then, it would possibly still be so today, for neither the technology nor the social organization of Europe in the sixteenth and seven-

teenth centuries had the capacity to maintain, of its own resources, outpost colonies thousands of miles from home. Incapable of conquering true wilderness, the Europeans were highly competent in the skill of conquering other peoples, and this they did. They did not settle a virgin land. They invaded and displaced a resident population.[1]

"All historians of the European colonies begin by describing the natives' reception of the newcomers," Jennings continues. "Yet, paradoxically, most of the same historians also repeat identical mythical phrases purporting that the land-starved people of Europe had found a magnificent opportunity to pioneer a savage wilderness and bring civilization to it. As a rationalization for the invasion and conquest of unoffending peoples, such phrases function to smother retroactive moral scruples that have been dismissed as irrelevant to objective history. Unfortunately, however, the price of repressing scruples has been suppression of the facts."[2]

As a consequence, a mythology has become firmly ensconced in the popular American consciousness which portrays traditional Native North America as consisting of tiny and widely scattered bands of stone-age hunter-gatherers wandering nomadically about the vastness of North America, leading a perpetually miserable hand-to-mouth existence until the more advanced invading culture of Europe came along to show them a better way of life.

Twentieth century academics have taught generations of students that only about one million natives resided within the North American vastness in the year 1500. This, it has been held by mainstream scholars allegedly knowledgeable in such matters, was the "peak level" of indigenous population prior to the present day.[3] The supposed "factual basis" for this wildly inaccurate estimate rests squarely in the pronouncements of two men, James M. Mooney and Alfred Louis Kroeber, both of them reputed "giants" of American anthropology. The methods they employed in arriving at their conclusions are instructive, illustrating as they do both the standards of accuracy attending much (even most) non-Indian research and writing about Native America, and the sorts of propaganda functions attending "responsible scholarship" in contemporary society more generally.

Mooney's work came first. An insight into his approach may be gleaned from a passage in his posthumously published book, *The Aboriginal Population of America North of Mexico*, in which he states: "The original Indian population of New England was probably about 25,000 or about one-half of what the historian [John Gorham] Palfrey makes it."[4] It is important to note that no explanation is offered as to why Mooney felt Palfrey's estimate was "exaggerated." Nor is any mention made of the fact that Palfrey himself had elected to arbitrarily slash the estimates of the indigenous New England population tendered in earlier sources, or that these sources had in turn diminished—again, with no explanation other than that the aboriginal native population "couldn't" have been so great—the counts of Indians recorded by the original New England colonists who encountered them.[5] Finally, no mention at all is made by any of this long string of pre-Mooney revisionists that the figures accruing from primary colonial sources failed to take into account the fact that the indigenous peoples of the North American Atlantic Coast had already been considerably reduced by epidemic disease prior to the commencement of European colonization in the region.[6]

Mooney appears to have followed the procedure of compiling existing, usually already well reduced, estimates with regard to each area of North America and then arbitrarily cutting them in half. The grand total of approximately 1,152,590 deriving from this process was then advanced as what his editor, Smithsonian anthropologist John Reed Swanton, described as a "provisional detailed estimate" for the entire continent when the result was published in 1928 (Mooney had died in 1921). Kroeber, heir apparent as leading luminary in the American anthropological scene, then took over, ultimately reclassifying Mooney's estimates according to a somewhat different "tribal typology" in his "definitive" *Cultural and Natural Areas of Native North America,* released in 1939. Kroeber, while accepting his predecessor's numbers overall, felt Mooney had been overly charitable with regard to the population of California, and therefore reduced his own aggregate continental estimate to 900,000. He then extrapolated a formulaic "hemispheric total" of about 8,400,000.[7]

As of 1948, the revised edition of Kroeber's general-utility text, *Anthropology,* was still assigned—absent any kind of comment or qualification—in many introductory university courses.[8] John Swanton weighed in during 1952 with his own highly popular textbook, *The Indian Tribes of North America,* affirming—without further research into the matter—the veracity of the Mooney/Kroeber calculations, entrenching them even more deeply in academic orthodoxy.[9] He was soon joined by Harold E. Driver, who published his own corroborative text, *The Indians of North America,* and collaborated with William C. Massey in producing *Comparative Studies of North American Indians,* a highly politicized "philosophical refutation" of those questioning any fundamental aspect of Kroeber's reasoning.[10] The lid was thus firmly affixed to the can of conventional Eurocentric wisdom. Today, the "million Indian estimate" has become so well established that—despite minor recent revisions—even so ostensibly anti-establishmentarian a group as the Revolutionary Communist Party, USA is prepared to regurgitate it as a "fundamental truth."[11]

Real Numbers

It's not that other scholars weren't arriving at rather different conclusions. As early as 1860, Emmanuel H. Domenech computed the precontact population of Native North America as having been sixteen to seventeen million.[12] At the same time Mooney's posthumous estimates were being published, H. J. Spinden, while articulating the results of a comprehensive hemispheric study suggesting that fifty to seventy-five million native people had lived in the Americas (*circa* 1200), argued on the basis of burial mound archaeology and other evidence that the population of the Ohio River Valley alone had been as great as Mooney's estimate for the entirety of North America.[13] By the early 1960s, California anthropologists Woodrow W.

Borah, Leslie B. Simpson, and Sherburn F. Cook had completed long and excruciatingly detailed analyses—focusing on anthropological evidence and known agricultural techniques, region by region—of pre-Columbian hemispheric demography
which led them to project a hemispheric total of some 100 million at the point of
first contact.[14] They were joined by Henry F. Dobyns who, working independently
and employing somewhat different techniques, arrived at a "tentative" hemispheric
estimate of ninety to 112 million, with about 12.5 million people living north of the
Río Grande in the year 1500.[15]

Hence, by 1970, more considered and methodologically refined efforts were
producing population estimates consistently running ten to fourteen times the
maximum numbers projected by Kroeber and still accepted as "sound" by the
academic establishment. The new work was largely discounted or ignored in the
latter circles, probably for reasons best elaborated by historian Wilbur R. Jacobs in
his influential essay, "The Tip of an Iceberg: Precolumbian Indian Demography and
Some Implications for Revisionism."[16] Meanwhile, the work of Borah, Cook,
Dobyns, and—somewhat belatedly—Carl O. Sauer,[17] began to have an increasing
effect on those sectors of American scholarship not sharing the interests and
therefore not committed to maintaining the mythologies of the U.S. socio-politico-
economic status quo.

Under such mounting pressure, even the Smithsonian Institution, that citadel
of orthodox anthropological "truth," was forced to engage in an exercise in intellectual containment, acknowledging for the first time that the Mooney/Kroeber
estimates might require some degree of "responsible revision." The task was left
largely to the institution's head physical anthropologist, Douglas Ubelaker, who
produced a region-by-region itemization, concluding that the precontact native
population of North America had been precisely 2,171,125. Ubelaker deduced,
through means which are not altogether clear, that 1,850,011 of these individuals
lived within the area now comprising the forty-eight coterminous states of the
United States. Another 73,326 "aboriginals" were assigned to Alaska, while Canada
was allotted 237,798 and Greenland 10,000.[18]

In 1983, Dobyns, who had by then completed more detailed studies of North
America, published his watershed book, *Their Numbers Become Thinned,* in which
he concluded that the northwest Pacific coastal region supported as many as
1,205,000 native people in precontact times, the Great Lakes region some 3,800,000,
and the Great Basin, Plateau, California, and Plains regions combined to support
another 2,772,000.[19]

> The southeastern portion of the continent was also thickly populated, with
> highest densities on or near the coast. The shores of the Gulf of Mexico from
> the Attakapa people east through the Apalachee [in east Texas] may have
> supported as many as 4.6 persons per square kilometer for a total of about
> 1,100,000 individuals. The Timucuan chiefdoms, the Calusa, and smaller
> groups inhabiting peninsular Florida numbered perhaps 697,000 persons, with
> an average density of 5.72 persons per square kilometer. The Atlantic coastal
> plain from Florida to Massachusetts afforded a favorable habitat to about

2,211,000 Native Americans. Records of early historic population density rose to as many as 13.77 people per square kilometer in southern New England. The Virginia-Maryland tidewater region was still another area of dense Native American settlement. Population densities might appear as high elsewhere in North America were the documentary record equally detailed for earlier Colonial years.[20]

Dobyns also advanced a population tally for "the great Mississippi River Valley, its major Missouri, Ohio, Kentucky, Tennessee, and Red River tributaries, and their affluents" of about 5,250,000, while estimating a total of 928,000 native inhabitants of the Senora Desert region.[21] Cumulatively, these regional calculations, along with certain mediations which served to adjust the aggregate total, caused him to extend "a continental estimate of approximately eighteen million Native Americans living north of civilized Mesoamerica in the early years of the sixteenth century," about sixteen million of them living within the area that is now the continental United States.[22] While anything approaching absolute precision in such efforts is of course impossible, as Dobyns readily admitted, no more painstakingly complete assessment of precontact indigenous demography in North America has been undertaken to date.

This time the establishment response came from Russell Thornton, a somewhat confused Cherokee demographer at the University of Minnesota (now at the University of California at Berkeley) who appears to have glimpsed an opportunity to acquire "academic credibility" through adding the weight of his "native voice" to the chorus of "respectable scholars" insistently low-counting native population. Although, in his 1987 book, *American Indian Holocaust and Survival,* Thornton claims to have arrived at conclusions "remarkably close" to Ubelaker's, the best he could do with the available evidence was hold his overall estimate of precontact Native North American population down to "five million plus" within the continental U.S. area, and another "2 million plus" in Canada and Alaska, for a combined continental total of seven to nine million.[23] This arithmetic, of course, more than tripled Ubelaker's reluctant doubling of the Mooney/Kroeber estimates, and has caused Thornton himself to come under attack from paleo-conservative polemicists such as David Henige, who vehemently defend the Smithsonian's current "two million thesis" (and would likely be more comfortable with continuation of Mooney's and Kroeber's one million as a hard and fast number).[24]

Some aspects of Thornton's critique of Dobyns—such as the latter's assumption that American Indian populations would have followed the Malthusian dictum of expanding to the limits of environmental carrying capacity—are likely correct. There is, in fact, appreciable evidence suggesting they remained a respectful distance below the level of saturation as a matter of course.[25] It is therefore probable that the actual precontact population fell 10 to 20 percent below Dobyns' maximal projection. Hence, it seems appropriate to follow author Kirkpatrick Sale in suggesting that a precontact North American Indian population of fifteen million is perhaps the best and most accurate "working number" available to us.[26] Of this total, it follows (based upon Dobyns' proportional calculations) that about twelve million resided within the present borders of the United States.

Implications of the Size of Aboriginal Native Population

The tenacity and increasing viciousness with which representatives of the Euroamerican academic establishment such as Allan Bloom, E.D. Hirsch, and former White House domestic policy analyst Dinesh D'Souza have defended persistent low-counting of the continent's original inhabitants has little to do with their oft professed desires to "revitalize liberal education."[27] Still less does it have to do with defending "meaningful history," "methodological accuracy," or any of the other noble-sounding rationalizations voiced by cruder propagandists like Jeffrey Hart, Charles Krauthammer, and former education secretary William Bennett to explain their revulsion at "multicultural" interpretations of reality more generally.[28] At base, the concerns of such champions of the status quo do not rest in the saving of any discernable "canonical truth" from "distortion" or "dilution" in the name of "political correctness." To the contrary, they are, at least in connection to indigenous demographics, devoted to preserving a specific and rather elaborately constructed lie—to preventing its "deconstruction," as it were—which constitutes the very core of their culture's pretensions to legitimacy in its assertion of "natural dominance" in North America.

The issue goes to the concept of the "Norman Yoke," an element of juridical philosophy arising among medieval Anglo-Saxons and subsequently incorporated into the British variants of the Doctrine of Discovery and Rights of Conquest.[29] In simplest terms, the concept, as it was eventually articulated in John Locke's philosophy of Natural Law, held that any "Christian" (read: European) happening upon "waste land"—most particularly land that was vacant or virtually vacant of human inhabitants—assumed not only a "natural right," but indeed *an obligation* to put such land to "productive use." Having thus performed "God's will" by "cultivating" and thereby "conquering" the former "wilderness," its "discoverer" can be said to "own" it.[30] It was upon this peculiar doctrine that Chief Justice of the Supreme Court John Marshall, in his 1823 opinion in the *Johnson v. McIntosh* case, based the notion that the U.S. holds "inherent and preeminent rights" over Indian lands.[31] This has been the basis of U.S. property law vis-à-vis American Indians—in effect, the country's claim to a moral and legal basis for its territorial existence—ever since.

For Marshall's utilization of the idea of the Norman Yoke to work out for the United States, it was/is necessary to believe that there were very few native people prior to the onset of the European invasion of North America. A substantial precontact native population would imply that the land was for all intents and purposes *not* vacant. In that event, the supposed rights of discovery and conquest Marshall wished to rely upon would be governed, under the then prevailing Laws of Nations, by certain fairly strict criteria pertaining to prosecution of "Just Wars."

To be sure, the conditions defined by these criteria—delineated in Chapter Two—were quite absent in North America.[32] All in all, it was much easier and more effective for U.S. colonizers to begin fabricating a complex of falsehoods concerning the extremely low population density of aboriginal North America, and the correspondingly extreme primitivism of this population's socio-economic and cultural circumstances, than it was to attempt to justify the prosecution of a lengthy series of unjust wars either before contemporaneous courts of international opinion, or in the eyes of their own posterity.[33]

It was necessary, once this justifying mythology had been advanced, that it be maintained and perfected. For Eurosupremacists, either historical or contemporary, to admit that the precontact Native North American population had been fifteen million rather than one or two million would compel their admission of a number of other uncomfortable facts. For instance, the larger population figure could only have been sustained by a primary reliance upon extensive agriculture rather than hunting and gathering. This, in turn, means that precontact American Indians were primarily "sedentary" rather than "nomadic," cultivators of the land, and residents of permanent towns rather than wandering occupants of a "barren wilderness." As Jack Weatherford puts it in his recent book, *Indian Givers:*

> Even though European settlers imposed new architectural styles and new ideas of urban planning on America, they usually built over existing Indian settlements rather than clearing out new areas of settlement. Subsequent generations of Americans usually forgot that their towns and cities had been founded by Indians. Myths arose about how the colonists literally carved their settlements out of the uninhabited forest,...The new settlers of America [merely] continued the same settlement patterns already firmly established by Indians...along the rivers and coasts, with only minimal settlement of the plains and mountains...Few Americans bother to mention that the city of Washington [D.C.] arose on top of Naconchtanke, the main trading town of the Conoy Indians.[34]

The native origins, and often the indigenous names, of most present townships within the present U.S.—places as diverse as Tallahasee, Oswego, Kansas City, Chicago, Seattle, and Roanoke—are equally apparent. Although many of these locations were villages in which only a hundred or fewer people resided, this was not always the case. The Cahokia site, near present-day St. Louis, was a city accommodating as many as 40,000 inhabitants, and it is only the most pronounced known example within the Mississippian culture it represents.[35] Towns of up to 10,000 were not especially uncommon in the great river basin areas east of the Mississippi.[36] Dobyns has estimated that perhaps 150 communities of 2,000 or more people existed in the year 1500 in the present state of Florida alone.[37] Even in the arid upper Sonoran region of the Southwest, the Hohokam culture of southern Arizona exhibited a population of some 30,000, while more northerly Anasazi urban centers such as Chaco Canyon housed populations that may well have exceeded 1,200 persons apiece.[38]

The agriculture system that supported all this was the most advanced and complex in the world. As Smithsonian anthropologist H.J. Spinden quietly admitted in a little-remarked 1929 report, "about four-sevenths of the agricultural production of the United States [is] in economic plants domesticated by the American Indian and taken over by the white man."[39] This was a conservative assessment:

> In actuality, fully two-thirds of all the vegetal foodstuffs now consumed by humanity were under cultivation in Native America—*and nowhere else*—at the moment Columbus first set foot on Hispañola. An instructive, but by no means exhaustive, list of crops includes corn, potatoes [about 3,000 varieties], yams, sweet potatoes, tomatoes, squash [about 600 varieties], pumpkins, most varieties of beans, all varieties of pepper except black, amaranth, manioc (tapioca), mustard and a number of other greens, sunflowers, cassava, some types of rice, artichokes, avocadoes, okra, chayotes, peanuts, cashews, walnuts, hickory nuts, pecans, pineapples, bread fruit, passion fruit, many melons, persimmons, choke cherries, papayas, cranberries, blueberries, blackberries, coffee, sassafras, vanilla, chocolate, and cocoa. In order to raise this proliferation of food items, American Indians had perfected elaborate and sophisticated agricultural technologies throughout the hemisphere long before the arrival of the first European. This included intricate and highly efficient irrigation systems, ecologically integrated and highly effective planting methods such as *milpa* and *conuco,* and the refinement of what amounted to botanical experimentation facilities, among other things.[40]

The methods employed in North America included planting rather than sowing seeds in the Old World fashion—a practice that allowed for seed selection and the perfection of specific plant strains—as well as crop rotation and fertilization.[41] Vast acreages were under cultivation at any given point, especially east of the Mississippi, but were never plowed under in the soil-destructive manner of Europe.[42] Fields themselves were also rotated in and out of cultivation in order that the balance between domesticated and natural flora not be radically altered.[43] Considerable surplus was typically generated through these means, a situation that led to construction of extensive food storage facilities and development of a continental (perhaps hemispheric) trade network with an attendant network of trails and roadways that form the basis for the contemporary U.S. highway system.[44] Destruction of the indigenous agricultural base was always an integral aspect of European and Euroamerican warfare against North American Indians, from the earliest forays at Roanoke, Virginia, through Kit Carson's campaign against the Navajos in 1863-64.[45]

Obviously, if *any* of this were to become popularly acknowledged as true, a complete reversal of the polarities of "American history" as it is now known would be in order. The entire predication for an intrinsic "rightness" to Eurosupremacy in North America would evaporate. The Roanoke, Plymouth, and Jamestown "settlers" would have found no "waste land" which they made productive and to which they and their descendants were innately and legitimately entitled. Instead, they would be marked forever with the indelible *wrongness* of having all along been some of history's most pathological thieves and murderers. Assuming *any* degree of integrity and desire for justice among the general Euroamerican population, such "revision" of the historical record as is sketched above might conceivably induce a massive cognitive dissonance leading to erosion of the social consensus allowing Eurosupremacy to function in its usual and accustomed fashion. This, in turn, might serve to alter the sorts of power relations that have increasingly prevailed between Indians and whites over the past 200 years. This, the status quo must avoid at all costs. Hence, the ongoing academic hegemony accorded low-counters and their colleagues.

Decimation by Disease

The destruction of North American Indian populations by contact, direct or indirect, with Europeans started well before the European invasion of the continent began in earnest. This was accomplished through introduction of a whole series of pathogenic viruses and bacteria—"smallpox, measles, the bubonic plague, cholera, typhoid, pleurisy, scarlet fever, diphtheria, mumps, whooping cough, colds, the venereal diseases gonorrhea and chancroid, pneumonia and some unusual respiratory diseases, quite probably typhus and venereal syphilis"—to which the natives had never been exposed, and to which they therefore had no acquired immunity.[46] In all probability, the first epidemics had already occurred in Florida, carried by Indians in contact with Spaniards invading the Caribbean Basin, at the time Ponce de Léon made his initial expedition into that area in 1513. In any event, the first smallpox pandemic was raging, not only among the peninsula's indigenous Timucuan population but across the whole continent within a decade of the Spanish arrival.This first pandemic, which lasted from 1520-24, may have reduced the native population of North America by as much as 75 percent.[47]

Such catastrophes were only beginning. Dobyns has chronicled forty-one separate smallpox epidemics and pandemics occurring in North America from 1520 through 1899; seventeen measles epidemics between 1531 and 1892; ten major epidemics and pandemics of influenza from 1559 through 1918; four plague epidemics between 1545 and 1707; five diphtheria epidemics between 1601 and 1890; four typhus epidemics from 1586 through 1742; three major outbreaks of cholera between 1832 and 1867; four scarlet fever epidemics beginning in 1637 and ending in 1865; and six epidemics of other diseases, including typhoid, between 1528 and 1833.[48]

The diseases did not merely spread among American Indians, kill them, and then disappear. On the contrary, they came, spread, and killed again and again and again. It has recently been calculated that there may have been as many as 93 serious epidemics and pandemics of Old World pathogens among North American Indians from the early sixteenth century to the beginning of the twentieth century. In other words, a "serious contagious disease causing significant mortality invaded North American peoples at intervals of four years and two and a half months, on the average, from 1520 to 1900."[49]

The decimation of Native North America by disease has been traditionally treated by conventional anthropologists and historians as a sort of "natural disaster," induced but never intended by Europeans. There is considerable evidence, however, that this was not always the case. For instance, the so-called King Philip's War between British colonists and the Wampanoag and Narragansett nations during 1675 and '76 appears to have been fought, in part, because the Indians were convinced the colonials had deliberately spread disease among them.[50] While this possible early instance of biological warfare is speculative, other examples are not. During 1763, while striving to defeat Pontiac's confederation of Ottawas and other peoples:

> Sir Jeffrey Amherst, commander-in-chief of the British forces, wrote in a postscript of a letter to Bouquet [a subordinate] that smallpox be sent among the disaffected tribes. Bouquet replied, also in a postscript, "I will try to [contaminate] them with some blankets that may fall into their hands, and take care not to get the disease myself"...To Bouquet's postscript Amherst replied, "You will do well to [infect] the Indians by means of blankets as well as to try every other method that can serve to extirpate this exorable race." On June 24, Captain Ecuyer, of the Royal Americans, noted in his journal: "...we gave them two blankets and a handkerchief out of the smallpox hospital. I hope it will have the desired effect."[51]

It did. The disease spread rapidly among the Mingo, Delaware, Shawnee, and other nations of the Ohio River Valley, killing perhaps 100,000 people and bringing about the collapse of Pontiac's military alliance.[52] The familiarity with which Amherst and his officers appear to have approached the techniques of inculcating smallpox among the Ottawas and their allies strongly suggest such methods had been used before, most probably with regard to at least two earlier but equally debilitating outbreaks of the disease under wartime conditions within the Haudenosaunee (Iroquois Six Nations Confederacy) and other nations:

> In 1717, a large Iroquois war expedition was "forced to return because smallpox broke out among them." In 1731-32, another epidemic caused them to flee in terror "in great numbers across the frontier and spread along the borders of Massachusetts and New Hampshire. By this Iroquois dispersal smallpox was spread among other American Indian tribes [such as the Huron, Neutral, Erie and Conestago], and it "attacked one tribe after another until, by 1733, it had caused great mortality among all the Six Nations." Smallpox also infected the Indians of New England as a result.[53]

Amherst's tactics may have been used by the fledgling United States against the Cherokees (who were allied with the British) in 1783: at any rate, the epidemic among them was very convenient for George Washington's rebel forces, and "broke their [the Cherokees'] last resistance."[54] Certainly, the distribution of smallpox-infected blankets by the U.S. Army to Mandans at Fort Clark, on the Missouri River in present-day South Dakota, was the causative factor in the pandemic of 1836-40.[55] By Russell Thornton's conservative calculations:

> The total numbers of American Indians thought to have died are overwhelming:

6,000 to 8,000 Blackfoot, Piegans, and Bloods; 2,000 Pawnee; virtually all of several thousand Mandan; one-half of the 4,500 Arikara and Minitaree; many Osage; one-third of the 3,000 Crow; 400 Yanktonai Dakota; over one-half of 8,000 Assiniboin; and three-fifths of the north-central California Indians...[The disease also affected Indians to the] south, where it infected the Choctaw, killing 400 to 500 of them...Specific numbers are not recorded, but the pox is known also to have killed many Chickasaw in 1838, as well as infecting other southern tribes and the Kiowa, the Apache, the Gros Ventre, the Winnebago...the Comanche, the Cayuse, and other New Mexico, Canada, and Alaska Indians.[56]

The death toll probably exceeded 100,000—and may have been several times that—a matter which undoubtedly made the subsequent U.S. conquest of the territory lying west of the Mississippi River far easier than it would otherwise have been. Nor is direct engagement in biological warfare *per se*, real or suspected, the only dimension of European and Euroamerican culpability regarding the decimation of the Native North American population by disease. Obviously, the above-mentioned military strategy of systematically destroying the indigenous agricultural base served to impose starvation conditions upon entire peoples, dramatically lowering their resistance to disease and increasing their susceptibility to epidemics. The same can be said of General Phil Sheridan's policy, applied mainly during the 1870s, of exterminating at least 60 million buffalo in order to deny a basis of subsistence to the Cheyenne, Lakota, and other peoples of the Great Plains.[57]

Even clearer instances in which the decimation of native people by disease stems from federal policy are those related to forced relocation and/or concentration. Probably the most notorious concerns the removal of the Cherokee Nation from its homeland in an area encompassing portions of the present states of Tennessee, Georgia, North Carolina, and Alabama to Oklahoma during 1838. Some 17,000 Cherokees were rounded up by U.S. troops and then force-marched at bayonet point up to 1,500 miles in order to clear the way for white settlement east of the Mississippi River. Even by Mooney's usual low-counting estimation, at least 25 percent of those compelled to walk the "Trail of Tears" died of disease, exposure, and malnutrition along the way.[58] Thornton's much more thorough computations reveal that approximately 8,000—or nearly 50 percent of the entire Cherokee population remaining after earlier epidemics had caused severe attrition—failed to survive the Trail.[59] As concerns the other four of the "Five Civilized Tribes" subjected to comparable forced relocation from the Southeast to Oklahoma during the same period:

> The Choctaws are said to have lost fifteen percent of their population, 6,000 out of 40,000; and the Chickasaw...surely suffered severe losses as well. By contrast the Creeks and Seminoles are said to have suffered about 50 percent mortality. For the Creeks, this came primarily in the period immediately after removal: for example, "of the 10,000 or more who were resettled in 1836-37...an incredible 3,500...died of 'bilious fevers.'"[60]

A somewhat lesser known example concerns the experience of the Navajo during the period 1864-68. This occurred as a result of the above-mentioned Kit Carson Campaign to destroy Navajo agricultural capacity, at the conclusion of which some 9,000 Navajos surrendered. After being gathered together at Fort Defiance, Arizona, the prisoners were then force-marched more than 300 miles—an ordeal called "The Long Walk" in Navajo tradition—to be interred at the Bosque Redondo, adjacent to Fort Sumner, southeast of Santa Fe.[61] The site had been selected as the location for "concentration and maintenance of all captive Indians [in] New Mexico Territory," but no preparations had been made to accommodate them.[62] Over the next four years, the Indians were forced to live under guard, in holes in the ground, on perpetually short rations, and with a paucity of medical attention.[63] As many as 3,500 of them died during their captivity.[64]

Genocide

Plainly, much of what has been described in the preceding section tends to merge with any reasonable definition of genocide. There are, however, even clearer illustrations of genocidal activities directed against the Native North American population, especially since the emergence of the U.S. as an independent state. The first of these concerns the so-called Indian Wars, which began at least as early as Francisco Vásquez de Coronado's invasion of what are now the states of New Mexico and Arizona in 1540-41, and a comparable expedition by Hernando de Soto into the Southeast during 1540-42.[65] Over the next two centuries, wars of outright extermination had been fought by British colonists against "the Indians of Virginia" and nations such as the Pequot (who were among those who had fed the Plymouth Colony on the first "Thanksgiving" in 1620). The latter group had been dispatched *en masse* on May 26, 1637 by being surrounded in their main village along the Mystic River and then burned alive or shot and hacked to pieces with axes and swords. An estimated 800 of the already seriously depleted Pequot population died in the half-hour long massacre.[66]

By the mid-19th century, U.S. policymakers and military commanders were stating—openly, frequently and in plain English—that their objective was no less than the "complete extermination" of any native people who resisted being dispossessed of their lands, subordinated to federal authority, and assimilated into the colonizing culture.[67] The country was as good as its word on the matter, perpetrating literally hundreds of massacres of Indians by military and paramilitary formations at points all over the West. A bare sampling of some of the worst must include the 1854 massacre of perhaps 150 Lakotas at Blue River (Nebraska), the 1863 Bear River (Idaho) Massacre of some 500 Western Shoshones, the 1864 Sand Creek (Colorado) Massacre of as many as 250 Cheyennes and Arapahoes, the 1868 massacre of another 300 Cheyennes at the Washita River (Oklahoma), the 1875 massacre of about seventy-five Cheyennes along the Sappa Creek (Kansas), the 1878 massacre of still another 100 Cheyennes at Camp Robinson (Nebraska), and the 1890 massacre of more than 300 Lakotas at Wounded Knee (South Dakota).[68] As the U.S. Bureau of the Census put it in 1894:

It has been estimated that since 1775, more than [8,500 Indians] have been killed in individual affairs with [whites]...The Indian wars under the government of the United States have been more than 40 in number. They have cost the lives of...about 30,000 Indians...The actual number of killed and wounded Indians must be very much greater than the number given, as they conceal, where possible, their actual loss in battle...Fifty percent additional would be a safe number to add to the numbers given.[69]

This comes to a minimum of 56,750 Indians killed outright by Euroamericans militarily pushing into native lands during a period roughly conforming to the century spanning the years 1775-1875. Thornton, who has examined the matter closely, suggests that the official number is far too low and might "easily" be doubled. He also addresses the fact that "American Indians were also killed by other Indians in intertribal wars resulting from European involvement in tribal relations."[70] He then poses the relevant questions:

As these deaths are added, the mortality figures become considerably more substantial: 150,000? 250,000? 500,000? We do not know. Suffice it to say, American Indians suffered substantial population loss due to warfare stemming from the European arrival and colonization.[71]

Such queries are not rhetorical. Their full significance begins to emerge when one considers just how low the government's estimate of 8,500 Indians dying in "individual affairs"—that is, being killed through other than official, military actions—actually is. Examples of this sort of killing are legion and span the entire geography of the United States, but the worst cases seem to have occurred in Texas and northern California/southern Oregon. In Texas, which once accommodated a greater diversity of native cultures than any other region of North America, "the facts of history are plain: Most Texas Indians were exterminated or brought to the brink of oblivion by Spaniards, Mexicans, Texans, and Americans who often had no more regard for the life of an Indian than they had for that of a dog, sometimes less."[72] From its inception, the Republic of Texas placed a bounty upon the scalp of any Indian brought in to a government office—man, woman, or child, no matter what "tribe"—no questions asked. The situation improved little, if at all, once Texas became a state.[73]

Under such conditions, the explorer Jean Louis Berlandier, who visited the area during 1828 and '29, reported that of the fifty-two separate indigenous nations encountered by René-Robert Cavelier de La Salle in 1685 only a scant handful remained in existence.[74] By 1890, after another sixty years of Texan and American "private enterprise," most of these were also gone. The 1890 U.S. Census found that the once populous Karankawans, Akokisa, Bidui, Tejas, and Coahuiltecans were entirely extinct. The Tonkawas, who had numbered over a thousand in 1800, were reduced to fifty-six. The Caddo had been reduced from 8,500 or more to barely 500; the Wichita from at least 3,500 to 358; the Kichai from as many as 1,000 to 66; the Lipan Apache from more than 500 to 60. The mighty Comanche Nation, which had numbered at least 7,000, could show no more than 1,598 survivors. Overall, the

19th century attrition of the indigenous population of Texas appears to have been in the mid-to-upper-80th percentile, much of it through the armed action of private individuals.[75] Further, simple computation shows the "body count" for Texas alone—at least 10,000 individuals, and more probably 15,000—to be greater than the entire U.S. aggregated estimate of native deaths by "individual affair" offered by the Bureau of the Census.

In California and Oregon, things were much worse. As Mooney acknowledged in 1910, "the enormous decrease [in California's native population] from about a quarter-million to less than 20,000 is due chiefly to the cruelties and wholesale massacres perpetrated by the miners and early settlers."[76] Actually, the original indigenous population of California was probably three times Mooney's estimate and still numbered about 300,000 in 1800. Sherburn F. Cook has compiled an excruciatingly detailed chronology of the actions of self-organized white "militias" in northern California, mostly along the Mad and Eel Rivers, for the years 1855-65. The standard technique was to surround an Indian village (or "rancheria," as they are called by Californians) in the dead of night, set it ablaze and, if possible, kill everyone inside.[77]

> Much of the killing in California and southern Oregon Territory resulted, directly and indirectly, from the discovery of gold in 1849 and the subsequent influx of miners and settlers. Newspaper accounts document the atrocities, as do oral histories of the California Indians today. It was not uncommon for small groups or villages to be attacked by immigrants...and virtually wiped out overnight.[78]

By 1864, Cook notes, "The policy was to wear the Indians down by 'keeping them moving, and preventing them from laying in supplies of food and ammunition.' Also by preventing the women and children from resting."[79] In reality, this was the tail end of the Californians' *ad hoc* extermination campaign, the main damage having already been done. Thornton has observed that, "Primarily because of the killings—which some scholars say had been...over 700,000—[the population] decreased almost by two-thirds in a single decade: from 100,000 in 1849 to 35,000 in 1860."[80] By 1900, the combined native population of California numbered only 15,377.[81] All told, perhaps 50,000 indigenous people had been systematically butchered during "individual affairs" in California during the second half of the 19th century. As Cook put it, "The record speaks for itself. No further commentary is necessary."[82]

Nadir and Recovery

In 1890, the federal government declared the period of conquest termed "Indian Wars" to be officially over. It also determined that only 248,253 identifiable Indians remained alive within its borders, with another 122,585 residing north of the border, in Canada.[83] After another decade of life under what amounted to martial law conditions, things had taken a marked turn for the worse in both countries: the census conducted in 1900 revealed only 237,196 Indians in the U.S., barely 101,000 in Canada.[84] By 1910, however, as the worst of the early reservation conditions passed in most locales, an overall population recovery became discernable: the U.S. Indian population for that year was recorded at 265,683, that of Canada at 108, 261.[85] The global flu epidemic of 1918 had a significant impact upon the U.S. native population, and is largely responsible for its decline to 244,437 by 1920.[86] However, by 1930, a surge to 333,397 had occurred, and the Native North American population has grown every decade since.[87]

It is impossible to ascertain the exact extent of indigenous population reduction reflected in these figures. Using Dobyns' maximal 18 million estimate of precontact Native North American people, the combined total of one-third of a million Indians alive in both the United States and Canada at the 1900 low point would indicate an overall attrition of over 99 percent. Kirkpatrick Sale's working number of 15 million produces a reduction figure in the 98th percentile. Thornton's minimum of 7 million yields a result of about 95 percent population loss between 1500 and 1900. Even the Mooney/Kroeber 1 million figure indicates a population loss of some two-thirds during the same 400 years. Surely, there can be no more monumental example of sustained genocide—certainly none involving a "race" of people as broad and complex as this—anywhere in the annals of human history.

Computing the extent of native population reduction at the hands of the United States per se is equally tricky. Dobyns offers little of use in this regard. Thornton asserts that only about 600,000 American Indians remained alive within the confines of the forty-eight states by 1800,[88] an estimate that would reflect an approximate two-thirds diminishment over the following century. His calculations in this regard are, however, suspect, not only on the basis of his general tendency to under-count, but because of his own earlier-quoted query as to whether a full half-million native people hadn't died as a result of the "Indian Wars" and more-or-less private campaigns of physical extermination. Following the proportional relationship (about 3:1) evident between his and Sale's precontact estimates, it is likely that somewhere between 1.5 and 1.8 million Indians still lived within the continental U.S. area at the time the "Founding Fathers" took over. The probability is thus that the U.S. destroyed 80 to 85 percent of "its" Indians during the first century of its existence.

Such dire numbers are readily borne out in the census data from states that still included substantial numbers of native people at the time of the American Revolution. In 1900, New Hampshire, for example, possessed a total Indian population of 22. Delaware could show only nine. Alabama had 177; Arkansas, 66; Connecticut, 153; Georgia, 19; Illinois, 16; Kentucky, 102; Massachusetts, 587; Ohio, 42; Rhode Island, 35; South Carolina, 121; Tennessee, 108; Texas, 470; and West Virginia, 12. There were five living Indians in New Jersey, and only three in Maryland.[89] By and large, such native people who remained had been confined to a dwindling quantity of reservation land—the total acreage dropped from about 150 million acres in 1885 to some 50 million acres in 1925—often left them because it was arid, semi-arid, or otherwise considered to be of little value to Euroamerican society. The Indian population of Arizona in 1900, for example, was recorded as being 26,480. South Dakota held another 19,834 Indians, while New Mexico contained 15,044 and Montana 11,343. 64,445 native people, representing at least 79 different indigenous nations, resided in the former "Permanent Indian Territory" of Oklahoma.[90]

During the second half of the 20th century, the aggregate Indian population within the United States has more-or-less regained its probable 1800 level. In 1950, the U.S. Bureau of the Census reported a total of 343,410 native people living in the forty-eight contiguous states and Alaska.[91] In 1960, the number had reached 523,591; by 1970, it had reached 792,730; and by 1980, it was about 1.4 million (see accompanying chart).[92] As of 1990, the unadjusted total of American Indians and Alaska natives exceeds 1.6 million.[93] Such resurgence does not, however, imply a reconstitution of traditional indigenous demographic patterns. Most noticeably, the deformities in physical circumstance imposed by colonial order have resulted in a situation in which formerly numerous peoples are now nonexistent or almost so, while some historically small peoples have become quite populous. For example, the Sioux (Lakota, Nakota, and Dakota combined), whose population was probably not greater than 35,000 in 1700, had increased to 78,588 by 1980. Similarly, the Chippewa, who may have numbered upwards of 40,000 in precontact times, had a population of 73,491 in the latter year. Other examples are even more spectacular. The Navajo, who are estimated to have numbered not more than 8,000 in 1680, had attained a population of 158,633.[94] The Cherokee, who are thought to have numbered perhaps 22,000 in 1650—albeit after being depleted by as much as 70 percent by smallpox and other diseases—had increased to more than 232,000 by 1980.[95]

Conversely, the Eastern Shawnee—who at their zenith probably numbered over 50,000—exhibited a 1980 population of just 335 (another 2,297 Absentee Shawnee are recorded). The Delaware, who were once at least as numerous as the Shawnee, weighed in with only 989 identified members. The Mandan, still at least 15,000 strong in 1738, and who numbered just 138 after the army-induced smallpox pandemic of 1837, were only up to 1,013 by 1980. In the same year, the Wyandotte, another formerly large people, could field only 440 identifiable members. The Miami showed only 350 members, the Ottawa a mere 336. At one time, there were probably upwards of 20,000 Peorias; in 1980, there were 355. The once populous Tonkawas of the Texas coast could claim only 212 members; the Iowas of the fertile Mississippi Basin, just 280. Other, smaller, peoples have also suffered dramatic and apparently permanent reduction: in 1980, the Walla Wallas had only 262 members remaining; the Kaws, 312; the Kallapuya, 65; the Modocs, 150; and the Yana had disappeared altogether.[96] Moreover, there are a minimum of 200 indigenous peoples who still exist to some extent, but who are not recognized as existing by the federal government. Their usually tiny memberships are consequently not tallied at all. Such persons are typically carried as "generic" Indians on census counts.[97]

Distribution of American Indians and Alaska
Natives by State, 1980

Alabama	7,502	Montana	37,598
Alaska	21,869	Nebraska	9,145
Arizona	152,498	Nevada	13,306
Arkansas	9,364	New Hampshire	1,297
California	198,275	New Jersey	8,176
Colorado	17,734	New Mexico	107,338
Connecticut	4,431	New York	38,967
Delaware	1,307	North Carolina	64,536
Florida	9,134	North Dakota	20,120
Georgia	7,442	Ohio	11,985
Hawaii	2,655	Oklahoma	169,292
Idaho	10,418	Oregon	26,591
Illinois	15,846	Pennsylvania	9,179
Indiana	7,682	Rhode Island	2,872
Iowa	5,369	South Carolina	5,665
Kansas	15,256	South Dakota	44,948
Kentucky	3,518	Tennessee	5,013
Louisiana	11,969	Texas	39,740
Maine	4,057	Utah	19,158
Maryland	7,823	Vermont	968
Massachusetts	7,100	Virginia	9,211
Michigan	39,734	Washington	58,186
Minnesota	34,831	West Virginia	1,555
Mississippi	6,131	Wisconsin	29,320
Missouri	12,129	Wyoming	7,057
		Washington, D.C.	996

Note: This information pertains only to *federally recognized Indians.*
Source: U.S. Bureau of the Census, *1980 Census of the Population, Supplementary Reports: American Indian Areas and Alaska Native Villages,* 1980, PC80-SI-13, U.S. Government Printing Office, Washington, D.C., 1984, Table 1, p. 14.

Dilution and Dispersal

Other factors strongly affect the demographic composition of contemporary Native North America. Chief among these are genetic and cultural dilution, and the extent of Indians' dispersal among non-Indian populations. In precontact times, of course, all natives of this continent were "full-blooded Indians," although the meaning of this is a bit nebulous. Insofar as indigenous North Americans defined themselves in terms of specific socio-cultural and political membership—that is, as Mohawks or Muscogees or Gros Ventres—rather than in terms of a racial category, the issue seems moot. This is all the more true in that "intertribal" marriages were always rather common, meaning that "mixed-bloodedness"—at least in traditional Indian terms—has always been normative. Traditional native societies were able to accommodate the regular influx of members of other indigenous nations, often adapting certain aspects of the newcomers' material and philosophical life to their own needs, without becoming culturally diluted. The mainstay of this timeless equilibrium had to do with the cohesion of Indian societies as discrete socio-cultural blocs, primarily because of the linkages of these blocs with specific geographical settings.

All of this changed with the European invasion, introduction of the concept of race as the definitive dimension of cultural membership, and obliteration of the traditional relationships between native peoples and the lands they occupied.[98] M. Annette Jaimes does a fine job of exposing the political and economic ramifications of the U.S. imposition of eugenics codes upon Native North America (see Chapter Four). As Russell Thornton frames the matter:

> During the twentieth century population recovery of American Indians there has been an increasing amount of mixture between them and non-Indian peoples. Data documenting this may be obtained from the 1910 and 1930 U.S. censuses of American Indians...In 1910 only 56.5 percent of American Indians enumerated in the United States were full-blood—150,053 out of 265,683— with the blood quantum of 8.4 percent (22,207) not reported...In the U.S. census of 1930, however, 46.3 percent—153,933 out of 332,397—were enumerated as full-bloods and 42.4 percent (141,101) were enumerated as mixed-bloods, with the degree of Indian blood of 11.2 percent (37,363) not reported. Thus, whereas American Indian population size increased by slightly over 66,000 from 1910 to 1930, the number of full-blood American Indians increased by only 4,000; most of the increase was among mixed-blood Indians.[99]

There was and is considerable disparity in full-blood/mixed-blood proportionality within specific indigenous nations. The Pimas, for example, showed a 98.6 percent proportion of full-bloods in 1910, and 97.9 percent proportion in 1930. The Arapaho, on the other hand, showed a 92.4 percent full-blood proportion in 1910, but this had dropped to 75.2 percent by 1930. 75.2 percent of Yokuts were full-bloods in 1910, but only 41.4 percent in 1930; while the Chippewas began in 1910 with only a 34.5 percent proportion of full-bloods, a proportion which had fallen to 18.7 percent by 1930.[100] These trends have, in most cases, continued for the past sixty years, as is evidenced by the high rates of marriage and childbearing between Indians and non-Indians. By 1970, an even 65 percent of all marriages of American Indian males were to non-Indian women; for native females, the rate of marriage to non-Indian men was 62 percent.[101] By 1980, more than half of all Indians above age sixteen were married to non-Indians (this is as compared to 1 percent of Euroamericans and 2 percent of African Americans married to members of other racial groups).[102] Further, as of 1970:

> [B]arely three-fifths of all births registered as Indian list both parents as Indians [of some degree of native blood]. More than one-fourth of the remaining Indian births had only an Indian mother, and 15 percent had only an Indian father...The number of Indian children born to two Indian parents declined from 66 percent in 1965 to 59 percent in 1968.[103]

Given continuation of only the *present* rates of intermarriage and birth among Indians and non-Indians—a rate that has been increasing throughout the 20th century—the proportion of the currently recognized Indian population with one-quarter or less "degree of Indian blood" may be expected to rise from 4 percent in 1980 to 59 percent in 2080.[104] What is tremendously important about this phenomenon is that quarter-blood is typically the level below which the federal government withdraws recognition that a person is Indian. This official posture is now reflected in the sensibilities of popular American culture and, unfortunately, among many native people as well.[105] Under such circumstances, as Jaimes notes in her essay, the prospect of the "statistical extermination" of Native North America has become very much a contemporary reality, replacing the more physically violent forms of genocide evidenced in earlier periods.

Further, the federal government has persistently and deliberately utilized the "full-blood/mixed-blood" dichotomy it has contrived as a means to destroy the unity and undermine the cultural integrity of indigenous societies. In simplest terms, this has amounted to a long-term policy of rewarding those of mixed racial ancestry, especially those of some Indian-white admixture, while penalizing those of fully Indian genetic composition. At least as early as its 1830 Treaty with the Sauk and Fox, the government began to extend special advantages to mixed-bloods; full-bloods were required to leave Illinois by the end of the decade while mixed bloods were not. In the 1858 Treaty with the Poncas, all full-bloods were required to relocate from their traditional homeland to a small reservation in Oklahoma while "their half-breed relatives" were not.[106] In its 1865 Treaty with the Blackfoot Nation of Indians, the government made it clear that:

> The half-breeds of the tribes, parties to the treaty, and those persons citizens of the United States, who have intermarried with Indian women, of said tribes, and continue to maintain domestic relations with them, shall not be compelled to remove to said reservation but shall be allowed to remain undisturbed upon the lands herein ceded and relinquished to the United States.

Under provision of the 1887 General Allotment Act, all full-bloods were tightly restricted to small land parcels and, as legally defined "incompetents," expressly denied control over them for a minimum of twenty-five years. Mixed-bloods, on the other hand, were often allotted much larger parcels, often in better areas, and with immediate full control over their property.[107] Such processes, which are ongoing in many ways, served to foster deep divisions within most native societies over the years. Moreover, such policies have always been intentionally deculturating. The message was and is clear: advantage (and sometimes even survival itself) lies in abandoning one's own traditions in favor of alignment with and ultimately becoming part of the dominant culture. While the correlation is hardly perfect, there is a pronounced correspondence between mixed-bloodedness and deculturation. The extent to which such "detribalization" has occurred may be detected in the fact that, by 1970, only 32 percent of all American Indians could claim any degree of fluency in their own languages.[108]

Propelling the dilution of Native North America during the late 20th century has been a complex of long-range federal policies forcing a massive dispersal of Indian population. Under the General Allotment Act, the reserved indigenous land base inside the U.S. was reduced to an area barely adequate to support the then existing native population. As the Indian population began to increase significantly during the 1920s and '30s, it rapidly began to outstrip the reservation acreage available to accommodate it, a matter which set off an initial "outflow" of Indians from the reservations, primarily into non-Indian rural areas.[109] Continued population increase and the imposition of military conscription upon native people during the Second World War escalated the outflow trend, but with its destination shifting toward urban areas.[110] Then, in the 1950s, with the onset of formal federal relocation programs, the flow became a flood.[111] The outflow trend has all along been reinforced by policies designed to make the living conditions of reservation Indians by far the worst of any ethnic group in North America.[112]

In 1890, the Census Bureau reported virtually no Indians living in cities, a figure that had changed little by 1900 (to 0.4 percent). By 1930, the proportion had jumped to 9.9 percent and was becoming significant. By 1950, it had risen to 13.4 percent. After the first decade of systematic federal relocation, more than a quarter of all Indians, 27.9 percent, were urban-dwellers. Another decade of such programming nearly doubled the total, bringing it up to 44.5 percent. Abandonment of the relocation effort during the 1970s caused a substantial drop-off in the rate at which Indians left their reservations, with the result that the 1980 urban total reflected an increase to 49 percent.[113] Still, by 1990, more than half of all American Indians live in urban areas where they are simply engulfed by vastly larger non-Indian populations.[114] As of 1980, the fifteen U.S. cities with the largest Native American populations were the Los Angeles Metropolitan Area (90,689), Tulsa (38,463), Oklahoma City (24,695), Phoenix (22,778), Albuquerque (20,721), San Francisco-Oakland (17,546), Minneapolis-St. Paul (15,831), Seattle Metropolitan Area (15,162), Tucson (14,880), San Diego (14,355), New York City (13,440), Detroit (12,372), Dallas-Ft. Worth (11,076), Sacramento (10,944), and Chicago (10,415).[115]

This federally contrived diaspora of native people does not tell the whole story. Even American Indian reservations are no longer enclaves within which indigenous cultures are necessarily safe from encroachment and dilution. As Indians have been increasingly forced to leave their reservations for cities during the late 20th century, non-Indians have been steadily moving in. By 1980, largely as a result of Bureau of

Indian Affairs leasing practices, non-Indians often outnumbered Indians—sometimes by considerable margins—on the reservations themselves. In the state of Washington, for example, only 20.8 percent of the 79,043 reservation residents were Indian. While some reservations such as Kalispel (92.5 percent Indian), Port Gamble (88.1 percent), and Shoalwater (84.8 percent) still evidenced decisive native majorities, others such as Puyallup (3.4 percent), Fort Madison (4.3 percent), Muckleshoot (12.5 percent), and Tulalip (15.2 percent) found Indians being numerically overwhelmed on their own land. Even the Yakima Reservation, the largest in Washington, had only a 19.6 percent Indian population.[116]

Elsewhere, the situation is often the same or worse. While, in 1980, 83.8 percent of Nevada's reservation residents were Indians, only 30.3 percent of those in California were. In Arizona the proportion was 88 percent Indian, and in New Mexico it was 72.9 percent—but in Wyoming it was only 18 percent, in Idaho, 17.2 percent, and in Utah, 31.2 percent. Only 12.1 percent of reservation residents in Oklahoma—traditionally the state with the greatest Indian population—were native people in 1980. In Louisiana, the figure was 15.2 percent, and in Michigan, it was only 5.9 percent. While 30 (90.9 percent) of Georgia's 33 reservation residents and 96.2 percent of Mississippi's 2,866 were Indians, only 36.3 percent of Florida's 3,593 reservation residents and 28.6 percent of Colorado's 6,877 were native people. In several "Indian" states such as South Dakota (58.4 percent), Oregon (61.1 percent) and North Dakota (60.1 percent), the proportion was almost equal. They were joined by New York, with 48.2 percent, and Connecticut, with 43.5 percent of its 62 inhabitants. Just 38.8 percent of Minnesota's sizable reservation population was Indian, however, and only 30 percent of Nebraska's. Wisconsin weighed in with 39 percent of 24,017 reservation residents, and Maine with 86.4 percent of 1,430.[117]

Manipulation and Confusion

The future of Native North America appears hazy in many ways. This is not accidental. As has been detailed elsewhere, deliberate low-counting is still going on through official census information-gathering, which has been carefully skewed away from recording Indians, even when they clearly meet the federal government's genetic criteria of "Indian-ness."[118] As the Bureau of the Census itself has acknowledged,

> The category 'white' includes persons who indicated their race as white, as well as persons who did not classify themselves in one of the specific race categories on the questionnaire but entered Mexican, Puerto Rican, or a response suggesting Indo-European stock...Persons of Spanish origin are those persons who indicated that their origin was Mexican, Puerto Rican, Cuban, Central or South American, or other Spanish origin...93.3 percent of all persons of Spanish origin were reported as white.[119]

In a survey carried out in March, 1971, the Census Bureau tells us that

> "white" includes almost all persons reporting Spanish origin. About 97 percent

of persons of Spanish origin, about 99 percent of persons of Mexican origin, and 96 percent of persons of Puerto Rican origin were classified white in this survey.[120]

Essentially, the remaining few percent were classified as "black," a designation reflecting the means of manipulating indigenous population counts in U.S. domestic locales such as North Carolina for generations.[121] In a 1979 census update, only 26,859 (0.3 percent) "Hispanic Surnamed" individuals were classified as Indians, with 23,172 of them having been born in the United States. A large portion of these were of the various Southwestern Pueblos, southern California Mission Bands (Juaneño, Luiseño, etc.), O'Odham Nation (Pima, Papago, etc.), and other indigenous North American peoples who had been endowed with the requisite names through earlier Spanish/Mexican colonization. Thus, just 3,678 of new "Spanish" arrivals in the U.S. were recognized as being Indian. Meanwhile, only 15,988 (1.9 percent) of all Mexican-American citizens or resident aliens were officially reported as being Indian by race.[122] The idea that "Mexicans," a population *primarily* deriving from Indian "stock"—only about 200,000 Europeans and 250,000 Africans having immigrated to Mexico by 1810, and almost none since—should be almost exclusively categorized as being of "Indo-European stock" in the United States tends to speak for itself.[123]

So too does it speak to notions that an Indian from north of the Río Grande marrying a person from south of that river has engaged in "interracial marriage," and that their children or children's children will inevitably become ethnic "non-Indians" if such intermarriage persists. Ultimately, there may have been more than 7 million Indians—by even the government's conservative definition—in the United States in 1980, rather than the less than 1.4 million evident in the "corrected" census for that year.[124] The real numbers may run far higher:

Since at least 1969, the Bureau of the Census, conspiring with the Office of Management and Budget and political special interests, has made a mess of understanding the "racial" character of the U.S. population and, as part of that process, has "lost" some six to eight million persons of Native American ancestry and appearance with a scientifically useless "Hispanic/Spanish" category. In addition, [as many as 7 million] persons of mixed African and Native American ancestry remain uncounted as such because of the way census questions were asked and answers tallied.[125]

While such statistical sleight of hand undoubtedly serves the interests of the status quo by way of its desire to avoid assuming the full burden of its obligations to contemporary American Indians in terms of social services, educational benefits and the like—as well as effectively negating the possibility of viable indigenous power blocs emerging within any off-reservation political arena—it has also engendered considerable confusion among native people themselves.[126] Indeed, in many modern Indian communities, it appears that far more time and energy has come to be spent endlessly debating exclusivist and divisive questions as to "who's Indian enough to be Indian"—that is, endlessly squabbling with one another in a way that diminishes our potential strength, both numerically and in terms of unity—than with confronting the governmental and corporate sources of our mutual oppression.

The Future of Native North America

In many ways, the future of Native North America hinges on the posing of a lengthy series of questions. The first, and perhaps most important, issue is whether American Indians will continue to allow themselves to be defined mainly by their colonizers, in exclusively racial/familial terms (as "tribes"), or whether they will (re)assume responsibility for advancing the more general and coherently political definition of themselves they once held, as *nations* defining membership/citizenship in terms of culture, socialization, and commitment to the good of the group. Put another way, the central question is whether Indians can recover in any meaningful way their age-old and inclusive traditions of bringing "outsiders"—whether from other native peoples, or from entirely different races—into their membership by way of marriage, birth, adoption, and naturalization.

If the answers to such queries are negative, then the coming century will surely see the disappearance of large portions of what is and has been recognizably Native North American from the panorama of humanity. Racialist definitions may perhaps be workable, at least to some extent, within the contexts presented by certain small and highly insular indigenous peoples such as the Havasupai, Pima, and Walapai, each of whom continues to exhibit more than 60 percent proportions of their populations with full blood (although whether this is full-blooded Havasupai, Pima, or Walapai, or simply "full-blooded Indian" of some sort is unclear). On the other hand, to make genetics the defining criterion for continuation of much larger peoples such as the Chippewa, whose overall proportion of full-bloods is now probably below 5 percent (certainly below 10 percent) no matter how the term is defined, would be quite literally suicidal.

Such considerations raise obvious questions concerning what will become of traditional native cultures, given a substantial influx of persons—including genetic Indians deculturated in urban environments—into the social settings necessary to their continued functioning. The answer, or part of it, may well lie in the experience of the Oklahoma Cherokees:

> In developing a new tribal constitution in the 1970s...the Cherokee Nation of Oklahoma, unlike [most others], established no minimum blood quantum for membership. Instead, one must only trace descent along Cherokee lines...This comparatively generous definition has expanded the Cherokee Nation of Oklahoma population: in the mid-1970s there were only about 12,000 enrolled Cherokee in the Cherokee Nation of Oklahoma; in 1985, there were over 64,300...There are still full-blood and traditional Cherokee, despite the myth in Oklahoma, and elsewhere, of Cherokee assimilation. In the 1960s there were approximately 9,500 Cherokee living in over 50 Cherokee settlements in northeastern Oklahoma, and some 2,000 more living in Indian enclaves in

towns and small cities. These people spoke mainly Cherokee, were extremely traditional in outlook, and kept alive important Cherokee ceremonies. They continue in the 1980s, insulated from American society by the much larger number of mixed bloods and less traditional Cherokee...The Oklahoma Cherokee, without a reservation land base, have thus been able to survive tribally by an inclusive definition of what it is to be Cherokee...This allowed the [nation] to reestablish itself after virtual "dissolution" and to achieve political power in Oklahoma. [The newly admitted membership] has protected a smaller group of full-blood, more traditional Cherokee from the American way of life.[127]

Hence, it is demonstrably possible to be inclusive without eradicating traditionalism. In fact, the principle of calculated inclusiveness would seem to be the only means by which to develop increasingly substantial polities, rather than smaller and smaller ones, informed by genuinely traditional American Indian perspectives (not the ersatz variety discussed by Wendy Rose in Chapter Fourteen). The question of land recovery is, of course, begged in the preceding observation. It is, to be sure, absolutely crucial to any broadly conceived strategy of inclusivity aimed at maintaining and revitalizing Native North America. Over the long run, no nation, Cherokee or otherwise, can sustain itself without a land base—and real control over the resources of that land base—adequate to support its people. But it is equally true that this rule applies as much to small peoples as to larger ones, and that U.S. colonialism has proven itself especially adept at relieving small groups of control over their territories. It seems self-evident that larger, more unified, native peoples stand a much better prospect of wresting their lands—reserved, treatied, and aboriginal—from the clutches of the Euroamerican status quo than small and fragmentary ones.

Instead of a final demise, it is entirely possible that the next 100 years could see a veritable rebirth of a Native North America, one that is autonomous, self-determining, and self-defining, one in which indigenous laws and the indigenous world view once again hold sway over the ways in which people inhabit the environment of this continent. It is a very long way from here to there, and the precise routes taken to the goal will unquestionably be many, perhaps as many as there are native peoples remaining in existence at the present time. The point is, however, that there is the possibility. Where there is possibility, there is hope that provides the core of motivation to struggle. In a way, this has been the history of the native peoples of this land for the past three centuries and more: always envisioning the possibilities that rest beyond the realm of the lies that have been imposed upon us, always struggling to attain a future for our children that is better and more true than the one we have been forced to inherit. Contrary to the non-Indian academics who have been predicting that we were on the verge of vanishing for the past 150 years, we are still here. We take pride in our survival against all odds. And we take heart in the vision which is our future.

Notes

1. Jennings, Francis, *The Invasion of America: Indians, Colonialism, and the Cant of Conquest*, W.W. Norton Company, New York, 1976, p. 15.
2. Ibid.
3. For analysis of the implications of this point, see Banks, James A., *Teaching Strategies for Ethnic Studies*, Allyn and Bacon, Inc., Boston/London/Sydney/Toronto, (fourth edition) 1987, pp. 57-79.
4. Mooney, James M., *The Aboriginal Population of America North of Mexico*, Smithsonian Miscellaneous Collections, LXXX, No. 7, Smithsonian Institution, Washington, D.C., 1928, p. 3.
5. Palfrey, John Gorham, *History of New England*, Vol. I, Stine Publishers, Boston, 1854-1890, p. 24.
6. An early assessment of the political implications of this may be found in Pearce, Roy Harvey, *The Savages of America: A Study of the Indian and the Idea of Civilization*, Johns Hopkins University Press, Baltimore, 1965. Also see Thomas, Peter A., "Contrastive Subsistence Strategies and Land Use as Factors for Understanding Indian-White Relations in New England," *Ethnohistory*, No. 23, 1976, pp. 1-18.
7. Kroeber, Alfred Louis, *Cultural and Natural Areas of Native North America*, University of California Publications in American Archaeology and Ethnology, No. 38, University of California Press, Berkeley, 1939. Further details concerning Kroeber's reduction of Mooney's California population estimates will be found in the former's preliminary study, "Native American Population," *American Anthropologist*, No. 36, 1925, pp. 1-25.
8. Kroeber, Alfred Louis, *Anthropology*, Macmillan Publishers, New York, 1948. For an elaboration of the author's more openly ideological motives in his handling of Native American demography, see his essay "Evolution, History and Culture," in Theodora Kroeber, ed., *A.L. Kroeber: An Anthropologist Looks at History*, University of California Press, Berkeley/Los Angeles, 1966.
9. Swanton, John Reed, *The Indian Tribes of North America*, Smithsonian Institution, Bureau of American Ethnology, Bulletin 145, U.S. Government Printing Office, Washington, D.C., 1952.
10. Driver, Harold E., *The Indians of North America*, University of Chicago Press, Chicago, 1961. Also see Driver, Harold E., and William C. Massey, *Comparative Studies of American Indians*, American Philosophical Society, Transactions, N.S., XLVII, 1957.
11. See Revolutionary Communist Party, USA, "In Search of the Second Harvest," in Ward Churchill, ed., *Marxism and Native Americans*, South End Press, Boston, 1983, pp. 35-58.
12. Domenech, Emmanuel Henri Dieudonné, *Seven Years Residence in the Great Deserts of North America*, Longman, Green, Longman and Roberts Publishers, London, 1860.
13. Spinden, Herbert J., "The Population of Ancient America," *Geographical Review*, No. 18, 1928, pp. 640-60.
14. The estimate accrues from Borah, Woodrow W., "America as Model: The Impact of European Expansion Upon the Non-European World," in *Actas y Memorias, XXXV Congreso Internacional de Americanistas, Mexico, 1962*, Vol. III, Editorial Libros de Mexico, Mexico City, 1964, pp. 379-87. For details on methodology, see Borah, Woodrow W., and Sherburn F. Cook, "The Aboriginal Population of Central Mexico on the Eve of the Spanish Conquest," *Ibero-Americana* No. 43, University of California Press, Berkeley, 1963; "New Demographic Research on the Sixteenth Century in Mexico," in Howard F. Cline, ed., *Latin American History: Essays on Its Study and Teaching, 1898-1965*, Vol. II, University of Texas Press, Austin, 1967, pp. 717-22; "Conquest and Population: A Demographic Approach to Mexican History," *Proceedings of the American Philosophical Society*, No. 113, 1969, pp. 177-83. Also see Cook, Sherburn F., and Leslie B. Simpson, "The Population of Central Mexico in the Sixteenth Century," *Ibero-Americana* No. 31, University of California Press, Berkeley, 1948.
15. Dobyns, Henry F., "Estimating Aboriginal American Population: An Appraisal of Techniques with a New Hemispheric Estimate," *Current Anthropology*, No. 7, 1966, pp. 395-416. For a comprehensive examination of demographic research on precontact Native America done up to the point of publication, see Dobyns, Henry F., *Native American Historical Demography: A Critical Bibliography*, Indiana University Press, Bloomington, 1976.
16. Jacobs, Wilbur R., "The Tip of an Iceberg: Precolumbian Indian Demography and Some

48 The State of Native America

Implications for Revisionism," *William and Mary Quarterly*, 3rd Series, No. 31, 1974, pp. 123-32.

17. See, for example, Sauer, Carl O., *Sixteenth Century North America*, University of California Press, Berkeley, 1971.
18. Ubelaker, Douglas H., "Prehistoric New World Population Size: Historical Review and Current Appraisal of North American Estimates," *American Journal of Physical Anthropology*, No. 45, 1976, pp. 661-6. Also see his "The Sources and Methodology for Mooney's Estimates of North American Indian Populations," in William H. Denevan, ed., *The Native Population of the Americas in 1492*, University of Wisconsin Press, Madison, 1976.
19. Dobyns, Henry F., *Their Numbers Become Thinned: Native American Population Dynamics in Eastern North America*, University of Tennessee Press, Knoxville, 1983. See especially the essay "The Native American Paradise Lost," pp. 34-45.
20. Ibid., p. 41.
21. Ibid., p. 42.
22. Ibid.
23. Thornton, Russell, *American Indian Holocaust and Survival: A Population History Since 1492*, University of Oklahoma Press, Norman, 1987; linkage to Ubelaker occurs at pp. 28-9, 5 million plus population estimate at p. xvii, Canada/Alaska estimate at p. 242. It is worth noting that Thornton has elsewhere conceded that the precontact indigenous population may well have been higher than that which he allows in his book; see his "American Indian Historical Demography: A Review Essay with Suggestions for Future Research," *American Indian Culture and Research Journal*, No. 3, 1979, pp. 69-74.
24. See Henige, David, "Their Numbers Become Thick: Native American Historical Demography as Expiation," in James E. Clifton, ed., *The Invented Indian: Cultural Fictions and Government Policies*, Transaction Books, Princeton University, 1990. Henige's qualifications to address Native American subject matters seem largely nonexistent: he is an *Africanist* librarian at the University of Wisconsin. He stole the idea for his title from Thornton, Russell, "But How Thick Were They? Review Essay on *Their Number Become Thinned*," *Contemporary Sociology*, No. 13, 1984, pp. 145-59.
25. For a sampling of such evidence, see Casteel, Richard W., "A Sample of Northern American Hunter-Gatherers and the Malthusian Thesis: An Explicitly Quantified Approach," in David L. Bowman, ed., *Early Native Americans*, Mouton Publishers, The Hague, Netherlands, 1980, pp. 301-19.
26. Sale, Kirkpatrick, *The Conquest of Paradise: Christopher Columbus and the Columbian Legacy*, Alfred A. Knopf Publishers, New York, 1990.
27. See Hirsch, E.D., *Cultural Literacy: What Every American Needs to Know*, Houghton-Mifflin Co., New York, 1987; and D'Souza, Dinesh, *Illiberal Education: The Politics of Race and Sex on Campus*, The Free Press, New York, 1991.
28. The notion that "non-Western" history is other than "meaningful" is often articulated quite straightforwardly by white supremacist "intellectuals." See, as examples, Hart, Jeffrey, "Discovering Columbus," *National Review*, October 15, 1990, pp. 56-7; and Krauthammer, Charles, "Hail Columbus, Dead White Male," *Time*, May 27, 1991, p. 74. For a recounting of Secretary Bennett's contribution to discourse on "scholarly methods and content," see McCurdy, Jack, "Bennett Calls Stanford Curriculum Revision Capitulation to Pressure," *The Chronicle of Higher Education*, April 27, 1988, p. A-2.
29. For the best explanation of the Norman Yoke concept within Anglo-Saxon international legal theory, see Williams, Robert A. Jr., *The American Indian in Western Legal Thought: The Discourses of Conquest*, Oxford University Press, London/New York, 1990, pp. 233-75.
30. Locke's elaboration on the Norman Yoke comes in his *Second Treatise of Government;* see Macpherson, Crawford Brough, *The Political Theory of Possessive Individualism: Hobbes to Locke*, Oxford University Press, London/New York, 1962.
31. On the philosophical threads in Marshall's *McIntosh* opinion, see Williams, op. cit., pp. 312-7.
32. The framework of understanding of "Just War," as intended here, accrues from the work of the Spanish legal theorist Franciscus de Victoria during the mid-16th century. See Scott, James Brown, *The Spanish Origin of International Law*, Oxford University Press, London/New York, 1934.
33. For an excellent elucidation of how the mythology evolved, see Drinnon, Richard, *Facing West: The Metaphysics of Indian Hating and Empire Building*, Schocken Books, New York, 1980.

34. Weatherford, Jack, *Indian Givers: How the Indians of the Americas Transformed the World*, Fawcett Columbine Publishers, New York, 1988, pp. 231-2.

35. Fowler, Melvin T., "A Pre-Columbian Urban Center on the Mississippi," *Scientific American*, No. 233, 1975, pp. 92-101.

36. O'Brien, Patricia, "Urbanism, Cahokia and Middle Mississippian," *Archaeology*, No. 25, 1972, pp. 188-97.

37. See "Settlement Demography," in *Their Numbers Become Thinned*, op. cit., pp. 190-211.

38. See Mays, Buddy, *Ancient Cities of the Southwest*, Chronicle Books, San Francisco, 1982. Also see Nabokov, Peter, and Robert Eastman, *Native American Architecture*, Oxford University Press, London/New York, 1988. For further information on the technical basis for these agricultural civilizations, see Masse, J.J., "Prehistoric Irrigation in the Salt River Valley, Arizona," *Science*, No. 214, 1981, p. 408; and Betancourt and Van Devender, "Holocene Vegetation in Chaco Canyon, New Mexico," *Science*, No. 214, 1981, p. 656.

39. Spinden, H.K., "Population of Ancient America," *Anthropological Report*, Smithsonian Institution, U.S. Government Printing Office, Washington, D.C., 1929.

40. Jaimes, M. Annette, "The Stone Age Revisited: An Indigenist View of Primitivism, Industrialism and the Labor Process," *New Studies on the Left*, Vol. XIV, No. 3, Winter 1990-1991, pp. 57-70. Also see Josephy, Alvin, *The Indian Heritage of America*, American Heritage Publishers, New York, 1968; and Holmes, G.K., "Aboriginal Agriculture—American Indians," L.H. Bailey, ed., *Cyclopedia of American Agriculture: A Popular Survey of Agricultural Conditions, Practices, and Ideals in the United States and Canada*, Vol. IV, New York, 1909.

41. On planting techniques and related matters, see "Indian Agricultural Technology," in Weatherford, op. cit., pp. 79-97. Also see Stea, Vikki, "High-Yield Corn from Ancient Seed Strains," *Christian Science Monitor*, August 20, 1989, p. 29.

42. See, for example, Herndon, G. Melvin, "Indian Agriculture in the Southern Colonies," *North Carolina Historical Review*, XLVI, 1967, pp. 283-97; and Russell, Howard S., "New England Indian Agriculture," *Bulletin of the Massachusetts Archaeological Society*, XXII, April-May 1961, pp. 58-91.

43. For elaboration of the basic principles involved, albeit in a somewhat different context, see Gleissman, S.R.R. Garcia, and M.F. Amador, "The Ecological Basis for Application of Traditional Agricultural Technology in the Management of Tropical Ecosystems," *Agro-Ecosystems*, No. 7, 1981.

44. On indigenous trading and highway systems in North America, see "The Pathfinders," in Weatherford, op. cit., pp. 235-48.

45. For the commencement of use of such tactics against the Conoy, Pamunkey, and other indigenous nations of the Virginia area, see Quinn, David Beers, ed., *The Two Roanoke Voyages, 1584-1590*, Haklyt Society Publications, 2d Ser., CIV-CV, London, 1955. On the Kit Carson Campaign, during which the Navajo orchards and other agricultural enterprises centered in Cañon De Chelly (Arizona) were deliberately destroyed, see Bailey, L.R., *The Long Walk*, Western Lore Press, Los Angeles, 1964; and Kelly, Lawrence, *Navajo Roundup*, Pruett Publishing Co., Boulder, CO, 1970. In his *Historical Recollections of Ohio*, published privately in two volumes, dated 1889 and 1891, respectively, the historian Henry Howe recounts how General George Rogers Clark, during a 1780 expedition, destroyed "five hundred acres...of corn and every species of edible vegetable...[serving as primary food source for]...two Shawnee towns, Chillicothe and Piqua." General "Mad Anthony" Wayne, after the battle of Fallen Timbers in 1794, reported doing a more thorough job on the Shawnees, burning "fifty miles" of corn fields laid out on either side of the Maumee River. At about the same time, General John Sullivan was conducting a scorched earth campaign against the Six Nations Iroquois Confederacy in up-state New York, during which "many thousands of acres" of Iroquois fields full of corn and other crops were burned. For further details of the process, see Cronon, William, *Changes in the Land: Indians, Colonists and the Ecology of New England*, Hill and Wang Publishers, New York, 1983.

46. *American Indian Holocaust and Survival*, op. cit., pp. 44-5. Also see Ashburn, Percy M., *The Ranks of Death* Coward and McCann Publishers, New York, 1947; and Marks, Geoffrey, and William K. Beatty, *Epidemics*, Charles Scribner's Sons, Publishers, New York, 1967.

47. *Their Numbers Become Thinned*, op. cit., pp. 9-16.

48. Ibid., pp. 15-23.

49. *American Indian Holocaust and Survival*, op. cit., p. 45. Thornton is quoting from *Their Numbers Become Thinned*, op. cit., p. 24.

50. See Cook, Sherburn F., "The Significance of Disease in the Extinction of the New England Indians," *Human Biology*, No. 45, 1973, pp. 485-508.
51. Stearn, E. Wagner, and Allen E. Stearn, *The Effects of Smallpox on the Destiny of the Amerindian*, Bruce Humphries, Inc., Boston, 1945, pp. 44-5.
52. Ibid., p. 45.
53. *American Indian Holocaust and Survival*, op. cit., p. 78. Thornton is quoting from Stearn and Stearn, op. cit., p. 38.
54. Stearn and Stearn, op. cit., p. 49. Also see Duffy, John, "Smallpox and the Indians in the American Colonies," *Bulletin of the History of Medicine*, No. 25, 1951, pp. 324-41; and *Epidemics in Colonial America*, Louisiana State University Press, Baton Rouge, 1953.
55. The blankets were taken from a U.S. Army infirmary in St. Louis and sent upriver on the steamer *St. Peter's*. They were distributed by army personnel on June 19, 1837. See Chardon, Francis A., *Journal at Fort Clark, 1834-39*, State Historical Society of South Dakota, Pierre, 1932.
56. *American Indian Holocaust and Survival*, op. cit., p. 95. He is relying mainly on Stearn and Stearn, op. cit., p. 94; and Schoolcraft, Henry R., *Personal Memoirs of a Residence of Thirty Years With the Indian Tribes of the Frontiers: With Brief Notes of Passing Events, Facts, and Opinions, A.D. 1812 to A.D. 1842*, Lippincott, Grambo & Co., Publishers, Philadelphia, 1851.
57. See Hornaday, William T., *Exterminating the American Bison*, Smithsonian Institution, U.S. Government Printing Office, Washington, D.C., 1899. Also see McHugh, Tom, with Victoria Hobson, *The Time of the Buffalo*, Alfred A. Knopf Publishers, New York, 1972.
58. Mooney, James, *Historical Sketch of the Cherokee*, Aldine Publishing Co., Chicago, (reprint of 1900 edition) 1975, p. 127.
59. Thornton, Russell, "Cherokee Population Losses During the Trail of Tears: A New Perspective and a New Estimate," *Ethnohistory*, No. 31, 1984, pp. 289-300.
60. Ibid., p. 293.
61. See Kelly, op. cit.
62. 1863 U.S. government policy pronouncement, quoted in Johnston, Denis Foster, *An Analysis of Sources of Information on the Population of the Navajo*, Bureau of American Ethnology, Bulletin No. 197, U.S. Government Printing Office, Washington, D.C., 1966, p. 23.
63. Salmon, Roberto Mario, "The Disease Complaint at Bosque Redondo (1864-68)," *The Indian Historian*, No. 9, 1976, pp. 1-7.
64. Johansson, S. Ryan, and S.H. Preston, "Tribal Demography: The Navajo and Hopi Populations as Seen Through Manuscripts from the 1900 U.S. Census," *Social Science History*, No. 3, 1978, pp. 1-33.
65. On the Coronado and de Soto expeditions, see Spicer, Edward, *A Short History of the Indians of the United States*, Van Nostrum Publishers, New York, 1960. Also see Gibson, Charles, ed., *The Spanish Tradition in America*, Harper and Row Publishers, New York, 1968.
66. The estimate of Pequot casualties derives from an extremely conservative source. See Utley, Robert M., and Wilcomb E. Washburn, *Indian Wars*, Houghton-Mifflin Co., Boston, 1977, p. 42.
67. For an excellent study of official language in this regard, see Svaldi, David, *Sand Creek and the Rhetoric of Extermination: A Case-Study in Indian-White Relations*, University Press of America, Lanham, MD, 1989.
68. On Blue River, see Sandoz, Mari, *Crazy Horse: Strange Man of the Oglalas*, University of Nebraska Press, Lincoln, 1961, pp. 63-85; on Bear River, see Madsen, Brigham D., *The Shoshone Frontier and the Bear River Massacre*, University of Utah Press, Salt Lake City, 1985; on Sand Creek, see Hoig, Stan, *The Sand Creek Massacre*, University of Oklahoma Press, Norman, 1961; on the Washita, see Hoig, Stan, *The Battle of the Washita: The Sheridan-Custer Campaign of 1868*, University of Nebraska Press, Lincoln, 1976; on Sappa Creek and Camp Robinson, see Sandoz, Mari, *Cheyenne Autumn*, Avon Books, New York, 1964, pp. 120-6, 190-228; on Wounded Knee, see Brown, Dee, *Bury My Heart At Wounded Knee: An Indian History of the American West*, Holt, Rinehart and Winston Publishers, New York, 1970, pp. 416-45.
69. U.S. Bureau of the Census, *Report on Indians Taxed and Indians Not Taxed in the United States (except Alaska) at the Eleventh U.S. Census: 1890*, U.S. Government Printing Office, Washington, D.C., 1894, pp. 637-8.
70. *American Indian Holocaust and Survival*, op. cit., p. 49.
71. Ibid.
72. Newcome, W.W. Jr., *The Indians of Texas*, University of Texas Press, Austin, 1961, p. 334.
73. Ewers, John C., "The Influence of Epidemics on the Indian Populations and Cultures of Texas,"

Plains Anthropologist, No. 18, 1973, pp. 104-15. Also see the various chapters on the indigenous peoples of Texas in Ortiz, Alfonso, ed., *Handbook of North American Indians,* Vols. 9 & 10, Smithsonian Institution, Washington, D.C., 1979 and 1983.

74. Berlandier, Jean Louis, *The Indians of Texas in 1830,* Smithsonian Institution, Washington, D.C., 1969, p. 100. Also see Aten, Lawrence E., *Indians of the Upper Texas Coast,* Academic Press, New York, 1983.

75. The census findings are summarized in Ewers, op. cit., p. 106.

76. Mooney, James, "Population," in Frederick W. Dodge, ed., *Handbook of the Indians North of Mexico,* Vol. 2, Bureau of American Ethnology, Bulletin No. 30, Smithsonian Institution, U.S. Government Printing Office, Washington, D.C., 1910, pp. 286-7.

77. Cook, Sherburn F., *The Conflict Between the California Indian and White Civilization,* University of California Press, Berkeley, 1976, pp. 282-4. He is drawing primarily from Bledsoe, Anthony J., *Indian Wars of the Northwest,* Bacon and Co. Publishers, San Francisco, 1885.

78. *American Indian Holocaust and Survival,* op. cit., p. 107. Also see Heizer, Robert F., ed., *The Destruction of the California Indians,* Peregrine Smith, Inc., Salt Lake City/Santa Barbara, 1974.

79. *The Conflict Between the California Indian and White Civilization,* op. cit., p. 284. Also see Coffer, William F., "Genocide of the California Indians," *The Indian Historian,* No. 10, 1977, pp. 8-15.

80. *American Indian Holocaust and Survival,* op. cit., p. 109.

81. U.S. Bureau of the Census, *Fifteenth Census of the United States, 1930: The Indian Population of the United States and Alaska,* U.S. Government Printing Office, Washington, D.C., 1937. See especially Table 2, "Indian Population by Divisions and States, 1890-1930," p. 3.

82. *The Conflict Between the California Indian and White Civilization,* op. cit., p. 284. For more on the history of the California/Oregon exterminations, see Caranco, Lynwood, and Estle Beard, *Genocide and Vendetta: The Round Valley Wars of Northern California,* University of Oklahoma Press, Norman, 1981; and Beckham, Steven Dow, *Requiem for a People: The Rogue River Indians and the Frontiersman,* University of Oklahoma Press, Norman, 1971.

83. The U.S. population figure accrues from *Fifteenth Census of the United States, 1930,* op. cit. The Canadian figure is taken from *Report on Indians Taxed and Indians Not Taxed,* op. cit.

84. The U.S. population figure accrues from *Fifteenth Census of the United States, 1930,* op. cit. The Canadian figure comes from Mooney's *The Aboriginal Population North of Mexico,* op. cit., p. 33. Mooney assigns a surviving native population of 54,200 to eastern Canada, 50,950 to central Canada, and 85,800 to British Columbia.

85. The U.S. population figure accrues from *Fifteenth Census of the United States, 1930,* op. cit. The Canadian figure comes from Mooney's *Population,* op. cit., p. 390. Also see U.S. Bureau of the Census, *Indian Population of the United States and Alaska, 1910,* U.S. Government Printing Office, Washington, D.C., 1915.

86. *Fifteenth Census of the United States, 1930,* op. cit. The 1918 world epidemic of influenza is estimated to have killed some 21 million people overall; see *The World Almanac and Book of Facts,* Newspaper Enterprise Association, New York, 1984; and Bunte, Pamela A., Robert Franklin, and Richard Stoffle, "Epidemics and Territorial Rearrangements: The San Juan Southern Paiutes and the 1918 Influenza Epidemic," unpublished paper presented at the 1083 National Historical Epidemiology Conference, Newberry Library, Chicago. Of further interest, see McNeill, William H., Plagues and Peoples, Anchor Doubleday Books, Garden City, NY, 1976.

87. Ibid. Figures pertaining to Indian population growth from 1940 through 1990 derive from each respective census.

88. *American Indian Holocaust and Survival,* op. cit., p. 90. Also see Thornton, Russell, and Joan Marsh-Thornton, "Estimating Prehistoric American Indian Population Size for the United States Area: Implications of the Nineteenth Century Population Decline and Nadir," *American Journal of Physical Anthropology,* No. 55, 1981, pp. 47-53.

89. *Fifteenth Census of the United States,* 1930, op. cit. Also see Prucha, Francis Paul, *Atlas of American Indian Affairs,* University of Nebraska Press, Lincoln, 1990.

90. *Fifteenth Census of the United States, 1930,* op. cit. Concerning diminishment of the reservation land base during the period in question, see McDonnell, Janet, *The Dispossession of the American Indian, 1887-1934,* Indiana University Press, Bloomington, 1991.

91. U.S. Bureau of the Census, *Census of 1950,* Vol. 2: *Characteristics of the Population,* Part 1: United States Summary, U.S. Government Printing Office, Washington, D.C., 1953.

92. U.S. Bureau of the Census, *United States Census of Population, 1960, General Population*

Characteristics, United States Summary U.S. Government Printing Office, Washington, D.C., 1961, esp. Table 56; U.S. Bureau of the Census, *1980 Census of Population, Supplementary Reports, Race of the Population by States, 1980*, U.S. Government Printing Office, Washington, D.C., 1981, esp. Table 3, "1970"; U.S. Bureau of the Census, *1980 Census of Population, Supplementary Report: American Indian Areas and Alaska Native Villages*, U.S. Government Printing Office, Washington, D.C., 1984, esp. Table 4.

93. U.S. Bureau of the Census, *1990 Census of the Population, Preliminary Report*, U.S. Government Printing Office, Washington, D.C., 1991.

94. On the Sioux and Chippewa, see *American Indian Holocaust and Survival*, op. cit., p. 161. On the Navajo, see Goodman, James M., *The Navajo Atlas*, University of Oklahoma Press, Norman, 1982, pp. 136-8.

95. *American Indian Holocaust and Survival*, op. cit., p. 115.

96. *Atlas of American Indian Affairs*, op. cit.; *American Indian Holocaust and Survival*, op. cit., pp. 96, 161.

97. See American Indian Policy Review Commission, Task Force Ten, *Report on Terminated and Nonfederally Recognized Tribes*, U.S. Government Printing Office, Washington, D.C., 1976.

98. For perhaps the best articulations of these racist themes in Euroamerican culture, see Horsman, Reginald, *Race and Manifest Destiny: The Origins of Racial Anglo-Saxonism*, Harvard University Press, Cambridge, MA, 1981. For a broader analysis, see Gist, Noel P., and Anthony G. Dworkin, *The Blending of Races: Marginality and Identity in World Perspective*, Wiley-Interscience Books, New York, 1972.

99. *American Indian Holocaust and Survival*, op. cit., pp. 174-5. For partial analysis, see Price, Edward T., "A Geographic Analysis of White-Indian-Negro Racial Mixtures in the Eastern United States," *Annals of the Association of American Geographers*, No. 43, 1953, pp. 138-55; and Posey, Darrell A., "Origin, Development and Maintenance of a Louisiana Mixed-Blood Community: The Ethnohistory of the Freejacks of the First Ward Settlement," *Ethnohistory*, No. 26, 1979, pp. 177-82.

100. Ibid. Also see *Indian Population of the United States and Alaska*, op. cit., p. 73.

101. U.S. Department of Health, Education and Welfare (DHEW), *A Study of Selected Socio-Economic Characteristics of Ethnic Minorities Based on the 1970 Census, Vol. 3: American Indians*, U.S. Government Printing Office, Washington, D.C., 1974, p. 36.

102. U.S. Congress, Office of Technology Assessment, *Indian Health Care* (OTA-H-290), U.S. Government Printing Office, Washington, D.C. 1986, p. 74.

103. DHEW, op. cit., p. 37.

104. *Indian Health Care*, op. cit., p. 78.

105. Explicit blood-quantum criteria for tribal membership and enrollment were built into many of the constitutions fashioned and imposed by Indian Commissioner John Collier's federal bureaucrats through implementation of the Indian Reorganization Act during the second half of the 1930s. Once the idea took hold on affected reservations, the Indians themselves often increased the quantum level involved in setting eligibility requirements. See, for example, *Constitution and Bylaws of the Confederated Salish and Kootenai Tribes of the Flathead Reservation* (1935) and *Amended Constitution and Bylaws of the Confederated Salish and Kootenai Tribes of the Flathead Reservation* (1960), analyzed in *American Indian Holocaust and Survival*, op. cit., pp. 196-8. For additional information, see Hargrett, Lester, *A Bibliography of the Constitutions and Laws of American Indians*, Harvard University Press, Cambridge, MA, 1947.

106. These and other treaties are analyzed according to their racial content in Editors, *Treaties and Agreements of the Indian Tribes of the Northern Plains* and *Treaties and Agreements of the Indian Tribes of the Pacific Northwest*, both from the Institute for the Development of Indian Law, Washington, D.C., no date. For background, see Bieder, Robert E., "Scientific Attitudes Towards Indian Mixed-Bloods in Early Nineteenth Century America," *Journal of Ethnic Studies*, No. 8, 1980, pp. 17-30.

107. For more on the racial content of the General Allotment Act, see Otis, D.S., *The Dawes Act and Allotment of Indian Lands*, University of Oklahoma Press, Norman, 1973.

108. See *1970 Census of the Population, Subject Report: American Indians*, op. cit., p.192; and *Indian Health Care*, op. cit., p. 48.

109. Thornton, Russell, Gary D. Sandefur, and Harold G. Grasmick, *The Urbanization of American*

Indians: A Critical Bibliography, Indiana University Press, Bloomington/Indianapolis, 1982, p. 14.
110. See Bernstein, Alison R., *American Indians and World War II*, University of Oklahoma Press, Norman, 1991, pp. 64-88.
111. On relocation, see Fixico, Donald L., *Termination and Relocation: Federal Indian Policy, 1945-1960*, University of New Mexico Press, Albuquerque, 1986.
112. According to the federal government's own data, reservation-based American Indians experience the lowest rate of employment and per capita income, highest infant mortality and malnutrition rates, and shortest life-expectancy of any ethnically identifiable population group in North America. This holds true despite their being, nominally at least, the largest per capita land owners, of some of the most mineral-rich acreage, on the continent. The difference between their potential wealth and their actual poverty rests squarely in the arena of federal policies regarding them and their land. See U.S. Department of Health, Education and Welfare, *A Statistical Portrait of the American Indian*, U.S. Government Printing Office, Washington, D.C., 1976. Also see U.S. Department of Health and Human Services, *Chart Series Book*, Public Health Service, Washington, D.C., 1988 (HE20.9409.988).
113. *American Indian Holocaust and Survival*, op. cit., p. 227. Also see U.S. Bureau of the Census, *General Social and Economic Characteristics: United States Summary*, U.S. Government Printing Office, Washington, D.C., 1983 (PC80-1-13), p. 92. Of further interest, see Sorkin, Alan L., *The Urban American Indian*, Lexington Books, Lexington, MA, 1978.
114. *1990 Census of the Population, Preliminary Report*, op. cit.
115. *Atlas of American Indian Affairs*, op. cit. The "Los Angeles Metro Area" includes, for purposes of the figure used here, not only Los Angeles-Long Beach, but Oxnard-Simi Valley-Ventura, Riverside-San Bernardino-Ontario, Santa Barbara-Santa Maria-Lompoc, and Santa Rosa as well.
116. *1980 Census of the Population, Supplementary Report: American Indian and Alaska Native Villages, 1980*, op. cit., pp. 22-4.
117. Ibid.
118. See Forbes, Jack D., "Undercounting Native Americans: The 1980 Census and the Manipulation of Racial Identity in the United States," *Wicazo Sa Review*, Vol. VI, No. 1, Spring 1990, pp. 2-26.
119. U.S. Bureau of the Census, *Subject Reports: Persons of Spanish Origin, 1970 Census of the Population*, (PC(2)-1C) Appendix C, U.S. Government Printing Office, Washington, D.C., 1973, pp. vii, ix.
120. U.S. Bureau of the Census, *Selected Characteristics of Persons and Families of Mexican, Puerto Rican and Other Spanish Origin: March 1971*, Ser. P-20, No. 224, U.S. Government Printing Office, Washington, D.C., 1971, p. 15.
121. See Forbes, Jack D., *Black Africans and Native Americans: Race, Color and Caste in the Evolution of Red-Black Peoples*, Oxford University Press, London/New York, 1988. Also see Berry, Brewton, *Almost White: A Study of Certain Racial Hybrids in the Eastern United States*, Macmillan Publishers, New York, 1963.
122. U.S. Bureau of the Census, *Current Population Report: Characteristics of the Population by Ethnic Origin, November 1979*, Ser. P-20, No. 221, U.S. Government Printing Office, Washington, D.C., 1979.
123. For European and African immigration totals relative to Mexico, see *Indians of North America*, op. cit., p. 602. Driver estimates that "more than 80 percent of the genes of the entire [modern Mexican] population are probably Indian, with the remainder divided equally between Negroes and Europeans." This would make the Mexican population less than 10 percent white, as compared to the Census Bureau's 90+ percent white categorization.
124. U.S. Bureau of the Census, *Ancestry of the Population by State, 1980*, Supp. Rep. PC80-SI-10, U.S. Government Printing Office, Washington, D.C., 1983, p. 2.
125. "Undercounting Native Americans," op. cit., p. 23.
126. A detailed study of this phenomenon in Los Angeles, the metropolitan area with the largest concentration of urban Indians in the U.S., may be found in Tucker, M. Belinda, Waddell M. Herron, Dan Nakasi, Luis Ortiz-Franco, and Lenore Stiffarm, *Ethnic Groups in Los Angeles: Quality of Life Indicators*, UCLA Ethnic Studies Centers, Los Angeles, 1987. More broadly, see Thornton, Russell, and Mary K. Grasmick, *Sociology of American Indians: A Critical Bibliography*, Indiana University Press, Bloomington/Indianapolis, 1980.
127. *American Indian Holocaust and Survival*, op. cit., pp. 199-200. Thornton is drawing upon the research and analysis embodied in Wahrhaftig, Albert L., and Robert K. Thomas, "Renaissance and Repression: The Oklahoma Cherokee," *Transaction*, No. 6, 1969, pp. 42-8.

Chapter II

International Law and Politics
Toward a Right to Self-Determination for Indigenous Peoples

Glenn T. Morris

We support the principles that indigenous peoples have the right to exist as distinct peoples of the world, and that they have a right to possession of their territories and the right to sovereign self-determination. We call upon the people of the world to join us in asserting that the genocide and dispossession of indigenous peoples is a matter of rightful concern to the world community, as are matters involving a consistent pattern of gross violations of the rights of the indigenous peoples and nations under principles established by international law, and that action must be taken by the world organizations and specifically the United Nations.

Statement of the Indigenous Peoples' Fourth Russell Tribunal on the
Rights of the Indians of the Americas, November 28, 1980

The historical operation of a system of legal norms and standards, ordained by a handful of states, and imposed upon the overwhelming majority of the world's peoples without their consent or input, is considered perverse and unjust by most indigenous peoples. This system, pretentiously known as "The Laws of Nations," continues to operate at the threshold of the 21st century without meaningful participation by hundreds of millions of the planet's indigenous peoples. This observation is not meant to suggest that all that has been, or continues to be, recognized as "The Laws of Nations" is either unjust or unacceptable. What it *is* intended to suggest is that, as is now readily acknowledged, colonial or settler states should not possess the right to impose their particular definition of just or equitable relations between peoples on the majority of humankind and call it "law."

Only in the past fifty years, or the past thirty for over a third of the states of the world, has self-determination been realized through the recognition that colonialism is abhorrent to the desired liberty of humankind. Through the acceptance of the U.N. charter and other human-rights instruments, self-determination of peoples is a universally accepted aspiration. Unfortunately, thousands of the world's peoples have yet to realize that aspiration. Indigenous peoples from Burma to Brazil, from the Arctic to Australia, continue to be denied the right to control their affairs in any effective and meaningful manner. In many of these countries, such as Guatemala, Bolivia, Greenland, and Ecuador, indigenous peoples comprise a majority of the total state population; yet, they often remain disenfranchised and subordinated by the descendants of the original settler or colonizing classes. Despite recent and tentative advances in the recognition of the rights of indigenous peoples in such places as Nicaragua, Greenland, and Panama, and despite some progress in certain international forums, the overwhelming majority of indigenous peoples are forced to struggle for their very existence against the enormous pressure of encroaching states surrounding them.

Through the application of international legal and political norms, many peoples under colonial domination have achieved some level of political self-determination. Many representatives of indigenous peoples and nations point to the example of the decolonization of southern Africa as an example to be emulated in the case of indigenous peoples elsewhere. Just as principles of self-determination have been applied to liberate the peoples of Zimbabwe or Namibia, where the idea of Black majority rule is accepted without question, so, too, should such principles apply to all indigenous peoples. This essay is devoted to the examination of why such principles have not been applied to indigenous peoples and how the operation of European and American legal doctrines has been used to maintain their colonial condition. One particular paradox in this examination will be the recognition that even by their own legal standards, the Euroamerican colonization of the Western hemisphere (and, by extension, other indigenous peoples' lands across the globe) was unjustified.

More important, the purpose here is to indicate that through the application of contemporary principles of international law, particularly in the area of decolonization and self-determination, indigenous peoples must ultimately be entitled to decide for themselves the dimensions of their political, economic, cultural, and social conditions. It must be emphasized that the construction of this position is not based in the supposition that because indigenous peoples constitute ethnic or cultural minorities in larger societies they must be protected due to that status. Rather, the position is that since Europeans first wandered into the Western hemisphere they have acknowledged the unique status of indigenous peoples qua indigenous peoples. That status is only now being reacknowledged through the application of evolving principles of positive and customary international law.

While such assertions may seem novel and untenable at present, it should be recalled that just forty years ago, tens of millions of people languished under the rule of colonial domination; today, they are politically independent. Central to their independence was the development and acceptance of the right to self-determination under international law. Despite such developments, many colonized peoples were forced by desperate conditions to engage in armed struggle to advance their legitimate aspirations. Similarly, for many indigenous peoples few viable options remain in their quest for control of their destinies. Consequently, a majority of the current armed conflicts in the world are not between established states, but between indigenous peoples and states that seek their subordination. Armed struggle for most indigenous peoples represents a desperate and untenable strategy for their survival. Nonetheless, it may remain an unavoidable option for many of them, because if their petitions seeking recognition of their rights in international forums are ignored, many indigenous peoples, quite literally, face extermination.

Although this chapter has implications for the status of all indigenous peoples, its concentration is primarily within the United States. This is because, in several ways, the status of indigenous nations within the U.S. is unique, and the policy of the United States toward indigenous nations has frequently been emulated by other states. The fact that a treaty relationship exists between the United States and indigenous nations, and the fact that indigenous nations within the U.S. retain defined and separate land bases and continue to exercise some degree of effective self-government, may contribute to the successful application of international standards in their cases. Also, given the size and relative power of the United States in international relations, and absent the unlikely independence of a majority-indigenous nation-state such as Guatemala or Greenland, the successful application of decolonization principles to indigenous nations within the U.S. could allow the extension of such applications to indigenous peoples in other parts of the planet.

One final introductory point: Indigenous peoples, as all colonized peoples, have come to realize the importance of semantics in their quest for self-determination. Consequently, the use of several key terms in this chapter is deliberate. The terms "indigenous peoples" or "indigenous nations" are used intentionally for the reason that, if nothing else, they accurately describe the original peoples of given territories. Ideally, the specific names of indigenous nations would be (and have been) used, but for the sake of clarity and brevity, that practice has been limited here. Although the term "nation" denotes a socio-political construct of European nature, the concept carries with it considerable importance in international debates. Fortunately, among the ranks of indigenous peoples a discussion has begun that calls into question the usefulness of forcing indigenous reality into the forms developed by Europeans. Consequently, new descriptions of the historical organization of indigenous societies, as well as indigenous aspirations, are being formulated. The result may be the evolution of completely novel international relationships between and among peoples. Despite this development, the term "nation" is deliberately used in this chapter. A reasonable explanation for the use of the term was provided by Oren Lyons of the Onondaga Nation:

> We are the original people on this land. We are the land keepers. We are not a minority within our own lands. One must understand that terminology is very important. How you address yourself is very important to [Euroamericans]. If you try and change that terminology, you will find out how important it is. So we must speak of ourselves as people...If you fall into the category of "tribes" or "bands," a gaggle of geese, a herd, a group...you're more than that. It's important not to call Indians "bands." You try to change [Euroamerican]

terminology,...they will not accept it because it is that important. That terminology is just as important to you. So, you should first of all represent yourself
as what you are. Nations are not according to size, nations are according to
culture. If there are twenty people left who are still representing their nation,
in the eyes of our people, they are a nation. Who are we to say less?[1]

Historical Rights of Indigenous Peoples

The historical antecedents of the legal rights of indigenous peoples may be found
centuries prior to the European arrival in the Western hemisphere. After the
establishment of the Holy Roman Empire, but prior to the colonial travels of
Europeans to the "New World," distinctions drawn by Europeans between the
various peoples of the known world were generally in terms of Christians and
"infidels."[2] With the expansion of Christianity, the acquisition of territory from
newly discovered peoples (such as those in Asia and Africa) or from familiar
peoples (particularly the Saracens and Turks) who were unwilling to accept Christian doctrines and who were therefore subject to "reconquest," was justified through
the extension of the Roman legal principle, *territorium (res) nullius*.[3] Under this
extension, a "discoverer" could legally occupy a territory that was already inhabited
(by "infidels") and extend Christian sovereignty over it.[4]

Eventually, this principle of effective occupation was rejected in favor of the
principles of conquest and effective possession. Under these new principles,
justification for extension of Christian sovereignty rested upon the attitude that
infidels were the enemies of Christian civilization and that non-believers could be
dispossessed of their territories justifiably by subjugation through wars of conquest.
They lost all rights to territorial integrity as separate and distinct peoples. Not all
Christian jurists or legal theorists of the time accepted the premises upon which the
principle of conquest was founded. Among the more notable defenders of the rights
of non-Christians to maintain control over their territories were Thomas Aquinas
(1227-1274)[5] and Sinibaldo Fiesco, who became Pope Innocent IV (1243-1254).[6]
Although the theories of these theologians and legal scholars characterized non-
Christians in pejorative terms, there was a fundamental acknowledgment of a
difference between the natural law of human-created institutions (*summa natura*)
and the divine law of God that distinguishes between the faithful and infidels.
According to Aquinas, although political society should disapprove of immoral
acts, i.e., spiritual infidelity, the state must make allowances for the "natural
sinfulness" of human beings.[7] In this way, the higher good fostered through the
promotion of a civilized, Christian society is maintained through the peaceful
integration and conversion of infidels, rather than through their violent subjugation
or destruction.

Spanish Colonial Law
Columbus' return to Europe after his first voyage to the Americas promoted
enormous debate regarding the status of the peoples he encountered. This debate

included the scope of authority of European states to extend themselves over the lands across the Atlantic. The first known European documents addressing the question of dominion over the "New World" were the Papal Bulls of Pope Alexander VI.[8] Signed on May 3 and 5, 1493, the Alexandrine Bulls acknowledged the right of the sovereigns of Castille and Aragon to acquire and Christianize the islands and *terra firma* of the new regions. The issuance of the bulls created immediate tensions between competing European powers concerning the new territories, tensions that would remain unresolved in Europe for over 300 years and that continue in the Americas today.[9] One interesting passage from the Bull *Inter Caetera* of May 4, 1493, represents the first European acknowledgment of the national character of the indigenous peoples of the New World:

> [Columbus] found certain remote islands and also mainlands, which had not been discovered before by others before [sic] in which dwell very many tribes, peacefully living, and, as it is asserted, going naked and not eating meat; and so far as your messengers are able to conjecture *these* nations living in the said islands and lands believe that there is one God and one Creator in the heavens (emphasis added).[10]

Subsequent to their initial contact with indigenous peoples in the Western hemisphere, the Europeans examined the source, depth, and legitimacy of their claims to the lands upon which they happened, vis-à-vis the nations already occupying the same lands. Ongoing discussion concerning Spanish claims in America took place in Paris in the early 16th century, primarily facilitated by John Mair (1469-1542) and his *Commentary on the Sentences of Pater Lombard*.[11] One of Mair's most prominent students was Franciscus de Victoria (1480-1546), a professor in Glasgow and Paris, widely recognized as "the father" of modern international law.[12] Mair's writings challenged the popular contention that the Pope possessed universal secular authority, suggesting instead that sovereign authority was vested in independent, secular political associations or kingdoms. Mair agreed with earlier theorists who taught that infidels (or indigenous peoples) could be subdued if they failed to convert to Christianity, but held there was no justification for conquest if conversion requirements were met. He also believed, in the Aristotelian tradition, that slavery is a natural state for some peoples, and that civilized nations have a natural right to rule the less civilized.[13]

In Spain, the development of legal doctrines regarding the lands and peoples of the Western hemisphere was stimulated by the sermons of Father Antonio de Montesinos in 1511, which castigated the Spanish for their enslavement and slaughter of the indigenous peoples of the Americas.[14] His sermons led to a convocation of legal theorists and theologians at Burgos in 1512. Two principal views emerged from the meeting, one represented by Juan López de Palacios Rubios (1450-1542) and the other by Matías de Paz (1468-1542).[15] Palacios Rubios advanced the position that the Alexandrine Bulls provided complete legal authority for the Spanish conquest of indigenous nations, since the Pope was heir to Christ's temporal and spiritual authority. According to Palacios Rubios, this authority enabled the Pope to assert control over all infidels and compelled their obedience to the rule of the Roman Catholic Church.[16] Rubios was also author of the infamous *Requirimiento,* an edict read (in Spanish) to the indigenous peoples of the Americas informing them of their obligation to convert to Roman Catholicism and to submit themselves to the sovereign authority of the Spanish Crown.[17] Failure to comply with the *Requirimiento* resulted in immediate attack by the Spaniards on recalcitrant communities and execution of resisters. It also provided the Spanish with what they believed to be legal authority to wage a "Just War" against indigenous nations and peoples.[18] This use of the *Requirimiento* as a mere rationalization has been viewed by some commentators as an "ironic, if not ridiculous, character of a formality intended to ease the conscience of the Spanish."[19]

Conversely, Matias de Paz, in his work *Concerning the Rule of the Kings of Spain Over the Indians,* was the first European scholar to repudiate the application of the Aristotelian theory of natural slavery to American Indians. While agreeing with the fundamental precept that the Pope and Church alone had authority to dominate the world, Matias went considerably further than Palacios Rubios in recognizing the humanity of non-Christians. Matias distinguished between those non-Christians who had been exposed to Christian teachings and rejected them and those, such as indigenous peoples, who had never known the "true faith." Matias de Paz suggested that American Indians, due to their ignorance of Christianity, could legally resist *any war* levied against them by the Spanish through the *Requirimiento* process. Since "wars cannot be just on both sides," either the Spanish possessed the right to levy a Just War, or the Indians had the legal right to resist.[20] Consequently, the Spanish were in his view without legal authority to enslave or dispossess indigenous nations. According to Matias de Paz, indigenous nations possessed the absolute right of self-defense, producing the logical conclusion that the Spanish wars were legally unjust and unjustifiable. Without a basis to wage a Just War, the Spanish had no legal right to dispossess indigenous nations of their lands or of their inherent sovereign authority to govern themselves.

The Burgos debates between Palacios Rubios and Matias de Paz were important for three reasons: first, they revealed dramatically divergent perspectives among European scholars regarding the rights of indigenous peoples. Second, they led to promulgation of the Laws of Burgos, theoretically regulating every aspect of Spanish colonial life in "New Spain" (in practice, of course, these laws were routinely violated or ignored). Third, they sowed the seeds for subsequent discussions of the same subject. The most critical of these subsequent debates took place at Vallodolid between Bartolomé de Las Casas (1474-1566) and Juan Ginés de Sepúlveda (1490-1573).[21]

Prior to the crucial Las Casas/Sepúlveda debates of 1550, the Spanish jurist Franciscus de Victoria authored several articles detailing the limits of papal and Spanish authority over indigenous peoples and their territories.[22] Victoria's conclusions were clear: indigenous nations of the Americas exercised true dominion over their property in both public and private matters, just like Christians, and...neither their princes nor private persons could be despoiled of their property on the ground of not being true owners. It would be hard to deny those who have never done any wrong, what we grant the Saracens and Jews, who are persistent enemies of Christianity. We do not deny that these latter peoples are true owners of their property, if they have not seized lands elsewhere belonging to Christians.[23]

He also concluded that because the Pope was not the lord of the entire world, there could be no exercise of papal authority over indigenous nations.[24] Further, Victoria asserted that Christians not only were without legal claim to already occupied lands of the Americas, but (as was previously recognized by Matias de Paz) they were without sufficient legal right to levy a Just War against indigenous peoples based on the claim that the new territories now belonged to Spain through papal donation, or based on the Indian's rejection of Christianity.[25] These conclusions effectively refute any European or Euro-derived claim to the Western hemisphere based on the so-called Rights of Conquest doctrine.[26]

Victoria was the first European theorist to suggest that indigenous nations in the Americas possessed the inherent sovereign power to make territorial cessions through voluntary and informed agreements in the form of international treaties. This principle was endorsed, though by no means universally, for the succeeding five centuries by various jurists, international legal scholars, and political leaders.[27] According to the noted U.S. legal theorist and historian Felix S. Cohen, the concept of treating between European states and indigenous nations, as first suggested by Victoria, was rooted in three basic assumptions:

1. that both parties to the treaty are sovereign powers;
2. that the Indian [nation] has a transferable title of some sort, to the land in question; and
3. that the acquisition of Indian lands could not safely be left to individual colonists, but must be controlled by government monopoly.[28]

Influenced by the writings and lectures of Victoria, Pope Paul III issued the Bull *Sublimus Deus* in 1537, instructing his Catholic subjects to view indigenous peoples as true humans. Further, he instructed European sovereigns that "the said Indians and all other people who have been or may later be discovered by Christians, are by no means to be deprived of their property, even though they be outside the faith of Jesus Christ; and that they may and should freely and legitimately enjoy their liberty and possession of their property; nor should they in any way be enslaved; should the contrary happen, it shall be null."[29] By 1540, reports of massacres of the indigenous peoples of the Americas by the Spaniards were becoming so common,[30] and were so troubling to Charles V of Spain, that he convened a council of jurists and legal scholars to discuss the rights and responsibilities of the Crown in the Western hemisphere.[31] A series of councils and debates took place in the succeeding years, culminating in the debate between Las Casas and Sepúlveda.[32] The latter, who had never traveled to the Americas, and who had seen American Indians only in the slave market in Seville, argued in favor of the Spanish conquest of indigenous peoples, whom he viewed as sub-human infidels:

> In defending the Spanish rule, Sepúlveda argued the superiority of Spaniards and the inferiority of Indians. A just war was one in which the barbarian enemy was offered an opportunity to yield peaceably, as in the *Requirimiento* procedure...He attacked the American Indians, and most particularly the Aztecs as stupid, inept, uncivilized, cruel, idolatrous and immoral. Indeed, they were "natural slaves."[33]

Las Casas, a Dominican missionary who had traveled and lived among indigenous nations throughout the Caribbean and Latin America between 1502 and 1547, argued fervently that native peoples could not be subjugated legally by the Spanish. He agreed with Victoria that the indigenous nations of the Western hemisphere were the rightful sovereigns of their territories, that Europeans had no cause to wage Just Wars, and that conquest of the region was "unlawful, tyrannical, and unjust."[34] Although the debate did not result in dramatic policy changes in Spain, the legal and political repercussions were felt in the Americas, at least temporarily. The Spanish had no intention of vacating their colonies, but the Crown did pass a number of laws, beginning in 1573, explicitly recognizing the territorial integrity of certain indigenous nations.[35] With the passage of these laws, the Spanish implicitly created a system of trusteeship for the indigenous peoples of New Spain.[36] This is not to suggest that the trust was consistently upheld, that the rights of indigenous nations were respected, or that the repression and subjugation of native peoples was diminished. It is intended, instead, to suggest that "the oppression was in defiance of, rather than pursuant to, the laws of Spain."[37] It also suggests, as the Papal Bulls and Spanish *Cedulas* themselves did, that violations of Spanish law should have rendered the extension of Spanish territorial sovereignty null and void.[38]

English Innovations

The Spanish debate concerning the rights of indigenous peoples was carried to northern Europe and influenced the legal and political practices of other European colonial powers (Spanish Catholic influence was extended to England, for instance, until 1558, when the Protestant Queen Elizabeth I ascended to the throne). English colonizing doctrines, perhaps the most enduring for indigenous peoples, were employed first on the Irish and then exported to the Western hemisphere. According to Robert Williams, this colonial style synthesized "medievally derived legal theories on the diminished status and rights of normatively divergent savage people, anti-Spanish religious and mercantile nationalism, and English innovations of Spanish colonizing practice."[39]

English justifications for the dispossession of North America from indigenous peoples derived from an Elizabethan Protestant doctrine declaring the English in covenant with God to bring "true" (as opposed to Spanish) Christianity to "heathen natives." The development of English legal doctrines regarding colonization was heavily influenced by George Peckham, who, in turn, relied on the writings of

Victoria. Peckham, however, used Victoria for his own purposes, primarily to justify English colonization under the Laws of Nations by asserting that English Christians had the lawful right to trade with indigenous peoples worldwide. According to Peckham, if infidels refused to trade, the English were then entitled to conquer the resisters and dispossess them of their lands.[40] By this reasoning, all that was required to wage a Just War was to come upon a people that was unwilling to trade or accept missionaries. The English claimed to—but probably did not—feel legally justified in conquering American Indians on this basis. In the example of the colonization of Virginia, English colonizers, cognizant of the questionable moral and legal justification for their invasion, engaged in self-deception, refusing any objective analysis of their actions:

> Instead, a strategy of silence, in order to suppress the arousal of any contrary discourse, was agreed on. The justice of the company's royally assigned title in America would operate simply on a presumption of English superior rights in America...Conquest of America itself would prove the superior right of the English to the Indians' America...By the early seventeenth century at least, Spaniards recognized as well as did the English that legal arguments had little to do with European "rights" in America.[41]

Hence, the imposition of the European presence in the Americas cannot reasonably be asserted to be the consequence of adherence to law, but rather the operation of sheer force. The *a priori* justifications of the English, while soothing to the conscience of those invaders who benefited, demand serious scrutiny because they constitute the legal cornerstone for all subsequent English settlement in the Western hemisphere. As often happens in the development of law affecting indigenous peoples, these early self-serving justifications of the English became enshrined and legitimized in legal precedent. The 1622 *Barkham's Case* held, despite contrary writings by Vattel and other legal authorities, that the legal and political authority of "heathen infidels" was necessarily abrogated when it came into contact with Christian sovereignty.[42] With such reasoning, expansion of English and U.S. colonization of indigenous peoples was inevitable.[43]

The Status of Indigenous Nations in the U.S.

The first sustained European settlements in the area now known as the United States were established in 1565 at St. Augustine, Florida; 1607 at Jamestown, Virginia; 1609 at New Amsterdam (New York) and Santa Fé, New Mexico; and 1620 at Plymouth, Massachusetts. Without exception, these colonists were greeted by native peoples with friendship and openness, as Columbus had been before them.[44] In return, indigenous nations were confronted with racism, massacres, religious bigotry, and systematic fraud.[45] As discussed above, by the time Europeans began colonizing the Americas, they had established and adhered to (at least among themselves) a number of accepted legal norms concerning territorial acquisition and possession. Among the most basic of these standards was the "right to use that which one had created, possessed or occupied without wrongfully taking [it] from another."[46] As concerns land, this principle was known as possession of *territorium nullius*, acknowledging the rights of those who had occupied territories over prolonged periods of time, under the principle of "immemorial possession."

Enforceable rights under immemorial possession were recognized by the legal theorists of the Middle Ages, as they had been by the Romans before them.[47] The doctrine of immemorial possession, combined with the recognition of the inherent sovereignty and possessory right of indigenous nations, was found to be so compelling by the Dutch that they began to negotiate treaties for land cessions from indigenous nations from their first contact with one another.[48] The Swedish soon followed the Dutch example, as did some English colonists,[49] reinforcing conclusions that the Doctrine of Discovery did not diminish the sovereign rights of indigenous peoples, but was a mechanism of controlling competing European states in their negotiations with indigenous nations regarding territorial cessions.[50]

After the 17th century, the discovery doctrine was generally understood not to limit or divest indigenous nations of any authority over their territories. The doctrine was developed as a regulatory mechanism between European sovereigns to prioritize their rights to engage in international relations with indigenous nations, and to preempt other European states from interacting with the same indigenous nation. The discovery doctrine and the limitations that Europeans knowingly placed on their claims to lands in the Americas were succinctly described by United States Supreme Court Chief Justice John Marshall:

> The principle, acknowledged by all Europeans, because it was in the self-interest of all to acknowledge it, gave to the nation making the discovery, as its inevitable consequence, the sole right of acquiring the title and of making settlements on it. It was an exclusive principle which shut out the right of competition among those who had agreed to it. It regulated rights given by discovery among the European discoverers; *but could not affect the rights of those already in possession*, either as aboriginal occupants or by virtue of discovery made before the memory of man. It gave the exclusive right of purchase, but did not found that right on a denial of the possessors to sell [emphasis added].[51]

European states fully understood the nature of their negotiations with the indigenous nations of the Americas. Indigenous governments acted as sovereigns, despite attempts to construct circumventions and rationalizations, with all the attendant authority of this status.[52] The years immediately preceding the American Revolution saw an effort, by both the British and the newly formed Continental Congress of the United States, to centralize their relations with indigenous nations.[53] This effort represented a deliberate decision to remove the power to negotiate with native nations from the individual colonies and vest it exclusively with the national government, thereby insuring the uniformity of negotiations between equal national sovereigns.[54] In an effort to enlist the support of indigenous nations for the Revolution, the Americans began to treat formally with native governments.[55] The first of these treaties[56] was later described by the U.S. Supreme Court as "the model of treaties between the crowned heads of Europe."[57]

The founding documents and laws of the United States remove any doubt that the nascent state recognized the national sovereignty of of indigenous nations; the intention to recognize indigenous sovereignty is clear.[58] Additional evidence may be obtained from the opinions of William Wirt, an early attorney general of the United States: "So long as a tribe exists and remains in possession of its lands, its title and possession are sovereign and exclusive. We treat with them as separate sovereignties, and while an Indian nation continues to exist within its acknowledged limits, we have no more right to enter upon their territory than we have to enter upon the territory of a foreign prince."[59]

> The point, then once conceded, that the Indians are independent to the purpose of treating, their independence is to that purpose as absolute as any other nation. Being competent to bind themselves by treaty, they are equally competent to bind the party who treats with them. Such party cannot take benefit of the treaty with the Indians, and then deny them the reciprocal benefits of the treaty on the grounds that they are not independent nations to all intents and purposes...Nor can it be conceded that their independence as a nation is a limited independence. *Like all other independent nations,* they have the absolute power of war and peace. *Like all other independent nations,* their territories are inviolable by any other sovereignty...As a nation, they are still free and independent. They are entirely self-governed, self-directed. They treat, or refuse to treat, at their pleasure; and there is no human power which can rightly control them in the exercise of their discretion in this respect [emphasis added].[60]

With this policy, the United States negotiated treaties with the sovereign indigenous peoples of North America. These treaties were, and continue to be, recognized under Article VI of the U.S. Constitution as the supreme law of the United States, and continue to warrant the same respect and enforcement as any other international treaty. Of equal importance is the principle of continued respect for the national sovereignty of the indigenous nations that entered into those treaties. In the previous section, evidence was advanced that European states were forced to acknowledge the objective sovereignty of indigenous nations. This recognition eventually translated into over a century of treaty-making by the governments of France, Spain, Sweden, Britain, the Netherlands, and the United States with various indigenous nations. Between 1778 and 1871, the United States entered into and ratified more than 370 treaties with indigenous peoples.[61] Between 1871 and 1902, new covenants between the governments were formalized in "agreements." As a practical matter, particularly as regards U.S. policy that continued to define indigenous nations as sovereign, the semantic difference between treaties and agreements was of limited importance.[62] The change reflected internal institutional conflicts between the U.S. Senate and House of Representatives over which would exert greater influence in the area of indigenous relations, but the overall perception of the United States toward native sovereignty was not altered.

As with all treaties, it would be reasonable to view the covenants between the United States and indigenous nations in an international context.[63] They should be reviewed in light of the norms and developments that govern all treaties in the international arena. One underlying assumption should be that treaties represent legal obligations by nations of people, entered into in good faith, the material parts of which must be honored by the parties to the accord. Treaties are, among other things, bilateral compacts between nations or states. The United States and indigenous nations entered into agreements on a co-equal legal footing, and the agreements should be accorded the same respect as other bilateral or multilateral treaties in the international community. U.S. courts have never upheld the claim that treaties between indigenous peoples and the U.S. are inferior to, or should be accorded any less respect, than any other treaty signed and ratified by the United States.

Treaties between the United States and indigenous governments remain in force, require compliance by all parties, and have not been diminished in their international character. It should be noted that the international dimensions of these treaties have been supplemented in two important respects by the courts of the United States. First, the canon of construction for these treaties requires that they are to be interpreted as the native negotiators and signatories would have understood them.[64] Second, treaties are to be interpreted liberally by the courts, with ambiguities resolved in favor of indigenous interpretations.[65] Additionally, U.S. courts will not find an implied abrogation of a treaty through subsequent treaty or legislation; the intent to abrogate the treaty must be expressly stated by the Congress.[66] Acceptance of these canons of construction in no way diminishes the nature or force of the treaties, but rather recognizes the unique character of the relationship—geographically and politically—between the United States and indigenous nations. These canons of construction also represent a recognition by the United States of the fraudulent and coercive techniques it often employed in securing indigenous agreement to the treaties.[67]

These principles notwithstanding, it has been asserted that the treaties between the United States and indigenous nations do not properly fall within the international definition of a treaty under international law.[68] Such assertions are disputed not only in U.S. case law—as Vine Deloria, Rebecca Robbins, and other contributors to this volume make abundantly clear—but they also find disfavor in principles advanced by international experts.[69] It cannot be denied that as the 20th century comes to a close many international legal scholars and jurists refuse to recognize an international status for indigenous peoples or for the treaties to which they are parties. This is at least partly a function of powerful states, the United States among them, that argue that relations between states and indigenous peoples are purely matters of internal, domestic jurisdiction. This position is shared by virtually every member state of the United Nations that is engaged in relations with indigenous peoples.

While it is true that the United States Congress has passed thousands of laws in the area of U.S.-indigenous affairs, to suggest that the unilateral acts of a legislature can diminish the national sovereignty of indigenous nations that are thousands of years old seems an unjustifiable conclusion. Although the United States claims that its national legislature possesses such rights under the "plenary power doctrine," its assertion is not unlike similar claims by other colonizing states that have maintained that their relations with colonized peoples are purely domestic issues.[70] Asserting such claims, however, does not accord them acceptance under law.[71] The roots of the assertion that the United States possesses exclusive domestic jurisdiction over its relations with indigenous nations can be found in U.S. case law and the self-serving legislation that often accompanied it.

U.S. Colonization of Indigenous Nations

Prior to the War of 1812, the military, economic, and political strength of the United States was inadequate to colonize all of the indigenous nations whose territories were found east of the Mississippi River. By the 1820s, however, the power of the United States had been consolidated considerably, to the extent that many indigenous nations were vulnerable to military invasion by U.S. forces. The expansion of the U.S. was fueled by the racist philosophy of Manifest Destiny. Under this philosophy, the Americans believed that through divine ordination and the natural superiority of the white race, they had a right (and indeed an obligation) to seize and occupy all of North America. Typical of the pronouncements from supporters of the philosophy, Senator Thomas Hart Benton proclaimed that Euroamericans "had alone received the divine command to subdue and replenish the earth," and indigenous people had no right to the land of the Americas because this land had been created for use...by the white races...according to the intentions of the Creator."[72] Several years later, racist sentiment had not tempered. On the floor of the United States Congress, the motives underlying the colonization of indigenous nations were made clear:

> Congress must apprise the Indian that he can no longer stand as a breakwater against the constant tide of civilization...An idle and thriftless race of savages cannot be permitted to stand guard at the treasure vaults of the nation which hold our gold and silver...the prospector and miner may enter and by enriching himself enrich the nation and bless the world by the result of his toil.[73]

During the 19th and 20th centuries, the philosophy of Manifest Destiny was accompanied by several pieces of legislation that accomplished under cover of law that which would not have been legally justifiable through military force. The legislation, discussed below, was invariably framed and adopted under the pretense of assistance to indigenous nations in making the transition to the U.S. brand of "civilized" society. The U.S. definition of civilization, not surprisingly, was a pungent combination of fundamentalist Christianity, unrepentant racism, and eco-

nomic Darwinism. President John Adams prefaced this philosophy in a letter to
Judge Tudor:

> What infinite pains have been taken and expenses incurred in treaties, presents,
> and stipulated sums of money, instruments of agriculture, education...to con-
> vert these poor savages to Christianity! And, alas! with how little success! The
> Indians are as bigoted to their religion as the Mohametans [sic] are to their
> Koran, the Hindoos are to their Shaster, the Chinese to Confucius, the Romans
> to the Saints and angels, or the Jews to Moses and the Prophets. It is a principle
> of religion, at bottom, which inspires the Indian with such invincible aversion
> both to Civilization and Christianity. The same principle has excited their
> perpetual hostilities against the colonists and the independent Americans.[74]

By 1848, the United States had consolidated its political, economic, and
military power sufficiently to abandon any remaining subtleties in its colonization
of indigenous peoples. In his report on the status of relations between the United
States and indigenous nations, as well as his prescription for a successful future
policy, Commissioner of Indian Affairs William Medill reported that he favored the
exercise of direct colonial power over the Indian nations:

> Apathy, barbarism, and heathenism must give way to energy, civilization and
> Christianity...The Policy already begun and relied on to accomplish objects so
> momentous and so desirable...is, as rapidly as it can safely and judiciously be
> done, to colonize our Indian tribes...within a small district of country, so that,
> as the game decreases and becomes scarce, the adults will eventually be
> compelled to resort to agriculture and other kinds of labor to obtain a subsis-
> tence...It may be said that we have commenced the establishment of two
> colonies for the Indian tribes that we have been compelled to remove; one north,
> on the headwaters of the Mississippi, and the other on the Western borders of
> Missouri and Arkansas in Oklahoma Territory.[75]

By its own admission, the U.S. had thus embraced a policy of colonizing
indigenous peoples, and it augmented its policy with additional legislation.
Through this policy, as Ward Churchill explains in Chapter Five, on land struggles,
indigenous nations were confined to enclaves a fraction of the size of their original
territories. Nor did U.S. expropriation of native land holdings end, as is popularly
imagined, during the early part of the 20th century. Between 1936 and 1976, over
1.8 million acres of land were removed from the control of indigenous nations by
the federal government.[76] Although these seizures were usually accorded some
monetary compensation, the cessions were not made voluntarily by the native
peoples involved. The damage inflicted upon the remaining territorial integrity of
the indigenous nations involved is unquantifiable, and, arguably, such transactions
constitute breaches of international standards of behavior.[77]

Political Colonization

While all this was going on, a series of statutes including the Major Crimes Act
(1885), General Allotment Act (1887), Indian Citizenship Act (1924), Indian Reor-

ganization Act (1934), and various termination and relocation acts during the 1950s and '60s—each of them discussed in this text by Rebecca Robbins and others—were subsequently passed in order to extend absolute U.S. control over jurisdiction, land tenure, national allegiance, and governance over even the residues of indigenous territoriality. The political colonization of indigenous nations becomes more complex as the process matures. As colonial administrations become more firmly entrenched, the comprador class on reservations refuses to acknowledge the role of the United States in the colonization of indigenous peoples at all.[78] Tribal regimes, ostensibly operated by indigenous peoples, are ultimately influenced by non-indigenous decisionmakers, usually in Washington, D.C. The appearance of self-determination is nothing more than colonial self-administration. In this way, as Voltaire stated, by maintaining the illusion of freedom, volition itself is captured, and subjugation becomes complete. Despite some recent changes in the way that the federal government views its relations with indigenous nations,[79] the ultimate decisionmaker concerning the parameters of indigenous self-determination is the U.S. In language that the U.S. considers benevolent, but that must ultimately be considered stifling to indigenous peoples, the U.S. policy of administering indigenous nations has been described in the following terms:

A [native nation] is free to maintain or establish its own form of government...[but periodically] Congress has by statute dictated the manner of choosing tribal officials or other aspects of the [Indian nation's] government...But if Congress intends to replace the authority of an established form of government, its intent must be clearly indicated and tribal authority will continue, to the extent that it can coexist with Congress' alterations.[80]

This attitude of administration resembles virtually any of the late colonial period. Certainly, it is similar to that of Portugal in its assertion of ultimate control over the governments of the colonized peoples of Angola and Mozambique.[81] Portugal also contended that the colonies were merely overseas provinces which, with Portugal itself, constituted a single, unitary state. Because, according to Portugal, the colonies were actually provinces, they were subject only to the municipal jurisdiction of Portugal. This nation-state adamantly refused to recognize the right of its colonies to independence and self-determination. Accordingly, it administered the colonies from Lisbon, allowing "self-government" only as defined by the colonial power, and ignoring the mandate of the United Nations to facilitate the independence of the colonies.[82] Portugal, like the United States and other states that must address indigenous issues, insisted that the entire matter of its relations with its colonies was purely domestic, not within the purview of international law or international organizations.

In another example with similarities to the U.S., the government of South Africa continued, until 1990, to dictate the form of government in Namibia. Just as the U.S. claims to hold indigenous lands in trust for the benefit of the various indigenous nations, so too did South Africa hold Namibia in what it called a "sacred trust." Fortunately for the Namibians, the international community saw through the self-serving pronouncements of South Africa and applied sufficient international pressure on this nation-state to insure Namibian independence.[83] The political colonization of indigenous nations within the U.S. is relatively easy to chronicle and comprehend. As with colonialism in other parts of the world, however, it represents only part of the equation. Economic colonization is not only often more insidious, but much more difficult to overcome than political subordination.

Economic Colonization

Domination can be achieved in many ways. It does not have to be the result of overt political control. If the economy of a small country is totally dependent upon a set of external factors, this is a form of domination as effective as anything that existed in classical colonial times. The effect of all economic factors adds up to a sort of cumulative *force majeure* from which there is no escape.[84] Given the multiplicity of indigenous nations in the U.S., and given the diversity of their populations, sizes, territories, and natural resource reserves, it is difficult to generalize about their economic colonization. Nevertheless, there are several common strategies that have been used by the United States to ensure the economic bondage of native peoples to the U.S. Also, some general economic statistics are useful in ascertaining the overall current economic condition of American Indians in the U.S.

Indigenous peoples are in the worst economic position of any racial or ethnic group in the U.S.[85] In 1970, President Nixon admitted that Indians were the most economically depressed of any group, a condition that has not changed to the present.[86] The economic condition of indigenous nations can be tied directly to the political and military policies of the federal government, as overseen by the Bureau of Indian Affairs (BIA) and the secretary of the interior.[87] In recent years, the BIA has become more indigenous in appearance, but ultimately, the secretary of interior makes all important decisions. To illustrate this power, the U.S. Commission on Civil Rights wrote:

> Federal law gives the Secretary of the Interior and the Commissioner for Indian Affairs [now the Assistant Secretary of Interior for Indian Affairs] broad powers over all Indian affairs and all matters arising out of Indian relations. This includes veto power over all tribal contracts. Although the Navajo Nation has an elected council, set up under non-traditional Anglo guidelines, virtually every significant action of this council must receive BIA approval before it can become law or acted upon by the the the tribe. That approval process is often unnecessarily protracted and obstructionist.[88]

After years of agitation and demands by indigenous governments, some changes have been realized in this relationship, resulting in relatively greater control of decisions on Indian reservations. Nevertheless, the federal government continues to insist that it, and not native peoples, is the ultimate arbiter of the degree of sovereignty exercised by indigenous nations. The importance of the exercise of U.S. control in Indian affairs becomes increasingly clear when one understands the considerable natural resource reserves found within the territories of indigenous nations—many of which are considered strategic by the United States.[89] In this respect, native peoples of the U.S. experience similar economic invasions and controls as other indigenous peoples—be they the Yanomamis of Brazil, the Crees of Alberta, or the Penans of Sarawak. States consistently claim that it is their prerogative to exploit indigenous natural resources for the "national security," and such matters are purely domestic in nature, beyond the scope of international scrutiny or rebuke.

What makes the economic condition of indigenous peoples in the U.S. somewhat unique is the judicially-created "trust relationship" that requires the U.S. to hold native lands and resources for the benefit of indigenous nations.[90] Although this trust can apparently be breached with impunity by the U.S.,[91] some legally enforceable rights for indigenous peoples do exist if the U.S. breaches its fiduciary obligation to them.[92] Even more interesting is the fact that the United States is a fiduciary under two trust obligations: one to the indigenous peoples it has colonized and who now live within territory claimed by the U.S., and one to the peoples of the Pacific Trust Territory, whose territories were placed in trust by the United Nations, with the U.S. as trustee. A significant difference between these two trust arrangements is that the peoples of the Pacific Trust Territory possess the absolute right to exercise self-determination when and if they choose to do so.[93] No such right currently exists under international law for indigenous nations within the U.S., and the main difference in the attachment of international rights and status has to do with geographical separation from the colonizing power. This requirement, and its implications for indigenous peoples, can best be understood upon examining the evolution of the right to self-determination in international law, and the attendant decisions about to whom the right is extended.

Decolonization and the Right to Self-Determination

Discussion of the rights of colonized peoples prior to World War I took place in the abstract, but serious discussion of limitations on the right of colonial powers to administer the colonies under their control was limited.[94] At the close of World War I, political leaders in the two major ideological camps—liberal capitalist republicanism and marxist socialism—began to recognize the inevitable decline of the system of European colonialism that had enveloped the world for the previous 400 years. Each side in this ideological struggle was determined to affect the evolution of the right to self-determination according to its particular perspective of human development and according to its own agenda for the future. Among the capitalist leadership, the most vocal in support of a right of colonized peoples to exercise self-determination was President Woodrow Wilson of the United States. In an address to Congress in 1917, Wilson condemned colonialism, and implicitly condoned wars of national liberation:

> No peace can last, or ought to last, which does not recognize or accept the principle that governments derive all their just powers from the consent of the

governed and that no right anywhere exists to hand people around from
sovereignty to sovereignty as if they were property.[95]

The following year, Wilson warned the colonial powers of the impending
movement of colonized peoples demanding their political self-determination:

> The rights of nations to self-determination is no mere phrase, it is an imperative
> principle of action which will be disregarded by statesmen in the future only
> at their own risk.[96]

Wilson's pronouncements, although consistent with his support of liberal
democracy, cannot be considered altruistic. At the time of his statements, European
socialism was spreading, and Wilson was interested in ensuring that a design for
self-determination that served Western interests would prevail. Simultaneously, V.I.
Lenin was constructing a political model that would soon transform the ancient
Russian empire into a new society more disturbing to the West than anything the
czars had ever dreamed of. A central theme to Lenin's plan, and one that he was
convinced would persuade colonized peoples to elaborate marxist socialism, was
his definition of self-determination.[97] He realized that the socialist model of
self-determination must embrace novel and expanded notions of the rights of
colonized peoples not addressed by Wilson or the West. Consequently, Lenin's
theory of self-determination embraced the aspirations of millions of colonized people:

> Victorious socialism must necessarily establish a full democracy and conse-
> quently, not only introduce full equality of nations, but also realize the right of
> oppressed nations to self determination, i.e., the right to free political separa-
> tion. Socialist parties which did not show by all their activities, both now,
> during the revolution and after its victory, that they would liberate the enslaved
> nations and build up relations with them on the basis of a free union—and free
> union is a false phrase without the right to secede—these parties would be
> betraying socialism.[98]

The Bolshevik Revolution of 1917 brought with it one of the first state declarations supporting the principle of self-determination. The Decree of Peace in 1917
declared that it was illegal for the Soviet Union to annex "small or weak peoples
without their clear, voluntary, express consent and desire."[99] Although nearly
seventy years elapsed before the Soviet Union took seriously Lenin's rhetoric
regarding the right of nations to genuine self-determination, its support for other
colonized peoples advanced the debate on decolonization dramatically in the
international arena.[100] Following World War I, the creation of the Mandated Territories under the League of Nations, later renamed the International Trusteeship
Council under the United Nations, began the process of supervising colonial
territories working toward the attainment of self-government and eventual independence. In 1950, over 20 million people lived under the UN trusteeship system in
eleven territories. Today, only one such territory remains: the Trust Territory of the
Pacific Islands, administered by the United States. All of the others have either

attained self-governance or independence or voluntarily consolidated their territories with neighboring nations or states.[101]

The United Nations

After World War II, a number of factors converged, leading to the disintegration of the global colonial system. Among these was the improved education and exposure to democratic principles and aspirations of political independence of colonized peoples.[102] This led to discontent and turmoil in the colonies, a factor compounded by the economic hardships experienced by the colonial powers as a consequence of the War, making it increasingly difficult to maintain distant, volatile territories.[103] Analysts have suggested that the Western countries allowed the demise of colonialism after World War II because their interest would be better protected through the containment of the Soviet Union and the Eastern bloc than through the maintenance of colonialism.[104]

With the founding of the United Nations in 1945, recognition of the right to self-determination was expressed in the United Nations charter itself.[105] According to Cristescu, the effect on customary international law resulting from reference to the right to self-determination in the charter "marks...the recognition of the concept as a legal principle and a principle of contemporary law."[106] Although some debate continues about the legal consequence of the mention of the right to self-determination in the charter,[107] state practice and subsequent U.N. resolutions have provided "ample evidence that there now exists a legal right to self-determination," under international law.[108]

Subsequent to the establishment of the United Nations and the ratification of its charter by the founding members, there was considerable debate over the substance of the rights flowing from the principle of self-determination. The elements of the right to self-determination were gradually outlined in a series of General Assembly resolutions.[109] The right also received prominent attention in the *International Covenant on Economic, Social and Cultural Rights* and the *International Covenant on Civil and Political Rights*.[110] Additionally, state practice indicates an overwhelming acceptance of the principle. Of the current members of the United Nations, over 100 were previously colonies, and have achieved their independence since the end of World War II.[111] Gudmundur Alfredsson concludes:

> The extent and general uniformity of actual state practice which has characterized the speedy dismantling of the colonial empire indicates for one thing that such *opinio juris* [on the right to self-determination] exists.[112]

The actions of the General Assembly and the Security Council have also been the subject of interpretation by the International Court of Justice (ICJ). In two relatively recent advisory opinions concerning rights to self-determination for the peoples of the Western Sahara and Namibia, the Court interpreted the law of decolonization in these terms:

> [T]he subsequent development of international law in regard to non-self-governing territories, as enshrined in the Charter of the United Nations, made

the principle of self-determination applicable to all of them. The concept of the sacred trust was confirmed and expanded to all "territories whose people have not yet attained a full measure of self-government" (Article 73). Thus it clearly embraced territories under a colonial regime.[113]

This discussion indicates that through the actions of the various bodies of the United Nations and the state members themselves, and through the confirmation of those actions in scholarly writings and judicial opinions, the law of decolonization and the right to self-determination exist as established rules of international law. This question settled, another fundamentally important one remains: who constitutes the "self" in self-determination? Under the law, who are to be the beneficiaries of the right? According to Alfredsson, the U.N. resolutions previously mentioned extend the right to colonies, non-self-governing territories, and former colonial territories integrated with the administering powers.[114] Colonies are defined through three basic criteria: 1. foreign domination, 2. the presence of a political/territorial entity in the colony, and 3. geographical separation from the colonizing power.[115] The only criterion that may be problematic for indigenous peoples to satisfy is the requirement for geographical separation from the colonizer. Because of the methods used by the "settler state" form of colonialism, most indigenous nations' territories were enveloped by encroaching powers, resulting in the colonized nations' territories being contiguous with, not separate from, that of their colonizers.

Non-self-governing territories are defined in Article 73 of the U.N. charter as "territories whose people have not yet attained the full measure of self-government." Though this category is subject to future clarification, certain characteristics are indicative of the status, namely that the colony is politically, economically, socially, and educationally underdeveloped relative to the colonizing power.[116] As discussed above, indigenous nations within the U.S. satisfy each of these criteria.[117] As with colonies, the prevailing view is that non-self-governing territories must be geographically separated from the colonizing power. This perspective, known as the "salt-water" or "blue-water" thesis of decolonization, requires that colonies be separated from the colonial power by a substantial body of water, preferably an ocean. This interpretation of decolonization was challenged by Belgium through its "Belgian Thesis," which contended that decolonization should extend to all colonized peoples, even if they are bound in enclaves entirely surrounded by colonizing states. The thesis specifically mentioned the enclave conditions of indigenous peoples for remedy.[118] Despite this attempt to extend decolonization to indigenous peoples, the "salt water thesis" has predominated in international debate.

The competence of the General Assembly to define non-self-governing territories is derived from Article 10 of the charter, and has been inferred by the ICJ in its *Western Sahara* opinion, in which the Court held that Spain "could not validly object to the General Assembly's exercise of its powers to deal with the decolonization of a non-self-governing territory."[119] Consequently, it appears to be within the competence of the General Assembly to extend the definition of non-self-governing territories to enclaves of indigenous nations. Convincing arguments to persuade the General Assembly to make such an extension can be derived from the fact that other enclaves, such as Lesotho and Gambia have been recognized as independent states without disrupting the territorial integrity of the states around them.

The final category in decolonization, colonial territories that have been integrated with the administering powers, is especially pertinent to the case of indigenous nations within the United States. Similar examples of colonial powers integrating colonies in circumvention of international law have been held to be illegal. The colonial rationale for integration schemes is explained by Alfredsson:

> [T]he practice by some colonizing states of integrating their colonial territories, even though such integration in many cases was pure constitutional fiction introduced in order to avoid international supervision by sheltering these territories under an umbrella of domestic jurisdiction, implies strongly that political decolonization appeared to the colonizers as a legal force and not just political rhetoric which they could have flatly rejected or more simply ignored.[120]

Such attempts by colonial governments to create the legal and political fiction of integration of their colonies, without the informed and willful consent of the colonized, "have failed however, and the territories involved have exercised their right to political decolonization...But the attempts provide one more compelling reason for a critical supervision and scrutiny of integration cases and for a strict adherence to the standards imposed by the United Nations for guaranteeing due process and equality."[121] Arguably, indigenous nations within the geography of the United States satisfy the criteria for decolonization if their unique conditions of original sovereignty, territory, and the nature of their colonization by the United States is considered. The primary obstacle to the recognition of their rights under decolonization principles appears to be the reluctance of states to redefine the constructs of self-determination to include indigenous enclaves.

Application of Self-Determining Right to Indigenous Peoples

Appeals by indigenous nations in international forums to secure the vindication of their rights as distinct and independent peoples is not new.[122] During the late 19th century, the Maori of Aotearoa (New Zealand) and the Aborigines of Australia, as well as various indigenous nations in Canada, submitted international petitions for resolution of territorial and jurisdictional conflicts.[123] In the 1920s, leaders from the Maori and Haudenosaunee (Iroquois) confederations petitioned the League of Nations to hear their cases for recognition under international law, but both were frustrated through the operation of diplomatic procedural rulings.[124] In the case of the Haudenosaunee, their leader, Deskaheh, spent over two years attempting to persuade the international community through the League to recognize the national status of his people, but without success.[125]

Subsequently, little attention was given indigenous issues until the adoption of the so-called Convention 107 by the International Labor Organization (ILO).[126] Formally called "The Convention of Indigenous Populations of 1957," Convention 107 fell far short of recognizing an indigenous right to self-determination. Nonetheless, for its time, the convention was a significant step forward in the contemporary recognition of the rights of indigenous peoples. The ILO recognized that indigenous peoples constitute distinct and separate peoples possessing protectable interests in their lands, cultures, and political structures.[127] The convention also laid the foundation for future progress in the area of indigenous peoples' rights. After several years of deliberation, ILO Convention 107 was deemed outdated and assimilationist in its perspective. Assimilation of indigenous peoples, while acceptable in international discourse in 1957, had fallen into disfavor since that time. The ILO began revising the convention in 1986 and concluded its revisions in 1989. The new document, known as Convention 169, updated the archaic provisions of 107 but was reviled by many native peoples as ignoring the legitimate aspirations of indigenous nations and continuing to protect states in their denial of native claims for self-determination.[128]

During the 1970s, several other events brought indigenous issues into international attention. In 1971, and again in 1977, the Declarations of Barbados, documents drafted by progressive anthropologists and indigenous representatives, called on the world to re-examine the colonial condition of indigenous peoples, and recognized the necessity of a hemispheric indigenous movement led by native peoples.[129] During this period, indigenous movements were growing and demanding recognition of their historic rights. By 1974, traditional native elders in North America called upon Russell Means, a leader of the American Indian Movement (AIM),[130] one of the most militant and prominent of the new organizations, to take their issues before the United Nations. Means and Jimmie Durham organized the International Indian Treaty Council (IITC) as the international diplomatic arm of AIM, receiving non-governmental organization (NGO) status at the United Nations in 1977. Other indigenous organizations later entered the arena and began constructing a global network of peoples, nations, and movements designed to secure the attention of international bodies.[131] In 1977 and 1981, this network convened two international conferences in Geneva and Rotterdam to examine the rights of indigenous peoples.[132]

In 1974, the United Nations Sub-Commission on Prevention of Discrimination and Protection of Minorities commissioned a study on the condition of indigenous peoples worldwide. *The Study of the Problem of Discrimination Against Indigenous Populations* by Special Rapporteur José R. Martinez Cobo consisted of ten years of extensive research on the global condition of indigenous peoples.[133] As a direct result of the study and the exhaustive work of indigenous nations themselves, the Sub-Commission voted to establish a Working Group on Indigenous Populations (WGIP) to meet annually in Geneva to provide native peoples with a voice in the international arena.[134] The WGIP has been extremely important in the indigenous quest for self-determination for several reasons. As already mentioned, it provides a forum through which native peoples can articulate their needs and aspirations, including demands for self-determination. Additionally, it exposes states to evolving and expanding debates concerning individual and group rights. In this regard, the draft proposal of the Chair of the Working Group, Erica-Irene A. Daes, for a U.N. declaration on indigenous rights provides a framework through which states can be impressed with the justness and inevitability of extending internationally recognized rights to indigenous peoples.[135]

Because Daes' draft declaration proposal does not explicitly mention the right to self-determination, some indigenous delegates to the WGIP have deemed it inadequate.136 However, despite explicit omission of the term, some benefits of the right to self-determination are clearly recognizable. For example, the draft recognizes certain collective rights—to physical and cultural integrity, traditional lands, and autonomous control of internal political, economic, and social institutions—and it requires states to honor all treaties and agreements made with indigenous nations. It therefore continues to fall short of full recognition of the right of indigenous peoples to determine their own status within the international community, to be recognized as having standing under international law other than as individuals in human rights proceedings, and to bring group claims of genocide or ethnocide. It therefore continues to recognize the supremacy of states in the ultimate determination of the rights and jurisdiction of indigenous nations, and it refuses to recognize the international nature of disputes between states and indigenous nations.

Despite these shortcomings, Daes' draft declaration provides an important step in the long, often tedious, process of transforming international legal standards. In conjunction with the draft declaration provided by indigenous NGOs, and inevitable future drafts, Daes' document can be utilized by the WGIP to educate states and alter their policies toward indigenous peoples. In addition to the draft declaration, the work of the WGIP has led directly to a study on the international status of treaties between indigenous nations and states. The study, led by WGIP member Miguel Alfonso Martinez, of Cuba, may provide native peoples with the impetus necessary to allow international adjudication or arbitration of treaty violations between indigenous peoples and states. To date, indigenous peoples have been left without any legal forums in their treaty disputes with states other than the domestic courts of the state with which they are a party in the treaty. This type of self-adjudication by states, not surprisingly, has led to many unjust interpretations of treaty provisions, to the detriment of indigenous peoples.

Conclusion

The historical denial of the extension of the right of self-determination to indigenous peoples and nations is rooted in the desire of states to protect what they perceive to be their interests. This, too, was the central motivation of some states in their refusal to accept decolonization principles. Fortunately for colonized peoples who were geographically separated from the colonizing states, the international community decided that the self-determination of peoples took priority over the right of states to hold colonies. Although the adoption of this standard was disruptive to the international status quo, advancement of world peace and freedom was considered to be more important. Similarly, a transformation in the attitudes of state actors toward the rights of indigenous peoples is under way. The major obstacle to the attainment of indigenous self-determination is the perceived sacredness of the territorial integrity of states. Recent dramatic developments in the Soviet republics and other countries of the world regarding the rights of national groups to exercise self-determination, including secession, presents an unprecedented opportunity to revisit questions considered long settled.

Of particular prominence in the discussion of indigenous self-determination is the objection that indigenous peoples, wherever they are found, constitute indivisible sectors of a unitary state. To allow indigenous peoples the ultimate expression of self determination, so goes the argument, would constitute secession, and a threat to the territorial integrity of the state in clear violation of the U.N. charter. To characterize indigenous expression of self-determination as secession, it first must be conceded that a nation has been legitimately integrated into a state. If not, it can hardly be argued that the state has a lawful right to maintain that nation in bondage. Most indigenous peoples argue that because their territories have been invaded and incorporated into states without indigenous consent, self-determination does not constitute secession, but merely the exercise of inherent sovereign powers that have never been relinquished.

Even if, for the sake of argument, the ultimate expression of indigenous self-determination *were* to constitute secession, would the recognition of such a right for indigenous peoples disrupt the desire of the international community for world peace and friendly relations between peoples? On the contrary, those aspirations would be enhanced. Professor Ved Nanda's discussion of this point is helpful.[137] Although he does not advocate secession, Nanda recognizes that national self-determination for enclave nations "appears to be an irrepressible feature of the contemporary world scene."[138] Consequently, he proposes the development of international institutional mechanisms to allow the self-determination of peoples who have been denied such rights because their aspirations were considered secessionist. According to Nanda, the legitimacy of the expression of self-determination should be governed by four criteria:

- A clearly identifiable group possessing genuine national characteristics;
- Satisfaction that the nature and the scope of the claim are compelling;
- Substantiation of the underlying historical reasons for the claim; and
- Proof of substantial deprivation of human rights.[139]

Using these criteria, many, if not most, indigenous nations in the Western hemisphere would be entitled to exercise the right. This brings us to another important point. Recognition of the right to self-determination does not compel a move to national independence. In applications of the right to non-self-governing territories, peoples may choose one of three options to express their self-determination. First, they may choose to pursue sovereign independence as a state; second, they may choose a relationship of free association with an independent state; or third, they may choose integration with an independent state. The assumption by states that indigenous peoples exercising a right to self-determination would automatically choose the first option appears unfounded. Given the difficult practical political and economic difficulties facing smaller states in the world today, most indigenous peoples may very well *not* opt for complete independent state status. Many would probably choose some type of autonomy or federation with existing states, preserving rights to internal self-governance and control as members of a larger state. Some however, may choose formal integration into a state, for reasons unique to their particular situation.

Regardless of which status an indigenous nation might choose, the movement toward recognizing each nation's right to make some choice other than unconsented to domination by a colonial or settler state appears consistent with historical notions of self-determination. To apply the conclusions of Nanda to indigenous circumstances, not only would the extension of the right to self-determination to indigenous nations, even if it meant secession, promote the expansion of rights in the world, it would also promote predictable international mechanisms of resolving disputes between indigenous nations and the states around them, leading to an overall expansion of global freedom, peace, and stability.[140] Without recognition of the right, the liberation and survival of indigenous nations remains questionable, and the majority of global conflicts in the world will remain unresolved.[141]

Notes

1. Committee on Native American Struggles, *Rethinking Indian Law,* New York, 1982, IV. For an excellent discussion of the distinctions between the terms "nation," "state," and "Fourth World" (indigenous peoples), see Nietschmann, Bernard, "The Third World War," *Cultural Survival Quarterly,* Vol. 11, No. 3, 1987.
2. Nys, Ernest, *Les Origines du Droit International,* Brussels/Paris, 1984, esp. Chapter Seven.
3. Maine, Henry, ed., *Ancient Law,* 13th edition, London, 1850, p. 257.
4. Nys, op. cit.
5. Aquinas, Thomas, *Summa Theologica Secunda Secundae,* Venetiis, 1593, Quarto 11, Article 10.
6. Nys, op. cit.
7. Post, Gaines, *Studies in Medieval Legal Thought,* Princeton University Press, Princeton, NJ, 1964, pp. 532-61.
8. Gottschalk, Paul, *Earliest Diplomatic Documents of America,* New York, 1978, p. 21. Also see Deloria, Vine Jr., *Behind the Trail of Broken Treaties: An Indian Declaration of Independence,* Delacourte Press, New York, 1974, p. 87.
9. These tensions resulted in the Treaty of Tordesillas on June 7, 1494, between Spain and Portugal, putatively dividing the planet into two equal parts. Other European States, particularly England, France, and Holland, ignored or militarily resisted the pontifical donations. Ultimately, whatever legal force was vested in the Bulls was replaced by the theory of effective occupation of territories by colonial powers. See Truyol y Serra, Antonio, "The Discovery of the New World and International Law," *Toledo Law Review,* No. 43, 1971, pp. 310-1.
10. Gottschalk, op. cit., p. 21.
11. Truyol y Serra, op. cit., p. 313.
12. See notes 22-28 and accompanying text. For a contrary opinion on Victoria, see Williams, Robert A., Jr., "The Medieval and Renaissance Origins of the Status of the American Indian in Western

Legal Thought," *Southern California Law Review*, Vol. 57, No. 1, 1983, pp. 1-99.
13. Truyol y Serra, op. cit., p. 315. Also see Hanke, Lewis, *Aristotle and the American Indians: A Study in Race Prejudice in the Modern World*, Indiana University Press, Bloomington/Indianapolis, 1959, pp. 14-15.
14. Hanke, Lewis, *All Mankind Is One: A Study of the Disputation Between Bartolomé de Las Casas and Juan Ginés de Sepúlveda in 1550 on the Intellectual and Religious Capacity of the American Indians*, Northern Illinois University Press, Dekalb, 1974, pp. 4-5.
15. *Aristotle and the Indians*, op. cit., p. 15. Also see Diaz, Jorge, "Los Doctrinas de Palacios Rubios y Matias de Paz ante la Conquista de America," in *Memoria de El Colegio Nacional*, Burgos, Spain, 1950, pp. 71-94.
16. See Bullon, Lewis, *El Doctor Palacios Rubios y Sus Obras*, Madrid, 1927.
17. See Hanke, Lewis, "The 'Requirimiento' and Its Interpreters," in *Sobretiro de la Revista de la Historia de America*, No. 1, 1938, pp. 25-34. Also see *All Mankind Is One*, op. cit., pp. 35-37. In part, the *Requirimiento* admonished the indigenous hosts that if they did not agree to convert to Catholicism and submit to the Europeans, the invaders would "take you and your wives and your children, and [we] shall make slaves of them and as such shall sell and dispose of them as their Highnesses may command; and we shall take away your goods, and we shall do all the harm and damage that we can as to vassals who do not obey...and we protest that the deaths and losses which shall accrue from this are your fault, and not that of their Highnesses, or ours, nor of these gentlemen who come with us."
18. "Just War" was a concept developed in Roman law that permitted nearly any military action for the purpose of defending the *patria*. Under medieval papal law, the war was considered just if it was for the defense "of the faith and the Church." Post, op. cit., p. 437. Later, Vattel would write that Just War can be employed only in the necessity of self defense, and that if a nation takes up arms when it has received no injury, nor is threatened with any, it undertakes an unjust war. Vattel, Emer, *The Law of Nations*, Book III, VII, Sec. 26, p. 302. Accordingly, it appears that, as regards the Spanish wars against the indigenous peoples of the Americas, the only legal right to wage a Just War belonged to the indigenous nations.
19. Truyol y Serra, op. cit., pp. 317-18.
20. Vattel, op. cit., p. 315.
21. Among those supporting Las Casas have been Balthazar Ayala, who believed that sovereignty was not exclusively a Christian right; Hugo Grotius (1583-1645) agreed that the Spanish had no right to wage a Just War in the Americas based on discovery and also believed in the equality of nations. His teachings have been extended to create the foundation for the current system of international law through the United Nations, embracing Christian and non-Christian nations alike (see Taylor, Robert, *International Public Law*, Metheun Publishers, London, 1901, pp. 75, 91). Samuel Puffendorf supported the principles of Las Casas, writing that "since every man is by nature equal to every man, and consequently not subject to the dominion of others, therefore, this bare seizing by force is not enough to found a lawful sovereignty over men" (cited in Lindley, Mark Frank, *The Acquisition and Government of Backward Country in International Law: A Treatise on the Law and Practice Relating to Colonial Expansion*, Longmans, Green Publishers, London, 1926, p. 14). The German theorists, Gunther, Kliber, and Heffter, agreed that no nation, regardless of its degree of civilization, has the right to take the property of another nation, "even savages or nomads" (Ibid., pp. 14-15). The French publisher Jeze argued in favor of the absolute right of indigenous nations to territorial and political sovereignty and held that land cessions by indigenous nations must be made freely, intelligently, and according to the customs of the indigenous nation (see Jeze, Gaston, *Etude Theoretique et Pratique Sur L'occupation Comme Mode d'Acquerir les Territoires en Droit International*, Paris, 1896). Those aligning themselves with Sepúlveda in his denial of indigenous rights to territorial and political sovereignty include the relatively modern publicists Westlake, Hall, Lawrence, and Marten Ferraro (see Lindley, op. cit., pp. 18-19). All of these men agreed with the proposition that due to the superior civilization of Europe, indigenous peoples could lose their territories without their consent through Euroamerican occupation. It should not pass unnoticed that all of these theorists hailed from states which, at the time of their publication, were holding vast tracts of territory that arguably belonged to indigenous nations.
22. Nys, Ernest, ed., *Franciscus de Victoria, De Indis et de Jure Belli: Relectiones*, Oceana Publishers, New York, 1917.
23. Ibid., Section 1, Title 4, p. 120.

24. Ibid., Section 7, Title 1-6, pp. 129-37.
25. Ibid., Section 2, Title 7-16, pp. 137-49.
26. Cohen, Felix S., *Handbook of Federal Indian Law*, University of New Mexico Press, Albuquerque (reprint of 1942 U.S. Government edition), n.d., p. 47.
27. Vattel, op. cit. Also see Kinney, Jay P., *A Continent Lost—A Civilization Won: Indian Land Tenure in America*, Johns Hopkins University Press, Baltimore, 1937, pp. 11-12, for a description of negotiations between Roger Williams, founder of the state of Rhode Island, and the Narragansett Nation; and Washburn, Wilcomb, *The Indian in America*, Harper and Row Publishers, New York, 1975, pp. 84-5, for a description of the negotiations between William Penn, founder of the state of Pennsylvania, and the indigenous nations of the region.
28. Cohen, op. cit., p. 47.
29. *Papal Bull Sublimis Deus*, in MacNutt, Francis Augustus, *Bartholomew de Las Casas: His Life, His Apostolate, and His Writings*, New York, 1909, p. 429. It should be noted that Papal Bulls were not considered cursory declarations, but carried with them the full force of law, particularly upon Catholic sovereigns. See Ullman, Walter, *The Church and the Laws in the Early Middle Ages: Selected Essays*, Metheun Publishers, London, 1975, pp. 131-2.
30. Las Casas reported the slaughter of over 20 million indigenous people in the Caribbean and Mexico before 1542. Las Casas, Fray Bartolomé de, "Cruelties of the Spaniards," in Charles Gibson, ed., *The Spanish Tradition in America*, Harper and Row Publishers, New York, 1968, pp. 106-08.
31. Las Casas, Fray Bartolomé de, "Disputa con Ginés de Sepúlveda Acerca de Lictud de las Conquistas de las Indias," in *Revista de Derecho Internacional y Political Exterior*, Madrid, 1908, Chapters LIX-LXI.
32. For a chronicle of the debate, see *All Mankind Is One*, op. cit.
33. Gibson, op. cit., pp. 113-20.
34. Lindley, op. cit., p. 12. Also see Las Casas, *In Defense of the Indians*, translated by S. Poole, Oxford University Press, London/New York, 1973.
35. Land grants to Spanish subjects to the prejudice of the indigenous peoples who had historically lived in the same area were prohibited. Any grant resulting in prejudice or injury to the indigenous nation was legally null, and full restitution was mandated. Not only was this a recognition of indigenous land rights, but it was also an admission that indigenous peoples possessed land rights previous to, and not subject to, the Crown. See Law of June 11, 1594, in *Recopilacion de Leyes de Los Reynos de las Indias*, Madrid, 1861, Bk. 4, title 12, law 9. See generally Taylor, John, *Spanish Law Concerning Discoveries, Pacifications, and Settlements Among the Indians*, University of Utah Press, Salt Lake City, 1980; and Hall, George, *Laws of Mexico*, Metheun Publishers, London, 1885.
36. Felix Cohen, "The Spanish Origin of Indian Rights in the Law of the United States," *Georgetown Law Review*, Vol. 31, No. 1, 1942, pp. 14-16. Also see Hanke, Lewis, *The Spanish Struggle for Justice in the Conquest of America*, University of Pennsylvania Press, Philadelphia, 1949.
37. Cohen, op. cit., p. 13.
38. See McNutt, op. cit., and Lindley, op. cit.
39. Williams, Robert A. Jr., *The American Indian in Western Legal Thought: The Discourses of Conquest*, Oxford University Press, London/New York, 1990, p. 136.
40. Ibid., pp. 165-71.
41. Ibid., p. 204.
42. Ibid., pp. 214-6.
43. For a comprehensive overview of these foundations, see ibid., pp. 151-334.
44. In describing his arrival in the Americas, Columbus characterized the indigenous people as "simple and honest, and exceedingly liberal with all they have...They exhibit great love towards all others in preference to themselves...They are men of great deference and kindness" (*The Columbus Letter of March 14, 1493*, University of Chicago Press, Chicago, 1953, pp. 6-10). In return "he resorted to a monstrous expedient of sending hundreds of the [Indians] overseas, to the slave market in Seville...the policy and acts of Columbus for which he was responsible began the depopulation of the terrestial paradise that was Hispaniola [sic]. Of the original natives [numbering at least 3,000,000 in 1492]...in 1548 Ovieda doubted whether 500 Indians remained" (Morison, Samuel Eliot, *Admiral of the Ocean Sea: A Life of Christopher Columbus*, Little, Brown Publishers, Boston, 1942, pp. 486-7, 492-3).
45. The subject of the initial European-Indian contact has been covered extensively elsewhere. See,

for example, Vogel, Virgil J., *This Country Was Ours: A Documentary History of the American Indian,* Harper and Row Publishers, New York, 1972, pp. 27, 52; Gibson, Arrell Morgan, *The American Indian: Prehistory to the Present,* D.C. Heath and Co., Publishers, Lexington, MA, 1985, p. 247; Brotherson, Gordon, *Image of the New World: The American Continent Portrayed in Native Texts,* Oxford University Press, London/New York, 1979; and Wrone, David R., and Russell S. Nelson, Jr., eds., *Who's the Savage?* Discus Books, New York, 1973.

46. Vattel, op. cit.

47. Maine, op. cit.

48. Broadhead, John R., "Documents Relative to the Colonial History of the State of New York," in Edmund Bailey O'Callaghan, ed., *Documents Relative to the Colonial History of the State of New York,* Vol. 1: Holland Documents II, No. 27, State Historical Society of New York, Albany, 1856, p. 99; cited in *Handbook of Federal Indian Law,* op. cit., p. 53.

49. Ibid.

50. Berman, Howard R., "The Concept of Aboriginal Rights in the Early History of the United States," *Buffalo Law Review,* No. 27, 1978, pp. 637, 653.

51. *Worcester v. Georgia,* at 542-543. Also see Coulter, Robert T., "United States Denial of Indian Property Rights: A Study in Lawless Power and Racial Discrimination," in *Rethinking Indian Law,* op. cit.

52. See Vaughan, Aldin T., *The New England Frontier: Puritans and Indians 1620-1675,* Little, Brown Publishers, Boston, 1965, pp. 109-120.

53. *Handbook of Federal Indian Law,* op. cit., pp. 56-58.

54. Ibid.

55. The Continental Congress created separate departments for its diplomatic relations with indigenous nations. Commissioners were appointed to serve essentially the same function as ambassadors, and the Congress explicitly acknowledged that "securing and preserving the friendship of Indian nations appears to be a subject of utmost moment to these colonies" (*Joint Continental Congress,* No. 2, [1795], p. 175). The British fully recognized the capacity of indigenous nations to harass, or decimate if they so chose, the Colonies. See Fey, Harold Edward, and D'Arcy McNickle, *Indians and Other Americans: Two Ways of Life Meet,* Harper and Brothers Publishers, New York, (revised edition) 1959, p. 55.

56. Treaty with the Delawares, September 17, 1778, 7 Stat. 13.

57. *Worcester v. Georgia,* at 550.

58. United States Constitution, Art. I, Sec. 8, cl. 2; Art. II, Sec. 2, cl. 1; The Trade and Intercourse Acts of 1790, 1 *Stat.* 137; 1793, 1 *Stat.* 329; 1796, 1 *Stat.* 469; 1802, 2 *Stat.* 139; and 1834, 4 *Stat.* 729.

59. Opinion rendered by Attorney General William Wirt (Op. Atty. Gen.), April 26, 1821, p. 345.

60. Op. Atty. Gen., 1828, pp. 613-18, 623-33:

61. Formal treaty making with indigenous nations was halted unilaterally by the United States with the Act of March 3, 1871, Ch. 120, sec. 1, 16 *Stat.* 544, 566. The statute explicitly states that "no obligation of any treaty previously satisfied shall be hereby invalidated or impaired."

62. See Margold, Nathan R., "Introduction," in Felix S. Cohen, *Handbook of Federal Indian Law,* U.S. Department of Interior, Washington, D.C., 1942, p. vii. Also see *Washington v. Washington State Commercial Passenger Fishing Vessel Association,* 443 U.S. 658, 675 (1979); *U.S. v. Forty-Three Gallons of Whiskey,* 93 U.S. (17 Wall.) 211, 242-3 (1872); *Worcester v. Georgia,* at 559.

63. See Barsh, Russel, "Indigenous North America and International Law," *Oregon Law Review,* No. 62, 1983, pp. 114-18.

64. *Choctaw Nation v. Oklahoma,* 397 U.S. 620, 631 (1970); *U.S. v. Shoshone Tribe,* 304 U.S. 111, 116 (1938); *Tulee v. Washington,* 315 U.S. 681, 684-85 (1942).

65. *McClanahan v. Arizona State Tax Commission,* 411 U.S. 164, 174 (1973); *Carpenter v. Shaw,* 280 U.S. 363 (1930); *Winters v. United States,* 207 U.S. 564.

66. *Washington v. Fishing Vessel Association; Menominee Tribe v. United States,* 391 U.S. 404 (1968). See generally, Wilkinson, Charles F., and John M. Volkman, "Judicial Review of Indian Treaty Abrogation. As Long As the Water Flows or Grass Grows Upon the Earth—How Long a Time Is That?" *California Law Review,* No. 63, 1975, pp. 601-61.

67. Referring to the treaties which preceded the forced removal of the indigenous nations of the southeastern United States in the 1830s, Vogel (op. cit., pp. 285-6) writes: "The treaties which preceded these expulsions...were masterpieces of intimidation, bribery, threats, and fraud.

Following these efforts to produce a fig leaf of legality for the operation, Indians were hunted down like animals, bound as prisoners, and confined in stockades to await removal. The conditions of the deportation were so barbarous that about one-third of the emigres died on the journey."

68. See *Island of Palmas Case*, Permanent Court of Arbitral Awards, 1928, pp. 44-5; Scott, James Brown, *Hague Court Reports*, The Hague, 2d Series, 1932, 84 et. seq. (115-116); "Cayuga Indian Claims Case," *Annual Digest of Public International Law Cases (1925-1926)*, pp. 237-38, 22 January 1926.

69. Rosenne, Shabati, *The Law of Treaties: A Guide to the Legislative History of the Vienna Convention*, Leyden, 1970, p. 108; *Harvard Research Draft Convention on the Law of Treaties*, Harvard University Press, Cambridge, MA, 1935, pp. 686-8; Report by J.L. Brierly, Special Rapporteur on the Law of Treaties, UN Doc. A/CN.4/23, 14 April 1950 (in *Yearbook of the International Law Commission* [YBILC] 1950 II, pp. 222-48); Crandell, Samuel Benjamin, *Treaties, Their Making and Enforcement*, Columbia University Press, New York (2d ed.) 1916, p. 76; Jencks, Wilfried C., *Law in the World Community*, Oxford University Press, London/New York, 1967, p. 143. Rosenne defined a treaty as follows: "Treaty means an international agreement concluded between states in written form and governed by international law, whether embodied in a single instrument or in two or more related instruments and whatever its particular designation."

70. For example, the case of Portugal's colonies. See note 81, below.

71. Rigo Sureda, Andres, *The Evolution of the Right of Self-Determination*, Leyden, 1973, p. 66: "It is doubtful whether states can claim domestic jurisdiction, since these constitutional changes purport to affect the international status of territories with respect of which they have pledged themselves to fulfill certain obligations." In 1989, The Economic and Social Council of the United Nations authorized a full study of the international scope, character, and status of treaties between indigenous nations and states. ECOSOC Res. 1989/77, U.N. Doc. E/1989/INF/7, at 154 (1989).

72. U.S. Senate, *Congressional Globe*, Appendix, 74, 27th Cong., 2d Sess., U.S. Government Printing Office, Washington, D.C., 1846.

73. U.S. Senate, *Congressional Record* 2462, 46th Cong., 2d Sess., U.S. Government Printing Office, Washington, D.C., 1880.

74. Cited in Drinnon, Richard, *Facing West: The Metaphysics of Indian-Hating and Empire Building*, University of Minnesota Press, Minneapolis, 1980.

75. John Medill, *Annual Report of the Commissioner of Indian Affairs*, in House Executive Document No. 1, Serial 537, 30th Cong., 2d Sess., U.S. Government Printing Office, Washington, D.C., 1848, pp. 385-89.

76. Johanson, Bruce, and Roberto Maestas, *Wasi'chu: The Continuing Indian Wars*, Monthly Review Press, New York, 1979, p. 31.

77. "Whoever agrees that robbery is a crime, and that we are not allowed to take forcible possession of our neighbor's property, will acknowledge, without any other proof, that no nation has a right to expel another people from the country they inhabit in order to settle in it herself" (Vattel, op. cit., p. 168).

78. The effects of this can be seen in Churchill, Ward, and Jim Vander Wall, *Agents of Repression: The FBI's Secret War Against the Black Panther Party and the American Indian Movement*, South End Press, Boston, 1988, pp. 103-97 .

79. These changes have included the Tribal Self-Governance Demonstration Project, P.L. 100-472 (1988), through which ten indigenous nations were allowed greater control over their affairs independent of the BIA. In 1990, seven nations were continuing the project, and moving toward complete separation from the BIA in their affairs. In addition, the U.S. Senate has begun seriously to entertain the idea, advocated many years ago by the American Indian Movement (AIM), of abolishing the BIA and allowing indigenous nations to exercise a more genuine brand of self-determination. See U.S. Senate, Select Committee on Indian Affairs, *Final Report and Legislative Recommendations, Report of the Special Committee on Investigations*, 101st Cong., 1st Sess., U.S. Government Printing Office, Washington, D.C., 1989, pp. 15-23.

80. *Handbook on Federal Indian Law*, op. cit., p. 247.

81. This refers particularly to the former colonies of Angola, Mozambique, Guinea-Bissau, Cape Verde, and Sao Tomé, which have attained their independence; and East Timor, which

continues its struggle to achieve its independence—now from Indonesia, which invaded the territory after Portugal withdrew.

82. See *Everyone's United Nations*, United Nations, New York, 1978, pp. 306-12.
83. Ibid., pp. 296-303.
84. Manley, Michael, *Jamaica: Struggle in the Periphery*, Monthly Review Press, New York, 1982, p. 217.
85. For a popular exposition on this theme, see "Fraud In Indian Country" (7 part series), *Arizona Republic*, October 4-11, 1987.
86. *Message from the President Transmitting Recommendations for Indian Policy*, H.R. Doc. 363, 91st Cong., 2d Sess. (1970). According to the National Indian Youth Council and the National Congress of American Indians, in the late 1980s, 60 percent of all indigenous people living on reservations lived in abject poverty. Rural unemployment was 80 percent, and the average indigenous person earned $7,200 per year less than the average U.S. citizen. Twenty-five percent of all indigenous children had been placed in non-Indian residences. Indigenous people have the highest per capita incidence of diabetes, heart disease, and infant mortality of any group in the U.S. and die from liver disease at ten times the U.S. rate. The alcoholism rate among indigenous youth between the ages 15 to 26 is eight times higher than the U.S. average, and one-third of all indigenous people in the U.S. die before reaching the age of 45. Incidences of hepatitis and teen age suicide are higher among indigenous peoples than any other group in the U.S. See *Miami Herald*, November 24, 1989.
87. Gibson, op. cit., pp. 443-56, 489-510, 517-21, 556-58. For a specific case study of the adverse influence of the BIA and Department of the Interior (DOI) on indigenous nations, see Moore, John H., "The Muskoke National Question in Oklahoma," *Science and Society*, Vol. 52, No. 2, 1988.
88. U.S. Commission on Civil Rights, *The Navajo Nation: An American Colony*, U.S. Government Printing Office, Washington, D.C., 1975.
89. These minerals include oil shale, gilsonite, uranium, gypsum, helium, copper, iron, zinc, lead, phosphate, asbestos, and bentonite. See Churchill, Ward, "The New Genocide: A Hidden Holocaust in the State of Native American Environments," *Research in Inequality and Social Conflict*, No. 1, 1989, and Jorgensen, Joseph, ed., *Native Americans and Energy Development II*, Anthropology Resource Center/Seventh Generation Fund, Boston, 1984. Despite the creation of such organizations as the Council of Energy Resource Tribes (CERT), ostensibly founded to survey and monitor energy resource exploitation on indigenous nations' lands, the theft of resources continues.
90. *Cherokee Nation v. Georgia*, at 17: "[Indigenous nations] are in a state of pupilage; their relation to the United States resembles that of a ward to his guardian."
91. *United States v. Mitchell* (Mitchell I), 445 U.S. 535 (1980); *Nevada v. United States*, 463 U.S. 110 (1983).
92. *United States v. Mitchell* (Mitchell II), 463 U.S. 206 (1983). Despite Mitchell II, the Court has never granted damages to indigenous peoples for breach of a general fiduciary obligation, such as is enforceable in the common law of trusts. See Chambers, Reid, "Judicial Enforcement of the Federal Trust Responsibility to Indians," *Stanford Law Review*, No. 27, 1975, p. 1213.
93. Cristescu, Aureliu, *The Right to Self-Determination: Historical and Current Developments on the Basis of United Nations Instruments*, U.N. Doc. E/CN.4/Sub.2/404/Rev.1, (1981), p. 46.
94. For an extensive listing of U.N. General Assembly and Security Council resolutions on the right to self determination, see Cristescu, Aureliu, *The Historical and Current Development of the Right to Self-Determination on the Basis of the Charter of the United Nations and Other Instruments Adopted by the United Nations Organs, With Particular Reference to the Promotion and Protection of Human Rights and Fundamental Freedoms*, U.N. Doc. E/CN.4/Sub.2/404, 2 June 1978, Vol. 1, pp. 66-9. For purposes of this paper, I have adopted the definitions developed by Alfredsson concerning "decolonization" and "self-determination": "The terms of political decolonization and external self-determination are closely interrelated and have in practice been used interchangeably. A discussion of one without extensive use of the other is practically impossible. Political decolonization can either be viewed as a separate rule of international law or as a sub-category of self-determination relating to the right of colonial territories to external self-determination...[S]elf determination can contain the right of potential beneficiaries to determine their international status, to live without foreign interference inside their own boundaries and to choose their own form of government or internal political organization, to

choose their government in a democratic manner, not to be oppressed by the majority of a State population, and to pursue their social and cultural development. Most recently, self-determination has played a role in the north-south dialogue about the distribution of wealth and control over natural resources." See Alfredsson, Gudmundur, "Greenland and the Law of Political Decolonization," *German Yearbook of International Law*, No. 25, 1982.

95. Quoted in Raschhofer, Hermann, "The Right of Self-Determination from the Western Viewpoint," *International Law and Diplomacy*, No. 31, 1962, pp. 25-36.

96. Ibid. Also see Pomerance, Michla, *Self-Determination in Law and Practice*, The Hague, 1982, pp. 1-8.

97. See Connor, Walker, *The National Question in Marxist-Leninist Theory and Strategy*, Princeton University Press, Princeton, NJ, 1984, pp. 33-8.

98. Lenin, V.I., *The Right of Nations to Self-Determination*, Progress Publishers, Moscow, 1974, p. 98.

99. Strausshenko, Gyorgy, *The Principle of National Self-Determination in Soviet Foreign Policy*, Progress Publishers, Moscow, 1969, p. 88.

100. Fein, Esther B., "Gorbachev Urges Lithuania to Stay Within Soviet Union," *New York Times*, January 12, 1990, p. 1. According to Yuri Maslyukov, a member of the Soviet Politburo and an associate of Soviet President Gorbachev, "It is only natural that Lithuanians have the right to decide their fate—to be within the Soviet Union or to leave the Soviet Union."

101. *Everyone's United Nations*, op. cit., p. 278.

102. Alfredsson, op. cit., pp. 5-6.

103. Ibid.

104. Claude, Inis L. Jr., *The Changing United Nations*, Anchor Books, New York, 1967.

105. U.N. Charter, Articles 1(2) and 55; also see Articles 73 and 76.

106. *The Right to Self-Determination*, op. cit., p. 86.

107. Crawford, op. cit., pp. 89-106. He suggests that self-determination is recognized in the charter as a principle of law, and as a right only after the unit of self-determination has been determined by the application of appropriate rules.

108. Higgins, Rosalyn, *The Development of International Law Through the Political Organs of the United Nations*, Oxford University Press, London/New York, 1963, p. 104.

109. General Assembly Resolution (GA Res.) 1514 (XV), U.N. Doc A/4684 (1960), in General Assembly Official Records (GAOR), 15th Sess., Supp. 16, pp. 66-67; GA Res. 2131 (XX), U.N. Doc. A/6014 (1965), in GAOR, 20th Sess. Supp. 14, pp. 11-12; GA Res 2625 (XXV), U.N. Doc. A/8082 (1970), in GAOR 25th Sess., Supp. 28, p. 121.

110. The two covenants, known together as the *U.N. Human Rights Covenants*, were approved by the General Assembly in 1966, and have been in force since 1976. See Alfredsson, op. cit., pp. 15-16. Also see Kelly, Joseph B., "National Minorities in International Law," *Denver Journal of International Law and Politics*, No. 3, 1973, p. 267; citing Summary Records of the Sub-Commission Meeting, 1972, U.N. Doc. E/CN 4/sub.2/SR647, p. 150.

111. Alfredsson, op. cit., p. 22.

112. Ibid.

113. *ICJ Reports*, 1971, p. 31; reaffirmed in *ICJ Reports*, 1975, p. 31.

114. Alfredsson, op. cit., pp. 43-61.

115. Ibid., p. 46.

116. Ibid., p. 51.

117. See generally, Deloria, Vine, Jr., and Clifford M. Lytle, *The Nations Within: The Past and Future of American Indian Sovereignty*, Pantheon Books, New York, 1984.

118. Barsh, Russel, op. cit. Also see *The Sacred Mission of Civilization: To Which Peoples Should the Benefit be Extended? The Belgian Thesis*, Belgium Government Information Center, New York, 1953, p. 3.

119. See generally, note 70, above.

120. Alfredsson, op. cit., p. 23.

121. Ibid., p. 59.

122. For a general discussion, see Independent Commission of International Humanitarian Issues, *Indigenous Peoples: A Global Quest For Justice*, Zed Press, London, 1987.

123. Sanders, Douglas, "The Re-Emergence of Indigenous Questions in International Law," *Canadian Human Rights Yearbook*, No. 3, 1983, p. 13.

124. Ibid., p. 14.

125. Editors, *A Basic Call to Consciousness*, Akwesasne Notes, Mohawk Nation via Rooseveltown, NY, 1978, pp. 19-35.

126. Convention Concerning the Protection and Integration of Indigenous and Other Tribal and Semi-tribal Populations in Independent Countries, adopted by the General Conference of the ILO, 26 June 1957; Convention No. 107, United Nations Treaty Series (UNTS) 238, p. 247.

127. Bennet, Gordon, *Aboriginal Rights in International Law*, Royal Anthropological Institute, London, 1978, p. 7985.

128. *The Indigenous and Tribal Peoples Convention*, International Labor Conf., 76th Sess., Prov. Rec. 25 (1989).

129. Dunbar Ortiz, Roxanne, *Indians of the Americas: Human Rights and Self-Determination*, Zed Press, London, 1984, pp. 27-70.

130. Weyler, Rex, *Blood of The Land: The U.S. Government and Corporate War Against the American Indian Movement*, Everest House Publishers, New York, 1982. Also see Churchill and Vander Wall, op. cit.

131. Among the more notable actors in this movement are the Indian Law Resource Center, Inuit Circumpolar Conference, National Indian Youth Council, Australian and Islander Legal Services, South American Indian Council, International Indian Treaty Council, Four Directions Council, and the World Council of Indigenous Peoples.

132. Ismaelillo and Robin Wright, eds., *Native Peoples in Struggle*, Akwesasne Notes, Mohawk Nation via Rooseveltown, NY, 1982; *A Basic Call To Consciousness*, op. cit.

133. Martinez Cobo, José R., *Study of the Problem of Discrimination Against Indigenous Populations*, U.N. Doc. E/CN.4/Sub.2/1987/Add.4.

134. U.N. Doc. E/CN.4/Sub. 2/1983/21, August 5, 1983. Also see Sanders, Douglas, "The UN Working Group on Indigenous Populations," *Human Rights Quarterly*, No. 11, 1989.

135. E/CN.4/Sub.2/1988/25, 212, June 1988; Appendix 1.

136. E/CN.4/Sub.2/AC.4/1985/WP.5; Appendix 2.

137. Nanda, Ved, "Self-Determination Under International Law: Validity of Claims to Secede," *Case Western Reserve Journal of International Law*, No. 13, 1981, p. 57.

138. Ibid., p. 278.

139. Ibid., p. 275.

140. Ibid., p. 279.

141. Nietschmann (op. cit., p. 7) notes that the vast majority of the world's armed conflicts are between indigenous nations struggling for some level of self-determination, and states that oppose such aspirations.

Chapter III

Self-Determination and Subordination
The Past, Present, and Future of American Indian Governance

Rebecca L. Robbins

[V]iewed in their totality, as one among many alternative routes that the course of Indian-white...history could have followed, the present status of [American Indians] presents an extraordinary spectacle of a variety of small cultural enclaves that have maintained better than anyone might have expected their culture, their aspirations, their land, and their autonomy after being overwhelmed by a tidal wave of invaders.

Wilcomb Washburn
Smithsonian Historian, 1985

How do we make permanent the understanding that [American Indian nations] are political entities? We are more than just unique little cultures. We are tired of educating the Congress and the government about this basic relationship.

LaDonna Harris
Comanche, 1986

The key to understanding the social, economic, and political status of contemporary Native North America rests in determining the form by which it is governed. Traditionally, the indigenous nations of this continent were entirely autonomous and self-regulating, having perfected highly complex and sophisticated governmental forms long before the European invasion of the hemisphere.[1] Indigenous governance in the Americas was far more refined than that evidenced across the Atlantic, at least until some point well into the 19th century. Certain of the structures and principles of indigenous governance, notably those drawn from the Haudenosaunee (Iroquois) Confederacy—consisting of the Mohawk, Onondaga, Seneca, Cayuga, Oneida, and Tuscarora nations, all located within the present state of New York and adjoining areas of Canada—were so advanced that they were consciously utilized as a primary model upon which the U.S. Constitution was formulated and the federal government created.[2]

As researcher Sharon O'Brien has framed the matter:

[S]ometime between A.D. 1000 and 1500, a great, visionary leader, Deganawidah, proposed that warring tribes form a confederacy—The Great Peace (known by whites as the Iroquois League, or Iroquois Confederacy) remains in existence. It was founded on the principles Deganewidah and his kinspeople cherished and nurtured: freedom, respect, tolerance, consensus, and brotherhood. These values contrasted sharply with the principles which underlay European governments at the time. In the 1500s, European governments were based on notions such as authoritarian rule by monarchs and the use of force and coercion to bring about unquestioning obedience.[3]

Under the terms and spirit of the *Ne Gayaneshagowa,* or "Great Binding Law," to which all parties pledged themselves:

[T]he confederacy's constitution provided for a governing council of fifty civil chiefs, the Council of Fifty [each member of which was appointed by, and could be recalled by, elder women known as Clan Mothers]. Each of the fifty seats was named, ranked, and associated with a particular duty or responsibility...Each year the Onondagas called together the Council of Fifty to discuss matters of mutual concern and resolve differences peacefully. Matters of interest strictly to one [nation] were handled by that [nation] individually, but anything involving two or more [nations] was discussed by the Council of Fifty...[T]he Onondagas were responsible for confirming [any] decision or subjecting it to further discussion. Ideally, all decisions were unanimous. All council members were to be of "one heart, one mind, one law." The system gave all [six] nations equal power.[4]

Nor were the Iroquois the only such example. With regard to the powerful Muscogee (Creek) Confederacy of the present states of Georgia and Alabama, O'Brien delineates an extremely complex structure balancing such matters as age and gender roles, civic and insular affairs, as well as secular and spiritual matters, through a "three-tiered system of advisors" that apportioned powers and responsibilities throughout society:

Harmony was so highly valued among the Muscogees that a special system was devised to maintain it even when a major issue could not be resolved to everyone's satisfaction. If a member or several members of a *talwa* [community] continued to disagree with the majority on a policy, they were free to move on and establish their own community, with the support—not the enmity—of those whose *talwa* they were leaving. When a dissident group established a new town (and also when a neighboring [nation] joined the Muscogee Confederacy), an ember from one of the mother [original] *talwas* was used to start the fire of the new settlement as a symbol of continuity and unity.[5]

The Lakota (Sioux) Nation of the northern Great Plains region, an entity that actually constituted a functioning confederation rather than a single homogeneous socio-political unit, developed an intricate localized structure known as the *tiyospaye* within which women exercised considerable practical influence by virtue of owning all real property and elders maintained not only an active advisory capacity with regard to the conduct of younger executives, but effective veto power over their decisions. The *tiyospaye* was manifested upward, to the national level. From there, this decentralized and inherently inclusive form of organization was inherently reflected by all seven participant nations—the Oglala, Sicangu (Brûlé), Minneconjou, Hunkpapa, Itazipco (Sans Arcs), Sihasapa (Blackfeet), and Oohinunpa (Two Kettles)—with regard to their overall participation in the confederacy.[6]

Many comparable examples of this refinement and sophistication were exhibited by traditional American Indian governments. These include the forms and structures evident among the various Pueblos of present day New Mexico and Arizona,[7] the Yaqui Confederation of the Sonoran Desert region,[8] those of the Yakimas and other nations of the Great Basin area,[9] and others. The point is that the indigenous peoples of North America required lessons in democratic governance from no one. To the contrary, their precontact attainments in this regard not only informed the establishment of the first modern democracy achieved by the European tradition (the United States), but they also exerted a noticeable influence on French Enlightenment philosophers such as Rousseau, whose thinking provided considerable impetus to the French Revolution.[10] To a certain extent at least, the same can be said with regard to such post-enlightenment European political thinkers as Karl Marx and Frederick Engels.[11]

Implications of U.S.-Indian Treaties

There can be no doubt that the United States formally recognized the fully sovereign national status and character of North American indigenous governments during the period following the American Revolution.[12] This was undoubtedly due in large part to the fact that native nations had held—and in many respects continued to hold for some time—the balance of military power all along the new republic's western border.[13] Additionally, as Vine Deloria, Jr., has pointed out, the Continental Congress, representing as it did an outlaw state, was desperate to establish its ability to comport itself responsibly and in accordance with the customs and conventions of diplomatic law.[14] Indian nations, many of which had already been formally recognized through treaties as legitimate sovereignties by various European Crowns, were in more of a position to recognize the legitimacy of the U.S. than the other way around.[15]

Correspondingly, U.S. relations with American Indians were legally restricted—in precisely the same fashion that relations were restricted with the European powers—to the level of interchange between the federal executive and various indigenous governments.[16] This is to say, the relationship was formally cast as being government-to-government in nature, a matter abundantly reflected in the fact that the U.S. Senate ratified not fewer than 371 separate treaties with Native American governments between 1778 and 1871.[17] These were complemented by a myriad of international agreements, unratified treaties, and other instruments of foreign affairs extending into the early 20th century.[18] At least as late as the Supreme Court's 1903 *Lonewolf v. Hitchcock* decision, federal authorities were still sending *de facto* treaty commissions into the field to negotiate with native leaders as the heads of nations entirely separate from the United States.[19]

Insofar as the federal government is constitutionally prohibited from entering into treaty relationships with any entity other than another fully sovereign national government, it follows that each treaty entered into by the United States with an Indian nation served the purpose of conveying formal federal recognition that the Indian nation involved was indeed a nation within the true legal and political meanings of the term. Further, given that these treaties remain on the books and thus are binding upon both parties, it follows that North American indigenous peoples continue to hold a clear legal entitlement—even under U.S. law—to conduct themselves as completely sovereign nations unless they themselves freely determine that things should be otherwise.[20] For this reason, they have been described as constituting "the nations within" the United States.[21] The native nations of North America are not presently allowed, however, to comport themselves as such.

The current reality is that American Indian governance within the United States has been converted into something very different from that which traditionally prevailed, or anything remotely resembling the exercise of national self-determination. Through the unilateral assertion of U.S. "plenary power" over Indian affairs, a doctrine forcefully articulated in the 1886 *United States v. Kagama* case, the status of indigenous national governments has been subordinated to that of the federal government. In other words, the sovereignty of native nations has been diminished without their consent to approximately the same level as that enjoyed by the states of the union. Under legislation such as Public Law 280, which emerged during the 1950s, the status of Indian nations has been in many cases again unilaterally lowered by the United States, this time to a level below that of the states, placing the indigenous governments affected by the change in approximately the same posture as counties.[22] Today, in a number of areas such as southern California, counties and even municipalities have extended jurisdictional prerogatives over indigenous people and their territories, eliminating the last pretenses that native peoples are intended to retain any residue of genuine sovereignty at all.[23]

In sum, it is accurate to observe, as has been noted elsewhere, that American Indian nations within the geography presently claimed by the United States exist in a condition of "internal colonization."[24] That is, their rights to self-government have been usurped by a foreign power, in this case one that claims their very homelands as its own, in order for that power to benefit from the resources their lands provide. Any serious effort on the part of Native Americans to change these circumstances will therefore necessarily assume the form of decolonization struggles.[25] And, as is usually the case in such situations, the process by which the colonial structure was created sheds considerable light on the means and methods that will necessarily attend such expressions of indigenous self-determination in the years ahead.

Effects of the "Indian Wars"

Once the United States had established and consolidated itself to the point where it could tip the balance of military power to its own advantage, it began a 100 year series of armed conflicts popularly known as the "Indian Wars." As Creek/Cherokee scholar Ward Churchill and others have observed, this description is a misnomer: "The term is revealing in itself. There is no historical record of any war between [Indian nations] and the United States which was initiated by the Indians. Each known outbreak of open warfare was predicated upon documentable invasion of defined (or definable) Indian lands by U.S. citizenry. The defensive nature of Indian participation in these wars is thus clear. Logically, they should thus be termed 'settler's wars' or, more accurately, 'wars of conquest.'"[26] It was mainly through this extended series of unprovoked assaults upon indigenous peoples that the United States expanded from its original territoriality along the Eastern Seaboard to encompass the area now comprising the "lower forty-eight" states.

Given the intended outcomes of this warfare on the part of the aggressors, it should come as no surprise that the United States often took native governments—and leaders upon which the effective functioning of these governments were perceived as depending—as primary targets.[27] At times such tactics took the approach of contriving situations in which individuals such as the great Shawnee leader, Tecumseh, who very nearly created a confederation of indigenous nations extending along the western U.S. border from Canada to the Gulf of Mexico, could be killed in battle.[28] On other occasions, outright assassination was employed, as in the cases of the Seminole leader, Osceola, in 1838,[29] and the Lakota "recalcitrants" Tesunke Witko (Crazy Horse) and Tatanka Yatanka (Sitting Bull), in 1877 and 1890, respectively.[30]

In still other instances, Indian leaders who had opposed the U.S. were executed after they had been defeated, as when President Abraham Lincoln ordered the mass hanging of thirty-eight Santee Dakota warriors at Mankato, Minnesota, in 1862.[31] A quarter-century later this was still going on, as is witnessed by the hanging—lynching would be a better word—of Kintpuash (Captain Jack), head of the northern California Modoc resistance, in 1873.[32] In addition, the federal government adopted a policy of imprisoning those Indian leaders who refused to bow to non-Indian authority in locations far from their lands and people. In this connection, the examples of Hinmaton Yalatkit (Chief Joseph) of the Nez Percé,[33] and Gothalay (Geronimo), the Chiricahua Apache "hold-out," spring readily to mind.[34]

The purpose of physically eliminating the strongest and most effective patriots among Native American leaders in nation after nation went beyond simply undercutting these nations' abilities to engage successfully in defensive war. The United States, with an eye to the aftermath, quickly developed a concomitant policy of recognizing or appointing "Indian leaders" of its own—usually individuals with little or no authority deriving from their own people, but upon whom the federal government could rely to comply with its needs and desires—to "represent the interests" of indigenous nations.[35] Such persons—many of whom were disgraced within their own societies by virtue of having become addicted to alcohol (a conscious U.S. effort against Indians that adds up to an early experiment in chemical warfare[36]), and most of whom were bribed by federal authorities—were routinely trotted out at treaty time to "accept" terms and provisions that had either been rejected by their nations or of which the latter remained unaware until after the fact.[37] These same traitorous individuals were typically installed as "official liaisons" to Army and Bureau of Indian Affairs (BIA) officials once their respective nations had been militarily defeated and consigned to administration by "Indian Agents."[38]

Plainly, an integral aspect of U.S. prosecution of wars against the native peoples of North America was the deliberate and systematic destruction, not only of indigenous governments, but of the Indian ability to self-govern in any meaningful way. Nations defeated in war possess an inherent ability to reconstitute themselves on their own terms afterwards, unless the victorious power undertakes concrete steps to prevent this from occurring. It is customary, and in many circumstances legally required, that the former rather than latter course be followed, even when "territorial adjustment" is the basis of conflict. The U.S. approach to "Indian fighting" was all along something entirely different. From the outset, it was designed to preclude any sort of autonomous reconstitution on the part of the vanquished. Instead, it consciously set the stage for the perpetual colonial subordination of Native America to the United States.

From Sovereignty to Subordination

By the mid-1880s, virtually all American Indians within the United States had ceased military resistance against U.S. expansion in North America.[39] In most cases, the native peoples west of the Mississippi River had withdrawn into portions of their traditional homelands reserved for their exclusive use and occupancy by the provisions of treaty agreements with the federal government; those originally resident to areas east of the river had also largely been relocated to the "permanent Indian territory" of Oklahoma by that point.[40] Typically, in exchange for their agreement to cease armed resistance and legally cede the remainder of their land base, these reserved territories were guaranteed permanent protection from further abridgement by non-Indians.[41] The right to native self-governance within these residual territories was also implicit to, and sometimes spelled out within, these arrangements.[42] Under such conditions, it seems likely that many—if not most—indigenous peoples might well have recovered their equilibrium, eventually reestablishing their collective self-sufficiency and vitality in the reservation context.

In 1885, however, the United States began to move in a serious fashion to eliminate all vestiges of genuine sovereignty among indigenous nations, bringing them directly within its own polity for the first time. The process started in earnest with the "Major Crimes Act" through which the federal government unilaterally extended its jurisdiction over felonies occurring among Indians in Indian territories, displacing traditional jurisprudence in such matters.[43] This initiated a process by which the United States ultimately enacted some 5,000 separate statutes usurping native jurisdiction—both criminal and civil—on reservations at every level.[44] The Major Crimes Act was followed, in 1887, by the General Allotment Act, which unilaterally negated Indian control over land tenure patterns within the reservations, forcibly replacing the traditional mode of collective use and occupancy with the Anglo-Saxon system of individual property ownership.[45] Not only was the cohesion of indigenous society dramatically disrupted by allotment, and traditional governmental prerogatives preempted, but it led directly to the loss of some two-thirds of all acreage still held by native people at the time it was passed.

The Allotment Act set forth that each American Indian recognized as such by the federal government would receive an allotment of land according to the following formula: 160 acres for family heads, eighty acres for single persons over eighteen years of age and orphans under eighteen, and forty acres for children under eighteen. "Mixed blood" Indians received title by fee simple patent; "full bloods" were issued "trust patents," meaning they had no control over their allotted property for a period of twenty-five years. Once each person recognized by the government as belonging to a given Indian nation had received his or her allotment, the "surplus" acreage was "opened" to non-Indian homesteading or conversion into the emerging system of national parks, forests, and grasslands. Thus, the potential for a resumption of Indian self-sufficiency was largely eliminated, setting the stage for a condition of permanent economic dependency among all native people within the United States.[46]

The purpose of all this was "assimilation," as federal policymakers described their intentions, or—to put the matter more unabashedly—to bring about the destruction and disappearance of American Indian peoples as such.[47] In the words of Francis E. Leupp, Commissioner of Indian Affairs from 1905 through 1909, the Allotment Act in particular should be viewed as a "mighty pulverizing engine for breaking up the tribal mass" which stood in the way of complete Euroamerican hegemony in North America.[48] Or, to quote Indian Commissioner Charles Burke a decade later, "[I]t is not desirable or consistent with the general welfare to promote [American Indian national] characteristics and organization."[49] Hence, one little-noted aspect of the General Allotment Act was that it required each "qualified" Indian (i.e., those of "mixed blood"), in order to receive the deed to his or her parcel of land, to accept U.S. citizenship, a circumstance which served to further confuse the already garbled identities and loyalties of recipients.[50] In 1924, Congress completed this process by passing a "clean-up" measure, the Indian Citizenship Act, unilaterally conferring American citizenship upon all native people—whether they desired it or not—who had not otherwise been nationalized as part of the U.S. population.[51]

A bit earlier, during the winter of 1919-20, a team of geologists employed by the Standard Oil Corporation had been exploring a section of the Navajo Reservation in northeastern Arizona. Deciding in 1921 that local rock formations suggested the probability of oil and natural gas deposits in the area, the group requested the U.S. Bureau of Indian Affairs (BIA) superintendent on the reservation to convene the traditional Diné (Navajo) government for purposes of authorizing the drilling of test holes to determine whether and to what extent the minerals were present.[52] Much to the surprise and consternation of both Standard and the BIA, the Diné elders declined, unanimously and unequivocally. This "unacceptable" outcome was bureaucratically altered by Commissioner Burke in early 1923 through promulgation of a set of *Regulations Relating to the Navajo Tribe of Indians*. This was done, according to Burke, in order to "promote better administration of the Navajo Tribe of Indians in conformity to law and particularly as to matters in which the Navajo tribe at large is concerned, such as oil, gas, coal and other mineral deposits."

The commissioner followed up by appointing, without consulting the Diné people themselves, what he termed a "Navajo Grand Council," composed entirely of young, hand-picked, white-educated Indians, and from which the traditional Diné leadership was excluded altogether. When the new council met for the first time on July 7, 1923, it immediately acknowledged that its primary allegiance was to the U.S. rather than to its own ostensible constituency. Its first act was to sign the leasing instruments that provided a veneer of legitimacy to the federal government's bringing of major corporate interests onto the reservation for the first time, over the express objections of the traditional Diné council.[53] Thereafter, the federally created council was the only "governmental" entity with which Washington would deal directly or recognize as holding authority on the reservation, a matter that has led to sustained profits for U.S. energy corporations and environmental catastrophe for the Diné themselves.[54]

"Reorganization"

During the early 1920s, a special "Committee of One Hundred" individuals selected by the interior secretary to study the U.S. "Indian problem" because of Indians' "prominence in the nation's civic, business and scholarly life" found the ongoing existence of indigenous peoples in North America to constitute an "intolerable financial burden" upon the United States. The committee recommended that dissolution of native nations and final absorption of their members into the U.S. polity be completed as rapidly as possible, allowing only for such restraints in timing and methods as might "be imposed by humane considerations."[55] These conclusions were contradicted, in 1928, by a study conducted by Lewis Meriam and his associates at the Institute for Government Research, a private think tank, which concluded that efficient utilization of mineral resources within reservation areas—by which the country might not only "recover the costs associated with its support" of the formerly self-sufficient native peoples it had so flagrantly dispossessed while creating its own economy, but turn a tidy profit as well—was being precluded by the fragmentation of land title inherent to the allotment policy.

The Meriam Report therefore recommended quite strongly that residual Indian lands (and thus "tribes") be maintained in block form, and that they be "governed" by outright corporate boards deriving their authority from, and being answerable to, the secretary of the interior.[56] From this perspective, the council prototype developed at the Navajo Reservation revealed such promise for the "beneficial" management of Indian land and resources that Meriam suggested its essential structure be replicated on as many reservations as possible. Meriam's recommendations quickly acquired powerful endorsers, both in Washington, D.C. and throughout the U.S. financial/industrial community. This became all the more true after the 1929 collapse of the stock market and onset of the Great Depression. Consequently, in 1934, Congress passed the Indian Reorganization Act (IRA), also called the "Wheeler-Howard Act," after its sponsors, Senator Burton K. Wheeler and Representative Edgar Howard. '

The IRA incorporated the Meriam council/board model of "tribal governance," and required that these be based, not in native traditions, but in "constitutions" and/or "charters" drafted by the BIA. All decisions of any consequence (in thirty-three separate areas of consideration) rendered by these "tribal councils" were made "subject to the approval of the Secretary of Interior or his delegate," the commissioner of Indian affairs. Worst of all, in some ways, the IRA decreed an electoral form of "democratic majority rule" which was and still is structurally antithetical to the consensual form of decision making and selection of leadership integral to most indigenous traditions.[57] The Reorganization Act was thus designed to undercut the unity marking traditional native societies, replacing it with a permanent divisiveness: "To vote for someone means you have to vote against somebody else," as Hopi leader David Monongye has put it.[58]

The democratic facade the federal government wished to foster through imposition of the IRA—a matter embodied in a requirement that members of each specific Indian nation be polled to determine whether or not they wished to be reorganized—caused certain problems in its implementation. Despite the allocation of an annual sum of $250,000 in "education funds" to assist the new governments in presenting an incentive to their ostensible constituents to go along with reorganization, as well as establishment of a $10 million revolving fund from which these governments might borrow for purposes of engaging in "cooperative ventures" with non-Indian corporations gearing up to do increased business in Indian Country (this was described as "economic development"), grassroots native resistance to the law was immediate, outspoken, and sustained. As the Cahuilla historian Rupert Costo recounts, after first quoting at length from the Oklahoma Quapaw traditional government rejecting the IRA and enforcement of its 1833 treaty with the United States:

> In hearings before the House of Representatives, the Flathead [of Montana asserted that] instead of new legislation they believed it would be better to insist on sovereign rights and treaty rights...On May 17, 1934, in hearings before the Senate, the...Yakima nation [of Washington], in a statement signed by their

chiefs and councilmen, said "We feel the best interests of the Indians can be preserved by the continuance of treaty laws and carried out in conformity with the treaty of 1855 entered into by the fathers of some of the undersigned chiefs and Governor Stevens of the territory of Washington." Now these are only a few of the examples of some of the testimony given by Indian witnesses and most of the tribes. Many refused to even consider the IRA and rejected it outright.[59]

As the Oneidas put it in a resolution presented to IRA sponsor Wheeler on April 17, 1934:

The Oneida nation firmly adheres to the terms of the Treaty of Canandaigua between our nation, our confederacy, and the U.S. on November 11, 1794. [We insist] that the laws of the U.S., the acts on Congress, and the customs and usages of the Oneida nation are the controlling provisions of Oneida basic law...the exponents of such basic law and the guides for the sachems, chiefs, headmen and warriors [are all bound to comply with the treaty].[60]

Such "recalcitrance" forced Indian Commissioner John Collier, who had championed the bill, to engage in extraordinary deception and manipulation of the referendum process in order to see it "accepted" by Indian nations. "Collier was vindictive and overbearing," Costo says. "He tolerated no dissent, neither from his staff nor from the tribes. He was a rank opportunist in politics, at once espousing and then rejecting one or another proposal. He did not hesitate to use informants and the FBI against Indian opponents. He habitually tampered with the truth in his dealings with Indians."[61] Recalling the struggle over the IRA in his own southern California region, Costo observes that:

In California, at Riverside, forty tribes were assembled. All but three voted against the proposed bill. Collier then reported [to Congress] that most of the California tribes were for [it]. The historical record was falsified...We were outraged at the provisions of the [IRA]...It is a curious fact that in all the ten meetings held with Indians across the country, in not one meeting was there a copy of the proposed legislation put before the people. We were asked to vote on the so-called explanations. The bill itself was withheld. We were told we need not vote but the meetings were only to discuss the explanations. In the end, however, we were required to vote. And I suppose you could call this maneuvering self-rule. I call it fraud.[62]

In the end, 258 separate referenda were conducted, exclusive of the Indian nations of Oklahoma and Alaska, which were reorganized *en masse* (and without consent) in an amendment to the IRA passed in 1936.[63] By 1938, 189 Indian nations (encompassing some 130,000 people) acquiesced to reorganization, while seventy-seven (representing approximately 90,000) rejected it outright, usually as a gross violation of their treaty-guaranteed sovereignty.[64] To obtain even this limited result, Collier had had to engage in a heavy-handed manipulation of the referenda themselves:

Although the IRA seemed to provide for tribal ratification of its terms, it did so in a way that effectively negated [Indian] wishes. Tribal members could vote to either accept or reject the IRA, but all abstentions (that is, the "votes" of anyone who didn't vote) were counted as votes in favor of the IRA...On several reservations, such as the Nez Percé and Coeur d'Alene [in Idaho], the majority of those voting voted against the act, but since abstentions were counted as votes for the act, it was ratified. On the Hopi Reservation [in Arizona], for example, traditionalists simply refused to recognize the BIA's authority, and thus most Hopis boycotted the election. Refusing to recognize the mass absten-tion for what it was—absolute nonacceptance of the act—the BIA counted the Hopi vote as favoring the act. Any [native nation] that failed to hold an election automatically came under the act's provisions.[65]

On the Pine Ridge (Oglala Lakota) Reservation in South Dakota, there weren't enough abstentions to carry the day against those voting against the IRA. It was subsequently discovered that a sufficient number of dead people had cast ballots to provide a pretext for ratification. Even after this was established to have been the case, the ratification was described as "binding" upon the Oglalas.[66] The same sort of situation pertained to the reorganization of the Cheyenne River (Minneconjou and Itazipko Lakota) Reservation and elsewhere.[67] Collier's most significant setback occurred when the Navajo Nation—outraged at the ruthlessness of a stock reduction program instituted against them by the BIA under provision of the 1934 Taylor Grazing Act (48 *Stat.* 1269), another piece of legislation advocated by the Indian commissioner—voted overwhelmingly to reject reorganization.[68] The point was largely moot, however, insofar as the Navajos had already undergone de facto reorganization by virtue of the earlier Grand Council imposition.

By 1940, the prevailing system of colonial governance on American Indian reservations was largely in place. Only the outbreak of World War II slowed the pace of corporate exploitation, a matter that retarded initiation of maximal "develop-ment" activities until the early 1950s.[69] By then, the questions concerning federal and corporate planners of the IRA-orientation had become somewhat technical: what to do with those indigenous nations which had refused reorganization? How to remove the portion of Indian population on even the reorganized reservations whose sheer physical presence served as a barrier to wholesale strip mining and other profitable enterprises anticipated by the U.S. business community? Such preoccupations overlapped noticeably with the desires of politicians and other individuals and organizations who remained committed to bringing about the outright and final disappearance of native peoples as a whole.

This has led to an ongoing tension and debate in federal and corporate sectors of the U.S. elites between those (often described as "assimilators" or "terminators") who wish to see an ultimate and "uncomplicated" consolidation of the country's internal territorial and politico-economic integrity on the one hand, and those (typically referred to as "IRA liberals") who perceive advantages to maintaining Indian nations as distinct, colonized entities on the other. Neither faction allowed in any way for realization of any aspect of the long and loudly voiced desire of most Indians to resume genuine self-government and other expressions of autonomous national life. The choice offered native people was and is either to endorse their

own colonization by aligning themselves with the liberals, or to risk total obliteration by engaging in what amounted to national liberation struggles.

Termination and Relocation

In December 1952, the BIA submitted a list to Congress enumerating specific
American Indian nations it felt were "ready to undergo...complete termination
of all federal services" and "an end to the exercise of federal trust responsibility
over their affairs."[70] Promoted as a measure to "liberate American Indian tribes from
federal domination," the concept of termination was really intended ultimately to
"do away with tribes [and their] reservations," at least those which had not been
amenable to conversion into resource and profit generators for the U.S. economy.[71]
Designated by the BIA as being ripe for immediate dissolution were the Nez Percé
and Coeur d'Alene, the Osage in Oklahoma, the Menominee in Wisconsin, the
Salish and Kootenai (Flathead) in Idaho, the Turtle Mountain Anishinabé (Chippewa) in North Dakota, the Six Nations and others in New York, the Potawatomi
and other nations in Iowa, the Klamath and other nations in Oregon, and all the
nations located within western Washington, Texas, Michigan, Kansas, Nebraska,
and Louisiana.[72]

The 1952 BIA proposal was nothing new. In May 1943, Oklahoma Senator
Elmer Davis had introduced a report, S-310, calling for the unilateral abrogation of
all treaties with Indian nations, withdrawal of federal recognition of their existence,
and abolition of the BIA itself.[73] Davis was publicly joined in these sentiments by
other legislators such as Senator Dennis Chavez of New Mexico and Idaho's Burton
K. Wheeler, cosponsor of the IRA.[74] With the resignation of John Collier as Indian
commissioner in January 1945, the search began for a replacement who would be
able to carry out such a policy. This resulted, in May 1950—after trial runs with
William A. Brophy (1945-49) and John Ralph Nichols (1949-50)—in the appointment of Dillon S. Myer, former head of the wartime internment program directed
against Japanese Americans.[75] Myer quickly set himself to the task of reorganizing
the BIA to oversee the destruction of targeted native societies, once and for all.[76]

The culmination of this process occurred with the approval of House Concurrent Resolution 108, otherwise known as the "Termination Act," on August 1, 1953.
Actually, this is something of a misnomer insofar as H.C.R. 108 did not itself bring
about termination. Instead it called for enactment of specific statutes that would
terminate selected Indian nations.[77]

> Major [termination] legislation affecting particular [nations] came out of the
> second session of the Eighty-third Congress in 1954. Among the [nations]
> involved were the comparatively large and wealthy Menominee of Wisconsin
> and the Klamath of Oregon—both owners of extensive timber resources. Also
> passed were acts to terminate...the Indians of western Oregon, small Paiute
> bands in Utah, and the mixed bloods of the Uintah and Ouray Reservations.
> Approved, too, was legislation to transfer administrative responsibility for the
> Alabama and Coushatta Indians to the state of Texas...Early in the first session

of the Eighty-fourth Congress, bills were submitted to [terminate the] Wyandotte, Ottawa, and Peoria [nations] of Oklahoma. These were finally enacted early in August of 1956, a month after passage of legislation directing the Colville Confederated Tribes of Washington to come up with a termination plan of their own...During the second administration of President Dwight D. Eisenhower, Congress enacted only three termination bills relating to specific [nations] or groups. Affected by this legislation were the Choctaw of Oklahoma, for whom the termination process was never completed, the Catawba of South Carolina, and the Indians of the southern California *rancherias*.[78]

All told, 109 indigenous nations, or portions of nations, were unilaterally dissolved by congressional action between 1953 and 1958.[79] Concomitantly, Congress passed the earlier-mentioned Public Law 280 in 1954, increasingly placing unterminated reservations under state jurisdictional authority, and, in 1956, Public Law 959, known as the "Relocation Act." The latter corresponded closely to a steadily diminishing congressional allocation of funds to the meeting of federal obligations to unterminated Indians, a matter resulting in the deterioration of such things as educational and health services (already very poor) on the reservations, spiraling unemployment among reservation Indians (already the highest of any population group), and a net decline in reservation per capita income (already the lowest in North America).[80]

P.L. 959 provided funding with which to underwrite moving expenses, establishment of a new residence, and a brief period of job training to any Native American willing to relocate "voluntarily" to one of a number of federally approved urban centers. Under the circumstances, this led to a sudden mass exodus of Indians from their reserved territories, with some 35,000 being relocated to such places as Los Angeles, San Francisco, Denver, Phoenix, Minneapolis, Seattle, Boston, and Chicago during the years 1957-59 alone.[81] Despite early (and ongoing) indications that the relocation experience was a disaster, both for the individuals involved and for their respective nations, by 1980 ongoing federal pressure had resulted in the "migration" to cities of slightly over half of all American Indians (about 880,000 of the approximately 1.6 million reflected in the 1980 census).[82] As Oglala Lakota activist Gerald One Feather has put it:

> The relocation program had an impact on our...government at Pine Ridge. Many people who could have provided [our] leadership were lost because they had motivation to go off the reservation to find employment or obtain an education. Relocation drained off a lot of our potential leadership.[83]

It is not that no resistance was mounted to termination and relocation. To the contrary, it was considerable and sustained. The Blackfeet of Montana, for example, acting in consultation with attorney Felix S. Cohen—whom they'd naturalized as a citizen of their nation and who had been a key member of John Collier's Indian Bureau during the formative phases of the IRA—physically occupied their tribal buildings against BIA impoundment and successfully argued on the basis of prior litigation to prevent Myer's policies from being implemented against them.[84] Similarly, the Oglala Lakotas of Pine Ridge—in a confrontational strategy described by Myer as "Communist inspired" (the Indian commissioner caused an FBI "subversive activities" investigation into the matter)—employed Cohen's advice to bar implementation of BIA termination efforts on their reservation.[85] Despite the fact that Myer came within a hair's breadth of having "A Bill to Authorize the Indian Bureau to Make Arrests Without Warrant for Violation of Indian Bureau Regulations" passed in collaboration with reactionary Senator Pat McCarran, these sorts of stand-offs continued throughout the 1950s.[86]

More broadly, the Association of American Indian Affairs (AAIA), spearheaded by articulate and determined spokespersons such as Avery Winnemucca (Pyramid Lake Piaute), Popavi Da (San Ildefonso Pueblo), Manuel Halcomb (Santa Clara Pueblo), Rufus Wallowing and John Wooden Legs (Northern Cheyenne), William V. Creager (Laguna Pueblo), Thomas Main (Gros Ventre), Servino Martinez and Paul Bernal (Taos Pueblo), and Ben Chief (Oglala Lakota), also in consultation with Cohen, put up a fierce fight centering on concentrated public relations and lobbying efforts. As a defense against further terminations, AAIA avidly endorsed IRA colonialism. It was joined in this posture by the National Congress of American Indians (NCAI), headed by Earl Old Person (Northern Cheyenne) and assisted by Cohen's associate (and fellow IRA liberal), attorney James E. Curry.[87] This response was effective, at least insofar as, by 1958, Interior Secretary Fred Seaton was willing to assert publicly that the Eisenhower administration would no longer support legislation "to terminate tribes without their consent."[88]

The IRA liberals had won, garnering a visible and subservient base of support in Indian Country that had been absent during the period of reorganization itself. This was accomplished even while they assisted their more reactionary counterparts in "clearing away much of the dead wood" represented by native nations that had earlier rejected colonial status and engineered reservation demography to allow increased utilization of the native land base by U.S. corporations. In the context of Indian activism that emerged during the 1960s and '70s, some of the worst results of the Eisenhower-era onslaught were rolled back. For instance, after protracted struggles, federal recognition of certain terminated nations, such as the Siletz of Oregon and the Menominees, was "restored."[89] Still, incalculable damage had been done, not only to those nations that were actually terminated, but to the willingness of most remaining native governments to challenge federal authority. To reinforce the latter circumstance, HCR 108 was left dangling like a Damoclean sword over Indian national decision making for another decade, until it was negated, at least in part, by the Indian Civil Rights Act of 1968. Relocation, meanwhile, continued full-force until "the BIA in 1980 finally shut down its urban employment centers."[90]

Activism and "Self-Determination"

As the 1960s dawned, much of Indian Country was in a furor concerning the threats to the very existence of indigenous nations posed by termination and other federal policies. While those involved in IRA-style tribal governance tended to be cowed into even greater measures of "cooperation," a bold new activist sensibility began to show itself in other quarters:

> Proud of their heritage and determined to protect their political, cultural and land rights, Indian people across the country organized, demonstrated and protested. In 1961, five hundred Indians representing sixty-seven [nations] met at the University of Chicago and adopted a Declaration of Indian Purpose. Later that year several of the younger participants from the Chicago conference [notably Clyde Warrior, a Ponca university student] formed the National Indian Youth Conference (NIYC). This group demonstrated against the denial of Indian rights, staged "fish-ins" to support Northwest...fishing rights claims, published studies and newspapers, and lobbied Congress. Five years later, the native peoples of Alaska formed the Alaska Federation of Natives to protect and preserve Alaskan native culture, land and resources.[91]

By the mid-60s, under the leadership of the young Lakota activist/law student Vine Deloria, Jr., even the historically staid National Congress of American Indians (NCAI) had adopted a much more "radical" and engaged approach to politics. By the end of the decade, Deloria had published *Custer Died for Your Sins,* a book widely viewed as a cornerstone statement of native resistance, followed shortly by *We Talk, You Listen,* sometimes described as "an American Indian Declaration of Independence."[92] These broadsides coincided with the founding of the first truly militant Indian rights organization, the American Indian Movement (AIM), in Minneapolis during 1968 and the extended occupation of Alcatraz Island by a coalition organization called Indians of All Tribes during 1969-70. By 1971, not only Alcatraz, but a series of physical confrontations between the Pit River Indians of northern California and the Pacific Gas and Electric Corporation (which claimed to own the Indians' land), repeated occupations of unused portions of the Fort Lawton military facility in Washington state, and highly publicized AIM demonstrations at the Mt. Rushmore National Monument and the Mayflower Replica had drawn considerable public attention to questions of Indian rights.[93]

This upsurge in Indian activism corresponded with a more generalized breakdown—manifested in the civil rights and Black liberation movements, student power and anti-war movements, and incipient Chicano rights and women's liberation movements—of the apparent consensus that had marked U.S. society during the 1950s.[94] By 1966, President Lyndon Johnson was somewhat desperately articulating a national policy he described as the formation of a "Great Society" designed to address the demands voiced by the entire range of "dissidents." One element of Johnson's attempt to defuse the situation was a speech entitled "The Forgotten American"—delivered in the wake of the release of a study he had commissioned to examine Native American issues—in which he renounced termination policy and promised Native America that "a new period in which Indian rights will be honored" was at hand.[95] This was followed, in short order, by passage of Public Law 89-635 (80 *Stat.* 880; codified at 28 U.S.C. 1362), the first section of which provided indigenous nations a clear standing upon which to sue the federal government for the first time. The hand of native governments was thus strengthened to a certain extent, at least in terms of their being able to defend themselves in court against some federal impositions.

P.L. 89-635 was followed, in 1968, by passage of the Indian Civil Rights Act, a law that effectively disallowed termination by spelling out in some detail the expectations of Congress with regard to the future functioning of Indian governments. Although much ballyhoo about "reinforcement of Indian rights" attended enactment of the civil rights bill, its purpose was ultimately cooptive (as was most Johnson-era legislation): to further integrate IRA-type governance into the functioning of the federal hierarchy itself.[96] Any questions as to whether the Indian Civil Rights Act might signify some new degree of federal acceptance of real indigenous autonomy and self-governance were subsequently put to rest with the passage of the Alaska Native Claims Settlement Act. This law, enacted in 1971, carried the logic of the IRA much further than had been the case in 1934:

> ANCSA...organized the Alaska natives into thirteen regional corporations, incorporated under state law, and various village corporations. It implemented the settlement [of Alaska native claims to territory and the right of self-government] "without establishing any permanent racially defined institutions, rights, privileges, or obligations, without creating a reservation system or lengthy wardship or trusteeship, and without adding to the categories of property and institutions engaging in special tax privileges."[97]

Meanwhile, beginning in 1969, as part of a strategy to "chill" forces for social change more generally, the administration of Richard M. Nixon took a very proactive approach to discrediting and otherwise neutralizing the political opposition. With regard to American Indian activism, one of Nixon's major initial tactics seems to have been to channel considerable federal support to a consortium composed of IRA government figures known as the National Tribal Chairman's Association (NTCA; presently renamed the National Tribal Chairman's Fund, or NTCF), the primary purpose of which was to provide a "native voice" endorsing the status quo in Indian affairs while publicly denouncing AIM and other assorted "sovereigntists" as "irresponsible, self-styled revolutionaries...renegades...and terrorists...without visible support among their own people."[98] Such federal tactics deepened already existing divisions between IRA-oriented "tribal leaders" (or "sell-outs," as AIM described them) and the traditionalists with whom the militants aligned on reservations across the country. They also placed AIM and the government itself on an outright collision course.

The conflict emerged in sharp relief during November 1972 when a sizable contingent of Indians, largely organized by AIM and describing themselves as "The Trail of Broken Treaties," arrived in Washington, D.C. on the eve of the U.S. presidential election. They carried with them a Twenty Point Program devoted to redefining the federal-Indian relationship on terms embodying elements of real self-determination for the latter, and demanded the program be negotiated by Nixon or his representatives prior to election day. A considerable portion of the Twenty Point Program was devoted to reassertion of Indian rights to full national sovereignty as implied by their treatied relationships with the federal government. As Vine Deloria, Jr., has summarized the matter:

> The first point dealt with a restoration of constitutional treaty-making authority...The second point proposed that a new treaty commission be established within the next year which could contract a new treaty relationship with the American Indian community on a tribal, regional, or multitribal basis...The fourth point (the third point had nothing to do with treaty rights) asked for a commission to review the treaty violations of the past and present and set up procedures for review of chronic treaty violations by both the states and the federal government...The resubmission of unratified treaties to the Senate for approval was the fifth of the Twenty Points...The sixth and perhaps most fundamental point, and one that would be later prominent at Wounded Knee, was a demand that all Indians be governed by treaty relations...The seventh point asked for mandatory relief from treaty violations by state governments...The eighth and final point dealing with the treaty relationship asked for judicial recognition by the government of Indians' right to interpret treaty provisions.[99]

To emphasize the seriousness of their agenda, Trail participants occupied the BIA's central headquarters in downtown Washington for several days, until White House aide John Ehrlichman delivered a promise from the president that he would be "open to discussion." Most of the Indians then left the capitol, taking the bulk of the BIA's internal documents with them when they left.[100] The administration tried to offset the impact of the Trail of Broken Treaties by bringing in NTCA head Webster Two Hawk, serving at the time as president of the IRA government on the Rosebud Sioux Reservation, to announce that "American Indians stand with President Nixon...We are disgusted with what happened" during the BIA takeover.[101] The gambit failed, however, mainly because Two Hawk was almost immediately unseated in a runoff election for the Rosebud tribal presidency by Robert Burnette, a major Trail organizer.[102] Worse, from the federal point of view, AIM had by then become locked in a toe-to-toe confrontation with the forces of Tribal President Richard Wilson, head of the IRA government on the Pine Ridge Sioux Reservation, and was garnering sufficient grassroots support to impeach him and replace his entire regime with a reconstituted version of the traditional Lakota Council of Elders.[103]

When the Justice Department rushed a large contingent of U.S. Marshals to Pine Ridge to support Wilson while he rigged the impeachment process, they merely exacerbated the situation, precipitating a sensational seventy-one-day armed confrontation at Wounded Knee, a hamlet on the reservation known mainly as the site of an 1890 massacre of Lakotas by the 7th Cavalry.[104] In the aftermath, AIM leader Russell Means challenged Wilson for the tribal presidency during the 1974 Pine Ridge general election and appears to have won, although what the U.S. Commission on Civil Rights termed "massive voter fraud" prevented him from being seated. On many other reservations as well, what might be seen as an "AIM sensibility" of desiring to depose IRA "puppet governments" in favor of more traditional forms was rapidly gaining ground.[105] The system of colonial governance of Indian Country so carefully developed by the United States over a lengthy period was showing signs of unraveling.

Federal response to the situation was essentially two-fold. First, an outright counterinsurgency campaign was launched against AIM—which was by then being described as "the shock troops of Indian sovereignty"—on Pine Ridge and elsewhere. In some ways, this represented a return to the 19th-century policy of assassinating the most patriotic and promising native leaders, as when Oglala Sioux Civil Rights Organization head Pedro Bissonette was murdered by BIA police on Pine Ridge during October 1973.[106] Second, with the activist core of Native America thus tied up in a protracted armed struggle which left scores of their number dead or imprisoned, the government itself adopted the rhetoric of indigenous liberation.[107] As early as 1970, seeing in such semantics a means of confusing or preempting the positions of the Indian opposition, Richard Nixon had delivered a message to Congress stating that he wished to see national Indian policy advanced within a vernacular framework of "self-determination."[108] In 1975, after Nixon had been driven from office by the "excesses" of Watergate, his desire was fulfilled with passage of the Indian Self-Determination and Educational Assistance Act.

Like the Indian Civil Rights Act before it, the Indian Self-Determination Act had little to do with its title. Contrary to accepted meanings of the term in international law, the federal legislation provided no hint that native peoples in the United States would at last be allowed to "freely determine their political status and freely pursue their economic, social and cultural development."[109] Instead, it called for increased Indian participation in staffing those programs implemented to carry out policies formulated by the federal government. Moreover, it placed a particular emphasis on "education" as a main vehicle by which Indians, as a whole, might eventually be indoctrinated to accept the idea that such subordination added up to freedom.[110] As Russell Means put it, "The so-called self-determination policy of the federal government was designed and intended to bolster rather than dismantle the whole structure of BIA/IRA colonialism. Only it calls upon us to administer our own colonization to a greater extent than we have before. Instead of labeling it as a 'Self-Determination Act,' they should have called this law the Self-*Administration* Act of 1975."[111]

Federal Reaction and Native Response

Follow-up to the Self-Determination Act came in the form of the final report of an American Indian Policy Review Commission, established by Congress in 1975 to formulate a federal strategy to accompany the new legislation, on May 17, 1977: "This report generally recommended a continuation of the federal policy [initiated in 1968] of protecting and strengthening tribal governments as permanent governmental units *in the federal system* [emphasis added]."[112] This conclusion was officially opposed by the commission's vice chairperson, reactionary Washington Representative Lloyd Meeds, who in his dissent argued vociferously that resolution of "the Indian problem" resided, not in the final incorporation of native nations into the federal structure, but in the expeditious abolition of all remaining vestiges of indigenous sovereignty:

> In our Federal system, as ordained and established by the United States Constitution, there are but two sovereignties: the United States and the States. This is obvious not only from an examination of the Constitution, its structure, and its amendments, but also in the express language of the 10th amendment which provides: The powers not delegated to the United States by the Constitution, nor prohibited by it to the States, are reserved to the States respectively, or to the peoples...The blunt fact of the matter is that American Indian tribes are not a third set of governments in the American federal system. They are not sovereigns.[113]

Meeds was swiftly joined by a broad assortment of paleo-conservatives who, for a variety of reasons extending from narrow self-interest to philosophical white supremacism, wished to see termination resumed and completed:

> After 1977, the political momentum for a fundamental change in the direction of federal Indian policy became intense. Organized political groups, like Montanans Opposed to Discrimination and the Interstate Congress for Equal Rights and Responsibilities, unsuccessfully lobbied Congress to extinguish Indian rights and force Indian assimilation. Others in Congress sought to go beyond Congressman Meeds' call...In 1977 H.R.J. Res. 1 was proposed to limit Indian treaty hunting and fishing rights. Then Congressman [Jack] Cunningham of Washington introduced H.R. 13329, 95th Cong., 2d Sess. (1978), Orwellianly entitled the Native American Equal Opportunity Act. If enacted, this bill would have, *inter alia*, directed the President within one year to abrogate all treaties entered into with Indians, terminated federal [recognition]...fully subjected all Indians to state jurisdiction, compelled Indian [nations] to distribute certain tribal assets on a per capita basis to their members, eliminated the restraints on alienation and tax immunities enjoyed by [reserved] tribal lands, and abrogated treaty-protected Indian hunting and fishing rights.[114]

The response from Indian Country to this onslaught was mixed. Those within the IRA government apparatus opted largely to protect their positions from the terminators by ever more ostentatious displays of the extent to which they embraced absorption into the federal domain as mere administrative entities. The accommodationist position was perhaps best framed by Robert Burnette, who, in the aftermath of winning a tribal presidency of his own, seems to have lost the militant native rights perspective he once carried along the Trail of Broken Treaties to Washington, D.C.:

> We are part of the United States of America. We are within its jurisdiction and subject to the plenary powers of Congress. So we are not, in a sense, sovereign, except that we do have treaties and the United States has usually tried to honor those treaties. The notion of tribal sovereignty is wishful thinking on the part of...modern day [Indian] leaders.[115]

Such assertions of fealty to federal power through inversion of historical and political realities was met head on by more traditionally oriented leaders such as Onondaga subchief Oren Lyons, whose nation had rejected the IRA in 1936: "We are not going to be part [of the federal system] because we are a separate sovereign nation."[116] Lyons and others consistently articulated a coherent vision of indigenous sovereignty, but it was left once again to the American Indian Movement to force the traditionals' message into the political arena. This time the mechanism employed was a process known as "The Longest Walk," initiated by AIM leader Dennis Banks and carried out by several hundred members of his organization. After spending several well-publicized months marching across the country from San Francisco to Washington, D.C., the AIM members held a mass rally at the Washington Monument on July 25, 1978. During the rally, they delivered a manifesto throwing down the gauntlet to the forces advocating a resumption of termination, challenging the federal definition of self-determination and the entire structure of IRA colonialism, and demanding acknowledgment of the right to unfettered expressions of sovereignty for all indigenous nations. These issues, they said, would be carried before the United Nations in short order. On July 27, California Representative Ron Dellums read the entire manifesto into the *Congressional Record*.[117]

AIM was true to its word with regard to the UN. In 1974, the traditional Lakota elders had called for a major meeting on the Standing Rock Sioux Reservation to discuss taking their treaties with the United States "before the family of nations" to seek review and enforcement. The meeting ended with AIM leader Russell Means accepting responsibility for carrying not only the Lakota treaties but all U.S.-Indian treaties, and "the human rights of the indigenous peoples of the entire hemisphere" into the international arena. Means named a Cherokee AIM member, Jimmie Durham, to establish and direct the movement's "international diplomatic arm," the International Indian Treaty Council (IITC), which was headquartered at United Nations Plaza in New York City.[118]

By 1977, Durham had secured United Nations Type II (Consultative) Non-Governmental Organization (NGO) status for IITC, making it the first indigenous entity in the world to assume such a role. He had also convinced the U.N. Commission on Human Rights to schedule a major hearing on the rights of American Indians at the Palace of Nations in Geneva, Switzerland. With support from the World Council of Churches, IITC was then able to bring representatives of ninety-eight indigenous nations from North, Central, and South America to testify.[119] In 1979, the Bertrand Russell International Tribunal on Human Rights conducted comparable hearings in Rotterdam.[120] The result was the creation in 1982 of a U.N. Working Group on Indigenous Populations, mandated to monitor and report on the interactions between various states and indigenous nations, undertake global studies of the politico-economic conditions in which native peoples now find themselves and the implications of treaty relationships between indigenous nations, and draft a Universal Declaration on the Rights of Indigenous Peoples.[121]

Since its formation, the Working Group on Indigenous Populations has scheduled two sessions annually at which native delegations provide input. Although IITC eventually collapsed as a viable entity (circa 1985-86), other indigenous organizations such as NIYC, the Indian Law Resource Center, Four Directions Council, Grand Council of the Crees, and the World Council of Indigenous Peoples had by then achieved NGO status. A separate NGO, the South American Indian Council (CISA), has emerged to represent the interests of the indigenous peoples of that continent. Further, the significance of American Indian participation in U.N. forums had also been amplified by the presence of native peoples from elsewhere, notably the Inuits of the circumpolar region, Native Hawaiians, Maoris of New Zealand, Kooris and other "Aboriginals" from Australia, and the Karins of Burma. By 1989, the Working Group was considering a second draft of its proposed Declaration,[122] while the International Labor Organization (ILO)—a specialized U.N. agency—adopted a *Convention on the Rights of Indigenous and Tribal Peoples* that is open to ratification by United Nations member states at the present time.[123] In a further development during the same year, the General Assembly of the Organization of American States resolved to "request the Inter-American Commission on Human Rights to prepare a juridical instrument relative to the rights of indigenous peoples, for adoption in 1992."[124]

All in all, the success of AIM's international initiatives has proven sufficient, not only to forestall the terminationist intentions of reactionaries like Meeds and Cunningham, but to subject the entire comportment of the federal government vis-à-vis Indians to a sort of international scrutiny it has never before encountered. This has prompted policymakers to proceed with far more caution than they have in the past. The tendency is bound to increase in the years ahead as the formal elements of international law designed to ensure indigenous rights are set in place. At this juncture, even organizations such as the Boulder, Colorado-based Native American Rights Fund (NARF, a federally funded legal firm exclusively devoted to handling cases for "recognized tribal governments")—long a leading proponent of the notion that subordination to federal dominion was "the best deal Indians can get," and which openly scoffed at IITC's efforts as being "AIMsters playing diplomat"—has queued up to obtain NGO status.[125]

In effect, AIM has to some extent reversed the Nixonian principle of inducing a "chilling effect" upon its opponents. This, in turn, has allowed a much greater degree of maneuvering room during the second half of the 1980s for those indigenous governments within the United States who wish to avail themselves of it. What will come of these changed circumstances remains to be seen, but an avenue of opportunity has been opened and preliminary indications are that there will be constructive results. As former NCAI Director Suzan Shown Harjo, herself no flaming radical, has put it, "Not enough attention has been paid to the Indian activism of the 1960s and the 1970s. The American Indian Movement, the second battle at Wounded Knee, and the occupation of the BIA building brought about tremendous change in Indian country. These events changed the way Indians are viewed and the way we view ourselves."[126]

Openings

In 1983, Russell Means made another bid for the tribal presidency at Pine Ridge. His platform, drafted by Colorado AIM leader Ward Churchill, was dubbed "The TREATY Program," and delineated a comprehensive plan to, among other things, rescind the reservation's IRA constitution, reinstate the traditional Oglala Lakota elders' councils as the primary level of government, pursue recovery of lands guaranteed the Lakota Nation under the 1868 Fort Laramie Treaty as a first national priority, and implement an economic development program based on bilateral/multilateral trade agreements with other nations.[127] The response from grassroots Pine Ridge communities was such that the BIA solicited a tribal council resolution disqualifying Means from the ballot because he had been convicted under a South Dakota "anarcho-syndicalism" statute during the late 1970s (he remains the only person ever sentenced for this nebulous offense in the history of the state).[128]

Although federal interference thus for a second time prevented Means from attempting to convert a contemporary native government into a vehicle for self-determination, the TREATY plan was widely circulated, its concepts studied and adapted to other settings. Before the end of the decade, AIM members such as Ted Means (at Pine Ridge) and Larry Anderson (at Navajo) had made their way onto their respective reservations' tribal councils, carrying "militant" notions of sovereignty with them as they went.[129] Others were even more successful, as is witnessed by the elections of Wilma Mankiller to head the Cherokee Nation of Oklahoma, Twila Martin at the Turtle Mountain Reservation in North Dakota, and Rubin Snake at the Winnebago Reservation in Nebraska.

The second half of the '80s also saw a stiffening of sovereigntist resolve even among some figures long associated with IRA colonialism. A notable instance is that of Joe DeLaCruz, chairperson of the Quinalt Nation on the outer coast of the Olympic Peninsula in Washington state, who has effected a tribal self-sufficiency program based largely in the salvage of redwood and cedar stumps left behind when major non-Indian timbering concerns logged the reservation during the 1930s. The manufacture of such items as shake shingles has not only provided an employment base among the Quinalt, but the proceeds have facilitated establishment of a tribal salmon hatchery and smoking plant, as well as a land consolidation program within the reservation's boundaries that is designed to undo the negative effects of allotment earlier in the century. DeLaCruz has also been instrumental in blocking completion of Coastal Highway 1—which begins at the Mexican border, is intended to end at the Canadian, and must cross Quinalt land in order to do so—until the state of Washington agrees to a jurisdictional arrangement acceptable to the Indians.[130]

Under steadily mounting pressure brought by Indian leaders of virtually every political persuasion, increasing public attention to U.S. Indian policy,[131] and public revelations concerning gross corruption within the BIA,[132] the federal government gave ground steadily with regard to native rights to self-government as the 1990s approached. On September 15, 1988, Congress amended the Indian Self-Determination Act (Public Law 100-472 301-306) to enable a self-selected group of ten indigenous nations—Quinalt, Rosebud Sioux, Lummi and the Jamestown Band of Klallam (both on Puget Sound), Mille Lacs and Red Lake Chippewa (both in northern Minnesota), Mescalero Apache (New Mexico), Hoopa (central California), Confederated Salish and Kootenai (Idaho), and Tlingit-Haida (southeastern Alaska)—to begin serious planning for self-governance on their own terms. From the model or models they develop during the five years of their pilot effort, it is expected that a broad extrapolation of the ways and means of achieving viable expressions of contemporary indigenous sovereignty may emerge.[133]

This potential is reinforced by the activities of the Special Committee on Investigations of the Senate Select Committee on Indian Affairs, chaired by Hawaii Senator Daniel Inouye. The special committee was formed in 1987 to investigate the above-mentioned allegations of rampant mismanagement and corruption in the BIA, and to tender recommendations on how the situation might be corrected. During the course of its investigation, the select committee took testimony and conducted on-site interviews with some 2,010 Indians and non-Indians concerned with Indian policy and examined a voluminous quantity of documentary material pertaining to federal Indian affairs. In its final report, published on November 20, 1989, the select committee called for a "New Era of Agreements" between the United States and indigenous nations within its borders. This "empowerment of tribal self-governance through formal, voluntary agreements" is, as the committee put it, contingent upon "mutual acceptance of four indispensable conditions":

1. The federal government must relinquish its current paternalistic controls over tribal affairs; in turn, the tribes must assume the full responsibilities of self-government;
2. Federal assets and annual appropriations must be transferred *in toto* to the tribes;
3. Formal agreements must be negotiated by tribal governments with written constitutions that have been democratically approved by each tribe; and
4. Tribal governmental officials must be held fully accountable and subject to fundamental federal laws against corruption. [134]

While it is clear that both the recent amendment to the Indian Self-Determination Act and the Select Committee's recommendations still retain the legally groundless presumption that Indian nations are somehow inherently subordinate to the United States, they combine to move in a direction that may serve to diminish the sorts of colonial control manifested in IRA liberalism. By transferring significant decisionmaking back to native governments, along with the assets to give them meaning, the federal government consciously and tangibly strengthens the former at the expense of its own hegemony for the first time in its history. Perhaps more importantly, the Select Committee's recommendation that future U.S.-Indian relations be predicated in "formal, voluntary agreements" is tantamount in many ways to a suggestion that treaty-making be resumed in every respect but the name and procedure for federal ratification.

The last point, of course, is hardly unimportant insofar as it denies Indian peoples the formal recognition of their national sovereignty implied by treaties, *per se.* Given the openings that are increasingly apparent, however, it may well be that this obstacle too can be overcome. The negotiating positions of native governments are in any event substantially enhanced. As things stand, the Indian rights agendas set forth in the 1972 Trail of Broken Treaties Twenty Point Program and the 1978 Longest Walk Manifesto may be seen as the benchmark articulations toward which federal policy is being steered (however grudgingly). As they are consummated, ideas such as those postulated in the 1983 TREATY Program may finally begin to be realized in a "real world" reservation context. It will be a long road from here to there, but it may now be said with a degree of confidence that at least some of the crucial groundwork for the national liberation of Native North America has been laid.

The Road Ahead

Nothing can adequately compensate American Indian nations for their experience at the hands of the United States over the past 200 years. Nothing can undo the legacy of the wars of extermination and dispossession the United States has waged against native peoples. Nothing can truly mend the damage done to indigenous societies by the systematic liquidation of their best leaders, the sustained and intentional suppression of their cultural and economic structures, the imposition of alien forms of governance and legal codes. There is no taking back the unrelenting trauma and suffering undergone by generations of native people forced to live in squalor as the wealth of their assets poured into the coffers of their oppressors. Nor can the extent of the lies, the seamless web of mendacity and duplicity, to which Euroamerica has subjected Native America since the first European "boat person" set foot in this hemisphere ever be retrieved. Probably, not even the damage done to the very treaty-guaranteed land that has been so ruthlessly stripped from native nations can at this point be fixed. Things will never be as they might have been.

Still, if things cannot be set exactly right, they *can* at least be made better. Native North America can at last be accorded its fundamental human right to self-determination. This need not be understood as meaning that each and every indigenous nation will automatically secede, becoming a sovereignty separate from the United States. Rather, it means that their intrinsic right to do so must be acknowledged, formally and unequivocally, by their colonizers. Only from this position—free from a dominating power unilaterally precluding certain of their options for its own reasons—can any nation "freely determine its political, social, and economic destiny," and hence the nature of its mode of governance. Viewed in any other way, the term "self-determination" is at best meaningless, at worst a subterfuge meant to mask its exact opposite, the continuation of a relationship between colonizer and colonized.

In the event, should the United States finally and simply admit what has been true all along, that native nations are absolutely entitled to complete national sovereignty, it is likely that few (if any) American Indian peoples would elect to exercise it fully. The Navajo nation, given the scale of its land base and population and the mineral resources available to it, might opt for complete independence. Similarly, should the Lakota Nation be able to recombine its territorality and population through recovery of all or most of what was once called "The Great Sioux Reservation," it might pursue such a course. In all probability, the remaining indigenous nations would select a commonwealth status vis-à-vis the United States, comparable to that occupied by some nations of the former British empire with regard to England, or a variation of the "home rule" status accorded by Denmark to its former "possessions" Iceland and Greenland. It is also possible that certain coastal or "trans-border tribes"—nations such as Blackfeet, Mohawk, and Haida (which are bisected by the U.S.-Canadian boundary), or Yaqui and Tohono O'Odham (bisected by the U.S.-Mexican border)—might wish to pursue some type of multinational arrangement. The point is that we will have thus been able to at last *decide for ourselves* the sort of relationship we wish to have with the United States, and other countries as well.

From this, it follows that we will finally be in a position to define for ourselves, nation by nation, the forms of governance best suited to our needs. Again, it is likely that very few native peoples will attempt a literal reconstitution of their traditional forms of government. In certain cases, such as the Haudenosaunee and the Hopi, where traditional governing bodies have continued to function (at Hopi, in parallel and in conflict with its IRA "replacement") throughout the periods of conquest and colonization, there may be exceptions. In most instances, however, the enforced rupture between past and present governmental forms has been too great, too much has been lost along the way. Nonetheless, it is also true that in virtually every case some degree of recollection of how traditional governments functioned, and why they approached things as they did, remains in place. Consequently, it is quite probable that most self-determining indigenous governments will exhibit a combination of traditional and non-traditional characteristics. There are a multiplicity of conceivable options relating to jurisdiction and definition and conditions of citizenry, legal codes and trade relations, social strictures and land use patterns. The possibilities of the forms that may be assumed by autonomous native governments are virtually endless.

What is necessary is no mere gestural concession on the part of the United States, but an actual relinquishment of its pretensions to preeminent rights over the lands and lives of others, lands and lives it has long professed to believe are its own, to do with as it will. For the self-determination of Native North America to be realized, the United States must be prodded into following through with the development of the "new relationships" with indigenous nations called for by Senator Inuoye's Select Committee, but it must be compelled to honor its past treaties with those nations in concrete ways. The treaty territories, or substantial portions of them, along with the resources associated with these lands, must be returned to native control if Indian Country is to possess the economic base from which to make self-governance practicable. Given what is at stake—a literal dismemberment of what is now seen as the internal territorial and economic integrity of the United States—the struggle will undoubtedly continue to be difficult, perhaps at times bloody. But it is well underway.

Altogether, despite the hurdles which remain to be cleared, the prospects for a revitalization of American Indian self-government and other aspects of self-determination are in many ways brighter than they have been since the conclusion of the "Indian Wars." The cycle of our prolonged battle for bare survival—a resistance to extinction emblemized by the sacrifices of Tecumseh and Osceola, Crazy Horse and Geronimo, Rupert Costo and Popavi Da, Anna Mae Aquash, Russell Means, and Dennis Banks—may be coming to a much overdue conclusion. Those of us who are indigenous to this land must now accept the responsibility of seizing every opportunity and doing the hard work necessary to achieve the potential for liberation they created. No less must non-Indians—regardless of their race, gender, ethnicity, sexual preference, or the story of how they got here—accept the responsibility of assisting us to succeed. For only in this way can we transcend the bitter legacy we have mutually inherited, forging instead a new heritage of respect, cooperation, and freedom. And only in this way can we transform the America that is into the America that could be.

Notes

1. See generally, Schusky, Ernest, ed., *Political Organization of Native North Americans*, University Press of America, Washington, D.C., 1970.
2. With regard to Iroquois influence on the U.S. Constitution and structure of the corresponding republic, see Grinde, Donald A. Jr., *The Iroquois in the Founding of the American Nation*, Indian Historian Press, San Francisco, 1977; Johansen, Bruce, *Forgotten Founders: How the American Indian Helped Shape Democracy*, The Harvard Common Press, Boston, 1982; and Johansen, Bruce, and Donald A. Grinde, Jr., *Exemplars of Liberty*, American Indian Studies Program, UCLA, 1991. Also see Burton, Bruce A., "Iroquois Confederate Law and the Origins of the U.S. Constitution," *Northeast Indian Quarterly*, Vol. 3, No. 2, Fall 1986, pp. 4-9; and Barriero, José, ed., *Indian Roots of American Democracy*, American Indian Program, Cornell University, Ithaca, NY, 1989.
3. O'Brien, Sharon, *American Indian Tribal Governments*, University of Oklahoma Press, Norman, 1989, pp. 17-18. She is relying heavily upon Colden, Cadwallader, *The History of the Five Indian Nations*, Cornell University Press, Ithaca, NY, 1958; Wallace, Anthony F.C., *The Death and Rebirth of the Seneca*, Alfred A. Knopf Publishers, New York, 1969; and Wilson, Edmund, *Apologies to the Iroquois*, Vintage Books, New York, 1960. An interesting and useful companion reading is Nammack, Georgiana C., *Fraud, Politics, and the Dispossession of the Indian: The Iroquois Land Frontier in the Colonial Period*, University of Oklahoma Press, Norman, 1969.
4. O'Brien, op. cit., pp. 18-19. Also see Jacobs, Wilbur, "Wampum: The Protocol of Indian Diplomacy, *William and Mary Quarterly*, 3rd Series, No. 6, October 1949, pp. 596-604; and Miles, George, "A Brief Study of Joseph Brant's Political Career in Relation to Iroquois Political Structure," *American Indian Journal*, No. 2, December 1976, pp. 12-20.
5. O'Brien, op. cit., p. 23. She relies upon Corkran, David H., *The Creek Frontier, 1540-1783*, University of Oklahoma Press, Norman, 1967; Debo, Angie, *The Road to Disappearance: A History of the Creek Indians*, University of Oklahoma Press, Norman, 1941; Green, Donald E., *The Politics of Indian Removal: Creek Government and Society in Crisis*, University of Nebraska Press, Lincoln, 1977; and Swanton, John R., "Early History of the Creek Indians and their

Neighbors," *Bureau of American Ethnology Bulletin,* No. 73, U.S. Government Printing Office, Washington, D.C., 1922. Also see Morton, Ohland, "The Government of the Creek Indians," Parts 1 and 2, *Chronicles of Oklahoma,* No. 8, March 1930, pp. 42-64; June 1930, pp. 189-225.

6. On the Lakota, see O'Brien, op. cit., pp. 23-6. Also see Pennington, Robert, "An Analysis of the Political Structure of the Teton Dakota Tribe of North America," *North Dakota History,* No. 20, July 1953, pp. 143-55; DeMallie, Raymond, *Lakota Society,* University of Nebraska Press, Lincoln, 1982; Hassrick, Royal B., *The Sioux: Life and Customs of a Warrior Society,* University of Oklahoma Press, Norman, 1964; and Vestal, Stanley, *Warpath and Council Fire: The Plains Indians' Struggle for Survival in War and Diplomacy, 1851-1891,* Random House Publishers, New York, 1948.

7. On the Pueblos, see O'Brien, op. cit., pp. 27-9. Also see Dozier, Edward P., *The Pueblo Indians,* Holt, Rinehart and Winston Publishers, New York, 1970; Jones, Oakah L. Jr., *Pueblo Warriors and Spanish Conquest,* University of Oklahoma Press, Norman, 1966; and Ortiz, Alfonso, ed., *New Perspectives on the Pueblos,* School of American Research, University of New Mexico, Albuquerque, 1972.

8. On the Yaquis, see Hu-DeHart, Evelyn, *Yaqui Resistance and Survival,* University of Wisconsin Press, Madison, 1984.

9. On the Yakimas, see O'Brien, op. cit., pp. 29-33. Also see Daugherty, Richard, *The Yakima People,* Indian Tribal Series, Phoenix, AZ, 1973; Guie, D.H., *Tribal Days of the Yakima,* Republic Publishers, North Yakima, WA, 1937; and MacWhorter, Lucuilus, *Crime Against the Yakima,* Republic Publishers, North Yakima, WA, 1913.

10. On the influence of Iroquois and other Indians upon the thought, not only of Rousseau, but British Enlightenment thinkers such as John Locke and Thomas Hobbes, see Johnansen, op. cit., pp. 14, 120-1. Also see Cohen, Felix S., "Americanizing the White Man," *American Scholar,* Vol. 21, No. 2, Summer 1952, pp. 177-91.

11. With regard to Iroquois influence on Marx and Engels, it plainly accrued through Marx's reading, between December of 1880 and March of 1881, of anthropologist Lewis Henry Morgan's 1871 book, *Ancient Society,* based in large part upon his earlier (1851) *The League of the Hau-de-no-sau-nee or Iroquois.* Marx took at least 98 pages of handwritten notes on the topic of traditional Iroquoian governance. After Marx's death, his collaborator, Frederick Engels, inherited these notes and converted them into a book entitled *The Origin of the Family, Private Property and the State,* originally subtitled *In Light of the Researches of Lewis H. Morgan.* The Engels exposition is included in *Marx and Engels: Selected Works,* International Publishers, New York, 1968.

12. The language of Article I, Section 10 of the U.S. Constitution prohibits the federal government from entering into treaty relationships with entities other than fully sovereign nations. A treaty, once ratified by the Senate, therefore represents formal recognition by the United States of the fully sovereign national status of the other party or parties to the agreement. Between 1778 and 1871, the Senate duly ratified at least 371 treaties with various American Indian peoples.

13. An examination of this consideration may be found in Graymont, Barbara, *The Iroquois in the American Revolution,* Syracuse University Press, Syracuse, NY, 1972. A broader perspective is offered in Tebbel, John, and Keith Jennison, *The American Indian Wars,* Harper and Brothers Publishers, New York, 1960. Also see Hall, Arthur H., "The Red Stick War: Creek Indian Affairs During the War of 1812," *Chronicles of Oklahoma,* No. 12, September 1934, pp. 264-93.

14. Deloria, Vine Jr., "Sovereignty," in Roxanne Dunbar Ortiz and Larry Emerson eds., *Economic Development in American Indian Reservations,* Native American Studies Center, University of New Mexico, Albuquerque, 1979. Also see DeMallie, Raymond, "American Indian Treaty Making: Motives and Meanings," *American Indian Journal,* No. 3, January 1977, pp. 2-10.

15. See Peckman, Howard, and Charles Gibson, eds., *Attitudes of the Colonial Powers Toward the American Indian,* University of Utah Press, Salt Lake City, 1969. Also see Schaaf, Gregory, *Wampum Belts and Peace Trees: George Morgan, Native Americans and Revolutionary Diplomacy,* Fulcrum Publishers, Golden, CO, 1990.

16. See Prucha, Francis Paul, *American Indian Policy in the Formative Years: The Indian Trade and Intercourse Acts, 1790-1834,* University of Nebraska Press, Lincoln, 1970; and *Documents of United States Indian Policy,* University of Nebraska Press, Lincoln, 1975.

17. For texts and other data, see Kappler, Charles J., *Indian Treaties, 1778-1883,* Interland Publishers, New York, 1972.

18. The Sioux legal scholar Vine Deloria, Jr., has collected some 1,400 pages of such material to

date, and believes several hundred additional pages exist.

19. This was true despite a rider attached to the Indian Appropriations Act of 1871 (ch. 120, 16 *Stat.* 544, 566) formally suspending federal treaty-making with indigenous nations.

20. This principle derives from a range of sources, but is embodied quite clearly in the United Nations Declaration on the Granting of Independence to Colonial Countries and Peoples (December 14, 1960), and the International Covenant on Civil and Political Rights (March 23, 1966). For a broad view, see Bennett, Gordon, *Aboriginal Rights in International Law,* Royal Anthropological Institute, London, 1978.

21. The term was coined by Deloria, Vine Jr., and Clifford M. Lytle, *The Nations Within: The Past and Future of American Indian Sovereignty,* Pantheon Books, New York, 1984.

22. See Goldberg, Carol E., "Public Law 280: The Limits of State Law over Indian Reservations," *UCLA Law Review,* No. 22, February 1975, pp. 535-94. More generally, see Fixico, Donald L., *Termination and Relocation: Federal Indian Policy, 1945-1960,* University of New Mexico Press, Albuquerque, 1986.

23. On the southern California Indians specifically, see Shipeck, Florence Connolly, *Pushed Into the Rocks: Southern California Indian Land Tenure, 1769-1986,* University of Nebraska Press, Lincoln, 1988.

24. See, for example, Churchill, Ward, "The Indigenous Peoples of North America: A Struggle Against Internal Colonialism," *The Black Scholar,* Vol. 16, No. 1, February 1985.

25. This position is consistent with the United Nations' Declaration of the Granting of Independence to Colonial Countries and Peoples (1960): "All peoples have the right to self-determination: by virtue of that right they freely determine their political status and freely pursue their economic, social and cultural development." For the full text, see Brownlie, Ian, *Basic Documents on Human Rights,* Oxford University Press, London/New York, 1971, pp. 28-30.

26. Churchill, Ward, "The 'Trial' of Leonard Peltier," preface to Jim Messerschmidt's *The Trial of Leonard Peltier,* South End Press, Boston, 1983, p. viii.

27. This practice should be contrasted to the rules of "civilized warfare" then pertaining among the European powers, in which it was held that heads of state—and usually government functionaries more generally—were exempt from being killed by military action. That the United States subscribed to these conventions is witnessed in its treatment of, among others, President Santa Ana in the wake of the 1846 Mexican-American War, and of Confederate President Jefferson Davis at the end of the American Civil War. The kind of warfare practiced against Native America was of a wholly different sort, and patently illegal, even by the standards of the day.

28. On Tecumseh, see Sugden, John, *Tecumseh's Last Stand,* University of Oklahoma Press, Norman, 1985, especially p. 180: "Most witnesses remembered Tecumseh's body on its back...the limbs drawn up...Then on October 6 the souvenir hunters got to work, and when the warrior had been stripped of his clothing...Kentuckians tore skin from his back and thigh...[T]he rapacious soldiery so thoroughly scalped the corpse that some of them came away with fragments of skin the size of a cent piece and endowed with a mere tuft of hair. When [one of them] was interviewed in 1886 he was able to display a piece of Tecumseh's skin."

29. On the imprisonment and subsequent murder of Osceola on January 27, 1838, after he attended—under protection of a white truce flag—a peace negotiation requested by U.S. officials, see Boyd, Mark F., "Asi-Yahola or Osceola," *Florida Historical Quarterly,* Vol. XXXIII, Nos. 1-2, January/April 1955.

30. On the assassination of Crazy Horse in 1877, see Sandoz, Mari, *Crazy Horse: Strange Man of the Oglalas,* University of Nebraska Press, Lincoln, 1942. Also see Clark, Robert, ed., *The Killing of Chief Crazy Horse,* University of Nebraska Press, Lincoln, 1976. On the assassination of Sitting Bull in 1890, see Vestal, Stanley, *Sitting Bull: Champion of the Sioux,* University of Oklahoma Press, Norman, 1957.

31. On the execution of the Santees at Mankato after the so-called Little Crow's War, see Carley, Kenneth, *The Sioux Uprising of 1862,* Minnesota Historical Society, St. Paul, 1961.

32. On the execution of Captain Jack on October 3, 1873, see Murray, Keith A., *The Modocs and Their War,* University of Oklahoma Press, Norman, 1959. Also see Riddell, Jeff C., *The Indian History of the Modoc War and the Causes That Led to It,* Pine Cone Publishers, Medford, OR, 1973.

33. On the fate of Chief Joseph, see Beal, Merril, *I Will Fight No More Forever: Chief Joseph and the Nez Percé War,* University of Washington Press, Seattle, 1963.

34. On Geronimo's incarceration, first in Florida at the same prison in which Osceola had been assassinated, and subsequently at Fort Sill, Oklahoma (until his death), see Barrett, S.M., ed., *Geronimo: His Own Story*, E.P. Dutton Co., New York, 1971.

35. A classic case of this relates to U.S. interactions with the Cherokee Nation during the period leading up the the forced removal of that people from its Georgia/Carolina/Tennessee homeland, beginning in 1833. See Wilkins, Thurman, *Cherokee Tragedy: The Story of the Ridge Family and the Decimation of a People*, Macmillan Publishers, New York, 1970.

36. For an examination of this issue, see Leland, Joy, *Firewater Myths: North American Indian Drinking and Drug Addiction*, Rutgers Center for Alcohol Studies, Rutgers University, New Brunswick, NJ, 1976. Also see French, Laurence, and Jim Hornbuckle, "Alcoholism Among Native Americans: An Analysis," *Social Work*, No. 25, July 1980, pp. 275-80; and Heidenreich, C. Adrian, "Alcohol and Drug Use and Abuse Among Indian-Americans: A Review of Issues and Sources," *Journal of Drug Issues*, No. 6, Summer 1976, pp. 256-72.

37. There are numerous examples of this practice. One of the more notorious concerns the 1861 "Treaty with the Cheyenne," by which the United States claimed the latter nation had voluntarily ceded some 90 percent of the territory recognized as belonging to it under the 1851 Fort Laramie Treaty. As it turned out, the bulk of the alleged Cheyenne signatories had not attended the treaty conference at which they supposedly agreed to the new arrangement. Those who had, declined to sign. The appearance is that the United States then enlisted the services of a group of Lakotas who had assembled for other reasons—and who appear to have thought the whole thing was simply a riotous joke on their Cheyenne cousins—to sign the document "in behalf of" various Cheyenne leaders. The implications were ultimately less than humorous, however: the terms of the 1861 treaty led directly to the Sand Creek Massacre and resulting "Indian War of 1864-1865." See generally, Hoig, Stan, *The Sand Creek Massacre*, University of Oklahoma Press, Norman, 1961. The conclusion that the signatories were probably Lakotas derives from an unpublished study of the 1861 treaty process undertaken by Cheyenne/Lakota historian Richard B. Williams.

38. The contours of this policy are readily evident in Schmeckebier, Laurence, *The Office of Indian Affairs: Its History, Activities and Organization*, Johns Hopkins University Press, Baltimore, 1927.

39. See Weems, John Edward, *Death Song: The Last of the Indian Wars*, Doubleday Publishers, Garden City, NY, 1976.

40. On the forced relocation of eastern Indians to points west of the Mississippi, see Foreman, Grant, *Advancing the Frontier, 1830-1860*, University of Oklahoma Press, Norman, 1933 and *Indian Removal: The Immigration of the Five Civilized Tribes*, University of Oklahoma Press, Norman, 1953. Also see Strickland, Rennard, *The Indians in Oklahoma*, University of Oklahoma Press, Norman, 1980; and Williams, Walter, ed., *Southeastern Indians Since the Removal Era*, University of Georgia Press, Athens, 1979. A good philosophical overview of the entire process may be found in Downs, Ernest, "How the East Was Lost," *American Indian Journal*, Vol. 1, No. 2, 1975, pp. 6-10.

41. In effect, this makes the treaties the basic real estate documents by which the United States is entitled to claim rights of legal occupancy in North America. No other legal basis exists, the United States having formally foresworn "rights of conquest" *per se* in early statutes such as the 1787 Northwest Ordinance. See Cohen, Felix S., "How We Bought the United States," *Colliers*, January 19, 1946, pp. 22-3, 62.

42. An interesting examination of the implications and dimensions of this understanding in Oklahoma may be found in Applen, Allen G., "An Attempted Indian State Government: The Okmulgee Constitution in Indian Territory, 1870-1876," *Kansas Quarterly*, No. 3, Fall 1971, pp. 89-99. For exploration of the dynamics which prevented the Okmulgee experiment and others from succeeding, see Miner, H. Craig, *The Corporation and the Indian: Tribal Sovereignty and Industrial Civilization in Indian Territory, 1865-1907*, University of Missouri Press, Columbia, 1976.

43. Act of March 3, 1885, 23 *Stat.* 385, amended as 18 USCA 1153. The problems inherent to the statute are examined in Lucke, Thomas W. Jr., "Indian Law: Recognition of a Field of Values," *The Indian Historian*, No. 10, Spring 1977, pp. 43-7. A more comprehensive examination of the philosophical questions at issue will be found in Hoebel, E. Adamson, *The Law of Primitive Man: A Study in Comparative Legal Dynamics*, Harvard University Press, Cambridge, MA, 1964.

44. See Deloria, Vine Jr., "Indian Law and the Reach of History," *Journal of Contemporary Law*, No.

4, Winter 1977, pp. 1-13. For other views, see Cohen, Felix S., "Indian Rights and the Federal Courts," *Minnesota Law Review*, No. 24, January 1940, pp. 145-200; as well as Clinton, Robert N., "Development of Criminal Jurisdiction over Indian Lands: The Historical Perspective," *Arizona Law Review*, Vol. 17, No. 4, 1975, pp. 951-91 and "Criminal Jurisdiction on Reservations: A Journey Through a Jurisdictional Maze," *Arizona Law Review*, Vol. 18, No. 3, 1976, pp. 503-83.

45. Act of February 8, 1887, 24 *Stat.* 388. See Otis, D.S., *The Dawes Act and the Allotment of Indian Land*, University of Oklahoma Press, Norman, 1973.

46. On the impact of allotment, see Kickingbird, Kirk, and Karen Ducheneaux, *One Hundred Million Acres*, Macmillan Publishers, New York, 1973. Also see McDonnell, Janet A., *The Dispossession of the American Indian, 1887-1934*, Indiana University Press, Bloomington/Indianapolis, 1991.

47. To place the matter in perspective, the expression of such intentions as a matter of state policy would become a "Crime Against Humanity," the penalty for perpetration of which is death, under the Convention on Punishment and Prevention of the Crime of Genocide (1948). It should be noted that a genocide conducted by such means does not have to be completely successful in order to be illegal. Attempting or conspiring to attempt such genocidal policies are also capital crimes under the 1948 Convention. For the complete text, see Brownlie, op. cit., pp. 31-4.

48. Leupp, Francis E., *The Indian and His Problem*, Charles Scribner's Sons, New York, 1910 (rpt: Arno Press, New York, 1971), p. 93. An examination of the attitudes involved, and their practical policy implications, may be found in Jackson, Curtis E., and Marcia J. Galli, *A History of the Bureau of Indian Affairs and Its Activities Among Indians*, R&E Research Associates, San Francisco, 1977.

49. Letter, Charles Burke to William Williamson, September 16, 1921; William Williamson Papers, Box 2, File—Indian Matters, Miscellaneous, I.D. Weeks Library, University of South Dakota, Vermillion. The articulation of similar sensibilities occurs throughout the history of the BIA; see Kvasnicka, Robert M., and Herman J. Viola, eds., *The Commissioners of Indian Affairs, 1824-1977*, University of Nebraska Press, Lincoln, 1979.

50. For a sociological perspective on this phenomenon, see Yinger, Milton J., and George E. Simpson, "The Integration of Americans of Indian Descent," *The Annals (AAPS)*, 436, March 1978, pp. 131-51.

51. 18 USCA 1401 (a) (2). For a summary of at least some of the effects, see Hertzberg, Hazel W., *The Search for an American Indian Identity: Modern Pan-Indian Movements*, Syracuse University Press, Syracuse, NY, 1971.

52. The geologists were present under provision of the 1918 Metalliferous Minerals Act, which allowed for exploitation of resources on Indian land—and required payment of a 5 percent royalty on the market value of extracted ores—but which required Indian consent prior to leases being let. The last matter is what brought about the meeting of the traditional Diné government.

53. See Parlow, Anita, *Cry, Sacred Ground: Big Mountain, USA*, Christic Institute, Washington, D.C., 1988, p. 30. Also see Kelly, Laurence C., *The Navajo Indians and Federal Indian Policy, 1900-1935*, University of Arizona Press, Tucson, 1968.

54. On this topic, see Wood, John, "The Navajo: A History of Dependence and Underdevelopment," *URPE*, No. 11, Summer 1979, pp. 25-43. Also see Ruffing, Lorraine Turner, "Navajo Mineral Development," *American Indian Journal*, No. 4, September 1978, pp. 2-15; and Whitson, Hollis, and Martha Roberge, "Moving Those Indians Into the Twentieth Century," *Technology Review*, July 1986.

55. U.S. House of Representatives, Committee of One Hundred, *The Indian Problem: Resolution of the Committee of One Hundred Appointed by the Secretary of Interior and Review of the Indian Problem*, H. Doc. 149 (Serial 8392), 68th Cong., 1st Sess., U.S. Government Printing Office, Washington, DC, 1925.

56. Merriam, Lewis, et al., *The Problem of Indian Administration*, Johns Hopkins University Press, Baltimore, 1928.

57. For itemization of the Reorganization Act's contents and its legislative history, see Deloria and Lytle, op. cit. For more contemporary assessments, see Nash, Jay Brian, *The New Deal for Indians: A Survey of the Workings of the Indian Reorganization Act of 1934*, Academy Press, New York, 1938; and Mckeel, Scudder, "An Appraisal of the Indian Reorganization Act," *American Anthropologist*, No. 46, April-June 1944, pp. 209-17.

58. Interview with elder David Monongye, village of Hotevilla, Hopi Reservation, Arizona, May 16, 1987 (tape on file).
59. Costo, Rupert, "Federal Indian Policy, 1933-1945," in Kenneth R. Philp, ed., *Indian Self-Rule: First-Hand Accounts of Indian-White Relations from Roosevelt to Reagan*, Howe Brothers Publishers, Salt Lake City, 1986, p. 49.
60. Quoted in ibid., p. 52. The Oneidas were joined by the rest of the Six Nations in adopting this position.
61. Ibid., pp. 28-9. Costo's assessment of Collier's tactics, especially in southern California, is borne out in the investigations of the matter by Yamasee historian Donald A. Crinde, Jr.; see his "Southern California Indians' Resistance to the Indian New Deal," unpublished draft essay presented at the Western Social Science Association annual conference, Reno, NV, April 1991.
62. Ibid., pp. 50-1.
63. Wright, Peter, "John Collier and the Oklahoma Indian Welfare Act of 1936," *Chronicles of Oklahoma*, No. 50, Autumn 1972, pp. 347-51. Also see Quinton, B.T., "Oklahoma Tribes, the Great Depression and the Indian Bureau," *Mid-America*, No. 49, January 1967, pp. 29-43.
64. Of those nations that reorganized, ninety-two were provided with BIA-written "constitutions" effectively converting them into business entities. Another seventy-two ended up with corporate charters, pure and simple. See Philp, Kenneth R., "The Indian Reorganization Act Fifty Years Later," in *Indian Self-Rule*, op. cit., p. 18.
65. O'Brien, op. cit., pp. 82-83. With regard to the travesty at Hopi, see Lummis, Charles, *Bullying the Hopi*, Prescott College Press, Prescott, AZ, 1968. Also see LaFarge, Oliver, *Running Narrative of the Organization of the Hopi Tribe of Indians*, in the LaFarge Collection, University of Texas at Austin.
66. See Taylor, Graham D., *The New Deal and American Indian Tribalism: The Administration of the Indian Reorganization Act, 1934-45*, University of Nebraska Press, Lincoln, 1980. Also see Stein, Gary, "Tribal Self-Government and the Indian Reorganization Act of 1934," *Michigan Law Review*, No. 70, April 1972, pp. 955-86.
67. See Ducheneaux, Franklin, "The Indian Reorganization Act and the Cheyenne River Sioux," *American Indian Journal*, No. 2, August 1976, pp. 8-14. More generally, see Kelly, William H., ed., *Indian Affairs and the Indian Reorganization Act: The Twenty Year Record*, University of Arizona Press, Tucson, 1954.
68. Concerning Navajo rejection of the IRA and the reasons for it, see Iverson, Peter, *The Navajo Nation*, Greenwood Press, Westport, CT, 1981. Also see Boyce, George A., *"When the Navajos Had Too Many Sheep": The 1940s*, Indian Historian Press, San Francisco, 1974.
69. This is covered in passing in Zimmerman, William Jr., "The Role of the Bureau of Indian Affairs Since 1933," *Annals of the American Academy of Political and Social Science*, No. 311, May 1957, pp. 31-40.
70. U.S. House of Representatives, Committee on Indian Affairs, *Investigation of the Bureau of Indian Affairs*, House Report 2053, 82d Cong., 2d Sess., U.S. Government Printing Office, Washington, D.C., 1952, pp. 161-78.
71. See Officer, James E., "Termination as Federal Policy: An Overview," in *Indian Self-Rule*, op. cit., p. 118.
72. *Investigation of the Bureau of Indian Affairs*, op. cit., pp. 28-30.
73. U.S. Senate, S. Rep. 310, 78th Cong., 1st Sess. (1943). The report is quoted in Philp, Kenneth R., *John Collier's Crusade for Indian Reform, 1920-1954*, University of Arizona Press, Tucson, 1977, p. 208.
74. See U.S. House of Representatives, Committee on Indian Affairs, *Investigation of the Bureau of Indian Affairs*, 78th Cong., 1st Sess., U.S. Government Printing Office, Washington, D.C., 1944, pp. 28-39. Also see Koppes, Clayton R., "From New Deal to Termination: Liberalism and Indian Policy, 1933-1953," *Pacific Historical Review*, No. 46, November 1977, pp. 543-66.
75. Brophy's main job was to usher in the Indian Claims Commission in 1946. Brophy retired due to ill health until Myer could come aboard. See *The Commissioners of Indian Affairs*, op. cit.
76. By far the best handling of Myer's character and career will be found in Drinnon, Richard, *Keeper of Concentration Camps: Dillon S. Myer and American Racism*, University of California Press, Berkeley, 1987. It should be noted that Myer was aided in his task by the passage, in 1952, of Public Law 82-291, a law authorizing transfer of "Indian services" from the BIA to other federal agencies where they could be incorporated into broader social services program-

ming. See Orfield, Gary, *A Study of Termination Policy,* National Congress of American Indians, Denver, 1965.

77. The complete text of H.R. 108 appears in Part II of Spicer, Edward H., *A Short History of the United States,* Van Nostrand Rinehold Co., New York, 1969.

78. Officer, op. cit., p. 125. The most comprehensive overview of the termination and relocation policies is to be found in Fixico, *Termination and Relocation,* op. cit. Also see LaFarge, Oliver, "Termination of Federal Supervision: Disintegration and the American Indian," *Annals of the American Academy of Political and Social Science,* No. 311, May 1975, pp. 56-70; and Stefon, Frederick J., "The Irony of Termination: 1943-1958," *The Indian Historian,* Vol. 3, No. 3, Summer 1978, pp. 3-14.

79. One dissolution, that of the Oklahoma Ponca, was delayed in committee and was not consummated until 1966. See Butler, Raymond V., "The Bureau of Indian Affairs: Activities Since 1945," *Annals of the American Academy of Political and Social Science,* No. 436, 1978, pp. 50-60.

80. For assessment of reservation economic conditions in the pre-termination period, see Project Committee on Indian Affairs, Commission on Organization of the Executive Branch of Government, *Report of the Committee on Indian Affairs to the Commission on Organization of the Executive Branch of Government,* 82d Cong., 2d Sess., U.S. Government Printing Office, Washington, D.C., October 1948. Also see Zimmerman, William Jr., "Economic Status of Indians in the United States," *Journal of Religious Thought,* Summer 1950 and Sorkin, Alan L., "The Economic and Social Status of the American Indian, 1940-1970," *Nebraska Journal of Economics,* No. 22, Spring 1974, pp. 33-50.

81. See O'Brien, op. cit., p. 86. Also see Burt, Larry W., *Tribalism in Crisis: Federal Indian Policy, 1953-1961,* University of New Mexico Press, Albuquerque, 1982; Ablon, Joan, "American Indian Relocation: Problems of Dependency and Management in the City," *Phylon,* No. 26, 1965, pp. 362-71.

82. On proportion of Indian population which is urban, see U.S. Bureau of the Census, *General Population Characteristics: United States Summary,* PC80-1-B1, Pt. 1, U.S. Government Printing Office, Washington, D.C., 1983. For use of the term "migrate," see Gundlach, James H., Nelson P. Reid and Alden E. Roberts, "Native American Indian Migration and Relocation," *Pacific Sociological Review,* No. 21, 1978, pp. 117-27.

83. Quoted in *Indian Self-Rule,* op. cit., p. 171.

84. *The Blackfeet Nation v. United States,* 81 Ct. Cl. 101 (1935). The matter is thoroughly discussed in Cohen, Felix S., "The Erosion of Indian Rights, 1950-53: A Case Study in Bureaucracy," *Yale Law Journal,* No. 62, February 1953, pp. 348-90.

85. See FBI serialization number 100-378472, January 10, 1952. On Cohen overall, see Haas, Theodore H., ed., *Felix S. Cohen: A Fighter for Justice,* Alumni of the City College of New York, Washington, D.C., 1956.

86. McCarran's draft bill, S. 2543, is contained in *The Congressional Record,* January 29, 1952.

87. Concerning the AAIA/NCAI counteroffensive, and Cohen's and Curry's parts in it, see Drinnon, op. cit., pp. 188-248.

88. Quoted in Officer, op. cit., p. 125.

89. On the Menominee restoration (Public Law 93-197 (1973), 87 *Stat.* 770, codified at 25 U.S.C. 903 *et seq.),* see Deer, Ada, "Menominee Restoration: How the Good Guys Won," *Journal of Intergroup Relations,* No. 3, 1974, pp. 41-50. Also see Shames, Deborah, ed., *Freedom With Reservation: The Menominee Struggle to Save Their Land and People,* National Committee to Save the Menominee People and Forest, Madison, WI, 1972, and Peroff, Nicholas, *Menominee DRUMS: Tribal Termination and Restoration, 1954-1974* University of Oklahoma Press, Norman, 1982. On the Siletz restoration (Public Law 95-195 (1977); 91 *Stat.* 1415, codified at 25 U.S.C. 711 *et seq.),* see Wilkinson, Charles F., and Eric R. Biggs, "The Evolution of the Termination Policy," *American Indian Law Review,* No. 5, 1977, pp. 139-84. Other nations that were "reinstated" during the 1970s (Public Law 95-281 (1978), 92 *Stat.* 246, codified at 25 U.S.C. 861 *et seq.)* included the Wyandotte, Peoria, Ottawa, and Modoc.

90. Officer, op. cit., p. 126.

91. O'Brien, op. cit., p. 87. For details on Clyde Warrior, the founding of NIYC, and the "fish-ins," see Steiner, Stan, *The New Indians,* Harper and Row Publishers, New York, 1968. Also see Berthrong, Donald J., *The American Indian: From Pacifism to Activism,* Forum Press, St. Charles, MO, 1973.

92. Deloria, Vine Jr., *Custer Died for Your Sins: An Indian Manifesto*, Macmillan Publishers, New York, 1969; reprinted by the University of Oklahoma Press, Norman, 1988; and *We Talk, You Listen: New Tribes, New Turf*, Macmillan Publishers, New York, 1970.

93. On the founding of AIM and its early demonstrations, see Churchill, Ward, and Jim Vander Wall, *Agents of Repression: The FBI's Secret Wars Against the Black Panther Party and the American Indian Movement*, South End Press, Boston, 1988. On the Alcatraz occupation, see Blue Cloud, Peter, *Alcatraz Is Not An Island*, Wingbow Press, Berkeley, CA, 1972. On the Pit River confrontations, see Jaimes, M. Annette, "The Pit River Indian Land Claim Dispute in Northern California," *Journal of Ethnic Studies*, Vol. 14, No. 4, Winter 1987.

94. See Albert, Stewart, and Judith Clavir-Albert, eds., *The Sixties Papers: Documents of a Rebellious Decade*, Praeger Publishers, New York, 1984.

95. The study in question is Brophie, William A., and Sophie E. Aberle, *The Indian, America's Unfinished Business: Report of the Commission on Rights, Liberties and Responsibilities of the American Indian*, University of Oklahoma Press, Norman, 1966. For the text of the Johnson speech, see *Public Papers of the Presidents, 1968-1969*, U.S. Government Printing Office, Washington, D.C., 1970, p. 335. For analysis of the speech and its policy context, see Clinton, Robert M., Nell Jessup Newton, and Monroe E. Price, *American Indian Law: Cases and Materials*, The Michie Co., Charlottesville, VA, 1991, p. 159.

96. See Burnett, Donald E., "An Historical Analysis of the 1968 'Indian Civil Rights' Act," *Harvard Journal of Legislation*, No. 9, May 1972, pp. 557-626. Also see Prucha, Francis Paul, "American Indian Policy in the Twentieth Century," *Western Historical Quarterly*, No. 15, January 1984, pp. 5-18.

97. Clinton, *et al.*, op. cit., p. 159.

98. The language is from a speech delivered by NTCA President Webster Two Hawks in Washington, D.C. on November 6, 1972; quoted in the *Washington Post* the same day. It should be noted that NTCA was supported by $100,000 in federal funds each year for fiscal years 1969-73, and that Two Hawks' trip to the capitol to make the speech in question was underwritten entirely by funds provided by Nixon's Committee to Reelect the President (CREEP).

99. Deloria, Vine Jr., *Behind the Trail of Broken Treaties: An Indian Declaration of Independence*, University of Texas Press, Austin, 2nd Edition, 1984, pp. 48-52.

100. The best account of the 1972 BIA building occupation may be found in Editors, *BIA, I'm Not Your Indian Anymore*, Akwesasne Notes, Mohawk Nation via Rooseveltown, NY, 1973. More generally, see *Behind the Trail of Broken Treaties*, op. cit., and Burnette, Robert, with John Koster, *The Road to Wounded Knee*, Bantam Books, New York, 1974. It should be noted that AIM's "liberation" of the BIA's internal documents revealed a broad range of questionable (and previously denied) federal practices involving the leasing of Indian lands. It also exposed a secret program of involuntary sterilization targeting native women.

101. See Churchill, Ward, "'Renegades, Terrorists and Revolutionaries': The U.S. Government's Propaganda War Against the American Indian Movement," *Propaganda Review*, No. 4, Spring 1989, pp. 12-16. Also see *BIA, I'm Not Your Indian Anymore*, op. cit.

102. Burnette and Koster, op. cit.

103. The circumstances leading up to the Wounded Knee Siege are covered in Holm, Tom, "The Crisis in Tribal Government," in Vine Deloria, Jr., ed., *American Indian Policy in the Twentieth Century*, University of Oklahoma Press, Norman, 1985, pp. 135-54. Also see U.S. Senate, Committee on Insular Affairs, Subcommittee on Indian Affairs, *The Occupation of Wounded Knee: Hearings Before the Subcommittee on Indian Affairs, June 16-17, 1973*, 93rd Cong., 1st Sess., U.S. Government Printing Office, Washington, D.C., 1973.

104. For the best single account of the Wounded Knee siege, see Editors, *Voices From Wounded Knee, 1973*, Akwesasne Notes, Mohawk Nation via Rooseveltown, NY, 1974. Also see *Agents of Repression*, op. cit., pp. 141-77.

105. See U.S. Commission on Civil Rights, *Report of Investigation: Oglala Sioux Tribe, General Election, 1974*, Rocky Mountain Regional Office, Denver, 1974.

106. On the assassination of Pedro Bissonette, see *Agents of Repression*, op. cit., pp. 200-3.

107. In addition to works already cited, interesting assessments of the government's counterinsurgency war against AIM may be found in Johansen, Bruce, and Roberto Maestas, *Wasi'chu: The Continuing Indian Wars*, Monthly Review Press, New York, 1979; and Weyler, Rex, *Blood of the Land: The U.S. Government and Corporate War Against the American Indian Movement*, Everest House Publishers, New York, 1983.

108. Analysis of Nixon's use of the term may be obtained in Forbes, Jack D., *Native Americans and Nixon: Presidential Politics and Minority Self-Determination,* American Indian Studies Center, UCLA, 1981.

109. This formulation accrues from Point 2 of the United Nations' 1960 Declaration on the Granting of Independence to Colonial Countries and Peoples, which the U.S.—as is usually the case with elements of international law pertaining to human rights—abstained from signing. The Declaration is reproduced verbatim in Brownlie, op. cit., pp. 28-30.

110. For cogent analysis of the Act's content, see Gross, Michael P., "Indian Self-Determination and Tribal Sovereignty: An Analysis of Recent Federal Indian Policy," *Texas Law Review,* No. 56, 1978, esp. p. 1195: "Even if it were an established fact...Indian control of [such agencies as] the BIA would not substitute for self-government."

111. Speech by Russell Means, July 25, 1978 (tape on file).

112. The commission was authorized under provision of 25 U.S.C. 174. Its findings, entitled *Report: American Indian Policy Review Commission Task Force,* were published in nine volumes U.S. Government Printing Office, Washington, D.C., 1977. The quote is taken from Clinton, et al., op. cit., p. 162.

113. Meeds is quoted from *Final Report: American Indian Policy Review Commission Task Force,* op. cit., p. 573.

114. Clinton, et al., op. cit., p. 162. For analysis, see Wilkinson, Charles F., "Shall the Islands be Protected?" *American West,* No. 41, 1979. Also see Clinton, Robert N., "Isolated in Their Own Country: A Defense of Federal Protection of Indian Autonomy and Self-Government," *Stanford Law Review,* No. 33, 1981.

115. Quoted in *Indian Self-Rule,* op. cit., p. 291. The "Indian governments as part of the federal hierarchy" theory has by now been worked out in a doctrinal sense, primarily by liberal non-Indian legal scholars such as Charles F. Wilkinson. For a full-bore display of such thinking, see his *Indians, Time and Law,* Yale University Press, New Haven, CT, 1987. For an "Indian" adaptation of the principles at issue, see American Indian Lawyer Training Program, *Indian Tribes as Sovereign Governments: A Sourcebook on Federal-Tribal History, Law and Policy,* American Indian Resources Institute Press, Oakland, CA, 1985.

116. Quoted in *Indian Self-Rule,* p. 287.

117. For discussion of the Longest Walk, and the full text of its manifesto, see Robbins, Rebecca L., "American Indian Self-Determination: Comparative Analysis and Rhetorical Criticism," *Issues in Radical Therapy/New Studies on the Left,* Vol. XIII, Nos. 3 and 4, Summer-Fall 1988, pp. 48-58. Also see "The Longest Walk," *Akwesasne Notes,* Mohawk Nation via Rooseveltown, NY, Vol. 10, No. 3, Summer 1978.

118. The Standing Rock conference and formation of IITC is covered in the updated version of *Behind the Trail of Broken Treaties,* op. cit. Corroboration has been obtained by direct interview of both Jimmie Durham and Russell Means during 1991. Portions of Durham's views on the process may also be found in his *Columbus Day,* West End Press, Minneapolis, 1982.

119. *Behind the Trail of Broken Treaties,* op. cit.

120. Russell Tribunal, *The Rights of the Indians of the Americas,* Fourth Russell Tribunal, Rotterdam, Netherlands, 1980.

121. On formation of the Working Group and its mandate (E.S.C. Res. 34, U.N. ESCOR Supp. (No. 1) at 26-27, U.N. Doc. E/1982/82 (1982)), see Anaya, James S., "The Rights of Indigenous Peoples and International Law in Historical and Contemporary Perspective," in Clinton, *et al.,* op. cit., pp. 1257-76. Also see Barsh, Russel, "Indigenous North America and Contemporary International Law," *Oregon Law Review,* No. 62, 1983.

122. For the text of the revised draft of the *International Declaration on the Rights of Indigenous Peoples,* see *Report of the Working Group on Indigenous Populations,* 7th Session, Annex II, U.N. Doc. E/CN.4/sub.2/1989/36, August 25, 1989.

123. The text of the ILO Convention, approved in June 1989, appears in "Report of the Committee on Convention 107," *Provisional Record,* No. 25, 76th Sess., 1989, pp. 25-33. For interpretation of its significance, see Anaya, op. cit.

124. The proposal for a new OAS instrument on indigenous rights, approved on November 18, 1989, is described in the *Annual Report of the Inter-American Commission on Human Rights, 1988-89,* OEA/Ser.L/v/II.76, Doc. 10, September 18, 1989.

125. During the summer of 1990, Colorado AIM Codirector Glenn T. Morris received a telephone call from a NARF staff attorney soliciting advice as to how go about obtaining NGO status.

126. Quoted in *Indian Self-Rule*, op. cit., p. 280.
127. The complete text of the Churchill/Means collaboration is forthcoming under the title *TREATY: A Program for American Indian Sovereignty*, from the Fourth World Center for Indigenous Law and Politics, University of Colorado at Denver, in early 1992.
128. On Means' 1978 conviction, see Amnesty International, *Proposal for a Commission of Inquiry into the Effect of Domestic Intelligence Activities on Criminal Trials in the United States of America*, Amnesty International, New York, 1980. AI was preparing to adopt Means as a "prisoner of conscience" at the time of his release from prison in 1979. The South Dakota anarcho-syndicalism statute under which the AIM leader was convicted has been subsequently repealed.
129. Anderson was a major leader of the resistance of traditional Diné to forced relocation from the Big Mountain area of the Navajo Nation during the period 1974-1986. See Weyler, op. cit. Also see Kammer, Jerry, *The Second Long Walk: The Navajo-Hopi Land Dispute*, University of New Mexico, Albuquerque, 1980.
130. For DeLaCruz's thinking on strategies that might lead to a resumption of genuine Indian sovereignty, see his "From Self-Determination to Self-Governance," in Minugh, Carol J., Glenn T. Morris, and Rudolph C. Ryser, eds., *Indian Self-Governance: Perspectives on the Political Status of Indian Nations in the United States of America*, Center for World Indigenous Studies, Kenmore, WA, 1989, pp. 1-14. For background on the Coastal Highway dispute and related matters, see Ryser, Rudolph C., ed., *Tribes and States in Conflict: A Tribal Proposal*, Intertribal Study Group on Tribal/State Relations, Rational Island Press, Seattle, 1981.
131. See Martinez Cobo, José R., *Study of the Problem of Discrimination Against Indigenous Populations, Final Report: Conclusions, Proposals and Recommendations*, U.N./ID # E/CN.4/Sub.2/1983/21/Add.83, September 1983. Also see Independent Commission on International Humanitarian Issues, *Indigenous Peoples: A Global Quest for Justice*, Zed Press, London, 1987.
132. With regard to the revelations on BIA mismanagement and related matters, see U.S. Senate, Select Committee on Indian Affairs, *Hearings Before the Committee on Investigations, January 30 and 31, 1989*, 101st Cong., 1st Sess., U.S. Government Printing Office, Washington, D.C., February 1, 1989.
133. The text of the relevant portions of P.L. 100-472 may be found in Minugh, et al., op. cit., pp. 122-5. Analysis of the law by three of the involved nations—Quinalt, Lummi and the Jamestown Band of Klallam—may be found on pp. 117-22.
134. U.S. Senate, Select Committee on Indian Affairs, *Final Report and Legislative Recommendations: A Report of the Special Committee on Investigations*, 101st Cong., 2d Sess., U.S. Government Printing Office, Washington, D.C., November 20, 1989, p. 17.

Chapter IV

Federal Indian Identification Policy
A Usurpation of Indigenous Sovereignty in North America

M. Annette Jaimes

I'm forever being asked not only my "tribe," but my "percentage of Indian blood." I've given the matter a lot of thought, and find I prefer to make the computation based on all of me rather than just the fluid coursing through my veins. Calculated in this way, I can report that I am precisely 52.5 pounds Indian—about 35 pounds Creek and the remainder Cherokee—88 pounds Teutonic, 43.5 pounds some sort of English, and the rest "undetermined." Maybe the last part should just be described as "human." It all seems rather silly as a means of assessing who I am, don't you think?

> Ward Churchill
> Creek/Cherokee Métis, 1991

The question of my "identity" often comes up. I think I must be a mixed-blood. I claim to be male, although only one of my parents was male.

> Jimmie Durham
> Cherokee, 1991

By all accepted standards of international jurisprudence and human decency, American Indian peoples whose territory lies within the borders of the United States hold compelling legal and moral rights to be treated as fully sovereign nations. It is axiomatic that any such national entity is inherently entitled to exercise the prerogative of determining for itself the criteria by which its citizenry, or "membership," is to be recognized by other sovereign nations. This is a principle that applies equally to superpowers such as the U.S. and to non-powers such as Grenada and Monaco. In fact, it is a tenet so widely understood and imbedded in international law, custom, and convention that it bears no particular elaboration here.

Contrary to virtually universal practice, the United States has opted to preempt unilaterally the rights of many North American indigenous nations to engage in this most fundamental level of internal decisionmaking. Instead, in pursuit of the interests of their own state rather than those of the nations that are thereby affected, federal policymakers have increasingly imposed "Indian identification standards" of their own design. Typically centering upon a notion of "blood quantum"—not especially different in its conception from the eugenics code once adopted by nazi Germany in its effort to achieve "racial purity," or currently utilized by South Africa to segregate Blacks and "coloreds"—this aspect of U.S. policy has increasingly wrought havoc with the American Indian sense of nationhood (and often the individual sense of self) over the past century. This chapter offers a brief analysis of the motivations underlying this federal usurpation of the American Indian expression of sovereignty and points out certain implications of it.

Federal Obligations

The more than 370 formally ratified treaties entered into by the United States with various Indian nations represent the basic real estate documents by which the federal government now claims legal title to most of its land base. In exchange for the lands ceded by Indians, the United States committed itself to the permanent provision of a range of services to Indian populations (i.e., the citizens of the Indian nations with which the treaty agreements were reached), which would assist them in adjusting their economies and ways of life to their newly constricted territories. For example, in the 1794 Treaty with the Oneida (also affecting the Tuscarora and Stockbridge Indians), the United States guaranteed provision of instruction "in the arts of the miller and sawyer," as well as regular annuities paid in goods and cash, in exchange for a portion of what is now the state of New York.[1] Similarly, the 1804 Treaty with the Delaware extended assurances of technical instruction in agriculture and the mechanical arts, as well as annuities.[2] As Evelyn C. Adams frames it:

> Treaties with the Indians varied widely, stipulating cash annuities to be paid over a specified period of time or perpetually; rations and clothing, farming implements and domestic animals, and instruction in agriculture along with other educational opportunities…[And eventually] the school supplemented the Federal program of practical teaching.[3]

The reciprocal nature of such agreements received considerable reinforcement when it was determined, early in the 19th century, that "the enlightenment and civilization of the Indian" might yield—quite aside from any need on the part of the United States to honor its international obligations—a certain utility in terms of subordinating North America's indigenous peoples to Euroamerican domination. Secretary of War John C. Calhoun articulated this quite clearly in 1818:

> By a proper combination of force and persuasion, of punishment and rewards, they [the Indians] ought to be brought within the pales of law and civilization. Left to themselves, they will never reach that desirable condition. Before the slow operation of reason and experience can convince them of its superior advantages, they must be overwhelmed by the mighty torrent of our population.

Such small bodies, with savage customs and character, cannot, and ought not, to be allowed to exist in an independent society. Our laws and manners ought to supersede their present savage manners and customs...their [treaty] annuities would constitute an ample school fund; and education, comprehending as well as the common arts of life, reading, writing, and arithmetic, ought not to be left discretionary with the parents...When sufficiently advanced in civilization, they would be permitted to participate in such civil and political rights as the respective States.[4]

The utter cynicism involved in Calhoun's position—that of intentionally using the treaty instruments by which the United States conveyed recognition of Indian sovereignty as the vehicle with which to destroy that same sovereignty—speaks for itself. The more important point for purposes of this study, however, is that by 1820 U.S. strategic interests had congealed around the notion of extending federal obligations to Indians. The tactic was therefore continued throughout the entirety of the period of U. S. internal territorial conquest and consolidation.[5] By 1900, the federal obligations to Indian nations were therefore quite extensive.

Financial Factors

As Vine Deloria, Jr., has observed:

The original relationship between the United States government and American Indian [nations] was one of treaties. Beginning with the establishment of federal policy toward Indians in the Northwest Ordinance of 1787, which pledged that the utmost good faith would be exercised toward the Indian [nations], and continuing through many treaties and statutes, the relationship has gradually evolved into a strange and stifling union in which the United States has become responsible for all the programs and policies affecting Indian communities.[6]

What this meant in practice was that the government was being required to underwrite the cost of a proliferating bureaucratic apparatus overseeing "service delivery" to Indians, a process initiated on April 16, 1818, with the passage of an act (*U.S. Statutes at Large*, 13:461) requiring the placement of a federal agent with each Indian nation, to serve as liaison and to "administer the discharge of Governmental obligations thereto." As the number of Indian groups with which the United States held relations had increased, so too had the number of "civilizing" programs and services undertaken, ostensibly in their behalf. This was all well and good during the time-span when it was seen as a politico-military requirement, but by the turn of the century this need had passed. The situation was compounded by the fact that the era of Indian population decline engendered by war and disease had also come to an end; the population eligible for per capita benefits, which had been reduced to a quarter-million by the 1890s, could be expected to rebound steadily in the 20th century. With its land base secured, the United States was casting about for a satisfactory mechanism to avoid paying the ongoing costs associated with its acquisition.

The most obvious route to this end, of course, lay in simply and overtly refusing to comply with the terms of the treaties, thus abrogating them.[7] The problems in this regard were, however, both two-fold and extreme. First, the deliberate invalidation of the U.S. treaties with the Indians would (obviously) tend to simultaneously invalidate the legitimacy which the country attributed to its occupancy of much of North America. Second, such a move would immediately negate the useful and carefully nurtured image the U.S. had cultivated of itself as a country of progressive laws rather than raw force. The federal government had to appear to continue to meet its commitments, while at the same time avoiding them, or at least containing them at some acceptable level. A devious approach to the issue was needed.

This was found in the so-called "blood quantum" or "degree of Indian blood" standard of American Indian identification which had been adopted by Congress in 1887 as part of the General Allotment Act. The function of this piece of legislation was to expedite the process of Indian "civilization" by unilaterally dissolving their collectively (i.e., nationally) held reservation land holdings. Reservation lands were reallocated in accordance with the "superior" (i.e., Euroamerican) concept of property: *individually* deeded land parcels, usually of 160 acres each. Each Indian, identified as being those documentably of *one-half or more Indian blood,* was entitled to receive title in fee of such a parcel; all others were simply disenfranchised altogether. Reserved Indian land which remained unallotted after all "blooded" Indians had received their individual parcels was to be declared "surplus" and opened up for non-Indian use and occupancy.

Needless to say, there were nowhere near enough Indians meeting the Act's genetic requirements to absorb by individual parcel the quantity of acreage involved in the formerly reserved land areas. Consequently, between 1887 and 1934, the aggregate Indian land base within the U.S. was "legally" reduced from about 138 million acres to about 48 million.[8] Moreover, the allotment process itself had been manipulated in such a way that the worst reservation acreage tended to be parceled out to Indians, while the best was opened to non-Indian homesteading and corporate use; nearly 20 million of the acres remaining in Indian hands by the latter year were arid or semi-arid, and thus marginal or useless for agricultural purposes.[9]

By the early 1900s, then, the eugenics mechanism of the blood quantum had already proven itself such a boon in the federal management of its Indian affairs that it was generally adapted as the "eligibility factor," triggering entitlement to any federal service from the issuance of commodity rations to health care, annuity payments, and educational benefits. If the government could not repeal its obligations to Indians, it could at least act to limit their number, thereby diminishing the cost associated with underwriting their entitlements on a per capita basis. Concomitantly, it must have seemed logical that if the overall number of Indians could be kept small, the administrative expenses involved in their service programs might also be held to a minimum. Much of the original impetus toward the federal preemption of the sovereign Indian prerogative of defining "who's Indian," and the standardization of the racist degree-of-blood method of Indian identification, derived from the budgetary considerations of a federal government anxious to avoid paying its bills.

Other Economic Factors

As the example of the General Allotment Act clearly demonstrates, economic determinants other than the mere outflow of cash from the federal treasury figure into the federal utilization of the blood quantum. The huge windfall of land expropriated by the United States as a result of the act was only the tip of the iceberg. For instance, in constricting the acknowledged size of Indian populations, the government could technically meet its obligations to reserve "first rights" to water usage for Indians while simultaneously siphoning off artificial "surpluses" to non-Indian agricultural, ranching, municipal, and industrial use in the arid west.[10] The same principle pertains to the assignment of fishing quotas in the Pacific Northwest, a matter directly related to the development of a lucrative non-Indian fishing industry there.[11]

By the 1920s, it was also becoming increasingly apparent that much of the agriculturally worthless terrain left to Indians after allotment lay astride rich deposits of natural resources such as coal, copper, oil, and natural gas; later in the century, it was revealed that some 60 percent of all "domestic" uranium reserves also lay beneath reservation lands. It was therefore becoming imperative, from the viewpoint of federal and corporate economic planners, to gain unhindered access to these assets. Given that it would have been just as problematic to simply seize the resources as it would have been to abrogate the treaties, another expedient was required. This assumed the form of legislation unilaterally extending the responsibilities of citizenship (though not all the rights; Indians are still regulated by about 5,000 more laws than other citizens) over all American Indians within the United States.

> Approximately two-thirds of the Indian population had citizenship conferred upon them under the 1877 Allotment Act, as a condition of the allotment of their holdings...[In 1924] an act of Congress [8 U.S.C.A. 1402 (a) (2)] declared all Indians to be citizens of the United States and of the states in which they resided...[12]

The Indian Citizenship Act greatly confused the circumstances even of many of the blooded and federally certified Indians insofar as it was held to bear legal force, and to carry legal obligations, whether or not any given Indian or group of Indians wished to be a U.S. citizen. As for the host of non-certified, mixed-blood people residing in the U.S., their status was finally "clarified"; they had been definitionally absorbed into the American mainstream at the stroke of the congressional pen. And, despite the fact that the act technically left certified Indians occupying the status of citizenship in their own indigenous nation as well as in the U.S. (a "dual form" of citizenship so awkward as to be sublime), the juridical door had been opened by which the weight of Indian obligations would begin to accrue more to the U.S. than to themselves. Resource negotiations would henceforth be conducted between "American citizens" rather than between representatives of separate nations, a context in which federal and corporate arguments "for the greater good" could be predicted to prevail.

In 1934, the effects of the citizenship act were augmented by the passage of the Indian Reorganization Act. The expressed purpose of this law was finally and completely to usurp the traditional mechanisms of American Indian governance (e.g., the traditional chiefs, council of elders, etc.), replacing them with a system of federally approved and regulated "tribal councils." These councils, in turn, were consciously structured more along the lines of corporate boards than of governmental entities. As Section 17 of the IRA, which spells out the council functions, puts the matter:

> [An IRA charter] may convey to the incorporated tribe the power to purchase, take by gift, or bequest, or otherwise, own, hold, manage, operate, and dispose of property of every description, real and personal, including the power to purchase restricted Indian lands and to issue in exchange for corporate property, and such further powers as may be incidental to the conduct of corporate business, not inconsistent with the law.

Indeed, since the exercise of such typical governmental attributes as jurisdiction over criminal law had already been stripped away from the councils by legislation such as the 1885 Major Crimes Act, there has been very little for the IRA form of Indian government to do *but* sign off on leasing and other business arrangements with external interests. The situation was and is compounded by the fact that grassroots Indian resistance to the act's "acceptance" on many reservations was overcome by federal manipulation of local referenda.[13] This has left the IRA governments in the position of owing Washington rather than their supposed constituents for whatever legitimacy they may possess. All in all, it was and is a situation made to order for the rubber-stamping of plans integral to U.S. economic development at the direct expense of Indian nations and individual Indian people. This is readily borne out by the fact that, as of 1984, American Indians received, on the average, less than 20 percent of the market royalty rates (i.e., the rates paid to non-Indians) for the extraction of minerals from their land. As Winona LaDuke observes:

> By official census counts, there are only about 1 1/2 million Indians in the United States. By conservative estimates a quarter of all the low sulphur coal in the United States lies under our reservation land. About 15 percent of all the oil and natural gas lies there, as well as two-thirds of the uranium. 100 percent of all U.S. uranium production since 1955 has been on Indian land. And we have a lot of copper, timber, water rights and other resources too. By any reasonable estimation, with this small number of people and vast amount of resources, we should be the richest group in the United States. But we are the poorest. Indians have the lowest per capita income of any population group in the U.S. We have the highest rate of unemployment and the lowest level of educational attainment. We have the highest rates of malnutrition, plague

disease, death by exposure and infant mortality. On the other hand, we have the shortest life-span. Now, I think this says it all. Indian wealth is going somewhere, and that somewhere is definitely not to Indians. I don't know your definition of colonialism, but this certainly fits into mine.[14]

In sum, the financial advantages incurred by the United States in its appropriation of the definition of Indian identity have been neatly joined to even more powerful economic motivators during this century. The previously noted reluctance of the federal government to pay its bills cannot be uncoupled from its desire to profit from the resources of others.

Contemporary Political Factors

The utilization of treaties as instruments by which to begin the subordination of American Indian nations to U.S. hegemony, as well as subsequent legislation, such as the Major Crime Act, the General Allotment Act, and the Termination Act, all carry remarkably clear political overtones. This, to be sure, is the language of the colonizer and the colonized, to borrow a phrase from Albert Memmi,[15] and in each case the federal manipulation of the question of American Indian identity has played its role. These examples, however, may rightly be perceived as being both historical and parts of the "grand scheme" of U.S. internal colonialism (or "Manifest Destiny," as it was once called).

Today, the function of the Indian identity question appears to reside at the less rarified level of maintaining the status quo. First, it goes to the matter of keeping the aggregate number of Indians at less than 1 percent of the overall U.S. population and thus devoid of any potential electoral power. Second, and perhaps of equal importance, it goes to the classic "divide and conquer" strategy of keeping Indians at odds with one another, even within their own communities. As Tim Giago, conservative editor of the *Lakota Times*, asks:

> Don't we have enough problems trying to unite without...additional headaches? Why must people be categorized as full-bloods, mixed-bloods, etc? Many years ago, the Bureau of Indian Affairs decided to establish blood quanta for the purpose of [tribal] enrollment. At that time, blood quantum was set at one-fourth degree for enrollment. Unfortunately, through the years this caused many people on the reservation to be categorized and labeled...[The] situation [is] created solely by the BIA, with the able assistance of the Department of Interior.[16]

What has occurred is that the limitation of federal resources allocated to meeting U.S. obligations to American Indians has become so severe that Indians themselves have increasingly begun to enforce the race codes excluding the genetically marginalized from both identification as Indian citizens and consequent entitlements. In theory, such a posture leaves greater per capita shares for all remaining "bona fide" Indians. But, as American Indian Movement activist Russell Means has pointed out:

The situation is absurd. Our treaties say nothing about your having to be such-and-such a degree of blood in order to be covered...when the federal government made its guarantees to our nations in exchange for our land, it committed to provide certain services to us as we defined ourselves. As nations, and as a *people*. This seems to have been forgotten. Now we have Indian people who spend most of their time trying to prevent other Indian people from being recognized as such, just so that a few more crumbs—crumbs from the federal table—may be available to them, personally. I don't have to tell you that this isn't the Indian way of doing things. The Indian way would be to get together and demand what is coming to each and every one of us, instead of trying to cancel each other out. We are acting like colonized peoples, like subject peoples...[17]

The nature of the dispute has followed the classic formulation of Frantz Fanon, wherein the colonizer contrives issues which pit the colonized against one another, fighting viciously for some presumed status within the colonial structure, never having time or audacity enough to confront their oppressors.[18] In the words of Stella Pretty Sounding Flute, a member of the Crow Creek band of Lakota, "My grand-mother used to say that Indian blood was getting all mixed up, and some day there would be a terrible mess...[Now] no matter which way we turn, the white man has taken over."[19]

The problem, of course, has been conscientiously exacerbated by the government through its policies of leasing individual reservation land parcels to non-Indians, increasingly "checkerboarding" tribal holdings since 1900. Immediate economic consequences aside, this has virtually ensured that a sufficient number of non-Indians would be residents in reservations, and that intermarriage would steadily result. During the 1950s, the federal relocation program—in which reservation-based Indians were subsidized to move to cities, where they might be anticipated as being subsumed within vastly larger non-Indian populations—accelerated the process of "biological hybridization." Taken in combination with the ongoing federal insistence that "Indianness" could be measured only by degree of blood, these policies tend to speak for themselves. Even in 1972 when, through the Indian Education Act (86 *Stat.* 334), the government seemed finally to be abandoning the blood quantum, there was a hidden agenda. As Lorelei DeCora (Means), a former Indian education program coordinator, put it:

The question was really one of control, whether Indians would ever be allowed to control the identification of their own group members or citizens. First there was this strict blood quantum thing, and it was enforced for a hundred years, over the strong objections of a lot of Indians. Then, when things were sufficiently screwed up because of that, the feds suddenly reverse themselves completely, saying it's all a matter of self-identification. Almost anybody who wants to can just walk in and announce that he or she is Indian—no familiarity with tribal history, or Indian affairs, community recognition, or anything else really required—and, under the law, there's not a lot that Indians can do about it. The whole thing is suddenly just...really out of control. At that point, you really did have a lot of people showing up claiming that one of their ancestors, seven steps removed, had been some sort of "Cherokee princess." And we were obliged to accept that, and provide services. Hell, if all of that was real, there are more Cherokees in the world than there are Chinese.[20]

Predictably, Indians of all perspectives on the identity question reacted strongly against such gratuitous dilution of themselves. The result was a broad rejection of what was perceived as "the federal attempt to convert us from being the citizens of our own sovereign nations into benign members of some sort of all-purpose U.S. "minority group," without sovereign rights."[21] For its part, the government, without so much as a pause to consider the connotations of the word "sovereign" in this connection, elected to view such statements as an *Indian* demand for resumption of the universal application of the blood-quantum standard. Consequently, the Reagan administration, during the 1980s, set out to gut the Indian Education Act[22] and to enforce degree-of-blood requirements for federal services, such as those of the Indian Health Service.[23]

An even clearer example of the contemporary reassertion of eugenics principles in federal Indian identification policies came under the Bush administration. On November 30, 1990, Public Law 101-644 (104 *Stat.* 4662) went into effect. Grotesquely described as "an Act to promote development of Indian arts and crafts," the statute legally restricts definition of American Indian artists to those possessing a federally issued "Certificate of Degree of Indian Blood"—derogatorally referred to as "pedigree slips" by opponents—or those certified as such by "federally recognized tribes" or the "Alaska Native Corporation." Excluded are not only those who fall below blood-quantum requirements, but anyone who has, for politico-philosophical reasons, refused to cooperate with federal pretensions to define for itself who will and who will not be considered a member and citizen of a recognized indigenous nation. Further, the entire populations of federally unrecognized nations such as the populous Lumbees of North Carolina, Abenakis of Vermont, and more than 200 others, are simply written out of existence even in terms of their internal membership identification as Indians.

In order to put "teeth" into the legislation, Congress imposed penalties of up to $1 million in fines and as much as fifteen years in a federal prison for anyone not meeting its definition to "offer to display for sale or to sell any good, with or without a Government trademark, which...suggests it is Indian produced." For galleries, museums, and other private concerns to display as "Indian arts or crafts" the work of any person not meeting the federal definition of Indian-ness, a fine of up to $5 million is imposed. Under such conditions, the Cherokee National Museum in Muskogee, Oklahoma was forced to close its doors when it was discovered that even the late Willard Stone—a talented sculptor, creator of the Great Seal of the Cherokee Nation, and a probable "full blood"—had never registered himself as a bona fide Indian according to federal standards.[24] At this juncture, things have become such a welter of confusion that:

> The Federal government, State governments and the census Bureau all have different criteria for defining "Indians" for statistical purposes, and even

Federal criteria are not consistent among Federal agencies. For example, a State desiring financial aid to assist Indian education receives the aid only for the number of people with one-quarter or more Indian blood. For preference in hiring, enrollment records from a Federally recognized tribe are required. Under regulations for law and order, anyone of "Indian descent" is counted as an Indian. If the Federal criteria are inconsistent, State guidelines are [at this point] even more chaotic. In the course of preparing this report, the Commission contacted several States with large Indian populations to determine their criteria. Two States accept the individual's own determination. Four accept individuals as Indian if they were "recognized in the community" as Native Americans. Five use residence on a reservation as criteria. One requires one-quarter blood, and still another uses the Census Bureau definition that Indians are who they say they are.[25]

This, without doubt, is a situation made to order for conflict, among Indians more than anyone else. Somehow, it is exceedingly difficult to imagine that the government would wish to see things turn out any other way.

Implications

The eventual outcome of federal blood-quantum policies can be described as little other than genocidal in their final implications. As historian Patricia Nelson Limerick recently summarized the process:

Set the blood quantum at one-quarter, hold to it as a rigid definition of Indians, let intermarriage proceed as it had for centuries, and eventually Indians will be defined out of existence. When that happens, the federal government will be freed of its persistent "Indian problem."[26]

Already, this conclusion receives considerable validation in the experience of the Indians of California, such as the Juaneño. Pursuant to the "Pit River Consolidated Land Settlement" of the 1970s, in which the government purported to "compensate" many of the small California bands for lands expropriated during the course of non-Indian "settlement" in that state (at less than 50 cents per acre), the Juaneño and a number of other "Mission Indians" were simply declared to be "extinct." This policy was pursed despite the fact that substantial numbers of such Indians were known to exist, and that the government was at the time issuing settlement checks to them. The tribal rolls were simply ordered closed to any new additions, despite the fact that many of the people involved were still bearing children, and their population might well have been expanding. It was even suggested in some instances that children born after an arbitrary cut-off date should be identified as "Hispanic" or "Mexican" in order that they benefit from federal and state services to minority groups.[27]

When attempting to come to grips with the issues raised by such federal policies, the recently "dissolved" California groups, as well as a number of previously unrecognized ones such as the Gay Head Wampanoags (long described as extinct), confronted a Catch-22 situation worthy of Joseph Heller. This rested in the federal criteria for recognition of Indian existence to the present day:

1. An Indian is a member of any federally recognized Indian Tribe. To be federally recognized, an Indian Tribe must be comprised of Indians.
2. To gain federal recognition, an Indian Tribe must have a land base. To secure a land base, an Indian Tribe must be federally recognized.[28]

As Shoshone activist Josephine C. Mills put it in 1964, "There is no longer any need to shoot down Indians in order to take away their rights and land [or to wipe them out]...legislation is sufficient to do the trick legally."[29]

The notion of genocidal implications in all this receives firm reinforcement from the increasing federal propensity to utilize residual Indian land bases as dumping grounds for many of the more virulently toxic by-products of its advanced technology and industry.[30] By the early '70s, this practice had become so pronounced that the Four Corners and Black Hills regions, two of the more heavily populated locales (by Indians) in the country, had been semi-officially designated as prospective "National Sacrifice Areas" in the interests of projected U.S. energy development.[31] This, in turn, provoked Russell Means to observe that such a move would turn the Lakota, Navajo, Laguna, and other native nations in to "national sacrifice peoples."[32]

American Indian Response

Of late, there have been encouraging signs that American Indians of many perspectives and political persuasions have begun to arrive at common conclusions regarding the use to which the federal government had been putting their identity and the compelling need for Indians to finally reassert complete control over this vital aspect of their lives. For instance, Dr. Frank Ryan, a liberal and rather establishmentarian Indian who has served as the director of the federal Office of Indian Education, began during the early 1980s to reach some rather hard conclusions about the policies of his employers. Describing the federal blood-quantum criteria for benefits eligibility in the educational arena as "a racist policy," Ryan went on to term it nothing more than "a shorthand method for denying Indian children admission to federal schools [and other programs]."[33] He concluded that, "The power to determine tribal membership has always been an essential attribute of inherent tribal sovereignty," and called for abolition of federal guidelines on the question of Indian identity without *any* lessening of federal obligations to the individuals and groups affected.[34] The question of the (re)adoption of blood-quantum standards by the Indian Health Service, proposed during the '80s by the Reagan administration, has served as even more of a catalyst. The National Congress of American Indians, never a bastion of radicalism, took up the issue at its 43rd Annual Convention, in October 1986. The NCAI produced a sharply worded statement rejecting federal identification policy:

> [T]he federal government, in an effort to erode tribal sovereignty and reduce the number of Indians to the point where they are politically, economically and

culturally insignificant, [is being censured by] many of the more than 500 Indian leaders [attending the convention].[35]

The statement went on to condemn:

...a proposal by the Indian Health Service to establish blood quotas for Indians, thus allowing the federal government to determine who is Indian and who is not, for the purpose of health care. Tribal leaders argue that *only* the individual tribe, not the federal government, should have this right, and many are concerned that this debate will overlap [as it has, long since] into Indian education and its regulation as well [emphasis added].[36]

Charles E. Dawes, Second Chief of the Ottawa Indian Tribe of Oklahoma, took the convention position much further at about the same time:

What could not be completed over a three hundred year span [by force of arms] may now be completed in our life-span by administrative law...What I am referring to is the continued and expanded use of blood quantum to determine eligibility of Indian people for government entitlement programs...[in] such areas as education, health care, management and economic assistance...[obligations] that the United States government imposed upon itself in treaties with sovereign Indian nations...We as tribal leaders made a serious mistake in accepting [genetic] limits in educational programs, and we must not make the same mistake again in health programs. On the contrary, we must fight any attempt to limit any program by blood quantum every time there is mention of such a possibility...we simply cannot give up on this issue—ever...Our commitment as tribal leaders must be to eliminate any possibility of *genocide* for our people by administrative law. We must dedicate our efforts to insuring that...Native American people[s] will be clearly identified without reference to blood quantum...and that our sovereign Indian Nations will be recognized as promised [emphasis added].[37]

On the Pine Ridge Reservation in South Dakota, the Oglala Lakota have become leaders in totally abandoning blood quantum as a criterion for tribal enrollment, opting instead to consider factors such as residency on the reservation, affinity to and knowledge of, as well as service to the Oglala people.[38] This follows the development of a recent "tradition" of Oglala militancy in which tribal members played a leading role in challenging federal conceptions of Indian identity during the 1972 Trail of Broken Treaties takeover of BIA headquarters in Washington, and seven non-Indian members of the Vietnam Veterans Against the War were naturalized as citizens of the "Independent Oglala Nation" during the 1973 siege of Wounded Knee.[39] In 1986, at a meeting of the United Sioux Tribes in Pierre, South Dakota, Oglala representatives lobbied the leaders of other Lakota reservations to broaden their own enrollment criteria beyond federal norms. This is so, despite recognition that "in the past fifty years, since the Indian Reorganization Act of 1934, tribal leaders have been reluctant to recognize blood from individuals from other tribes [or any one else]."[40]

In Alaska, the Haida have produced a new draft constitution which offers a full expression of indigenous sovereignty, at least insofar as the identity of citizenry is concerned. The Haida draft begins with those who are now acknowledged as members of the Haida nation and posits that all those who marry Haidas will also be considered eligible for naturalized citizenship (just as in any other nation). The children of such unions would also be Haida citizens from birth, regardless of their degree of Indian blood, and children adopted by Haidas would also be considered citizens.[41] On Pine Ridge, a similar "naturalization" plank had surfaced in the 1983 TREATY platform upon which Russell Means attempted to run for the Oglala Lakota tribal presidency before being disqualified at the insistence of the BIA.[42]

An obvious problem that might be associated with this trend is that even though Indian nations have begun to recognize their citizens by their own standards rather than those of the federal government, the government may well refuse to recognize the entitlement of unblooded tribal members to the same services and benefits as any other. In fact, there is every indication that this is the federal intent, and such a disparity of "status" stands to heighten tensions among Indians, destroying their fragile rebirth of unity and solidarity before it gets off the ground. Federal policy in this regard is, however, also being challenged.

Most immediately, this concerns the case of Dianne Zarr, an enrolled member of the Sherwood Valley Pomo Band of Indians, who is of less than one-quarter degree of Indian blood. On September 11, 1980, Zarr filed an application for higher educational grant benefits, and was shortly rejected as not meeting quantum requirements. Zarr went through all appropriate appeal procedures before filing, on July 15, 1983, a suit in federal court, seeking to compel award of her benefits. This was denied by the district court on April 2, 1985. Zarr appealed and, on September 26, 1985, the lower court was reversed on the basis of the "Snyder Act" (25 U.S.C. S297), which precludes discrimination based solely on racial criteria.[43] Zarr received her grant, setting a very useful precedent for the future.

Still, realizing that the utility of the U.S. courts will necessarily be limited, a number of Indian organizations have recently begun to seek to bring international pressure to bear on the federal government. The Indian Law Resource Center, National Indian Youth Council, and, for a time, the International Indian Treaty Council, have repeatedly taken Native American issues before the United Nations Working Group on Indigenous Populations (a component of the U.N. Commission on Human Rights) in Geneva, Switzerland, since 1977. Another forum that has been utilized for this purpose has been the Fourth Russell International Tribunal on the Rights of the Indians of the Americas, held in Rotterdam, Netherlands, in 1980. Additionally, delegations from various Indian nations and organizations have visited, often under auspices of the host governments, more than thirty countries during the past decade.[44]

Conclusion

The history of the U.S. imposition of its standards of identification upon American Indians is particularly ugly. Its cost to Indians has involved millions of acres of land, the water by which to make much of this land agriculturally useful, control over vast mineral resources that might have afforded them a comfortable standard of living, and the ability to form themselves into viable and meaningful political blocks at any level. Worse, it has played a prominent role in bringing about their generalized psychic disempowerment; if one is not allowed even to determine for one's self, or within one's peer group, the answer to the all-important question "Who am I?," what possible personal power can one feel s/he possesses? The negative impact, both physically and psychologically, of this process upon succeeding generations of Native Americans in the United States is simply incalculable.

The blood-quantum mechanism most typically used by the federal government to assign identification to individuals over the years is as racist as any conceivable policy. It has brought about the systematic marginalization and eventual exclusion of many more Indians from their own cultural/national designation than it has retained. This is all the more apparent when one considers that, while one-quarter degree of blood has been the norm used in defining *Indian-ness,* the quantum has varied from time to time and place to place; one-half blood was the standard utilized in the case of the Mississippi Choctaws and adopted in the Wheeler-Howard Act; one sixty-fourth was utilized in establishing the Santee rolls in Nebraska. It is hardly unnatural, under the circumstances, that federal policy has set off a ridiculous game of one-upmanship in Indian Country: "I'm more Indian than you" and "You aren't Indian enough to say (or do, or think) that" have become common assertions during the second half of the 20th century.

The restriction of federal entitlement funds to cover only the relatively few Indians who meet quantum requirements, essentially a cost-cutting policy at its inception, has served to exacerbate tensions over the identity issue among Indians. It has established a scenario in which it has been perceived as profitable for one Indian to cancel the identity of her/his neighbor as means of receiving her/his entitlement. Thus, a bitter divisiveness has been built into Indian communities and national policies, sufficient to preclude our achieving the internal unity necessary to offer any serious challenge to the status quo. At every turn, U.S. practice vis-à-vis American Indians is indicative of an advanced and extremely successful system of colonialism.

Fortunately, increasing numbers of Indians are waking up to the fact that this is the case. The recent analysis and positions assumed by such politically diverse Indian nations, organizations, and individuals as Frank Ryan and Russell Means, the National Congress of American Indians and the Indian Law Resource Center, the Haida and the Oglala, are a very favorable sign. The willingness of the latter two nations simply to defy federal standards and adopt identification and enrollment policies in line with their own interests and traditions is particularly important. Recent U.S. court decisions, such as that in the *Zarr* case, and growing international attention and concern over the circumstances of Native Americans are also hopeful indicators that things may be at long last changing for the better.

We are currently at a crossroads. If American Indians are able to continue the positive trend in which we reassert our sovereign prerogative to control the criteria of our own membership, we may reasonably assume that we will be able to move onward, into a true process of decolonization and reestablishment of ourselves as functioning national entities. The alternative, of course, is that we will fail, continue to be duped into bickering over the question of "who's Indian" in light of federal guidelines, and thus facilitate not only our own continued subordination, expropriation, and colonization, but ultimately our own statistical extermination.

Notes

1. Kappler, Charles J., ed., *Indian Treaties, 1778-1883,* Interland Publishing Co., New York, (Second Printing) 1973, pp. 3-5.
2. Ibid., pp. 7-9.
3. Adams, Evelyn C., *American Indian Education: Government Schools and Economic Progress,* King's Crown Press, New York, 1946, pp. 30-31.
4. Calhoun is quoted in *American State Papers: Indian Affairs* (Volume II), Wilmington, Delaware, 1972, pp. 183-4.
5. The bulk of the obligations in question were established prior to Congress' 1871 suspension of treaty-making with "the tribes" (Title 25, Section 71, U.S. Code). Additional obligations were undertaken by the federal government thereafter by "agreement" and as part of its ongoing agenda of completing the socio-political subordination of Indians, with an eye toward their eventual "assimilation" into the dominant culture and polity.
6. Deloria, Vine Jr., "The Place of Indians In Contemporary Education," *American Indian Journal,* Vol. 2, No. 21, February, 1976, p. 2.
7. This strategy was actually tried in the wake of the passage of the House Concurrent Resolution 108 in June 1953. Predictably, the federal dissolution of American Indian nations such as the Klamath and Menominee so tarnished the U.S. image that implementation of the policy was shortly suspended (albeit the law remains on the books).
8. Collier, John, *Memorandum, Hearings on H.R. 7902 Before the House Committee on Indian Affairs,* (73rd Cong., 2d Sess.), U.S. Department of the Interior, Washington, D.C., 1934, pp. 16-18.
9. Deloria, Vine, Jr., and Clifford M. Lytle, *American Indians, American Justice,* University of Texas Press, Austin, 1983, p. 10.
10. See Hundley, Norris C. Jr., "The Dark and Bloody Ground of Indian Water Rights," in Roxanne Dunbar Ortiz and Larry Emerson, eds., *Economic Development in Indian Reservations,* University of New Mexico Press, Albuquerque, 1979.
11. See American Friends Service Committee, *Uncommon Controversy: Fishing Rights of the Muckleshoot, Puyallup, and Nisqually Indians,* University of Washington Press, Seattle, 1970. Also see Cohen, Fay G., *Treaties on Trial: The Continuing Controversy over Northwest Indian Fishing Rights,* University of Washington Press, Seattle, 1986.
12. League of Women Voters, *Indian Country,* Publication No. 605, Washington, D.C., 1977, p. 24.
13. Probably the best overview of the IRA process may be found in Deloria, Vine Jr., and Clifford M. Lytle, *The Nations Within: The Past and Future of American Indian Sovereignty,* Pantheon Press, New York, 1984; on referenda fraud, see Chapter 11.
14. LaDuke, Winona, presentation at International Women's Week activities, University of Colorado at Boulder, March 13, 1984; tape on file.
15. Memmi, Albert, *The Colonizer and the Colonized,* Beacon Press, Boston, 1967.
16. Giago, Tim, "Blood Quantum Is a Degree of Discrimination," *Notes From Indian Country,* Vol. 1, State Publishing Co., Pierre, SD, 1984, p. 337.
17. Means, Russell, speech at the law school of the University of Colorado at Boulder, April 19, 1985; tape on file.
18. See Fanon, Frantz, *The Wretched of the Earth,* Grove Press, New York, 1966.
19. Quoted in Martz, Ron, "Indians decry verification plan for federally-funded heath care," *Cox News Service,* Pierre, SD, October 7, 1986.

20. DeCora (Means), Lorelei, statement on radio station KILI, Porcupine, SD, October 12, 1986.
21. Means, Ted, statement before the South Dakota Indian Education Association, Pierre, SD, November 16, 1975.
22. See Jones, Richard, *American Indian Policy: Selected Major Issues in the 98th Congress,* Issue Brief No. 1B83083, Library of Congress, Government Division, Washington, D.C. (updated version, February 6, 1984), pp. 3-4.
23. Martz, op. cit.
24. Nichols, Lyn, "New Indian Art Regulations Shut Down Muskogee Museum," *San Francisco Examiner,* December 3, 1990.
25. American Indian Policy Review Commission, *Final Report,* Vol. 1, May 17, 1977, U.S. Government Printing Office, Washington, D.C., 1977, p. 89.
26. Limerick, Patricia Nelson, *The Legacy of Conquest: The Unbroken Past of the American West,* W. W. Norton and Co., New York, 1987, p. 338.
27. The author is an enrolled Juaneño, as is her eldest son. Her younger son, born after the closing of the Juaneño rolls, is not "federally recognized" as an Indian, despite the fact that his genealogy, cultural background, etc., is identical to that of his brother. The "suggestions" mentioned in the text were made to the author by a federal employee in 1979. The Juaneño band in California, in the 1990s, is initiating federal recognition prodecures.
28. Native American Consultants, Inc., *Indian Definition Study,* contracted pursuant to P.L. 95-561, Title IV, Section 1147, submitted to the Office of the Assistant Secretary of Education, U. S. Department of Education, Washington, D.C., January 1980, p. 2.
29. Quoted in Armstrong, Virginia I., *I Have Spoken: American History Through the Voices of Indians,* Pocket Books, New York, 1975, p. 175.
30. See Churchill, Ward, "American Indian Lands: The Native Ethic amid Resource Development," *Environment,* Vol. 28, No. 6, July/August 1986, pp. 12-7, 28-33.
31. Ibid.
32. Means, Russell, "The Same Old Song," in Ward Churchill, ed., *Marxism and Native Americans,* South End Press, Boston, 1983, p. 25.
33. Ryan, Frank A., *A Working Paper Prepared for the National Advisory Committee on Indian Education,* Paper No. 071279, Harvard American Indian Education Program, Harvard University Graduate School of Education, Cambridge, MA, July 18, 1979, p. 3.
34. Ibid., pp. 41-44.
35. Quoted in Martz, Ron, "Indians maintain U.S. trying to erode tribal sovereignty: cultural insignificance said to be goal," *Cox News Service,* Pierre, SD, October 26, 1986.
36. Quoted in Martz, Ron, "Indians decry verification plan for federally-funded health care," *Cox News Service,* Pierre, SD, October 26, 1986.
37. Dawes, Charles E., "Tribal leaders see danger in use of blood quantum as eligibility standard," *The Uset Calumet,* Nashville, TN, February/March, 1986, pp. 7-8.
38. "Indians decry verification plan for federally-funded health care," op. cit.
39. On the Trail of Broken Treaties challenge, see Editors, *BIA, I'm Not Your Indian Any More, Akwesasne Notes,* Mohawk Nation via Rooseveltown, NY, 1973., p. 78. On VVAW naturalization, see Burnette, Robert, and John Koster, *The Road to Wounded Knee,* Bantam Books, New York, 1974, p. 238.
40. "Indians maintain U.S. trying to erode tribal sovereignty," op. cit.
41. Draft, Haida Constitution, circa 1982, xerox copy provided to the author by Pam Colorado.
42. *TREATY: The Campaign of Russell Means for the Presidency of the Oglala Sioux Tribe,* Porcupine, SD, 1982, p. 3.
43. *Zarr v. Barlow, et al.,* No. 85-2170, U.S. Ninth Circuit Court of Appeals, District Court for the Northern District of California, Judge John P. Vukasin presiding.
44. These have included Austria, Cuba, Nicaragua, Poland, East Germany, Hungary, Rumania, Switzerland, Algeria, Grenada, El Salvador, Colombia, Tunisia, Libya, Syria, Jordan, Iran, the Maori of New Zealand, New Aotara (Australia), Belize, Mexico, Costa Rica, Guinea, Kenya, Micronesia, the USSR, Finland, Norway, Sweden, Canada, Great Britain, Netherlands, France, Belgium, Japan, West Germany, Bulgaria, Yugoslavia, and Papua (New Guinea). The list here is undoubtedly incomplete.

Chapter V

The Earth is Our Mother
Struggles for American Indian Land and Liberation in the Contemporary United States

Ward Churchill

The inhabitants of your country districts regard—wrongfully, it is true—Indians and forests as natural enemies which must be exterminated by fire and sword and brandy, in order that they may seize their territory. They regard themselves, themselves and their posterity, as collateral heirs to all the magnificent portion of land which God has created from Cumberland and Ohio to the Pacific Ocean.

Pierre Samuel Du Pont de Nemours
letter to Thomas Jefferson, December 17, 1801

Of course our whole national history has been one of expansion...That the barbarians recede or are conquered, with the attendant fact that peace follows their retrogression or conquest, is due solely to the power of the mighty civilized races which have not lost their fighting instinct, and which by their expansion are gradually bringing peace into the red wastes where the barbarian peoples of the world hold sway.

Theodore Roosevelt
The Strenuous Life, 1901

Since the inception of the U.S. republic, and before, control of land and the resources within it has been the essential source of conflict between the Euroamerican settler population and indigenous nations. In effect, contentions over land usage and ownership have served to define the totality of U.S.-Indian relationships from the first moment to the present day, shaping not only the historical flow of interactions between invader and invaded, but the nature of ongoing domination of native peoples in areas such as governance and jurisdiction, identification, recognition, and education. The issue of a proprietary interest of non-Indians in the American Indian land base has also been and remains the fundament of popular (mis)conceptions of who and what Indians were and are, whether they continue to exist, and even whether they ever really existed. All indications are that these circumstances will continue to prevail over the foreseeable future.

The situation was prefigured in the period of planning for Columbus' first voyage, which—according to the Great Discoverer's own journals—was never about discovery or scientific inquisitiveness as such, always about seizing wealth belonging to others for his sponsors and himself.[1] But, as Glenn T. Morris details in Chapter Two, this is not to imply that Columbus enjoyed an entirely free hand. Contrary to current orthodoxy, there were even then laws concerning how such wealth, especially land, might be legitimately acquired by mercenary adventurers like Columbus and the various European Crowns which fielded them. Primary among these were the so-called Doctrine of Discovery and pursuant Rights of Conquest. Such elements of the Laws of Nations are much misunderstood in North America today, largely as a result of their systematic misinterpretation over the past century by Eurocentric academics and the U.S. Supreme Court. In its actual formulation, however, the Doctrine of Discovery never conveyed title to discoverers over any lands already occupied at the time of the discovery.[2]

> [The doctrine's] basic tenet—that the European nation which first discovered and settled lands previously unknown to Europeans thereby gained the right to acquire those lands from their inhabitants—became part of the early body of international law dealing with aboriginal peoples...[B]y the time Europeans settled in North America, it was well-established international law that natives had property rights which could not be lawfully denied by the discovering European nation...The right of discovery served mainly to regulate the relations between European nations. It did not limit the powers or rights of Indian nations in their homelands; its major limitation was to prohibit Indians from diplomatic dealings with all but the discovering European nation—Moreover, the right of discovery gave a European nation the right to extinguish Indian land title only when the Indians consented to it by treaty.[3]

Conquest rights were also quite restrictive, pertaining only to the results of Just Wars, conflicts fought as the result of unprovoked Indian aggression against their supposed discoverers.[4] Hence, although the Laws of Nations were—as was certainly the case with Columbus—plainly broken from time to time:[5]

> As a matter of both legal principle and practicality, European nations dealt with Indian nations as they did other nations in the world. In general, Indian lands were acquired by agreement, through the use of international diplomacy—specifically, through formal treaties of cession. Indian lands were seldom acquired by military conquest or fiat, and the practices of Spain, France, [England, Portugal] and the Netherlands did not differ in this regard.[6]

The reality of colonial North America was that indigenous nations tended to be militarily superior to their would-be colonizers, or at least held the balance of military power between European states such as England and France.[7] The matter was of such concern in London that, in 1763, King George III—specifically to retain the allegiance of the powerful Haudenosaunee (Iroquois) and Muscogee (Creek) Confederacies vis-à-vis England's French rivals—issued a proclamation prohibiting acquisition of lands west of a line drawn along the Allegheny and Appalachian mountain chains.[8] This, probably more than taxation without representation, was a major contributing factor in sparking the extended decolonization struggle that resulted in the independence of the original thirteen U.S. states.[9] George Washington, Thomas Jefferson, John Adams, James Madison, Anthony Wayne, and numerous others among the "Founding Fathers" all had considerable speculative investments in westerly Indian lands at the time the 1763 edict was handed down. The rank-and-file soldiers who fought in their revolutionary army arguably did so, not for abstract ideals of freedom and equality, but because of promises made by their leaders that their services would be rewarded with grants of Indian land in the West after victory had been secured.[10]

U.S. Theory and Practice

As Vine Deloria, Jr., has observed, the United States emerged from its successful war against the British Crown (perhaps the most serious offense imaginable under prevailing law) as a pariah, an outlaw state that was considered utterly illegitimate by almost all other countries and therefore shunned by them, both politically and economically. Survival of the new nation was entirely dependent upon the ability of its initial government to change such perceptions and thereby end its isolation. Desperate to establish itself as a respectable entity, and lacking other alternatives with which to demonstrate its sense of international legality, the government was virtually compelled to present the appearance of adhering to the strictest of protocols in its dealings with Indians.[11] Indeed, what the Continental Congress needed more than anything at the time was for indigenous nations—many of whose formal national integrity and legitimacy had already been recognized by the European powers through treaties—to convey a comparable recognition upon the fledgling U.S. by entering into treaty relationships with *it*.

Consequently, both the Articles of Confederation and the Constitution of the United States contain clauses reserving interactions with Indian peoples, as recognized foreign powers, to the federal government. The U.S. also officially renounced, in the 1789 Northwest Ordinance and elsewhere, any aggressive intent concerning these nations, especially with regard to their land base. As it was put in the Ordinance:

> The utmost good faith shall always be observed towards the Indian; their land property shall never be taken from them without their consent; and in their property, rights, and liberty, they shall never be invaded or disturbed—but laws founded in justice and humanity shall from time to time be made, for wrongs being done to them, and for preserving peace and friendship with them.

Such lofty-sounding (and legally correct) rhetoric was, of course, belied by the actualities of U.S. performance. As Chief Justice of the Supreme Court John Marshall pointed out rather early on, almost every white-held land title in the country—New England, New York, New Jersey, Pennsylvania, Maryland, Virginia, and parts of the Carolinas—would have been clouded had the standards of international law truly been applied.[12] More, title to the pre-revolutionary acquisitions west of the 1763 demarcation line made by the new North American politico-economic elite would have been negated, along with all the thousands of grants of land in that region bestowed by Congress upon those who had fought against the Crown. Not coincidental to Marshall's concern in the matter was the fact that he and his father had each received 10,000-acre grants of such land in what is now West Virginia.[13] Obviously, a country that had been founded largely on the basis of a lust to possess native lands was not about to relinquish its pretensions to ownership of them, no matter what the law said. Moreover, the balance of military power between Indians and whites east of the Mississippi River began to change rapidly in favor of the latter during the post-revolutionary period. It was becoming technically possible for the U.S. simply to seize native lands at will.[14]

Still, the requirements of international diplomacy dictated that things seem otherwise. Marshall's singular task, then, was to forge a juridical doctrine that preserved the image of enlightened U.S. furtherance of accepted international legality in its relations with Indians on the one hand, while accommodating a pattern of illegally aggressive federal expropriations of Indian land on the other. This he did in opinions rendered in a series of cases, delineated in Table: Key Indian Laws and Cases at the front of this volume, beginning with *Fletcher v. Peck* (1810) and extending through *Johnson v. McIntosh* (1822) to *Cherokee Nation v. Georgia* (1831) and *Worcester v. Georgia* (1832).[15] By the end of this sequence of decisions, Marshall had completely inverted international law, custom, and convention, finding that the Doctrine of Discovery imparted preeminent title over North America to Europeans—the mantle of which implicitly passed to the U.S. when England quit-claimed its thirteen dissident Atlantic colonies—mainly because Indian-held lands were effectively "vacant" when Europeans found them. The chief justice was forced to coin a whole new politico-legal expression—that of domestic, dependent nations—to encompass the unprecedented status, neither fish nor fowl, he needed native people to occupy.[16]

Within this convoluted and falsely premised reasoning, Indian nations were entitled to keep their land, but only so long as the intrinsically superior U.S. agreed to their doing so. Given this, Indians could be legally construed as committing aggression whenever they resisted invasion by the United States, a matter which rendered literally any military action the U.S. chose to pursue against native people, no matter how unprovoked, a "Just War." With all this worked out, Marshall argued that the U.S. should nonetheless follow accepted European practice wherever possible, obtaining by formal treaty negotiations involving purchase and other considerations, native "consent" to land cessions. This, he felt, would complete the veneer of "reason and moderation" attending international perceptions of federal expropriations of Indian land. Ultimately, Marshall's position reduced to the notion that indigenous nations inherently possessed sufficient sovereign rights "for purposes of treating" to hand over legal title to their territories, but never enough to retain any tract of land the U.S. wanted as its own.

The carefully balanced logical contradictions embedded in the "Marshall Doctrine," which allowed the U.S. to pursue one course of action with regard to Indian land while purporting to do the exact opposite, formed the theoretical basis for the entire statutory body of what is now called "Indian Law" in this country. Through a lengthy series of subsequent "interpretive" decisions—especially *Ex Parte Crow Dog* (1883), *U.S. v. Kagama* (1886), *Lonewolf v. Hitchcock* (1903), *Tee-Hit-Ton v. United States* (1955) and *Dann v. United States* (1985)—the Supreme Court extended Marshall's unfounded concept of native nations occupying a status of subordinate or "limited" sovereignty to include the idea that the U.S. enjoyed an inherent "plenary" (full and absolute) power over them in such crucial domains as governance and jurisdiction.[17] An aspect of this self-assigned power, articulated most clearly in *Lonewolf*, is that Congress has the prerogative to unilaterally abrogate aspects of U.S. treaties with Indian nations that it found inconvenient or burdensome while continuing to hold the Indians to those provisions of the treaties by which they agreed to cede land.[18]

In these decisions, the high court also extended Marshall's baseless notion that self-sufficient indigenous nations were somehow "dependent" upon the U.S. to include the idea that the federal government thereby inherited a "trust responsibility" to Indians—actually *control* over their remaining property—in the "management of their affairs." While the "Trust Doctrine" has been used as a device to offset and soften impressions created by exercise of the "Rights of Plenary Power" over indigenous people, it has in reality served as an instrument through which that power is administered.

> [U]nder United States law, the government has no legal trusteeship duties toward Indians except those it imposes upon itself. Stripped of its legal trappings, the Indian trust relationship becomes simply an assertion of unrestrained political power over Indians, power that may be exercised without Indian consent and without substantial legal restraint. An early twentieth century critic of the European colonial "trusteeship for civilization" [in Africa and Asia], which is closely related to the American model, summed it up as "an impudent act of self assertion."[19]

While the U.S. judiciary was thus busily collaborating with the federal legislature in creating a body of "settled law" to serve as "the perfect instrument of empire," the federal government was also consistently engaged in creating the physical fact of that empire, all the while declaring itself in the most vociferous possible terms to be devoutly *anti*-imperial.[20] This was done by the conducting of at least forty "Indian Wars"[21]—each of which was packaged as a campaign to defend U.S. citizens from the "depredations" of "savage natives" resisting the invasion of their homelands or comparable abuse—and negotiation of several hundred treaties and agreements with indigenous nations.[22] Together with an assortment of unilateral executive and congressional actions, these wars and negotiated arrangements resulted by the early 20th century in Native America being constricted to about 2.5 percent of its original two billion acre land base within the forty-eight contiguous states of the union.[23] And federal control over even this residue was virtually complete. Under such circumstances—in combination with those revealed by the extent of indigenous population reduction detailed by Lenore Stiffarm and Phil Lane, Jr., in Chapter One—it is not difficult to see why Indians were viewed, often hopefully, as a "vanishing race" during this period.[24]

The Indian Claims Commission

At the turn of the century, Indian efforts to maintain what little real property was left to them or to receive compensation for lands that were still being arbitrarily seized by the government were ridiculed and largely dismissed out of hand.[25] Although native people were supposedly entitled to due process under U.S. law after a district court in Nebraska recognized them as "persons" during the 1879 *Standing Bear v. Crook* case, the import was largely meaningless.[26] From 1881 to 1918, only thirty-one claims involving the illegal taking of native land were accepted by federal courts; fourteen resulted in recoveries of land adding up to less than 10,000 acres.[27] In 1928, a government commission termed even this degree of judicial recourse to be "burdensome and unfair" to non-Indians.[28] Meanwhile, some 100 million acres—about two-thirds of all land native people had left at the conclusion of the period of their military resistance—was stripped away under provision of the 1887 General Allotment Act.[29] Power and possession, the rule of thugs as it were, constituted all of the law in North America where Indian land rights were concerned.

Throughout most of the first half of the 20th century, the U.S. devoted itself to perfecting the mechanisms through which it would administer the tiny residual fragments of Indian Country for its own purposes. Nothing beyond the most *pro forma* gesture was made to address the fact that a considerable proportion of the land that was said to have passed from native ownership during the previous 150 years had been transferred in direct contravention of every known form of legality, including even the patently self-serving theories of U.S.-Indian property relations developed by the United States itself. In 1924, federal courts accepted a mere five native land claims cases; in 1925, there were seven; in 1926, there were ten; in 1927, the total was fifteen. Most of these were dismissed in the early stages; none resulted in land recovery or payment of significant compensation.[30] Things might have remained locked firmly in this mode were it not for geopolitical considerations emerging in the context of World War II.

As part of an overall strategy to advance U.S. interests in its planned post-war role as a hegemonic global power, the United States set out to project an enhanced image of itself as a "white knight" to the world's oppressed peoples. At least temporarily, until its own preferred style of neocolonialism could become entrenched as the dominant force in international affairs, the U.S. needed to be widely perceived as a beneficent and staunchly democratic alternative, not only to the "totalitarian impulse" represented by fascism and communism, but to the classic colonial orders maintained in Third World locales by France, Great Britain, and other American allies. A part of this ploy resided within President Franklin D. Roosevelt's wartime opposition to reconstitution of the old European empires of the French and Dutch in Africa and Asia after the conclusion of hostilities (this trend was shortly reversed by Roosevelt's successor, Harry Truman, as part of his Cold War policy of prioritizing "containment of communism" above all else).[31]

The centerpiece of the entire international public relations gambit, however, rested in the U.S. assumption of the decisive role in formulating and implementing the "Nuremberg Doctrine" under which the surviving leadership of nazi Germany was accused, tried, convicted, and in most cases executed or imprisoned, for having engaged in "Crimes Against the Peace," "Aggressive War," and "Crimes Against Humanity."[32] The primary messages intended for popular consumption in the U.S. performance against the defendants were that behavior such as that displayed by the nazis was considered criminal and intolerable by all "civilized peoples," and that the United States—first and foremost—would stand as guarantor that all governments would be held accountable to the standards of comportment established at Nuremberg. The nazi leaders were to stand forever as the symbol of the principle that international aggression would be punished, not rewarded (this is, of course, precisely the same line trotted out by George Bush in explaining the rather interesting U.S. behavior against Iraq during 1990-91).[33]

A primary flaw in this otherwise noble-seeming U.S. posture on international human rights law was (and is) that no less prominent a nazi than Adolf Hitler had long since made it quite clear he had based many of his more repugnant policies directly on earlier U.S. conduct against Native America. Hitler's conception of *lebensraumpolitik*—the idea that Germans were innately entitled by virtue of their racial and cultural superiority to land belonging to others, and that they were thus morally free to take it by aggressive military action—obviously had much in common with the 19th century American sense of "Manifest Destiny."[34] Further, his notion of how to attain this "living room"—the "clearing of inferior racial stock" from their land base in order that vacated areas might be "settled by ethnic Germans"—followed closely from such U.S. precedents as the 1830 Indian Removal Act and subsequent military campaigns against the indigenous nations of the Great Plains, Great Basin, and Sonora Desert Regions. Even the nazi tactic of concentrating "undesirables" prior to their forced "relocation or reduction" was drawn from actual U.S. examples, including internment of the Cherokees and other "Civilized Tribes" during the 1830s, before the devastatingly lethal Trail of Tears was forced upon them, and the comparable experience of the Navajo people at the Bosque Redondo during the period 1864-68.[35]

This potential embarrassment to U.S. pretensions abroad precipitated something of a sea change in the country's approach to indigenous issues. Seeking to distance its own history from comparison to that of the Germans it was even then prosecuting—and thus to stand accused of conducting an exercise in mere "victor's justice" at Nuremberg—the federal government was for the first time prepared to admit openly that "unfortunate and sometimes tragic errors" had been made in the process of its continental expansion. Unlike nazi Germany, federal spokespersons intoned, the U.S. had never held aggressive territorial intentions against Indians or anyone else; the Indian Wars notwithstanding, the U.S. had always bought, rather than conquered, the land it occupied. As proof of this thesis, it was announced that a formal mechanism was being created for purposes of "resolving any lingering issues" among Native Americans concerning the legitimacy of U.S. title to its territory.[36] The book, which had been closed on Indian land claims for a full generation and more, was suddenly opened again.

What was ultimately established, on August 13, 1946, was a quasi-judicial entity, dubbed the "Indian Claims Commission," of the sort long desired by those who had followed the wisdom of Chief Justice Marshall's enjoiner that appearances demanded that a veneer of legality, even one applied *post hoc*, be affixed to all U.S. expropriations of native territory. As early as 1910, Indian Commissioner Francis E. Leupp had suggested "a special court, or the addition of a branch to the present United States Court of Claims, to be charged with the adjudication of Indian claims exclusively."[37] He was followed by Assistant Commissioner Edgar B. Merritt, who recommended in 1913 that a special commission be empaneled to investigate the extent to which native lands had been taken without legal justification or rationalization and what would be necessary to attain retroactive legitimization in such instances.[38] In 1928, the Meriam Commission had recommended a similar expedient.[39] Congress had persistently balked at the ideas of acknowledging that the U.S. had effectively stolen much of its territory, and/or of belatedly making even token payments for what had been taken.[40]

The new commission was charged with investigating all native claims contesting U.S. title, defining precisely the territory involved in each case, and determining whether legal procedures verging on outright conquest had ever been applied to its transfer out of Indian hands. In instances where it was concluded that there was no existing legal basis for non-Indian ownership of contested lands, or where the price originally paid for such lands was deemed "unconscionably low," the commission was responsible for fixing what might have been a "fair market price" (according to the buyers, not the sellers) *at the time the land was taken*. Corresponding sums were then paid by Congress—$29.1 million (about 47¢ per acre) for the entire state of California in the 1964 "Pit River Land Claim Settlement," for example—as "just compensation" to indigenous nations for their loss of property.[41] At the point such payment was accepted by an Indian people, the title at issue in its land claim was said to be "quieted" and "justice served."

In reality, as Jack Forbes and others have pointed out, non-Indian titles were being *created* where none had existed before.[42] As even the Chair of the Senate Subcommittee on Indian Affairs, Henry M. Jackson, put it at the time: "[Any other course of action would] perpetuate clouds upon white men's title that interfere with development of our public domain."[13] The stated presumptions underlying the commission's mandate were simply a continuation of the Marshall Doctrine that preeminent rights over Indian Country were inherently vested in the U.S., and that native nations had in any event always wished to sell their lands to the federal government. The unstated premise, of course, was that Indians had no choice in the matter anyway. Even if they had desired to convert their property into cash by the late 1940s, the commission was not authorized other than in a very narrow range of circumstances to award payment of interest on retroactive land "sales," although the "bills" owed by the government were in many instances more than a century overdue.[44] In no event was the commission authorized to return land to native claimants, no matter *how* it had been taken from them.[45] Hence, during the 1950s, the commission served as a perfect "liberal" counterpart to the more extremist ("conservative") federal termination policies discussed by Rebecca Robbins in Chapter Three.

Nonetheless, the existence of the Indian Claims Commission afforded native people a forum in which they might clarify the factual nature of their grievances for the first time. Consequently, by the end of 1951, more than 600 cases (only twenty-six of which were adjudicated at that point) had been docketed.[46] Things continued to move grudgingly, a matter which caused the process to be extended.[47] During the first fifteen years of its operation, the commission completed only eighty cases, dismissing thirty outright, and finding "validity" to only fifteen. Its awards of monetary compensation totalled only $17.1 million by 1959. The "civil rights era" of the 1960s saw something of a surge in performance, with 250 cases completed (another $111 million in awards) and 347 pending (of which forty-two had still seen no action at all).[48] During the early '70s, Indians began increasingly to appeal the commission's rulings to federal courts; of 206 such appeals filed by 1975, the commission was affirmed in ninety-six, partially affirmed in thirty-one, and overruled in seventy-nine.[49] At the end of its life on September 30, 1978, the Claims Commission had sixty-eight docketed cases (plus an indeterminate number of emerging appeals) still pending. These were turned over to the U.S. Court of Claims.[50]

Cracks in the Empire

While it is clear that the Indian Claims Commission functioned mainly as a subterfuge designed to cast an undeserved mantle of humanitarianism and legitimacy over U.S. territorial integrity,[51] it inadvertently served indigenous interests as well. As a result of its lengthy exploration of the factual record, necessary to its mission of nailing down federal land title in every area of the country, the commission revealed the full extent to which the United States had occupied areas to which it had no lawful title. Indeed, one cumulative result of the commission's endeavor was to catalogue the fact that, according to the last known U.S. judicial rulings and legislative actions in each respective instance, legal title to more than

35 percent of the continental United States remained in the hands of native nations (see Map I).

> The fact is that about half the land area of the country was purchased by treaty or agreement at an average price of less than a dollar an acre; another third of a [billion] acres, mainly in the West, were confiscated without compensation; another two-thirds of a [billion] acres were claimed by the United States without pretense of a unilateral action extinguishing native title.[52]

Indians were quick to seize upon the implications of this, arguing that the commission process had no bearing at all on land title other than to resolve questions concerning who held lawful rights to precisely which parts of the U.S., and to provide a means by which the government could provide native owners with "back rent" on lands which had been "borrowed" by the United States for generations. The "underbrush of confusion as to who owns what" having been finally cleared away, it is appropriate in this view for Indians inside the U.S. to begin reasserting their national property rights over the approximately 750 million acres of North America that remain theirs by accepted legal definition.[53] Such knowledge has fueled a resurgent indigenous national militancy which, beginning in the early 1970s with the emergence of the American Indian Movement (AIM), has led to a series of spectacular extra-legal confrontations over land and liberty (several of them covered in Chapters Three and Ten) with federal authorities. These, in turn, have commanded the very sort of international attention to U.S. territorial claims, and Indian policy more generally, that the Claims Commission was supposed to avert.

Beginning in the late '70s, Native North Americans—spearheaded by AIM's "diplomatic arm," the International Indian Treaty Council (IITC)—were able to escalate this trend by establishing a place for themselves within the United Nations structure and entering annual reports concerning the conduct of both the U.S. and Canadian governments vis-à-vis native peoples and their lands. In this changing context, the federal government has once again begun to engage in "damage control," allowing a calculated range of concessions in order to preserve what it seeks to project as its image abroad. Notably, in 1974, the U.S. Supreme Court announced for the first time that Indians had a right to pursue actual recovery of stolen land through the federal judiciary.[54] Although resort to the courts of the conqueror is hardly an ideal solution to the issues raised by Indian nations, it does provide another tool with which they can now pursue their rights. And it has resulted in measurable gains for some of them over the past fifteen years.

Probably the best example of this is the suit, first entered in 1972 under auspices of a sponsoring organization, of the basically landless Passamaquoddy and Pennobscot Nations in present-day Maine claiming some 12 million acres that were acknowledged as theirs in a series of letters dating from the 1790s and signed by George Washington.[55] Since it was demonstrated that no ratified treaty existed by which the Indians had ceded their land, U.S. District Judge Edward T. Gignoux ordered a settlement acceptable to the majority of the native people involved.[56] This resulted in the recovery, in 1980, of some 300,000 acres of land, and payment of $27

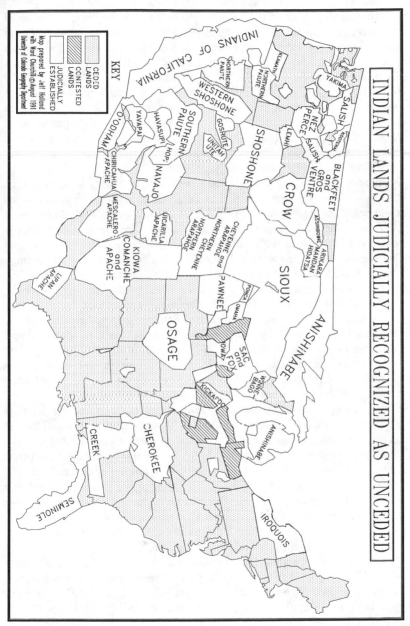

Map I

INDIAN LANDS JUDICIALLY RECOGNIZED AS UNCEDED

KEY

CEDED LANDS
CONTESTED LANDS
JUDICIALLY ESTABLISHED

Map prepared by Jeff Holland
with Ward Churchill (c)August 1991
University of Colorado Geography Department

million in compensatory damages by the federal government.[57] In a similarly argued case, the Narragansetts of Rhode Island—not previously recognized by the government as still existing—were in 1978 able to win not only recognition, but recovery of 1,800 acres of the remaining 3,200 stripped from them in 1880 by unilateral action of the state.[58] In another example, the Mashantucket Pequot people of Connecticut filed suit in 1976 to recover 800 of the 2,000 acres comprising their original reservation, created by the Connecticut Colony in 1686 but reduced to 184 acres by the state of Connecticut after the American Revolution.[59] Pursuant to a settlement agreement arrived at with the state in 1982, Congress passed an act providing funds to acquire the desired acreage. It was promptly vetoed by Ronald Reagan on April 11, 1983.[60] Only after the Senate Select Committee on Indian Affairs convened hearings on the matter did Reagan agree to a slight revision of the statute, finally affixing his signature on October 18 the same year.[61]

Other nations, however, have not fared as well, even in an atmosphere in which the U.S. has sometimes proven more than usually willing to compromise as a means to contain questions of native land rights. The Wampanoags of the Mashpee area of Cape Cod, for instance, filed suit in 1974 in an attempt to recover about 17,000—later reduced to 11,000—of the 23,000 acres that were historically acknowledged as being theirs (the Commonwealth of Massachusetts having unilaterally declared their reservation a "township" in 1870). At trial, the all-white jury, all of whom had property interests in the Mashpee area, were asked to determine whether the Wampanoag plaintiffs were "a tribe within the meaning of the law." After deliberating for twenty-one hours, the jury returned with the absurd finding that they were not such an entity in 1790, 1869, and 1870 (the years that were key to the Indians' case), but that they *were* in 1834 and 1832 (years during which it was important they were "a tribe" for purposes of ceding land to the government). Their claim was then denied by District Judge Walter J. Skinner.[62] An appeal to the U.S. First Circuit Court failed, and the U.S. Supreme Court refused to review the case.[63]

Still pending land claims cases include those of the presently landless Schaghticoke and Mohegan peoples of Connecticut, each of whom is attempting to recover approximately 1,000 acres lost to unilateral state actions during the 19th century.[64] Another is that of the Catawbas of South Carolina, who filed suit in 1980 for recovery of their original 144,000-acre reservation, created by George III in 1760 and 1763, and acknowledged by the fledgling U.S. before being dissolved in a fraudulent treaty negotiated by South Carolina and ratified by the Senate.[65] In 1981, the state, arguing that federal termination of the Catawbas in 1959 invalidated their right to sue, asked for and received a dismissal of the case. On appeal in 1983, however, the Fourth Circuit Court reinstated the case.[66]

Given such mixed results, it is plain that justice in native land claims cases cannot really be expected to accrue through the federal court system. Eventual resolution must inevitably reside within bodies such as the United Nations Working Group on Indigenous Populations (a sub-part of the Commission on Human Rights), which is even now engaged in drafting a new element of international law entitled

"The Universal Declaration of the Rights of Indigenous Peoples," and the World Court, which must interpret and render opinions based in such law.[67] From there, it may be that international scrutiny and pressure, as well as changed sentiments in a growing portion of the U.S. body politic, will force the United States to edge ever closer to a fair and equitable handling of indigenous rights.

In the meantime, nearly every litigation of land claims within the federal system adds to the weight of evidence supporting the international case presented by native people: when they win, it proves they were entitled to the land all along; when they lose, it proves that the "due process rights" that the U.S. insists protect their interests are, at most, inconsistently available to them. Either way, these legalistic endeavors force cracks in the ideological matrix of the American empire. In combination with extra-legal efforts such as the refusal of Indian traditionals to leave their homes and physical occupations of contested areas by groups like AIM, as well as the increasing extent of international work undertaken by indigenous delegations, they comprise the core of the ongoing land struggles that represent the future survival of Native North America.

Current Land Struggles

Aside from those already mentioned, there is no shortage of ongoing struggles for their land rights undertaken by native people within the United States today, any or all of which are admirably suited to illustrate various aspects of the phenomenon. In Florida, the descendants of a group of Seminole (Miccosukee) "recalcitrants," who had managed to avoid forced relocation to Oklahoma during the 1830s by taking refuge in the Everglades, simply "squatted" in their homeland for more than 130 years, never agreeing to a "peace accord" with the U.S. until the mid-1960s. Because of their unswerving resistance to moving, the state of Florida finally agreed to create a small reservation for these people and Congress concurred by statute in 1982.[68] In Minnesota, there is the struggle of Anishinabé Akeeng (People's Land Organization) to reassert indigenous control over the remaining 20 percent—250,000 acres—of the White Earth Chippewa Reservation, and to recover some portion of the additional 1 million acres reserved as part of White Earth under an 1854 treaty with the U.S., but declared "surplus" through the General Allotment Act in 1906.[69]

In southern Arizona, the Tohono O'Odham (Papago) Nation continues its efforts to secure the entirety of its sacred Baboquivari Mountain Range, acknowledged by the government to be part of the Papago Reservation in 1916, but opened to non-Indian "mineral development interests"—especially those concerned with mining copper—both before and since.[70] In the northern portion of the same state, there are ongoing struggles by both the Hopis and Diné (Navajos) to block U.S. Forest Service scheme to convert San Francisco Peaks, a site sacred to both peoples, into a ski resort complex.[71] And, of course, there is the grueling and government-instigated land struggle occurring between the tribal councils of these same two peoples within what was until recently called the "Navajo-Hopi Joint Use Area." The matter is bound up in energy development issues—primarily the strip mining of an estimated 24 billion tons of readily accessible low-sulphur coal—and entails a program to forcibly relocate as many as 13,500 traditional Diné who have refused to leave their land.[72]

In Massachusetts, the Gayhead Wampanoags, proceeding slowly and carefully so as to avoid the pitfalls encountered by their cousins at Mashpee, are preparing litigation to regain control over ancestral lands.[73] In Alaska, struggles to preserve some measure of sovereign indigenous (Indian, Aleut, and Inuit) control over some 40 million oil-rich acres corporatized by the 1971 Alaska Native Claims Settlement Act are sharpening steadily.[74] In Hawaii, the native owners of the islands, having rejected a proffered cash settlement for relinquishment of their historic land rights in 1974,[75] are pursuing a legislative remedy that would both pay monetary compensation for loss of use of their territory and restore a portion of it.[76] The fact of the matter is that wherever there are indigenous people within the United States, land claims struggles are occurring with increasing frequency and intensity.

In order to convey a sense of the texture of these ongoing battles over land, it is useful to consider a small selection of examples in a depth not possible for every case that has been cited. For this purpose, the claims of the Iroquois Confederacy in upstate New York, the Lakota Black Hills Land Claim in South Dakota, and the Western Shoshone claims, primarily in Nevada, should serve quite well. Although they are hardly unique in many of their characteristics—and are thus able to represent the generalities of a broad range of comparable struggles—they are among the most sustained and intensively pursued of such efforts.

The Iroquois Land Claims

One of the longest and most complicated land claim struggles in the U.S. is that of the Haudenosaunee, or Iroquois Six Nations Confederacy. While the 1782 Treaty of Paris ended hostilities between the British Crown and its secessionist subjects in the thirteen colonies, it had no direct effect upon the state of war existing between those subjects and indigenous nations allied with the Crown. Similarly, while George III quit-claimed by treaty his property rights under the Doctrine of Discovery to the affected portion of North America, it was the opinion of Thomas Jefferson and others that this had done nothing to vest title to these lands in the newly born United States.[77] On both counts, the Continental Congress found it imperative to enter into treaty arrangements with Indian nations as expeditiously as possible. A very high priority in this regard was accorded the Iroquois Confederacy, four members of which—the Mohawks, Senecas, Cayugas, and Onondagas—had fought with the British (the remaining two, the Oneidas and Tuscaroras, had remained largely neutral but occasionally provided assistance to the colonists).[78]

During October 1784, the government conducted extensive negotiations with representatives of the Six Nations at Fort Stanwix, the result being a treaty by which the Indians relinquished claim to all lands lying west of a north-south line running from Niagara to the border of Pennsylvania—territory within the Ohio Valley (this

Map II

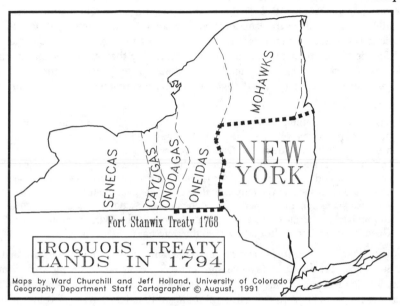

Fort Stanwix Treaty 1768

IROQUOIS TREATY
LANDS IN 1794

Maps by Ward Churchill and Jeff Holland, University of Colorado
Geography Department Staff Cartographer © August, 1991

was a provision reinforced in the 1789 Treaty of Fort Harmar)—and the land on which Fort Oswego had been built. In exchange, the U.S. guaranteed three of the four hostile nations the bulk of their traditional homelands. The Oneida and Tuscarora were also "secured in the possession of the lands on which they are now settled." Altogether, the area in question came to about 6 million acres, or half of the present state of New York (see Map II). The agreement, while meeting most of the Indians' needs, was quite useful to the U.S. central government:

> First...in order to sell [land in the Ohio River area] and settle it, the Continental Congress needed to extinguish Indian title, including any claims by the Iroquois [nations] of New York. Second, the commissioners wanted to punish the...Senecas. Thus they forced the Senecas to surrender most of their land in [Pennsylvania] to the United States...Third, the United States...wanted to secure peace by confirming to the [nations] their remaining lands. Fourth, the United States was anxious to protect its frontier from the British in Canada by securing land for forts and roads along lakes Erie and Ontario.[79]

New York state, needless to say, was rather less enthusiastic about the terms of the treaty, and had already attempted, unsuccessfully, to obtain additional land cessions from the Iroquois during meetings conducted prior to arrival of the federal delegation at Fort Stanwix.[80] Further such efforts by the state were barred by Article IX of the Articles of Confederation—and subsequently by Article I (Section 10) and the Commerce Clause of the Constitution—all of which combined to render treaty-making and outright purchases of Indian land by states illegal. New York then resorted to subterfuge, securing a series of twenty-six "leases," many of them for 999 years, on almost all native territory within its boundaries. The Haudenosaunee initially agreed to these transactions because of Governor Robert N. Clinton's duplicitous assurances that leases represented a way for them to *keep* their land, and for his government to "extend its protection over their property against the dealings of unscrupulous white land speculators" in the private sector. The first such arrangement was forged with the Oneidas. In a meeting begun at Fort Schuyler on August 28, 1788:

> The New York commissioners...led them to believe that they had [already] lost all their land to the New York Genesee Company, and that the commissioners were there to restore title. The Oneidas expressed confusion over this since they had never signed any instruments to that effect, but Governor Clinton just waved that aside...Thus the Oneidas agreed to the lease arrangement with the state because it seemed the only way they could get back their land. The state received some five million acres for $2,000 in cash, $2,000 in clothing, $1,000 in provisions, and $600 in annual rental. So complete was the deception that Good Peter [an Oneida leader] thanked the governor for his efforts.[81]

Leasing of the Tuscaroras' land occurred the same day, by a parallel instrument.[82] On September 12, the Onondagas leased almost all their land to New York under virtually identical conditions.[83] The Cayugas followed suit on February 25, 1789, in exchange for payment of $500 in silver, plus an additional $1,625 the next June and a $500 annuity."[84] New York's flagrant circumvention of constitutional restrictions on non-federal acquisitions of Indian land was a major factor in congressional tightening of its mechanisms of control over such activities in the first of the so-called Indian Trade and Intercourse Acts in 1790 (1 *Stat.* 37).[85] Clinton, however, simply shifted to a different ruse, back-dating his maneuvers and announcing in 1791 that the state would honor a 999-year lease negotiated in 1787 by a private speculator named John Livingston. The lease covered 800,000 acres of mainly Mohawk land, but had been declared null and void by the state legislature in 1788.[86]

Concerned that such dealings by New York might push the Iroquois, the largely landless Senecas in particular, into joining the Shawnee leader Tecumseh's alliance resisting further U.S. expansion into the Ohio Valley, the federal government sent a new commission to meet with the Haudenosaunee leadership at the principle Seneca town of Canandaigua in 1794. In exchange for the Indians' pledge not to bear arms against the U.S., their ownership of the lands guaranteed them at Fort Stanwix was reaffirmed, the state's leases notwithstanding, and the bulk of the Seneca territory in Pennsylvania was restored.[87] New York nonetheless began parceling out sections of the leased lands in sub-leases to the very "unscrupulous whites" it had pledged to guard against. On September 15, 1797, the Holland Land Company—in which many members of the state government had invested—assumed control over all but ten tracts of land, totalling 397 square miles, of the Fort Stanwix Treaty area. The leasing instrument purportedly "extinguished" native title to the land.[88] (See Map III.)

Map III

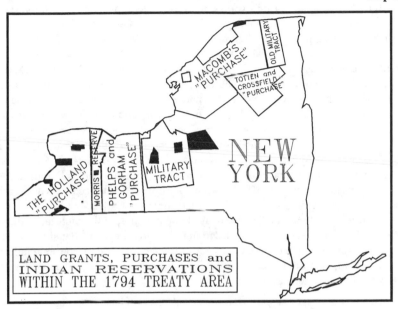

LAND GRANTS, PURCHASES and
INDIAN RESERVATIONS
WITHIN THE 1794 TREATY AREA

Given the diminishing military importance of the Six Nations after Tecumseh's 1794 defeat at Fallen Timbers, Washington did nothing to correct the situation despite Iroquois protests. New York was thus emboldened to proceed with its appropriations of native territory. In 1810, the Holland Company sold some 200,000 acres of its holdings in Conoca and Tuscarora land to its accountant, David A. Ogden, at a price of 50¢ per acre. Ogden then issued shares against development of this area, many of them to Albany politicians. Thus capitalized, he was able to push through a deal in 1826 to buy a further 81,000 acres of previously unleased reservation land at 53¢ per acre. A federal investigation into the affair was quashed by Secretary of War Peter B. Porter, himself a major stockholder in the Ogden Land Company, in 1828.[89] Under such circumstances, most of the Oneidas requested in 1831 that what was left of their New York holdings, which they were sure they would lose anyway, be exchanged for a 500,000 acre parcel purchased from the Menominees in Wisconsin. President Andrew Jackson, at the time pursuing his policy of general Indian removal to points west of the Mississippi, readily agreed.[90]

In the climate of removal, Washington officials actively colluded with the speculators. On January 15, 1838, federal commissioners oversaw the signing of the Treaty of Buffalo Creek, wherein 102,069 acres of Seneca land was "ceded" directly to the Ogden Company. The $202,000 purchase price was divided almost evenly between the government (to be held "in trust" for the Indians), and individual non-Indians seeking to buy and "improve" plots in the former reservation area. At the same time, what was left of the Cayuga, Oneida, Onondaga and Tuscarora holdings was wiped out, at an aggregate cost of $400,000 to Ogden.[91] The Iroquois were told they should relocate *en masse* to Missouri. Although the Six Nations never consented to the treaty, and it was never properly ratified by the Senate, President Martin Van Buren proclaimed it to be the law of the land on April 4, 1840.[92]

By 1841, Iroquois complaints about the Buffalo Creek Treaty were being joined by increasing numbers of non-Indians outraged not so much by the Indians' loss of land as by the obvious corruption involved in its terms.[93] Consequently, in 1842, a second Treaty of Buffalo Creek was negotiated. Under its provisions, the U.S. again acknowledged the Haudenosaunee right to reside in New York and restored small areas as the Allegheny and Cattaraugus Seneca reservations. The Onondaga Reservation was also reconstituted on a 7,300-acre land base, the Tuscarora Reservation on about 2,500 acres. The Ogden Company was allowed to keep the rest.[94] The Tonawanda Seneca Band immediately filed a formal protest of these terms with the Senate,[95] and, in 1857, received a $256,000 "award" *of their own money* from a "trust" account with which to "buy back" a minor portion of their former territory from Ogden.[96]

Beginning in 1855, the Erie Railway Company entered the picture, setting out to lease significant portions of both Cattaraugus and Allegheny. Sensing the depth of the then-prevailing federal support for railroad construction, the state judiciary seized the opportunity to cast an aura of legitimacy upon all of New York's other illicit leasing arrangements:

> Though the leases were ratified by New York, the state's supreme court in 1875 invalidated them. In recognition of this action, the New York legislature passed a concurrent resolution [a century after the fact] that state action was not sufficient to ratify leases because "Congress alone possesses the power to deal with and for the Indians." Instead of setting aside the leases, Congress in 1875 passed an act authorizing [them]. The state now made leases renewable for twelve years, and by an amendment in 1890 the years were extended to ninety-nine. Later the Supreme Court of New York deemed them perpetual.[97]

As a result, by 1889, 80 percent of all Iroquois reservation land in New York was under lease to non-Indian interests and individuals. The same year, a commission was appointed by Albany to examine the state's "Indian Problem." Rather than "suggesting that the leasing of four-fifths of their land had deterred Indian welfare, the commission criticized the Indians for not growing enough to feed themselves," thereby placing an "undue burden" on those profiting from their land. Chancellor C.N. Sims of Syracuse University, a commission member, argued strongly that only "obliteration of the tribes, conferral of citizenship, and allotment of lands" would set things right.[98] Washington duly set out to undertake allotment, but was stunned to discover it was stymied by the "underlying title" to much of the reserved Iroquois land it had allowed the Ogden Company to obtain over the years. In 1895, Congress passed a bill authorizing a buy-out of the Ogden interest (again at taxpayer expense), but the company upped its asking price for the desired acreage from $50,000 to $270,000. Negotiations thereupon collapsed, and the Six Nations were spared the trauma (and further land loss) of the allotment process.[99]

Not that the state didn't keep trying. In 1900, Governor Theodore Roosevelt created a commission to reexamine the matter. This led to introduction of another bill (HR 12270) in 1902 aimed at allotting the Seneca reservations (with 50,000 in all, they were by far the largest remaining Iroquois land areas) by paying Ogden $200,000 of the Indians' "trust funds" to abandon its claims on Allegheny and Cattaraugus.[100] The Senecas retained attorney John Van Voorhis to argue that the Ogden claim was invalid because, for more than 100 years, the company had not been compelled to pay so much as a nickle of tax on the acreage it professed to "own." By this, VanVoorhis contended, both Ogden and the government had all along admitted—for purposes of federal law—that the land was really still the property of "Indians not taxed." The new bill was withdrawn in some confusion at this point, and allotment was again averted.[101] In 1905, the Senecas carried the tax issue into court in an attempt to clear their land title, but the case was dismissed under the premise that they had "no legal standing to sue" non-Indians.[102]

A third attempt to allot the Six Nations reservations (HR 18735) foundered in 1914, as did a New York state constitutional amendment, proposed in 1915, to effectively abolish the reservations. Even worse, from New York's viewpoint, in 1919 the U.S. Justice Department for the first time acted in behalf of the Iroquois, filing a suit which (re)established a thirty-two acre "reservation" in the state for the Oneidas.[103] The state legislature responded by creating yet another commission, this one headed by attorney Edward A. Everett, to conduct a comprehensive study of land title questions in New York and to make recommendations as to how they might be cleared up across the board, once and for all.[104] After more than two years of hearings and intensive research, Everett handed in a totally unanticipated conclusion: The Six Nations still possessed legal title to all 6 million acres of the Fort Stanwix treaty area:

> He cited international law to the effect that there are only two ways to take a country away from a people possessing it—purchase or conquest. The Europeans who came here did recognize that the Indians were in possession and so, in his opinion, thus recognized their status as nations...If then, the Indians did hold fee to the land, how did they lose it?...[T]he Indians were [again] recognized by George Washington as a nation at the Treaty of 1784. Hence, they were as of 1922 owners of all the land [reserved by] them in that treaty unless they had ceded it by a treaty equally valid and binding.[105]

Everett reinforced his basic finding with reference to the Treaties of Fort Harmar and Canandaigua, discounted both Buffalo Creek Treaties as fraudulent and rejected both the leases of the state and those taken by entities such as the Holland and Ogden Companies as having no legal validity at all.[106] The Albany government quickly shelved the report rather than publishing it, but it couldn't prevent the implications from being discussed throughout the Six Nations. On August 21, 1922, a council meeting was held at Onondaga for purposes of retaining Mrs. Lulu G. Stillman, Everett's secretary, to do research on the exact boundaries of the Fort Stanwix treaty area.[107] The Iroquois land claim struggle had shifted from dogged resistance to dispossession to the offensive strategy of land recovery, and the first test case, *James Deere v. St. Lawrence River Power Company* (32 F.2d 550), was filed on June 26, 1925 in an attempt to regain a portion of the St. Regis Mohawk Reservation taken by New York. The federal government declined to intervene in the Mohawks' behalf—as it was its "trust responsibility" to do—and the suit was dismissed by a district court judge on October 10, 1927. The dismissal was upheld on appeal in April 1929.[108]

Things remained quiet on the land claims front during the 1930s, as the Haudenosaunee were mainly preoccupied with preventing the supplanting of their traditional Longhouse form of government by "tribal councils" sponsored by the Bureau of Indian Affairs via the Indian Reorganization Act of 1934. Probably as a means of coaxing them into a more favorable view of federal intentions under the IRA, Indian Commissioner John Collier agreed toward the end of the decade that his agency would finally provide at least limited support to Iroquois claims litigation. This resulted, in 1941, in the Justice Department's filing of *U.S. v. Forness* (125 F.2d 928) in behalf of the Allegheny Senecas. The suit—ostensibly aimed at eviction of an individual who had refused to pay his $4-per-year rent to the Indians for eight years—actually sought to enforce a resolution of the Seneca Nation cancelling hundreds of low-cost ninety-nine year leases taken in the city of Salamanca, on the reservation, in 1892. Intervening for the defendants was the Salamanca Trust Corporation, a mortgage institution holding much of the paper at issue. Although the case was ultimately unsuccessful in its primary objective, it did clarify that New York law had no bearing on Indian leasing arrangements.[109]

This was partly "corrected," in the state view, on July 2, 1948 and September 13, 1950, when Congress passed bills placing the Six Nations under New York jurisdiction in first criminal and then civil matters.[110] Federal responsibility to assist Indians in pursuing treaty-based land claims was nonetheless explicitly preserved.[111] Washington, of course, elected to treat this obligation in its usual cavalier fashion, plunging ahead during the 1950s—while the Indians were mired in efforts to prevent termination of their federal recognition altogether—with the flooding of 130 acres of the St. Regis Reservation near Messena (and about 1,300 acres of the Caughnawaga Mohawk Reserve in Canada) as part of the St. Lawrence Seaway Project.[112] The government also proceeded with plans to flood more than 9,000 acres of the Allegheny Reservation as a by-product of constructing the Kinzua Dam in Pennsylvania. Although studies revealed that an alternative siting of the dam would not only spare the Seneca land from flooding but better serve "the greater public good" for which it was supposedly intended, Congress pushed ahead.[113] The Senecas protested the project as a clear violation of the Fort Stanwix guarantees, a position with which lower federal courts agreed, but the Supreme Court declined to review the question and Army Corps of Engineers completed the dam in 1967.[114]

Meanwhile, the New York State Power Authority was attempting to seize more than half (1,383 acres) of the Tuscarora Reservation, near Buffalo, as a reservoir for the Niagara Power Project. In April 1958, the Tuscaroras physically blocked access by construction workers to the site and several were arrested (charges were later dropped). A federal district judge entered a temporary restraining order against the state, but the appellate court ruled that congressional issuance of a license to the Federal Power Commission constituted sufficient grounds for the state to "exercise eminent domain" over native property.[115] The Supreme Court again refused to hear the resulting Haudenosaunee appeal. A "compromise" was then implemented in which the state flooded "only" 560 acres, or about one-eighth of the remaining Tuscarora land.[116]

By the early 1960s, it had become apparent that the Iroquois, because their territory fell "within the boundaries of one of the original thirteen states," would be disallowed from seeking redress through the Indian Claims Commission.[117] The decade was largely devoted to a protracted series of discussions between state officials and various sectors of the Iroquois leadership. Agreements were reached in areas related to education, housing, and revenue sharing, but on the issues of land claims and jurisdiction, the position of Longhouse traditionals was unflinching. In their view, the state holds no rights over the Iroquois in either sphere.[118] Their point was punctuated on May 13, 1974, when Mohawks from St. Regis and Caughnawaga occupied an area at Ganiekeh (Moss Lake), in the Adirondack Mountains. They proclaimed the site to be sovereign Mohawk territory under the Fort Stanwix Treaty—"[We] represent a cloud of title not only to [this] 612.7 acres in Herkimer County but to all of northeastern New York"—and set out to defend it (and themselves) by force of arms.[119]

After a pair of local vigilantes engaged in harassing the Indians were wounded by return gunfire in October, the state filed for eviction in federal court. The matter was bounced back on the premise that it was not a federal issue, and the New York attorney general—undoubtedly discomfited at the publicity prospects entailed in an armed confrontation on the scale of the 1973 Wounded Knee siege—let the case die.[120] Alternatively, the state dispatched a negotiating team headed by future governor Mario Cuomo. In May 1977, the "Moss Lake Agreement" was reached, and the Mohawks assumed permanent possession of a land parcel at Miner Lake, in the town of Altona, and another in the McComb Reforestation Area.[121] Mohawk possession of the sites remains ongoing in 1991, a circumstance that has prompted others among the Six Nations to pursue land recovery through a broader range of tactics and, perhaps, with greater vigor than they might have otherwise (for example, Mohawk actions taken in Canada, concerning a land dispute at the Oka Reserve, near Montreal, during 1990).

As all this was going on, the Oneidas had, in 1970, filed the first of the really significant Iroquois land claims suits. The case, *Oneida Indian Nation of New York v. County of Oneida* (70-CV-35 (N.D.N.Y.)), charged that the transfer of 100,000 acres of Oneida land to New York via a 1795 lease engineered by Governor Clinton was fraudulent and invalid on both constitutional grounds and because it violated the 1790 Trade and Intercourse Act. The case was dismissed because of the usual "Indians lack legal standing" argument, but reinstated by the Supreme Court in

1974.[122] Compelled actually to examine the merits of the case for the first time, the U.S. District Court agreed with the Indians (and the Everett Report) that title still rested with the Oneidas.

> The plaintiffs have established a claim for violation of the Nonintercourse Act. Unless the Act is to be considered nugatory, it must be concluded that the plaintiff's right of occupancy and possession of the land in question was not alienated. By the deed of 1795, the State acquired no rights against the plaintiffs; consequently, its successors, the defendant counties, are in no better position.[123]

Terming the Oneidas a "legal fiction," and the lower courts' rulings "racist," attorney Allan Van Gestel appealed to the Supreme Court.[124] On October 1, 1984, the high court ruled against Van Gestel and ordered his clients to work out an accommodation, indemnified by the state, including land restoration, compensation and rent on unrecovered areas.[125] Van Gestel continued to howl that "the common people" of Oneida and Madison Counties were being "held hostage," but as the Oneidas' attorney, Arlinda Locklear, put it in 1986:

> One final word about responsibility for the Oneida claims. It is true that the original sin here was committed by the United States and the state of New York. It is also no doubt true that there are a number of innocent landowners in the area, i.e., individuals who acquired their land with no knowledge of the Oneida claim to it. But those facts alone do not end the inquiry respecting ultimate responsibility. Whatever the knowledge of the claims before then, the landowners have certainly been aware of the Oneida claims since 1970 when the first suit was filed. Since that time, the landowners have done nothing to seek a speedy and just resolution of the claims. Instead, they have as a point of principle denied the validity of the claims and pursued the litigation, determined to prove the claims to be frivolous. Now that the landowners have failed in that effort, they loudly protest their innocence in the entire matter. The Oneidas, on the other hand, have since 1970 repeatedly expressed their preference for an out-of-court resolution of their claims. Had the landowners joined with the Oneidas sixteen years ago in seeking a just resolution, the claims would no doubt be resolved today. For that reason, the landowners share in the responsibility for the situation in which they find themselves today.[126]

Others would do well to heed these words because, as Locklear pointed out, the Oneida case "paved the legal way for other Indian land claims."[127] Not least of these are other suits by the Oneidas themselves. In 1978, the New York Oneidas filed for adjudication of title to the entirety of their Fort Stanwix claim—about 4.5 million acres—a case effecting not only Oneida and Madison Counties, but Broome, Chenango, Cortland, Herkimer, Jefferson, Lewis, Onondaga, Oswego, St. Lawrence, and Tiago Counties as well (this matter was shelved, pending final resolution of the first Oneida claims litigation).[128] In December 1979, the Oneida Nation of Wisconsin and the Thames Band of Southgold, Ontario joined in an action pursuing rights in the same claim area, but naming the state rather than individual counties as defendant.[129] The Cayuga Nation, landless throughout the 20th century, has also filed suit against Cayuga and Seneca Counties for recovery of 64,015 acres taken during Clinton's leasing foray of 1789 (See Map IV).[130]

Map IV

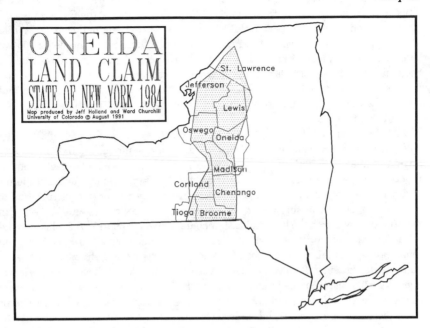

The latter case, filed on November 19, 1980, resulted from attempts by the Cayugas to negotiate some sort of land base and compensation for themselves with federal, state, and county officials from the mid-1970s onward. By August 1979, they had worked out a tentative agreement that would have provided them with the 1,852 acre Sampson Park area in southern Seneca County, the 3,620-acre Hector Land Use Area in the same county, and an $8 million trust account established by the Secretary of Interior (up to $2.5 million of which would be used to buy additional land).[131] Although not one square inch of their holdings was threatened by the arrangement, the response of the local non-Indian population was rabid. To quote Paul D. Moonan, Sr., president of the local Monroe Title and Abstract Company: "The Cayugas have no moral or legal justification for their claim." Wisner Kinne, a farmer near the town of Ovid, immediately founded the Seneca County Liberation Organization (SCLO), premised on virulent anti-Indianism. SCLO attracted several hundred highly vocal members from the sparsely populated county.

A bill to authorize the settlement subsequently failed due to this "white backlash," and so the Cayugas went to court to obtain a much larger area, eviction of 7,000 county residents and $350 million in trespass damages. Attempts by attorneys for SCLO to have the suit dismissed failed in 1982, as did a 1984 compromise offer initiated by Representative Frank Horton. The latter, which might well have been accepted by the Cayugas, would have provided them with the 3,200 acre Howland Game Management Reserve along the Seneca River, a 2,850-acre parcel on Lake Ontario (owned by the Rochester Gas and Electric Company), and a 2,000 acre parcel adjoining Sampson State Park. Additionally, the Cayugas would have received "well in excess" of the $8 million they had originally sought. While SCLO appears to have decided acquiescence was by this point the better part of valor, the proposal came under heavy attack from non-Indian environmentalists "concerned about the animals in the Howland Reserve." Ultimately, it was nixed by Ronald Reagan in 1987, not because he was concerned with area fauna, but because he was angry with Horton for voting against aid to the Nicaraguan "contras." The suit is therefore ongoing.[132]

At the town of Salamanca, the leases to which expire at the end of 1991, the Allegheny Senecas also undertook decisive action during the second half of the '80s. Beginning as early as 1986, they stipulated the intent not to renew and to begin eviction proceedings against non-Indian lease and mortgage holders in the area, unless the terms of any new arrangement were considerably recast in their favor (i.e., clarification of Seneca title, shorter leasing period, fair rates for property rental, and "preeminent jurisdiction" over both the land and cash income derived from it).[133] A further precondition to lease renewal was that compensation be made for all non-payment and underpayment of fair rental values of Seneca property accruing from the last lease. Although these demands unleashed a storm of protest from local whites—who, as usual, argued vociferously that the Indian owners of the land held no rights to it—they were unsuccessful in both court and Congress.[134] At this juncture, all essential Seneca terms have been met, and Congress has passed the Seneca Nation Settlement Act of 1990, including a settlement award of $60 million (the cost of which is to be shared by federal, state, and local non-Indian governments) for rental monies the Seneca should have received over the past ninety-nine years, but didn't.[135]

The Black Hills Land Claim

A much more harshly fought struggle, at least in terms of physical combat, has been the battle waged by the Lakota ("Western Sioux") Nation to retain their spiritual heartland, the Black Hills. In 1851, in exchange for right-of-way to California and Oregon along what was called the Platte River Road, the government entered into the first Fort Laramie Treaty with the Lakota. The treaty recognized Lakota ownership of and sovereignty within a vast area amounting to approximately 5 percent of the continental United States (see Map V).[136] By 1864, however, silver had been discovered in Montana, and the U.S., seeking the shortest route to the mines, violated the treaty by attempting to establish the "Bozeman Trail" directly through Lakota territory. This led to the so-called Red Cloud War of 1866-68, in which the Lakota formed a politico-military alliance with the Cheyenne and Arapaho Nations, laid siege to U.S. military posts along the trail, and defeated the Army several times in the field. For the first time in its history, the government sued for peace. All Lakota terms were agreed to in a second Fort Laramie Treaty, signed during the spring of 1868, in exchange for which the U.S. was allowed to withdraw its remaining soldiers without further damage.[137]

The provisions of the 1868 Fort Laramie Treaty were clear and unequivocal. All land from the east bank of the Missouri River westward within the present boundaries of the state of South Dakota was recognized by the U.S. as a "Great Sioux Reservation," exclusively for Indian use and occupancy. Contiguous portions of North Dakota and Montana and about a third of Wyoming were also recognized as being "Unceded Indian Territory" belonging to the "Greater Sioux Nation," and all of Nebraska north of the North Platte River was perpetually reserved as hunting territory. A stipulation in the 1868 treaty acknowledged that its terms would not impair any Lakota land rights reserved under any earlier treaties, and the U.S. pledged to use its military to prevent its citizens from trespassing again in Lakota territory.[138] Finally, the way in which any future transfer of Lakota title might occur was spelled out:

> No [subsequent] treaty for cession of any portion of the reservation herein described which may be held in common shall be of any validity or force as against said Indians, unless executed and signed by at least three-fourths of all adult male Indians, occupying or interested in the same.[139]

In 1873, a Catholic priest named Jean de Smet, after sojourning illegally in the Black Hills, reported the presence of gold there. In short order, this incentive proved sufficient to cause Washington to violate the new treaty, sending Lieutenant Colonel George Armstrong Custer and his elite 7th Cavalry Regiment (heavily reinforced) to explore the Hills. When Custer, during the summer of 1874, reported that he too had found gold, the government dispatched a commission to purchase the region from the Lakotas while developing contingency plans for a military seizure in the event that negotiations were unsuccessful.[140] During the fall of 1875, the commission reported failure, and "Sioux Affairs" were shifted to the War Department.[141] The latter announced that all Lakotas who failed to congregate by mid-January at Army posts—where they could be taken under military command—would be henceforth considered "hostile" and subject to "punishment" the following summer. In Washington, the refusal of most Lakotas to comply with this command was publicized as an "Act of War" against the United States.[142]

Seeking to compensate for its earlier humiliation at the hands of these same Indians, the Army launched a huge three-pronged invasion, involving several thousand troops, of the Powder River sector of Unceded Indian Territory during the spring of 1876. The idea was to catch all the "Sioux recalcitrants" in a giant vise, overwhelm them, and then—with the Lakota military capacity destroyed—simply take whatever land area the U.S. desired. Things did not work out so quickly or so easily. First, on June 17, the southern command (a force of about 1,500 under General George Crook) was met and decisively defeated along the Rosebud Creek by several hundred warriors led by the Oglala Lakota, Crazy Horse.[143] Then, on June 25, Custer and a portion of his 7th Cavalry (part of the eastern command) were annihilated in the valley of the Little Big Horn River by a combined force of perhaps 1,000 led by Crazy Horse and Gall, a Hunkpapa Lakota.[144] The balance of the U.S. troops spent the rest of the summer and fall chasing Indians they could never quite catch.[145]

In the end, the Army was forced to resort to "total war" expedients, pursuing a winter campaign of the type developed on the southern plains with the 1864 Sand Creek Massacre and Custer's massacre at the Washita River in 1868. An expert in such operations, Colonel Ranald McKenzie, was imported for the task and spent the snowy months of 1876-77 tracking down one village after another, killing women, children, and ponies as he went.[146] By the spring of 1877, all Lakota groups other than a portion of the Hunkpapas led by Sitting Bull and Gall, and a segment of the Oglalas led by Crazy Horse, had surrendered. The Hunkpapas sought asylum in Canada, while U.S. negotiators tricked Crazy Horse into standing down in May.[147] The great Oglala leader was assassinated on September 5, 1877.[148]

With the Lakotas increasingly disarmed, dismounted, and under guard, Congress felt confident in taking possession of the westernmost portion of the Great Sioux Reservation, in which the Black Hills are located. On August 15, 1876, it had passed an act (Ch. 289, 19 *Stat.* 176, 192) announcing that the Lakota Nation had given up its claim to the desired territory. Concerned that this appear to be a legitimate transfer of title rather than outright conquest, however, the bill was written so as not to take effect until such time as Lakota "consent" was obtained. Another commission, this one headed by George Manypenny, was dispatched for this purpose. When even noncombatant Lakota men refused to cooperate, rations for the captive people as a whole were suspended. Ultimately, some 10 percent of all "adult Lakota males" signed the cession instrument in order to feed their families. Although this was a far cry from the 75 percent express consent required by the 1868 treaty to make the matter legal, Congress decided the gesture was sufficient. Meanwhile, on February 28, 1877, the legislators followed up with another law (19 *Stat.* 254) stripping away the Unceded Indian Territory. Since the 1851 treaty boundaries were simply ignored, the Great Sioux Nation had shrunk, almost overnight, from approximately 134 million acres to less than fifteen million.[149]

Beginning in 1882, the U.S. began to impose an "Assimilation Policy" upon the Lakota Nation, outlawing key spiritual practices such as the Sun Dance, extending its jurisdiction over Lakota territory through the 1885 Major Crimes Act, and systematically removing children to remote boarding schools at which their language and cultural practices were not only prohibited, but replaced with those of their conquerors.[150] As part of this concerted drive to destroy the sociocultural integrity of the Lakotas, allotment of the Great Sioux Reservation was undertaken, starting in 1889, with the consequence that some 80 percent of the remaining Lakota land base was declared surplus by unilateral action of the federal government over the next twenty years. Resulting land losses—about seven million acres—caused separation of the various Lakota bands from one another for the first time, through emergence of a "complex" of much smaller reservations (i.e., Pine Ridge for the Oglala, Rosebud for the Sicangu ["Brûlé"], Standing Rock for the Hunkpapa and Minneconju, and Cheyenne River for the Itazipco ["Sans Arcs"], Sihasapa ["Blackfeet"] and Oohinunpa ["Two Kettles"]; see Map V).[151]

By 1890, despair at such circumstances among the Indians was so great that there was widespread adoption of the Ghost Dance religion; its adherents believed

Map V

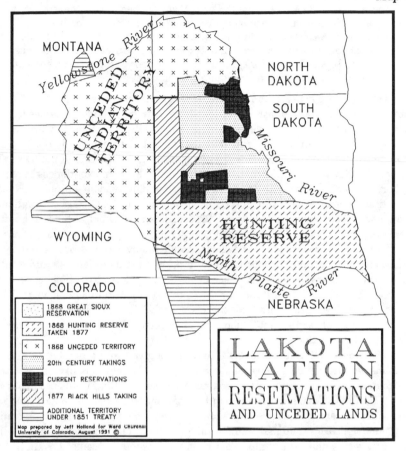

Map prepared by Jeff Holland for Ward Churchill
University of Colorado, August 1991 ©

Legend:
- 1868 GREAT SIOUX RESERVATION
- 1868 HUNTING RESERVE TAKEN 1877
- 1868 UNCEDED TERRITORY
- 20th CENTURY TAKINGS
- CURRENT RESERVATIONS
- 1877 BLACK HILLS TAKING
- ADDITIONAL TERRITORY UNDER 1851 TREATY

LAKOTA NATION RESERVATIONS AND UNCEDED LANDS

that performance of specified rituals would cause a return of the buffalo and people killed by the Army, as well as disappearance of the invaders. Deliberately misconstruing the Ghost Dance as evidence of "an incipient uprising," local Indian agents seized the opportunity to rid themselves of those most resistant to the new order they were seeking to install. A special police unit was used to murder Sitting Bull—who had returned from Canada in 1881—at his home on December 15, 1890. On December 28, four companies of the reconstituted 7th Cavalry were used to massacre some 350 followers of Big Foot, a Minneconjou leader, along Wounded Knee Creek. In Washington, it was generally believed "the recalcitrant Sioux" and other "Indian troublemakers" had finally "gotten the message" concerning the permanent and unconditional nature of their subordination.[152] The government felt free to consolidate its grip over even the last residue of land left nominally in native hands:

In 1891 an amendment was made to the General Allotment Act...that allowed the secretary of interior to lease the lands of any allottee who, in the secretary's opinion, "by reason of age or other disability," could not "personally and with benefit to himself occupy or improve his allotment or any part thereof." In effect this amendment gave almost dictatorial powers over the use of allotments since, if the local agent disagreed with the use to which lands were being put, he could intervene and lease the land to whomsoever he pleased.[153]

During the early part of the 20th century, virtually every useful parcel of Lakota land had been let in this fashion on long-term, extremely low-cost leases ($1 per acre, per year for ninety-nine years was typical).[154] At the same time, however, Sioux resistance surfaced in another form. A young Santee Dakota named Charles Eastman began to publish books including, among other things, accounts of the means by which the Black Hills had been expropriated and of his own experiences as part of a burial detail at Wounded Knee. These were widely read in Europe.[155] Hence, questions on such topics were posed to U.S. observers at the Geneva convention of newly founded League of Nations in 1919. (There is a school of thought holding that Congress refused to allow formal U.S. participation in the League because, at least in part, it was aware that federal Indian policy would never stand up to international scrutiny). Always inclined to paste a patina of fairness and legality over even its most murderous misdeeds, the U.S. responded to this embarrassment with an act (41 *Stat.* 738) authorizing the Lakotas to file suit in federal court if they felt they had been dealt with "less than honorably." The thinking was apparently that an "equitable settlement"—consisting of a relatively minor amount of cash—would end the matter.

No consideration at all seems to have been given to the possibility that the Indians would have other ideas about what "equity" might look like. In 1923 they pitched the U.S. government a curve, entering the first Black Hills case with the U.S. Court of Claims, premised on land restoration rather than monetary compensation. Bewildered by this unexpected turn of events, the claims court simply stalled for nineteen years, endlessly entertaining motions and counter-motions while professing to "study" the matter. Finally, in 1942, when it became absolutely clear that the Lakota Nation would not accept cash in lieu of land, the court simply dismissed the case, asserting the situation was a "moral issue" rather than a constitutional question over which it held jurisdiction.[156] In 1943, the U.S. Supreme Court refused to review the claims court decision.[157]

Although the litigational route appeared stalemated at this point, passage of the Indian Claims Commission Act in 1946 revived the Lakotas' judicial strategy. A case was filed with the commission in 1950, but was deemed by the commissioners to have been "retired" by the earlier claims court dismissal and Supreme Court denial of *certiorari*. Thus, the commission also dismissed the case in 1954.[158] Undeterred, the Lakota entered an appeal that was denied and refiled. In 1958, the Black Hills claim was reinstated on the basis of a ruling that the Indians had been represented by "inadequate counsel" during the 1920s and '30s. The Justice Department then attempted to have the whole issue simply set aside, submitting a *writ of mandamus* in 1961 that requested "extraordinary relief" from continued Lakota litigation. The government's argument was rejected by the U.S. Court of Claims later in the same year.[159] Thus, the claims commission was compelled to consider the case.[160]

After another long hiatus, the commission entered an opinion in 1974 that Congress had been merely exercising its "power of eminent domain" in taking the Lakota land, and that such action was therefore "justified." On the other hand, the commission held, it was constitutionally required that the Indians be "justly compensated" for their loss.[161] The Justice Department responded immediately by filing an appeal to minimize any cash award. This resulted, in 1975, in the government's securing of a *res judicata* prohibition against payment of public funds "in excess of the value of said property at the time it was taken."[162] By official estimation, this came to exactly $17.1 million, against which the Department of Interior levied an "offset" of $3,484 for rations issued to its captives in 1877.[163] The Lakotas attempted an appeal to the Supreme Court, but once again the justices declined to review the matter.[164]

As all this was going on, the frustrations of grassroots Lakotas finally boiled over in a way that radically altered the extra-legal context in which their Black Hills claim was situated. Early in 1973, traditionals on the Pine Ridge Reservation requested assistance from AIM in confronting the corrupt (and federally installed) tribal government, in part to block another illegal land transfer. At issue was the uranium-rich northwestern one-eighth of Pine Ridge—known as the Sheep Mountain Gunnery Range—which the Department of Interior wished to incorporate into the adjoining Badlands National Monument. AIM's physical intervention resulted in its being besieged for seventy-one days in the symbolic hamlet of Wounded Knee by massive federal forces. By the time the spectacular armed confrontation had ended, international attention was riveted on U.S. Indian affairs as never before. In an attempt to contain the situation, the government—as Jim Vander Wall explains in Chapter Ten—fought a veritable counterinsurgency war against AIM and the traditional Oglalas of Pine Ridge during the three years following Wounded Knee.[165]

By the time the Gunnery Range was finally transferred in 1976, the Oglalas—who had sustained at least sixty-nine fatalities and nearly 350 serious physical assaults on their reservation during the period of federal repression—were in no mood to accept further abuse.[166] They not only mounted a storm of protest that caused a partial reversal of the transfer, but also rallied the rest of their nation to demand that the three-fourths express-consent clause of the 1868 treaty (now including adult women as well as men) be applied to the claims commission award. Organizing a referendum on the matter under the slogan "The Black Hills Are Not For Sale," the United Sioux Tribes of South Dakota voted overwhelmingly in 1977 to refuse the settlement.[167] Meanwhile, AIM had created the IITC and managed to have Lakota treaty issues (as well as other indigenous rights questions) docketed with the United Nations Commission on Human Rights.[168]

Under these circumstances, Congress once again backpedaled, passing an act in 1978 that set aside all judicial decisions leading up to the 1977 award amount, and ordering *pro novo* review by the claims court on the question of how much the Lakota compensation package should be.[169] The following year, the court determined that 5 percent simple annual interest should pertain to the Claims Commission's award of principal, a factor that upped the amount offered the Lakota to $122.5 million.[170] The Justice Department appealed this outcome to the Supreme Court, a circumstance that prompted the high court—after denying Indian requests for nearly forty years—finally to examine the Black Hills case:

> In 1980, the Supreme Court, on *writ of certiorari* from the Court of Claims, held that the 1877 act did not effect a "mere change of form in investment in Indian tribal property," but, rather, effected a taking of tribal property which had been set aside by the treaty of Fort Laramie for the Sioux's exclusive occupation, which taking implied an obligation on the government's part to make just compensation, including an award of interest, to the Sioux. Justice Rehnquist filed a blistering dissenting opinion in which he charged the majority had been led astray by "revisionist historians."[171]

The Lakota remained entirely unsatisfied. Opponents to monetary settlement pointed out that Homestake Corporation alone had removed about $18 *billion* in gold from one site near the Black Hills towns of Lead and Deadwood since 1877. They also noted a 1979 poll of the reservations, which showed that the great bulk of residents, although being among the most impoverished people in North America, were no more willing to accept the new offer than they were the old one.[172] In July 1980—while a week-long "Survival Gathering" attended by 10,000 people was occurring just across the fence from the Strategic Air Command's Ellsworth Air Force Base, ten miles from the Hills—the Oglalas filed a new suit demanding return of significant acreage and $11 billion in damages.[173] Although the case was dismissed by a federal district judge in September of the same year on the premise that "the matter has already been resolved," and subsequently was denied on appeal, the point had been made.[174]

It was punctuated in April 1981 when AIM leader Russell Means led a group to an 880-acre site in the Black Hills about thirteen miles outside Rapid City, named it "Yellow Thunder Camp," and announced it was "the first step in the physical reoccupation of Paha Sapa," as the Hills are known in the Lakota language. The U.S. Forest Service, which claimed the land on which Yellow Thunder Camp was situated, filed suit for eviction and requested federal marshals to carry it out. When it became apparent that AIM was prepared to offer physical resistance as it had at Wounded Knee, a district judge in the state capitol of Pierre issued a restraining order on federal authorities.[175] During the following summer, several other occupation camps sprang up, some of them sponsored by usually more timid tribal council governments.[176] Although they were mostly short-lived, the AIM occupation was continuous for nearly five years.

The Forest Service eviction suit was litigated before U.S. District Judge Robert O'Brien. AIM countersued, arguing that the federal government was in violation of the 1868 treaty, the 1978 American Indian Religious Freedom Act (AIRFA), and several of its own anti-discrimination statutes. In 1985, the government was stunned when O'Brien upheld AIM's contentions, entering a potential landmark opinion that whole geographical areas and specific locations might be considered "sacred lands" within the meaning of AIRFA, and enjoining the Forest Service from further harassing Yellow Thunder occupants.[177] The decision was reversed by the Eighth Circuit Court in 1988, however, in the wake of the Supreme Court's decision in the *Lyng* case analyzed by Vine Deloria, Jr. in Chapter Nine. By that time, the government had deposited the Lakota settlement monies in an escrow account at an Albuquerque bank, where it continues to draw interest (reportedly, it now totals slightly more than $200 million, no Lakota having accepted a disbursement check).[178]

Throughout the first half of the 1980s, IITC reported developments in the Black Hills struggle annually to the U.N. Working Group on Indigenous Populations, formed by the Human Rights Commission in 1982.[179] The U.S. United Nations delegation was forced to file formal responses to information provided through this medium, a circumstance that caused ever greater international exposure of the inner workings of federal Indian policy. This, in combination with the persistence of Lakota litigation efforts and physical confrontations, precipitated an unprecedented governmental initiative to resolve the Black Hills issue during the late '80s. It took the form of a bill, S.1453, first introduced by New Jersey Senator Bill Bradley in 1987, to "reconvey title"—including water and mineral rights—of over 750,000 acres of forest land within the Paha Sapa to the Lakota Nation. Additionally, specified sacred sites adding up to several thousand acres and a 50,000-acre "Sioux Park," would be retitled without mineral rights. A "Sioux National Council," drawn from all Lakota reservations, would share jurisdictional and policymaking prerogatives—as well as revenues from leasing, royalties, etc.—over the balance of the original Great Sioux Reservation with federal and state authorities. Finally, the 1980 claims court award, plus subsequently accrued interest, would be converted into compensation for damages rather than payment for land *per se*.[180]

Although the Bradley Bill hardly afforded a full measure of Lakota rights to land and sovereignty, it was the sort of substantive compromise arrangement that the bulk of Lakotas might have accepted as workable. Certainly, Lakota support for the bill had become pronounced by 1988, even as a local white backlash—whipped up in part by South Dakota Senator Larry Pressler and former governor William Janklow—mounted steadily. If enacted in some form, it might have created a viable model for eventual indigenous land rights resolutions throughout North America. Unfortunately, the bill was withdrawn by its sponsor in 1990, after a two-year period of highly publicized anti-Bradley agitation by an individual named Phil Stevens, previously unknown to the Indians but purporting to be "Great Chief of all the Sioux." At present, Lakota land claim efforts are primarily devoted to resuscitating the bill, or developing a reasonable variant of it.[181]

The Western Shoshone Land Claims

A different and lesser known struggle for land has been waged by the Western Shoshone, mainly in the Nevada desert region. In 1863, the U.S. entered into the Treaty of Ruby Valley (13 *Stat.* 663) with the Newe (Western Shoshone) Nation,

Map VI

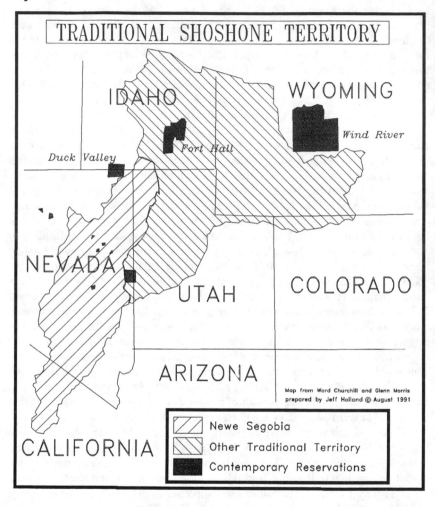

TRADITIONAL SHOSHONE TERRITORY

IDAHO

WYOMING

Wind River

Duck Valley

Fort Hall

NEVADA

UTAH

COLORADO

ARIZONA

Map from Ward Churchill and Glenn Morris
prepared by Jeff Holland © August 1991

CALIFORNIA

Newe Segobia
Other Traditional Territory
Contemporary Reservations

agreeing—in exchange for Indian commitments of peace and friendship, willingness to provide right-of-way through their lands, and the granting of assorted trade licenses—to recognize the boundaries encompassing the approximately 24.5 million acres of the traditional Western Shoshone homeland, known in their language as Newe Segobia (see Map VI).[182] The U.S. also agreed to pay the Newes $100,000 in restitution for environmental disruptions anticipated as a result of Euroamerican "commerce" in the area. As researcher Rudolph C. Ryser has observed:

> Nothing in the Treaty of Ruby Valley ever sold, traded or gave away any part of the Newe Country to the United States of America. Nothing in this treaty said

that the United States could establish counties or smaller states within Newe Country. Nothing in this treaty said the United States could establish settlements of U.S. citizens who would be engaged in any activity other than mining, agriculture, milling and ranching.[183]

From the signing of the treaty until the mid-20th century, no action was taken by either Congress or federal courts to extinguish native title to Newe Segobia.[184] Essentially, the land was an area in which the U.S. was not much interested. Still, relatively small but steadily growing numbers of non-Indians did move into Newe territory, a situation which was generally accommodated by the Indians so long as the newcomers did not become overly presumptuous. By the late 1920s, however, conflicts over land use had begun to sharpen. Things worsened after 1934, when the federal government installed a tribal council form of government—desired by Washington but rejected by traditional Newes—under provision of the Indian Reorganization Act.[185] It was to the IRA council heading one of the Western Shoshone bands, the Temoak, that attorney Ernest Wilkinson went with a proposal in early 1946.

Wilkinson was senior partner in the Washington-based law firm Wilkinson, Cragun and Barker, commissioned by Congress toward the end of World War II to draft legislation creating the Indian Claims Commission. The idea he presented to the Temoak council was that his firm be retained to "represent their interests" before the commission.[186] Ostensibly, his objective was to secure the band's title to its portion of the 1863 treaty area. Much more likely, given subsequent events, his purpose was to secure title for non-Indian interests in Nevada, and to collect the 10 percent attorney's fee he and his colleagues had written into the Claims Commission Act as pertaining to any compensation awarded to native clients.[187] In any event, the Temoaks agreed, and a contract between Wilkinson and the council was approved by the BIA in 1947.[188] Wilkinson followed up, in 1951, with a petition to the claims commission that his representation of the Temoaks be construed as representing the interests of the entire Newe Nation. The commission concurred, despite protests from the bulk of the people involved.[189]

From the outset, Wilkinson's pleadings led directly away from Newe rights over the Ruby Valley Treaty Territory. As Glenn T. Morris has framed the matter in what is probably the best article on the Western Shoshone land struggle to date:

> In 1962, the commission conceded that it "was unable to discover any formal extinguishment" of Western Shoshone title to lands in Nevada, and could not establish a date of taking, but nonetheless ruled that the lands were taken at some point in the past. It did rule that approximately two million acres of Newe land in California was taken on March 3, 1853 [contrary to the Treaty of Ruby Valley, which would have supplanted any such taking], but without documenting what specific Act of Congress extinguished the title. Without the consent of the Western Shoshone Nation, on February 11, 1966, Wilkinson and the U.S. lawyers arbitrarily stipulated that the date of valuation for government extinguishment of Western Shoshone title to over 22 million acres of land in Nevada occurred on July 1, 1872. This lawyers' agreement, entered without the knowl-

edge or consent of the Shoshone people, served as the ultimate loophole through which the U.S. would allege that the Newe had lost their land.[190]

By 1872 prices, the award of compensation to the Newe for the "historic loss" of their territory was calculated, in 1972, at $21,350,000, an amount revised upward to $26,154,600 (against which the government levied an offset of $9,410.11 for "goods" delivered in the 1870s) and certified on December 19, 1979.[191] In the interim, by 1976, even the Temoaks had joined the other Newe bands in maintaining that Wilkinson did not represent their interests; they fired him, but the BIA continued to renew his contract "in their behalf" until the claims commission itself was concluded in 1980.[192] Meanwhile, the Newes had retained other counsel and filed a motion to suspend commission proceedings with regard to their case. This was denied on August 15, 1977, appealed, but upheld by the U.S. Court of Claims on the basis that if the Newe desired "to avert extinguishment of their land claims, they should go to Congress" rather than the courts for redress; $26,145,189.89 was then placed in a trust account with the U.S. Treasury Department in order to absolve the U.S. of further responsibility in the matter.[193]

One analyst of the case suggests that "if the United States were honest in its valuation date of the taking of Newe land, the date would be December 19, 1979—the date of the ICC award—since the [commission] could point to no other extinguishment date. The U.S. should thus compensate the Shoshone in 1979 land values and not those of 1872." Consequently, the value of the land

> that would be more realistic, assuming the Western Shoshone were prepared to ignore violations of the Ruby Valley Treaty, would be in the neighborhood of $40 billion. On a per capita basis of distribution, the United States would be paying each Shoshone roughly $20 million...The [U.S.] has already received billions of dollars in resources and use from Newe territory in the past 125 years. Despite this obvious benefit, the U.S. government is only prepared to pay the Shoshone less than a penny of actual value for each acre of Newe territory.[194]

The Newes as a whole have refused to accept payment for their land, under the premise articulated by Raymond Yowell, Chair of the Western Shoshone Sacred Lands Association: "We entered into the Treaty of Ruby Valley as co-equal sovereign nations...The land to the traditional Shoshone is sacred. It is the basis of our lives. To take away the land is to take away the lives of the people."[195] Giving form to this sentiment, two sisters—Mary and Carrie Dann, refused eviction from their homes by the U.S. Bureau of Land Management, which claimed by that point to own property that had been in their family for generations—and challenged all U.S. title contentions within the Newe treaty area when the Bureau attempted to enforce its position in court. The litigation has caused federal courts to flounder about in disarray ever since.

In 1977, the federal district court for Nevada ruled that the Danns were "trespassers" because the claims commission had resolved all title questions. This decision was reversed on appeal to the Ninth Circuit Court in 1978 because, in its view, the question of land title "had not been litigated, and has not been decided."[196]

On remand, the district court waited until the claims commission award had been paid into the treasury and then ruled against them in 1980. The court, however, in attempting to rationalize both its present decision and its past reversal, observed that, "Western Shoshone Indians retained unextinguished title to their aboriginal lands *until December of 1979*, when the Indian Claims Commission judgment became final (emphasis added)."[197] This, of course, demolished the basis for the commission's award amount. It also pointed to the fact that the commission had comported itself illegally in the Western Shoshone case insofar as the Indian Claims Commission Act explicitly disallowed the commissioners (never mind attorneys representing the Indians) from extinguishing previously unextinguished land titles. Thus armed, the Danns went back to the Ninth Circuit Court and obtained another reversal.[198]

The government appealed the circuit court's ruling to the Supreme Court and, entering yet *another* official (and exceedingly ambiguous) estimation of when Newe title was supposed to have been extinguished, the justices reversed the circuit court's reversal of the district court's last ruling. Having thus served the government's interest on appeal, the high court declined in 1990 to hear an appeal from the Danns concerning the question of whether they might retain individual aboriginal property rights based on continuous occupancy even if the collective rights of the Newes were denied.[199] As of this writing, despite their adverse experiences with the federal judiciary, the Dann sisters remain on their land in defiance of federal authority. Their physical resistance, directly supported by most Newes, forms the core of whatever will come next.

One route open to the Indians—and undoubtedly the locus of much of the intensity with which the government has rejected their land claims—rests in the fact that most U.S. nuclear weapons testing facilities lie squarely in the heart of Newe territory. According to geographer Bernard Nietschmann, the U.S. detonation of 651 atomic weapons there since 1963 makes Newe Segobia "the most bombed country in the world."[200] The Newe portion of Nevada was also the area specified for siting of the MX missile system, and, currently, the government is planning to store a variety of nuclear wastes in repositories bored into Yucca Mountain, in the southwestern sector of Newe treaty land. For obvious reasons, the Newes oppose both nuclear testing and the dumping of such wastes in their homeland. Given this, it may be possible that their land rights can be fruitfully pursued through the emergence of a broad coalition with non-Indian environmental, anti-war, and anti-nuclear organizations. That such a potential is not far from the minds of Newe strategists is witnessed by the wording of a permit issued to all protesters arriving to oppose nuclear experiments at military bases in the area: "The Western Shoshone Nation is calling upon citizens of the United States, as well as the world community of nations, to demand that the United States terminate its invasion of our lands for the evil purpose of testing nuclear bombs and other weapons of war."[201]

Where Do We Go From Here?

The question that inevitably arises with regard to indigenous land claims, especially in the U.S., is whether they are "realistic." The answer, of course, is "no they are not." Further, no form of decolonization has ever been realistic when viewed within the construct of a colonialist paradigm. It wasn't realistic at the time to expect George Washington's rag-tag militia to defeat the British military during the American Revolution. Just ask the British. It wasn't realistic, as the French could tell you, for the Vietnamese to defeat U.S.-backed France in 1954, or for the Algerians to follow in their footsteps. Surely, it wasn't reasonable to predict that Fidel Castro's pitiful handful of guerrillas would overcome Batista's regime in Cuba, another U.S. client, after only a few years in the mountains. And the Sandinistas, to be sure, had no prayer of attaining victory over Somoza twenty years later.

The point is that in each case, in order to begin their struggles at all, anti-colonial fighters around the world have had to abandon orthodox realism in favor of what they knew (and their opponents knew) to be right. To paraphrase Daniel Cohn-Bendit, they accepted as their agenda a redefinition of reality in terms deemed quite impossible within the conventional wisdom of their oppressors. And, in each case, they succeeded in their immediate quest for liberation.[202] The fact that all but one (Cuba) of these former colonies subsequently turned out to hold colonizing pretensions of its own does not alter the truth of this—or alter the appropriateness of their efforts to decolonize themselves. It simply means that decolonization has yet to run its course, that much remains to be done.

The battles waged by native nations in North America to free themselves, and the lands upon which they depend for ongoing existence as discernable peoples, from the grip of U.S. (and Canadian) internal colonialism are plainly part of this process of liberation. Given that our very survival depends upon our perseverance in the face of all apparent odds, American Indians have no real alternative but to carry on. We must struggle, and where there is struggle there is always hope. Moreover, the unrealistic or "romantic" dimensions of our aspiration to quite literally dismantle the territorial corpus of the U.S. state begin to erode when one considers that federal domination of Native America is utterly contingent upon maintenance of a perceived confluence of interest between prevailing governmental/corporate elites and common non-Indian citizens. Herein lies the prospect of long-term success. It is entirely possible that the consensus of opinion concerning non-Indian "rights" to exploit the land and resources of indigenous nations can be eroded, and that large numbers of non-Indians will join in the struggle to decolonize Native North America.

Few non-Indians wish to identify with or defend the naziesque characteristics of U.S. history. To the contrary, most seek to deny it in rather vociferous fashion. All things being equal, they are uncomfortable with many of the resulting federal positions and—in substantial numbers—actively oppose one or more of these, so long as such politics do not intrude into a certain range of closely guarded self-interest. This is where the crunch comes in the realm of Indian rights issues. Most non-Indians (of all races and ethnicities and both genders) have been indoctrinated to believe the officially contrived notion that, in the event "the Indians get their land back," or even if the extent of present federal domination is relaxed, native people will do unto their occupiers exactly as has been done to them: Mass dispossession and eviction of non-Indians, especially Euroamericans, is expected to ensue.

Hence, even those progressives who are most eloquently inclined to condemn U.S. imperialism abroad and racism and sexism at home tend to deliver a blank stare or profess open disinterest when indigenous land rights are mentioned. Instead of attempting to come to grips with this most fundamental of all issues on the continent upon which they reside, the more sophisticated among them seek to divert discussion into "higher priority" or "more important" topics like " issues of class and gender equity" in which "justice" becomes synonymous with a redistribution of the power and loot deriving from the occupation of Native North America, even while the occupation continues (presumably permanently). Sometimes, Indians are even slated to receive "their fair share" in the division of spoils accruing from expropriation of their resources. Always, such things are couched—and typically seen—in terms of some "greater good" than decolonizing the 0.6 percent of the U.S. population that is indigenous.[203] Some marxist and environmentalist groups have taken the argument so far as to deny that Indians possess *any* rights distinguishable from those of their conquerors.[204] Russell Means snapped the picture into sharp focus when he observed in 1987 that

> So-called radicals in the United States claiming that Indians are obligated to give up their rights because a much larger group of non-Indians "need" their resources is exactly the same as Ronald Reagan and Elliot Abrams asserting that the rights of 250 million North Americans outweighs the rights of a couple million Nicaraguans. Colonialist attitudes are colonialist attitudes, and it doesn't make one damn bit of difference whether they come from the left or the right.[205]

Leaving aside the pronounced and pervasive hypocrisy permeating their positions, which add up to a phenomenon elsewhere described as "settler state colonialism,"[206] the fact is that the specter driving even most radical non-Indians into lockstep with the federal government on questions of native land rights is largely illusory. The alternative *reality* posed by native liberation struggles is actually much different:

- While government propagandists are wont to trumpet—as they did during the Maine and Black Hills land disputes of the '70s—that an Indian win would mean individual non-Indian property owners losing everything, the native position has always been the exact opposite. Overwhelmingly, the lands sought for actual recovery have been governmentally and corporately held. Eviction of small land owners has been pursued only in instances where they have banded together—as they have during certain of the Iroquois claims cases—to prevent Indians from recovering any land at all, and to otherwise deny native rights.
- Official sources contend this is inconsistent with the fact that all non-Indian title to any portion of North America could be called into question. Once "the dike is breached," they argue, it is just a matter of

time before "everybody has to start swimming back to Europe, or Africa, or wherever."[207] Although there is considerable accuracy to admissions that all non-Indian title to North America is illegitimate, Indians have by and large indicated they would be content to honor the cession agreements entered into by their ancestors even though the U.S. has long since defaulted. This would leave somewhere close to two-thirds of the continental U.S. in non-Indian hands, with the real rather than pretended consent of native people. The remaining one third, the areas delineated in Map I to which the U.S. never acquired title at all, would be recovered by its rightful owners.

- The government holds that there is no longer sufficient land available for unceded lands, or their equivalent, to be returned. In fact, the government itself still directly controls more than one-third of the total U.S. land area, about 770 million acres. Each of the states also "owns" large tracts, totalling about 78 million acres. It is thus quite possible—and always has been—for *all* native claims to be met in full without the loss to non-Indians of a single acre of privately held land. When it is considered that about 250 million acres of the "privately" held total are now in the hands of major corporate entities, the real dimension of the "threat" to small land holders (or, more accurately, lack of it) stands revealed.[208]

- Government spokespersons have pointed out that the disposition of public lands does not always conform to treaty areas. While this is true, it in no way precludes some process of negotiated land exchange wherein the boundaries of indigenous nations are redrawn by mutual consent. All that is needed is an honest, open and binding forum—such as a new bilateral treaty process—in which to proceed. In fact, numerous native peoples have, for a long time, repeatedly and in a variety of ways, expressed a desire to do just that (see Chapter Three).

- Nonetheless, it is argued, there will still be at least some non-Indians "trapped" within such restored areas. Actually, they would not be trapped at all. The federally imposed genetic criteria of "Indian-ness" discussed by Annette Jaimes in Chapter Four notwithstanding, indigenous nations have the same rights as any other to define citizenry by allegiance (naturalization) rather than by race. Non-Indians could apply for citizenship, or for some form of landed alien status that would allow them to retain their property until they die. In the event they could not reconcile themselves to living under any jurisdiction other than that of the U.S., they would obviously have the right to leave, and they should have the right to compensation from their own government (which got them into the mess in the first place).[209]

- Finally, and one suspects this is the real crux of the matter from the government/corporate perspective, any such restoration of land and attendant sovereign prerogatives to native nations would result in a truly massive loss of "domestic" resources to the U.S., thereby impairing the country's economic and military capacities (see Chapter Eight). For everyone who queued up to wave flags and tie yellow ribbons during America's recent imperial adventure in the Persian Gulf, this prospect may induce a certain psychic trauma. But, for progressives, at least, it should be precisely the point.

When we think about it like this, the great mass of non-Indians in North America *really* have much to gain, and almost nothing to lose, from native people succeeding in struggles to reclaim the land which is rightfully ours. The tangible diminishment of U.S. material power that is integral to our victories in this sphere stands to pave the way for realization of most other agendas—from anti-imperialism to environmentalism, from African-American liberation to feminism, from gay rights to the ending of class privilege—pursued by progressives on this continent. Conversely, succeeding with any or even *all* these other agendas would still represent an inherently oppressive situation if their realization is contingent upon an ongoing occupation of Native North America without the consent of Indian people. Any North American revolution which failed to free indigenous territory from non-Indian domination would be simply a continuation of colonialism in another form.

Regardless of the angle from which you view the matter, the liberation of Native North America, liberation of the land first and foremost, is *the* key to fundamental and positive social changes of many other sorts. One thing, as they say, leads to another. The question has always been, of course, which "thing" is to be first in the sequence. A preliminary formulation for those serious about achieving (rather than merely theorizing and endlessly debating) radical change in the United States might be "First Priority to First Americans." Put another way, this would mean, "U.S. Out of Indian Country." Inevitably, the logic leads to what we've all been so desperately seeking: The U.S.—at least as we've come to know it—out of North America altogether. From there, it can be permanently banished from the planet. In its stead, surely we can join hands to create something new and infinitely better. That's *our* vision of "impossible realism." Isn't it time we *all* went to work on attaining it?

Notes

1. See Morison, Samuel Eliot, ed. and trans., *Journals and Other Documents on the Life and Voyages of Christopher Columbus,* Heritage Publishers, New York, 1963. For context, see Parry, John Horace, *The Establishment of European Hegemony, 1415-1713,* Harper and Row Publishers, New York (revised edition), 1966.
2. See Vattel, M.D., *The Laws of Nations,* T. & J.W. Johnson Publishers, Philadelphia, 1855, pp. 160-1. Vattel is drawing on the mid-16th century discourses of Spanish legal theorist Franciscus de Victoria, published as *De Indis et De Jure Belli Reflectiones* by the Carnegie Institution in 1917. Also see Scott, James Brown, *The Spanish Origin of International Law,* Clarendon Press, Oxford, 1934 and Nussbaum, Alfred, *A Concise History of the Laws of Nations,* Macmillan Publishers, New York, (revised edition) 1954.
3. Coulter, Robert T., and Steven M. Tullberg, "Indian Land Rights," in Cadwalader, Sandra L., and Vine Deloria, Jr. eds., *The Aggressions of Civilization: Federal Indian Policy Since the 1880s,* Temple University Press, Philadelphia, 1984, pp. 185-213, quote at pp. 190-1. Additional information may be obtained from Parry, John Horace, *The Spanish Theory of Empire in the Sixteenth Century,* Cambridge University Press, Cambridge, MA. 1940.
4. Victoria, following Saint Augustine, framed the conditions for "Just Wars" by Europeans against Indians in 1577. For articulation and analysis, see Williams, Robert A. Jr., *The American Indian*

in *Western Legal Thought: The Discourses of Conquest,* Oxford University Press, New York, 1990, pp. 96-108. With regard to England *per se,* see Knorr, K., *British Colonial Theories, 1570-1850,* University of Toronto Press, Toronto, 1944. On the Augustinian formulation, see Deane, Herbert Andrew, *The Political and Social Ideas of St. Augustine,* Columbia University Press, New York, 1963.

5. On Columbus' violation of prevailing laws, both international and Spanish, see Floyd, Trof, *The Columbus Dynasty in the Caribbean, 1492-1526,* University of New Mexico Press, Albuquerque, 1973. Also see Sale, Kirkpatrick, *The Conquest of Paradise: Christopher Columbus and the Columbian Legacy,* Alfred A. Knopf Publishers, New York, 1990.

6. Coulter and Tullberg, op. cit., p. 191. The authors are drawing on Oppenheim, L., *International Law,* Vol. I, Longmans, Green and Co. Publishers, London, 1955, pp. 588-9. For a comprehensive overview, see Peckman, Howard, and Charles Gibson, eds., *Attitudes of the Colonial Powers Towards American Indians,* University of Utah Press, Salt Lake City, 1969. On evolution of the British tradition in this respect, see Quinn, David Beers, *England and the Discovery of America, 1481-1620,* Alfred A. Knopf Publishers, New York, 1974. Excellent collections of the actual treaty texts at issue may be found in Davenport, Francis Gardiner, ed., *European Treaties Bearing on the History of the United States and Its Dependencies* (2 Vols.), Carnegie Institution of Washington, Washington, D.C., 1917 and Vaughan, Alden T., *Early American Indian Documents: Treaties and Laws, 1607-1789,* University Publications of America, Washington, D.C., 1979.

7. For examination of the military balance, see Peckman, Howard Henry, *Pontiac and the Indian Uprising,* Russell and Russell Publishers, New York, 1970. For deeper background, see Porter, Harry Culverwell, *The Inconstant Savage: England and the American Indian, 1500-1600,* Duckworth Publishers, London, 1979.

8. On the British military alliance with the Iroquois Confederacy, see Flexner, James Thomas, *Lord of the Mohawks: A Biography of Sir William Johnson,* Little, Brown Publishers, Boston, 1979. On the Muscogee, see Robinson, Walter Stilt, *The Southern Colonial Frontier, 1607-1763,* University of New Mexico Press, Albuquerque, 1979. Overall, see Jacobs, Wilbur, *Dispossessing the American Indian: Indians and Whites on the Colonial Frontier,* Charles Scribner Publishers, New York, 1972.

9. This thesis is brought forward quite forcefully in Jensen, Merrill, *Founding of a Nation: A History of the American Revolution, 1763-1776,* Oxford University Press, London/New York, 1968, pp. 3-35. Also see Abernathy, Thomas Perkins, *Western Lands and the American Revolution,* Russell and Russell Publishers, New York, 1959 and Bailyn, Bernard, *The Ideological Origins of the American Revolution,* Harvard University Press, Cambridge, MA, 1967.

10. In general, see Jensen, Merrill, *The Articles of Confederation: An Interpretation of the Socio-Constitutional History of the American Revolution, 1774-1778,* University of Wisconsin Press, Madison, 1940, especially pp. 154-62, 190-232. Also see Wood, Gordon, *The Creation of the American Republic, 1776-1787,* University of North Carolina Press, Chapel Hill, 1969 and Lewis, Gordon, *The Indiana Company, 1763-1798,* Clark Publishers, Glendale, CA, 1941.

11. Deloria, Vine Jr., "Sovereignty," in Roxanne Dunbar Ortiz and Larry Emerson, eds., *Economic Development in American Indian Reservations,* Native American Studies Center, University of New Mexico, Albuquerque, 1979. For context, see Mohr, Walter Harrison, *Federal Indian Relations, 1774-1788,* University of Pennsylvania Press, Philadelphia, 1933.

12. The case at issue is *Johnson v. McIntosh* (1822); see legal table in this volume.

13. Baker, L., *John Marshall: A Life in Law,* Macmillan Publishers, New York, p. 80.

14. See Horsman, Reginald, *Expansion and American Indian Policy, 1783-1812,* Michigan State University Press, East Lansing, 1967.

15. For further discussion of Marshall's and others' thinking during this period, see Berman, Howard R., "The Concept of Aboriginal Rights in the Early Legal History of the United States," *Buffalo Law Review,* No. 28, 1978, pp. 637-67. Also see Cohen, Felix S., "Original Indian Title," *Minnesota Law Review,* No. 32, 1947, pp. 28-59.

16. Interesting analysis of Marshall's emerging doctrine may be found in Barsh, Russel, and James Youngblood Henderson, *The Road: Indian Tribes and Political Liberty,* University of California Press, Berkeley, 1980.

17. See Harvey, C., "Constitutional Law: Congressional Plenary Power Over Indian Affairs—A Doctrine Rooted in Prejudice," *American Indian Law Review,* No. 10, 1982, pp. 117-50.

18. See Estin, Ann Laquer, "*Lonewolf v. Hitchcock:* The Long Shadow," in Cadwalader and Deloria, op. cit., pp. 215-45. Also see Wilkinson, Charles F., and John M. Volkman, "Judicial Review of

Treaty Abrogation: 'As Long as the Water Flows, or Grass Grows upon the Earth'—How Long a Time is That?" *California Law Review*, No. 63, May 1975, pp. 601-61.

19. Coulter and Tullberg, op. cit., p. 203. The authors are quoting from Hobson, J.A., *Imperialism: A Study*, University of Michigan Press, Ann Arbor, 1965, p. 240. Also see Coulter, Robert T., "The Denial of Legal Remedies to Indian Nations Under U.S. Law," *American Indian Law Journal*, Vol. 9, No. 3, 1977, pp. 5-9.

20. Professions of formal U.S. anti-imperialism began to be put forward in serious fashion by government propagandists in 1823, the year in which the Monroe Doctrine was articulated (that is, within one year of the *Johnson v. McIntosh* opinion in which John Marshall began his project of legitimizing wholesale conquest and colonization of Native America). It was always used as a cover for North American economic and political domination. See Pearce, Jenny, *Under the Eagle: U.S. Intervention in Central America and the Caribbean*, South End Press, Boston, 1982.

21. The count of forty Indian Wars is the conservative official view. See U.S. Bureau of the Census, *Report on Indians Taxed and Indians Not Taxed in the United States (except Alaska) at the Eleventh Census: 1890*, U.S. Government Printing Office, Washington, D.C., 1894, p. 637.

22. The standard count has been that the U.S. Senate ratified 371 treaties with various indigenous nations between 1778 and 1868. The texts of these are reproduced verbatim in Kappler, Charles J., *Indian Treaties, 1778-1883*, Interland Publishing Co., New York, 1973. In addition, the Sioux scholar Vine Deloria, Jr. has collected the texts of an additional nine ratified treaties not contained in Kappler, as well as the texts of some 300 additional treaty instruments negotiated by the federal executive, and upon which the U.S. now professes to anchor title to assorted chunks of territory, although they were never ratified. For further background, see Jones, Dorothy V., *License for Empire: Colonialism by Treaty in Early America*, University of Chicago Press, Chicago, 1982. Also see Worcester, Donald, ed., *Forked Tongues and Broken Treaties*, Caxton Publishers, Caldwell, ID, 1975.

23. The official record of the cumulative reductions in native land base leading to this result may be found in Royce, Charles C., *Indian Land Cessions in the United States: 18th Annual Report, 1896-97* (2 Vols.), Smithsonian Institution, Bureau of American Ethnography, Washington, D.C., 1899. The 2.5 percent figure derives from computing 50 million acres against the total acreage.

24. For use of the term during the period at issue, see Wanamaker, Rodman, *The Vanishing Race: A Record in Picture and Story of the Last Great Indian Council, Including the Indians' Story of the Custer Fight*, Crown Publishers, New York, 1913.

25. In 1903, the U.S. Supreme Court opined in the *Lonewolf v. Hitchcock* case that Indians had no right either to block the wholesale transfer of their reserved and treaty-guaranteed lands to non-Indians under the 1887 General Allotment Act, or to receive compensation for the loss of such lands. The high court held that federal plenary power over native property was absolute, and that Indians had no right to sue the government for breach of its concomitant trust responsibility in such matters. See Cohen, Felix S., *Handbook on Federal Indian Law*, University of New Mexico Press, Albuquerque (reprint of 1942 U.S. Government Printing Office Edition n.d., p. 96.

26. See Jackson, Helen Hunt, *A Century of Dishonor*, Harper Torchbooks, New York (reprint of the 1881 edition by A.F. Rolfe Publishers, 1965,) p. 204.

27. U.S. House of Representatives, Committee on Interior and Insular Affairs, *Indirect Services and Expenditures by the Federal Government for the American Indian*, 86th Cong., 1st Sess., U.S. Government Printing Office, Washington, D.C., 1959, pp. 11-14.

28. Meriam, Lewis, *et al.*, *Problems of Indian Administration*, Johns Hopkins University Press, Baltimore, 1928, pp. 805-11.

29. On the effects of the General Allotment Act, or "Dawes Act" as it is often known, see McDonnell, Janet A., *The Dispossession of the American Indian, 1887-1934*, Indiana University Press, Bloomington/Indianapolis, 1991. Also see Otis, D.S., *The Dawes Act and the Allotment of Indian Land*, University of Oklahoma Press, Norman, 1973.

30. Ehrenfeld, Alice, and Robert W. Barker, comps., *Legislative Material on the Indian Claims Commission Act of 1946*, unpublished study, Washington, D.C., n.d.

31. An interesting handling of the geopolitical dynamics involved during the Roosevelt era may be found in Varg, Paul A., *America: From Client State to World Power*, University of Oklahoma Press, Norman, 1990, especially pp. 167-207. Also see Isaacson, Walter, and Evan Thomas, *The Wise Men: Six Friends and the World They Made*, Simon and Schuster Publishers, New York, 1986. On Truman's shift, see Chomsky, Noam, *Towards a New Cold War: Essays on the Current*

Crisis and How We Got There, Pantheon Books, New York, 1982.

32. On the formulation of Nuremberg Doctrine, and the primacy of the U.S. role in that regard, see Smith, Bradley F., *The Road to Nuremberg*, Basic Books, New York, 1981.

33. On the handling of the Nuremberg Trials, and the messages embodied in it, see Smith, Bradley F., *Reaching Judgment at Nuremberg: The Untold Story of How the nazi War Criminals Were Judged*, Basic Books, New York, 1977. Also see Davidson, Eugene, *The Trial of the Germans: Nuremberg, 1945-1946*, Macmillan Publishers, New York, 1966. Concerning George Bush's recent use of Nuremberg rhetoric, see Cheney, George, "'Talking War': Symbols, Strategies, and Images," *New Studies on the Left*, Vol. XIV, No. 3, Winter 1990-91, pp. 8-16.

34. For detailed analysis of the American concept, see Merk, Frederick, *Manifest Destiny and Mission in American Life*, Vintage Books, New York, 1966 and Horsman, Reginald, *Race and Manifest Destiny*, Harvard University Press, Cambridge, MA, 1981. To sample the philosophy at issue from the proverbial horse's mouth, see Fiske, John, "Manifest Destiny," in *American Political Ideas Viewed from the Standpoint of Universal History*, Houghton-Mifflin Publishers, New York, 1885. For purposes of comparison to nazi ideology, see Koehl, Robert L., *German Resettlement and Population Policy, 1939-1945*, Harvard University Press, Cambridge, MA, 1957.

35. See Hitler, Adolf, *Hitler's Secret Conversations*, Signet Books, New York, 1961 and *Hitler's Secret Book*, Grove Press, New York, 1961. The nazi leader's attributions to U.S. policy are also remarked in Hoffman, Heinrich, *Hitler Was My Friend*, Burke Publishers, London, 1955; Toland, John, *Adolf Hitler*, (2 Vols.) Doubleday Publishers, Garden City, NJ, 1976; and elsewhere. For detail on nazi policy applications, see Dallin, Alexander, *German Rule in Russia, 1941-1944*, Macmillan Publishers, London, 1957. Concerning the Trail of Tears, Bosque Redondo, etc., see the Chapter One and accompanying notes.

36. Discussion of such measures began in Congress in the fall of 1944, at the same time that planning for Nuremberg was entering its final stages. See Smith, Bradley F., *The American Road to Nuremberg: The Documentary Record*, Stanford University Press, Palo Alto, CA, 1981. For summative discussion of the mechanism to be used in retiring Indian claims and the motives for creating it, see U.S. House of Representatives, Committee on Indian Affairs, *Hearings on H.R. 1198 and H.R. 1341*, 79th Cong., 1st Sess., U.S. Government Printing Office, Washington, D.C., 1945.

37. Leupp, Francis E., *The Indian and His Problem*, Charles Scribner's Sons Publishers, New York, 1910, pp. 194-6. For an overview of such sentiments, see Vance, John T., "The Congressional Mandate and the Indian Claims Commission," *North Dakota Law Review*, No. 45, 1969, pp. 325-36.

38. U.S. House of Representatives, Committee on Indian Affairs, *Hearings on the Appropriation Bill of 1914*, 64th Cong., 2d Sess., U.S. Government Printing Office, Washington, D.C., 1913, p. 99.

39. Meriam, *et al.*, op. cit., pp. 805-11.

40. See, as examples, U.S. Senate, Committee on Interior and Insular Affairs, Subcommittee on Indian Affairs, *Hearings on S. 2731*, 74th Cong., 1st Sess., U.S. Government Printing Office, Washington, D.C., 1935 and U.S. House of Representatives, Committee on Indian Affairs, *Hearings on H.R. 7837*, 74th Cong., 1st Sess., U.S. Government Printing Office, Washington, D.C., 1935.

41. The case involved was *Thompson v. United States*, 13 Ind. Cl. Comm. 369 (1964). For further information, see Jaimes, M. Annette, "The Pit River Indian Land Claim Dispute in Northern California," *Journal of Ethnic Studies*, Vol. 4, No. 4, Winter 1987. In the California case, Indian resistance was vocal and involved a land occupation in the northern part of the state.

42. Forbes, Jack, "'The Public Domain' of Nevada and Its Relationship to Indian Property Rights," *Nevada State Bar Journal*, No. 30, 1965, pp. 16-47.

43. *Congressional Record*, May 20, 1946, p. 5312.

44. The exception here involved claims entered under provision of the Fifth Amendment, of which there were almost none. Interest was denied as a matter of course in other types of claim, based on the outcome of the *Loyal Creek* case (1 Ind. Cl. Comm. 22). See LaDuc, Thomas, "The Work of the Indian Claims Commission Under the Act of 1946," *Pacific Historical Review*, No. 26, 1957, pp. 1-16.

45. Actually, there is one exception. In 1965, the Claims Commission recommended (15 Ind. Cl. Comm. 666) restoration of 130,000 acres of the Blue Lake area to Taos Pueblo (see Gordon-Mc-Cutchan, R.C., *The Taos Indians and the Battle for Blue Lake*, Red Crane Books, Santa Fe, NM, 1991). In 1970, Congress followed up by restoring a total of 48,000 acres (85 *Stat.* 1437). For

further information, see Nielson, Richard A., "American Indian Land Claims: Land versus Money as a Remedy," *University of Florida Law Review*, Vol. 19, No. 3, 1973, pp. 308-26.

46. U.S. House of Representatives, Committee on Indian Affairs, *Providing a One-Year Extension of the Five-Year Limitation on the Time for Presenting Indian Claims to the Indian Claims Commission*, H. Rep. 692, 82d Cong., 1st Sess., U.S. Government Printing Office, Washington, D.C., 1951, pp. 593-601.

47. The Claims Commission was initially authorized for ten years. In 1956, it was extended for a further five years. The process was repeated in 1961, 1967, 1972, and 1976. See U.S. House and Senate, Joint Committee on Appropriations, *Hearings on Appropriations for the Department of Interior*, 94th Cong., 1st Sess., U.S. Government Printing Office, Washington, D.C., 1976.

48. U.S. Senate, Committee on Interior and Insular Affairs, Subcommmittee on Indian Affairs, *Hearings on S. 307*, 90th Cong., 1st Sess., U.S. Government Printing Office, Washington, D.C., 1967.

49. U.S. Senate, Committee on Interior and Insular Affairs, Subcommittee on Indian Affairs, *Hearings on S. 876*, 94th Cong., 1st Sess., U.S. Government Printing Office, Washington, D.C., 1975.

50. Indian Claims Commission, *Final Report*, U.S. Government Printing Office, Washington, D.C., 1978.

51. For a prime example of the sort of academic apologetics for U.S. conduct engendered by the Claims Commission process, see Sutton, Imre, ed., *Irredeemable America: The Indians' Estate and Land Tenure*, University of New Mexico Press, Albuquerque, 1985.

52. Barsh, Russel, "Indian Land Claims Policy in the United States," *North Dakota Law Review*, No. 58, 1982, pp. 1-82.

53. See, for instance, Deloria, Vine Jr., *A Better Day for Indians*, Field Foundation, New York, 1977. For official quantification of the acreage involved, see Public Land Law Review Commission, *One-Third of the Nation's Land*, U.S. Department of Interior, Washington, D.C., 1970.

54. *Oneida Indian Nation v. County of Oneida*, 414 U.S. 661 (1974). For background on the strategy involved in such litigation, see Kellogg, Mark, "Indian Rights: Fighting Back With White Man's Weapons," *Saturday Review*, November 1978, pp. 24-30.

55. The letters were found in an old trunk by an elderly Passamaquoddy woman in 1957 and turned over to township governor John Stevens. It took the Indians fifteen years to bring the matter to court, largely because it was denied they had "legal standing" to do so. See Brodeur, Paul, *Restitution: The Land Claims of the Mashpee, Passamaquoddy, and Penobscot Indians of New England*, Northeastern University Press, Boston, 1985.

56. *Passamaquoddy Tribe v. Morton*, 528 F.2d, 370 (1975). For additional background, see O'Toole, Francis J., and Thomas N. Tureen, "State Power and the Passamaquoddy Tribe: A Gross National Hypocrisy?" *Maine Law Review*, Vol. 23, No. 1, 1971, pp. 1-39.

57. Maine Indian Land Claims Settlement Act of 1980, 94 *Stat.* 1785.

58. The case is *Narragansett Tribe of Indians v. S.R.I. Land Development Corporation*, 418 F. Supp. 803 (1978). The decision was followed by the Rhode Island Indian Claims Settlement Act of 1978, 94 *Stat.* 3498.

59. *Western Pequot Tribe of Indians v. Holdridge Enterprises, Inc.*, Civ. No. 76-193 (1976).

60. The Mashantucket Pequot Indian Claims Settlement Act (S.366) was passed by Congress in December 1982. Reagan's veto is covered in the *Congressional Quarterly*, Vol. 41, No. 14, pp. 710-1.

61. The revised version of the Mashantucket Pequot Indian Claims Settlement Act (S.1499) was signed on October 18, 1983.

62. *Mashpee Tribe v. Town of Mashpee*, 447 F. Supp. 940 (1978).

63. *Mashpee Tribe v. New Seabury Corporation*, 592 F.2d (1st Cir.) 575 (1979), *cert.* denied (1980). For further information, see Wallace, Harry B., "Indian Sovereignty and the Eastern Indian Land Claims," *New York University Law School Law Review*, No. 27, 1982, pp. 921-50. Also see Brodeur, op. cit.

64. *Mohegan Tribe v. Connecticut*, 483 F. Supp. 597 (D. Conn. 1980) and *Schaghticoke Tribe v. Kent School Corporation*, 423 F. Supp. 780 (D. Conn. 1983).

65. By the 1840 Treaty of Nation Ford, the Catawbas agreed to relinquish the reservation in exchange for a $5,000 acquisition of replacement lands. The state defaulted on the agreement, and the Catawbas were left entirely homeless for two years. Finally, in 1842, South Carolina spent $2,000 to buy 630 acres (apparently from itself) of the former reservation for "Catawba use and occupancy." See Hudson, Charles M., "The Catawba Indians of South Carolina: A Question of Ethnic Survival," in Walter L. William, ed., *Southeastern Indians Since the Removal Era*, University of Georgia Press, Athens, 1979, pp. 110-20.

66. *Catawba Indian Tribe of South Carolina v. State of South Carolina*, October 11, 1983.

67. For an assessment of the progress made in this arena, see Anaya, S. James, "The Rights of Indigenous Peoples and International Law in Historical and Contemporary Perspective," in Robert N. Clinton, Nell Jessup Newton, and Monroe E. Price, eds., *American Indian Law: Cases and Materials*, The Michie Co., Law Publishers, Charlottesville, VA, 1991, pp. 1257-76. For the principles involved in resolving issues of this sort through such means, see Lillich, Richard B., *International Claims: Their Adjudication by National Commission*, Syracuse University Press, Syracuse, NY, 1962.

68. Florida Indian Land Claim Settlement Act, 96 *Stat.* 2012 (1982). For background, see Coulter, Robert T., *et al.*, "Seminole Land Rights in Florida and the Award of the Indian Claims Commission," *American Indian Journal*, Vol. 4, No. 3, August 1978, pp. 2-27.

69. See LaDuke, Winona, "The White Earth Land Struggle," in Ward Churchill, ed., *Critical Issues in Native North America*, Doc. 63, International Work Group on Indigenous Affairs, Copenhagen, 1989, pp. 55-71 and "White Earth: The Struggle Continues," in Ward Churchill, ed., *Critical Issues in Native North America*, Vol. II, Doc. 68, International Work Group on Indigenous Affairs, Copenhagen, 1991, pp. 99-103. Also see Peterson, E.M. Jr., "The So-Called Warranty Deed: Clouded Land Titles on the White Earth Reservation in Minnesota," *North Dakota Law Review*, No. 59, 1983, pp. 159-81.

70. See McCool, Daniel, "Federal Indian Policy and the Sacred Mountains of the Papago Indians," *Journal of Ethnic Studies*, Vol. 9, No. 3, 1981, pp. 57-69.

71. See Lovett, Richard A., "The Role of the Forest Service in Ski Resort Development: An Economic Approach to Public Lands Management," *Ecology Law Review*, No. 10, 1983, pp. 507-78. Also see Lubick, George, "Sacred Mountains, Kachinas, and Skiers: The Controversy Over the San Francisco Peaks," in R. Lora, ed., *The American West: Essays in Honor of W. Eugene Hollan*, University of Toledo Press, Toledo, OH, 1980, pp. 133-53.

72. See Churchill, Ward, "Genocide in Arizona? The Navajo-Hopi Land Dispute in Perspective," in *Critical Issues in Native North America*, Vol. II, op. cit., pp. 104-46.

73. See Campisi, Jack, "The Trade and Intercourse Acts: Indian Land Claims on the Eastern Seaboard," in Sutton, op. cit., pp. 337-62.

74. For the basis of this struggle, see Berry, M.C., *The Alaska Pipeline: The Politics of Oil and Native Land Claims*, Indiana University Press, Bloomington/Indianapolis, 1975. Also see Berger, John, *Report from the Frontier: The State of the World's Indigenous Peoples*, Zed Press, London, 1987.

75. On the rejection, see U.S. House of Representatives, *House Report 15066*, 94th Cong., 1st Sess., U.S. Government Printing Office, Washington, D.C., 1974. In 1980, Congress passed an act (94 *Stat.* 3321 mandating formation of a Native Hawaiians Study Commission (six federal officials and three Hawaiians) to find out "what the natives really want." The answer, predictably, was land.

76. For the basis of the native argument here, see Cannelora, L., *The Origin of Hawaiian Land Titles and the Rights of Native Tenants*, Security Title Corporation, Honolulu, 1974.

77. Jefferson and other "radicals" held that U.S. sovereignty accrued from the country itself and did not "devolve" from the British Crown. Hence, U.S. land title could not devolve from the Crown. Put another way, Jefferson—in contrast to John Marshall—held that Britain's asserted discovery rights in North America had no bearing on U.S. rights to occupancy on the continent. See Wood, Gordon, op. cit., pp. 162-96.

78. See generally, Graymont, Barbara, *The Iroquois in the American Revolution*, Syracuse University Press, Syracuse, NY, 1975. The concern felt by Congress with regard to the Iroquois as a military threat, and the consequent need to reach an accommodation with them, is expressed often in early official correspondence. See Ford, Washington C., *et al.*, eds. and comps., *Journals of the Continental Congress, 1774-1789* (34 Vols.), U.S. Government Printing Office, Washington, D.C., 1904-1937.

79. Campisi, Jack, "From Fort Stanwix to Canandaigua: National Policy, States' Rights and Indian Land," in Christopher Vescey and William A. Starna, eds., *Iroquois Land Claims*, Syracuse University Press, Syracuse, NY, 1988, pp. 49-65, quote from p. 55. Also see Manley, Henry M., *The Treaty of Fort Stanwix, 1784*, Rome Sentinel Publications, Rome, NY, 1932.

80. For an account of these meetings, conducted by New York's Governor Clinton during August and September 1784, see Hough, Franklin B., ed., *Proceedings of the Commissioners of Indian Affairs, Appointed by Law for Extinguishment of Indian Titles in the State of New York* (2 Vols.), John Munsell Publishers, Albany, NY, 1861, pp. 41-63.

81. Campisi, op. cit., p. 59. Clinton lied, bold faced. New York's references to the Genesee Company concerned a bid by that group of land speculators to lease Oneida land which the Indians had

not only rejected, but which the state legislature had refused to approve. In effect, the Oneidas had lost no land and were unlikely to, and the governor knew it.

82. See Clinton, George, *Public Papers of George Clinton: First Governor of New York*, Vol. 8, Albany, NY, 1904.

83. The price paid by New York for the Onondaga lease was "1,000 French Crowns, 200 pounds in clothing, plus a $500 annuity." See Upton, Helen M., *The Everett Report in Historical Perspective: The Indians of New York*, New York State Bicentennial Commission, Albany, 1980, p. 35.

84. Ibid., p. 38.

85. The relevant portion of the statute's text reads: "[N]o sale of lands made by any Indians, or any nation or tribe of Indians within the United States, shall be valid to any person or persons, or to any state, whether having the right of pre-emption to such lands or not, unless the same shall be made and duly executed at some public treaty, held under the authority of the United States."

86. Upton, op. cit., p. 40.

87. For ratification discussion on the meaning of the Treaty of Canandaigua, see *American State Papers: Documents, Legislative and Executive of the Congress of the United States, from the First Session to the Third Session of the Thirteenth Congress, Inclusive* (Vol. 4), Gales and Seaton Publishers, Washington, D.C., 1832, pp. 545-70. On Tecumseh's alliance, see Edmunds, R. David, *Tecumseh and the Quest for Indian Leadership*, Little, Brown and Company Publishers, Boston, 1984.

88. See Edwards, Paul D., *The Holland Company*, Buffalo Historical Society, Buffalo, NY, 1924.

89. See Nammack, Georgiana C., *Fraud, Politics, and the Dispossession of the Indians: The Iroquois Frontier and the Colonial Period*, University of Oklahoma Press, Norman, 1969. Also see Manley, Henry S., "Red Jacket's Last Campaign," *New York History*, No. 21, April 1950.

90. See Manley, Henry S., "Buying Buffalo from the Indians," *New York History*, No. 28, July 1947.

91. Kappler, op. cit., pp. 374-8. Also see Society of Friends (Hicksite), *The Case of the Seneca Indians in the State of New York*, Earl E. Coleman Publisher, Stanfordville, NY (reprint of 1840 edition), 1979.

92. Most principle leaders of the Six Nations never signed the Buffalo Creek Treaty. Each of the three consecutive votes taken in the Senate on ratification (requiring two-thirds affirmation to be lawful) resulted in a tie, broken only by the "aye" vote of Vice President Richard Johnson. See Manley, "Buying Buffalo from the Indians," op. cit.

93. U.S. House of Representatives, H. Doc. 66, 26th Cong., 2d Sess., January 6, 1841.

94. Kappler, op. cit., p. 397.

95. The Tonawanda protest appears as U.S. Senate, S. Doc. 273, 29th Cong., 2d Sess., April 2, 1842.

96. On the award, made on November 5, 1857, see *Documents of the Assembly of the State of New York*, 112th Sess., Doc. 51, Albany, 1889, pp. 167-70.

97. Upton, op. cit., p. 53. The New York Supreme Court's invalidation of the leases is covered in *U.S. v. Forness*, 125 F.2d 928 (1942). On the Court's deeming of the leases to be perpetual, see U.S. House of Representatives, Committee on Indian Affairs, *Hearings in Favor of House Bill No. 12270*, 57th Cong., 2d Sess., U.S. Government Printing Office, Washington, D.C., 1902.

98. Assembly Doc. 51, op. cit., pp. 43, 408.

99. 28 *Stat.* 887, March 2, 1895.

100. *Hearings in Favor of House Bill No. 12270*, op. cit. p. 23.

101. Ibid., p. 66.

102. The original case is *Seneca Nation v. Appleby*, 127 AD 770 (1905). It was appealed as *Seneca Nation v. Appleby*, 196 NY 318 (1906).

103. The case, *United States v. Boylan*, 265 Fed. 165 (2d Cir. 1920), is important not because of the paltry quantity of land restored, but because it was the first time the federal judiciary formally acknowledged New York had never acquired legal title to Iroquois land. It was also one of the very few times in American history when non-Indians were actually evicted in order that Indians might recover illegally taken property.

104. New York State Indian Commission Act, Chapter 590, Laws of New York, May 12, 1919.

105. Upton, op. cit., p. 99.

106. The document is Everett, Edward A., *Report of the New York State Indian Commission*, Albany, NY, March 17, 1922 (unpublished), pp. 308-9, 322-30.

107. Stenographic record of August 21, 1922 meeting, Stillman files.

108. Upton, op. cit., pp. 124-9.

109. The total amount to be paid the Senecas for rental of their Salamanca property was $6,000 per year, much of which had gone unpaid since the mid-1930s. The judges found the federal

government to have defaulted on its obligation to regulate state and private leases of Seneca land, and instructed it to take an active role in the future. See Hauptman, Laurence M., "The Historical Background to the Present-Day Seneca Nation-Salamanca Lease Controversy," in *Iroquois Land Claims*, op. cit., pp. 101-22. Also see Merrill, Arch, "The Salamanca Lease Settlement," *American Indian*, No. 1, 1944.

110. These laws, which were replicated in Kansas and Iowa during 1952, predate the more general application of state jurisdiction to Indians embodied in Public Law 280, passed in August 1953. U.S. Congress, Joint Legislative Committee, *Report* (Leg. Doc. 74), 83rd Cong., 1st Sess., U.S. Government Printing Office, Washington, D.C., 1953.

111. This was based on a finding in *United States v. Minnesota* (270 U.S. 181 (1926), s.c. 271 U.S. 648) that state statutes of limitations do not apply to federal action in Indian rights cases.

112. See Campisi, Jack, "National Policy, States' Rights, and Indian Sovereignty: The Case of the New York Iroquois," in Michael K. Foster, Jack Campisi, and Marianne Mithun, eds., *Extending the Rafters: Interdisciplinary Approaches to Iroquoian Studies*, State University of New York Press, Albany, 1984.

113. For the congressional position and commentary on the independent study of alternative sites undertaken by Dr. Arthur Morgan see U.S. Senate, Committee on Interior and Insular Affairs, *Hearings Before the Committee on Interior and Insular Affairs: Kinzua Dam Project, Pennsylvania*, 88th Cong., 1st Sess., U.S. Government Printing Office, Washington, D.C., May-December 1963.

114. For further detail on the struggle around Kinzua Dam, see Hauptman, Lawrence M., *The Iroquois Struggle for Survival: World War II to Red Power*, Syracuse University Press, Syracuse, NY, 1986.

115. *Tuscarora Indians v. New York State Power Authority*, 257 F.2d 885 (1958).

116. On the compromise acreage, see Hauptman, Laurence M., "Iroquois Land Claims Issues: At Odds with the 'Family of New York,'" in *Iroquois Land Claims*, op. cit., pp. 67-86.

117. It took another ten years for this to be spelled out definitively; *Oneida Indian Nation v. United States*, 37 Ind. Cl. Comm. 522 (1971).

118. For a detailed account of the discussions, agreements, and various factions within the process, see Upton, op. cit., pp. 139-61.

119. See Treur, Margaret, "Ganiekeh: An Alternative to the Reservation System and Public Trust," *American Indian Journal*, Vol. 5, No. 5, 1979, pp. 22-6.

120. *State of New York v. Danny White, et al.*, Civ. No. 74-CV-370 (N.D.N.Y.), April 1976; *State of New York v. Danny White, et al.*, Civ. No. 74-CV-370, Memorandum Decision and Order, 23 March 1977.

121. On the Moss Lake Agreement, see Kwartler, Richard, "'This Is Our Land': Mohawk Indians v. The State of New York," in Robert B. Goldman, ed., *Roundtable Justice: Case Studies in Conflict Resolution*, Westview Press, Boulder, CO, 1980.

122. *Oneida Indian Nation of New York v. County of Oneida*, 14 U.S. 661 (1974).

123. *Oneida Indian Nation of New York v. County of Oneida*, 434 F. Supp. 527, 548 (N.D.N.Y. 1979).

124. Van Gestel, Allan, "New York Indian Land Claims: The Modern Landowner as Hostage," in *Iroquois Land Claims*, op. cit., pp. 123-39. Also see the revision, published as "When Fictions Take Hostages," in James E. Clifton, ed., *The Invented Indian: Cultural Fictions and Government Policies*, Transaction Books, New Brunswick, NJ, 1990, pp. 291-312 and "The New York Indian Land Claims: An Overview and a Warning," *New York State Bar Journal*, April 1981.

125. *County of Oneida v. Oneida Indian Nation of New York*, 84 L.Ed.2d 169, 191 (1984).

126. Locklear, Arlinda, "The Oneida Land Claims: A Legal Overview," in *Iroquois Land Claims*, op. cit., pp. 141-53.

127. Ibid., p. 148.

128. This suit was later recast to name the state rather than the counties as primary defendant, and enlarged to encompass 6 million acres. It was challenged, but upheld on appeal; *Oneida Indian Nation of New York v. State of New York*, 691 F.2d 1070 (1982). Dismissed by a district judge four years later (Brennan, Claire, "Oneida Claim to 6 Million Acres Voided," *Syracuse Post-Standard*, November 22, 1986), it was reinstated by the Second Circuit Court in 1988 (*Oneida Indian Nation of New York v. State of New York*, 860 F.2d 1145), and is ongoing as of this writing.

129. *Oneida Nation of Indians of Wisconsin v. State of New York*, 85 F.D.R. 701, 703 (N.Y.D.C. 1980).

130. New York has attempted various arguments to obtain dismissal of the Cayuga suit. In 1990, the state's contention that it had obtained bona fide land title to the disputed area in leases obtained in 1795 and 1801 was overruled at the district court level (*Cayuga Indian Nation of New York v. Cuomo*, 730 F. Supp. 485). In 1991, an "interpretation" by the state attorney general that

reservation of land by the Six Nations in the Fort Stanwix Treaty "did not really" invest recognizable title in them was similarly overruled (*Cayuga Indian Nation of New York v. Cuomo*, 758 F. Supp. 107). Finally, in 1991, a state contention that only a special railroad reorganization would have jurisdiction to litigate claims involving areas leased to railroads was overruled (*Cayuga Indian Nation of New York v. Cuomo*, 762 F. Supp. 30). The suit is ongoing.

131. The terms of the agreement were published in *Finger Lakes Times*, August 18, 1979.

132. For further details, see Lavin, Chris, "The Cayuga Land Claims," in *Iroquois Land Claims*, op. cit., pp. 87-100.

133. The one jurisdictional exception is that the Second Circuit Court ruled in 1988 that a federal statute passed in 1875 empowers the city of Salamanca, rather than the Senecas, to regulate zoning within the leased area so long as the leases exist (*John v. City of Salamanca*, 845 F.2d 37).

134. The non-Indian city government of Salamanca, a sub-part of which is the Salamanca Lease Authority, filed suit in 1990 to block settlement of the Seneca claim as "unconstitutional," and to compel a new ninety-nine year lease on its own terms (*Salamanca Indian Lease Authority v. Seneca Indian Nation*, Civ. No. 1300, Docket 91-7086). They lost and appealed. The lower court decision was affirmed by the Second Circuit Court on March 15, 1991, on the basis that the Senecas enjoy "sovereign immunity" from any further such suits.

135. Public Law 101-503, 104 *Stat.* 1179.

136. For the treaty text, see Kappler, op. cit., pp. 594-6. For background, see Nadeau, Remi, *Fort Laramie and the Sioux*, University of Nebraska Press, Lincoln, 1967 and Hafen, LeRoy R., and Francis Marion Young, *Fort Laramie and the Pageant of the West, 1834-1890*, University of Nebraska Press, Lincoln, 1938.

137. See Brown, Dee, *Fort Phil Kearny: An American Saga*, University of Nebraska Press, Lincoln, 1971. Also see Hebard, Grace, and E.A. Brindenstool, *The Bozeman Trail* (2 Vols.), Arthur H. Clark Publishers, Cleveland, 1922.

138. The treaty text will be found in Kappler, op. cit.. Lakota territorality is spelled out in Articles 2 and 16 of the Constitution, non-abrogation of 1851 treaty land provisions in Article 17.

139. Ibid., Article 12. The gender provision is of U.S. rather than Lakota origin.

140. See Jackson, Donald, *Custer's Gold: The United States Cavalry Expedition of 1874*, University of Nebraska Press, Lincoln, 1966. Also see U.S. Department of Interior (William Ludlow), *Report of a Reconnaissance of the Black Hills of Dakota*, U.S. Government Printing Office, Washington, D.C., 1875. Prior to the outbreak of hostilities in 1876, a second U.S. invasion of Lakota territory—the 1875 "Jenny Expedition"—was sent into the Black Hills to corroborate Custer's findings. See U.S. Department of Interior (Walter P. Jenny), *Report to Congress on the Mineral Wealth, Climate and Rainfall, and Natural Resources of the Black Hills of South Dakota* (Exec. Doc. 51), 44th Cong., 1st Sess., U.S. Government Printing Office, Washington, D.C., 1876. The Lakota responded militarily to neither violation of the treaty.

141. U.S. Department of Interior, Bureau of Indian Affairs, *Annual Report of the Commissioner of Indian Affairs, 1875*, U.S. Government Printing Office, Washington, D.C., 1875.

142. U.S. Department of War, *Annual Report of the Secretary of War*, 43rd Cong., 2d Sess., U.S. Government Printing Office, Washington, D.C., 1876, p. 441. Also see Olsen, James C., *Red Cloud and the Sioux Problem*, University of Nebraska Press, Lincoln, 1965.

143. See Vaughn, J.W., *With Crook at the Rosebud*, University of Nebraska Press, Lincoln, 1956.

144. On the Custer fight, see Sandoz, Mari, *The Battle of the Little Big Horn*, Curtis Books, New York, 1966. Another excellent reading is Ambrose, Stephen E., *Crazy Horse and Custer: The Parallel Lives of Two American Warriors*, Doubleday Publishers, Garden City, NY, 1975.

145. Gray, John S., *Centennial Campaign: The Sioux Wars of 1876*, University of Oklahoma Press, Norman, 1988.

146. For a detailed account of one of these slaughters, see Greene, Jerome, *Slim Buttes, 1877: An Episode in the Great Sioux War*, University of Oklahoma Press, Norman, 1982. For more on McKenzie, who had made his reputation in a winter attack upon a Comanche village in Palo Duro Canyon (Texas) in 1874, see Fehrenbach, T.R., *Comanches: The Destruction of a People*, Alfred A. Knopf Publishers, New York, 1975, pp. 516-21.

147. On the Hunkpapa evasion to Canada, see Vestal, Stanley, *Sitting Bull: Champion of the Sioux*, University of Oklahoma Press, Norman, 1932. On the false promises made to Crazy Horse (through Red Cloud), see Brown, Dee, *Bury My Heart at Wounded Knee: An Indian History of the American West*, Holt, Rinehart and Winston Publishers, New York, 1970, pp. 308-10.

148. For first-hand accounts, see Clark, Robert A., ed., *The Killing of Chief Crazy Horse*, University

of Nebraska Press, Lincoln, 1976.

149. This legislative history is covered in "1986 Black Hills Hearing on S.1453, Introduction," prepared by the staff of Senator Daniel Inouye, Chair of the Senate Select Committee on Indian Affairs, for *Wicazo Sa Review*, Vol. IV, No. 1, Spring 1988. Total "Sioux" treaty territory—including that of the Nakota ("Prairie Sioux") and Dakota ("Woodland Sioux") east of the Missouri River—added up to 160 to 175 million acres according to the Indian Claims Commission (*Final Report*, op. cit.)

150. See Fritz, Henry E., *The Movement for Indian Assimilation, 1860-1890*, University of Pennsylvania Press, Philadelphia, 1963.

151. See *Sioux Tribe v. United States* (2 Ind. Cl. Comm. 671) for computation of acreage.

152. For a good dose of the propaganda prevailing at the time, see Welsh, Herbert, "The Meaning of the Dakota Outbreak," *Scribner's Magazine*, April 1891, pp. 439-52. A more comprehensive and considered topical view, albeit one generally conforming to ideological requirements, is Mooney, James M., *The Ghost-Dance Religion and the Sioux Outbreak of 1890*, Smithsonian Institution, Bureau of American Ethnology, U.S. Government Printing Office, Washington, D.C., 1896. The most balanced and accurate account may be found in *Bury My Heart at Wounded Knee*, op. cit.

153. Deloria, Vine Jr., and Clifford M. Lytle, *American Indians, American Justice*, University of Texas Press, Austin, 1983, p. 10.

154. For an official assessment of this situation, see the memorandum of Indian Commissioner John Collier; U.S. House of Representatives, Committee on Indian Affairs, *Hearings on HR 7902 before the House Committee on Indian Affairs*, 73rd Cong., 2d Sess., U.S. Government Printing Office, Washington, D.C., 1934, pp. 16-8.

155. Eastman's books include *Old Indian Days*, McClure Publishers, New York, 1907; *The Soul of the Indian: An Interpretation*, Johnson Reprint Corp., New York, 1971, originally published in 1911; *From Deep Woods to Civilization: Chapters in an Autobiography of an Indian*, Little, Brown Publishers, Boston, 1916; and *Indian Heroes and Great Chieftains*, Little, Brown Publishers, Boston, 1918.

156. *Sioux Tribe v. United States*, 97 Ct. Cl. 613 (1942).

157. *Sioux Tribe v. United States*, 318 U.S. 789, *cert.* denied (1943).

158. *Sioux Tribe v. United States*, 2 Ind. Cl. Comm. (1956).

159. *Wicazo Sa Review*, op. cit., pp. 10-1.

160. *United States v. Sioux Nation of Indians*, 448 U.S. 371, 385 (1968). The grounds, however, were exceedingly narrow. The commission was charged only with discovering: 1) What, if any, land rights vis-à-vis the Black Hills had been acquired in 1877; 2) What consideration had been given by the U.S. in exchange for these lands; and 3) If no consideration had been given, had the U.S. made any payments which might offset its obligation to provide consideration?

161. *Sioux Nation v. United States*, 33 Ind. Cl. Comm. 151 (1974); the decision was of course legally absurd. The U.S. holds "eminent domain" powers over the property of *no* foreign nation, such as the Lakota had to be in order for the 1868 treaty to be consummated. Fifth Amendment compensation hardly provides redress to an invaded country. See Meinhart, Nick, and Diane Payne, "Reviewing U.S. Commitments to the Lakota Nation," *American Indian Journal*, No. 13, November-December 1975, pp. 15-17.

162. *United States v. Sioux Nation of Indians*, 207 Ct. Cl. 234, 518 F.2d 1293 (1975).

163. *Wicazo Sa Review*, op. cit., p. 12. On the concept of government "offsets," see White, John R., "Barmecide Revisited: The Gratuitous Offset in Indian Claims Cases," *Ethnohistory*, No. 25, 1978, pp. 179-92.

164. *Sioux Nation of Indians v. United States*, 423 U.S. 1016, *cert.* denied (1975).

165. For additional information, see Matthiessen, Peter, *In the Spirit of Crazy Horse*, Viking Press, New York (2d edition), 1991. Also see Churchill, Ward, and Jim Vander Wall, *Agents of Repression: The FBI's Secret Wars Against the Black Panther Party and the American Indian Movement*, South End Press, Boston, 1988.

166. The transfer instrument, entitled *Memorandum of Agreement Between the Oglala Sioux Tribe of South Dakota and the National Park Service of the Department of Interior to Facilitate Establishment, Development, Administration and Public Use of the Oglala Sioux Tribal Lands, Badlands National Monument*, was signed secretly by Tribal President Richard Wilson on January 2, 1976. Although the arrangement hardly conformed to the provisions for Lakota land cessions in the still-binding 1868 treaty, Congress acted as it had in 1877, quickly passing Public Law 90-468 to take possession of the property. When Lakota protest became too great, the act was amended to allow the Indians to recover the surface rights any time they elected to do so

by referendum (thus inverting the treaty requirements), but *not* the mineral rights (thus removing any question as to whether the whole thing hadn't been about taking the Lakota uranium rather than enlarging a national park). See Huber, Jacqueline, *et al.*, *The Gunnery Range Report*, Oglala Sioux Tribe, Office of the Tribal President, Pine Ridge, SD, 1981.

167. "The Black Hills Are Not For Sale," *Native American Support Committee (NASC) Newsletter*, Vol. V, No. 10, October 1977.

168. On the building of IITC, see Weyler, Rex, *Blood of the Land: The U.S. Government and Corporate War Against the American Indian Movement*, Everest House Publishers, New York, 1982, pp. 213-6.

169. Public Law 95-243, 25 U.S.C. #70s (Supp. II, 1978).

170. *Sioux Nation of Indians v. United States*, 220 Ct. Cl. 442, 601 F.2d 1157 (1979).

171. Washburn, Wilcomb E., "Land Claims in the Mainstream," in Sutton, op. cit., pp. 21-33, quote from p. 26. The opinion is *Sioux Nation of Indians v. United States*, 448 U.S. 371 (1980). For a sample of Rehnquist's own extremely inaccurate and highly politicized historical revisionism, see his opinion in the 1978 *Oliphant* case.

172. Means, Russell, "'The Black Hills: They're Still Not For Sale!" *Oyate Wicaho*, May 1980. Also see Hanson, Steven C., "*United States v. Sioux Nation:* Political Questions, Moral Imperative and National Honor," *American Indian Law Review*, Vol. 8, No. 2, 1980, pp. 459-84.

173. On the 1980 Black Hills Survival Gathering, see Anonymous, *Keystone for Survival*, Black Hills Alliance, Rapid City, SD, 1981. Also see Tabb, Bill, "Marx versus Marxism," in Ward Churchill, ed., *Marxism and Native Americans*, South End Press, Boston, 1983, pp. 159-74.

174. *Oglala Sioux Tribe v. United States*, Cir. No. 85-062, W.D.N.D. 1980; 448 U.S. 371, cert. denied (1980).

175. For analysis of the AIM strategy in the Yellow Thunder occupation, see Churchill, Ward, "Yellow Thunder *Tiyospaye:* Misadventure or Watershed Action?" *Policy Perspectives*, Vol. 2, No. 2, Spring 1982. Also see Weyler, op. cit., especially Chapter 8, "Yellow Thunder," pp. 251-64.

176. The Oglala Sioux Tribal Council, for example, sponsored what was called Crazy Horse Camp, in Wind Cave State Park, from July through September 1981. The Cheyenne River Sioux established a camp at Craven Canyon, deep in the Black Hills, during the same period.

177. *United States v. Means, et al.*, Civ. No. 81-5131, D.S.D., December 9, 1985.

178. The deposit was made pursuant to a claims court ruling, *Sioux Tribe v. United States*, 7 Cl. Cl. 80 (1985).

179. On establishment of the Working Group and its mandate, see Anaya, op. cit.

180. Further delineation of the Bradley Bill, and comprehensive analysis of its implications, will be found in *Wicazo Sa Review*, op. cit.

181. Stevens was a successful Defense Department contractor in the Los Angeles area who retired and sold off his company at a reputed $60 million profit during the early '80s. He then allegedly discovered he was in some part Lakota, traveled to South Dakota, and announced "his people" were entitled to much more than was being offered in the Bradley Bill (which, of course, was true). He stipulated that if he were named "Great Chief of all the Sioux" (a position that has never existed), he would be able—based on his executive expertise—to negotiate a multi-billion dollar settlement and recover the whole 1868 reservation area. Some Lakotas endorsed this strategy. Tellingly, once S.1453 was withdrawn, Stevens also withdrew, and has not been much heard from since. It is widely suspected he was an operative for anti-Indian interests. For details, see *Lakota Times*, 1988-89, inclusive.

182. The full treaty text may be found in Kappler, op. cit.

183. Ryser, Rudolph C., *Newe Segobia and the United States of America*, Occasional Paper, Center for World Indigenous Studies, Kenmore, WA, 1985. Also see Matthiessen, Peter, *Indian Country*, Viking Press, New York, 1984, pp. 261-89.

184. Actually, under U.S. law, a specific Act of Congress is required to extinguish aboriginal title; *United States ex rel. Hualapi Indians v. Santa Fe Railroad*, 314, U.S. 339, 354 (1941). On Newe use of the land during this period, see Clemmer, Richard O., "Land Use Patterns and Aboriginal Rights: Northern and Eastern Nevada, 1858-1971," *The Indian Historian*, Vol. 7, No. 1, 1974, pp. 24-41, 47-9.

185. Ryser, op. cit., pp. 15-6.

186. Wilkinson had already entered into negotiations to represent the Temoak before the Claims Commission Act was passed; Ibid., p. 13, n. 1.

187. The Temoaks have said consistently that Wilkinson always represented the claim to them as being for land rather than money. The firm is known to have run the same scam on other Indian

clients; Ibid., pp. 16-7.
188. Ibid., p. 16. Also see Coulter, op. cit., and Coulter and Tullberg, op. cit.
189. See Morris, Glenn T., "The Battle for Newe Segobia: The Western Shoshone Land Rights Struggle," in *Critical Issues in Native North America*, Vol. II, op. cit., pp. 86-98.
190. Ibid., p. 90. The case is *Western Shoshone Identifiable Group v. United States*, 11 Ind. Cl. Comm. 387, 416 (1962). The whole issue is well covered in Forbes, Jack D., "The 'Public Domain' in Nevada and Its Relationship to Indian Property Rights," *Nevada State Bar Journal*, No. 30, 1965, pp. 16-47.
191. The first award amount appears in *Western Shoshone Identifiable Group v. United States*, 29 Ind. Cl. Comm. 5 (1972), p. 124. The second award appears in *Western Shoshone Identifiable Group v. United States*, 40 Ind. Cl. Comm. 305 (1977).
192. The final Court of Claims order for Wilkinson's retention in *Western Shoshone Identifiable Group v. United States*, 593 F.2d 994 (1979). Also see "Excerpts from a Memorandum from the Duckwater Shoshone Tribe, Battle Mountain Indian Community, and the Western Shoshone Sacred Lands Association in Opposition to the Motion and Petition for Attorney Fees and Expenses, July 15, 1980," in *Rethinking Indian Law*, op. cit., pp. 68-9.
193. *Western Shoshone Identifiable Group v. United States*, 40 Ind. Cl. Comm. 311 (1977).
194. Morris, quoting Ryser, op. cit., p. 8, n. 4.
195. Quoted in Ryser, op. cit., p. 20.
196. *United States v. Dann*, 572 F.2d 222 (1978). For background, see Foot, Kristine L., "*United States v. Dann:* What It Portends for Ownership of Millions of Acres in the Western United States," *Public Land Law Review*, No. 5, 1984, pp. 183-91.
197. *United States v. Dann*, Civ. No. R-74-60, April 25, 1980.
198. *United States v. Dann*, 706 F.2d 919, 926 (1983).
199. Morris, op. cit., p. 94.
200. Nietschmann, Bernard, and William Le Bon, "Nuclear States and Fourth World Nations," *Cultural Survival Quarterly*, Vol. 11, No. 4, 1988, pp. 4-7. Also see Knack, Martha C., "MX Issues for Native American Communities," in Francis Hartigan, ed., *MX in Nevada: A Humanistic Perspective*, Nevada Humanities Press, Reno, 1980, pp. 59-66.
201. Nietschmann and Le Bon, op. cit., p. 7.
202. The actual quote, used as a slogan during the French student rebellion of 1968, is "Be realistic, demand the impossible." For details, see Cohn-Bendit, Daniel, *Obsolete Communism: The Left-Wing Alternative*, McGraw-Hill Books, New York, 1968.
203. See, for example, Sutton, Imre, "Indian Land Rights and the Sagebrush Rebellion," *Geographical Review*, No. 72, 1982, pp. 357-9. Also see Lyons, David, "The New Indian Claims and Original Rights to Land," *Social Theory and Practice*, No. 4, 1977, pp. 249-72 and Clayton, Richard D., "The Sagebrush Rebellion: Who Would Control Public Lands?," *Utah Law Review*, No. 68, 1980, pp. 505-33.
204. For some environmentalist arguments, see Watkins, T.H., "Ancient Wrongs and Public Rights," *Sierra Club Bulletin*, Vol. 59, No. 8, 1974, pp. 15-6, 37-9; Blumm, M.C., "Fulfilling the Parity Promise: A Perspective on Scientific Proof, Economic Cost and Indian Treaty Rights in the Approval of the Columbia Fish and Wildlife Program," *Environmental Law*, Vol. 13, No. 1, 1982, pp. 103-59; and every issue of *Earth First!* from 1986-89. For marxist articulations, see Revolutionary Communist Party, U.S.A., "Searching for the Second Harvest," in *Marxism and Native Americans*, op. cit., pp. 35-58 and Muga, David, "Native Americans and the Nationalities Question: Premises for a Marxist Approach to Ethnicity and Self-Determination," *Nature, Society, Thought*, Vol. 1, No. 1, 1987.
205. Means, Russell, speech at the University of Colorado at Denver, April 1986 (tape on file).
206. For use of the term, and explanation, see Stock, David, "The Settler State and the U.S. Left," *Forward Motion*, Vol. 9, No. 4, January 1991, pp. 53-61.
207. The quote is attributed to paleo-conservative pundit Patrick J. Buchanan, delivered on the CNN talk show *Crossfire*, 1987.
208. See Ensworth, Laurie, "Native American Free Exercise Rights to the Use of Public Lands," *Boston University Law Review*, No. 63, 1983, pp. 141-79. Also see Hooker, Barbara, "Surplus Lands for Indians: One Road to Self-Determination," *Vital Issues*, Vol. 22, No. 1, 1972 and Hodge, R.A., "Getting Back the Land: How Native Americans Can Acquire Excess and Surplus Federal Property," *North Dakota Law Review*, Vol. 49, No. 2, 1973, pp. 333-42.
209. This is taken up in some detail in Means, Russell, and Ward Churchill, *TREATY: A Program for the Liberation of Native North America*, forthcoming from the Fourth World Center for Indigenous Law and Politics, University of Colorado at Denver, 1992.

Chapter VI

American Indian Water Rights
The Blood of Life in Native North America

Marianna Guerrero

The basic element is survival. No matter what color you are, you get thirsty.
Cecil Williams
Papago Tribal Chair, 1979

During the period in which the native peoples of North America were engaged in the process of ceding portions of their territory to the United States in exchange for guarantees of their remaining land bases, the question of their rights to the water in or flowing into these reserved areas seldom arose. Both parties to the treaties and other agreements by which the cessions and reservations occurred implicitly accepted the premise that water, like trees, grass, and air, was integral to the concept of "land" under discussion, and required no specific language setting it aside for Indian usage within reservation boundaries. This concept corresponds quite well with the U.S. juridical doctrines holding that indigenous people retain all rights they have not freely relinquished or that Congress has not expressly removed from them by statute,[1] and that disputes over the meaning of treaty language should be resolved in favor of the Indian understandings of them.[2]

Over the years, however, especially in the arid and semi-arid regions of the West, a variety of forces have sought to separate land and water rights. While conceding that American Indians retain clear title to the acreage encompassed within their reservations, it is argued that water—particularly water such as rivers, streams, and aquifers not completely bounded by reserved territory—is another matter. The thrust of this thinking, and the policies which devolve from it, is to leave native peoples in possession of their residual land holdings (thus upholding "the letter of the law"), while diverting to non-Indian use and profit the water necessary to support enterprise, and in some cases life itself, on that land. Contemporary federal water policies vis-à-vis Indians thus hold much in common with such earlier exercises in colonial governance as the "general allotment" program by which the most valuable reservation land was transferred to non-Indians while native people were restricted to the most barren areas of their homelands (see Chapters Four and Five). They also bear more than passing resemblance to more recent policies of leaving what is left of the reservations in place while systematically expropriating the resources within them (see Chapter Eight).

Origins of the Water Rights Conflict

In 1855, several indigenous nations of the Great Plains entered into a treaty with the United States that reserved approximately 17.5 million acres of what is now the state of Montana for their joint use and exclusive occupancy. Called the "Great Blackfeet Reservation," this huge parcel was subsequently reduced by about 80 percent and broken up into individual "tribal" reservations through a series of congressional actions in the 1880s.[3] The Gros Ventre and Assiniboine nations, for example, agreed in 1888 to cede all but about 600,000 acres of their portion of the great reserve in exchange for federal guarantees of the permanence of their new boundaries, centering on Fort Belknap, and provision of housing, livestock, medical care and farming implements.[4]

Water was not a point of contention in Indian-white relations on the Great Plains during the period in which the Montana reservations were established, the non-Indian population of the area being very sparse. This began to change in 1890 when the first railroads pushed into the region, bringing with them the first major development interests and a substantial wave of settlers eager for the free or extremely low cost farming and ranching parcels available under the 1862 Homestead Act and other legislation.[5] This increasing non-Indian presence on Great Plains required—as it did elsewhere in the West—the creation of a costly hydraulic infrastructure for irrigation and other purposes, an expense the federal government was loath to undertake. Hence, in 1894 the Carey Act was passed, under which the U.S. gave some 9.75 million acres impounded from Indians under the General Allotment Act to various western states. The states were expected to sell this land to private parties, thereby raising the capital needed to solve their respective water problems on their own.[6]

By 1900, it had become apparent that the Carey program was a "dismal and discouraging failure".[7] In addition, it was running head-on into an emerging consolidation of sentiment in Washington, D.C. concerning resource conservation and "reclamation" of desert lands. Adherents to the latter view followed the thinking of Major John Wesley Powell, first articulated in his 1878 *Report on the Lands of the Arid Region,* that the West could be efficiently "developed" only through a "coordinated, communal effort" at the national level.[8] In 1902, President Theodore Roosevelt, comparing what he had in mind to a civilian counterpart to the Army Corps of Engineers, went on record stating, "It is right for the National Government to make the streams and rivers of the arid regions useful by engineering works for water storage."[9]

Centralized federal control over water resources was (and remains) crucial to any development scheme, a matter that conflicted fundamentally with the "states' rights" sentiments fostered under the Carey Act and earlier statutes with regard to water and other matters.[10] Consequently, when the National Reclamation Act (43 U.S.C. 391) was passed in 1902, Congress attempted to create the desired federal coordinating mechanism for water development while simultaneously providing a balm to the sensibilities of "states' rightsers." Section 8 of the law reads:

> [N]othing in this Act shall be construed as affecting or intended to affect or in any way interfere with the laws of any State or Territory relating to the control, appropriation, use, or distribution of water used in irrigation, or in any vested right acquired thereunder...the Secretary of Interior, in carrying out the provisions of this Act, shall proceed in conformity with such laws, and nothing herein shall in any way affect any right of any State or of the Federal Government or of any land owner, appropriator, or user of water in, to or from any interstate stream or the waters thereof. Provided, that the right to the use of water acquired under the provisions of this Act shall be appurtenant to the land irrigated, and beneficial use shall be the basis, the measure, and the limit of the right.[11]

Such compromise legislation, of course, satisfied no one. Even before the bill was enacted, Representative Gerald Ray of New York was complaining vociferously that, although federal funds were to be used in western water development initiatives, "the United States surrenders all control. Congress surrenders all control. The laws of the several states are in control."[12] On the other side, a speaker at the 1906 National Irrigation Congress warned that "any plan or scheme that seeks to transfer the control and administration of irrigation affairs, from the several States to the general government at Washington, is regarded as an encroachment upon the rights of the State and an interference with the individual prerogative acquired under local custom or law, and meets with more or less hostility from those largely interested in irrigation affairs."[13] Meanwhile, the first annual report of the newly created federal Reclamation Service (later Bureau of Reclamation) observed, "It appears probable that in some of the States radical changes in the laws must be made before important projects can be undertaken."[14]

This problem increased dramatically from the federal perspective in 1907 when the *Kansas v. Colorado* case (206 U.S. 46) was decided by the Supreme Court to the effect that, under existing laws, the central government had virtually no legal basis to exert control over non-navigable waters within its borders. It was perceived in Washington that resolving the issue by amendment of the Reclamation Act simply to override state laws by federal authority would be impossible. Not only would such federal action provoke a vast political backlash against western lawmakers in their home districts, but it would precipitate a potential constitutional crisis. Some other means, ostensibly "neutral," was needed to cut through the knot of conflicting rights and interests, leaving the federal government in *de facto* control over all—or a decisive portion of—western water. The blade by which this was accomplished was found at Fort Belknap.

Actually, no one had been paying much attention to the idea of Indian water rights throughout the entire struggle over federal versus state control of the vital fluid. One result was that white settlers had moved into the area of the Milk River north of the reservation and increasingly diverted its flow for their own irrigation needs. In 1905, Fort Belknap experienced its first water shortage because of this practice. Almost immediately, Assistant U.S. Attorney Carl Rasch was instructed by the Justice Department to enter a suit in behalf of the Indians.[15] In his argument to the federal court, Rasch contended that water rights were implicitly reserved for the reservation under the 1855 treaty and reaffirmed by the 1888 agreement. He further argued that, in any event, the Gros Ventres and Assiniboines possessed a "riparian right" to the Milk River water that superseded the "prior use doctrine" applied in Montana state law. The latter, an English Common Law practice that prevailed in states east of the Mississippi, was a direct assault upon the western states'-rights position.

In the concept of riparian rights, title to land abutting a stream carries with it a right to withdraw from that stream any amount of water necessary for "reasonable use." Riparian rights are not quantified. In order for this to work, the rights of all users along a stream must be such that no user is entitled to alter the flow of water in ways which will disrupt his or her neighbors' use. In times of shortage, all users share equally. Riparian rights are permanent and not subject to loss through non-use, since title inheres in the land.[16] By contrast, the statutory codes of western states all conform to the principle that water is allocated through a strict hierarchy of rights based in the chronological order in which users obtain permits to appropriate water from a given source. The right is limited to a specific "quantified" amount for an officially approved "beneficial use." Non-use of the right for specified periods results in its loss, and in times of shortage users high on the list continue to receive their full quota while those low on the list may receive no water at all.[17]

At trial in late 1905, the U.S. District Court for Montana immediately found in favor of the Indians, and issued an injunction against non-Indian diversion of water necessary to reservation life and economy. Interestingly, the court rejected Rasch's argument concerning the applicability of riparian rights per se, basing its conclusion expressly upon treaty rights: "[The] Indians...reserved the right to the use of the waters of the Milk River, at least to the extent reasonably necessary to irrigate their lands."[18] With this stated, however, the judge promptly borrowed from the riparian tradition by leaving both the quantity of water to which the Gros Ventres and Assiniboines were entitled and the period for which they were entitled to it unspecified, a matter that made their rights virtually open-ended and overriding those of area non-Indians.[19] In effect, a new legal doctrine had been created.

The settlers quickly filed an appeal with the Ninth Circuit Court, arguing that the lower court decision should be set aside and Indian water rights judicially abolished. In this effort, they were sorely disappointed. In 1906, the circuit court not only affirmed the earlier decision, but added a significant piece to the emerging doctrine by using state legal principles against themselves to complete the demolition of their applicability to Indian water rights. If "first use" were really at issue, the appeals court held, then the 1888 agreement—and perhaps the 1855 treaty as well—should be construed as the Indians' "application" to appropriate water. Since these predated any non-Indian application by ten to forty-three years, the point worked in favor of the Indians rather than the settlers. Altogether, the circuit court concluded, the district court's ruling had been a "true interpretation of the treaty of May 1, 1888."[20] An appeal of what was by then called *Winters v. U.S.* was next filed with the Supreme Court. Again, in 1908, the lower court decision was affirmed.[21]

> In upholding the circuit court decision, the Supreme Court agreed (1) that in keeping with the western states' water rights, the date a reservation was established was to be considered as the date the waters were reserved (thus making Indians the senior appropriators on many western streams since most reservations were founded from the 1850s through the 1880s); but (2) that unlike state-appropriation doctrine, the reserved right was not liable to extinction through non-use; and (3) the right need not be quantified if the appropriated waters are used to fulfill the reservation's purpose.[22]

Left unstated, perhaps deliberately so, in the high court's final articulation of what became known as the "*Winters* Doctrine" was whether it was the federal government or the Indians themselves who were considered as having reserved these rights through the treaty-making process. This was and is an important distinction when it comes to making decisions on water use. In any event, given the Supreme Court's then recent assertion of absolute U.S. "plenary power" over Indian property in the *Lonewolf v. Hitchcock* case (1904), it is plain that the justices saw their decision as placing the waters at issue in *Winters* under federal rather than Indian control. It was a policymaker's dream come true: the government could proceed with centralized development of water resources throughout the West, while its indigenous "wards" could be blamed for the assorted usurpations of states' rights that would necessarily occur along the way.

Early Responses to *Winters*

The first response of the Milk River settlers to the *Winters* decision was undertaken well before the high court reached it, and is entirely consistent with Euroamerican behavior at all historical junctures in which native people were found to possess something they wanted: they tried to make the Indians "disappear," albeit legislatively in this instance rather than through physical extermination.

> By the time of the *Winters* decision the settlers in the Milk River Valley had organized into two interest groups: the Upper and Lower Milk River Valley Water Users Associations. When they lost in district court they turned to their senator, Thomas Carter, for relief. Their strategy was simple: if the water belonged to the reservation, they would obtain the reservation. Acquiescing, Senator Carter introduced a bill in 1906—one month before the case was to go to the appeals court. His bill provided for the opening of the northern part of the Fort Belknap Reservation—that is, the section that bordered the Milk River.

It was thought that this would deprive the reservation of its reserved water right. A similar bill was proposed as an amendment to a bill opening the Blackfeet Reservation [also in Montana, further up the Milk, where another water rights case was developing]. This bill, however, went even further; it proposed that all suits by the federal government that might enjoin settlers from diverting water be suspended and no future suits of like character be initiated.[23]

Despite active support from railroad magnate J.J. Hill, the bills failed to pass. Over the next decade and a half—in 1910, 1911, 1916, and 1923—the settlers continued their efforts to have all or part of Fort Belknap abolished through bills introduced by Carter and his replacement, Senator Jason Myers.

A number of "schemes" generated by the persistent settlers of Milk River were [also] reported by the project engineer on the Fort Belknap Reservation in 1920, among them a plan to apply state law to the Indians and a proposal to limit each Indian to forty acres of irrigable land and open the remaining "surplus" land to whites.[24]

Ultimately, no laws bearing upon the substance of the *Winters* decision were to be passed during the first half of the 20th century, evidence that Congress was quite content to utilize the federal power attendant to the ambiguous situation created by the courts while allowing its western state members to slide off the political hook by "fighting the good fight," and introducing one bill after another at their constituents' behest. Meanwhile, on the judicial front, the scope of federal power over western water was being steadily enlarged. In 1908, the Ninth Circuit Court heard *Conrad Investment Co. v. U.S.* (161 F.2d 829), in which it amplified *Winters* by holding that Indians on the Blackfeet Reservation possessed a paramount right not simply to the water necessary to meet their present needs, but future needs as well. This was followed, in 1921, by a Ninth Circuit decision in *Skeem v. U.S.* (273 F.2d 93) that native water rights pertained to entire reservations rather than simply the acreage abutting rivers or streams, and that Indians held the right to lease these rights whenever they leased portions of their land.[25] In other words, the undefined extent of "Indian" water under direct federal control could not be diminished under *any* circumstances.

The ways in which the government intended to apply its new-found power to allocate western water—and the extent of its real concern with native rights—was shortly demonstrated on the Yakima Reservation in eastern Washington state, established by treaty in 1859:

By 1906...non-Indian diversions of water were sufficiently extensive to deprive the Indians of their customary usage of water. A long and bitter struggle ensued for control of the waters of the Yakima River. The white settlers in the area sent "various petitions" to Washington in hopes of persuading Congress to give them clear title to the water...The dispute dragged on for years...Being upstream, the non-Indian irrigators exercised the right of possession and left the Indians with little or no water in dry months. Finally, in 1913 the secretary of interior arbitrarily divided the water between the [Yakimas] and [a] reclamation project.

The amount he awarded the Indians was insufficient to irrigate most of the lands they had historically [used].[26]

Although the *Winters* precedent provided an ample basis for litigation on behalf of the Yakimas, Congress provided a "legislative remedy" in 1915, enacting a bill appropriating funds to buy water from its own Reclamation Service to meet the reservation's needs.

The new law enraged the settlers in the area and did not put an end to the Indians' water rights difficulties. In 1915 the chief engineer for the BIA [Bureau of Indian Affairs] wrote that the situation at Yakima was "delicate and might blow up like a powder magazine at almost any time." Disputes and litigation continued for years, the BIA chief of irrigation concluding in his 1917 annual report that in the Yakima Valley "the ownership of irrigation water apparently will always be subject to more or less successful assaults." Today [1991] the Yakima [Nation] and non-Indian irrigators are still locked in bitter conflict.[27]

Comparable situations were developing throughout the West. At about the same time the Yakima situation was unfolding, the Pima and Maricopa O'Odham peoples of the Gila River Reservation, established in southern Arizona in 1869, were in a similar circumstance.

The [Pimas and Maricopas] had a long history of irrigated farming and were quite prosperous until settlers moved in and diverted the Gila River. The government did nothing to stop these diversions and by the turn of the century, this once prosperous [people] was starving and destitute. The [nation's] fortunes plummeted so rapidly that the first decade of the twentieth century is known as the "black decade."[28]

The Reclamation Service, with BIA endorsement, responded to the Indians' "plight" (a plight is something natural and unavoidable; the Indians' problems were deliberately and humanly caused), not by challenging the settlers' expropriation of Pima-Maricopa water, but by advocating what the government wanted done in Arizona anyway. In 1915, it was recommended to Congress that a dam—a smaller complement to the Roosevelt Dam, which had been built in 1911—be built on the Gila River. The suggestion was quickly approved, but was not funded until 1924. The structure was completed in 1929,[29] with half its contents allocated to federally approved non-Indian users. The remaining half was maintained primarily as a federal water reserve under the premise that the relative trickle released for native use was one of the "first important steps which had been done for these Pima Indians for the 30 or 40 years their water supply has been encroached upon by whites."[30] The extent to which this was true has been described by journalist James Bishop, Jr., writing in 1991.

Have you been to the Gila River lately? Its upper reaches have been dammed and diverted for mining, agricultural, and urban uses, and by the time you cross it on the reservation on Interstate 10, you're on a big bridge over a gulch of sand. This has been the true story of the development of Arizona.[31]

While all this was getting under way, the Gros Ventres and Assiniboines of Fort Belknap, having served their purpose as props with which the federal government staged its capture of a preeminent position vis-à-vis the states in regard to control over western water, had been left to languish. In 1915, seven years after the *Winters* decision was rendered, only 7,670 of their 34,000 readily irrigable acres were under any sort of cultivation because, as the local BIA superintendent cabled the commissioner of Indian affairs, the entire flow of the Milk River was still being diverted by non-Indians upstream.[32] In 1920, the farm foreman at Fort Belknap reported the situation was essentially the same. In 1928, the BIA requested that the Justice Department take action to ensure that at least some of the water ostensibly available to the Indians of Fort Belknap under *Winters* actually would be provided them. An on-site investigation the same year concluded that this would be "impossible."[33] A BIA irrigation project begun at the time—using Indian funds, for which they were to be "reimbursed"[34]—was never completed and, by 1977, had fallen into almost total disrepair.[35] Nor was the money used to construct it ever repaid. Although reimbursement was finally authorized by Congress in 1985, it was opposed by BIA head Ross Swimmer and ultimately pocket-vetoed by Ronald Reagan.[36]

The *Winters* Doctrine in Practice

The ways in which the glowing Indian rights phraseology embedded in *Winters* was manipulated by the federal bureaucracy to its own ends, most usually at the direct expense of native people, have been both simple and sordid. As it has been put elsewhere:

> An enduring, intractable, and—from the standpoint of legal ethics—morally indefensible conflict of interest pervaded [enforcement of native water rights] and continues to do so to this day. The Interior Department, which through its Bureau of Reclamation (BuRec) was encouraging the rapid appropriation and development of water resources by non-Indian users...was also responsible through its [BIA] for protection of the Indians' reserved rights in the federal courts. Sadly but predictably, Interior was far more active and successful in discharging its former responsibility than its latter one...Without the political power necessary to get budgetary appropriations for Indian [projects], the tribes were incapable of converting the *Winters* rights guaranteed them by the Supreme Court into actual beneficial use of their waters. Meanwhile, the remaining water resources were rapidly being appropriated by non-Indians, with BuRec acquiescence and support [to federally approved users].[37]

A large part of how this has worked has had to do with tight interlocks—called "iron triangles" by one recent researcher—between the Bureau of Reclamation, state officials, and major corporate interests.[38] Once federal authority was firmly established as the controlling voice in western water issues, state governments adopted a more "cooperative" approach to dealing with the Bureau. In 1922, the seven Colorado River Basin states negotiated a compact on water apportionment among themselves.[39] Representatives of the indigenous nations lying within the same area were excluded from both participation and apportionment. The state of Arizona also declined to agree to the compact's terms. Nonetheless, BuRec strongly endorsed the compact, and it was ratified by Congress in 1928.[40] With this compact in hand, the governors of all seven states joined BuRec Director Elwood Mead in 1932 to form the National Reclamation Association (later the National Water Resources Association—NWRA).[41] The NWRA has historically been funded, partially on the basis of state legislative appropriations and partially through contributions from substantial corporate interests such as the western chambers of commerce, utilities and other businesses that profit heavily from utilization of water in certain ways.[42] Working in tandem with other organizations, such as the American Public Power Association, NWRA has been described as "the most powerful water lobby in the nation."[43]

There have always been plenty of incentives for corporate participation in the interlock. BuRec has never functioned as a construction enterprise, per se. Instead, it has supervised building on a grand scale, awarding contracts amounting to billions of dollars since 1930. Primary beneficiaries of this largesse have been the Six Companies, Inc., a consortium of a half-dozen of the largest construction firms in the world (Utah Construction of Salt Lake City; the W.A. Bechtel, J.H. Kaiser, and McDonald & Kahn Corporations of San Francisco; J.F. Shae and Pacific Bridge Corporations of Portland, Oregon; and Morrison-Knudson Corporation of Boise, Idaho).[44] By 1979, this combination of firms, as well as a scattering of lesser actors, had completed irrigation of eleven million acres of western land, all of it designated for non-Indian usage, with another nine million acres to be irrigated upon comple- tion of projects then in process. They had also built fifty power plants with six million kilowatts of power "on line" and another 4.5 million kilowatt capacity under construction. About 14,590 miles of canals, 990 miles of pipelines, 230 miles of tunnels, 35,160 miles of laterals, 15,750 miles of project drains and 16,236 miles of transmission systems had been constructed. In addition, 345 diversion dams had been completed, providing 3.5 million acre-feet of municipal and industrial water delivery each year, with another 1.6 million acro-feet of capacity under way.[45]

In order to appreciate the true extent of water development for non-Indian use, much of it for commercial or corporate purposes, one must also look beyond BuRec to that quasi-autonomous governmental construction firm, the Army Corps of Engineers. By 1976, the Corps reported it had completed more than 4,000 projects valued at $88 billion.[46] These included the building of some 19,000 miles of waterways, 500 harbors, 350 reservoirs, 9,000 miles of flood control structures, 7,500 miles of "improved" channels, and fifty hydropower facilities with a gener- ating capacity of twelve million kilowatts.[47] Although much of this does not relate to water consumption or directly affect reservation land, a sizable portion of it does. The Kinzua Dam in Pennsylvania, for instance, flooded most of the Seneca national territory.[48] Moreover, when BuRec and the Corps of Engineers were brought together in 1978 under the Senate Subcommittee for Water Resources (Committee on Environment and Public Works), a sort of governmental "super group" was created with which to approach such tasks in an even "more coordinated, efficient and industrious" manner.[49]

Indication of what this phrase means for Indians may best be illustrated by the effects of the so-called "Pick-Sloan Plan," a massive complex of 107 dams built jointly by BuRec and the Corps of Engineers along the Missouri River during the 1950s and '60s to generate hydroelectrical power and facilitate water diversion. As concerns the Fort Berthold Reservation, shared by the Arikara, Mandan, and Hidatsa peoples of the upper Missouri, "One-fourth of the reservation was flooded, including the best and most valuable and productive land on the reservation—the bottom lands along the river where most of the people lived."[50]

> Fort Berthold was not the only reservation to be flooded by the Corps of Engineers on the Missouri River. Five different Sioux reservations [Standing Rock, Cheyenne River, Crow Creek, Cherry Creek, and Yankton] also lost land. Again, the impact was quite severe: over one-third of the family members of [the] reservations were relocated. The dams destroyed nearly 90 percent of the tribes' timberland, 75 percent of the wild game, and the best agricultural lands.[51]

Ultimately, the Pick-Sloan Plan cost the indigenous nations of the Missouri River Valley an estimated 350,000 acres of their best land—including a number of burial and other sacred sites—as well as further impoverishment and severe cultural and emotional trauma.[52] Virtually every drop of the water accruing from the finished Missouri River Basin Development Program (MRDP) was consigned to non-Indian use. A guarantee, used to rationalize the plan in the first place, that some 216,000 acres of Indian land would be irrigated was simply scrapped as the project neared completion.[53] As researcher Bernard Shanks has put it:

> [MRDP] replaced the subsistence economy of the Missouri River Indians...with a welfare economy...As a result of the project, the Indians bore a disproportionate share of the social cost of water development, while having no share in the benefits.[54]

By contrast to this vast emphasis upon the needs of non-Indians, almost nothing was done to provide water to Indian users, real or potential, during the sixty years following *Winters*. As of 1968, it was officially estimated that only about percent of all potential agricultural land on western reservations had been irrigated.[55] One reason for this was, as James Officer, a former associate commissioner of indian affairs, noted in 1983:

> I found getting appropriations for Indian irrigation projects to be the most difficult task I had to face. The appropriations committees, as well as the representatives of the Budget Bureau [now Office of Management and Budget], could find dozens of reasons for denying money...for Indian irrigation projects, while endorsing gigantic sums to fund reclamation projects [for non-Indians] with much worse cost-benefit ratios in the districts of influential congressmen.[56]

The problem was particularly acute in extremely arid locales like southern

Arizona, where the non-Indian population was burgeoning. The city of Tucson, for example, underwent a near 400 percent population increase—from 45,000 to 213,000—between 1950 and 1960. By 1970, an additional 50,000 had been added, and the same growth rate has been sustained thereafter.[57] Much the same pattern, on an even larger scale, has prevailed in Phoenix, 120 miles to the north. This rapidly expanding urban sprawl (within one of the continent's least suitable areas for cities) had spawned a proliferation of administrative entities euphemistically titled "water conservation districts" designed to deliver a maximum quantity of water for residential and industrial consumption to enterprises such as the Salt River Project. By 1991, the latter entity alone was utilizing 133 miles of canals and 1,132 miles of ditches and laterals to provide Phoenix with water belonging to eight separate Indian reservations.[58]

Beginning in the early 1960s, the *de facto* federal freeze on water development devoted to native use finally thawed somewhat, but only as a variation on the scenario played out in *Winters,* with Indian rights used as a device by which to coerce an acceptably compliant posture on the part of western states. The issue concerned interstate squabbling—specifically a suit repeatedly filed by Arizona to diminish or deny California's share of Colorado River water—which threatened the orderly functioning of federal/state/corporate planning and development. Initially filed in 1931, the suit was dismissed in federal court in 1933, a circumstance that provoked the governor of Arizona to call out the state's National Guard in an attempt to physically block diversion of water to California. Under federal pressure, Arizona grudgingly joined the interstate compact in 1944, but reinstated its suit in 1951 as part of an effort to increase the quantity of water available for its Central Arizona Project CAP (designed to divert a portion of the Colorado River to Phoenix and Tucson. The project has consumed billions of dollars and is still unfinished.)[59]

It was twelve years before the Supreme Court finally rendered its decision in the case. In its opinion, written by Justice Hugo Black, the high court denied Arizona's contentions before shifting focus to the fact that no Indian allocations had been included in the compact's division of Colorado River water. It thereupon ordered each of the participating states' apportionments reduced by the amount necessary to service "all practicably irrigable acreage" on regional reservations.[60] Although the court's decision provided a measurement of what this meant in terms of actual water volume with regard to only a handful of small groups located on the Fort Mohave, Chemehuevi, Cocopah, and Fort Yuma Reservations, the clear implication was that all indigenous water rights within the compact states were to be quantified, and at a maximum feasible level with regard to agriculture. By the end of the '80s, this was computed as totaling approximately 45.9 million acre-feet per year, or about four times the total annual flow of the Colorado River.[61] Put another way, the 1963 *Arizona v. California* decision removed every drop of water in the West from local control. The message to the western states was plain enough: "Either play ball with federal planners, or face very severe penalties."

The central government punctuated its point by initiating what it called the

"Navajo Indian Irrigation Project" (NIIP). The viability of such an effort had previously been ascertained by federal engineers during the early 1940s.[62] Despite the obvious desperate need of the Diné (Navajos) for the sort of economic boost irrigation might have provided, however, nothing at all was done with the idea until Washington perceived it as a way of disciplining recalcitrant state governments and consolidating its own grip on water-use decisionmaking. Having accomplished this objective by the early '60s, the government then used the project as a double-edged sword, a means by which to begin obliterating legal recognition of the very native water rights under the *Winters* Doctrine it had itself traded upon for more than fifty years.

Authorized by Congress in 1962, the plan called for diversion of a half-million acre-feet per year from the San Juan River, a tributary of the Colorado, to fields surrounding the reservation town of Shiprock, New Mexico. Funding for construction was slated to be incremental, allocated in "phases" as the project moved along over a twenty year period.[63] Commencement of the undertaking was, however, left contingent upon the Diné acquiring approval from the compact states.[64] This placed the Indians in the position of having to negotiate an arrangement acceptable to parties who had been systematically stealing their water for decades if they were to receive any portion of their resource at all. BuRec, of course, volunteered to "assist" in these "delicate discussions." The results have been described elsewhere:

> First, New Mexico agreed to support the Navajo proposal if its authorizing legislation provided for the construction of a companion project to water the San Juan and into the greater Rio Grande watershed for non-Indian use within New Mexico. Second, the Navajo Tribal Council agreed to the guaranteed delivery of 508,000 acre-feet of water annually through its proposed project in exchange for sharing water resources during dry years with other San Juan water users. *They also agreed that during drought years they would not assert senior rights based on the 1868 founding date of the Navajo Reservation* [emphasis added].[65]

Thus, Washington neatly reversed its historical casting of Indians as "heavies" vis-à-vis state water rights by having the states play exactly the same part with regard to native rights. For their part, the Diné were forced to set a paradoxical precedent wherein Indians could exercise rights under the *Winters* Doctrine only by "voluntarily" relinquishing them, establishing the current federally preferred model of "negotiated settlements" between states and indigenous nations whenever the latter's reserved rights are at issue. Further, the NIIP affords a perfect example of exactly what native peoples might expect to receive in exchange for entering into procedures in which they are expected to be so "reasonable" as to legitimate the expropriation of their property as a *quid pro quo* before they are allowed to use some portion of it themselves.

While the NIIP and New Mexico's San Juan-Chama Project were authorized under the same act, with the latter ostensibly due only to existence of the former, Congress appropriated funds for their completion in precisely reverse order. By

1970, NIIP was about 17 percent completed while the state project was more than 65 percent operational.[66] In 1974, the Interior Department "corrected" the problem by unilaterally reducing the water volume allocated to the NIIP from 508,000 to 370,000 acre-feet per year—the BIA had computed the actual Diné entitlement within the San Juan watershed at 787,000 annual acre-feet in 1943—while leaving all Indian obligations and relinquishments under the arrangement unchanged.[67] As of this writing, although the San Juan-Chama irrigation system has been fully functional for nearly a decade, the Diné have still received only a fraction of even their reduced entitlement.[68]

The Post-*Winters* Context

In some ways, the federal government misjudged the situation when it entered into its post-*Winters* strategy in the aftermath of *Arizona v. California.* For one thing, the policy shift occurred at the onset of a wave of increasing indigenous militancy ushered in by fishing rights confrontations in the Pacific Northwest (see Chapter Seven) and culminating in pitched battles between members of the American Indian Movement (AIM) and the federal government a decade later (see Chapter Ten). AIM's tactics emerged within a much wider panorama of direct action deployed by an array of movements for social justice—from African-Americans' civil rights and black liberation movements, to anti-war activism, to gay rights and women's liberation struggles—which, temporarily at least, impaired the ability of the U.S. status quo to function as it liked.

Additionally, this social ferment coincided with the maturation of the first generation of American Indian political strategists and attorneys ready, willing, and able to engage in a sort of policymaking and juridical "ju jitsu" with the "rules of the game" enunciated by Congress and the federal courts. Not just treaty rights, but statutes like the Clean Water Act (33 U.S.C. 1251, *et seq.*), Resource Conservation and Recovery Act (42 U.S.C. 6901) and the Safe Water Drinking Act (42 U.S.C. 300f) were therefore brought increasingly to bear in litigation and negotiation of indigenous water rights. Similarly, beginning in 1977, Native Americans began to gain increasing access to international forums such as the United Nations, through which new and sometimes effective sorts of pressure can be brought to bear upon the U.S. (see Chapters Three and Five). All of this added up, between 1965 and 1980, to a radical alteration of the context in which indigenous water rights were pursued.

One of the methods employed in this regard has been to attempt to figuratively bury the judiciary in water rights lawsuits. In 1984, Secretary of the Interior William Clark estimated that there had been at least 4,000 native water rights cases brought before federal courts since 1908, the bulk of them after 1970. He also noted that the rate at which they were being filed appeared to be increasing, and that they were of an ever more complex nature.[69] Many—perhaps most—of these suits have accomplished little in and of themselves. Indeed, some have led to adverse decisions as Reagan-appointed Supreme Court justices began to make their presence felt during the 1980s. For example, in *Montana v. U.S.* (450 U.S. 544 (1981)), a case

involving ownership of the bed of the Little Big Horn River on the Northern
Cheyenne Reservation:

> In a decision remarkable for its abandonment of traditional doctrines of treaty
> interpretation, the Court held that creation of an Indian reservation fails to
> establish riverbed ownership [of an indigenous nation] unless the language of
> the treaty, agreement, or executive order establishing the reservation specifies
> [this].[70]

The purpose of litigation, however, is not always so much to score a "win" in
court as it is to extend the threat that you *might*, and that you can in any event tie
up your opponent's use of water in whole or in part for the duration of the case.
Both factors tend to better the bargaining position of the party filing the suit, can be
used to facilitate the development of political alliances useful in extra-legal action
and often serve as vehicles for public education campaigns.[71] Such multifaceted
approaches have begun to yield mixed but sometimes favorable results for indigenous nations pursuing water rights for the first time in U.S. history. One measure
of this is that irrigated reservation acreage has increased by more than 750 percent
since 1968.[72] Another is that native nations have in some cases been able to end or
at least curtail non-Indian water-use patterns that negatively impact traditional
cultures and economies. Yet another has been instances in which Indians have been
able to sell or lease some portion of their water rights to non-Indian users without
waiving their broader reserved rights.

An illustration of how this has worked in practice concerns the Pyramid Lake
Paiutes of Nevada who filed a suit in 1973 to set aside the so-called Orr Ditch Decree
of 1944, apportioning water between the Paiutes and a range of non-Indian users.
The Indian contention was that federal agreement in their behalf (but without their
consent) to receipt of a very small share of the annual flow from the Truckee River
was unconscionable, both because it effectively voided their reserved water rights
and because it had led to the rapid depletion of Pyramid Lake, the Lahontan trout
from which formed the core of their economy.[73] In 1983, the Supreme Court rejected
this argument, not on its merits but because the "Court did not want to set a
precedent of reopening cases already settled by judicial-consent decrees, even if
those settlements seemed unjust by contemporary standards."[74] The Paiutes immediately announced they would file new suits in an attempt to change this grossly
unfair ruling, a course of action which stood to enjoin further water development
in the Truckee watershed indefinitely. The federal government, which had plans to
engage in a major regional project for non-Indian consumption, thereupon decided
it was time to abandon the Orr Decree itself.

> By 1989 a settlement had been fashioned that would empower the Interior
> Secretary to buy up water rights...to maintain habitats in state and federal
> wildlife preserves as well as in Pyramid Lake. As embodied in legislation
> submitted to Congress in 1989, the agreement also authorized water rights
> exchange and sharing agreements. The [Paiutes] would dismiss pending law-
> suits and the federal government would restore [their] fisheries habitat...Con-

gress would also set aside a $75 million trust fund for tribal economic development.[75]

Comparable examples have emerged in the Northwest. In Oregon, the Umatilla Confederated Tribes filed a successful 1977 suit arguing that the Army Corps of Engineers, which constructed the Chief Joseph Dam, illegally interfered with the water flow necessary to the spawning of salmon and steelhead trout that were the basis of their economy.[76] At about the same time, in Washington state, the Colville Confederated Tribes filed a similar suit, upheld by the Ninth Circuit Court, with regard to the Corps' Catherine Creek Lake Dam.[77] In both cases, the courts ordered the devising of a plan "in the public interest" that would correct the problem. This led to the evolution of an unlikely alliance between Indians, environmental activists, the non-Indian sport-fishing industry and the U.S. Forest Service, which, by 1991, appears to be headed toward achieving removal of at least one, and perhaps both, of the dams within two years.[78] The positive environmental effects of such an outcome are undeniable.

Murkier illustrations of the same trend are evident in Florida and California. In Florida, the Seminoles brought a quiet-title suit against Everglades-area landholders in 1978 that led directly to questions of both surface and ground water rights.[79] A negotiated settlement, arrived at in 1987 and ratified by statute the same year, resulted in the Indians' relinquishing a portion of their land rights in exchange for clarification of their water entitlements within their remaining territory, monetary compensation, and a voice in local water-use policy, which may have a beneficial impact upon the Everglades Ecological Disaster Area.[80] A year later, the tiny Mission Bands (Juaneños, Luiseños, Digueños, Rincóns, La Jollas, and others) of southern California, many of them restricted to "reservations" as small as a single acre, were collectively able to obtain a water rights settlement agreement in which they were assured of 14,000 acre-feet annually.[81] What is most interesting about the arrangement is that it was centered in a conservation measure requiring major agribusiness interests in the California Central Valley to retrofit the eighty-year-old All American Canal with a lining to reduce water loss during distribution.[82] The Indians' share of water is projected to accrue from the savings, and a $30 million federal trust fund was established to finance native administration of some portions of the project. What is troubling is that a *quid pro quo* was established wherein the Indians were forced to foreswear further claims to reserved water rights the federal government had illegally brokered away in 1914 and 1924.[83]

In some instances, the results of negotiation have been far worse. For example, there is the case of the Ak Chin O'Odham Indian Community, located in the Santa Cruz River Basin, about fifty miles south of Phoenix. In 1978, confronted with the possibility of a massive Ak Chin water rights suit, Congress engineered an alternative proposal in which the Ak Chin would relinquish all reserved rights to ground water (confirmed by *U.S. v. Cappaert* in 1974)[84] in exchange for an annual guarantee of 60,000 acre-feet provided from federal sources and a $40 million allocation to build the required distribution system.[85] As it turned out, the project required an additional $50 million in allocations due to miscalculations of the cost of the required technology. In 1983, a bill to implement a revised plan and appropriate the corresponding sum was vetoed by Ronald Reagan under a premise that the matter was a "purely local problem," requiring considerable contributions from the state, Phoenix, and the surrounding suburbs.[86] The Reagan administration also demanded a clearer renunciation of Ak Chin reserved rights before agreeing to provide any water at all. Eventually, this was accommodated by a clause—accepted by the Ak Chins—providing cash compensation in the event the government failed to deliver on its promises in any given year. This legitimated the placing of a higher priority on the needs of non-Indian users than of the Ak Chins, even with water directly allocated to the reservation.[87]

Similarly, the administration balked on finalizing a 1982 agreement between Arizona, the city of Tucson, and the Tohono O'Odham (Papago) Nation until the state and city agreed to make substantial financial contributions toward meeting federal obligations, and the Indians agreed not only to less than the 160,000 annual acre-feet of water to which they were entitled, but to waive all reserved water rights as well.[88] The state agreed under the pressure produced by the outcome of a federal case brought by the San Carlos (Chiricahua) Apaches, suggesting that indigenous water rights claims might subsequently have to be satisfied through state courts with no federal participation at all.[89] The city went along because it was using its own groundwater—virtually the only source available until CAP pipelines reach it some time early in the next century—three times faster than it is naturally replenished.[90] Although their bargaining position was theoretically very strong, the Tohonos were convinced by Morris Udall, the "friendly" Arizona representative who heads the House Committee on Interior and Insular Affairs, that if they refused the deal their water would simply be expropriated (this was probably untrue, as is shown below in the Salt River Pima-Maricopa example).

> The [Tohonos] agreed to abandon their *Winters* Doctrine claims to the ground-water underlying the eastern districts of the reservation in return for delivery of close to [76,000] acre-feet of agricultural-quality water to its lands [40,000 acre-feet to the main Papago Reservation and about 36,000 to the smaller San Xavier Reservation] through the uncompleted Central Arizona Project and/or through the Interior Secretary's purchase of water and water rights from willing sellers. The Indians also agreed to accept money damages [$5 million per year] instead of wet water in the event the Central Arizona Project was not completed or the agreement proved otherwise unfeasible...[Even then, the] bill escaped a veto...because Congressman Udall attached it as a rider to a piece of legislation the president wanted—an amendment to the reclamation act allowing large landholders (e.g., agribusiness interests in California's Central Valley) easier access to cheap water from federal reclamation projects.[91]

The Reaganites' manipulation of the Ak Chin and Tohono settlement acts for purposes entirely contrary to Indian interests illuminated what was to become the standard administration position on Indian water rights negotiations throughout the '80s. The emergent "Reagan Doctrine" was to pursue "comprehensive settle-ments" which would negate indigenous reserved rights, preferably in ways making such water as was actually committed to Indian use of more benefit to area whites than to native people themselves, while laying off as much of the attendant cost as possible upon cities and states. A classic example is the accord accepted by the Southern Utes and Ute Mountain Utes of Colorado in 1988. Although both peoples were in a perfect position to "gain a substantial entitlement from [a] lawsuit and also tie up everybody else's rights in the region for years,"[92] Representative Ben Nighthorse Campbell—the only "Indian" in Congress —the tribal councils involved to drop litigation in favor of a "compromise agreement." Colorado Ute reserved rights were then permanently forfeited in exchange for what may amount to nothing at all.[93]

> As adopted in September of 1988, the [Colorado Ute Indian Water Rights Settlement Act] provided for 70,000 acre-feet of water to the Southern Ute and Ute Mountain tribes through the partially completed Delores Project and the as-yet-unconstructed Animas-La Plata Project...[It is] unquestionable that the primary beneficiaries will be non-Indian farmers.[94]

In Montana, meanwhile, a cluster of five promising suits finally forced the state to enter into negotiations with the indigenous nations to whom it had been systematically and illegally denying water since 1908.[95] With federal assistance, however, Montana was able to push through an instrument, first accepted in 1985 by the tribal council of the Fort Peck Reservation (occupied by Assiniboines and Yanktonai Dakotas), which involved abandonment of the very reserved rights upon which the suits were based, and which had been theoretically won in the same state seventy-seven years earlier. In exchange, 525,236 acre-feet of water per year, as well as the right to regulate it (subject to approval of their water codes by the secretary of interior), were "guaranteed" to the indigenous nations of Montana, but no funds with which to construct irrigation and other distribution systems or compensation in the event the water was never delivered. In principle, the necessary money is to derive exclusively from sales of up to 50,000 acre-feet of water per year to non-Indian users, a complete default on its obligations by the U.S.[96] Continuing its traditional style, the Montana Euroamerican population proved itself as virulently racist as ever, even in response to this patent abrogation of native water rights. Two stridently anti-Indian organizations—the Citizens' Rights Organization and Montanans Opposed to Discrimination—had already been formed to try to block the settlement, and the Montana Cattlemen's Association passed a resolution demanding abolition of the reservations rather than an agreement of any sort.[97]

Having learned from such disasters by mid-decade, some native nations were able to forge better terms for themselves during the second half of the '80s. The Salt River Pima-Maricopa Community, for instance, adopted a much different negotiating stance than had their Ak Chin and Tohono O'Odham relatives only a few years previously. Having filed a successful 1983 suit arguing that both the 1911 Roosevelt Dam (the oldest reclamation structure in the country) and the subsequent Granite Reef diversion dam on the Salt River represented illegal takings of reservation water,[98] the Indians simply refused to sign *any* agreement legitimizing consumption by nearby Phoenix until provisions acceptable to themselves formed the basis of

206
The State of Native America

the arrangement. With important surface water sources in jeopardy, the state and area cities came around fairly rapidly, and a deal was ratified by Congress in 1988.[99]

> This exceedingly complex agreement provides for water exchanges among various user groups in the Salt River valley, involving Central Arizona Project water and a variety of other sources...Under the agreement, water resources accruing to the Indian community total just over 120,000 acre-feet per year...Although the payment of money damages to [the Indians] is contemplated in the event the agreement fails, [they are] not barred from relitigating in the event the federal or state governments fail to honor the bargain [they thus retain reserved rights]. The [reservation] is specifically empowered to sell water at a rate fixed in the agreement to surrounding cities in the Phoenix metropolitan area...The federal government agreed to contribute a total of $58 million to implement the settlement, some of which [is] deposited in a $29 million trust fund, with interest also used to implement the act...the state and Phoenix area cities will contribute $28 million to implementation of the agreement (the Indians will contribute $2 million) and as much as an additional $96 million worth of water.[100]

Another striking victory was attained in Utah, where the very idea that the Ouray and Uintah Utes might pursue protracted suits tying up non-Indian water use in the wake of *Arizona v. California* prompted state officials to enter into multilateral negotiations with both the Indians and the federal government. Although the process was quite lengthy, ultimately taking more than twenty years, it finally resulted in a 1989 agreement by which the two reservations were jointly guaranteed 250,000 acre-feet of water per year, plus allocation of $515 million to provide for a water delivery infrastructure and capitalization for Ute economic development programs. In effect, the Utah Utes ultimately agreed in principle to waive reserved rights, but only in exchange for an apportionment of water equivalent to the amount required by their own estimates to service irrigable reservation acreage, and with retention of the right to sue in the event of any default by federal or state governments.[101]

At this point, the largest of all Arizona water cases is before the courts. Known in aggregate as the "Gila River Adjudication," it involves rights to the effluent from all six watersheds within the state and more than 65,000 separate claims by the federal government (for Luke Air Force Base, the Army's Fort Huachuca, the Bureau of Land Management and U.S. Forest Service, national parks and monuments, and assorted fish and wildlife refuges), municipalities such as Phoenix and Tucson, as well as corporations like Phelps Dodge, utilities, agricultural districts, water companies, and a variety of private parties. Primary litigants have been the peoples of twelve Indian reservations, only two of whom have reached settlements, both patterned after that achieved by the Salt River Pima-Maricopas. The first is the Fort McDowell Indian (Yavapai) Community, located on the Verde River, east of Scottsdale, "although some final details have yet to be ironed out."[102] As to the second:

> Now pending in Congress is the San Carlos Apache Indian Water Rights Act of 1991. Both the House and Senate bills call for 152,000 acre-feet for the [Indians], and cash development funds of some $39 million, payable...over the next three years.[103]

The sentiment prevailing among remaining native litigants in the Gila River action is perhaps best illustrated by the posture of the White Mountain (Chiricahua) Apaches, who filed a suit to block the Interior and Justice Departments from representing their interests in 1983, the moment a waiver of reserved water rights was mentioned by a federal representative.[104] A similar perspective is evident among indigenous nations who have entered, or are preparing to enter, major water rights suits in California, New Mexico, western Oklahoma, North Dakota, Idaho, and Washington.[105] These proverbial chickens hatched under the historical denial of indigenous water rights by the U.S. and its settler population are finally beginning to come home to roost with a vengeance. As Jennele Morris O'Hair, assistant city attorney for Glendale, a wealthy Phoenix suburb, has complained, "What most people don't realize is that when the final decree comes down, there will be a drastic reallocation of water. Non-Indians will still have some use of the water, but the Indians will have rights to most of it. They'll lease it back, but we'll pay much more for it."[106]

Lloyd Burton, a careful Euroamerican researcher of the issue, takes a different view:

> The often-heard lamentation over the absence of a free lunch is certainly nowhere more applicable than to the dilemma over American Indian water rights. The debt to [native nations] incurred and ignored by our fathers must be paid, either by us or by our children. That payment may be in lost water, as the doctrine of federal reserved rights inevitably makes preemptive inroads into state water law...For over eight decades now American society has had the moral satisfaction of knowing the Supreme Court in *Winters v. U.S.* did the right thing in protecting Indian water rights in theory; but we have not taken the fiscal responsibility for acknowledging those rights in fact. With the current onslaught of litigation over water rights, the debt has come due. And in one coin or another, it must be paid.[107]

Looking Forward

Burton also observes that, "many American Indian [nations] feel at this juncture conflict (water rights litigation) and not cooperation is the key to their survival as cultural and national entities. The survival instinct in the arid West is not drawing Indian and non-Indian peoples together; it is driving them apart. Until the Euro-American culture can convincingly demonstrate the ability of cooperative effort to insure the survival of all peoples in the West, the Indians will have no reason to make peace."[108] William Swan, an attorney involved in western water rights litigation for the Interior Department, concurs: "The last chapter of the Indian wars hasn't been written yet. This time, it's not being fought with Winchesters, axes, bows and arrows, but between lawyers in courtrooms."[109] Neither individual overstates the situation, a matter confirmed by Madonna Thunderhawk, a Hunkpapa Lakota AIM member, one of the group that founded Women of All Red Nations (WARN), and long-time water rights activist on the Standing Rock Reservation in North Dakota.

> Water is the life blood, the key to the whole thing. Without water, our land rights struggles—even if we were to win back every square inch of our unceded

lands—would be meaningless. With the water which is ours by aboriginal right, by treaty right, and by simple moral right, we Indians can recover our self-sufficiency and our self-determination. Without that water, we are condemned to perpetual poverty, erosion of our land base, our culture, our population itself. If we do not recover our water rights, we are dooming ourselves to extinction. It's that simple. And so I say that the very front line of the Indian liberation struggle, at least in the plains and desert regions, is the battle for control over our water.[110]

Indeed, it is far more than a question of drinking and bathing. One aspect is that there are deep spiritual and cultural considerations involved with the destruction of irreplaceable portions of indigenous sacred geography through non-Indian water prioritization and concomitant construction of facilities such as the aforementioned Pick-Sloan dams, the Glen Canyon in southern Utah, and the Tellico Dam in eastern Tennessee.[111] Another is that with even a fraction of the water to which they are entitled throughout the West, indigenous nations could at last reestablish the agricultural economies that, in many cases, are central to their heritage.[112] It would then be possible for them to feed their peoples and free themselves from subsistence dependency on federal commodities and welfare programs, and create an alternative to the sorts of deadly extractive and transient industries described in Chapter Eight. With anything approaching the full quota of water to which they are entitled, native nations could actually begin to market it to non-Indian users in much the same way other resources like oil, natural gas, and various minerals are now marketable.

This would truly form the basis for achieving the native self-sufficiency and self-determination called for by Thunderhawk. The ramifications, however, extend much further. With control over their water, indigenous nations would be in a position to substantially increase the price per acre-foot throughout the West, or even withhold water altogether from certain uses.[113] This would have an immediate and unequivocally positive effect upon the extent to which the immigrant population could devote itself to watering the myriad lawns and golf course turfs, all of them sodded with alien grasses imported from humid zones, with which it has burdened the arid ecosphere of the western plains and deserts. Doubtless, millions of swimming pools and "Big Surf" recreation centers in places like Phoenix, Albuquerque, and Denver would have to stand empty. Such accoutrements of "civilization" as drive-through car washes would quickly become cost-prohibitive.

In turn, these "deprivations" would undoubtedly do much to end the cancer-like population growth patterns which have been increasingly apparent over the past few decades in such waterless or nearly waterless locales as southern Arizona and California, northern New Mexico and the Colorado front range. Probably, they would result in an outright reversal of the present demographic trend, eventually paring down the sheer numbers of human residents in the West to a level sustainable by plains and desert habitats, leaving a residual populace composed of persons who genuinely appreciate the harsh environments in which they live.[114] As water consumption levels are lowered, both by alterations in use patterns and by corresponding diminishment of population density, the western ecology, so seriously disrupted since 1950, can begin revitalizing and recharging itself. Perhaps ironically, the kind of dramatic population reduction in the West at issue makes not only ecological, but *economic* sense.[115]

Nor do the favorable ripple effects end there. Any reversal of the displacement of people from the already overpopulated eastern regions of the U.S. can only result in an increasing awareness on the part of the population as a whole of what indigenous people and other astute observers have known for a long time: There have come to be far, far too many people on the continent overall.[116] The much-vaunted "American quality of life" is most probably not possible over the long haul in any event (and, for that matter, was never possible for most people in the first place) and can only be approximated in the years ahead on the basis of a steady decline rather than perpetual increase in the numbers of people pursuing it. The U.S., to borrow an oft-repeated phrase used by most radicals and progressives (and practiced by almost none of them), "must learn to live within its means," a cognitive consideration that leads unerringly to a fundamental redefinition of what "quality of life" really means.[117] Plainly, the realization of indegenous water rights in the West is a vital key to any genuine reconceptualization of priorities among the wider population.

In the alternative, the process in which we are now enmeshed will continue to its next logical level of destructiveness. If past denials of native water rights can be said to have led directly to what amounts to a "hydrological engineering" of the West by the Bureau of Reclamation and Army Corps of Engineers—with all the diversion of tax dollars to corporate profits, human misery, and environmental degradation this implies—planned "solutions" to the problems created by such policies thus far are truly staggering. They amount to a comparable re-engineering of the ecosystem of the entire continent. This assumes the form of the North American Water and Power Alliance (NAWAPA), called by *Newsweek* the "greatest, the most colossal, stupendous, supersplendificent public-works project in history."[118] The scheme, devised by the Ralph M. Parsons Company of Los Angeles during the 1960s, is "to divert 36 trillion trillion gallons of water [per year] from the Yukon River in Alaska [through the Great Bear and Great Slave Lakes, southward] to thirty-three states, seven Canadian provinces, and northern Mexico."[119]

> The Rocky Mountain Trench, Peace River, Lesser Slave Lake, Athabasca River, North Saskatchewan River, Qu'Appell River, Columbia River, Fraser River, Nelson River, Lake Winnipeg, and the Hudson and James Bays as well as many of the tributaries of these are all treated in the NAWAPA plan and its variants as part of a gigantic, interlocked hydrological "feeder system" pumping Canadian fluids down to more southerly consumers.[120]

Part of the current, most comprehensive version of the NAWAPA plan entails bringing vast quantities of Alaskan and western Canadian water all the way down into the southern Río Grande watershed, watering assorted plains and desert states along the way, to develop the agricultural economy of the northern Sonora and Chihuahua provinces in Mexico under U.S. auspices.[121] A second part concerns channeling another huge flow into western Lake Superior as an expedient to boosting hydroelectric generating capacity and "flushing" industrial pollutants dumped into the

Great Lakes outward into the Atlantic Ocean.[122] A third section is concerned with converting much of northern Québec and Ontario into little more than hydroelectrical providers serving the east coast U.S. megalopolis, from Maine to Miami.[123]

Indications that all this is not hallucinatory are abundant. The James Bay I Project, completed during the early '70s in Québec, flooded an 11,000-square-kilometer area and pumps nearly 90 percent of its hydroelectrical output directly into the northeastern U.S. and Ohio. The James Bay II Project—currently underway in Ontario and projected eventually to incorporate more than eighty dams, divert at least three major rivers and dozens of tributaries, and flood an aggregate area about the size of West Germany (all of it traditional Cree territory)—will again deliver the near entirety of its "product" to U.S. consumers.[124] To the west, in British Columbia, the Bennett Dam, completed in 1971, created a reservoir more than ninety miles long. A second dam, completed at Moran Canyon on the Fraser in 1976, backed up water into a 170 mile "lake." Since then, another score of dams have been built along the Columbia River, and twenty-five more along the Fraser. Another thirteen have been built along the Thompson River, and as many as thirty more are either in progress or planned for the immediate future.[125] In the Prairie Provinces (Manitoba, Alberta, and Saskatchewan), the PRIME Project sets forth the mechanics by which the same sorts of construction will occur there as soon as funds permit.[126]

The infrastructure by which NAWAPA can be implemented is plainly being created. The consequences to subarctic ecosystems, already quite severe, could well become globally catastrophic in the event the project is consummated. As the matter has been framed elsewhere:

> What must be understood is that the Canadian north—like the Antarctic, the Amazon Basin in Brazil, and a few other portions of the globe—is absolutely essential to ecological survival. If it is destroyed, eventually everything else will be destroyed. We are all running out of "alternatives" and places to hide from the grim reality which now stalks us, regardless of where and how we live.[127]

It may be—as it will undoubtedly be argued in many non-Indian quarters—that assertion of native water rights in the fashion described in the concluding section of this essay will prove insufficient to avert the sort of incipient disaster represented by NAWAPA. Perhaps. But it must be said that there is really no other viable point of departure. American Indians, and they alone, occupy the first and best position, both legally and morally, from which to fight back. We have struggled for generations, usually all but alone, against the very mentality which has culminated in NAWAPA. As a result, Indian people have, far more than any other sector of the North American population, accumulated the mass of skills and experience necessary to use the U.S. legal system against itself in altering federal water policy. Should our sacrifice and juridical savvy at last be matched by recognition on the part of some substantial segment of the non-Indian population that indigenous nations' fight for control over western water serves not only legitimate native interests, but the interests of nearly everyone else as well, then the sort of political vision necessary to defeat the "NAWAPA Syndrome" *is* possible.

Paradoxically, then, the very issue which now most sharply divides Indians and non-Indians in arid regions could well be the mechanism that ultimately brings us together, not only in the West, but everywhere. This will require that non-Indians—radicals and progressives, at least—abandon for the first time in their history the pretension to superior rights over native lands and resources they have always shared with U.S. elites, finally making indigenous rights the number-one priority in North America they *should* have been all along. As the problems generated by the Euroamerican status quo crystalize more and more into questions of sheer survival for the general populace, this prospect for meaningful cooperation on the basis of common interest becomes an ever greater potentiality. Either way, it can be asserted with confidence that American Indians will not only continue to fight for control of water, but will adopt an ever harder line in doing so. Whether anyone joins us or not, we know beyond questioning that our survival, and yours, depends on it.

Notes

1. This concept was perhaps best articulated in *Wall v. Williamson* (8 Ala. 48, 51 (1845)): "It is only by positive enactments, even in the case of conquered and subdued nations, that their laws can be changed by the conqueror." This has led to passage of numerous statutes specifically diminishing native rights in the U.S.
2. In a concurring opinion authored in *Worcester v. Georgia* (1832), Justice McLean offered the idea that "the language used in treaties with the Indians should never be construed to their prejudice...How the words of the treaty were understood by this unlettered people, rather than their critical meaning, should form the rule of construction." As the principle is framed in *Carpenter v. Shaw* (280 U.S. 363, 367 (1930)): "Doubtful expressions are to be resolved in favor of the weak and defenseless people who are wards of the nation, dependent upon its protection and good faith." Of course, it is left to Congress, rather than the Indians, to decide what constitutes a "just resolution" in each dispute.
3. This series of transactions is covered quite well in Hundley, Norris, "The *Winters* Decision and Indian Water Rights: A Mystery Reexamined," *Western Historical Quarterly,* No. 13, 1982.
4. 25 *Stat.* 113 (1889).
5. See Gates, Paul, *The History of Public Land Law Development,* Zenger Publishing Co., Washington, D.C., 1968.
6. 28 *Stat.* 166 (1894). For more on the Carey Act, see Glass, Mary Ellen, *Water for Nevada: The Reclamation Controversy, 1885-1902,* University of Nevada Press, Reno, 1964.
7. Worcester, Donald, *Rivers of Empire,* Pantheon Books, New York, 1985, p. 157.
8. Excerpts from Powell's report and a broad exposition of his thinking on the matter are contained in Powell, John Wesley, *Canyons of the Colorado,* Flood and Vincent Publishers, New York, 1985 (reprinted as *The Exploration of the Colorado River and Its Canyons,* Dover Books, New York, 1961).
9. Quoted in Hays, Samuel P., *Conservation and the Gospel of Efficiency,* Harvard University Press, Cambridge, MA, 1959, p. 104.
10. The earlier statutes leading in the same direction as the Carey Act are the Homestead Act (12 Stat. 392, May 29, 1862), the Mining Act (14 *Stat.* 253, July 26, 1866), the Act of July 9, 1870 (16 *Stat.* 377), the Desert Lands Act (19 *Stat.* 377, 1877), and the Act of March 3, 1891 (26 *Stat.* 989). In addition, there were three statutes passed shortly after the Carey Act (29 *Stat.* 598, February 26, 1897; 29 *Stat.* 603, March 2, 1897; and 30 *Stat.* 11, June 4, 1897).
11. U.S. Congress, *Congressional Record,* U.S. Government Printing Office, Washington, D.C., 1902, p. 6777.
12. Ibid., p. 6766.
13. National Irrigation Congress, "Proceedings, 1905-1911," *National Journal,* April 9, 1977 (1906), p. 65.
14. U.S. Department of Interior, Reclamation Service, *Annual Report, 1902-1903,* U.S. Government Printing Office, Washington, D.C., 1903, p. 33.

15. In an undated Justice Department memorandum sent some time in December 1905, Rasch was instructed to "take promptly such action as may be necessary to protect the interests of the Indians against interference by subsequent appropriators of the Milk River."

16. See Clark, Ronald, ed., *Waters and Water Rights*, Smith and Co. Publishers, Indianapolis, 1978, Sec. 50.

17. Ibid.

18. *U.S. v. Mose Anderson, et al.*, Memorandum Order (December 1905).

19. Ibid.

20. *Winters, et al. v. United States*, 143 F.2d 743, 749 (1906). In 1939, the Ninth Circuit Court held that reserved water rights pertain to reservations created by executive order as well as those established by treaty or agreement. See *United States v. Walker River Irrigation District*, 104 F.2d 234.

21. *Winters v. United States*, 207 U.S. 564 (1908).

22. Burton, Lloyd, *American Indian Water Rights and the Limits of the Law*, University Press of Kansas, Lawrence, 1991, p. 21.

23. McCool, Daniel, *Command of the Waters: Iron Triangles, Federal Water Development, and Indian Water*, University of California Press, Berkeley, 1987, p. 51.

24. Ibid., p. 53.

25. The cases are analyzed in Andrews, Barbara T., and Marie Sansone, *Who Runs the Rivers? Dams and Decisions in the New West*, Stanford Environmental Law Society, Palo Alto, CA, 1983.

26. McCool, op. cit., p. 57. The author is drawing on McWhorter, Lucius, *Crime Against the Yakimas*, Republic Publishers, North Yakima, WA, 1913.

27. McCool, op. cit., p. 58.

28. Ibid., pp. 58-9. The author is drawing on Bowden, Charles, *Killing the Hidden Waters*, University of Texas Press, Austin, 1977, p. 85.

29. For background on the Pimas and the Roosevelt Dam project, see Folke-Williams, John, *What Indian Water Means to the West: A Sourcebook*, Western Network, Santa Fe, NM, 1982, pp. 36-9.

30. U.S. Department of Interior, Bureau of Indian Affairs, *Annual Report of the Commissioner of Indian Affairs, 1916*, U.S. Government Printing Office, Washington, D.C., 1916, p. 43.

31. Bishop, James Jr., "'Wet Water' Wars," *Phoenix Magazine*, June 1991, pp. 80-7. The term "wet water" refers to surface water, as opposed to the "ground water" deposited naturally in subterranean aquifers.

32. Abbott, F.H., "Brief on Indian Irrigation," *National Archives*, n.d. (circa 1915), R.G. 75, Irrigation Division, General Correspondence, 1901-1931, Special Topics, Miscellaneous.

33. U.S. Senate, Committee on Indian Affairs, Subcommittee on Resolution 79, *Survey of Conditions of the Indians in the United States*, 71st Cong., 2d Sess., U.S. Government Printing Office, Washington, D.C., 1930.

34. Reimbursement for such expenses was legally mandated by the Leavitt Act (47 *Stat.* 737, July 1, 1932).

35. U.S. House of Representatives, Committee on Appropriations, Subcommittee on the Department of Interior and Related Agencies, *Appropriations for 1978*, Part II, 95th Cong., 1st Sess., U.S. Government Printing Office, Washington, D.C., 1977, Section 4, p. 130: "[M]any areas of the [Fort Belknap irrigation project] are in need of rehabilitation. Laterals, drains, and old concrete structures are badly deteriorated."

36. McCool, op. cit., pp. 257-8.

37. Burton, op. cit., p. 23. He is relying on Folke-Williams, op. cit., pp. 7-8.

38. McCool, op. cit.

39. Participating states were Arizona, California, Colorado, Nevada, New Mexico, Utah, and Wyoming. The apportionment was that the upper basin states (north of the Grand Canyon) would claim 7.5 million acre-feet of Colorado River water each year, while the lower basin states would take another 7.5 million. An acre-foot is the amount of water—43,560 cubic feet or 325,851 gallons—required to cover a one-acre area with one foot of water.

40. The Colorado River Compact, *Congressional Record*, No. 324, U.S. Government Printing Office, Washington, D.C., 1928; ratified as the Boulder Canyon Project Act, 43 U.S.C.S. 617 (1) (1976).

41. Warne, William E., *The Bureau of Reclamation*, Praeger Publishers, New York, 1973, pp. 191-2.

42. Ibid., pp. 192-3.

43. Harrison, David C., *Do We Need a National Water Policy?* National Academy of Public Administration, Washington, D.C., 1981, p. S-11.

44. Warne, op. cit., pp. 29-31.

45. U.S. House of Representatives, Committee on Appropriations, Subcommittee on Public Works, *Appropriations for 1980*, Part I, 95th Cong., 2d Sess., U.S. Government Printing Office, Washington, D.C., 1979, Section 4, p. 3.

46. U.S. Army Corps of Engineers, *The Corps in Perspective since 1775*, U.S. Government Printing Office, Washington, D.C., 1976.

47. U.S. Army Corps of Engineers, *Historical Highlights of the United States Army Corps of Engineers*, Department of Defense Publication EP360-1-2, Washington, D.C., 1973, pp. 25-6.

48. Levine, Stuart, and Nancy O. Lurie, eds., *The American Indian Today*, Everett and Edwards Publishers, Deland, Fl., 1965, p. 68.

49. McCool, op. cit., p. 89.

50. Ibid., p. 177. Also see Berman, Terry, "For the Taking: The Garrison Dam and the Tribal Taking Area," *Cultural Survival Quarterly*, Vol. 12, No. 2, 1989.

51. McCool, op. cit., p. 178. He is relying upon Lawson, Michael, *Dammed Indians: The Pick-Sloan Plan and the Missouri River Sioux*, University of Oklahoma Press, Norman, 1982.

52. See Shanks, Bernard, "The American Indian and Missouri River Water Development," *Water Resources Bulletin*, No. 10, June 1974, p. 576. On burial and sacred sites, see Vine Deloria, Jr.'s introduction in Lawson, op. cit.

53. McCool, op. cit., p. 177.

54. Shanks, Bernard, "Dams and Disasters: The Social Problems of Water Development Policies," in John Baden and Richard L. Shoup, eds., *Bureaucracy vs. Environment*, University of Michigan Press, Ann Arbor, 1982, p. 116. It should be noted that in his quasi-official polemic on behalf of the Pick-Sloan Project, *The Dammed Missouri Valley*, Alfred A. Knopf Publishers, New York, 1951, p. 115. Richard Baumhoff suggests this outcome was intentional: "It is possible that these projects for dams and reservoirs may be of real service in *forcing* a long step toward [moving] Indians into *normal* society (emphasis added)."

55. Bishop, op. cit., p. 84.

56. Quoted in McCool, op. cit., p. 140.

57. Sonnichsen, Carl, *Tucson: The Life and Times of an American City*, University of Oklahoma Press, Norman, 1982, p. 280.

58. Bishop, op. cit., p. 84. For more on the Salt River Project, see Hart, Athia L., ed., *Arizona Waterline*, Salt River Project, Phoenix, 1990.

59. For a fuller depiction of these Arizona-California confrontations, see Hundley, Norris, *Water and the West*, University of California Press, Berkeley, 1975.

60. Black was following the recommendations of a Special Master appointed to investigate the practical realities of the issue prior to the Supreme Court's reaching its decision. See "Report of the Special Master," *Arizona v. California* (1960), referenced in full in *Arizona v. California*, 373 U.S. 340 (1963).

61. Bishop, op. cit., p. 86.

62. The plan is mentioned in the Colorado River Basin Compact, ratified as 63 *Stat*. 31, April 6, 1949.

63. Act of June 13, 1962, 76 *Stat*. 96; as amended, 43 USCS 615, *et seq*. (1976).

64. See Price, Monroe, and Gary Weatherford, "Indian Water Rights in Theory and Practice," in Lawrence Rosen, ed., *American Indians and the Law*, Transaction Books, New Brunswick, NJ, 1976, pp. 97-131.

65. Burton, op. cit., p. 31.

66. U.S. Senate, Committee on Appropriations, *Hearings on H.R. 17619 Before a Subcommittee of the Senate Committee on Appropriations*, 91st Cong., 2d Sess., U.S. Government Printing Office, Washington, D.C., 1970, p. 2021.

67. Memorandum from David E. Lundgren, Deputy Solicitor for the U.S. Department of Interior, to John C. Whittaker, Undersecretary of Interior, entitled "Navajo Indian Irrigation—Water Entitlement of the Navajo Tribe," December 6, 1974.

68. Burton, op. cit., p. 31.

69. Quoted in the *Denver Post*, June 3, 1984, p. 6b.

70. McCool, op. cit., p. 45. In a follow-up case argued before its own bench, *Montana, et al. v. Northern Cheyenne Tribe of the Northern Cheyenne Reservation, et al.* (103 S.Ct. 3201 (1983)), the state revealed the extent of its weighty motivations in going to the Supreme Court to challenge ownership of the Little Big Horn riverbed; it awarded itself the right to regulate and license—and thus collect fees from—non-Indians fly-casting on the reservation portion of the river. Other cases that have gone decidedly against indigenous water rights since the Reagan

era began include *Arizona v. California* (103 S.Ct. 1382 (1983)), *Arizona, et al. v. San Carlos Apache Tribe* (103 S.Ct. 3201 (1983)) and *Nevada v. U.S.* (103 S.Ct. 2906 (1983)).

71. Notable examples drawn from the last decade in which native water rights litigation has been approached in this fashion include *Swinomish Tribal Council v. FERC* (627 F.2d 499 (D.C. Cir. 1980)), *Lower Elwha Tribal Community, et al. v. Reagan* (520 F. Supp. 334 (W.D. Wash. 1981)), *Puget Sound Power & Light v. FERC; Muckleshoot Tribe v. Puget Sound Power & Light* (454 U.S. 1053, cert denied (1981)), *U.S. v. Anderson* (450 U.S. 920, cert. denied (1981)), *South Dakota v. Rippling Water Ranch* (531 F. Supp. 449 (D.S.D. 1982)), *U.S. v. Big Horn Low Line Canal, et al.* (rev'd 463 U.S. 545 (1983)), *Puyallup Tribe of Indians v. Port of Tacoma* (465 U.S. 1049, cert. denied (1984)), *Yankton Sioux Tribe v. Adair* (107 S.Ct. 3228, cert denied (1987)).

72. As was noted earlier, approximately 1 percent of reservation land was irrigated in 1968. According to a comprehensive study completed in 1984, the figure had risen to a little over 7 percent (Western States Water Council, *Indian Water Rights in the West*, Western Governors' Association, May 1984, p. 93). By 1991, it is estimated that another 1.5 percent of the total acreage has been added.

73. *Pyramid Lake Tribe of Paiute Indians v. Truckee-Carson Irrigation District, et al.*, 463 U.S. 110 (1983).

74. Burton, op. cit., p. 42.

75. Ibid., p. 78. The bill was S. 536, 101st Cong., 1st Sess., 1989.

76. *Confederated Tribes of the Umatilla Reservation v. Alexander*, 440 F. Supp. 553 (Dist. Ct. Ore. 1977).

77. *Colville Confederated Tribe v. Walton*, 460 F. Supp. 1320 (E.D. Wash. 1978); 647 F.2d 42 (9th Cir. 1981).

78. CNN news broadcast, August 5, 1991.

79. In common with other eastern water rights cases, the Seminole position is based exclusively in the doctrine of riparian rights. There was thus never an issue of their waiving reserved water rights involved in the negotiating process.

80. Seminole Indian Land Claims Settlement Act of 1987, 101 *Stat.* 1556 (1987). The term "Everglades Ecological Disaster Area" is used because, over the past fifty years, non-Indian water-use patterns in southern Florida have so contaminated and depleted the regional wetlands that the ecology of even those portions designated as parks and National Wilderness Areas is obviously on the verge of extinction. Once destroyed, the unique environment of the Everglades—found nowhere else in the world—can never be restored. For background, see Matthiessen, Peter, *Indian Country*, Viking Press, New York, 1984, pp. 15-63.

81. San Luis Rey Indian Water Rights Settlement Act, 102 *Stat.* 4000 (1988).

82. The plan was based in a study done by environmental economist Zach Willey during the early '80s. See Willey, Zach, *Economic Development and Environmental Quality in California's Water System*, Institute for Governmental Studies, University of California at Berkeley, 1985.

83. For background on Mission Indian litigation since 1914, see U.S. Senate, Select Committee on Indian Affairs, *Senate Report 100-47*, 100th Cong., 1st Sess., U.S. Government Printing Office, Washington, D.C., 1987.

84. *U.S. v. Cappaert* (375 F. Supp. 456 (D. Nev. 1974)) was the first case to confirm that indigenous reserved rights pertain to sub-surface as well as surface water. This was reaffirmed in *Gila River Pima-Maricopa Indian Community v. U.S.*, 9. Cl. Ct. 660 (1986).

85. Ak Chin Indian Community Settlement Act, 92 *Stat.* 409 (1978). The original plan, introduced by Representative Morris Udall, called for water to be provided from adjacent, federally controlled, groundwater sources. When these proved insufficient, the plan was revised to draw down on the Central Arizona Project, a much more expensive proposition.

86. For an historical overview of Reagan's role, see U.S. House of Representatives, Committee on Interior and Insular Affairs, *Report No. 98-1026*, 98th Cong., 2d Sess., U.S. Government Printing Office, Washington, D.C., 1984, p. 6.

87. Ak Chin Indian Community Settlement Act (amended), 98 *Stat.* 885 (1984).

88. On Reagan's role, see U.S. Senate, Select Committee on Indian Affairs, *Senate Report No. 97-375*, 97th Cong., 2d Sess., U.S. Government Printing Office, Washington, D.C., 1982, p. 33. It should be noted that nearly one-third of the main Papago Reservation's three million acres are officially assessed as irrigable, while San Xavier holds another 10,000-plus irrigable acres. Under the Supreme Court's apportionment guideline, established in *Arizona v. California* (1963), this would make the entitlement of San Xavier alone about 55,000 acre-feet of water per year.

89. *San Carlos Apache Tribe v. State of Arizona*, 484 F. Supp. 778 (1979); 668 F.2d 1093 (CA9 1982).

90. See *Tucson Urban Study*, Draft of Regional Water Supply Appendix, unpublished study

commissioned by the Tucson City Council, December 1981. The city draws less than 5 percent of its water supply from a small reservoir on the Santa Cruz River; the other 95 percent-plus comes from wells.

91. Burton, op. cit., pp. 72-3. Southern Arizona Water Rights Settlement Act of 1982 (Title III, 96 *Stat.* 1274); the federal contribution to resolving this problem for which it itself was primarily responsible was $35 million (about which Reagan complained vehemently) of the estimated $112 million involved. The bill was attached as a rider to the Reclamation Reform Act of 1982 (P.L. 97-293; S. 1409). For analysis of recent problems with implementation, see McGuire, Thomas R., "Indian Water Rights Settlements: A Case Study in the Rhetoric of Implementation," *American Indian Culture and Research Journal,* Vol. 15, No. 2, Summer 1991, pp. 139-69.

92. Burton, op. cit., p. 75.

93. See, for example, the comments of California Representative George Miller, *Congressional Record,* October 3, 1988.

94. Burton, op. cit., p. 76, analyzing the Colorado Ute Indian Water Settlement Act, 102 Stat. 2973 (1988). Actually, the Ute agreement may have been used as a means of selling the Animas-La Plata Project—which Reagan very much wanted—to liberal sectors of Congress that were resistant to allocating its estimated $380 million in costs to serve primarily corporate needs. The "Ute" portion of the whole, which will service mainly non-Indian farmers and ranchers, comes to an additional $60 million, a substantial portion of which is provided by the state of Colorado. Given the priority structure of the whole arrangement, it is unlikely the Utes will ever see any significant portion of their water allocation delivered. Meanwhile, they have permanently waived their right to sue.

95. The cases were *U.S. v. Big Horn Low Line Canal, et al.; U.S. v. Aegeson; U.S. v. Aasheim; U.S. v. Abell;* and *U.S. v. AMS Ranch* (combined as rev'd 463 U.S. 545 (1983)),

96. Fort Peck-Montana Water Compact, 89 *Stat.* 2203 (1985). The federal contribution to making this work is essentially zilch.

97. On formation of the Citizens' Rights Organization and Montanans Opposed to Discrimination, see the *Billings Gazette,* April 16 and May 21, 1977. The Cattlemen's Association resolution is covered in the same paper, November 20, 1977.

98. *Salt River Pima-Maricopa Indian Community v. State of Arizona,* rev'd 463 U.S. 545 (1983).

99. Salt River Pima-Maricopa Indian Community Water Rights Settlement Act of 1988, 102 *Stat.* 2555.

100. Burton, op. cit., pp. 73-4.

101. U.S. Senate, Committee on Energy and Natural Resources, Senate Select Committee on Indian Affairs, *Ute Indian Water Compact,* 101st Cong., 1st Sess., U.S. Government Printing Office, Washington, D.C., 1989.

102. Bishop, op. cit., p. 87. This is the best single source presently available on the overall adjudication.

103. Ibid.

104. *White Mountain Apache Tribe v. William French Smith and James Watt,* 51 USLW 3932 (1983).

105. Most of these cases remain in preparation and are thus unavailable for citation.

106. Quoted in Bishop, op. cit., p. 83. It is interesting to note that Mr. O'Hair is a registered Republican, a staunch advocate of "property rights," and a strong supporter of Reagan-style "free market" economics. Yet his complaint is really that if American Indians are allowed to exercise rights over their water (property), selling or leasing it on an open market, Glendale's upper-middle-class, "politically conservative" and overwhelmingly white residents might be compelled to shell out $2,500 or more per acre-foot of water they sprinkle on their lawns and pour into their swimming pools. This is as opposed to the $9.50 per acre-foot systematic denial of indigenous property rights, as well as centralized government controls and huge subsidies, made possible in southern Arizona.

107. Burton, op. cit., pp. 140-1.

108. Ibid., p. 140.

109. Quoted in Bishop, op. cit., p. 80.

110. Talk at the University of Colorado at Boulder, October 1985 (tape on file).

111. The Glen Canyon Dam, built by the Reclamation Bureau on the Colorado River, was unsuccessfully opposed by both the Diné and Hopi nations in the *Badoni v. Higginson* (see Table of Key Indian Laws and Cases). It was completed in 1982 and submerged sacred sites at Rainbow Bridge beneath Lake Powell, a huge, 500-feet-deep reservoir that environmentalist writer Edward Abbey once described as "the biggest sewage lagoon in the American Southwest" (*Beyond the Wall,* Holt, Rinehart and Winston Publishers, New York, 1984, p. 102); for a definitive treatment, see Martin, Russell, *A Story that Stands Like a Dam: Glen Canyon and the Struggle for the Soul of the West,* Henry Holt Publishers, New York, 1989. The Tellico Dam, built by the Tennessee Valley Authority

on the Little Tennessee (formerly Cherokee) River and completed in 1980 despite arguments that it would cause extinction of a fish species known as the snail darter, turned out to be totally unnecessary. Its reservoir, meanwhile, flooded the sites of all seven principle villages that comprised the core of the Cherokee Nation until that people's removal in the 1830s, as well as numerous burial and other sacred sites (see *Indian Country,* op. cit., pp. 105-26).

112. Every people indigenous to the arid West had an economy traditionally incorporating agriculture to one degree or another. Many, such as the various Puebloan cultures and the O'Odhams, were primarily agricultural.

113. See note 106, above.

114. Interestingly, the logic of this idea has come to appeal not only to American Indians, but to such fundamentally anti-Indian "redneck" types as Edward Abbey. See, for example, his *Desert Solitaire: A Season in the Wilderness* (Simon and Schuster Publishers, New York, 1968), and *Abbey's Road: Take the Other* (E.P. Dutton Publishers, New York, 1979).

115. Lately, Frank and Deborah Popper, a husband-wife team at Rutgers specializing in urban planning and economics, have completed an unprecedented study of the Great Plains region in which they establish incontrovertibly that perhaps 80 percent of the entire area has been maintained on the basis of a net economic loss to everyone except selected corporations since it was first "settled." They are presently working on a book in which they advocate that most of the West be evacuated by non-Indians on economic grounds. Sioux scholar Vine Deloria, Jr. and others have endorsed the concept, recommending that vast portions of what is now subsidized farm and ranch land on the plains be allowed to return to buffalo graze.

116. Noted ecological demographer William R. Catton, Jr., in *Overshoot: The Ecological Basis for Revolutionary Change* (University of Illinois Press, Urbana, 1982), has estimated that the North American continent had reached its maximum sustainable population density in about 1840, when the number of humans was approximately one-quarter of present figures. He warns that if such "overshoot" continues, humanity will inevitably experience a "crash" (massive, uncontrollable die-off).

117. For a sample of this thinking, see Kahn, Herman, William Brown, and Leon Martel, *The Next 200 Years: A Scenario for America and the World,* William Morrow Publishers, New York, 1976.

118. *Newsweek,* February 22, 1965, p. 53. In the same article, Secretary of Interior Stewart Udall is quoted as saying, "I'm for this type of thinking. I'm glad the engineers talk so much about it."

119. McCool, op. cit., pp. 107-8. For further information, see Reisner, Mark, *Cadillac Desert: The American West and Its Disappearing Water,* Viking Press, New York, 1986, pp. 506-13.

120. Dam the Dams Project and the Institute for Natural Progress, "The Water Plot: Hydrological Rape in Northern Canada," in Ward Churchill, ed., *Critical Issues in Native North America,* IWGIA Document 62, International Work Group on Indigenous Affairs, Copenhagen, 1989, pp. 137-51; quote from p. 142.

121. Evidence that things are moving right along in this regard is perhaps indicated by George Bush's recent and successful interest in forging a new "cooperative free-trade agreement" with Mexico concerning precisely these provinces.

122. The plan effectively transforms Canada—always economically subordinate to its southerly neighbor—into a *de facto* colony of the U.S. As early as 1966, Canadian General A.G.L. McNaughton warned that if schemes like NAWAPA were actually realized, "Jurisdiction and control...although nominally international, would in reality be dominated by [the U.S., which] would thereby acquire a formidable vested interest in the national waters of Canada...it is obvious that if we make a bargain to divert water to the United States, we cannot ever discontinue or we shall face force to compel continuance." McNaughton's statements are excerpted in *Water Resources of Canada,* Royal Society of Canada, Ottawa, 1968.

123. Overall, see Alberta Department of Agriculture, Water Resources Division, Development Planning Branch, *Water Diversion Proposals of North America,* Canadian Council of Resource Ministers, Ottawa, 1968. Analysis may be found in Welsh, Frank, *How to Create a Water Crisis,* Johnson Publishing, Boulder, CO, 1985, pp. 105-8.

124. On the James Bay Projects, see Higgins, James, "Hydro-Québec and Native People," *Cultural Survival Quarterly,* Vol. 11, No. 3, 1987. Also see LaDuke, Winona, "James Bay," *Spirit of Crazy Horse,* August-September 1991, pp. 5, 10.

125. Covered in *Water Diversion Proposals of North America,* op. cit.

126. "The Water Plot," op. cit., p. 144.

127. Ibid., p. 150.

Chapter VII

In Usual and Accustomed Places
Contemporary American Indian Fishing Rights Struggles

The Institute for Natural Progress

The right to resort to the fishing places in controversy was a part of the larger rights possessed by the Indians, upon which there was not a shadow of impediment and which were not much less necessary to the existence of the Indians than the atmosphere they breathed. New conditions came into existence, to which these rights had to be accommodated. Only a limitation of them, however, was necessary and intended, not a taking away. In other words, the treaties [were] not a granting of rights to them but a grant of rights from them [and] a reservation of those not granted. Citizens might share it, but the Indians were secured in its employment by special provisions of means for its exercise.

U.S. v. Winans
1905

A mong the more crucial battles fought by native people in North America have been those involving preservation or restoration of their traditional economies. Such struggles have been especially sharp over the past several decades with regard to treaty-guaranteed fishing rights in the Pacific Northwest and the state of Wisconsin. While the latter confrontations are rather recent, and a correspondingly minor amount of material is therefore currently in print about them, detailed analyses of the situation in the Pacific Northwest may be found in several books, notably *Uncommon Controversy: Fishing Rights of the Muckleshoot, Puyallup and Nisqually Indians* (1970); *Indian Tribes: A Continuing Quest for Survival* (1981); and *Treaties on Trial: The Continuing Controversy over Northwest Indian Fishing Rights* (1986).[1]

In the Northwest, despite clear treaty language permanently ensuring such prerogatives, treatied peoples suffered more than a century of systematic deprivation of their rights to fish. Consequences, not just to indigenous economies, but to social and cultural practices, have been pronounced. Beginning in the late 1950s, a series of increasingly severe clashes with federal and local authorities (and area non-Indian commercial and "sport" fishers), as well as a lengthy series of court cases, challenged the denial of native fishing rights, especially in the state of Washington. One result has been the emergence of a pattern of bilateral negotiations by which some of the most extravagant abuses of Indian rights have been ended. Although the issues associated with Northwest Indian fishing rights are by no means entirely resolved, terms like "co-management" and "cooperative resource management" are now regularly used in discussions of "the fishing industry" between state planners and the representatives of native nations in Washington, Oregon, and Idaho.[2]

Hopefully, the process forged in the Northwest will not only fulfill its promise in that region, but provide a basis upon which the crisis in Wisconsin can be remedied as well. If so, then perhaps the *de facto* negotiation of modern treaties developed with regard to fishing rights can serve as a model by which to address other Indian "reserved rights" such as those pertaining to hunting and the gathering of wild rice in the years ahead.[3] This essay seeks to explore not only the nature of the fishing rights struggles *per se*, but these other potentials as well.

Disinheritance in the Pacific Northwest

As even the U.S. courts have recognized, fish have always been "not much less necessary than the atmosphere they breathed" for the indigenous peoples of the Pacific Northwest.[4] The Indians of this region traditionally centered both their diet and their way of life around the great runs of anadromous fish, the salmon and steelhead trout, that return each year from the open sea to spawn along rivers as far inland as central Idaho.[5] It has been estimated that upwards of 60 percent of the nutrients consumed by these once wealthy peoples derived directly from the fish.[6] Hence, when native nations of the Northwest negotiated treaties with the United States government during the 1850s and '60s, they were far more concerned with reserving perpetual access to their customary fishing sites along the coasts and interior waterways than with demarcating significant territorial units. In large part, they ceded the land itself (a total of about 64 million acres), retaining only small parcels for their own exclusive use and occupancy, in exchange for cash payments, other aid and solemn guarantees of their fishing rights (see Map I).

Within the state of Washington, the U.S. recognized through the signing and ratification of treaties some twenty-six indigenous nations. Of these, by the 1960s, "the Puyallups' reservation had thirty-three acres of tribal-owned land; the Snohomish had sixteen acres; the Suquamish had forty-one; and the Muckleshoot [Nation's] 300 members shared a tribal-owned reservation of one-quarter of an acre."[7] "This paper secures your fish," the Indians were repeatedly assured by federal negotiators as the U.S. assumed title to their territories.[8] As it was put in Article 3 of the Treaty of Medicine Creek with the Nisqually, Puyallup, and other indigenous nations in 1854:

> The right of taking fish, at *all* usual and accustomed grounds and stations, is further secured to said Indians in common with all other citizens of the Territory, and of erecting temporary houses for the purpose of curing them,

Map I

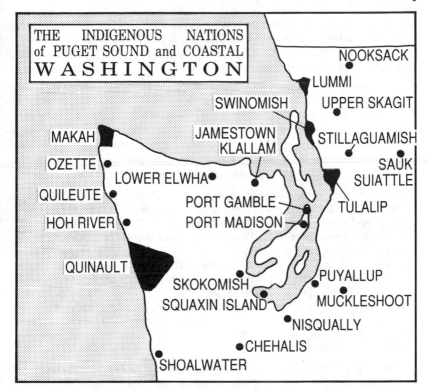

THE INDIGENOUS NATIONS of PUGET SOUND and COASTAL WASHINGTON

NOOKSACK
LUMMI
SWINOMISH
UPPER SKAGIT
MAKAH
JAMESTOWN KLALLAM
STILLAGUAMISH
OZETTE
LOWER ELWHA
SAUK
SUIATTLE
QUILEUTE
PORT GAMBLE
TULALIP
HOH RIVER
PORT MADISON
QUINAULT
SKOKOMISH
SQUAXIN ISLAND
PUYALLUP
MUCKLESHOOT
NISQUALLY
CHEHALIS
SHOALWATER

together with the privileges of hunting, gathering roots and berries, and pasturing their horses on open and unclaimed lands (emphasis added).[9]

For a while, it appeared as if the treaties might be honored, since the early U.S. settler population was interested primarily in agriculture, secondarily in timbering and mining. However, as the U.S. commercial fishing fleet grew during the late 1800s, Indian fishing rights underwent a marked and rapid erosion. State regulations, enacted in direct contravention of the treaties, abolished or closely restricted native use of traditional fishing techniques such as salmon spearing and limited Indians to fishing within the confines of their tiny reservations.

In 1913 Indians began being arrested by state authorities for fishing activities, even on their own federally-supervised lands. The Washington fish and game commission shared responsibility for commercial and sports fishing, and acted under state laws to suppress the Indians. In 1929, Washington state denied the Quinalt [Nation] the right to fish, choosing to lease their rights to a private company of Bakers Bay for a $63,000 fee.[10]

Indigenous people throughout the Northwest were forbidden to fish in many rivers and tributaries they had utilized since time immemorial. State governments also prohibited net fishing for steelhead, a traditional source of winter food and a staple of the trade that afforded the Indians a cash economy (necessary, once their land bases had been constricted by white settlement).[11] These state-level treaty violations were coupled to those of the federal government itself, which, as part of the overall policy of Indian assimilation remarked on by other contributors to this volume, began a campaign during the same period to eradicate the Potlatch ("give away") ceremonies that formed the core of area native spirituality and ensured that no one in traditional societies went hungry.[12] Despite a federal court ruling in the 1905 *Winans* case that native fishing rights had never been forfeited, both the states and the U.S. Department of Interior continued their policies. An endemic empoverishment "and in some cases outright starvation" of Northwest Indians resulted.[13] As a Nisqually elder explained the process:

> The white man, he took over, see, after he saw there was money in fish. He just took over, you know, just steal like stealing off the Indian. And that's how they got it. And that's why they don't want the Indian to fish, because there's big money for them. Now you even have to get permission to gather nuts and things from the mountains and from the desert. They didn't plant these trees here. They didn't bring the deer here. They didn't bring the fish here, and yet they say, "We give you" the right to fish here—"we give you." They had nothing to give in the first place. They were beggars. They were paupers. They came to this country looking for freedom of speech and to worship the way they wanted to. But when they got here they forgot when it came to the Indian. This country was built on total aggression. There was room for everyone. But now [the white man] wants to take the rest of us—he wants to take away everything we have.[14]

The problem was exacerbated throughout the first half of the 20th century, as farming, industrialization, and dramatic expansion of the logging business degraded rivers and estuaries and caused a concomitant diminishment in the numbers of salmon. The states acted consistently to decrease the portion of even this declining fish population which Indians were allowed to catch. By mid-century, most of the fishing peoples were completely destitute.[15] Even this was not enough for the state of Washington:

> Judicially, 109 years after it had been signed, the Supreme Court of Washington State decided to take a look at the Treaty of Medicine Creek. And, in effect, it nullified the treaty. "None of the signatories of the original treaty contemplated fishing with a 600 foot nylon gill net, which could prevent the escapement of any fish for spawning purposes," the court decreed, in December, 1963..."Legally," the treaty must be broken. That's what happens when progress pushes forward, declared Thor Tollefson, the director of State Fisheries. He was merely obeying the law by breaking the treaty, he said.[16]

As of 1964, although federal investigators concluded that native people were engaged in wholesale violation of state fishing regulations in a desperate effort to feed their families, it was estimated that Indians were taking only about 5 percent of the total annual fish "harvest."[17] On the other hand, official estimates also revealed that the non-Indian commercial fishing industry had by that point become so over-developed that 30 to 50 percent of the boats then employed were unnecessary to catch the depleted number of fish available.[18]

The "Fish-Ins"

B eginning in March 1964, the Northwest nations responded to this perpetual crisis and the total absence of due process options available to them to address it by intitiating a series of "fish-ins" in western Washington and along the Columbia River. The idea apparently originated among the Makah elders, or at least it was they who issued an appeal for participation of fifty indigenous nations (more than forty came) in a planning meeting for the first demonstration during February of the same year. Support was also provided by the newly formed National Indian Youth Council—which committed key organizers like Robert Satiacum, Mel Thom, and Bruce Wilkie to the fray for the duration.[19] The sentiments of the gathering were voiced by a young Tulalip named Janet McCloud, who was to emerge as one of the major native resistance leaders of her generation:

> They promised us that we could fish...as "long as the mountain stands, the grass grows green and the sun shines." But now the State of Washington has declared the steelhead trout a "white man's fish." They must think the steelhead swam over behind the *Mayflower.*[20]

Organizing not only to eat, but to express their defiance of the regulations that abridged their rights, they fished at times and places forbidden by state law (but guaranteed under provision of the treaties), facing repeated arrest, jail, confiscation of gear, and frequent physical violence. The first such action on the Quillayute Reservation has been described by Stan Steiner:

> Hundreds of Indians stood on the banks of the river, watching the fishermen row out. The winds of Puget Sound tore at them. On the Quillayute River the Indians were uneasy. The tribe was small. It had never done anything this bold; for fishing off the reservation, without licenses, was an act of civil disobedience to the game laws, and to the State Supreme Court decisions that confined net fishing by Indians to their reservations. And the wardens were white with wrath...[But] before it ended the hundreds of Indians had swelled to thousands. There were Fish-Ins on half a dozen rivers. There were dozens of arrests, war dances on the steps of the capitol rotunda, an Indian protest meeting of several thousand at the state capitol. There were Treaty Treks on the streets of the cities and Canoe treks, of sixty miles, through Puget sound. There was a gathering of more than a thousand Indians from fifty-six [nations] throughout the country— Seminoles of Florida, Winnebagos of Nebraska, Navajos of New Mexico, Blackfeet of Montana, Potawatamis of Michigan, Iroquois of New York, Shoshone of Wyoming, Sioux of the Dakotas, Kiowas and Poncas of Oklahoma, Nez Percés and Couer d'Alenes of Idaho—who came to join the Northwest activists.[21]

State response was predictably brutal:

[At Frank's Landing] officials of Washington, in open opposition to Supreme Court rulings, arrested Indians for "illegal" fishing, using tear gas, blackjacks, and excessive violence to subdue two dozen Indian men, women and children. A series of night attacks by state officials followed, using terrorist tactics against old men and women, and violence against the very young. Many people were hospitalized.[22]

At first the Yakimas, a relatively well-landed and conservative group, declined to join the fish-in movement. The Warm Springs Confederation and other Columbia River nations followed suit. The situation changed in 1965, however, when state fish and game personnel, running amok, made the mistake of arresting more than a dozen elderly Yakimas peacefully going about their business—as they had all their lives—in time-honored fishing locations along the river.

When the jailings began [despite their "moderation"] the Yakimas felt betrayed. They took up arms. Young men of the tribe put on their discarded Marine Corps and Army uniforms and shouldered their M-1 rifles. The armed Yakimas patrolled the banks of the rivers, guarding the tribal fishermen. There were guns along the rivers for the first time since the Yakima Wars, one hundred years before. Rifles in hand, the Yakimas cast their nets.[23]

The earlier fish-ins and state responses had undoubtedly discomfited federal officials in a public relations sense, especially after celebrities such as Marlon Brando, Dick Gregory and Jane Fonda began to articulate the Indians' message before a mass audience. All things being equal, however, it is likely the status quo would nonetheless have prevailed.[24] The Yakima action riveted federal attention in a far more serious fashion. This was because of the location of a critical Atomic Energy Commission facility at Hanford, on the Yakima Reservation (see Chapter Eight). The prospect of armed Indians assaulting and perhaps damaging a primary manufacturing center of U.S. nuclear weapons as a form of retribution for violation of their fishing rights was more than national security experts cared to contend with. Although anti-Indian violence would continue for several more years, culminating in the near-fatal wounding of activist leader Hank Adams in January 1971, the battle had already been decided.[25] From the moment the first Yakima picked up the first gun, the state of Washington was defeated. The inevitability of a federally imposed compromise had been set by 1966. The only real question was the form it would assume.

The express intent of those pursuing fish-in tactics was to force the U.S. finally to live up to some measure of its treaty obligations by putting the states in line. In this sense, the fishing rights activists plainly foreshadowed the American Indian Movement and other militant organizations of the 1970s.[26] Vine Deloria, Jr. and Clifford M. Lytle have described the importance of the fish-ins in the contemporary struggle for Indian rights:

Indian activism was certainly an invention of [traditional] Indians. They devoutly believed that whites in positions of authority would give them justice if only they knew the conditions under which [they] lived. They were absolutely fearless in exercising their treaty rights and believed implicitly in the

neutral operation of a kind of abstract justice they felt would uphold them...The
first activist events of the sixties were the "fish-ins" in the Pacific Northwest.[27]

Litigation

It was in this context that the first modern fishing rights cases were accepted by
the U.S. Supreme Court. During the late 1960s and on into the '70s, a "cluster"
of three cases addressed the rights of the Puyallup Nation to engage in net fishing
on the Puyallup River in Washington state. They clarified the coastal nations' rights
to take fish, but left fishing techniques under state regulatory authority.[28] Another
case, *Sohappy v. Smith* (later consolidated with *U.S. v. Oregon*) was initially decided
in the federal district court for Oregon and was upheld on appeal. It reaffirmed the
Columbia River nations' right to a "fair and equitable" portion of all fish passing
through their traditional on-reservation fishing places, but failed to define what this
meant in terms of actual quantity.[29] *U.S. v. Washington*, a pivotal case involving
Indian treaty rights to fish at locations off the reservations and clarification of what
portion of annual fish harvests rightly belonged to native nations was first heard
in the District Court for Washington by Judge George H. Boldt.[30] A second phase,
still pending, questions whether hatchery-bred or other artificially propagated
fish—intended to replace fish lost to non-Indian industrial and agricultural pollution—fall within native allocations and whether the treaties might be construed as
protecting the fish themselves against destruction of their habitat.[31]

Boldt's "Phase I" interpretation of the relevant treaty language, rendered in
1974, held that Indian peoples possess an unequivocal right to fish at *all* "usual and
accustomed places," whether on or off present reservations, and an equivalent right
to participate in regional fisheries management. The judge also declared that a fair
and equitable portion of the annual fish harvest, within the meaning of the Northwest treaties, must be construed as *half* of all fish taken each year (or *ten times* what
the state of Washington claimed Indians had been "stealing" from non-Indians). He
then elaborated guidelines by which the Indian portion of each year's catch should
be ascertained. Over the next five years, state officials, often in collusion with the
commercial fishing lobby, along with regional and national "sportsmen's associations," engaged in serious obstruction while appealing Boldt's decision.[32] In 1977,
federal marshals had to be called in to attempt implementation of the judge's orders.
Meanwhile, the Interior and Justice Departments—under heavy pressure from
lobbyists of the virulently racist Interstate Congress for Equal Rights and Responsibilities (ICERR)—attempted to subvert the ruling, forming a joint task force to
"mediate" the dispute by suggesting an arrangement that would have reduced the
Indians' proportionate rights and undercut their management authority.[33]

Native people attempting to exercise their fishing rights anywhere beyond
reservation boundaries reported massive intimidation and frequent physical assaults. Judge Boldt himself came in for considerable abuse; he was targeted by an
anti-Indian coalition including state and local officials, the ICERR, local and
national "sporting" organizations, the commercial fishing industry, the John Birch

Society, and the Ku Klux Klan.[34] For more than a year, he was the focus of protest demonstrations, newspaper editorials, petition drives calling for his impeachment, and bill boards and bumper stickers reading "NUTS TO BOLDT!"[35] In 1978, the Ninth Circuit Court of Appeals—even as Washington Representative Jack Cunningham was introducing a bill designed to abrogate the treaties upon which Indian fishing rights are based—went on record comparing the situation in the Northwest to that earlier experienced during the Civil Rights era in Georgia, Mississippi and Alabama: "Except for some desegregation cases, the district court has faced the most concerted official and private efforts to frustrate the decree of a federal court witnessed in this century."[36]

Finally, with the Supreme Court's affirmation of the bulk of the *Boldt* Decision in 1979, the state governments were compelled in large part to back down. As it had in the third *Puyallup* case, however, the high court opted to leave methods by which the Indian portion of annual fish harvests might be obtained under state regulation.[37] This was a political compromise of no small magnitude and might well have opened the door to a different sort of state-level scuttling of indigenous rights, had it not been for Congress' belated passage of two environmental protection acts in 1980.[38] These statutes effectively forced the states rather than the Indians to alter their fishing posture and called for a new state-Indian management arrangement. The results can be measured in fish, as is reflected in Table I, depicting the harvest of salmon among Washington's coastal peoples over the past decades. Table II shows the annual harvests of treated nations along the Columbia River for the period 1973-1987.[39]

Although the main impact of the favorable change in native fish harvesting has obviously been economic, benefits have been even more far-reaching and pervasive. Andy Fernando, former chairperson of the Upper Skagit Community in Washington, has assessed the impact of *U.S. v. Washington*:

> Decades of decay in many Indian communities have given succeeding genera-
> tions fewer reasons to follow the traditions and to remain active in tribal society.
> The *Boldt* decision has acted as a catalyst to change that. In years past, most
> talented Indian people left the reservations. Driven away by lack of jobs or a
> future, they fled to opportunities in the cities. Their exodus sapped strength
> from the reservations. The fishing right assured by the *Boldt* decision has
> reversed the trend. The elation and positive feeling of pulling a fifty-pound
> salmon into the boat is being translated into social change and activity in more
> than two dozen Indian communities. Following the 1974 decision, many young
> Indian people returned to their [nations] at first only to fish. But now they stay
> on because they see renewed activity in their tribal communities. Those people
> bringing skills have found welcoming tribal councils and communities eager
> to tap their knowledge and experience. Those willing to learn have found new
> opportunities, training, and employment in tribally operated housing, health,
> and service programs, in the many tribally owned businesses that have emerged
> in recent years, and in the tribal salmon management programs created under
> the *Boldt* decision. No one is suggesting that the *Boldt* decision has solved all
> the problems in Indian country, but the opportunities created directly or

Table I.

Indian and Non-Indian Catch in *U.S. v. Washington* Case Area* 1970—1987				
	Indian		*Non-Indian*	
Year	Catch	% of Total	Catch	% of Total
1970-73 (avg)	328,888	5.0	6,231,044	95.0
1974	688,582	11.9	5,845,482	88.1
1975	827,356	12.1	5,987,374	87.9
1976	986,153	13.8	5,600,131	86.2
1977	1,360,399	16.9	6,691,223	83.1
1978	1,391,890	27.2	3,727,355	72.8
1979	1,938,388	22.4	6,742,089	77.7
1980	1,526,571	42.9	2,030,845	57.1
1981	2,784,158	33.8	5,450,628	66.2
1982	3,019,250	45.7	3,590,968	54.3
1983	2,145,373	43.3	2,809,077	53.7
1984	2,033,362	49.0	2,112,526	51.0
1985	5,344,962	49.8	5,381,181	50.2
1986	3,221,409	48.9	3,494,930	52.0
1987	4,200,061	49.9	4,209,002	50.1

* Catches include marine areas 1 through 13.
Source: Northwest Indian Fisheries Commission, Annual Report, FY1988, p. 23.

Table II.

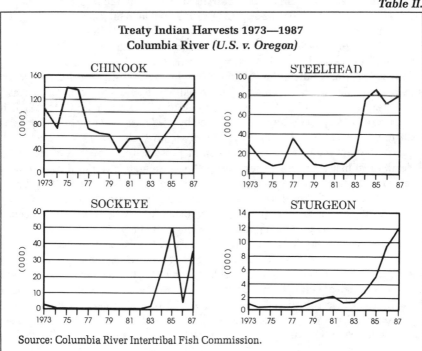

Treaty Indian Harvests 1973—1987
Columbia River *(U.S. v. Oregon)*

Source: Columbia River Intertribal Fish Commission.

indirectly from the legally secured right to fish are the difference between staying and leaving for many young Indian families. Today, when young Indians leave the reservation for college or to learn a skill, most intend to return and use their knowledge close to home. And many of those young people will return, to stay and build a future.[40]

The sort of management structure worked out under federal auspices between indigenous nations and the state of Washington in particular, in which Indian governments have a say in decisions affecting their economic, social, and cultural destinies, is encouraging. Although, as will be seen in the next section, neither federal nor state governments have by any means given up their presumption of "preeminent jurisdiction" over Indian fishing, it may well be that the emerging management structure has created a tentative basis upon which the sorts of genuine self-governing prerogatives called for by Rebecca Robbins in Chapter Three can begin to be realized in the years ahead. In any event, as the fishing rights battles of the 1960s and '70s were left behind, the *Boldt* Decision gave impetus to new Indian initiatives in the Northwest during the 1980s.

The *Sohappy* Case

A t least some elements of non-Indian government remain prepared to go to extreme lengths to circumvent or at least contain Indian rights in the Northwest. During the fall of 1981 and spring of 1982, native fishing activities along the Columbia River were the subject of an intensive campaign conducted by the National Marine Fisheries Service in cooperation with Washington and Oregon fish and game officials and the FBI. A "sting" operation was initiated in which nineteen traditional Yakimas—including veteran fishing rights activist David Sohappy, Sr. and his son, David, Jr.—were arrested for selling to undercover agents a small number of salmon that had been caught under tribally issued permits to take fish for ceremonial purposes. They were indicted by a federal grand jury on October 21, 1982 under the Lacey Act (16 U.S.C. 3371, *et seq.*), which makes it a crime to sell, receive, or purchase fish or wildlife taken or possessed in violation of any state, federal, or Indian tribal law or regulation. A year later, thirteen of those indicted were convicted on at least one count each in a combined case titled *U.S. v. David Sohappy, Sr., et al.*[41] This case raised questions of jurisdiction over native fishing in the Northwest (and, consequently, of the extent to which native people could really avail themselves of the rights acknowledged by Judge Boldt).

On appeal to the the Ninth Circuit Court, the defendants relied upon the language of Article 3 of the 1855 Treaty with the Yakima Confederacy, in which the Indians ceded some ten million acres of land to the U.S. in exchange for guarantees of their "exclusive right of taking fish in all the streams, where running through or bordering [their] reservation [and] also the right of taking fish at all usual and accustomed places [off the reservation]."[42] It was pointed out that the Supreme Court, in its *Winans* opinion, had interpreted the article as meaning:

The right to resort to the fishing places in controversy was part of a larger right possessed by the Indians, upon which there was *not a shadow of impediment,* and which were not much less necessary to the existence of the Indians than the atmosphere they breathed (emphasis added).[43]

It was also noted that this interpretation had been upheld by the high court as recently as 1979, with the case of *State of Washington v. Washington State Commercial Passenger Fishing Vessel Association* (443 U.S. 681),[44] and that the minutes of the 1855 treaty negotiations revealed that both the Yakimas and the U.S. had understood the Indians to be reserving all jurisdiction over their affairs unto themselves.[45] Furthermore, the Lacey Act itself specifically states that "nothing in this chapter shall be construed as repealing, superseding, or modifying any right, privilege, or immunity...reserved or established pursuant to a treaty." Nonetheless, relying on the logical loophole created by the Supreme Court in *Puyallup III,* and left standing in *U.S. v. Washington,* the Ninth Circuit upheld the convictions by determining there was nothing inconsistent in the imposition of state and federal fishing regulations over *Indian* fishing. Worse, the court concluded there was nothing wrong with using federal authority, methods, and personnel to enforce Indian fishing regulations in reservation areas: "[T]he exercise of federal jurisdiction under the Lacey Act is *not particularly disruptive* of tribal authority, for rather than overturning basic tribal regulations, it supports the tribal laws by authorizing federal penalties for violations [emphasis added]."[46]

This interpretation of "legitimate" non-Indian control over the Yakima national regulatory structure was sufficient to cause the Yakima Nation itself, under whose rules the defendants were supposedly culpable in part, to enter an *amicus curiae* brief supporting the Sohappy group's Supreme Court appeal in 1986.[47] Arguing for the Yakimas, tribal attorney James B. Hovis contended the circuit court had misunderstood the idea of salmon and steelhead being shared "in common" between Indians and non-Indians as suggesting a single jurisdiction pertaining to fishing. Following Judge Boldt, Hovis insisted instead that the concept meant only that each side was entitled to its own equal and distinct portion of the annual "fish crop." Each side was therefore entitled to exercise its own jurisdiction over its portion of fish: "There is no basis in law or fact for the Ninth Circuit's contrary opinion in this action."[48]

> There is no standard that allows "not particularly disruptive" laws to upset tribal sovereignty. Clearly the application of the Lacey Act *is* disruptive and cannot stand...[I]f the opinion...stands, the federal government can potentially convert every tribal misdemeanor into a federal felony—including catching *one* (1) fish over the number allowed on a ceremonial permit, as that is technically a violation of "tribal law." The Yakima Nation now faces a Hobson's choice— must it repeal all of its tribal laws to protect its members from unfair or unjust federal prosecution?[49]

Despite such active opposition to the lower court rulings by the Yakima government itself, the Rehnquist court refused in 1986 to review the convictions.[50] Already imprisoned, the thirteen defendants ultimately served nearly five years

228 The State of Native America

before parole. The elder Sohappy remained incarcerated even after suffering a near-fatal heart attack. During the fall of 1990, less than a year after he was finally released from prison, he suffered another and died. In the interim, his circumstances and the case that bore his name became something of a *cause célèbre* among native rights activists throughout the United States and abroad, largely replacing the earlier fish-in movement as the cutting edge of the fishing rights struggle.[51] The transparent contortions and contradictions of juridical reasoning forced upon federal courts in rationalizing and defending governmental controls over the exercise of Indian rights—and broad public awareness of these defects resulting from the publicity attracted by the case—could perhaps prove to be the anvil upon which some broad restoration of indigenous jurisdiction is eventually forged.

Gaining Ground

In the wake of the *Boldt* Decision, and in the glare of publicity attending the *Sohappy* case, several of the treatied nations of the Northwest have made significant progress toward resurrecting modern equivalents of their traditional fishing economies. For instance, both state and federal authorities have become increasingly hesitant to interfere with the issuance of Indian fishing licenses, enforcement of native regulatory codes, and so on. Once their right to take fish was clarified, some nations—such as the Quinalt, on the outer Olympic Peninsula—have been able to establish comprehensive and relatively autonomous fisheries systems, complete with commercial smoking and marketing facilities of their own. Others, such as the Skagit System Cooperative and the Point No Point Treaty Council, have undertaken collaborative multinational efforts to accomplish the same thing. Map I illustrates the location of such enterprises among native peoples of coastal Washington. Map II illustrates the same pattern among nations of the Columbia River region.

Contemporary Northwest Indian fishing is a striking amalgamation of traditional patterns and modern technologies. Many of the same communities that gather each year to participate in the First Salmon Ceremony—welcoming the returning fish and honoring the natural cycle of life—also rely on sons and daughters sent to universities to learn biology in order to run state-of-the-art hatcheries. While native people once again fish for subsistence, with consumption of salmon and steelhead now composing almost as much of the diet in some areas as in pre-treaty days, consortia like the Northwest Indian Fisheries Commission in western Washington and the Columbia River Intertribal Fish Commission in Oregon rely on high-powered computers to compile harvest data for commercial purposes. These latter entities, as well as representatives of the various regional native governments, interact regularly and directly with state, national, and international fisheries management boards, on which Indians now hold several key positions.

Things have moved a considerable distance from the days in the late '60s when the federal government professed to "lack the resources" to assist indigenous nations of the Pacific Northwest in rebuilding their shattered fishing economies

Map II

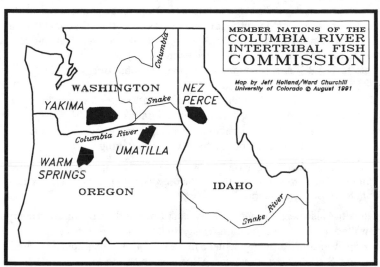

MEMBER NATIONS OF THE
COLUMBIA RIVER
INTERTRIBAL FISH
COMMISSION

Map by Jeff Holland/Ward Churchill
University of Colorado © August 1991

(while, as part of its "hearts and minds" program in Southeast Asia, it was providing Vietnamese fishermen with 10,000 outboard motors, 50,000 sets of fishing gear, 27 million fingerlings for stocking purposes, and sixteen complete fishing piers).[52] Gone too are the days when the Federal Bureau of Commercial Fisheries could decline a $100,000-grant request from the Quinaults to begin development of economic self-sufficiency based in fishing while providing double that amount to bolster the already solvent non-Indian fishing industry in the same area.[53]

Native American extra-legal and legal offensives have, of course, been of fundamental importance in bringing about such changes. As Marci Golde of the Washington Environmental Council put it in 1987, "People may not have seen the light, but they felt the fire."[54] Other factors, corporate self-interest among them, have also occasionally worked to the Indians' advantage. Norman Dale, in his article "Getting to Co-Management: Social Learning in the Redesign of Fisheries Management," suggests that the court decisions in the Northwest combined with other factors to establish a context for "social learning," wherein a fundamental shift in the framework of organizational attitudes and interorganizational behavior has taken place.[55] The emerging situation has been characterized by a drift in state policy from confrontation to litigation to negotiation, and by the development of an array of working relationships between indigenous, governmental, industrial, and environmental groups.[56]

The formation and strategy of the Northwest Water Resources Committee (NWRC) offers a useful illustration of how the process has evolved. Created in 1981 by major timber, utility and banking concerns, NWRC set out to assess the implications of a 1980 ruling in *U.S. v. Washington (Phase II),* which endorsed the concept of environmental protection for native fisheries. NWRC was concerned about the limits such protection might place on future development and about the uncertainty it could engender among potential investors. The committee hired James Waldo, an attorney experienced in treaty litigation, to study the matter. His analysis high-lighted the record of legal losses suffered by treaty opponents, outlined the options available to NWRC, and recommended direct negotiations with indigenous na-tions.[57] The corporations agreed.

Negotiations have had positive results beyond improvements in native eco-nomic and political positioning. These include finalization of a very effective Puget Sound Management Plan for salmon in 1985. Anadronomous-fish expert William Clark has described the result of this first-ever undertaking:

> Puget Sound salmon management is a success overall, at least in the author's opinion. Some problems remain, but the prospects for solving them are better than for most other fisheries.[58]

There has also been formation of an Indian/non-Indian coalition to complete a long-awaited U.S./Canada Salmon Treaty in 1985 and the development of the Timber, Fish and Wildlife Agreement in 1987 that led to important changes in Washington State forestry practices. Moreover, the state and several indigenous nations negotiated a hunting agreement that took effect in the fall of 1988. On the Columbia River, a new fish management plan was agreed upon by Oregon, Wash-ington, the U.S., and four indigenous nations in 1988. As Michael Blumm, editor of the *Anadromous Fish Law Memo,* has put it:

> Recognition of the tribes as managers as well as harvesters has, while compli-cating management, also induced better decision making by requiring better data and more publicly accountable decisions. The treaty right even fostered an international agreement to better manage harvests and national legislation designed to double run sizes. There is little question that the beneficiaries of the treaty right to fish are not limited to the signatory Indian tribes.[59]

On August 4, 1989, as part of the state's bicentennial, the state of Washington and the treaty peoples signed the Centennial Accord, which outlines key principles of the relationship between the two sides. A ceremony and celebration was held at the Burke Museum on the University of Washington campus. For the occasion, Washington Governor Booth Gardner declared: "This accord sets the pace for the rest of the nation. Once and for all, let us recognize the mutual benefits of government-to-government relations."[60] Despite the remarkable changes that have occurred in the last decade, there continue to be problems requiring resolution. One issue involves rights to harvest shellfish. Over the past several years, representatives of state agencies and indigenous nations have attempted to resolve the question of Indian rights to this vital resource. These negotiations have thus far proven unsuccessful. Native people also continue to express concern about environmental issues affecting the fish. The Yakima Nation recently drew attention to the threat posed by pollution of the Columbia River system by pulp and paper mills. *The Columbia River Intertribal Fish Commission News* reported that EPA and industry studies indicate that dioxin is present in some Columbia

Map III

River fish, including sturgeon and salmon, giving rise to apprehension over the use of these fish in the Indian diet and in commerce.[61]

And, of course, there is the perpetual problem of white backlash. The 1988 Washington state gubernatorial race incumbent, Booth Gardner, a proponent of cooperative management, was seriously challenged by Bob White, advocate of a return of all natural resource management authority to state agencies. Although his position was clearly untenable under the current legal mandate, and he was solidly defeated in the election, White commanded support from a substantial segment of the non-Indian population opposed to Indian treaty rights. Anti-treaty organizations—such as ICERR; S/SPAWN (Salmon/Steelhead Protective Association and Wildlife Network), based in Washington; STA (Stop Treaty Abuse); and PARR (Protect America's Rights and Resources), based in Wisconsin—continue to challenge implementation of legally affirmed Indian treaty rights. This threat is currently most evident in the conflict surrounding Anishinabé treaty rights in northern Wisconsin.

The Battle in Wisconsin

The Great Lakes Chippewa (Anishinabé) bands in the U.S. are indigenous to the very center of North America. The region is defined by Lake Michigan, Lake Superior, and Lake Huron, and is dotted with thousands of smaller lakes, in the present states of Michigan, Minnesota, and Wisconsin (see Map III). The treaty rights of Indians in all three states have been the subject of important lawsuits in recent years: *Minnesota Chippewa Tribe v. United States* (315 F.2d 906, 911 (Ct. Cl. 1962)),

Menominee Tribe v. United States (391 U.S. 404 (1968)), *People v. LaBlanc* (399 Mich. 31, 248 N.W.2d 199 (1976)), and *United States v. Michigan* (623 F.2d 448, 450 (6th Cir. 1980)). This discussion, however, deals primarily with the Anishinabé of Wisconsin.[62]

Although the Anishinabé were partially agricultural and engaged in a significant amount of trade, their traditional economy also incorporated considerable hunting, fishing, and gathering: "The Chippewa harvested virtually everything on the landscape. They had some use or uses for all flora and fauna in their environment, whether for food, clothing, shelter, religious, commercial or other purposes."[63] By the mid-19th century, the Anishinabé had ceded much of their vast lands through treaties with the United States and Canada, but they reserved rights to the resources in these ceded territories. Anishinabé activist Winona LaDuke observes that:

> Beginning at Fort MacIntosh in 1785, and ending in 1923 at Georgian Bay, the U.S. and Canadian governments (or the Crown of England, during the early period) entered into more than 40 treaties with the Anishinabé. These treaties were an interpretation of Anishinabé legal rights in relationship to the U.S., England and Canada. They were also the basis for some of the largest land transactions in world history.[64]

As concerns the Anishinabés of Wisconsin in particular, the right of "hunting, fishing and gathering wild rice, upon the lands, the rivers and lakes included in the territory ceded," were reserved under Article 5 of the Treaty of 1837. The reservation of such rights was, however, qualified by inclusion of the language "during the pleasure of the President of the United States." In 1842, a second treaty, by which the Anishinabé ceded a portion of their remaining Wisconsin territory, was negotiated. Article 2 of that treaty also reserved "the right of hunting on that territory, along with the usual rights of occupancy, until required to remove them by the President of the United States."[65] Although the Indians had been led to believe that a presidential revocation of their hunting and fishing rights was unlikely ever to occur, it was ordered by President Millard Fillmore on February 6, 1850.[66] The revocation was shortly reversed at the request of the secretary of interior when it was discovered that the Wisconsin area might be used as a sort of swap for Anishinabé consent to cede a mineral-rich tract in Minnesota, east of the Mississippi River:

> [I]t may be necessary to permit them all to remain, in order to acquire a cession of the large tract of country they still own east of the Mississippi, which, on account of its great mineral resources, is an object of material importance to obtain.[67]

Consequently, in the Treaty of LaPointe, concluded on September 30, 1854, the Wisconsin reservations—along with unrestricted usufructary rights, including entitlement to hunt and fish in previously ceded areas—were reinstated under Articles 2 and 11. This was the final transaction between the federal government and Anishinabés of Wisconsin, so all should have been well. But, as in the Northwest, state restrictions severely eroded these treaty guarantees before the end of the 19th century. By the mid-20th century, native fishing and hunting rights had been effectively confined to demarcated reservation areas, and traditional fishing techniques, such as spearing and gill-netting, were prohibited even there.[68] As a result, the Anishinabé of Wisconsin were among the poorest people in North America and were particularly susceptible to the government's relocation programs of the 1950s and '60s.[69] Those who remained on the reservations had little alternative but to defy state game regulations or starve.

On March 8, 1974, two Anishinabé men from the Lac Courte Oreilles Reservation were arrested by wardens of the Wisconsin Department of Natural Resources (WDNR) while engaged in subsistence ice fishing at Chief Lake, an off-reservation location. They were charged with several offenses, including possession of a fishing spear and occupation of a fish shanty without a state permit, convicted and heavily fined.[70] A year later, the Lac Courte Oreilles Ojibway (as these Anishinabés are officially known) filed suit against Lester P. Voight, director of the WDNR, for "systematic interference in the exercise of Indian off-reservation fishing, hunting and other rights."[71]

> After a long period of litigation, on January 25, 1983, a three-judge panel of the U.S. Court of Appeals for the Seventh Circuit ruled that the Lake Superior Ojibway [of which the Anishinabés of Wisconsin are part] retained the right to hunt, fish and forage on lands ceded to the United States in the treaties of 1837 and 1842…encompassing nearly the entire northern third of Wisconsin. The court remanded the case to Judge James Doyle in Madison to consider "the permissible scope of State regulation of the ceded lands." In July 1983 Wisconsin appealed the case to the United States Supreme Court, which on October 3 denied its appeal, letting the lower court's ruling stand and leaving the state to work out the details.[72]

For their part, the six Wisconsin bands of Anishinabé joined with the four Lake Superior Minnesota bands to form the Voight Inter-Tribal Task Force, chaired by attorney James H. Schlender, an officer in the Lac Courte Oreilles government. The purpose of this entity was to coordinate environmental assessments, plan for Indian enforcement of unified native hunting and fishing regulations in both on- and off-reservation settings, manage and develop resources, and negotiate directly with state officials concerning ways and means of implementing the exercise of indigenous usufructary rights.[73] By mid-1984, the latter process had produced agreements with regard to deer hunting, ice fishing, trapping, and open-water fishing. The WDNR had publicly announced it would no longer attempt to enforce state regulations over Indians engaged in treaty-protected subsistence activities, including spear fishing and netting,

This brought a tremendous outcry from both anti-Indian political organizations, and "sporting groups" represented by the National Rifle Association and periodicals like *Field and Stream*.[74] At first, emphasis was placed on the "threat" of the native "running wild" and "exterminating" Wisconsin's deer population.

When it was revealed that Indians had taken fewer than 700 deer in 1984—about 0.3 percent of the total kill in Wisconsin that year—the focus was shifted to the "unfair advantage" enjoyed by indigenous people using traditional fishing techniques while non-Indians were restricted to fly fishing.[75] STA and PARR commenced a viciously racist campaign utilizing slogans such as "SAVE A WALLEYE — SPEAR AN INDIAN!" in an effort to whip up a climate of violence against native people and designed to intimidate them into foregoing their rights.[76] Beginning in 1985, substantial groups of non-Indian protesters—mainly, but not exclusively, white—responded to such cues by gathering at landings of lakes used by Indians engaged in fishing to harass them both physically and psychologically.

> The peaceful harvest of muskellunge and walleye [pike] by the Chippewa is threatened by non-Indians who barrage the peaceful fishers with rocks and insults, and who use large motorboats trailing anchors to capsize the boats of fishers. Because of this, the State of Wisconsin has pressured the Chippewa to give up their ancient rights to fish off of their reservation and has pressured them to do so immediately. This pressure has sometimes been applied indirectly, sometimes directly, but always upon the Chippewa. And all because a small group creates a disturbance in opposition to the Chippewas' federally recognized legal rights.[77]

By 1989, PARR had published a list assigning "points" in ascending quantity to anyone bringing in proof that he or she had killed various "types" of Indian: a "basic" Indian was said to be worth five points, a fisher worth ten, a native attorney worth twenty, and a "pregnant squaw" worth fifty points.[78] Although the "contest" has been sloughed off by authorities as a "sick joke," shots have been fired at Indians, several cases of arson have occurred, and numerous beatings of native people— some of them quite severe—have been reported. In its document *Moving Beyond Argument: Racism and Treaty Rights,* the Great Lakes Indian Fish and Wildlife Commission describes the growth of anti-Indian violence in northern Wisconsin as "a fearsome phenomenon," unchecked by area law enforcement personnel.[79] The Center for World Indigenous Studies, based in Washington state, has expressed concern that STA and related groups may be converging with right-wing extremists who have coherent neo-nazi aspirations.[80]

The Anishinabé have responded to this situation by soliciting advice and support from the indigenous nations of the Pacific Northwest, Indian organizations such as AIM, and sympathetic non-Indian groups like the Left Green Network and Midwest Treaty Network.[81] They have also undertaken a concerted litigational offensive designed to expand upon the range of practical rights acknowledged as theirs under the treaties, compel enforcement of these rights by officials and agencies of the state of Wisconsin, and bring direct federal intervention in the conflict in the event the state defaults on its responsibilities in this regard.[82] At present, the results of these initiatives are not in. However, as James Horton of Washington's Klallam Nation observed during a recent visit to Wisconsin, "We've gone through all of the things you're going through."[83]

The extent to which the experience of the indigenous nations of the Pacific Northwest may in fact be applicable to those of Wisconsin remains to be seen. Certainly, there are numerous differences in cultural context, land use and tenure patterns, geography, and the nature of the fisheries themselves.[84] Additionally, there are marked differences in the timing by which maximum non-Indian violence has occurred in relation to judicial decisions on native rights. Still, most of the elements of "social learning" by which appreciable gains have been made by Indians in the Northwest are present in Wisconsin at this point. And it is clear that the Anishinabé of that state, like the Indians of Washington and Oregon, are prepared to stay the course of their struggle, regardless of how long it lasts.

Conclusion

After decades of conflict, the treatied peoples of the United States are moving closer to regaining their rights to harvest and manage fish and other resources. In recent years, strong legal rulings have confirmed their claims to the natural resources upon which they depended since time immemorial. The translation of rights guaranteed by federal treaty into the practical realities of contemporary politics has been very difficult, distorted and sometimes blocked by state actions or inactions and by the opposition of private non-Indian entities that perceive their interests to be threatened. The sharing of resources, policymaking, and management prerogatives are all part of a system of government-to-government relations that can and must replace the structure of internal colonial domination that has defined the U.S.-Indian relationship for the past two centuries. The Pacific Northwest experience amply demonstrates that confrontation can, to the benefit of all parties concerned, be replaced by patterns of cooperation and coordination. The same principle applies to Wisconsin and every other area of the United States.

Such sharing is itself a key concept underlying the treaties in both the northwest and Wisconsin, at least from the indigenous point of view. The Northwest treaties spoke of "fishing in common," a matter which was and is perfectly acceptable to the native nations of that area. In Wisconsin, various court rulings also state that Indian rights are held in common with those of non-Indians.[85] Historically, indigenous nations of both regions have long traditions of sharing with non-Indians. This pattern is reflected in the recent statement of Nick Hockings, member of the Wa-Swa-Gon Association in Wisconsin, an organization to support treaty rights among the Lac du Flambeau Anishinabé Band: "We want to share with non-Indians, we really do, we always have."[86] But, of course, sharing is a two-way street, based in mutual respect and acknowledgment by each side of the rights and needs of the other. In the end, there is no other basis for dignity and justice among human beings.

American Indians and non-Indians who work with them on cooperative programs frequently speak of another essential motivation for development of a bona fide system of sharing at every level. This is their common concern for the resources at issue. There is increasing awareness, especially among non-Indians (native people having never really abandoned such knowledge), of the fragility of the environment, the need for conservation, and of the goal of sustainable resource use.[87] In this context, the environmental dimension of Indian treaty rights becomes particularly important. Michael Blumm and others have argued that a legal obligation to our mutual habitat almost certainly exists, even though it has not yet been defined in court rulings.[88] This "environmental right," which may provide for environmental rehabilitation, clean water, and other shared benefits, is another basis—indeed, an imperative—for Indian and non-Indian cooperation at the most fundamental levels. Until this cooperation is finally actualized between the indigenous people of North America and those whose heritage is one of immigration, the native struggle on this continent must and will continue.

Notes

1. American Friends Service Committee, *Uncommon Controversy: Fishing Rights of the Muckleshoot, Puyallup and Nisqually Indians,* University of Washington Press, Seattle, 1970; U.S. Commission on Civil Rights, *Indian Tribes: A Continuing Quest for Survival,* U.S. Government Printing Office, Washington, D.C., 1981; Cohen, Faye G., *Treaties on Trial: The Continuing Controversy Over Northwest Fishing Rights,* University of Washington Press, Seattle, 1986.
2. Interview with staff at Northwest Renewable Center, Seattle, March 17, 1989; quoted in Cohen, Faye G., "American Indian Fishing Rights: A Legacy of Conflict," in Ward Churchill, ed., *Critical Issues in Native North America,* Vol. II, International Work Group on Indigenous Affairs (IWGIA), Copenhagen, 1991, pp. 154-73.
3. See Vennum, Thomas Jr., *Wild Rice and the Ojibway People,* Minnesota Historical Society Press, St. Paul, 1988.
4. *U.S. v. Winans,* p. 381. It is estimated by most reputable anthropologists that the fishing cultures of the Pacific Northwest are at least 30,000 years old.
5. Anadromous fish are born in fresh water, migrate to the ocean where they reach their maturity, and complete their life cycle by returning on one or more occasions to the place where they were born to spawn.
6. See Drucker, Philip, *Cultures of the Northwest Coast,* Chandler Publishers, San Francisco, 1965.
7. Steiner, Stan, *The New Indians,* Harper and Row Publishers, New York, 1968, p. 54. For a recounting of the process by which the reservations, tiny to begin with, were diminished to this size, see Deloria, Vine Jr., *Indians of the Pacific Northwest: From the Coming of the White Man to the Present Day,* Doubleday Publishers, Garden City, NY, 1977 (esp. Chapter 10).
8. Record of the council proceedings wherein the Treaty of Point No Point was negotiated and executed, January 26, 1855, Exh. PL-15, Joint Appendix to *U.S. v. Washington,* 384 F. Supp. 312 (W.D. Wash. 1974), p. 331.
9. The Treaty of Port Elliot, signed with the Muckleshoot in the same year, reads exactly the same way. Subsequent treaties signed with the Yakima, Flatheads (Salish), Kutenai and others also contain almost identical language.
10. Meyer, William, *Native Americans: The New Indian Resistance,* International Publishers, New York, 1971, p. 70.
11. *Treaties on Trial,* op. cit., p. 58.
12. See Cole, Douglas, and Ira Chaikan, *An Iron Hand Upon the People: The Law Against Potlatch on the Northwest Coast,* University of Washington Press, Seattle, 1990.
13. "American Indian Fishing Rights," op. cit.
14. Quoted in O'Brien, Sharon, *American Indian Tribal Governments,* University of Oklahoma Press, Norman, 1989, p. 286.
15. See Wolf, Roger, "Needed: A System of Low Income Maintenance for Indians," *Arizona Law Review,* No. 10, 1968.
16. Steiner, op. cit., p. 56.
17. U.S. Senate, Committee on Interior and Insular Affairs, Subcommittee on Indian Affairs, *Indian Fishing Rights: Hearings on S.J.R. 170 and S.J.R. 171,* 88th Cong., 2d Sess., U.S. Government Printing Office, Washington, D.C., August 5-6, 1964, p. 23.

18. Royce, W., *et al.*, *Salmon Gear Limitations in Northern Washington Waters*, University of Washington Publications in Fisheries, N.S. 2, No. 2, 1963.
19. See Steiner, op. cit., pp. 48-64. Also see Thom, Mel, "Indian War, 1963-1964," *American Aborigine*, Vol. 2, No. 1, 1965.
20. Quoted in ibid., p. 55.
21. Ibid., pp. 50-1. Also see "Fish-Ins: The Whys and Wherefores," *NCAI Sentinel*, Vol. 10, No. 5, December 1965 and McCloud, Janet, "Fisher Indians in Fight for Treaty," *The Indian Historian*, Vol. 4, Nos. 1-2, Winter 1966/Spring 1967.
22. Meyer, op. cit., p. 71.
23. Steiner, op. cit., pp. 52-3.
24. Brando is quoted in ibid., p. 57. On Gregory's participation and arrest, see Deloria, op. cit., p. 164.
25. Adams, a "displaced Assiniboin-Sioux" who was raised on the Quinalt Reservation and is director of Survival of American Indians, Inc. (a fishing rights organization), was shot in the stomach by two white men with a rifle who fired through the open window of his car. Tacoma police investigators labored mightily to establish that the wound was "self-inflicted." See Meyer, op. cit., p. 72.
26. Certain of the more important AIM leaders of the early '70s, such as Janet McCloud and Sid Mills, a Yakima, came directly from the fishing rights struggle. A significant element of the grassroots membership—notably the Northwest AIM Group, of which Leonard Peltier, Bob and Jim Robideau, Joe Stuntz, and Dino Butler were a part—was also forged in that crucible.
27. Deloria, Vine Jr., and Clifford M. Lytle, *The Nations Within: The Past and Future of American Indian Sovereignty*, Pantheon Books, NY, 1984, p. 234.
28. *Puyallup Tribe v. Department of Game, et al.*, 391 U.S. 392 (1968); *Puyallup Tribe v. Department of Game, et al.*, 414 U.S. 441 (1973); *Puyallup Tribe v. Department of Game, et al.*, 433 U.S. 165 (1977).
29. *Sohappy v. Smith*, 302 F. Supp. 899 (1986); also known as *United States. v. Oregon*, 657 F.2d 1009 (1982); 717 F.2d 299 (9 Cir. 1983); 699 F. Supp. 1456 (D. Or. 1988).
30. *U.S. v. Washington* (Phase I), 384 F. Supp. 312 (1974).
31. *U.S. v. Washington* (Phase II), 506 F. Supp. 187 (1980).
32. See Schmidhauser, Eric, "The Struggle for Cultural Survival: The Fishing Rights of the Treaty Tribes of the Pacific Northwest," *Notre Dame Law Review*, No. 52, 1976 and Reynolds, Norman J., "Indian Hunting and Fishing Rights: The Role of Tribal Sovereignty and Preemption," *North Carolina Law Review*, No. 62, 1984.
33. On the ICERR, see Wright, Carol, "What People Have Formed Backlash Groups?" *Yakima Nation Review*, Special Autumn Supplement, 1977.
34. See Talbot, Steve, *The Roots of Oppression. The American Indian Question*, International Publishers, New York, 1981, pp. 184-6. He is drawing heavily on Wright, op. cit., and an unpublished manuscript by Harvard economist Eilene M. Stillwagon entitled "Anti-Indian Agitation and Economic Interests in the 1980s."
35. *Treaties on Trial*, op. cit., pp. 100-1.
36. *Puget Sound Gillnetters Association v. United States District Court*, 573 F. 2d 1123 (1978), p. 1126. The Cunningham draft bill is contained in H.R. 13329, 95th Cong., 2d Sess. (1978).
37. On *Puyallup III*, see Johnson, Ralph, "The State versus Indian Off-Reservation Fishing: A United States Supreme Court Error," *Washington Law Review*, No. 47, 1972.
38. The U.S. Congress passed the Salmon and Steelhead Conservation and Enhancement Act of 1980 and the Pacific Northwest Power Planning and Conservation Act of 1980, which contained provisions for the protection, enhancement, and mitigation of fish populations affected by Columbia River power developments.
39. The system of harvest sharing on the Columbia River differs from that in western Washington. It is based on separate treaty and non-treaty fishing zones and on the allocation framework in the Columbia River Management Plan. See *Treaties on Trial*, op. cit., Chapter Ten.
40. Quoted in the introduction to ibid., pp. xxiv-xxv.
41. *United States v. David Sohappy, Sr., et al.*, 770 F.2d 816 (9th Cir. 1985). The defendants were charged not only with specific violation(s) of the Lacey Act, but with conspiring to violate it. All were acquitted on the conspiracy charge.
42. 12 *Stat.* 951 (1855), at 953.
43. *United States v. Winans*, at 381.

44. Similar interpretations occur in *Seufert Bros. Co. v. United States* (249 U.S. 194 (1918)) and *Tulee v. State of Washington* (315 U.S. 681 (1941)).

45. See *A True Copy of the Record of the Official Proceedings of the Council in the Walla Walla Valley, 1855*, Ye Galleon Press, Yakima, WA, 1985, pp. 39-40.

46. *U.S. v. Sohappy*, at 819-20. This is directly contrary to specific precedents established by the Ninth Circuit Court itself; see *Settler v. Lameer* (507 F.2d 231 (9th Cir. 1974)). It is also contrary to the principles embodied in Supreme Court rulings such as those in *Williams v. Lee* (358 U.S. 217 (1959)) and *New Mexico v. Mescalero Apache Tribe* (462 U.S. 324 (1983)).

47. *David Sohappy, Sr., et al. v. United States*, No. 85-6581, October Term, 1985; brief submitted, April 23, 1986.

48. Brief, at 7.

49. Ibid., at 9-10.

50. *United States v. David Sohappy, Sr., et al.*, 477 U.S. 906 (1986), *cert.* denied.

51. A sample of the sort of non-Indian activist attention attracted to Indian fishing rights by the Sohappy case may be found in Anonymous, *To Fish in Common: Fishing Rights in the Northwest*, Native American Solidarity Committee (NASC), Seattle, 1978; revised and reprinted in 1988.

52. Steiner, op. cit., p. 62.

53. See Office of the Director, *American Indian Resources Study, 1967*, National Congress of the American Indian (NCAI), Washington, D.C., November 1966.

54. Quoted in "Implementing Indian Treaty Fishing Rights," op. cit., p. 160.

55. Dale, Norman, "Getting to Co-Management: Social Learning in the Redesign of Fisheries Management," in Evelyn Pinkerton, ed., *Cooperative Management of Local Fisheries: New Directions for Improved Management and Community Development*, University of British Columbia Press, Vancouver, 1989, pp. 49-72.

56. Ibid., pp. 62-6.

57. Waldo, James, "*U.S. v. Washington* (Phase II): Analysis and Recommendations," prepared for the Northwest Water Resources Committee, Seattle, 1981 (unpublished).

58. Clark, William, "Fishing in a Sea of Court Orders: Puget Sound Salmon Management 10 Years After the Boldt Decision," *North American Journal of Fisheries Management*, No. 5, 1985, pp. 417-34 (esp. p. 417).

59. Blumm, Michael, "Native Fishing Rights and Environmental Protection in North America and New Zealand: A Comparative Analysis," *Anadromous Fish Law Memo*, No. 48, Lewis and Clark Law School, Portland, OR, January 1989.

60. Quoted on invitations to the signing ceremony.

61. Columbia River Inter-Tribal Fishing Commission, "Dioxin: Yakimas Take a Stand Against Pollution," *CRITF News*, February 1990, pp. 2-3.

62. For a discussion of the Wisconsin cases, see Strickland, Rennard, Stephan J. Hertzberg, and Steven R. Owens, "Keeping Our Word: Indian Treaty Rights and Public Responsibilities, A Report on a Recommended Federal Role Following Wisconsin's Request for Federal Assistance," April 16, 1990 (presently unpublished). At p. 10, Strickland, *et al.*, point out that although the cases refer to treaty rights, the rights predate the treaties. The courts recognize that the rights always belonged to the Anishinabé and were reserved by them in the treaties. Some Anishinabé object to the term "treaty rights" since it implies that the rights were actually created by the treaties, rather than simply acknowledged within them.

63. *Lac Courte Oreilles Band of Lake Superior Chippewa Indians v. State of Wisconsin*, 653 F. Supp. 1420 (1987), p. 1424. Also see Hickerson, Harold, *The Chippewa and Their Neighbors: A Study in Ethnohistory*, Holt, Rinehart and Winston Publishers, New York, 1970.

64. LaDuke, Winona, "The White Earth Land Struggle," in Ward Churchill, ed., *Critical Issues in Native North America*, International Work Group on Indigenous Affairs (IWGIA), Copenhagen, 1989, pp. 55-71; quote from p. 55.

65. The history of treaty-making is recounted in *Lac Courte Oreilles Band of Lake Superior Chippewa Indians v. State of Wisconsin*, 700 F.2d 341 (7th Cir. 1983).

66. As a white trader who had witnessed the 1842 treaty proceedings first-hand later put it, "No conversation that was held gave the Indians an inkling or caused them to mistrust that they were ceding away their lands, but supposed that they were simply selling their pine and minerals, as they had in 1837." See Armstrong, Benjamin G., *Early Life Among the Indians*, A.W. Bowron Publishers, Ashland, WI, 1892.

67. U.S. Department of War, Office of Indian Affairs, *Annual Report of the Commissioner of Indian Affairs*, 33d Cong., 2d Sess., U.S. Government Printing Office, Washington, D.C., November 1854.
68. See Hawley, Brian A., "Treaty Interpretation of Off Reservation Rights," *Hamline Law Review*, No. 4, January 1981, pp. 373-89.
69. See Fixico, Donald E., *Termination and Relocation: Federal Indian Policy, 1945-1960*, University of New Mexico Press, Albuquerque, 1986.
70. Vennum, op. cit., pp. 275-6.
71. *Lac Courte Oreilles Band of Lake Superior Chippewa Indians v. Voight* (1974), discussed in 700 F.2d (7th Cir. 1983).
72. Vennum, op. cit., p. 276.
73. Ibid., pp. 276-7. Also see Hawley, op. cit.
74. The NRA has used its various publications, such as *American Rifleman*, to editorialize consistently against Indian treaty rights since 1985. On the early stages of anti-Indian backlash in Wisconsin, see the coverage in *Newsweek*, September 30, 1985, p. 35.
75. The totals on deer kill were provided by the WDNR; they have not varied appreciably since 1984, with the Indian total still running at less than 1 percent of the Wisconsin total in 1990.
76. See Wisconsin Advisory Committee to the U.S. Commission on Civil Rights, *Discrimination Against Chippewa Indians in Northern Wisconsin: A Summary Report*, Milwaukee, December 1989, p. 13 (unpublished).
77. Strickland, et al., op. cit., p. 1.
78. *Discrimination Against Chippewa Indians*, op. cit. Also see *Lac Court Oreilles Band of Lake Superior Chippewa Indians v. State of Wisconsin*, 707 F. Supp. 10346 (1989), at 1054.
79. Great Lakes Indian Fish and Wildlife Commission, *Moving Beyond Argument: Racism and Treaty Rights*, Public Information Office, Odanah, WI, n.d., p. 6.
80. Center for World Indigenous Studies, "Study on Competing Sovereignties and the Anti-Indian Movement," in *Insights Into Racism*, a special supplement to *Masinaigan: Newspaper of the Great Lakes Indian Fish and Game Commission*, July 1988, p. 11.
81. See Grossman, Zoltan "Wisconsin Treaty Conflict: No End in Sight," *Z Magazine*, July-August 1990, pp. 124-8.
82. The cases are *Lac Courte Oreilles Band of Lake Superior Chippewa Indians v. Wisconsin* (668 F. Supp. 1233 (W.D. Wis. 1987)), *Lac Courte Oreilles Band of Lake Superior Chippewa Indians v. Wisconsin* (663 F. Supp. 682 (W.D. Wis. 1987)), *Lac Court Oreilles Band of Lake Superior Chippewa Indians v. Wisconsin* (653 F. Supp. 1420 (W.D. Wis. 1987)), *Lac Courte Oreilles Band of Lake Superior Chippewa Indians v. Wisconsin*, 686 F. Supp. 226 (W.D. Wis. 1988)), and *Lac Courte Oreilles Band of Lake Superior Chippewa Indians v. Wisconsin*, 707 F. Supp. 1034 (W.D. Wis 1989)).
83. Quoted in "The Chronicle of the Lake Superior Chippewa," *Masinaigan*, 1989 Spring Spearing Edition, Odanah, WI, p. 16. Also see Strickland, et al., op. cit., p. 10.
84. *Lac Court Oreilles Band of Lake Superior Chippewa Indians v. State of Wisconsin* (1989), op. cit., p. 1053 emphasizes the differences between the Wisconsin situation and that of the Northwest fisheries. Another difference involves the nature and implications of competing resource use in Wisconsin, particularly with regard to mining (*Minewatch Briefing*. No. 5, June 1990).
85. *Lac Court Oreilles Band of Lake Superior Chippewa Indians v. State of Wisconsin* (1987), op. cit., p. 1429; *U.S. v. Bourchard*, 464 F. Supp. 1316, 1338 (1978).
86. Quoted in Strickland, et al., op. cit., p. 26.
87. See, for example, World Commission on Environment and Development, *Our Common Future*, Oxford University Press, London/New York, 1987, pp. 114-16.
88. Blumm, op. cit., pp. 4-5.

Chapter VIII

Native North America
The Political Economy of Radioactive Colonialism

Ward Churchill and Winona LaDuke

[O]ur defeat was always implicit in the history of others; our wealth has always generated our poverty by nourishing the prosperity of others, the empires and their native overseers...In the colonial and neocolonial alchemy, gold changes to scrap metal and food into poison...[We]have become painfully aware of the mortality of wealth which nature bestows and imperialism appropriates.

Eduardo Galeano
Open Veins of Latin America

L and has always been the issue central to North American politics and econom-ics. Those who control the land are those who control the resources within and upon it. Whether the resource at issue is oil, natural gas, uranium, or other minerals; water or agriculture; or land ownership, social control and all the other aggregate components of power are fundamentally interrelated. At some levels, such a situation seems universal, but in this hemisphere, given the peculiarities of a contemporary socioeconomic apparatus of power that has been literally imported in its entirety, the equation seems all the more acute.

Within North America, American Indian reservations—or "reserves," as they are called in Canada—constitute a small but crucial "piece of the rock." Approximately one-third of all western U.S. low-sulphur coal, 20 percent of known U.S. reserves of oil and natural gas, and over one-half of all U.S. uranium deposits lie under the reservations.[1] Other important minerals such as bauxite and zeolites are also located there in substantial quantities, and a considerable proportion of western U.S. water resources are subject to American Indian priority use through various treaty stipulations. A comparable, if somewhat less pronounced, situation prevails in Canada.[2] Even these figures are misleadingly small. Past (1890-1920) and more recent (1930-1990) land expropriations undertaken by corporate interests, such as railroads, agribusiness, and mining concerns, as well as "land withdrawals" from indigenous nations orchestrated by the federal government under the provisions of the Allotment Act, the Homestead Act, the Termination Act, and other legislation must be considered in any rational assessment.[3] If the areas stripped away from tribal ownership and control in direct violation of standing international agreements are included, the amount of contemporary American Indian resources is suddenly jolted to a much higher level than is conventionally perceived.[4]

One example of this is the southern Arizona copper belt, a deposit yielding fully two-thirds of all U.S. copper ore. The bulk of the area was a part of the Papago Reservation until the copper was discovered during the 1920s. The ore-bearing portion was subsequently removed from the Papago domain by unilateral decree ("statute") of the U.S. Congress.[5] Similarly, the bulk of the massive Fort Union coal deposit of Wyoming, Montana, and North Dakota does not fall within current reservation boundaries but does underlie the territory reserved by the Lakota, Cheyenne, and Arapaho nations under the terms of the Fort Laramie Treaty of 1868. Although some 90 percent of the original treaty area has now "passed" from Indian control, the treaty in question remains an internationally binding document conferring ownership to the signatory indigenous peoples in perpetuity.[6]

Aside from the mining interests that have made huge contemporary inroads into what amounts to unceded Indian territory, another focal point of any examination of Indian resources must concern water rights (see Chapter Six). In the arid but energy-rich western U.S., water is both prerequisite and integral to all forms of corporate development. The preponderance of western water is legally owned (by virtue of treaties) by various Indian nations. Hypothetically, even if a given nation could not retain control over a portion of its territorality, it could still shape the nature and extent of corporate exploitation of the land through assertion of its water rights. Of course, the federal government has acted systematically to diminish or effectively void most Indian exercise of water rights prerogatives, even while pretending to uphold them (see Chapter Six).[7]

A final factor worthy of consideration concerns not resource distribution and control, but the distribution of production itself. For instance, while Indians technically "own" only about half of U.S. uranium resources, production statistics relative to reservation areas are *much* higher. In 1974, 100 percent of all federally controlled uranium production accrued from the contemporary reservation land base.[8] In 1975, there were some 380 leases concerning uranium extraction on reservation lands, as compared to a total of *four* on *both* public and acquired land. In Canada, the data are quite similar,[9] indicating that while North American Indian resources are perhaps not overwhelmingly large on a global scale, production certainly is.

The pattern of colonization prevalent in South America and noted in the quotation from Eduardo Galeano at the beginning of this chapter seems appropriate to conditions currently existing in the North as well. Internal colonialism—the colonization of indigenous peoples—is a prominent, if little discussed, fact of life within both the United States and Canada (and Mexico as well). The centrality of the issue of colonization of such Fourth World peoples to any reasonable strategy of global anti-imperialism appears much more evident in the North than in the South, not for moral reasons, but for pragmatic ones.[10] North America, the United States in particular, is the seat of the most comprehensive system of imperialism ever witnessed by humanity. Increasingly, it is a system fueled by nuclear capabilities, fed by uranium. The relationship of the reservations to that uranium is clear. Likewise, the United States and Canada lead the world in "food production"; needless to say, they have a huge stake in maintaining this position of dominance. Again, the relationship of the American Indian treaty lands to primary North American agricultural areas is readily observable. The same can be said relative to a range of crucial resources. Such issues, the internal integrity and hegemony of North American imperialism, and the colonial stranglehold over the resources of native sovereignties it implies, are the subject of this essay.

Internal Colonialism

A distinction must be made between property in its economic and legal aspects and property considered as a social institution. The territorial question of American Indian peoples in the United States is fundamentally an economic question, that is as the source of livelihood, but also involves the survival of human societies, and is, therefore, a question of human rights, and a nationalities question. A people cannot continue as a people without a land base, an economic base, and political independence, as distinguished from a religious group or an ethnic minority of fundamentally the same historical character as the majority society.

United Nations Subcommittee on Racism,
Racial Discrimination, Apartheid and Decolonization,
Final Report, 1977

American Indian nations in North America are today constrained to occupation of approximately 2.5 percent of their original land base.[11] Nonetheless, this land, if carefully managed or, in some cases, expanded to reconcile with legally posited treaty boundaries, provides a viable basis for national survival. The Navajo Nation, as one example, holds territory comparable to that of Belgium, the Netherlands, or Denmark. It is considerably larger than such European sovereignties as Luxemburg, Lichtenstein, or Monaco. Its natural resource base is far greater than that of these nations combined.[12] The Lakota or "Great Sioux" Reservation of the Dakotas, prior to its patently illegal dismemberment under the Allotment and Homestead Acts (1890-1920), provides an even more striking example. The Menominees of Wisconsin were almost entirely self-sufficient despite radical reductions of their land base, with a replenishable economy based on timbering, when the nation was unilaterally "dissolved" by congressional fiat in 1955. The peoples of the Pacific Northwest, the "Five Civilized Tribes" (Creek, Cherokee, Chickasaw, Choctaw, and Seminole, relocated from the Southeast to Oklahoma by federal force during the 1830s), the

Tohono O'Odham (Papago) of Arizona, the Cheyenne and Crow of Montana—and the list could go on and on—all possess a treaty-sanctioned and demonstrably viable economic basis for national existence. In Canada, the situation is much the same.

The *foreign* interests represented by the United States and Canadian national governments, however, have not been content with past land confiscations. Throughout this century, and into the present moment, each has proceeded with entirely insidious and mercenary policies. A classic vehicle of neocolonialism was created under the so-called Indian Reorganization Act (1934), whereby the United States imposed a system of "tribal council" governments on each reservation, a mechanism designed to replace traditional (and resistant) Indian governmental forms with an apparatus approved by and owing its allegiance to Washington, D.C. (See Chapter Three).

Recognized by the United States after 1934 as the sole governing body of Indian reservations (and peoples), the tribal council system rapidly circumvented or usurped the authority of traditional Indian governments such as the councils of chiefs. The U.S. rationale was and is readily apparent. The new "governments" were charged with responsibilities for "economic planning": mineral lease negotiations, contracting with external corporate agencies, long-term agricultural and ranching leasing, water rights negotiations, land transfers, and so on, all of which required direct approval from Bureau of Indian Affairs (BIA) representatives prior to consummation, and most of which had long been staunchly resisted by the traditional leadership.[13] The "reorganization" created a structure within which U.S. "developmental" policies could be implemented through a formalized agency *composed of the Indians themselves.* Canada followed suit with a similar ploy during the 1930s.

With the consolidation of political power on this blatantly neocolonial principle, modern internal colonialism became possible in North America. To inaugurate this fact, federal land management authorities acted immediately (in 1934) to begin the inversion of the extant tribal economies that had evolved to accommodate both traditional needs and the constrictions of reservation conditions. Stock reduction programs were initiated to alleviate what was termed "overgrazing" of reservation areas by individually and tribally owned cattle. These programs rapidly became permanent—as applied against Indians, not against non-Indian ranchers leasing reservation land for grazing purposes—and, since 1935, more than one-half of all Indian livestock resources have been eliminated as a result.

The effects of such a policy were predictable and immediate: the economic infrastructure of North American indigenous nations was dramatically undercut. On the Navajo Reservation, for instance, 58 percent of the people derived a livelihood from stock raising (mostly sheep) and agriculture (mostly gardening) in 1940. By 1958, less than 10 percent were able to do so.[14] Correspondingly, secondary and tertiary aspects of the tribal economy—such as the wool derived from sheep raising, and the blankets derived from wool—were dislocated. Concurrent with this marked and externally imposed reduction in self-sufficiency was the systematic transfer of economic power to the neocolonial structure lodged in the U.S./tribal council relationship: "developmental aid" from the United States, implementation of an "educational system" geared to training for the cruder labor needs of industrialism, employment contracts with mining and other resource extraction concerns, "housing programs" to provide appropriate workforce concentrations, and—eventually—actualization of cooptive social control mechanisms such as unemployment and welfare for newly dependent Indian citizens.

On the Navajo Reservation in 1978, approximately 35 percent of the working-age population was employed year-round. Of those employed, 57.7 percent worked as a result of government subsidies, 29.3 percent received their salaries from private non-Navajo enterprises, and only 13 percent worked in wholly Navajo operations of all types. This, of course, left Navajo unemployment at approximately 65 percent. Hence, Navajo self-sufficiency may be estimated as accommodating some 4.3 percent of the work-age population, down from 100 percent in 1920.[15] Such a single-generational transition from self-sufficiency to destitution would seem the strongest possible testimony to the negative effects of U.S. internal colonialism on indigenous populations, but it is not: At the Pine Ridge Lakota Reservation in South Dakota, to list but one example, unemployment currently hovers over 90 percent and self-sufficiency is unknown.[16]

Overall, reservation unemployment in both the United States and Canada runs at about 65 percent (making the Navajo example somewhat normal).[17] Subsistence is gleaned from a sort of federal per capita payment system that keeps the bulk of the population alive but abjectly dependent. Two Canadian researchers, Mark Zannis and Robert Davis, analyzed the welfare system in Canada and found that:

> The welfare system is a form of pacification. Combined with political and physical repression it keeps people alive at a subsistence level but blunts any attempt at revolt while turning them into captive consumers of industrial products...For the past 2-3 decades, a kind of enclosure movement has taken place, brought on by the very nature of the welfare system and the dictates of corporate profits.[18]

Zannis and Davis go on to note that residential requirements are integral to any form of welfare—nuclear families and individuals receive this sort of income as opposed to groups (i.e., "clans" or extended families, the traditional Indian form of social organization). Coupled with the educational system, the result is that "without children, adults are deprived of the essential labor to carry out traditional economic activities. This creates the need for more welfare," and continues the "reorganization" of Indian societies mandated by the act of 1934.

In recent years, it has become obvious that the social and economic disruption inflicted upon many indigenous nations results from needs peculiar to energy corporations. For example, when Peabody Coal requires 400,000 acres of Indian land for a strip-mining operation, not only is the tribal infrastructure (land use, employment, and the like) affected, but the physical distribution of the people as well. Relocation of people—as is happening at Big Mountain, Hopi and elsewhere—forces transformations of familial integrity, community organization, etc.[19] The phased destruction of tribal entities undertaken as "reorganization" in the 1930s has greatly accelerated with the advent of the world "energy crisis" in the 1970s.

Compounding this problem in the 1980s and on into the '90s are the budgetary cutbacks in social service spending undertaken by the "supply-siders" of the Reagan and Bush administrations. As the federal government defaults on the reservations, native people are driven for bare sustenance into the arms of the very corporations with which they are purportedly to "negotiate" over use of their land and extraction of their resources. Clearly, prostration is a poor bargaining position from which to proceed, but a half-century of neocolonial rule has resulted in little else. Despite the obvious and abundant wealth of land and resources they nominally retain mentioned above, North American Indian populations suffer virtually the full range of conditions observable in the most depressed of Third World areas. Theirs is the highest rate of infant mortality on the continent, the shortest life expectancy, the greatest incidence of malnutrition, the highest rate of death by exposure, the highest unemployment, the lowest per capita income, the highest rate of communicable or plague diseases, the lowest level of formal educational attainment, and so on.[20]

Since such data indicate that the federal government has failed abjectly in promoting Indian well-being as promised by the Reorganization Act, there is a strong feeling in many quarters of Indian Country that the turn to the corporations now being necessitated by Reaganite policies is not such a bad idea. Despite the poor bargaining position through which indigenous nations are securing extraction royalty rates in the 2 to 5 percent (of market) range, a pittance in the world market, internal production distribution within North America is such that the sheer quantity of mining and other corporate activities likely to occur over the next twenty years will generate a huge cash flow into the hands of the tribal councils.[21] It is this cash flow, real and potential, which the U.S. government, the tribal governments, and the corporations are all banking on to offset—in the short run at least—the cumulative effects of internal colonialism on American Indians.

Western energy- and resource-rich reservations in particular are faced with a political and economic turning point at least as vast in its implications as the reorganization of the 1930s, or even the 19th-century transitions to reservation status. Should they embrace and participate in the process of industrializing the reservations after the fashion of "developing" Third World nations, or pursue a Fourth World strategy of attempting to disengage from dominant processes and procedures altogether?[22] The results of this decision will undoubtedly shape the futures of American Indian peoples irrevocably. At this juncture, even many of the tribal councils are beginning to realize what is at stake, and some are expressing consternation as a result. To date, however, no tribal council member has been able to articulate a clear position favoring disengagement as opposed to "development." A number have attempted to articulate plans favoring both approaches, a stance that has proven so contradictory as to be untenable. Whether some will ultimately break ranks with the federally promulgated vision of "progress" remains to be seen, but will no doubt prove crucial to the number and magnitude of factional splits among native peoples themselves over the next decade.

The New Colonialism

Simply stated, the difference between the economics of the old colonialism, with its reliance on territorial conquest and manpower, and the "new colonialism," with its reliance on technologically oriented resource extraction and transportation to the metropolitan centers, is the expendable relationship of subject peoples to multinational corporations. This fact has implications for both the new ways in which genocide is committed, and the new kind of dependence created. Under the old colonialism, the economy of subject peoples was more or less incorporated into the colonial system in a fashion which altered the subject people as little as possible. The economic base commodities were extracted and semiprocessed, in part, by the subject people. These people were expected to maintain their own subsistence economy basically intact...Under new style colonialism, the subsistence economy is not a matter of great concern to the corporations. The raw material they wish to process is usually not organic, nor does it require "heavy labor." The multinational corporation today does not see any relationship between what they want (mineral wealth) and the local economy (organic wealth).

Robert Davis and Mark Zannis
The Genocide Machine in Canada

Spurred by the advice of the Bureau of Indian Affairs and corporate promises of jobs and royalties, the Navajo Tribal Council approved a mineral extraction agreement with the Kerr-McGee Corporation in 1952. In return for access to uranium deposits near the town of Shiprock on the reservation, and to fulfill risk-free contracts with the U.S. Atomic Energy Commission, Kerr-McGee employed 100 Diné men in underground mining operations.[23] Wages for these nonunion Diné miners were low, averaging $1.60 per hour or approximately two-thirds of the then prevailing off-reservation rate.[24] Additionally, the corporation cut operating costs significantly by virtue of lax enforcement of worker safety regulations at its Shiprock site. In 1952, a federal mine inspector found that ventilation units in the mine's primary shaft were not in operation.[25] In 1954, the inspector discovered the ventilation was still not functioning properly, with the fan operating only during the first half of each shift. When the inspector returned in 1955, the ventilation blower ran out of gas during his visit.[26] One report, dating from 1959, noted that radiation levels in the Kerr-McGee shaft had been allowed to reach ninety times the "permissible" limit.[27]

For the corporation, low wages, a guaranteed labor force, privileged contract status, virtually nonexistent severance taxes, and nonexistent safety regulations provided a great incentive to maintain and expand operations on the reservation. However, by 1979 Kerr-McGee had exhausted the easily recoverable uranium deposits at Shiprock, both in geological and financial terms. Uranium extraction technology at the time was such that further profitable recovery—under *any* conditions—was rendered unlikely. Further, the Atomic Energy Commission was in the process of phasing out its ore-buying program, the factor that had made the entire mining venture feasible in the first place. The Shiprock facility was closed in early 1980.

For the Diné people, Kerr-McGee's abrupt departure shed light upon the "diseconomies" of uranium development. First, the corporation simply abandoned some seventy-one acres of "raw" uranium tailings at the mining site. These tailings constitute waste by-products of uranium ore refinement, but retain 85 percent of the original radioactivity of the ore.[28] This huge tailing pile begins approximately sixty feet from the San Juan River, the only significant surface water source within the Shiprock area.[29] The obvious result has been a considerable dispersal of radioactive contamination to a number of downstream communities that, of necessity, draw upon the river for potable water.[30]

The price of Kerr-McGee's "development" at Shiprock, in terms of life lost in this generation and in generations yet to come, cannot be calculated by any financial/economic yardstick. Of the 150-odd Diné miners who worked underground at the Shiprock facility during the eighteen years of its operation, eighteen had died of radiation-induced lung cancer by 1975 (not the "oat cell" variety associated with cigarette smoking) and another twenty-one were feared dying.[31] By 1980, twenty of these twenty-one miners were dead, and another ninety-five had contracted similar respiratory ailments and cancers.[32] Birth defects such as cleft palate, leukemia, and other diseases commonly linked to increased radiation exposure have risen dramatically both at Shiprock and in the downstream communities of the San Juan watershed.[33] Since 1970, such diseases have come to be the greatest health concerns of the Navajo Nation.

Nonetheless, by 1980, under the leadership of Tribal Chairman Peter McDonald—a staunch advocate of energy development and founder of the Council of Energy Resource Tribes (CERT)—the Navajo council had allowed forty-two uranium mines and seven uranium mills to be located on or immediately adjacent to the reservation.[34] Some fifteen new uranium-oriented projects were in the construction stages on Navajo land. Additionally, four coal-stripping operations, averaging approximately 30,000 acres each, and five coal-fired power plants have been built on the reservation. Much more is in the planning stages. As the U.S. uranium industry undergoes a temporary depression in the early '90s, such nonnuclear energy facilities will remain and burgeon, continuing the development of infrastructure upon which "the new colonialism" depends.

The extent of infrastructural development that is to be continued is indicated by the means through which energy corporations are seeking to address the chronic Navajo unemployment spawned by reorganization. In an article entitled "Manpower Gap at the Uranium Mines," *Business Week* observed:

> Currently, 3,200 miners work underground and 900 more are in open pit operations. By 1990, the industry will need 18,400 underground miners and 4,000 above ground...once on the job, Kerr-McGee estimates that it costs $80,000 per miner in training, salary and benefits, as well as the costs for the trainees who quit. Kerr-McGee is now operating a training program at its Churchrock mine on the Navajo Reservation. The $2 million program is financed by the U.S. Labor Department, and is expected to turn out 100 miners annually. Labor Department sponsors hope the program will help alleviate the tribe's chronic unemployment.[35]

The training program is still in effect and has been successful in employing a number of Diné in "practical applications" of their new-found skills. In the case of the Navajo Nation, which now has more trained and educated persons per capita than any reservation in North America, the form of education within financial reach clearly does not encourage questioning of the desirability of reliance on energy resource exploitation as a means to "self-sufficiency," nor does it explore the cumulative effects of radioactive contamination.Yet there are lessons to be learned by those who can manage to be de-educated. It seems axiomatic that the "solution" to unemployment being offered by the energy corporations (in direct collusion with the federal government) is—as in the case of the Shiprock miners—lethal. The consequences to the surrounding habitat and inhabitants will be similar to those at Shiprock. Tuba City, Arizona—another location on the Navajo Reservation—has been left with raw tailings piles comparable to those at Shiprock and with entirely similar effects.[36] Until recently, the Kerr-McGee mine at Churchrock discharged some 80,000 gallons of radioactive water from its primary shaft ("dewatering") per day, contamination which was introduced directly into local and downstream potable water supplies.[37]

In July 1979, the United Nuclear uranium mill, also located at Churchrock, was the site of an enormous accident. The adjacent mill tailings dam broke under pressure and released more than 100 million gallons of highly radioactive water into the Río Puerco River. Kerr-McGee style safety standards, similar in principle to the ventilation system at Shiprock, were the cause. Although United Nuclear had known of cracks within the dam structure at least two months prior to the break, no repairs were made (or attempted). Seventeen hundred Diné people were immediately affected, their single water source hopelessly contaminated. More than 1,000 sheep and other livestock, which ingested Río Puerco water in the aftermath, died.[38]

As a token of the "expendability" of the indigenous population under the new colonialism referred to by Davis and Zannis, when the Churchrock community attempted to seek compensation—including emergency water and food supplies for directly affected community members—United Nuclear stonewalled. Through an array of evasions and obfuscations, the corporation was able to avoid any form of redress for *over a year,* finally making a minimal out-of-court settlement when a class-action suit was filed in behalf of the town. By then, of course, the immediate life-and-death situation had passed (long-term effects being, as yet, unknown). The potential outrage of the local citizenry was, however, a bit constrained. Between the aforementioned Kerr-McGee plant and training program, the United Nuclear facility, and several other energy corporations operating in the area, well over half the jobs and nearly 80 percent of income at Churchrock were derived from uranium production. Dependency, in its most virulent colonial manifestation, had effectively converted Churchrock into an "economic hostage"—and an expendable hostage at that—of the uranium industry.

But Churchrock and Shiprock are only sample cases of the radioactive colonization prevailing across the face of the Navajo Nation (the full extent of the situation

Map I

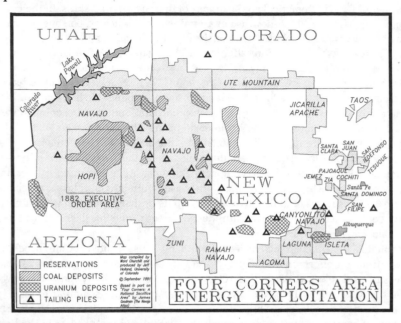

Map compiled by Ward Churchill and produced by Jeff Holand, University of Colorado © September 1991. Based in part on "Four Corners: A National Sacrifice Area" by James Goodman (The Navajo Atlas)

RESERVATIONS
COAL DEPOSITS
URANIUM DEPOSITS
TAILING PILES

FOUR CORNERS AREA
ENERGY EXPLOITATION

is revealed by Map I). Nor should the Diné be considered unique in their experience of radioactive colonization. To the north, within what, in 1977, the Supreme Court of the United States ruled was rightly the land base of the Lakota people, some 40 energy corporations are currently vying for position within an extremely rich "resource belt."[39] Central to the Lakota territory legally defined by the Fort Laramie Treaty of 1868 is the Black Hills region. As of August 1979, some 5,163 uranium claims were held in the Black Hills National Forest alone (a claim generally extends over about twenty acres); 218,747 acres of "private" land in the area are also under mining leases.[40]

In addition to uranium, coal is a major factor within Lakota territory. The huge Fort Union coal deposit underlies approximately half the land, including the whole of both the current Crow and Northern Cheyenne Reservations in Montana, the Fort Berthold Reservation in North Dakota, and substantial portions of the Standing Rock and Cheyenne River Lakota Reservations near the North Dakota-South Dakota state line. According to Henry Wasserman:

> Overall, the plans for industrializing the Black Hills are staggering. They include a gigantic energy park featuring more than a score of 10,000 megawatt coal-fired plants, a dozen nuclear reactors, huge coal slurry pipelines designed to use millions of gallons of water to move crushed coal thousands of miles, and at least 14 major uranium mines.[41]

Water may be the most immediately crucial issue. The plans for just one mine, Burdock, call for the "depressurization" of aquifers prior to commencement of mining per se. This would entail the pumping of some 675 gallons per minute from the area's quite limited ground water resources. As depressurization must be maintained for the duration of mining activities—projected over a full decade in the case of Burdock—the quantity of water at issue is not trivial. Compounded by the number of mines anticipated as being operational during the same period, the quantity becomes truly astronomical. The reason for the ten-year limitation on Burdock projections has little to do with depletion of mineral resources, but with the anticipated total exhaustion of regional ground water supplies by the end of the century. The pumped-off water is slated to be used in operations such as the Energy Transportation Systems, Inc. (ETSI) pipeline, intended to provide a fluid coal transportation system from the Dakotas to the southeastern United States.

Although development and consolidation of the uranium industry within the Lakota territory is not as pronounced as in the Navajo territory, the sorts of environmental phenomena occurring there are similar. On June 11, 1962, 200 tons of radioactive mill tailings washed into the Cheyenne River, an indirect source of potable water for the Pine Ridge Reservation.[42] In June 1980, the Indian Health Service announced that well water at the reservation community of Slim Buttes contained gross alpha levels at least three times the national safety standard.[43] A new well at Slim Buttes, moreover, tested at seventy picocuries (pCi) per liter. This is *fourteen times* the standard. Similarly, sub-surface water on Pine Ridge's Red Shirt Table tested at several times "acceptable" limits of radioactivity, and tests conducted at the towns of Manderson and Oglala revealed comparable results. The distribution of these locations is such as to indicate that the water sources for the entire reservation have been affected.[44]

Stanley Looking Elk, then tribal president, requested that $175,000 of the $200,000 federal allocation for reservation water management be committed to securing emergency (uncontaminated) water supplies. In a response strikingly similar to that of United Nuclear at Churchrock in its implications of the "expendability" of the indigenous population, the BIA stipulated that such alternative water supplies could be secured on Pine Ridge, *but only for consumption by cattle.*[45] Perhaps the reason underlying the government's stonewalling on the issue of radioactive contamination on Pine Ridge is that much worse is yet to come. Not the least cause of this could be the circumstance brought out in a situation report carried in *Akwesasne Notes:*

> The Air Force retained an area near which residents have sighted large containers being flown in by helicopter. These reports have raised strong suspicions that the Gunnery Range was being used as a dump for high-level military nuclear waste, which may be leaking radioactivity into the [Oglala] Aquifer. In the same area, the rate of stillborn or deformed calves has skyrocketed. Northeast of this area are 12 nuclear missile sites whose radioactive effects are unknown.[46]

The "Gunnery Range" is an area within the northwestern quadrant of the Pine Ridge Reservation "borrowed" from the Oglala Lakotas in 1942 for use in training Army Air Corps gunners. It was to be returned upon conclusion of World War II, but never was. In 1975, in "secret negotiations," former Tribal Chairman Dick Wilson assigned legal title over the area to the federal government (after thirty-three years of boldfaced expropriation by the federal government), ostensibly so that it could become a formal part of the Badlands National Monument.[47] Area residents have felt all along that the area was being used as a convenient dumping ground for virulently toxic nuclear waste, away from large concentrations of "mainstream" U.S. citizens.[48]

Whether or not the government is engaged in such a classified operation, it is known that earlier uranium mining and milling activities at the former army ordnance depot at Igloo, South Dakota left something on the order of 3.5 million tons of exposed tailings lining the banks of the Cheyenne River and Cottonwood Creek, one of the river's tributaries, in the downtown area of nearby Edgemont.[49] While it is known that wind and erosion are carrying significant quantities of this radioactive contaminant into these sources of potable water, it is considered "cost prohibitive" to clean up the wastes.[50] During the period 1987-89, the government purportedly "fixed" the tailings problem at Edgemont by digging up the material piled all through the center of Edgemont and redumping them in an open area a few miles outside the village limits. This new "disposal site" is protected by nothing more than signs adorning a chain-link fence.

Meanwhile, the same governmental/corporate entities which announced the commencement of uranium mining at Edgemont, circa 1955, carried with it "no public health hazard" are now proclaiming the area so thoroughly contaminated by radiation that there is nothing for it but to use the site as a *national* nuclear waste dump.[51] The cancer death rate among longtime Edgemont residents is currently spiraling, but government/corporate spokespersons have recently asserted that the situation of the dump site in the southern Black Hills area presents "no health danger" to surrounding communities.[52] Former South Dakota governor William Janklow, who campaigned on a platform of not allowing dump sites within the state, now advocates location of a dump in Edgemont as a "boon" to the depressed local economy.

What is not stated publicly by either federal or corporate officials is that such a site, and Black Hills uranium production in general, all but inevitably causes radioactive leaching into the Madison Formation, the primary ground water source of the region (and the same water which it is proposed will be transported to the Southeast via coal slurries). The U.S. Department of the Interior itself quietly summed up this problem in a 1979 report, cited in *Akwesasne Notes,* concerning uranium tailing ponds:

> Contamination is well beyond the safe limit for animals. Escape by infiltration into the water table or by breakout to stream drainages could cause contamination by dangerous levels of radioactivity. Stock or humans using water from wells down gradient from tailing ponds would be exposed. Plants and animals encountering contaminated flows or contaminated sediments deposited in drainage channels would be exposed. Increasing the danger is the nondegradable and accumulative nature of this type of contamination.[53]

The same, of course, would pertain to the types of material commonly disposed of in nuclear dumping operations. What the government report does not bring out is that not only *could* this happen but, in all probability, it already *has*—as is testified to both by the earlier cited 1962 "spill" at Edgemont, and by reported groundwater radiation levels at Pine Ridge. Correspondingly, a preliminary study conducted by Women of All Red Nations on Pine Ridge indicates a marked increase in such radiation-associated phenomena as stillbirths, infant deformations such as cleft palate, and cancer deaths among reservation residents since 1970.[54] The relationship between this situation and the disaster at Edgemont seems clear enough, and underscores the cynicism of government/corporate contentions that a continued development of the uranium industry holds no ill effects for area communities. The Greater Sioux Nation, like the Navajo Nation, has effectively become another radioactive colony within the schema of the new colonialism.[55] Again, the data presented are but a narrow sample of the prevailing situation within the aggregate Lakota treaty territory. A fairer portrait is offered by Map II (see next page).

A more candid (and accurate) appraisal of the situation at Navajo and Sioux Nation, in view both of current circumstances and of developmental projections, came from the Nixon administration in 1972. At that time, in conjunction with studies of U.S. energy development needs and planning undertaken by the Trilateral Commission, the government secretly termed and sought to designate both the Four Corners region and the impacted region of the Dakotas, Wyoming and Montana as "National Sacrifice Areas." That is, areas rendered uninhabitable through the deliberate elimination of the total water supplies for industrial purposes (the aquifers are estimated to take from 5,000 to 50,000 years to replenish themselves) and rampant nuclear contamination (much of which carries a lethal half-life from a quarter- to a half-million years). In other words, the destruction anticipated is effectively permanent.[56]

Needless to say, consummation of such plans would immediately eradicate Navajo and the so-called Sioux Complex as reservations. The largest block of landholdings remaining to American Indians within the United States would thus be lost utterly and irrevocably. The same situation would pertain to smaller reservations such as Hopi and most other Pueblos, Northern Cheyenne, Crow and possibly Wind River, which lie within the "sacrifice areas." The great likelihood is that the peoples involved, to the extent that they are not physically exterminated by the projected extraction processes, would cease to function as peoples, once severed from their land bases. Like the Klamath, who were "terminated" in the 1950s and never recovered their Oregon homeland, these newly landless nations would in all probability disintegrate rapidly, dissolving into the mists of history. By conventional English definition, such a prospect and such a process can only be termed genocide.[57]

Nor is the situation in Canada appreciably different, in spirit if not in quantity and intensity. The James Bay power project undertaken through conjoint governmental and corporate efforts, for example, threatens to utterly demolish the habitat,

Map II

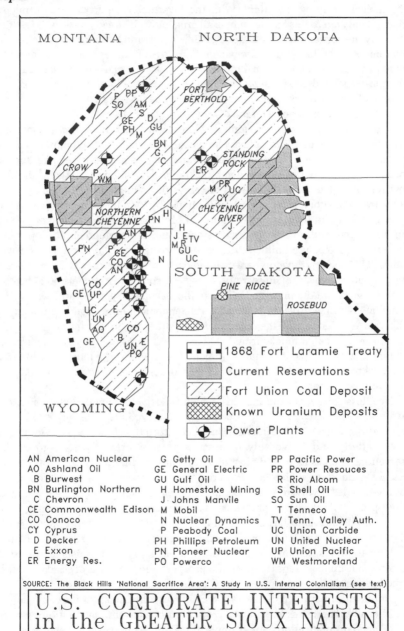

MONTANA   NORTH DAKOTA

FORT
BERTHOLD

STANDING
ROCK

CROW

NORTHERN
CHEYENNE

CHEYENNE
RIVER

SOUTH DAKOTA

PINE RIDGE

ROSEBUD

WYOMING

▪▪▪▪ 1868 Fort Laramie Treaty

░░ Current Reservations

/// Fort Union Coal Deposit

▨ Known Uranium Deposits

◉ Power Plants

AN American Nuclear	G Getty Oil	PP Pacific Power
AO Ashland Oil	GE General Electric	PR Power Resouces
B Burwest	GU Gulf Oil	R Rio Alcom
BN Burlington Northern	H Homestake Mining	S Shell Oil
C Chevron	J Johns Manvile	SO Sun Oil
CE Commonwealth Edison	M Mobil	T Tenneco
CO Conoco	N Nuclear Dynamics	TV Tenn. Valley Auth.
CY Cyprus	P Peabody Coal	UC Union Carbide
D Decker	PH Phillips Petroleum	UN United Nuclear
E Exxon	PN Pioneer Nuclear	UP Union Pacific
ER Energy Res.	PO Powerco	WM Westmoreland

SOURCE: The Black Hills 'National Sacrifice Area': A Study in U.S. Internal Colonialism (see text)

U.S. CORPORATE INTERESTS
in the GREATER SIOUX NATION

lifeways and self-sufficiency of the Cree people in that area.[58] Comparable sorts of activity in virtually every province of Canada—notably intensive mining of super-high grade uranium ore in the area of Yellow Knife and Wolleston in the District of McKenzie and northern Alberta respectively—harbor the same results for various indigenous peoples.[59] The native peoples of the entire northern half of the Americas stand in imminent danger of being swallowed up and eliminated entirely by the broader societies that have engulfed their land.

For American Indians to opt for the processes described within this section—to embrace transient extractive industrialism as a "solution" to the sorts of problems they now confront, problems brought into being and fostered by the representative institutions of industrial control and consolidation itself—seems to be at best a self-defeating strategy. More likely, it promises participation in a route to self-liquidation or, to borrow a phrase from certain analysts of the recent holocaust in Kampuchea and to place it within a rather more accurate framework, "auto-genocide."[60] Whatever the short-run benefits in terms of diminishing the, by now, all but perpetual cycle of American Indian disease, malnutrition, and despair generated by neocolonialism, the looming longer-term costs vastly outweigh them. In the next section, however, we shall examine whether even the short-term benefits perceived by such agencies of American Indian "progress" as CERT and many tribal councils are more real or illusory in their immediate potentials for prosperity and self-determination.

Radioactive Colonialism

When years before they had first come to the people living on the Cebolleta land grant they had not said what kind of mineral it was. They were driving U.S. Government cars, and they paid the land grant association five thousand dollars not to ask questions about the test holes they were drilling...Early in the spring of 1943, the mine began to flood with water from the subterranean springs. They hauled in big pumps and compressors from Albuquerque...But later in the summer the mine flooded again, and this time no pumps or compressors were sent. They had enough of what they needed, and the mine was closed, but the barbed wire fences and the guards remained until August 1945. By then they had other sources of uranium, and it was not top secret anymore...He had been so close to it, caught up in it for so long that its simplicity struck him deep inside his chest: Trinity site, where they exploded the first atomic bomb, was only three hundred miles to the southeast, at White Sands. And the top-secret laboratories where the bomb had been created were deep in the Jemez mountains, on land the Government took from Cochiti Pueblo: Los Alamos, only a hundred miles northeast of him now, still surrounded by high electric fences...There was no end to it; it knew no boundaries; and he had arrived at the point of convergence where the fate of all living things, and even the earth, had been laid. From the jungles of his dreaming he recognized why the Japanese voices had merged with the Laguna voices...converging in the middle of witchery's final ceremonial sand painting. From that time on, human beings were one clan again, united by the fate the destroyers had planned for all of them, for all living things; united by a circle of death that

devoured people in cities twelve thousand miles away, victims who had never
known these mesas, who had never seen the delicate colors of the rocks which
boiled up their slaughter.

Leslie Marmon Silko
Ceremony

Economic and labor analysts have argued on numerous occasions that improved
labor relations and altered mineral development policies could, or would, tip the
cost-benefit balance to the favorable side of the scale for American Indians. Careful
examination of such contentions and information available through the Oil, Chemical and Atomic Workers Union (Denver, CO) combine with any fundamental
understanding of the general environment in uranium producing regions to dispute
notions that adjusting or "tuning" the production scenario will do much of anything
to offset negative factors over either the long or short terms. The Diné experience at
Shiprock, Churchrock, Tuba City, and elsewhere and, in a slightly different sense,
the experiences of the Lakota to the north are not anomalies. There is, and can be,
no "safe" uranium mining, processing, or waste disposal, either now or in the
foreseeable future. Such facts can be denied, they can be argued with debater's
points or the exclusivity of narrow ranges of technical "expertise," but they cannot
be made to go away in the real world where people and environments become
contaminated, sicken, and die.

We have already seen how the energy corporations and the government use
local Indian workforces at the lowest possible wages, paying little if any heed to
community safety, avoiding both severance taxes to cover the community costs
incurred by their presence and land reclamation costs to cover even the most lethal
of their damages upon departure, and paying the absolute minimum rate in royalties
for the milled ore they ship. We have also seen that the nature of the destruction
they create as an integral aspect of their "productive process" is such that there can
be *no* further tribal development, once mining is completed. It is unlikely that much
beyond the level of amoeba will be able to survive in a National Sacrifice Area. In
other words, long-term consequences foreclose upon short-term advantages where
the uranium production process is concerned. Of course, the "right" Indian negotiator might be able to bargain the royalty rates to a higher, more "acceptable" level;
say two, or five, or ten times the going rate in Indian Country. But, to what avail?
This short-run "gain" is a mirage. No matter what magnitude of cash flow is
generated from such resource sales by tribal/managerial elites, it can only be
"invested" in a homeland that is soon to be uninhabitable, a people soon to be
extinguished. Cash can *never* be sufficient to replace either the homeland or the
people. Adjustments to the rate of exchange are thus ultimately irrelevant to the
issue at hand, whether over the next two decades or the next twenty.

The only possibility of even short-term benefits, then, lies in the improbable
possibility that a preponderance of tribal members—people who, despite personal
identity confusion and a grinding poverty lasting for generations, have clung
steadfastly to overall notions of Indianness and maintained a firm embrace of their

homelands—are somehow now prepared to abandon these things for the external reality of the dominant culture. In order for even this dubious prospect to be more than mere illusion, however, the uranium development option (and other energy development options as well) must be both survivable *to the participants* (which includes, from an Indian perspective, the ability to bear healthy children, the "unborn generations" leading to familial and tribal survival) and offer them not only a cash reserve, but the skills and employment through which to successfully enter the "mainstream."

The question thus becomes whether in fact there are means available to meet these short-run needs, assuming that Indians desire them. In this connection, it would seem that unionization might provide a key to success. The Oil, Chemical and Atomic Workers Union (OCAW) is the largest and most influential worker's force within the uranium industry. Although not all miners are unionized, within the Grants Uranium Belt of the Southwest, the OCAW has been somewhat successful in pressuring the overall uranium industry. To begin with, the union has essentially achieved standardization of conditions for all miners within the area—union or non-union, brown, red, black, or white.

As a result, conditions such as those prevailing in the Shiprock mine during the 1950s are now uncommon, even exceptional. Yet the industry, by OCAW's estimation, remains one of the most dangerous in every phase.[61] The union has devoted its primary concern and many actions to improving worker safety conditions within the mines. In one year, 525 men were seriously injured in the mines of New Mexico alone; seven of them died. But these are problems which prevail across the mining industry as a whole. The more insidious hazards associated with uranium mining—and the ones which claim the heaviest toll—are those involving chemical and radiation contamination.

In this regard, the OCAW has been active in opposing the "bonus system," the practice by which corporations reward miners financially for operating in "hot spots" or working higher-grade ore than is normally handled. In essence, the union argues that such sustained exposure as is expected of miners performing under the bonus system virtually guarantees contamination (and an early death), and that the corporations intentionally downplay the risks involved. The OCAW has also held that "worker rotation systems" for working hot spots and super-rich ore—often without the benefits of extra pay—fail to solve the contamination problem, serving instead to spread potentially lethal concentrations of radiation (on the order of 6.5 times maximum "safe" dosages) throughout the entire work force.[62]

In some respects then, OCAW might be viewed as affording a means by which initial steps have been taken to provide tangible worker safety. In addition, the union has proven quite successful in attaining real wage increases for miners across the board, whether or not they belong to OCAW. But, in fairness, it must be said that while the union has succeeded in eliminating the most extreme forms of abuse routinely conducted by management (such as operating deep shafts without ventilation), it has merely exposed, rather than corrected, the more generic varieties. In this sense, while it is certainly a more humane and progressive entity than the corporations it confronts, it represents no *solution* to the problems with which it deals. Additionally, many of the strategies through which the union has proposed to force wage increases and improved safety standards are much better suited to the usual, highly mobile mine labor force than to "reservation-bound" Indian miners.

Similarly, a number of improvements attained by the OCAW in behalf of its miner constituency have, perversely, worked to the detriment of the Indian miners' home communities. Consider the matter of mine ventilation: the uniform installation of proper ventilating blowers within mine shafts is unquestionably a major gain for miners. For transient miners, this is essentially the end of the story: a gain. But, for those whose intention it is to live out their lives within the mining community, and to have their children and their children's children live out their lives in the community as well, the question of what becomes of radioactive dust blown from the mine shafts assumes a critical importance.

The answer, of course, is into the air of the community, from which it settles upon the community. Hence, the gain to the Indian miner in terms of increased workplace safety for him/herself is incurred at the direct expense of his/her permanent habitat. The Gulf-operated Mt. Taylor mine located in San Mateo, New Mexico is an example of such problems. It is but one of many. The town of Questa, New Mexico has its elementary school built upon a dry tailings pond, at the foot of a tailing pile, situated near shaft ventilators. The OCAW maintains, perhaps rightly, that such matters are beyond its purview. But this leaves the concept of unionization voided in a very important respect for Indian miners and their communities. Short-run considerations of the ultimate survivability of uranium production would thus seem heavily skewed to the negative, both for participating miners and for participating communities. In view of this fact, concerns with short-term income (wage) benefits seem rather beside the point. There is obviously little advantage to be gained from achieving a short-term economic "security" from an occupation that is not only directly and rapidly killing you, but your family and offspring as well.

All uranium-producing American Indian nations, and the individuals who comprise them, are in the position typified by Navajo's Churchrock community: They are economic hostages of the new colonialism. For example, approximately 7,000 acres of the 418,000-acre Laguna Pueblo land-holding is leased to the Anaconda Corporation. The tribal goal in entering into the leasing agreement was to secure royalty revenues for the group and jobs for individuals within the group. In effect, the land has passed into Anaconda's eminent domain. Anaconda operated a uranium stripping operation at Laguna from 1952 until 1981 when, as in the case of Kerr-McGee's Shiprock mine, profitably extractible ore was used up. During the operating years, the Laguna Tribal Council negotiated an agreement with the corporation whereby tribal applicants would receive priority in hiring to work in the reservation mine. The practice was quite successful, with some 93 percent of the Anaconda labor force ultimately accruing from the pueblo. As the mining operation expanded over the years, so did the workforce, from 350 in 1952 to a peak of 650 in 1979.[63]

Wages to miners, relative to average per capita incomes on reservations, are quite high, and the high concentration of miners within the tiny Laguna population established it as one of the "richer" all-round native groups in the country by the early- to mid-1960s.[64] Throughout the 1970s, unemployment within the tribal membership averaged approximately 25 percent—high by non-Indian standards but less than half the prevailing average reservation rate nationally. Further, royalty payments and other mechanisms allowed the Lagunas symbolically to break out of certain important aspects of reorganization-fostered dependency upon the federal government. By 1979, former Laguna governor Floyd Correa was able to state in an interview that, of the tribal unemployed, only twelve were collecting unemployment benefits (as compared to the estimated 20 percent of the total labor force collecting benefits on most reservations at any given moment). Upon superficial examination, the Lagunas seemed well on the road to recovering the self-sufficiency that had long since passed from the grasp of most North American indigenous nations.

The bubble burst when Anaconda abruptly pulled up stakes and left the husk of their mining operation: a gaping crater and, of course, piles of virulently radioactive slag. Over the years, the Lagunas' negotiating position had steadily deteriorated as the absolute centrality of the Anaconda operation became apparent to the people—and to the corporation. Consequently, very little provision was built into lease renewals for clean-up and land reclamation upon conclusion of mining activities. It will probably cost the pueblo more to repair environmental havoc wrought by the corporation than it earned during the life of the mining contract.[65] And, unlike Anaconda, the Laguna people as a whole cannot simply move away, leaving the mess behind. Nor can individual workers. The sudden departure of Anaconda left the preponderance of the reservation's income earners instantly jobless. Here, a cruel lesson was learned. The skills imparted through training and employment in uranium mining are not readily translatable to other forms of employment, nor are they particularly transferable without dissolution of the tribal group itself (i.e., miners and their families moving away from the pueblo in order to secure employment elsewhere). Meanwhile, the steady thirty-year gravitation of the Laguna population toward mining as a livelihood caused a corresponding atrophy of the skills and occupations that had enabled the pueblo to remain essentially self-sufficient for centuries.

Whether or not the former Anaconda employees can "adjust" to their new circumstances and either make a sort of reverse transition to more traditional occupations or secure adequate alternative employment proximate to the reservation may in some respects be a moot point. While not as pronounced as in the deep-shaft mining areas on the Navajo Nation, the pattern of increasing early deaths from respiratory cancer and similar ailments—as well as congenital birth defects—has become steadily more apparent on the reservation.[66] Most of the afflicted no longer retain the insurance coverage, once a part of the corporate employment package, through which to offset the costs of their illness (and those suffered by relatives within the extended family structures by which the pueblo is organized).

Thus, the ghost of Anaconda is eating the personal as well as tribal savings accruing from the mining experience.

It seems safe enough to observe that the short-term benefits perceived at Laguna were more illusory than real. Although a temporary sense of economic security was imparted by the presence of a regular paycheck, and the "stability" of a "big time" employer, there was never time to consolidate the apparent profits. Costs swiftly overtook gains, although the tribal government was not necessarily immediately aware of the change of circumstances. In the final analysis, the people may well end up much more destitute, and in an infinitely worse environmental position, than they ever were in the past. As if to underscore the point, water has become a major problem at Laguna, one which may eventually outweigh all the others brought about by its relatively brief relationship with Anaconda. The Río Paguate River, which once provided the basis for irrigation and a potentially thriving local agriculture, now runs through the unreclaimed ruins of corporate flight. As early as 1973, the federal Environmental Protection Agency (EPA) discovered that the Anaconda strip-mining operation was contaminating the Laguna water supply.[67]

With agricultural and cattle raising production withering under the glare of higher-paying and more "glamorous" work in the mine, the pueblo converted to ground water in meeting all, rather than a portion, of its water needs. In 1975, however, the EPA returned to find widespread ground water contamination throughout the Grants Mineral Belt, including that under Laguna.[68] In 1978, the EPA was back again, this time to inform the Indians that *all* of their available water sources were dangerously contaminated by radioactivity, and that the tribal council building, community center, and newly constructed Jackpile Housing—paid for in substantial proportion by royalty monies—were all radioactive as well.[69] Additionally, Anaconda had used *low-grade uranium ore* to "improve" the road system leading to the mine and village.[70]

Hence, even were the Lagunas able to reclaim the land directly associated with what was once the world's largest open-pit uranium mine (preceding Namibia's Rossing Mine for this dubious distinction), no small feat in itself, and even if they were somehow able to avert the seemingly impending carcinogenic and genetic crises, restore an adequate measure of employment and tribal income, and clear up at least the direct sources of contamination to the Río Paguate, they would *still be* faced with the insurmountable problem of contaminated ground water (which can accrue from quite far-flung locations). And, if they have had enough of such "progress" and wish to attempt a return to the agriculture and animal husbandry that stood them in such good stead for generations? Then they will still have to contend with the factor of disrupted ore bodies that persist in leaching out into otherwise reclaimed soil.

When such leaching occurs, radioactive contaminants are drawn into the roots of plants. Animals, whether human or otherwise, consuming contaminated plants likewise become contaminated. This too may well be an unsurmountable problem. It seems likely that the damage is done and irreparable, that the way of life the

Lagunas have known, and with which they identify and represent themselves as a people, is gone forever. And in exchange? Nothing. At least nothing of value, unless one wishes to place a value on radioactive community centers and road repairs. Or unless one wishes to consider as valuable the bitter legacy and lessons learned as an example on which to base future plans and future actions.

Laguna is not unique in its experience. The examples earlier drawn from the Navajo Nation and the Lakota territory should be sufficient to demonstrate that. Dozens, scores, even hundreds of additional examples might be cited from the Hopi, Zuñi, Acoma, Isleta, Crow, Northern Cheyenne and other native nations in the United States, and from the Cree, Métis, Athabasca, and other native peoples of Canada. One other example within the United States might be drawn upon to nail things down. This concerns the Department of Energy's nuclear facility at Hanford, on the boundary of the Yakima Nation in central Washington state. Designed on the same pattern as the ill-fated Soviet plant at Chernobyl, Hanford was used for forty years to produce weapons-grade fissionable material. Finally closed down in 1987, when officials became concerned that a Chernobyl-style disaster might occur there, Hanford was still described by the federal government (in response to growing local concerns about health hazards inherent to the plant) as having functioned in a "safe and essentially accident-free fashion" throughout its operational existence. Finally, in July 1990, government spokespersons admitted that the weapons facility had been, since the early '50s, secretly dumping radioactive wastes into the environment at a level at least 2,000 times greater than those officially deemed "safe."[71]

A year later, in April 1991, this was spelled out as meaning that 444 *billion* gallons of water laced with plutonium, strontium, tritium, ruthenium, cesium, and assorted rare earth elements had simply been poured into a hole in the ground over the years. Officials admitted that these materials had long since seeped into local ground water sources, and estimated that the contamination will reach the Columbia River by the end of the decade (the local populace needn't worry about health hazards, however; "progressive" legislators have managed to prohibit cigarette smoking in all the buildings located above the dump site as a means of sparing health-conscious citizens the hazards of breathing such "air pollution.")[72] In sum, the residents of Yakima and the surrounding area have been exposed to greater concentrations of radiation—*as a matter of course*—than were those Soviet citizens living in or near Chernobyl during the near melt-down of the reactor there. Further, they, unlike their counterparts in the USSR, had been unknowingly exposed to the contamination for decades.

It should by now be plain that there is neither short- nor long-term advantage to be gained by indigenous nations in entering into energy resource extraction agreements. Advantage accrues only to the corporate and governmental representatives of a colonizing and dominant industrial culture. Occasionally it accrues momentarily, and in limited fashion, to the "Vichy" tribal governments they have reorganized into doing their bidding. For the people, there is only expendability, destruction, and grief under this new colonization. Ironically, the situation was spelled out in the clearest possible terms by the Los Alamos Scientific Laboratory, the site of the birth of "controlled" nuclear fission, in its February 1978 *Mini-Report:*

> Perhaps the solution to the radon emission problem is to zone the land into uranium mining and milling districts so as to forbid human habitation.

Viewed in this light, the choices for uranium-rich, land-locked reservation populations are clearly defined. For some, there is cause for immediate retreat from engagement in the uranium extraction process. For others, it is a matter of avoiding a problem not yet begun. In either case, such a choice will necessitate an active resistance to the demands and impositions of the new colonizers.

It seems certain that those who would claim "their" uranium to fuel the engines of empire, both at home and abroad, will be unlikely to accept a polite (if firm) "no" in response to their desires. Strategies must be found through which this "no" may be enforced. Perhaps, as Leslie Silko put it, "human beings will be one clan again" when they are united finally by "the circle of death" which ultimately confronts us all—united in putting an end to such insanity. Until that time, however, American Indians, those who have been selected by the dynamics of radioactive colonization to be the first 20th century national sacrifice peoples, must stand alone, or with their immediate allies, for a common survival. It is a gamble, no doubt, but a gamble that is clearly warranted. The alternative is virtual species suicide.

Notes

1. See Garrity, Michael, "The U.S. Colonial Empire is as Close as the Nearest Reservation," in Holly Sklar, ed., *Trilateralism: The Trilateral Commission and Elite Planning for World Management,* South End Press, Boston, 1980, pp. 238-68.
2. For an overview on the similarities of the situations prevailing in the United States and Canada, see Getty, Ian L., and Donald B. Smith, *One Century Later: Western Canadian Reserve Indians Since Treaty 7,* University of British Columbia Press, Vancouver, 1978. A more specific historical case study is provided in Fisher, Robin, *Contact and Conflict: Indian-European Relations in British Columbia, 1774-1890,* University of British Columbia Press, Vancouver, 1977.
3. See Deloria, Vine Jr., and Clifford M. Lytle, *American Indians, American Justice,* University of Texas Press, Austin, 1984.
4. LaDuke, Winona, "Indian Land Claims and Treaty Areas of North America: Succeeding into Native North America," *CoEvolution Quarterly,* No. 32, Winter 1981, pp. 64-65.
5. Cruz, Roberto, "U.S. Forced Cessions of Papago Land and Resources During the 20th Century," unpublished paper prepared at the Harvard School of Economics, Cambridge, MA, 1978, pp. 17-18.
6. See the map of Lakota (forced) cessions of 1868 treaty land contained in Dunbar Ortiz, Roxanne, ed., *The Great Sioux Nation: Sitting in Judgment on America,* International Indian Treaty Council/Moon Books, New York/San Francisco, 1977, p. 94.
7. See Clinton, Robert N., Nell Jessup Newton, and Monroe E. Price, *American Indian Law: Cases and Materials,* Michie Co. Law Publishers, Charlottesville, VA, 1991. Also see Deloria and Lytle, op. cit.
8. Internal Council of Energy Resource Tribes memorandum, Smith to McDonald, June 12, 1977.
9. *One Century Later,* op. cit.
10. The term "Fourth World" may be unfamiliar to some readers. In essence, the concept derives from the conventional notion that geopolitical reality assumes the configuration of having an industrially developed capitalist order (the First World) counterposed to an industrially developed socialist order (the Second World). Hovering between these two poles is a mass of former colonies now pursuing a course of more or less "independent" industrial development (the Third World). Those who have attempted to place traditional tribal peoples—peoples who

have never adopted, or who have come to reject the industrial ethos—within this tidy three-part spectrum have been left frustrated. In terms of traditional indigenous populations, the conventional definitions explain little. This has led to the evolution of the theory that there is a Fourth World or, perhaps more appropriately stated, a Host World of indigenous cultures and societies upon which the various variants of industrialism have been built.

11. See Map I in Chapter Five.

12. U.S. Commission on Civil Rights, *The Navajo Nation: An American Colony*, U.S. Government Printing Office, Washington, D.C., 1976.

13. On the formation of the first "modern tribal council," that of the Navajo Nation, see Chapter Three.

14. *The Navajo Nation*, op. cit.

15. Ibid.

16. See *TREATY* (True Revolution for Elders, Ancestors, Treaties and Youth), a campaign document produced by the Dakota American Indian Movement, Porcupine, SD, 1983.

17. See DHEW/U.S. Bureau of the Census, *A Statistical Portrait of the American Indian*, U.S. Government Printing Office, Washington, D.C., 1976, p. 19; data not appreciably changed during intervening seven years according to statement by U.S. Secretary of the Interior James Watt on May 19, 1982. Circumstances in Canada are brought out in *One Century Later*, op. cit.

18. Davis, Mark, and Robert Zannis, *The Genocide Machine in Canada: The Pacification of the North*, Black Rose Books, Toronto, Canada, 1973, p. 93.

19. See *Report of the Ad Hoc Committee Investigating Circumstances Surrounding Forced Relocation of Diné and Hopi People Within the Navajo/Hopi Joint Use Area, Arizona*, Big Mountain Legal Defense/Offense Committee, Flagstaff, AZ, 1984. Also see *Report to the Kikmongwe*, American Indian Law Resource Center, Washington, D.C., 1979.

20. See *A Statistical Portrait of the American Indian*, op. cit. For purposes of this chapter, "North" America is not considered to include Mexico or Central American areas.

21. Durham, Jimmie, "Native Americans and Colonialism," *The Guardian*, March 28, 1979, p. 40.

22. The Fourth World continues to exist, essentially intact, despite the imposition of various industrialized structures upon it. According to the International Work Group for Indigenous Affairs, "The Fourth World is the name given to the indigenous peoples descended from a country's aboriginal population and who today are completely or partly deprived of the right to their territory and riches…" Conceptualization of means to preserve and revitalize the Fourth World/Host World has led lately to a stream of theory and activism loosely termed as "indigenism." Among the better sources available about the Fourth World are the final chapter of Weyler, Rex, *Blood of the Land: The FBI and Corporate War Against the American Indian Movement*, Everest House Publishers, New York, 1982; and Diabo, J.R., "The Emergence of Fourth World Politics in the International Arena" (unpublished paper presented at the 1984 Western Social Science Association Conference in San Diego, CA). See also Borg, Peter, "Devolving Beyond Global Monoculture," *CoEvolution Quarterly*, No. 38, Winter 1981, pp. 24-30. For a dissenting view on pursuit of a Fourth World ideology see Dunbar Ortiz, Roxanne, "The Fourth World and Indigenism: Isolation and Alternatives," *Journal of Ethnic Studies*, Vol. 12, No. 1, Spring 1984.

23. In addition to the Diné employed as underground miners by Kerr-McGee during this period, somewhere between 300 and 500 more were involved in "independent" or Small Business Administration-backed operations going after shallow (50 ft. or less) deposits of rich uranium ore that was sold in small lots to an Atomic Energy Commission buying station located at the Kerr-McGee milling facility. They left behind between one and two hundred open shafts. See Tso, Harold, and Laura Mangum Shields, "Navajo Mining Operations: Early Hazards and Recent Interventions," *New Mexico Journal of Science*, Vol. 20, No. 1, June 1980, p. 13.

24. See LaDuke, Winona, "The Council of Energy Resource Tribes: An Outsider's View In," in Joseph Joregson, ed., *Native Americans and Energy Development II*, Anthropological Resource Center/Seventh Generation Fund, Cambridge, MA, 1984.

25. Sorenson, J.B., "Radiation Issues: Government Decision Making and Uranium Expansion in Northern New Mexico," *San Juan Basin Regional Uranium Study Working Paper No. 14*, Albuquerque, NM, 1978, p. 39. Also see LaDuke, Winona, "The History of Uranium Mining," *Black Hills/Paha Sapa Report*, Vol. 1, No. 1, 1979, p. 2 and McCleod, Christopher, "New Mexico's Nuclear Fiasco," *Minnesota Daily*, August 8, 1979, p. 5.

26. Best, Michael, and William Connally, "An Environmental Paradox," *The Progressive*, October, 1976, p. 20. Also see Wagoner, J.K., "Uranium, The U.S. Experience," *Testimony*, April 1980.

27. Barry, Tom, "Bury My Lungs at Red Rock," *The Progressive*, February 1979, pp. 25-27. Also see McCleod, Christopher, *The Four Corners: A National Sacrifice Area?* Earth Image Films, San Francisco, CA, 1981.

28. "Navajo Uranium Operations: Early Hazards and Recent Interventions," op. cit., pp. 12-13. Also see Ford, Bacon, and Davis Utah, Inc., *Phase II, Title I, Engineering Assessment of Inactive Uranium Tailings*, Shiprock Site, Shiprock, MN, March 1977.

29. The authors measured this distance by pacing it off. As Tso and Shields note in their 1980 publication ("Navajo Uranium Operations," op. cit.), "This tailings site is also within one mile of a day care center, the public schools...the Shiprock business district and cultivated farmlands." Also see Administrator's *Guide for Siting and Operation of Uranium Mining and Milling Facilities*, Stone and Webster Corporation, Denver, CO, 1978 and LaDuke, Winona, "How Much Development?" *Akwesasne Notes*, Late Winter 1979, p. 5.

30. As Michael Garrity has pointed out (op. cit., p. 258), the Kerr-McGee position on all this was summed up by corporate spokesman Bill Phillips when he told a Washington, D.C. reporter that, "I couldn't tell you what happened at some small mines on an Indian Reservation. We have uranium interests all over the world." For its part, the U.S. government chose to stonewall the matter as well. Amanda Spake of *Mother Jones* found, when inquiring about Shiprock in Atomic Energy Commission circles, that only one government official was even prepared to acknowledge that he was aware of the issue, and he denied the existence of the mines altogether.

31. As Sorenson points out, for populations living in close proximity to mill tailings, the risk of lung cancer doubles; among shaft miners the rate is much higher. V. Archer disclosed (in a presentation titled "Uranium Miners: Clinical Considerations") in a 1980 symposium on uranium conducted in Farmington, NM that, by that year, more than 200 miners had died of lung cancer across the Colorado plateau as a whole. At the same symposium, Larry Gottleib, an Indian Health Service physician, demonstrated that 40 percent of these miners who had died of the disease were under forty years of age. Also see Samet, J.M., *et al.*, "Uranium Mining and Lung Cancer in Navajo Men," *New England Journal of Medicine*, No. 310, 1984, pp. 1481-84.

32. In his symposium presentation, Gottleib indicated that "heart defects" had also become a recent leading contender among terminal illnesses prevailing among miners and those otherwise exposed to mining operations in the Shiprock area. Also see Nafziger, Rich, "Indian Uranium Profits and Perils," *Americans for Indian Opportunity*, Red Paper, Albuquerque, 1976.

33. According to Laura Mangum Shields and Alan B. Goodman, "Outcome of 13,300 Navajo Births from 1964-1981 in the Shiprock Uranium Mining Area," an unpublished paper presented at the May 25, 1984 American Association of Atomic Scientists symposium in New York, the rate of birth defects among Navajo newborns near Shiprock during the period 1964-74 was two to eight times as high as the national average. Microcephaly occurred at fifteen times the normal rate. They also note that male/female birth ratios may have become somewhat unbalanced during this period in areas associated with uranium mining and milling operations. Shields and Goodman indicate that the rate of birth anomalies seems to have diminished substantially after 1975, although it continues to run well above normal. They tentatively correlate this improvement to four industrially related factors: 1) the covering of a forty-acre, previously exposed tailings pile near Shiprock; 2)the marked decline of uranium mining and milling activities in the area after 1974; 3) improvement of electrostatic precipitators at the nearby Four Corners Power Plant; 4) closure of the Shiprock electronics plant that had chronically exposed Navajo women to a range of organic and inorganic chemicals including Cobalt-60 and Krypton-85. This information corresponds well with that of Marjane Ambler, who found in a *High Country News* feature (Vol. 12, No. 2, January 25, 1980, pp. 3-5) that the rate of infant birth defects, including a pronounced increase in Down's syndrome, at Grand Junction, Colorado (where more than 300,000 tons of raw tailings were utilized in construction projects) had tripled since the commencement of uranium mining/milling activities there.

34. Internal CERT memorandum, staff report to the director (Peter McDonald), February 9, 1980.

35. "Manpower Gap in the Uranium Mines," *Business Week*, November 1, 1977, cited in Garrity, op. cit., pp. 258-59. It should be noted that the domestic uranium market has since gone "bust" due to the termination of the Atomic Energy Commission's ore buying program in 1979. "South African" (i.e., Namibian), Canadian and Australian uranium ores were by then also underselling the U.S. variety by a considerable margin, rendering U.S. production largely unprofitable in commercial markets worldwide. The *Business Week* quotation remains nonetheless instructive concerning what will happen when the uranium "boom" resumes (as surely

it must, given present U.S. defense policies and other factors).

36. See Schwagin, Anthony S. and Thomas Hollbacher, "Lung Cancer Among Uranium Miners," *The Nuclear Fuel Cycle*, Union of Concerned Scientists, Cambridge, MA, 1973. Also see Shields and Goodman, op. cit., p. 4; and Rankin, Bob, "Congress Debates Cleanup of Uranium Mill Wastes." *Congressional Quarterly*, August 19, 1978, p. 2180.

37. Churchill, Ward, "Nuclear Contamination Resultant from Extraction Processes in the Southwestern United States," unpublished paper presented at the 1983 International Indian Treaty Council conference, Okema, OK (finding resultant from interviews). The contamination conclusion is largely borne out in a memorandum/news release of the New Mexico Environmental Improvement Agency dated May 21, 1980 made in conjunction with the area office of the Indian Health Service. In these documents, released upon completion of investigations into the 1979 "Churchrock Spill", Indian Health Service Director William Mohler observed that downstream animals tested for spill-related contamination revealed higher tissue levels of Lead-210 and Polonium-210 (not associated with tailings) than of Thorium-230 and Radium-236 (released in the spill). While this comment was no doubt intended to be reassuring to downstream residents, what it really meant was that animals along the Río Puerco were already heavily contaminated by nuclear wastes—what Dr. Laura M. Shields has termed "chronic environmental exposures"—prior to the Churchrock disaster.

38. In the memoranda/news releases mentioned in the preceding note, the Indian Health Service actually suggested that Churchrock area residents go ahead and eat their animals—after having delineated the nature and degree of contamination discovered in samples of the same animal's tissues—but recommended against consumption (typical among Diné) of organs such as sheep kidneys and livers as these tissues "tend to concentrate radioactive materials to a greater extent than other parts of the animal." As Christopher McCleod reveals in his "Kerr-McGee's Last Stand" (*Mother Jones*, December 1980), Churchrock sheepherders were still having difficulty finding commercial or governmental agency buyers for their contaminated animals three years after the spill. In other words, the animals were all right for consumption by Diné, but not by non-Indians in New York, Tokyo, and London.

39. "Rancher Bud Hollenbach...testified at the Edgemont [South Dakota] TVA Hearing on March 1, 1979 that the production of a flowing well two miles from the [Burdock] mine was cut in half by a two-week pumping test in 1977" (*Black Hills/Paha Sapa Report*, Vol. 1, No. 1, July 1979, p. 4).

40. Irvin, Amelia, "Energy Development and the Effects of Mining on the Lakota Nation," *Journal of Ethnic Studies*, Vol. 10, No. 1, Spring 1982.

41. Wasserman, Harvey, "The Sioux's Last Fight for the Black Hills," *Rocky Mt. News*, August 24, 1980.

42. *Black Hills/Paha Sapa Report*, op. cit., p. 4.

43. Indian Health Service Circular, Aberdeen (SD) Area Office, Pine Ridge District, June 1980.

44. Gilbert (Thunderhawk), Madonna, "Radioactive Water Contamination on the Red Shirt Table, Pine Ridge Reservation, South Dakota," unpublished report to Women of All Red Nations, Porcupine, SD, March 1980.

45. Women of All Red Nations, "Radiation: Dangerous to Pine Ridge Women," *Akwesasne Notes*, Spring 1980.

46. Irvin, op. cit., p. 99.

47. Messerschmidt, Jim, *The Trial of Leonard Peltier*, South End Press, Boston, 1983, p. 4. The area, located around the Sheep Mountain portion of Pine Ridge, also turned out to be rich in uranium in its own right. See U.S. Department of Interior, Bureau of Indian Affairs (J.P. Gries), *Status of Mineral Resource Information on the Pine Ridge Indian Reservation*, South Dakota, BIA Report No. 12, U.S. Department of Interior, Washington, D.C., 1976. Congress formalized illegal—under provision of the Fort Laramie Treaty of 1868—transfer of the Gunnery Range through P.L. 90-468. For further information, see Huber, Jacqueline, et al., *The Gunnery Range Report*, Oglala Sioux Tribe, Office of the President, Pine Ridge, SD, 1981.

48. "Radiation: Dangerous to Pine Ridge Women," op. cit.

49. *Black Hills/Paha Sapa Report*, op. cit., p. 1. Also see Matthiessen, Peter, *Indian Country*, Viking Press, New York, 1984, pp. 203-218.

50. Robert A. Taft Sanitary Engineering Center, *Technical Report W62-12*, U.S. Department of Health, Education and Welfare, U.S. Government Printing Office, Washington, D.C., 1979, p. 31.

51. "Nuclear Waste Facility Proposed Near Edgemont," *Rapid City Journal*, November 19, 1982.

52. It is a standing area "joke" that an Edgemont resident not killed in a car crash or hunting accident

will ultimately die of cancer. For typical governmental/corporate assertions that locating a nuclear waste facility there is "completely safe" see "Edgemont Waste Facility No Health Hazard Says Chem-Nuclear Corp.," *Rapid City Journal,* December 10, 1982, p. 5.

53. "Radiation: Dangerous to Pine Ridge Women," op. cit. WARN's contention is well corroborated within "mainstream" scientific literature. See, for example, Lindrop, Patricia J., and J. Rotblat, "Radiation Pollution in the Environment," *Bulletin of Atomic Scientists,* September 1981 (especially p. 18). Also see U.S. Department of Interior, Environmental Protection Agency, "National Revised Primary Drinking Water Regulations," *Federal Register,* Vol. 48, October 5, 1983, pp. 45502-21.

54. "Radiation: Dangerous to Pine Ridge Women," op. cit. Again, WARN's concern is hardly "paranoid," as is borne out in surveying reputable scientific literature on the issue. See, as but two examples, Tamplin, Arthur R., and John W. Gofman, *Population Control Through Nuclear Pollution,* Nelson-Hall Publishers, Chicago, 1971, and Reynolds, Earl E., "Irradiation and Human Evolution" in *The Process of Ongoing Human Evolution,* Wayne State University Press, Detroit, 1960; especially p. 92. For a more popular non-Indian view of the same general subject matter, see Ibser, H.W., "The Nuclear Energy Game: Nuclear Roulette," *The Progressive,* January 1976.

55. U.S. Department of Energy, Federal Energy Administration, Office of Strategic Analysis, *Project Independence: A Summary,* U.S. Government Printing Office, Washington, D.C., November 1, 1974.

56. Perhaps the best single study of aquifer contamination and depletion is Bowden, Charles, *Killing the Hidden Waters,* University of Texas Press, Austin, 1977. Also of interest is "Comments on Proposed Cleanup Standards for Inactive Uranium Processing Sites," memorandum to the U.S. Environmental Protection Agency from Dr. E.A. Martell, Docket Number A-79-25, June 16, 1980.

57. Article II of the 1948 United Nations Convention on Genocide defines the following as acts of genocide when directed against specific, identifiable racial, ethnic or religious groups: a) killing members of the group; b) causing serious bodily or mental harm to members of the group; c) deliberately inflicting on the group conditions of life calculated to bring about its physical destruction in whole or in part; d) imposing measures intended to prevent births within the group; e) forcibly transferring children of the group to another group. It is no doubt instructive to note that the United States was one of the very few "civilized nations" to refrain from signing this crucial piece of U.N. legislation.

58. *The Genocide Machine in Canada,* op. cit., pp. 183-187.

59. *One Century Later,* op. cit. Concerning uranium mining on indigenous lands in Canada, see Goldstick, Miles, *Wollaston: People Resisting Genocide,* Black Rose Books, Montréal, 1987. Also see Hardin, Jim, "Indigenous Rights and Uranium Mining in Northern Saskatchewan," in Ward Churchill, ed., *Critical Issues in Native North America,* Doc. 63, International Work Group on Indigenous Affairs, Copenhagen, 1989, pp. 116-36.

60. For a full discussion of the use and implications of the term "auto-genocide," see Chomsky, Noam, and Edward S. Herman, *After the Cataclysm: Postwar Indochina and the Reconstruction of Imperial Ideology,* South End Press, Boston, 1979, pp. 135-300.

61. *Worker Safety and Health Working Papers,* Oil, Chemical and Atomic Workers Union, Denver, 1978.

62. Ibid. Also see "Economic Data for Nuclear Industry Bargaining Units," *OCAW Position Paper,* Oil, Chemical and Atomic Workers Union, Denver, 1977.

63. Seib, Gerald F., "Indians Awaken to their Lands' Energy Riches and Seek to Wrest Development from Companies," *Wall Street Journal,* September 20, 1979, p. 40.

64. Owens, Nancy J., "Can Tribes Control Energy Development?" in *Native Americans and Energy Development,* Anthropological Resources Center, Cambridge, MA, 1978, p. 53.

65. *Akwesasne Notes,* Late Winter 1979, p. 6; Summer 1979, p. 31.

66. *Newsletter of the Native American Solidarity Committee,* Berkeley, CA, Spring 1979, pp. 12-13. See also Garrity, op. cit., p. 256.

67. Hoppe, Richard, "A stretch of desert along Route 66—the Grants Belt—is chief locale for U.S. uranium," *Engineering and Mining Journal,* November 1978, pp. 73-93.

68. Environmental Protection Agency, unpublished field report, number deleted, filed with Southwest Information Resource Center, Albuquerque, NM, June 1973.

69. Hoppe, op. cit. Also see *NASC Newsletter,* op. cit., and *Akwesasne Notes,* Summer 1979, op. cit.

70. *Akwesasne Notes,* Late Winter, 1979, op. cit.

71. *Cable News Network* report, July 17, 1990.

72. See Schumacher, Elouise, "440 billion gallons: Hanford wastes would fill 900 King Domes," *Seattle Times,* April 13, 1991.

Chapter IX

Trouble In High Places
Erosion of American Indian Rights to Religious Freedom in the United States

Vine Deloria, Jr.

The First Amendment to the Constitution declares that Congress shall make no law respecting the establishment of religion or prohibiting the free *exercise* thereof. The Fourteenth Amendment has rendered the legislatures of the states as incompetent as Congress to enact such laws. The constitutional inhibition on the subject of religion has a double aspect. On the one hand, it forestalls compulsion by law of the acceptance of any creed or the practice of any form of worship. Freedom of conscience and freedom to adhere to such religious organization or form of worship as the individual may choose cannot be restricted by law. On the other hand, it safeguards the *free exercise of the chosen form of religion.* Thus the amendment[s] embrace two concepts—freedom to believe and freedom to *act* (emphasis added).

Cantwell v. Connecticut
310 U.S. 296, 1940

Two recent Supreme Court cases, *Lyng v. Northwest Indian Cemetery Protective Association* (108 S. Ct. 1319 (1988)) and *Employment Division, Department of Human Resources of Oregon v. Smith* (110 S. Ct. 1595 (1990)), have stripped American Indians of the protection of the federal courts and the American Constitution insofar as the practice of traditional religions is concerned. Although the two cases are viewed in tandem as attacks on Indian rights, they only coincidentally come together. *Lyng* attempts to deal with Indian rights as defined following the passage of the American Indian Religious Freedom Resolution, and *Smith* confronts the question of the relationship of religion and the state. Thus, while *Lyng* can be cited as precedent in federal Indian law, *Smith* examines much broader questions of constitutional law. The latter case was considered in order to determine whether the state of Oregon held a constitutional right to impose either civil or criminal penalties upon members of the Native American Church for their traditional use of sacramental peyote simply because use of the substance was legally denied to everyone else. The high court held that the state did in fact possess such rights. But, as the dissenting justices put it in *Smith:*

> The Court today—interprets the [Free Exercise] Clause to permit the government to prohibit, without justification, conduct mandated by an individual's religious beliefs, so long as the prohibition is generally applicable. But a law that prohibits certain conduct—conduct that happens to be an act of worship for someone— manifestly does prohibit that person's free exercise of his religion. A person who is barred from engaging in religiously motivated conduct is barred from freely exercising his religion. Moreover, that person is barred from freely exercising his religion regardless of whether the law prohibits the conduct only when engaged in for religious reasons, only by members of that religion, or by all persons.[1]

The high court opinion in *Smith* therefore voids long-settled interpretations of the constitutional protections extended over the free exercise of religion—not only with regard to Indians, but to everyone else as well—and throws them in the same "community standards" arena covering pornography and other forms of obscenity.[2] *Lyng,* on the other hand, provides an opportunity to examine the three major paths that federal Indian law has taken in the course of American history: 1) the treaty relationship, 2) the Trust Doctrine, and 3) property ownership of the public domain by the federal government. Many practitioners of federal Indian law, including, unfortunately, most of the judges and justices who write decisions, tend to use these ideas interchangeably or as complementary theories that bolster a vague belief that Indians are and must always be at the mercy of the United States government. But these interpretations of the Indian relationship are actually exclusive of one another, and therefore any effort to combine them in a decision or legal brief inevitably adds to rather than reduces the confusion and mystery of federal Indian law.

The Treaty Relationship

It was the custom of European powers to enter into diplomatic relationships with powerful Indian peoples who controlled large areas of the interior of the continent. Since there was intense rivalry between the colonizing powers, no nation seeking possessions in the New World dared deal with native peoples in a manner that would leave open the question of legality for another nation to exploit.[3] With the exception of Spain—which conquered the Indians of Central and South America, including Mexico—Great Britain, France, and even Russia[4] sought some kind of legal formality in their relations with the Indians.[5] Dutch settlers in New York ensured that they had a deed, properly signed by the local Indian leaders before they began land speculation, and as late as 1847 a colony of German settlers in Texas entered into a formal agreement with the Comanches.[6] Spain and later Mexico signed numerous treaties with indigenous nations occupying the Gulf coast, Texas, and the American Southwest.

Treaties gave institutional structure to the expanding field of international law, which started to emerge in the generation after the discovery of the New World. Debates among Spanish theologians inspired thinkers of other countries particularly the Dutch, to articulate principles that should govern nations in their relations with one another.[7] European history became a fertile source of data for deriving these principles, and since small nations and minor principalities had often been the subject of larger territorial and dynastic wars, it was not unusual for large and small states to have agreed upon peaceful arrangements that would govern their activities even though it was apparent to all that the larger nation could easily seize and absorb the smaller one.[8]

Once such status had been recognized for small nations, it was no problem to transfer that concept to the North American situation and make it applicable to Indian nations.[9] Consequently, formal diplomatic relations were established with the various indigenous peoples and international political status was accorded them. The difficulty, however, was one of perception. European mini-states had family relationships with the rulers of larger nations, they were contiguous to the powerful countries of Europe, and they represented long-standing historical traditions going back to the time of original settlement when the barbaric tribes had divided the Roman Empire.[10] Indians could not claim this history and since they were of a different "race," and had different religions, languages, and cultures altogether, their political rights, even when phrased in European terms, were always considered to be intellectually suspect.[11]

France adopted the Indian custom of holding councils, reaching an agreement, and holding to the agreement until conditions changed and another council was warranted. Russia, Spain, and England, with some bureaucratic perversity, insisted on written documents to mark the negotiations with the Indians. The early colonial treaties are actually transcripts of councils held and discussions undertaken to clarify the points of conflict. The United States, after following this format for the first three years of the Revolution, in 1778 adopted the formal written document as evidence of the treaty and, consequently, the vast majority of diplomatic documents recording American relations with Indians fall into a formal set of legal instruments.[12]

From 1778 to the present time, the United States has generally used a diplomatic format with carefully worded texts and has not regarded the actual discussions and presentations made during the negotiations as part of the agreement, except insofar as courts have allowed transcripts to be entered into evidence to indicate the intent of the negotiators.[13] With this obsession with legality, the three branches of government have had to devise a vocabulary with which to interpret the status of the treaties and agreements. Here the legislative and judicial branches looked to the judiciary for guidance and the lower federal courts produced two interpretations of the status of treaties that have since been adopted by the federal government (with the exception of reactionary politicians and bureaucrats who have convinced themselves that Indians have no rights whatsoever).[14]

In *Turner v. American Baptist Missionary Union* (24 Fed. Cas. No. 14251 (C.C. Mich. 1852)), a Michigan federal district court rebutted the argument that Indian treaties had a different status than did those made with larger and foreign countries:

> It is contended that a treaty with Indian tribes has not the same dignity or effect
> as a treaty with a foreign and independent nation. This distinction is not
> authorized by the constitution. Since the commencement of the government,
> treaties have been made with the Indians, and the treaty-making power has
> been exercised in making them. They are treaties, within the meaning of the
> constitution, and as such are the supreme laws of the land (emphasis added).[15]

Thus, whatever other arguments might be made by the people seeking to dilute Indian rights, attacking the right articulated by a treaty or agreement is not within the realm of legality. The only alternative to granting the rights and privileges spelled out in treaties is to invoke another doctrine or to use rhetorical arguments to change the meaning of words, narrowing the content of ideas to a restricted, technical legal sense. Both of these tactics have been used on occasion but the general principle holds: treaties and agreements made with the Indians are the supreme law of the land.

The other major doctrine of interpretation relating to the diplomatic documents dealing with Indians was articulated in *U.S. v. Winans* (1905) by the Supreme Court. "The treaty was not a grant of rights *to* the Indians, but *a grant of rights from them*—a reservation of those not granted (emphasis added)."[16] This doctrine means that unless a specific subject matter becomes part of the negotiations and the exercise of powers relating to it is allocated to the United States, or occasionally to a private party, as in the case of education and other social services, the subject matter *and* the power to deal with it remain with the Indians.

The treaty or agreement with the Indians thus has precisely the same effect on the relationship of Indians to the United States as does the Tenth Amendment to the Constitution, which states: "The powers not delegated to the United States by the Constitution, nor prohibited by it to the States, are reserved to the States, respectively, or to the people." There are, consequently, some very large areas in which it is believed that a political vacuum occurs, and the federal government and the states often try to rush in and lay claim, arguing that nature abhors a vacuum, and that if a political power is not being exercised it does not exist or that they have the right and responsibility to fill it.[17] But such actions are a violation of the law since the subject matter and the power to deal with it must pass from the Indians to the federal government only as a matter of negotiated agreement.

In recent decades, Congress has adopted the format of the negotiated "settlement act" as a vehicle for resolving disputes that would otherwise involve extensive and prolonged litigation on the part of Indians, states, and the federal government.[18] These "settlements," in which the contending parties bring their proposed solution to Congress for final adjustment and approval, range from ancient land claims[19] to water rights[20] and child welfare agreements.[21] Except for the formalities of giving presents and being restricted to approval by the United States Senate alone, these settlement acts have all the status and legality of the old treaties and agreements. There is no question that the government should have informed the Indians in the

Lyng case of their right to seek a legislative solution in the same manner as did the Taos Pueblo, which secured return of its sacred Blue Lake area in 1970.[22]

It is important to bear in mind that formulating a settlement for use of the sacred California "High Country" at issue in *Lyng* was a reasonable and logical alternative to the litigation that took place. But it was apparent that the emphasis on the Trust Doctrine precluded all other considerations—by the Indians, by their attorneys, and by the federal agencies involved. Since settlement was never suggested at any time during the controversy, we must turn to the Trust Doctrine itself to see if it provided protections more reliable than a negotiated settlement.

The "Trust" Doctrine

The so-called Trust Doctrine is a strange creature composed of long-standing themes prevalent during the first century of "discovery" of the "New World": the need to find some operative principle to describe the internal location of Indian nations within the area claimed by the United States and for a practical guideline for the administration of services promised to the Indians in treaties and agreements. No single source can be found for the Trust Doctrine outside of the historical and political situations in which it has been invoked as a measure of federal performance. Consequently, it stands outside the constitutional framework as a moral presence much as does the idea of freedom with respect to American citizenship.

The justification for laying claim to lands in the Western hemisphere and for entering into political relationships with inhabitants was grounded in the idea that the Pope was Christ's representative in matters spiritual and temporal, and that all institutions were justified and validated if they functioned within the broad moral framework of Christian religion. The Pope could therefore "grant" rights to lands in the Western hemisphere to Christian sovereigns with the condition that they bring the natives thereof to a full understanding and acceptance of Christianity."[23] Although the Pope's authority was rejected by Protestant countries a few decades after this pronouncement, all European nations based their colonial claims on the "pagan" status of the natives of lands they were discovering, and some effort, however sporadic and minimal, was made to provide Christian religious teachings to people they were busy subduing.[24]

A series of what were virtually world wars originating in European dynastic struggles meant a juggling of claims in North America, and it was presumed that as the losing nations ceded their colonial possessions, their rights to exclusive intercourse with the natives were also transferred.[25] The alleged "Doctrine of Discovery," as the mature form of this practice came to be known, was interpreted by European colonial powers as vesting in the discovering country the legal right to acquire title over the lands described in the process of exploration.[26] Thus an explorer, landing on a remote headland of a North American coast, might claim all acquisition rights to lands encompassed by the watershed of the river at whose mouth he stood for his sovereign. It was then up to the sovereign to provide for the settlers and for administrative officials to establish the presence of the nation in that locale. As long as the natives did not eject the colonists, the claim was supposed to be respected by other European nations during times of peace. The Spanish, for example, landed on and claimed Cape Flattery but were rudely dispelled by the Makahs, and hence their claim came to naught.[27]

Following the Treaty of Paris (8 *Stat.* 80, September 3, 1783), which closed the American Revolution, Americans believed they had inherited the discovery claims of Great Britain to that area of North America where the British had recognized their independence—the Atlantic seaboard and vaguely identified areas of the Ohio Valley, excluding the region of Canada and some of the Great Lakes shorelines. The Indians were left in a diplomatic wasteland between 1783 and 1815 because they were able to make treaties, and did with *both* the United States and Great Britain, and yet lived within the territory now claimed by the United States as its own.[28] There is no question about the international status of Indians during this period, since Spain was also making treaties with the Indian nations living in the southeastern United States.[29]

In 1823, in a strange case involving the validity of a land sale made while Great Britain was the primary sovereign west of the Mississippi, *Johnson v. McIntosh,* the Supreme Court outlined its own version of the Doctrine of Discovery, which it admitted was illogical and preposterous but, since it was maintained by force, was the operative law regarding land titles. Therefore, according to the Supreme Court, "the Indian inhabitants are to be considered as merely occupants, to be protected, indeed, while in peace, in the possession of their lands, but to be deemed incapable of transferring the absolute title to others."[30] The perceived legal incapacity to transfer land title then gave justification for the federal government to assert that it held the legal title, that the Indians possessed the equitable title, and that a kind of trust existed within the relationship.[31]

John Marshall, in writing his two *Cherokee* opinions less than a decade later, sought to transfer the concept of incomplete title to lands to the political status of Indians as well. We can see in retrospect that Marshall was placed in an untenable position from which he had to extricate himself. In 1829 and 1830, the state of Georgia passed a series of statutes purporting to give the state jurisdiction within the borders of Cherokee Nation thereby nullifying Cherokee laws and political existence. The Cherokees filed an original action in the Supreme Court seeking to secure a writ of prohibition blocking enforcement of these Georgia laws. The choice was clear: accepting the Cherokee petition and granting relief would have opened the Supreme Court to numerous future filings by a wide variety of Indian nations, some not even as large as the Euroamerican's backwoods settlements. Marshall therefore described the status of Indians and the United States as resembling that of a ward and guardian relationship, referring perhaps to the handicap he had already imposed upon Indians in reference to the passage of valid land titles.[32]

Thus, the initial approach of the Cherokees was thwarted. A year later Reverend Samuel Worcester and a group of missionaries, convicted under a Georgia statute, approached the court with the argument that they had been active within Cherokee

Nation and had followed Cherokee laws because of the U.S. treaty relationship with the Cherokees, and because their services were understood as authorized activities under a federal statute. Faced now with the question of ruling whether a federal law, passed in accordance with the Commerce Clause that gave exclusive jurisdiction to Congress, overruled or took precedence over a state statute, the Chief Justice immediately ruled in favor of the federal position.[33] Unfortunately, subsequent Supreme Courts and lower federal courts seized upon the phrases "ward" and "guardian" and elaborated on them to suggest that a rigid "trust" relationship exists between the United States and American Indian nations.

Application of this doctrine varies considerably, however, depending on the forum in which it is presented. When Indians sued the United States in the Court of Claims and Indian Claims Commission, consistent application of the Trust Doctrine would have meant the awarding of exceedingly high sums as compensation for the many land cessions made during the 19th century. Again, the difficulty was conceptual. The United States wore two hats in the claims process: it had been the trustee of the Indian nations and, at the same time, was supposed to be making some land purchases as an impartial buyer. In general, the Indian Claims Commission took the position that the government was the buyer in good faith in a series of transactions in which the Indians acted as wholly competent legal sellers.[34]

Today the Trust Doctrine has been cited as the basis for providing a wide variety of social services to Indians, and is also cited as the excuse for high-handed bureaucratic manipulations of reservation resources. Most often the doctrine is brought into play when tribal governments wish to use their lands in a manner that conflicts with policies of the Bureau of Indian Affairs (BIA). Then the excuse is that Indian governments, under the supervision of the federal government, must secure the highest cash income from their resources, rather than use them in alternative ways that might be more beneficial and productive over the long term—particularly for the Indians, themselves. "Trust" thus leads directly to the question of property law and ultimately to the conflict between legal and equitable titles to public domain lands.

The Power of Property Rights

In 1883, the Supreme Court was faced with the question of determining the nature of criminal jurisdiction over crimes committed by one Indian against another on an Indian reservation.[35] *Revised Statutes,* Sections 2145 and 2146, passed in 1873, gave the basic jurisdiction to the federal government but preserved jurisdiction to an Indian nation that had, through treaty negotiations, reserved such powers to itself. In 1881 Crow Dog, a Brûlé Lakota, had killed Spotted Tail, a chief of the Brûlés and a favorite of the government. Resolving the killing through traditional Lakota condolence procedures, by compensating Spotted Tail's family, Crow Dog was neither in prison nor sentenced to death. The BIA, which had been agitating for extension of federal criminal jurisdiction for over a decade, immediately secured a special congressional appropriation to take the case to the Supreme Court. Crow

Dog, indicted and convicted in the Dakota Territory federal district court, became somewhat of a national celebrity as a result.

The Supreme Court upheld the *Revised Statutes* since it was clear that this situation had been adequately examined and approved by Congress. The ensuing outcry of the newspapers upon hearing the decision, coupled with intense lobbying by the Interior Department, resulted in the passage of the "Seven Major Crimes Act" in 1885. Actually, this radical change in criminal jurisdiction was not given proper hearing by Congress. It was, instead, attached to the annual appropriation act for the Bureau of Indian Affairs as a small paragraph purporting to extend federal jurisdiction over all reservations. In fact, it was never applied to the Five Civilized Tribes in Oklahoma or to smaller, scattered groups in other parts of the country. But, was the act constitutional in view of the previous reluctance of Congress to take such a step,[36] and in view of the treaty relationship that already defined the matter of jurisdiction quite adequately, particularly with respect to the Lakota poeple of the Great Plains ?[37]

The answer was not long in coming. Then pending from the California district court was an appeal dealing with a murder conviction of two Indians on the Hoopa Reservation. The district court had certified six questions to the Supreme Court, the third and sixth of which referred specifically to the recently passed statute. The decision in *United States v. Kagama* (1886) is so illogical that it should be reproduced, at least in part:

> The mention of Indians in the Constitution which has received the most attention is that found in the clause which gives Congress "power to regulate commerce with foreign nations and among the several States, and with the Indian tribes." This clause is relied on in the argument in the present case, the proposition being that the statute under consideration is a regulation of commerce with the Indian tribes. But we think it would be a very strained construction of this clause, that a system of criminal laws for Indians living peaceably in their reservations, which left out the entire code of trade and intercourse laws justly enacted under that provision, and established punishments for the common-law crimes of murder, manslaughter, arson, burglary, larceny, and the like, without any reference to their relation to any kind of commerce, was authorized by the grant of power to regulate commerce with the Indian tribes. While we are not able to see, in either of these clauses [the taxation clause being the other clause cited in the argument] of the Constitution and its amendments, any delegation of power to enact a code of criminal law for the punishment of the worst class of crimes known to civilized life when committed by Indians...[38]

Departing from all previous case law, the high court rejected the tax and representation clause of the First Article and Fourteenth Amendment, as well as the Commerce Clause, which had previously been the major constitutional moorings enabling Congress to deal with Indians. Instead Justice Miller, writing the unanimous opinion, went back to geography, noting that "Indians are within the geographical limits of the United States. The soil and the people within these limits are under the political control of the Government of the United States, or of the States of the Union."[39] Moreover, Miller then argued that:

> [T]his power of Congress to organize territorial governments, and make laws for their inhabitants, arises not so much from the clause in the Constitution, in regard to disposing of and making rules and regulations concerning the Territory and other property of the United States, as from the ownership of the country in which the Territories are, and the right of exclusive sovereignty which must exist in the National Government and can be found nowhere else.[40]

In support of this novel reasoning, which suggested that a federal statute could be constitutional by appealing to a power or attribute outside the Constitution, Justice Miller cited Chief Justice Marshall's opinion in *American Insurance Co. v. Canter* (1 Pet. 511 (1827)). This dealt with the territorial status of the people of Florida after it had been acquired by the United States: "Perhaps the power of governing a Territory belonging to the United States, which has not by becoming a State, acquired the means of self-government, may result necessarily from the fact that it is not within the jurisdiction of any particular State. The right to govern may be the inevitable consequence of the right to acquire Territory. Whichever may be the source whence the power is derived, the possession of it is unquestioned."[41]

Miller, like many of his successors, was irretrievably lost in the complexities of American history. Florida was acquired from Spain in 1819 by purchase and treaty, and the United States then acquired *political jurisdiction* over the territory. It was not acting in the capacity of a private landowner. Thus the property rights argument, when applied to the United States in any of its constitutional capacities, does not bring with it political powers that originate outside the Constitution in the *fact* of landownership, and which are not subject to limitations imposed by the Constitution. To argue otherwise would vest the federal government in a set of ultra-constitutional powers of unlimited scope. Additionally, the United States holds its lands, the public domain, on behalf of its citizens, and this ownership is not held against the citizens as if the United States were a competing private landholder.

The *Lyng* Case

The *Lyng* case is typical of much contemporary litigation over the use of federal lands. The Forest Service, which managed the Six Rivers National Forest, primarily for the benefit of the timber industry, proposed to build a six-mile paved road—known as the "G-O Road"—that would link two existing roads leading respectively to Gasquet and Orleans, California. The proposed road would run through the Chimney Rock section of the forest and would severely disrupt the solitude of a remote area known to the Yurok, Karok, and Tolowa Indians as the "High Country," a place used for untold hundreds of years for Vision Quests, gathering of medicine roots, and other ceremonial purposes. Prior to the controversy generated by the Forest Service proposal, the religious leaders of these Indian groups had conducted their religious ceremonies without disturbance or interruption.

A number of non-Indian conservation and environmental groups were also interested in this area and wanted it kept as a wilderness. Consequently, when the case was filed in the Northern District federal court in California, an impressive number of plaintiffs joined suit. In addition to an Indian coalition called the Northwest Indian Cemetery Protective Association, the Sierra Club, the Wilderness Society, California Trout, Siskiyou Mountain Resource Council, Redwood Audubon Society, Northcoast Environmental Society, and State of California acting through and by the Native American Heritage Commission and State Resources Agency all became plaintiffs. It is very difficult to determine, without being privy to pre-litigation conferences among the respective plaintiffs, whether the Indians initiated the suit or were drawn into it by other groups. The question is interesting in this respect: if the Indians initiated the suit, their theory of the spiritual value of the lands should have been the primary argument; if not, the secular perspective of the other plaintiffs may have determined the arguments that were used. Thus, the religious question might or might not have been foremost in the minds of the attorneys who directed the litigation.

At any rate, the complaint against the Forest Service should have made its director blush and withdraw the proposal immediately. The agency was accused of violating the First Amendment (Indian religious freedom exercise), the American Indian Religious Freedom Act, the National Environmental Policy Act, the National Historic Preservation Act, the Federal Water Quality Control Act, the Porter-Cologne Water Quality Control Act (a California state statute), Hoopa Indian Water and Fishing Rights (allegedly protected under the self-proclaimed "trust responsibility" of the federal government), the Wilderness Act, the Administrative Procedure Act, the National Forest Management Act of 1976, and the Multiple Use, Sustained Yield Act. This impressive list of federal and state statutes is in some ways more indicative of the inability of the United States Congress to adopt an intelligent comprehensive plan for management of public resources than it is an indictment of Forest Service practices. One could, however, argue that this endless list of efforts actually footnotes the indifference found in federal agencies fulfilling their responsibilities.

Now we enter the twilight world of administrative procedures and entrenched attitudes. The Forest Service had authorized a study of the impact of the proposed road on Indian religious beliefs and practices and had made an effort to devise an alternative route that would have minimized the impact both visually and audibly. Ten different routes were considered, including the possibility of not building the road at all. The Forest Service had also prepared two reports for the Advisory Council on Historic Preservation and had held a meeting at its request. In arguments before the courts, it was pointed out that aside from not building the road, none of the plaintiffs had suggested a route that had been neglected or overlooked by its study. Yet, the Forest Service frankly admitted that it had something of a trust responsibility to the Indians.

Prior to the trial, the district court denied the motion for a preliminary injunction with the understanding that the road would not be started until a full hearing could be held on the merits of the argument.[42] The trial then commenced, and during the course of the presentations the religious arguments began to have some weight. A document entitled the *Theodoratus Report,* which dealt with Indian religious practices, had outlined a comprehensive understanding of what the Indians did ceremonially and also pointed out that the ultimate plan was to build 200 miles of logging roads in the vicinity of the sacred area, close to their three most important mountains: Chimney Rock, Doctor Rock, and Peak #8.[43]

There was no question that the proposed road and ultimate management plan would destroy the area for religious and recreational purposes, dump an unknown quantity of dirt and gravel into streams (thereby destroying local salmon spawning beds) and serve little useful purpose by simply eliminating this part of an old forest. Under then-prevailing case law, the Forest Service was required to demonstrate a "compelling interest" to the federal government, at least sufficiently important to justify substantially burdening the practice of religion. But the court could find only miniscule bureaucratic justifications for the proposed road. It is useful to recount the Forest Service's understanding of what constitutes a compelling interest because it illustrates the difficulties involved in applying constitutional tests to the actions of federal agencies. The justifications were:

- The road would increase the quantity of timber accessible for harvest.
- It would stimulate employment in the regional timber industry.
- It would provide recreational access to the Blue Creek unit.
- It would allow for further efficient administration of Six Rivers National Forest.
- It would increase the price of the bids on future timber sales by decreasing the cost of hauling timber to the mills.
- It would increase timber production, thereby stimulating the timber industry.[44]

It does not take a genius to survey this list and realize that it is a set of excuses rather than compelling interests. The values of Forest Service personnel who rank possible increases in future timber bids and ease of administration against Indian rights, and the welfare of the forest itself, tend to speak for themselves. The courts, once they are allowed into the process, can do little but credit this reasoning and the commercial values represented by the Forest Service and its clients with a higher purpose.

The three possible theories of Indian relationship to the federal government—treaty, trust, and property—now come into focus. In order to use the treaty relationship, it would have been necessary for the Indians to approach Congress when the Forest Service first began its survey and seek special congressional action to set aside that part of the Six Rivers National Forest for their use. The Taos Pueblo effort at Blue Lake could have been cited as a precedent, and even if no legislation had been passed immediately, raising the issue of the preservation of sacred sites while the *Theodoratus Report* was being written would have radically changed the emphasis in that document, giving the Indians considerably more leverage in articulating their point of view.

The Forest Service admitted the existence of a trust relationship in its first court appearance, but the nature of this trust was not adequately explained by either the Indians or the Forest Service during the actual trial. The decision in 1983 favored the Indians. Yet, as we shall see when we discuss the appeals, this issue quickly fell by the wayside. What is important to note at this point, however, is that "trust" exists as a viable factor only at the very highest level of the administrative pyramid, that is, at the secretarial and presidential level, as part of the "climate" of responsibility. When trust appears at the lowest administrative level, it becomes merely one factor of many to be considered. And since the efficient and generally acceptable way of doing business is the real context within which administrative decisions are made, the trust responsibility is far too abstract a notion to have impact on the decisions made by forest managers.

Congress has had to confront this propensity of bureaucrats to sidestep policy considerations and the plenitude of other federal acts, which the Forest Service had been accused of violating, requiring that various steps be taken so that the intangible factors of forest preservation, historic preservation, clean water, and other goals be considered in the management of the national forests. However, these requirements are generally viewed by bureaucrats as mere stumbling blocks, hurdles to be surmounted in their quest for managerial control over lands and trees they consider to be their own property. Under existing federal law, while the Forest Service is required to file environmental impact statements and deal with the question of historic preservation, its personnel are really the directors of all administrative procedures. They, consequently, are in a position to determine the content and ultimate conclusions of all these reports and formal statements. Once a federal agency has decided on a course of action, litigation is a farce because the important issues that might have weighed heavily in the minds of judges and justices have already been neatly packaged in language that the federal agency has created.

At trial, however, the Forest Service did not do so well. It conceded the road construction would not materially improve access to timber resources.[45] It became abundantly clear that the road would not increase the number of jobs in the timber industry.[46] Increased recreational use of the area meant increased environmental degradation.[47] The road would increase sediment in Blue Creek, thus reducing the salmon spawning grounds and violating the trust responsibility for Indians downstream at the Hoopa Reservation.[48] It also became apparent that the Forest Service actions since 1960 had created a situation in which the construction of the road seemed inevitable— the "administrative symmetry" argument.[49] The six factors cited by the Forest Service as constituting the "compelling" federal interest devolved down to the simple proposition that the agency wanted to build the road. Period.

The federal district court therefore issued a permanent injunction against the building of the road and prohibited the Forest Service from engaging in any actions that would allow commercial timber harvesting in the High Country until a supplemental Environmental Impact Statement (EIS) could be made and circulated for public comment. Indians and environmental groups breathed easier with this ruling but the real meaning of it was again only too clear. The Forest Service had not done an adequate job of burying the arguments raised by the other side and, therefore, needed to go back and put some more nails in the coffin. Thus, as 1983 closed, the larger issues of an ancient forest, the religious freedom of three groups of American Indians, the national historic heritage, and concern for the environment were now prisoners of a process of technical readjustment to an environmental impact statement *that was to be written by the Forest Service.*

The case went to the Ninth Circuit Court of Appeals in July 1984, and was decided in June 1985. The Forest Service had raised three issues the court felt bound to address:

- Whether the district court erred in enjoining road construction and timbering in the High Country of the Blue Creek unit on the ground that such activity would impermissibly burden the Indian plaintiffs' first amendment right to free exercise of their religion;
- Whether the district court erred in holding that the EISs prepared for the road and the land management plans failed adequately to discuss the effects on water quality of the proposed actions;
- Whether the district court erred in holding that the Forest Service's proposed actions would violate the Federal Water Pollution Control Act and state water quality standard.[50]

Two of these issues, dealing with the technical aspects of water, were obviously close calls since predictions concerning the improvement or degradation of water constitute an inexact science subject to alteration as political and other considerations warrant. Thus, the real question on appeal was the religious freedom issue. And the key to this issue was whether the proposed actions would "impermissibly burden" the Indian's free exercise of religion. The Forest Service clearly did not prevail when it attacked the religious rights of the three Indian groups. Its basic argument was that the government's action *had* to penalize a religious belief or practice. The nuance here is that the action had aspects of deliberate intent which could be better satisfied with some other procedure. Here the Indians were rescued by the holding in the *Sherbert* case in which the Supreme Court ruled that an injury might be described as indirect, that is, without a clear intent to commit injury but having the effect of an injury.[51]

The discussion of the Establishment Clause was more enlightening. The Forest Service argued that managing the forest so that it would not intrude on the practice of Indian religion would be tantamount to establishing a religious shrine. While the appeals court also rejected that argument, pointing out to the Forest Service that it had far overstepped its own logical conclusions, the response noted that only one of the proposed uses of this part of the national forest—commercial harvesting of timber—was rejected. Other purposes, including outdoor recreation, range, watershed, wildlife, fish habitat, and wilderness uses were all upheld.[52] Presumably the establishment of a religious preserve for a single group, which is how the Forest Service described the religious argument, would exclude all of these other uses entirely.

The Forest Service logic really ended abruptly at this juncture, and it is useful to note that the other multiple uses—recreation, various habitats, and wilderness— actually had no more standing or value in that agency's perspective than did the Indian religious use. While the agency was bound to consider all of these other uses, and the multitude of federal laws cited by the plaintiffs in their initial appearance in court testified to the intent of Congress with respect to public lands, the fact is that federal lands are managed for the benefit of private commercial parties. The average citizen, informed that one of many uses he or she wanted to see on a tract of land was prohibited, might be content to exclude that use and get on with enjoyment and care of the land. Not so the Forest Service, since the agency's actions following this decision—*not* existing laws or congressional intent—define its real sense of purpose and mission.

Dealing with the violation of environmental laws at the circuit level was merely a matter of reviewing the procedures used by the Forest Service. Tiptoeing carefully among the various findings of the district court regarding the Basic Management Plan and the Environmental Impact Statement, the circuit court vacated the portion of the injunction that precluded timber harvesting or construction and upheld the rest of the decree.[53] The decision pleased no one and the case was given a rehearing in July 1986. At issue were the religious freedom arguments of the Indians, the portions of the EIS that had been found inadequate, and whether or not the National Environmental Policy Act and Wilderness Act required the Forest Service to evaluate the impact of the road on the wilderness potential of the region.[54]

If the logic of the case seemed to be established—pitting the congressional intent of protecting Indian religious freedom and ensuring that wilderness areas receive special consideration in the management of federal lands against the mission and administrative practices of the Forest Service in spite of its clear preference for commercial timber harvesting over the many other more benign uses of the area—it would have required a sophisticated judge or justice to decide the case. Coincident with this prolonged litigation, however, was an unexpected development that surely had the potential to moot the question of road construction. In 1984, Congress had passed the California Wilderness Act (98 *Stat.* 1619), which placed in a wilderness status about 19,000 acres of the Eightmile Creek area and 26,000 acres of the Blue Creek area—areas closely adjacent to sacred sites important to the Indians. But with a perversity known only in a government too large to be coordinated, this act had preserved the corridor in which the proposed road was to be located until other decisions were made regarding construction.

Thus, external events had created a novel situation. Obviously wilderness had become a primary value for both Congress and the state of California. According to popular definitions of wilderness, its primary value is as an area in its pristine natural state, because this represents some intangible and difficult-to-define spiritual aspect of nature that has a superior value to commercial use of the area. In a sense, we have a generalized secular use, albeit one that represents a recognition of intangible values no matter how shallow they might be emotionally, now holding a greater value than a specific religious use of the same region. The question here is whether the Indian argument is to be considered inferior to the wilderness argument because of a racial distinction.

Unfortunately, at the circuit court level and later with the Supreme Court, the close parallel in motive and perspective was neither recognized nor understood. This neglect should be a warning to Indians and non-Indians alike that the popular belief prevailing that non-Indians can somehow absorb the philosophical worldview of American Indians and inculcate "reverence" for the land into their intellectual and emotional perspectives is blatantly false. Inherent in the very definition of "wilderness" is contained the gulf between the understandings of the two cultures. Indians do not see the natural world as a wilderness. In contrast, Europeans and Euroamericans see a big difference between lands they have "settled" and lands they have left alone. As long as this difference is believed to be real by non-Indians, it is impossible to close the perceptual gap, and the substance of the two views will remain in conflict.

The rehearing of the case was basically a rehash of the previous hearing except that Judge Canby dealt a bit more thoroughly with the establishment question. But his language was not clear, as evidenced by his treatment of the articulation of the government's "paramount interests" in building the road:

> There was testimony that completion of the road and logging in the high country would increase employment in Del Norte County, but that this benefit would simply represent a shift of work from elsewhere in the state. Thus, there would be no statewide net gain in employment. There was evidence that forest management functions would be made easier by the road. There was evidence that the road would also provide greater recreational access to the area, but the projected use was not large.[55]

This was a fine analysis, but what was the real bottom line to be drawn? Canby needed to conclude that nothing was to be gained by this road, that its impact would simply be to rearrange pre-existing activities in a minor fashion so that even predictions of benefits were suspect. Consequently, the real issue was whether or not the Forest Service could act apart from the rest of the federal government. The Forest Service obviously has no argument to be considered if Canby's decision spells out what is actually at issue in this case.

Mild as Canby's opinion was, it drew a dissent from Judge Beezer, who otherwise agreed with his conclusions regarding the environmental issues. Yet, he felt that the Indians had not established a first amendment violation satisfactorily. Culling his objections from recently published law review articles that called into question some of the Indian arguments, Beezer concentrated on the *Theodoratus Report* and sought to distinguish between the actual presence of the road and the audible and visual side-effects that the road would create. This method of attack was reminiscent of the logic of the last century in which federal courts divided commerce into its constituent parts, arguing that there was no violation of the Commerce Clause by shipment of goods across country because the goods were always in one state or another, and hence subject to state regulation wherever they were located.

Beezer would have allowed construction of the road, assuming that no important archaeological sites were disturbed, and then encouraged the Indians to seek an injunction against the logging if it placed a burden on their religious practices. But then Beezer argued that logging activities were irrelevant to the analysis anyway because the issue was the construction of the road.[56] How the road, whose sole purpose for existence was commercial logging, could have been separated from logging for purposes of analysis and then put back together for purposes of administration without becoming a ludicrous exercise in abstract logic was never explained by the judge.

About all the rehearing had produced was a dissenting judge, a further fragmentation of substantial arguments into smaller subsets of complaints, and the identification of the religious issue as one to be decided by the Supreme Court if it wished to take the case. Judge Beezer had clearly identified the issue under consideration with respect to the federal-Indian relationship. If this decision was upheld, it would mark the first time since the passage of the American Indian Religious Freedom Resolution that Indian religious freedom could be used to enjoin development of the public lands.[57] The Indians and the environmental groups were unable to get the Ninth Circuit Court to look at the California Wilderness Act as an intervening statement by Congress that the whole area was to be treated as a wilderness, regardless of the Indian religious freedom issue. All previous efforts to put teeth into the Religious Freedom Resolution had failed because the question was that of the protection of spiritual activities as weighed against the investment made by federal agencies. In this case alone was there intervening evidence that Congress had a broader policy concern that mooted the question of building the road.

Here the specificity of the California Wilderness Act gave the case a bizarre twist. The section of land through which the road was to be built was preserved from wilderness until the pending case was resolved. Consequently, Congress was sending a mixed message: there *would be* a wilderness designation but there *could be* a road. The most obvious interpretation of the situation was that Congress did not want to deal with the politics of the road and hoped that things would be resolved locally without any further direction or involvement at the Washington level. Since the federal government is often perceived as a monolithic creature with a central, coordinated purpose, the confusion left by the vagueness of the California Wilderness Act meant that the property argument, which could be construed as ultra-constitutional, would become a powerful presence in the subsequent Supreme Court examination of the case.

Enter the Reagan Court

The Forest Service appealed the Ninth Circuit Court ruling and the case, now known formally, with replacement of Max Petersen with Lyng as head of the Forest Service, as *Lyng v. Northwest Indian Cemetery Protective Association* (108 S.

Ct. 1319 (1988)), was handed down in 1988. The high court had granted *certiorari* on the basis that the lower courts had not clearly explained whether they had determined a decision based on the First Amendment was necessary because this might have given the Indians relief beyond what they could have expected from the statutory claims they had made.[58] Such reasoning seemed to place minor statutory relief above the freedoms granted by the Bill of Rights and, therefore, gave prophetic forecast to how the majority would view and resolve the issue.

Justice Sandra Day O'Connor, writing the majority opinion, put the construction of the road in perspective; it was the final link of a seventy-five-mile paved road that had been gradually completed over the years by the Forest Service. Leaving the road unfinished would then have left two segments coming to a dead end in what was now a designated federal wilderness area with timber harvesting prohibited in much of the area. The majority of the Ninth Circuit Court had upheld the religious freedom claims, but the fact that there was a dissenting judge encouraged O'Connor to use that dissent to imply a degree of slippage the Supreme Court could not overlook: "These differences in wording suggest, without absolutely implying, that an injunction covering the Chimney Rock area would in some way have been conditional, or narrower in scope, if the district court had not decided the First Amendment as it did."[59] But what would have made the injunction "narrower in scope" apart from the First Amendment? Every other factor was environmental in nature and involved possible degradation of the area. So, O'Connor identified a nonexistent danger and promptly sought to deal with it.

The majority opinion then went down the line of traditional reasoning that government activities could not be disrupted by the religious claims of citizens because of the great variety of possible religious beliefs and activities inherent in American society. The basic "threat" perceived by the high court was that of a "sudden revelation" of sacredness to individuals, as well as the equally necessary task of recognizing and accommodating beliefs. O'Connor seized on the most remote possibility, a revelation at the Lincoln Memorial to one individual, and pretended that this was comparable to the continuing religious practices of three groups of Indians which extended back perhaps thousands of years. Her basic logical structure appeared to be: "Socrates is a man. Socrates is insane. All men are therefore insane." Such thinking is applicable perhaps to the netherworld inhabited by the current Supreme Court justices, but is hardly relevant to the issue at hand.

The thrust of O'Connor's opinion was aimed directly at the previous holding in *Sherbert v. Verner,* the indirect but easily identifiable burden on religion. "Whatever may be the exact line between unconstitutional prohibitions on the free exercise of religion and the legitimate conduct by the government of its own affairs," O'Connor argued, "the location of the line cannot depend on measuring the effects of a governmental action on a religious objector's spiritual development."[60] The measuring test, however, was precisely the line that *had* to be drawn, and when O'Connor admitted that "the government does not dispute, and we have no reason to doubt, that the logging and road-building projects at issue in this case could have devastating effects on traditional Indian religious practices," the issue should have been resolved.[61] As Justice Brennan put it in a dissent in which he was joined by Justices Marshall and Blackmun:

> The Court does not for one minute suggest that the interests served by the G-O Road are in any way compelling, or that they outweigh the destructive effect construction of the road will have on [the Indians'] religious practices. Instead, the Court embraces the Government's contention that its prerogative as land-owner should always take precedence over a claim that a particular use of federal property infringes religious practices. Attempting to justify this rule, the Court argues that the First Amendment bars only outright prohibitions, indirect coercion and penalties on the free exercise of religion. All other "incidental effects of government programs," it concludes, even those "which may make it difficult to practice certain religions but which have no tendency to coerce individuals into acting contrary to their religious beliefs," simply do not give rise to constitutional concerns. [Ever since] our recognition nearly half a century ago that restraints on religious conduct implicate the concerns of the Free Exercise Clause, [this Court has] never suggested that the protections of the guarantee are limited to so narrow a scope.[62]

At this point in discussing the opinion, it is important to note that O'Connor was using what is called the "old fact situation" to justify her reasoning, since the California Wilderness Act had rendered moot the question of whether or not there would be logging in the area: there would not be. With commercial logging virtually eliminated as a justification for building the road, the issue then became simply a question of whether the Forest Service had to give Indian religious freedom its due. O'Connor decided negatively on this point, arguing that the federal government as a landowner had certain rights that could not be infringed upon by either its wards or its citizens.[63]

In this, O'Connor finally committed the high court to a formal position on a question it had studiously avoided addressing through a whole series of cases involving Indian spiritual rights to land during the past half-century. Examples include the submersion of traditional Cherokee burial grounds in the Tennessee Valley behind the Tellico Dam,[64] flooding of much of the Allegheny Seneca Reservation in Pennsylvania behind the Kinzua Dam,[65] flooding of Lakota burial sites on the Standing Rock Reservation as part of the Missouri River Project,[66] submersion of the Rainbow Bridge formation, sacred to both the Navajo and the Hopi, behind the Glen Canyon Dam in southern Utah,[67] and destruction of Hopi and Navajo sacred sites on the San Francisco Peaks (near Flagstaff, Arizona) during construction of a ski resort.[68] Further, the Supreme Court's ruling in *Lyng* destroyed the basis for several promising religious freedom cases brought by Indians during the 1980s in the effort to protect or regain use of sacred lands. Notable in this regard were Lakota efforts to ensure unrestricted access to and spiritual use of the Black Hills,[69] and litigation designed to prevent wholesale strip mining of sacred areas within the former Navajo-Hopi Joint Use Area in northeastern Arizona.[70] At this point, such endeavors in attaining due process through U.S. courts appear to have been gutted by the "G-O Road Decision."

Stripped of peripheral issues, the matter before the high court was to weigh the government's trust responsibility toward Indians against its right to manage its own affairs. Undeniably, part of those affairs, a very important part, was execution of the trust responsibility itself. Hence, the question *should* have been academic. But the context in which trust responsibility was conceived to be important was back at the local level with the *Theodoratus Report.* When the Forest Service decided to proceed in spite of the religious question, then the integrity—and independence—of federal agency decision-making powers became the issue and the Supreme Court felt impelled to protect them.[71] To quote Brennan:

> "[T]he Free Exercise Clause," the Court explains today, "is written in terms of what the government cannot do to the [group or] individual, not in terms of what the individual [or group] can exact from the government." [Claiming] fidelity to the unremarkable constitutional principle, the Court concludes that even where the government uses federal land in a manner which threatens the very existence of a Native American religion, the government is simply not "doing" anything to the practitioners of that faith. Instead, the Court believes that Native Americans who request that the government refrain from destroying their religion effectively seek to exact from the government de facto beneficial ownership of federal property. These two astonishing conclusions follow naturally from the Court's determination that federal land-use decisions that render the practice of a given religion impossible do not burden that religion in a manner cognizable under the Free Exercise Clause.[72]

Once the idea of trust responsibility was negated, and this neutralization could only occur by conceiving of the Indians as a private party petitioning the government, rather than as a people to whom a trust responsibility is owed, it became necessary to attack the practice of religion itself. Consequently, O'Connor had to destroy the religious issue in order to deny the Indians. The minority opinion dwelled a bit on Indians and then defended previous doctrine on religious freedom. The dissenting justices objected to the twist that O'Connor had given to constitutional law. "The court's coercion test turns on a distinction between governmental actions that compel affirmative conduct inconsistent with religious belief and those governmental actions that prevent conduct consistent with religious belief," Brennan argued.[73] The distinction is important. With this new test the federal government, state, or municipality can deliberately oppress a minority religion as long as it is not apparent in the legislative record that there was an overt attempt to do so. *Lyng* thus leads directly to *Smith* and the variety of cases following *Smith* that place the religious body, of whatever persuasion, under the auspices of the state.

Felix S. Cohen once remarked that Indians serve as a sort of miner's canary on the American domestic scene. The idea is that oppression of indigenous peoples indicates at an early stage the general tightening of the administration of justice to exclude and restrict the rights of all citizens.[74] The basis for this statement is the nature of the trust responsibility. Trust requires that the United States act with the highest moral standards in its treatment of a small group of people who have placed themselves or have been placed under its protection. If a special and specific responsibility cannot be discerned and met, there is not much hope that broader and more universal responsibilities are going to be upheld. The minority opinion adequately described the meaning of the *Lyng* decision in its closing remarks: "[T]oday's ruling sacrifices a religion at least as old as the Nation itself, along with the spiritual well-being of its approximately 5,000 adherents, so that the Forest Service can build a 6-mile segment of road that two lower courts had found had only the most marginal and speculative utility, both to the Government itself and to the private lumber interests that might conceivably use it."[75]

Trouble in High Places

The tremendous irony of *Lyng* is that the road construction was later abandoned, as it should have been, so that the case need never have been heard in its own right. In upholding the principle that no citizen or group of citizens—or "wards," if that is what the Indians are—can tell a federal agency through court injunction how it is supposed to manage public lands, the Supreme Court has openly elevated the federal government to a dictatorial position over its citizens, legitimizing it as an entity with oppressive powers instead of a government of, by, and for the people. Three major questions arise from this litigation: 1) What is the nature of the trust responsibility of the federal government toward American Indians and what primacy does it have in the pyramid of federal values and decision making? 2) What is the nature of the relationship between the practice of religion and the administration of government? 3) What is the real nature of government in the United States today? The first question involves Indians primarily and non-Indians only secondarily, but the second and third questions are pivotal inquiries that must be resolved if American citizens are to maintain (or recover) their individual and collective freedoms.[76]

For American Indians, the message is especially clear. With the shunting aside of the trust responsibility in the *Lyng* case and the propensity of federal courts to interject the property doctrine when it is most convenient as a defense for the actions of government agencies, the most fruitful course of dealing with the U.S. government now seems to be in negotiated settlements. In other words, what is required is a modernization of the old diplomatic treaty relationship between Washington and the various Indian nations. *Lyng* may have been a necessary step in replacing the Trust Doctrine with the treaty settlement process, thus reversing a century-long trend of making the treaty right a function of the willingness of the federal entity to fulfill its promises. To the extent that this materializes over the next few years, and there is some indication that it will, *Lyng* may ultimately be remembered as an positive legal landmark by Indian people, regardless of the Supreme Court's intent in rendering its decision in the case.[77]

However, the high court's property argument is far greater than its application to Indians. Charged with multiple-use responsibilities for the Six Rivers National Forest, the Forest Service promptly opted for its traditional client, the timber industry, thus making public lands a reserved resource for private exploiters. Conservation and ecological groups, concerned about federal land management must now articulate their interests in a much more aggressive manner than has previously been the case. They must confront the emotional reality of federal agency existence, which is that government bureaucrats and employees deeply believe that the property they are charged with managing belongs to them *personally,* and that any effort by the public to participate in management is a personal affront. The more than 35 percent of the United States that is comprised of public lands belongs, in theory at least, to the public as a whole, not to federal employees and their favored clientele.[78] Until we can force a clear statement regarding limitations on the rights and powers that property ownership bestows on the federal government, we will *all* have the sword of Damocles hanging over our heads.

Notes

1. The opinion is reprinted in full in Clinton, Robert N., Nell Jessup Newton, and Monroe E. Price, eds., *American Indian Law: Cases and Materials,* The Michie Co. Law Publishers, Charlottesville, VA, 1991, pp. 46-65; quote from p. 55.
2. As concerns Indian peyote use specifically, *Smith* reversed the precedent that this was a protected activity established in *People v. Woody* (61 Cal. 2d 716, 394 P.2d 813, 40 Cal. Rptr. 69 (1964)).
3. See Lindley, Mark Frank, *The Acquisition and Government of Backward Territory in International Law,* Longmans Green Publishers, London, 1926.
4. An interesting reading in this connection is Belch, Stanislaus F., *Paulus Vladamiri and His Doctrine Concerning International Law and Politics,* Mouton Publishers, The Hague, 1965.
5. Several examples may be found in Davenport, Francis Gardener, ed., *European Treaties Bearing on the History of the United States and Its Dependencies,* Vols. I and II, Carnegie Institution of Washington, Washington, D.C., 1917.
6. See Neighbors, Kenneth, "The German-Comanche Treaty of 1847," *Southwestern Historical Quarterly,* No. 52, July 1948, pp. 32-48.
7. See generally, Williams, Robert A., *The American Indian in Western Legal Thought: The Discourses of Conquest,* Oxford University Press, London/New York, 1990 for background information. Also see Washburn, Wilcomb E., *Red Man's Land, White Man's Law,* Charles Scribner's Sons Publishers, New York, 1971 (esp. first two chapters).
8. See von Gierke, Otto Friedrich, *Natural Law and the Theory of Society, 1500-1800,* Cambridge University Press, Cambridge, MA, 1934 and *The Development of Political Theory,* W.W. Norton Publishers, New York, 1939.
9. See, for example, Canny, Nicholas P., "The Ideology of English Colonization: From Ireland to America," *William and Mary Quarterly,* No. 30, October 1973, pp. 575-98.
10. This is well covered in the introductory chapters of Bullough, Donald A., *The Age of Charlemagne,* Elek Books, London, 1965. Also see Hay, Denys, *Europe: The Emergence of an Idea,* University of Edinburgh Press, Edinburgh, 1968.
11. Although there are numerous examples of smaller states aligning themselves with larger states in the European example, the geographical setting of the New World plus the cultural differences made it impossible for Europeans to attribute political status of any substance to Indians. Justice Johnson in the first *Cherokee* case tried to establish an incipient or expectant status for the Cherokees akin to the Israelites wandering in the wilderness (i.e., a people *about* to achieve national and international status—but not yet).
12. The most instructive example of the use of treaty negotiations to indicate intent of the principals was in the *United States v. Washington* (384 F. Supp. 312 (W.D. Wash. 1974)) fishing rights case when anthropologist Barbara Lane gave extensive testimony on what fishing meant to the Northwest Indians and the role as commercial supplier of fish to the settlers that Isaac Stevens intended to play. Otherwise, the tendency of the courts has been to accuse Indians of having such a vested interest in the outcome of a case that they would lie to affect the course of a trial, an accusation that has never remotely been proven.
13. One need only compare the Treaty of Pittsburg (September and October 1775) between the U.S.

and the Iroquois Six Nations, Delawares, and Shawnees with the 1778 Delaware Treaty. The 1775 treaty consists of more than 100 pages of dialogue, primarily discussions concerning each point in contention. The 1778 treaty is several pages long and has sterile articles written in legal language that clearly outline benefits and responsibilities. The 1775 treaty can be found in Downes, Randolph C., *Council Fires on the Upper Ohio*, University of Pittsburg Press, Pittsburg, 1940, pp. 25-127. The text of the 1778 treaty appears as the first entry in Kappler, Charles J., *Indian Treaties, 1778-1883*, Interland Publishers, New York, 1973.

14. Good readings in this regard may be found in Cohen, Felix S., *The Legal Conscience: Selected Papers*, Yale University Press, New Haven, CT, 1960.

15. *Turner v. American Baptist Missionary Union*, at 346.

16. *United States v. Winans*, at 380-1.

17. This sequence of reasoning is what is really at stake in cases involving exercise of Indian self-governing rights although it is technically classified as an "infringement test" in *Williams v. Lee*, 358 U.S. 217 (1959).

18. This act first became an acceptable way of resolving Indian claims with the Alaska Native Claims Settlement Act in 1970. It was understood as a means of avoiding prolonged and complicated litigation. Thereafter, when confronted with complex claims and rights and the prospect of decades of litigation, both Indians and the federal and state governments decided to work out compromises and have them approved by Congress. The prospect of settlement is now an increasingly popular way of handling disputes that covers subjects of major importance as well as small annoyances.

19. See Rhode Island Indian Claims Settlement Act of 1978, P.L. 95-395, 92 *Stat.* 813.

20. See Southern Arizona Water Rights Settlement Act of 1982, P.L. 97-243, 96 *Stat.* 1274.

21. As of 1991, more than twenty indigenous nations have signed agreements under provision of the Indian Child Welfare Act of 1978.

22. Act of December 15, 1970, P.L. 91-550, 84 *Stat.* 1437. For context, see Gordon-McCutchan, R.C., *The Taos Indians and the Battle for Blue Lake*, Red Crane Books, Sante Fe, NM, 1991.

23. For discussion of these ideas, see Hanke, Lewis, *The Spanish Struggle for Justice in the Conquest of America*, University of Pennsylvania Press, Philadelphia, 1949.

24. See Quinn, David Beers, *England and the Discovery of America, 1481-1620*, Alfred A. Knopf Publishers, New York, 1974.

25. France, through a clever scheme, ceded Louisiana to Spain at some point before it signed the peace treaty with Great Britain closing the last of the "French and Indian Wars" (1756-1763). Later, Spain ceded Louisiana back to France and, in 1803, Napoleon sold it to the United States. But what the U.S. actually received in this purchase was the exclusive right to buy land within the boundaries of the Louisiana territory from the various Indian nations which owned it. Thus, many treaties after 1803 dealing with the Transmississippi West are purchase treaties wherein Indians sell some portion of their lands to the U.S. See Alvord, Clarence Walworth, *The Mississippi Valley in British Politics: A Study of the Trade, Land Speculation and Experiments in Imperialism Culminating in the American Revolution* (2 Vols.), Russell and Russell Publishers, New York, 1959.

26. Marshall used a variant of this treaty to void a land sale made by Indians at a public transaction conducted by the British a year before the American Revolution broke out. His application, in *Johnson v. McIntosh*, was to claim that the United States had good legal title in spite of British-Indian activity. Perhaps more strange, British-Indian land transactions in the Great Lakes region were almost always held to be valid even though some of them took place *after* the 1783 Treaty of Paris by which England admitted defeat at the hands of its dissident North American colonists.

27. The only remaining trace of Spanish presence in the area is a name, the Strait of Juan de Fuca.

28. The Treaty of Ghent (8 *Stat.* 218, TS 109, December 24, 1814), ending the War of 1812, required the United States and Great Britain to make peace treaties with the Indian allies of the other party so as to foreclose intertribal warfare started as a result of Indian nations aligning with one or another of the larger warring states, and to ensure that each of the larger countries would treat its former enemies justly. For background, see Horsman, Reginald, *Expansion and American Indian Policy, 1783-1812*, Michigan State University Press, Lansing, 1967.

29. See, for example, the treaty between Spain and the Creek Confederacy (May 20-June 1, 1784) at Pensacola, Florida, in *American State Papers: Foreign Affairs*, Vol. I, U.S. Government Printing Office, Washington, D.C., pp. 278-9. In fact, after the independence of the United States,

Spain and/or representatives of the King of Spain made some thirty treaties with Indian nations now regarded as domestic to the U.S. The indigenous principals in these international agreements ranged from the Choctaw, Creek, and Chickasaw of the Southeast, to the Comanches, Navajos, and Apaches of the Southwest, to several peoples in the San Francisco Bay area.

30. For a full elaboration, see *Johnson v. McIntosh* at 591-2.

31. Further discussion may be found in Cohen, Felix S., "Original Indian Title," *Minnesota Law Review*, No. 32, 1947, pp. 28-59.

32. *Cherokee Nation v. Georgia* (1831) gives a broad view of Marshall's use of the term. It was an analogy he was not quite capable of completing since it would have raised substantial questions about the amount of money the U.S. was offering Indians for their lands. Therefore, the comparison is qualified by use of the word "resembles," which, in this and other contexts, can mean almost anything.

33. In *Worcester v. Georgia* (1832), Marshall bolstered the status of federal statutes permitting missionaries to enter Cherokee lands, under Cherokee laws. In doing so, he brought the full measure of constitutional citation to bear (at 559): "[T]hat instrument confers on Congress the powers of war and peace; of making treaties; and of regulating commerce with foreign nations, and among the several States, and with the Indian tribes. They are not limited by any restrictions on their free actions; the shackles imposed on this power, in the confederation, are discarded."

34. See Vance, John T., "The Congressional Mandate and the Indian Claims Commission," *North Dakota Law Review*, No. 45, 1969, pp. 325-36.

35. *Ex Parte Crow Dog* (1883).

36. The BIA had tried but failed to get Congress to enact a similar law for nearly a decade. On May 20, 1874, the Senate Committee on Indian Affairs rejected the Bureau's overtures, stating, "The Indians, while their tribal relations subsist, generally maintain laws, customs, and usages of their own for the punishment of offenses. They have no knowledge of the laws of the United States and the attempt to enforce their own ordinances might bring them in direct conflict with existing statutes and subject them to prosecutions for their violation." See U.S. Senate, Committee on Indian Affairs, *Senate Report 367*, Vol. II, 43rd Cong., 1st Sess., U.S. Government Printing Office, Washington, D.C., 1874.

37. Article 1 of the 1868 Fort Laramie Treaty between the U.S. and the Lakota, Cheyenne and Arapaho nations made specific provisions for criminal jurisdiction to remain with the Indians. The latter agreed to surrender a person who committed a crime against non-Indians, or pay compensation for his or her crime, but the U.S. had no jurisdiction of its own within the boundaries of the "Great Sioux Nation."

38. *United States v. Kagama*, at 378-9.

39. Ibid., at 379.

40. Ibid., at 380.

41. *American Insurance Co. v. Canter* at 542.

42. *Northwest Indian Cemetery Protective Association v. Petersen*, 552 F. Supp. 951 (1982).

43. *Northwest Indian Cemetery Protective Association v. Petersen*, 565 F. Supp. 586, 592 (1983).

44. Ibid., at 595.

45. Ibid.

46. Ibid., at 595-6.

47. Ibid., at 596.

48. Ibid., at 605.

49. Ibid., at 601 (footnote).

50. *Northwest Indian Cemetery Protective Association v. Petersen*, 764 F.2d 581, 585 (1985).

51. *Sherbert v. Verner*, 374 U.S. 398 (1963).

52. *Northwest Indian Cemetery Protective Association v. Petersen*, 764 F.2d 581, 586 (1985).

53. *Northwest Indian Cemetery Protective Association v. Petersen*, 795 F.2d 688 (9th Cir. 1986).

54. Ibid., at 589.

55. *Northwest Indian Cemetery Protective Association v. Petersen*, 795 F.2d 688, 695 (1986).

56. Ibid., at 702.

57. Ibid., at 701.

58. *Lyng v. Northwest Indian Cemetery Protective Association*, at 1320.

59. Ibid., at 1324.

60. Ibid., at 1326.

61. Ibid.

62. Ibid., at 1338.
63. Ibid., at 1339.
64. On Tellico Dam, see Ensworth, Laurie, "Native American Free Exercise Rights to the Use of Public Lands," *Boston University Law Review,* No. 63, 1983, pp. 141-79. Also see Matthiessen, Peter, *Indian Country,* Viking Press, New York, 1984, pp. 103-126.
65. On Kinzua Dam, see U.S. Senate, Committee on Interior and Insular Affairs, *Hearings Before the Committee on Interior and Insular Affairs: Kinzua Dam Project, Pennsylvania,* 88th Cong., 1st Sess., U.S. Government Printing Office, Washington, D.C., May-December 1963.
66. On the Missouri River Project, see Lawson, Michael L., *Dammed Indians: The Pick-Sloan Plan and the Missouri River Sioux, 1944-1980,* University of Oklahoma Press, Norman, 1982.
67. This is the *Badoni* case; see "Table of Key Indian Laws and Cases" in this volume. Also see Ensworth, op. cit.
68. On San Francisco Peaks, see Lovett, Richard A., "The Role of the Forest Service in Ski Resort Development: An Economic Approach to Public Lands Management," *Ecology Law Quarterly,* No. 10, 1983, pp. 507-78.
69. *United States v. Means, et al.,* Civ. No. 81-5131, D.S.D. December 9, 1985.
70. One such suit, *Manybeads v. United States,* was dismissed by U.S. District Judge Earl Carroll on October 20, 1989, largely because of the high court ruling in *Lyng.*
71. An interesting discussion of the unsavory principles enshrined as doctrine by the *Lyng* decision may be found in Chambers, Reid D., "Discharge of Federal Trust Responsibility to Enforce Claims of Indian Tribes: Case Studies of Bureaucratic Conflict of Interest," *American Indian Law Newsletter,* Vol. 4, No. 15, 1980, pp. 1-20.
72. *Lyng,* op. cit., at 1336.
73. Ibid., at 1335. For further discussion, see Morris, Glenn T., "The 'G-O Road Decision': A Frontal Assault on American Indian Religious Freedom," in Ward Churchill, ed., *Critical Issues in Native North America,* International Work Group on Indigenous Affairs (IWGIA), Copenhagen, 1989, pp. 77-8.
74. Cohen, Felix S., "The Erosion of Indian Rights, 1950-53: A Case Study in Bureaucracy," *Yale Law Journal,* No. 62, 1953, p. 390.
75. *Lyng,* op. cit.
76. An interesting discussion of certain of the issues raised may be found in Clayton, Richard P., "The Sagebrush Rebellion: Who Should Control Public Lands?" *Utah Law Review,* 1980, pp. 505-33.
77. In any event, resumption of *de facto* treaty-making was one of the recommendations advanced by Senator Daniel Inouye's Special Committee on Investigations in its 1989 final report. See U.S. Senate, Select Committee on Indian Affairs, *Final Report and Legislative Recommendations: A Report of the Special Committee on Investigations,* 101st Cong., 2d Sess., U.S. Government Printing Office, Washington, D.C., November 20, 1989, p. 17.
78. For background, see Public Land Review Commission, *One Third of the Nation's Land,* Public Land Review Commission, Washington, D.C., 1970.

Chapter X

A Warrior Caged
The Continuing Struggle of
Leonard Peltier

Jim Vander Wall

> how many have come before?
> and I wonder how many more
> must be lost to the Indian wars...
>
> Jim Page
> *Leonard Peltier*

Leonard Peltier is a prisoner of war, one of the many victims of a covert war waged by the U.S. government against the American Indian Movement (AIM) and its supporters. This operation, conducted by America's secret political police—the Federal Bureau of Investigation (FBI)—during the mid-1970s, left scores of activists dead, hundreds injured, and many of the survivors imprisoned. Peltier, an AIM activist, is now serving two consecutive life sentences in Leavenworth federal prison for the alleged murder of two FBI agents. The two were killed in a June 26, 1975 firefight on the Pine Ridge Sioux Reservation in the state of South Dakota. Both the charges on which he is incarcerated and the evidence on which his conviction was obtained are complete fabrications of the FBI.

Peltier, an Anishinabé-Lakota, was born in 1944 in North Dakota and grew up on the Turtle Mountain Reservation there. In 1958, during a period when the United States was attempting to "terminate" reservations and relocate Indians to urban ghettos, he joined his relatives in the Pacific Northwest, living in Seattle and Portland. Peltier first became involved with AIM-style politics when he participated in the 1970 occupation of Fort Lawton, an abandoned military base that was legally Indian land. It was at Fort Lawton that Peltier first became acquainted with AIM organizers.[1]

After the occupation ended, Peltier became increasingly involved in AIM activities. In 1972, he was Milwaukee organizer for the Trail of Broken Treaties, a caravan from reservations across the country to the U.S. government's Bureau of

Indian Affairs (BIA) building in Washington, D.C., intended to focus public attention on the oppression of Indian people. When the caravan reached Washington on November 3, Peltier was one of those chosen to direct security. While Trail leaders were attempting to negotiate with BIA officials on a twenty-point program of reforms, supporters waiting in the lobby of the BIA building were attacked by club-wielding police. The police were overpowered and thrown out. What started as an attempt to evict the Indians turned into an occupation as the doors were barricaded to prevent the police from re-entering, and remaining BIA employees left via the windows. Indians held the building until November 9, when the government agreed to an amnesty for the occupiers and to respond to the twenty points. The occupiers returned to their homes, taking with them, in some cases, BIA records documenting its program of systematic expropriation of Indian lands and resources.[2]

It was apparently following the Trail of Broken Treaties that Leonard Peltier was targeted for "neutralization" by the FBI. On November 22, 1972, he was attacked in a Milwaukee diner by two off-duty policemen, beaten severely, and then charged with attempted murder of one of the cops. Peltier spent five months in jail before he could make bail, and went underground soon after he was released. He was eventually tried and acquitted on the charges. During the trial one of the policemen's former girlfriends testified that around the time of the incident he had shown her a picture of Peltier and boasted of "catching a big one for the FBI."[3]

A Reign of Terror on Pine Ridge

In 1972, as the Trail of Broken Treaties marched on Washington, Richard "Dick" Wilson was elected as Pine Ridge's tribal president, becoming head of a colonial regime created by the United States to administer the reservation for the benefit of non-Indian ranchers and corporations. Pine Ridge was the scene of a growing activism on the part of its more traditional Oglala Lakota residents (i.e., those who attempt to follow the spiritual and cultural ways of their ancestors) to regain control of the land—much of it thought to be resource-rich by federal authorities—guaranteed them by the 1868 Fort Laramie Treaty. It was Dick Wilson's primary objective to suppress this movement. To this end he created a private army, called the GOONs (Guardians Of the Oglala Nation), equipped and funded by the U.S. government. As the GOONs began a campaign of terrorism directed against traditionals and activists returning home from the Trail of Broken Treaties, the FBI—responsible for the investigation of serious crimes on Indian reservations—consistently ignored complaints of civil rights violations, harassment of activists, and assaults. The FBI's inaction, in light of the increasingly serious nature of the charges, gave rise to suspicions that the GOONs were acting in collusion with, if not at the direction of, federal authorities. Complaints filed with the BIA police bore even less fruit. This was hardly surprising, since there was considerable overlap in personnel between the GOONs and the BIA police who, in any case, acted under Wilson's direction.[4]

In February 1973, traditional Oglalas asked the AIM for assistance in dealing with GOON violence. On the February 28, following a meeting near Pine Ridge village, a caravan of several hundred traditionals, AIM members, and supporters drove to Wounded Knee and occupied the tiny village as a symbolic gesture of protest. They awoke the next morning to find themselves surrounded by scores of heavily armed FBI agents, U.S. marshals, GOONs, and white vigilantes. The occupiers issued a statement demanding hearings on treaties and an investigation of the BIA, and gave the government the choice of negotiating with them or removing them by force. The besiegers soon reinforced their positions with additional personnel and weaponry. Thus began the seventy-one-day siege of Wounded Knee, which focused world attention on the Pine Ridge Reservation.

U.S. military "advisors" were directly and illegally involved in the siege from its inception, and military weaponry poured onto the reservation. Tank-like vehicles called "armored personnel carriers," Bell "Huey" helicopters, .50 calibre heavy machine guns, M-79 grenade launchers, and M-16 assault rifles were brought to bear on the occupiers. The hundreds of thousands of rounds of ammunition fired into the hamlet claimed the lives of two warriors—Frank Clearwater and Buddy Lamont—and wounded dozens more. A number of supporters who were backpacking supplies into the village at night through the federal siege lines simply disappeared. It is generally believed they were murdered by GOON patrols and were buried somewhere on the reservation. The siege ended in May 1973 with an agreement by the U.S. government to negotiate on treaty issues.[5]

The Wounded Knee confrontation led to the arrest of 562 people, of whom 185 were indicted, for the most part on charges that were completely groundless and eventually dismissed. Only fifteen people were ever convicted on charges stemming from Wounded Knee, most on minor offenses such as interfering with a federal officer or on "collateral" charges such as "contempt" resulting from the trials themselves.[6] The judicial proceedings in the cases that went to trial were riddled with government misconduct. The "Wounded Knee Leadership Trial" of Russell Means and Dennis Banks is a classic example of the use of the courts to pursue political ends. Charges in this case were dismissed by Judge Fred Nichol after the government was found to have knowingly presented false evidence, infiltrated the defense team with an FBI informant, and lied to the judge about both issues. In dismissing the case, an angry Judge Nichol wrote:

> I am forced to conclude that the prosecution acted in bad faith at various times throughout the trial and was seeking convictions at the expense of justice...The fact that incidents of misconduct formed a pattern throughout the course of the trial leads me to the belief that this case was not prosecuted in good faith or in the spirit of justice. The waters of justice have been polluted, and dismissal, I believe, is the appropriate cure for the pollution.[7]

Nichol later stated that he believed "that the FBI were determined to get the AIM movement and completely destroy it." A similar pattern of misconduct would emerge in the trials of many AIM activists over the next four years, but, unfortunately, few federal judges had the integrity of Judge Nichol.[8]

While Wounded Knee cases dragged on in the courts, violence escalated on Pine Ridge. In the two years following the beginning of the occupation, more than sixty AIM members and supporters died at the hands of the GOONs, and hundreds were victims of assaults and harassment. Dick Wilson was returned to office in 1974 in an election described by the U.S. Commission on Civil Rights as being "permeated with fraud."[9] Government inaction on Wilson's abuses was taken by Wilson as license to physically destroy AIM. In the first five months of 1975, the Commission on Civil Rights recorded eighteen homicides on Pine Ridge, and the situation had become so tense that few dared to leave their homes without carrying guns. The rate of political murders on the reservation for the period 1972-1976 was 170 per 100,000, almost exactly the rate for Chile in the three years following the U.S.-supported coup of Augusto Pinochet.[10]

Throughout this entire period, the FBI failed to obtain a single conviction for the murder of an AIM activist, and complaints of assault and harassment went uninvestigated. Confronted with this singular absence of success in carrying out their legally mandated mission, the FBI asserted that "lack of manpower" prevented them from investigating complaints. Yet a brief look at FBI force levels during the same period shows that, between mid-1972 and mid-1973, the personnel assigned to the Rapid City resident agency—whose attention at that time focused almost exclusively on Pine Ridge—increased from three to eleven. In 1973 a ten-member Special Weapons and Tactics (SWAT) team was assigned to the village of Pine Ridge, giving the reservation the highest ratio of agents to citizens of any area in the U.S.[11] Clearly, it was not a lack of "manpower" which impaired investigation of crimes against AIM members and supporters, but a conscious policy of selective prosecution. While the FBI compiled massive files on AIM members and jailed them for even minor offenses, the most serious crimes committed by the GOONs—murder, rape, and felony assault—were not so much as investigated. In effect, open season was declared on AIM and its supporters.

During 1973 and 1974, Peltier and the Northwest AIM group to which he belonged had become increasingly involved in providing security support for local people while operating from an encampment on the land of the Jumping Bull family, near the Pine Ridge village of Oglala. They came at the request of local organizers and traditional elders to protect the community from GOON attacks which had been particularly intense in the Oglala area, regarded as a bastion of traditionalism. During the late spring of 1974, GOON activity decreased around Oglala due to the AIM presence. The camp became a center of spiritual activities, attracting local youth who were preparing for the Sun Dance.[12] During the same period, however, there were increasingly numerous indications of FBI interest in the AIM camp. During the first week of June 1975, an FBI memo noted "there are pockets of Indian population which consist almost exclusively of American Indian Movement...members and their supporters on the Reservation."[13] The memo went on to state, falsely, that fortified enclaves had been built that would require armored vehicles to successfully assault. No such fortifications actually existed, but such disinformation had the effect of "psyching-up" agents for an armed confrontation with AIM.

The Oglala Firefight

On June 25, 1975, FBI Special Agents (SAs) Ronald Williams and Jack Coler entered the Jumping Bull Compound, ostensibly searching for a young Oglala named Jimmy Eagle, on the charges of "kidnapping, aggravated assault and aggravated robbery." The accusations stemmed from a brawl involving Eagle and some other teenagers who had been drinking together. During the altercation, Eagle and his friends had taken a pair of cowboy boots from one of the other boys, who later filed a complaint. The only warrant issued for Eagle, dated two weeks later, was for robbery. So, with dozens of murders of AIM members and supporters uninvestigated due to "lack of manpower," two FBI agents were assigned to look for a teenager, suspected, at most, of the theft of a pair of used cowboy boots. Later the same day, three youths from the AIM camp were detained and questioned by the FBI on suspicion of being Jimmy Eagle. Interestingly, they were questioned not about Eagle, but about who was at the camp.[14]

By the next morning, June 26, it was clear something ominous was in the offing. Oglala residents noted that large numbers of paramilitary troops—GOONs, BIA police, state troopers, U.S. marshals, and FBI SWAT teams—were massing in the area. Around 11:30 a.m., two AIM members drove into the Jumping Bull Compound in a red pickup truck on their way to a meeting of the Northwest AIM group. They stopped at a residence (at the north end of the compound) to talk to Wallace "June" Little, Jr. Shortly thereafter, they observed two cars turn off Highway 18 and head toward them. The vehicles were driven by SAs Jack Coler and Ron Williams, who the FBI would later claim had come to "carry out an arrest under warrant" of Jimmy Eagle. As the cars approached, the AIM members got back into their pickup and headed south across a meadow toward the AIM camp. When Coler and Williams followed them, they got out of the truck carrying their weapons. According to one of the truck's occupants, the agents stopped and got out of their vehicles, guns drawn, and one of the agents—believed to be Coler—fired on them with a rifle. The AIM members returned fire and, as the agents took cover behind their cars, got back in their pickup and drove east to the compound. The agents continued to fire on them as they drove away.[15]

Hearing gunfire from the direction of the compound, occupants of the AIM camp believed themselves to be under attack from GOONs or vigilantes. They ran toward the sound of the firing, weapons in hand, and, observing two white men in civilian clothes shooting at the houses, joined in the return fire. Almost immediately, federal reinforcements began to enter the Jumping Bull property. Radio transmissions from Williams indicate the agents expected just such rapid support. Unfortunately for them, one of the teenagers from the camp had managed to position himself to cover the approach to the compound, and shot out the tires of the first two cars to arrive, driven by SA J. Gary Adams and Fred Two Bulls, a BIA police officer and known GOON. Pinned down by gunfire, they were unable to help Coler and Williams, who were subsequently seriously wounded.[16]

When it became clear they were surrounded by a large number of heavily armed police, Northwest AIM members Bob Robideau, Darelle "Dino" Butler, and Leonard Peltier decided to take the wounded agents hostage to use as a bargaining chip with the besieging forces. To this purpose, they circled around to the west, in the trees along White Clay Creek, and approached the agents from behind. When they were about fifty yards from the agents' cars, they observed the red pickup approach the cars and stop. They heard several shots from the vicinity of the agents, after which the red pickup drove off. When Robideau, Butler, and Peltier reached the agents, they found both of them were dead. In the cars, they found equipment marked "FBI DENVER." It was not until that point that the Northwest AIM members knew their attackers were federal agents.[17]

It was later revealed that the two AIM members in the red pickup had approached Coler and Williams, also hoping to capture them. The driver stopped the truck near the agents and his companion got out with an AR-15 rifle and walked toward them. According to this man, SA Williams raised his revolver and fired at him, missing at very close range. The AIM member responded by opening fire, killing both agents. He then got back into the pickup, and was driven off the Jumping Bull property, past Adams and Two Bulls, who were still pinned down by rifle fire.[18] FBI radio logs indicate the pickup left the area at 12:18 p.m.[19]

By early afternoon, police forces involved in the firefight had increased to nearly 200. They faced a group of eight or so adults and teenagers from the AIM camp.[20] At about 4:30 p.m. the FBI, further reinforced by SWAT teams flown in from Minneapolis and Chicago, decided they had sufficient personnel to undertake an assault. At this time, Edgar Bear Runner, a local AIM supporter, was sent into the compound to try to negotiate a surrender. When Bear Runner returned and reported that agents Coler and Williams were dead and that the defenders had disappeared, the FBI began its assault, gassing the Jumping Bull's houses and shooting everything in sight.[21]

Also killed in the firefight was AIM member Joe Stuntz Killsright, who, according to official reports, died from a bullet, fired at long range by a police sniper, that struck him in the forehead. Conflicting stories of the nature of Killsright's wounds have given rise to the suspicion that he may have been wounded during the firefight and then executed by the FBI. In contrast to the Bureau's intensive investigation into the deaths of Coler and Williams, the death of Joe Stuntz Killsright was never investigated.[22]

The Invasion of Pine Ridge

Although the deaths of agents Coler and Williams were probably an unintended consequence, provocation of the firefight achieved its intended objective: the justification of a massive paramilitary assault on AIM. By the following day, there were more than 180 FBI agents on Pine Ridge, headed by one of the FBI's foremost experts in political repression, Richard G. Held.[23] Held brought with him a number of other specialists and technicians in such matters, including his son, Richard W. Held, who had recently coordinated the Bureau's lethal counterintelligence operations against the Black Panther Party in Los Angeles; SA Thomas Greene, leader of the Chicago SWAT team and specialist in "antiterrorist" operations; and Norman Zigrossi, assigned to take operational control of the Rapid City FBI office.[24]

Along with U.S. marshals, BIA police and GOONs, FBI personnel carried out military-style sweeps for the next three months, both on Pine Ridge and on the adjacent Rosebud Reservation, which were clearly designed to terrorize AIM members and supporters. Assault teams were equipped with the full panoply of counterinsurgency weaponry—M-16 assault rifles, M-79 grenade launchers, "Huey" helicopters, armored personnel carriers, fixed-wing aircraft, and tracking dogs. With the excuse of searching for participants in the firefight, they broke into homes, conducted warrantless searches and illegal seizures, destroyed private property, harassed and threatened residents, and arrested people on illegal "John Doe" warrants. A report of the U.S. Commission of Civil Rights noted "numerous reports and complaints of threats, harassment, and search procedures conducted without due process of law." The chairman of the Civil Rights Commission, Arthur J. Flemming, characterized the operation as "an over-reaction which takes on aspects of a vendetta...a full-scale military type invasion." He went on to say:

> [The presence of such a massive force] has created a deep resentment on the part of many reservation residents who feel that such a procedure would not be tolerated in any non-Indian community in the United States. They point out that little has been done to solve numerous murders on the reservation, but when two white men are killed "troops" are brought in from all over the country at a cost of hundreds of millions of dollars.[25]

The Bureau's sweeping operations resulted in the death of at least one Oglala, an elderly man named James Brings Yellow, who was frightened into a fatal heart attack when a team of raiders headed by J. Gary Adams sneaked up to his home and abruptly kicked in his door.[26] Such tactics were also coupled to another method of intimidation, an open-ended "grand jury probe" of AIM, used as a means to jail selected organizational members and supporters—arbitrarily and for indefinite periods—who expressed the "contempt" of failing to cooperate with the Bureau's agenda. One victim of this process, Joanna LeDeaux, pregnant at the time of her incarceration, spent eight months behind bars without being charged with any crime. Her child, of course, was born in prison.[27] Another, Angie Long Visitor, was sent to lock-up for "refusing to respond to questions" while her husband was driven into hiding in order to avoid the same fate. The situation left their several small children effectively parentless for an extended period. In the end, it became plain that neither Long Visitor had known anything that might have been of value to the FBI.[28]

To assure public acquiescence in such massive violations of constitutional rights, the Bureau conducted an extensive disinformation campaign. Banner headlines across the U.S. proclaimed the FBI's story of how the helpless agents, carrying out their lawfully appointed duties, had been "ambushed" at "Wounded Knee" by AIM guerrillas from sophisticated "bunkers." Newspapers that had shown no interest whatsoever in the systematic murder of dozens of AIM members on Pine Ridge now printed detailed descriptions of how the agents were supposedly executed while pleading for their lives, their bodies riddled with machine-gun bullets. At least one publication announced the agents had been scalped. Retractions of these claims a few days later by FBI Director Clarence Kelley were run on the back pages.

The technique was so effective that even the "liberal media" denounced the victims, rather than the perpetrators, of this large-scale terrorist operation.[29]

The Arrests, Cedar Rapids Trial, and Extradition of Leonard Peltier

From an original list of some thirty known or suspected participants in the firefight, the FBI targeted four for prosecution as the slayers of SAs Coler and Williams. One of these, Jimmy Eagle, was apparently included simply to justify the presence of the agents on the Jumping Bull property. There was no demonstrable connection between Eagle and the agents' deaths, and eventually the charges against him were simply dropped. Not surprisingly, the other three indictments—on two counts of first-degree murder and "aiding and abetting"—were against what the FBI had decided was the leadership of the Northwest AIM Group: Bob Robideau, Dino Butler, and Leonard Peltier.[30] Butler was arrested in a September 5 pre-dawn air assault on "Crow Dog's Paradise," the home of Brûlé spiritual leader Leonard Crow Dog. More than 100 heavily armed FBI SWAT personnel descended on the medicine man's home in Huey helicopters, ostensibly to "investigate a fist fight" between teenagers. Bob Robideau was arrested in Wichita, Kansas on September 10 when his car caught fire and exploded on the Kansas Turnpike. Peltier, in the meantime, had fled to Canada. He was arrested on February 6, 1976 by the Royal Canadian Mounted Police at the camp of traditional Cree chief Robert Smallboy near Hinton, Alberta.[31]

Butler and Robideau were tried in Cedar Rapids, Iowa in June 1976 before Judge Edward McManus. McManus was certainly no friend of AIM, having earned the nickname "Speedie Eddie" for convicting and sentencing three AIM members on Wounded Knee charges in one week. Nevertheless, he allowed the defendants to argue that they had acted in self-defense in the shootout. Although the prosecution resorted to the use of doctored testimony, defense witnesses established that the atmosphere of terror existing on the reservation—a situation for which the FBI was responsible, at least, in part—contributed directly to the firefight.[32] Presented with a picture of wholesale violence on Pine Ridge and FBI duplicity, the jury acquitted the defendants, concluding:

> that an atmosphere of fear and violence exists on the reservation, and that the defendants arguably could have been shooting in self-defense. While it was shown that the defendants were firing guns in the direction of the agents, it was held that this was not excessive in the heat of passion.[33]

Jury foreman Robert Bolen later observed that, placed in context, much of the government's case had simply not been believable to him and his colleagues.[34] Faced with this bitter defeat, the FBI and federal prosecutors vowed to convict the remaining AIM defendant, Leonard Peltier, by any means, legal or otherwise. Charges against Eagle were dropped "so that the full prosecutive weight of the Government [could] be directed against Leonard Peltier."[35] Showing as little regard for the sovereignty of Canada as for that of indigenous nations, the United States violated the extradition treaty between the two countries by fraudulently extraditing

Peltier. At the extradition proceedings, the United States presented an affidavit signed by a woman named Myrtle Poor Bear—one of three mutually contradictory accounts of the matter signed by her—which falsely stated she had personally seen Peltier murder Coler and Williams. Based upon this deliberate deception, Canada ordered Peltier to be extradited, and he was returned to the United States on December 16, 1976.[36]

Poor Bear, it is worth noting, had a long history of treatment for a psychological disorder. Her statements concerning Peltier's "guilt" were obtained by SAs David Price and William Wood during a period when they had essentially kidnapped her and were holding her incommunicado at the Hacienda Motel, in Gordon, Nebraska. She was apparently threatened with death unless she "cooperated" with the FBI by signing a series of documents, prepared by the agents, incriminating Peltier. Tellingly, the first two Poor Bear affidavits—the existence of which were concealed from the Canadian court during extradition proceedings—contend she was *not* an eyewitness to the deaths of Coler and Williams. Instead, they state that she was Peltier's "girlfriend," and that he confessed he was "a murderer" to her in a bar.[37] This was precisely the content of the testimony—that she was the girlfriend of the accused, and that he'd confessed his guilt to her in a bar—Poor Bear was simultaneously presenting against a completely different AIM member, Richard Marshall, in an unrelated murder case. This testimony was, according to the jury, a primary factor in Marshall's subsequent conviction and life sentence.[38] Poor Bear later recanted, admitting under oath that she'd never so much as met either Peltier or Marshall, and stating that the only reason she'd entered false evidence against the two men was that she'd been terrified of what Price and Wood might do to her if she failed to say exactly what they told her to.[39]

While the Peltier extradition was in progress in Canada, the FBI was making a careful analysis of what had gone wrong during the Cedar Rapids trial, the results of which were outlined in a memorandum dated July 20, 1976. It noted that: 1) "...the defense was allowed freedom of questioning witnesses;" 2) the court allowed testimony concerning the FBI's illegal counterintelligence operations against other dissidents; 3) the government was forced to turn over agents' reports concerning the incident, and the defense was allowed to cross-examine agents on discrepancies between their testimony and written reports; 4) the defense was allowed to present evidence that the "...FBI had created a climate of fear on the reservation which precipitated the murders;" 5) the defense was uncontrolled in its dealings with the media; 6) the jury was not sequestered; 7) the jury was "confused" by "irrelevant" information presented by the defense (i.e., testimony concerning massive FBI misconduct on Pine Ridge).[40]

The Trial of Leonard Peltier

Its analysis completed, the FBI then went shopping for a judge who was likely to be more cooperative with the prosecution than Judge McManus. They found one in Judge Paul Benson, a Nixon appointee. Peltier's trial began on March 21, 1977 in Fargo, North Dakota. It can hardly be a coincidence that Benson ruled: 1) since Peltier would be tried as the principal—i.e., the person responsible for shooting the agents at close range—a self-defense argument would not be allowed; 2) as a consequence, the defense's ability to question witnesses would be restricted: evidence concerning the atmosphere of terror on Pine Ridge and the FBI's role in creating it would not be allowed; 3) therefore, no testimony concerning the FBI's other similar illegal operations would be permitted; 4) defense attorneys would not be allowed to question agents on discrepancies between their written reports and their testimony; 5) there would be a media blackout on the trial; 6) the jury would be sequestered; and 7) when the defense attempted to call Myrtle Poor Bear as a witness to describe how she had been coerced by the FBI into signing false affidavits implicating Peltier, Judge Benson would not allow it. He ruled that "to allow her testimony to go to the jury would be confusing the issues, may mislead the jury, and could be highly prejudicial [to the government]." These rulings sealed Leonard Peltier's legal fate before the trial even began. Prevented from presenting a reasonable defense, his conviction was inevitable and successful appeal rendered unlikely.[41]

In the end, the government's case rested on a weak chain of circumstantial evidence:

- The prosecutor's claim that the slain agents had reported they were following a red and white van, not a red pickup, when the firefight began. Peltier was known to drive a red and white van, a matter which appeared to "place" him in the midst of the shooting from the moment the first round was fired.[42]
- Mutually contradictory coroner's reports on the autopsies of the slain agents were presented. These indicated only that both men had been hit by bullets fired at close range from a small-caliber, high-velocity weapon of an unspecified type. No slugs were recovered, either from the dead agents' bodies or from the ground beneath them.[43]
- A spent .223 (5.56 mm) caliber cartridge casing—a small-caliber, high-velocity bullet—was allegedly recovered from the trunk of SA Coler's automobile. Its pedigree, however, was greatly suspect, since conflicting FBI documents and testimony indicated that it was found by two different agents on two different days. Further, the Bureau could not verify to whom this "most critical piece of evidence" had been given, or how it arrived at the FBI Crime Lab in Washington, D.C., regardless of who supposedly found it.[44]
- A Colt AR-15 rifle—which fires a .223 caliber round—was recovered from Bob Robideau's exploded car near Wichita, and linked by the prosecution, in an extremely questionable manner, to the firefight.[45]
- The cartridge was then linked to the Wichita AR-15 by FBI Firearms and Toolmarks expert Evan Hodge. Hodge testified that based on extractor markings, the .223 caliber cartridge casing had been loaded into and extracted from the Wichita AR-15. He said that a more definitive firing-pin test had been performed but that it was "inconclusive." Since an

AR-15 cannot eject cartridges more than about five meters, it was inferred that the cartridge had been fired near the agents' cars (i.e., near where the agents' bodies had been found).[46]

- Hodge also testified that ballistics evidence revealed only one AR-15 had been used by AIM during the firefight. Ipso facto, whoever could be shown to have carried an AR-15 rifle on the fatal day would appear as "the murderer."[47]

- All that was left was to have eyewitnesses testify that Peltier was seen carrying an AR-15 rifle on the day of the firefight. This eyewitness testimony was suspect, to say the least. For example, one of the witnesses, FBI agent Fred Coward, testified he identified Peltier (whom he had never seen before) through a 2x7-power rifle scope at a distance of more that 800 meters, and while Peltier was allegedly running away at an angle oblique to the observer (making identification in profile necessary) and carrying an AR-15. Such an identification was shown to be impossible under even ideal circumstances, never mind the conditions of severe atmospheric distortion known to have prevailed during the firefight. Other eyewitnesses later testified they had entered false testimony, having been threatened and coerced to do so by prosecutors and the FBI.[48]

The government then argued that the agents had been killed with an AR-15 fired at close range, that such a weapon linked to Peltier had been fired close to the location of the agents' bodies, and since that weapon was the only AR-15 used in the firefight, Leonard Peltier must have used it to slay SAs Coler and Williams. As prosecutor Lynn Crooks put it in his closing argument to the jury:

Apparently Special Agent Williams was killed first. He was struck in the face and hand by a bullet...probably begging for his life, and he was shot. The back of his head was blown off by a high powered rifle...Leonard Peltier then turned, as the evidence indicates, to Jack Coler lying on the ground, helpless. He shoots him in the top of the head. Apparently feeling he hasn't done a good enough job, he shoots him again through the jaw, and his face explodes. No shell comes out, just explodes. The whole bottom of his chin is blown out by the force of the concussion. He dies. Blood splattered against the side of the car.[49]

There was little the defense could do to counter this argument, since Judge Benson would not allow agents to be cross-examined concerning discrepancies between their testimony and either their prior sworn statements or written communications. Based upon this flimsy chain of circumstantial evidence and Crooks' inflammatory closing statements, the all-white jury found Peltier guilty of two counts of first-degree murder on April 18, 1977. He was sentenced by Judge Benson to serve two consecutive life terms. Despite the fact that he had no prior felony convictions, he was sent to the infamous "super-maximum security" prison at Marion, Illinois. This prison, ostensibly the final stop for the most dangerous criminals in the federal penal system, has been increasingly used to intern political prisoners under the most severe conditions.[50]

The Appeals

Somehow, I now think, in the back of my mind there was a lingering belief that, with fearless and bright lawyers, it would be possible to use the contradictions of the law to defeat them even in their own courts...In my mind, in a recess, there must have lingered a phantom of a group of dispassionate appeals judges—white United States-ers, to be sure, but nonetheless fair and distant—cooly weighing the facts of the crystal clear law.

Imari Obadele
RNA 11 Defendant

An appeal of Peltier's conviction based on documented FBI misconduct, such as the Myrtle Poor Bear affair, was rejected by the U.S. Eighth Circuit Court of Appeals. One of the members of the three-judge panel, Judge Donald Ross, commented in reference to the Poor Bear affidavits:

But can't you see...that what happened happened in such a way that it gives some credence to the claim of the...Indian people that the United States is willing to resort to *any* tactic in order to bring somebody back to the United States from Canada. And if they are willing to do that, they must be willing to fabricate other evidence as well.[51]

The court, however, while expressing "discomfort" with its own reasoning, opted to ignore evidence of FBI crimes and, citing the particular importance of the ballistics evidence, upheld Peltier's conviction. At about the same time, the Eighth Circuit Court's Chief Judge, William Webster—who had headed the Peltier appeal panel through most of its deliberations—left the bench to assume a new position as *director of the FBI*. An appeal was filed with the U.S. Supreme Court. On February 11, 1979, the high court refused without comment to hear the case.

In 1981, as a result of a Freedom of Information Act (FOIA) suit, 12,000 pages of FBI documents pertaining to Leonard Peltier were released to his appeal team. Another 6,000 pages were withheld on the grounds of "national security."[52] The documents directly contradicted, on several points, testimony given by FBI agents and other prosecution witnesses during the Peltier trial. The most serious contradiction was a Bureau teletype dated October 2, 1975, indicating that Evan Hodge had performed a firing-pin test on the Wichita AR-15 immediately after he received it and compared it to the cartridges found at the scene. Contrary to his trial testimony that the test was inconclusive, this memo conclusively stated that the rifle contained "a *different firing-pin*" from the weapon used in the firefight.[53] In other words, the memo called into question the validity of what the prosecutor deemed—and the courts agreed—was the most important piece of evidence in the case. Based upon precedents that any withholding of exculpatory evidence by the prosecution was grounds for a retrial, the appeal team filed a motion for a new trial with Judge Benson in April 1982. Since the FOIA documents also revealed what were arguably improper pretrial meetings between the prosecution, the FBI, and Judge Benson, the latter was asked to remove himself from the case. Given his previous record in the matter, few were surprised when Benson rejected both of these motions on December 30, 1982.

Upon dismissal of the motions, an appeal was again filed with the U.S. Eighth Circuit Court. In April 1984, the appeals court reversed Judge Benson's decision. Citing the apparent contradiction implied by the October 2 teletype and the critical nature of the .223 cartridge casing to the government's case, the court ordered Benson to hold a hearing on the ballistics evidence. This was conducted in Bismarck, North Dakota at the end of October 1984. A very nervous Evan Hodge explained that the conflict between his testimony and the October 2, 1975 teletype arose from a "misinterpretation." The teletype, he asserted, referred to comparison of the Wichita rifle to cartridge casings from *other* AR-15s found at the scene of the firefight, not to the .223 casing from SA Coler's trunk.[54]

When questioned as to why he had not tested that cartridge against the Wichita AR-15 immediately, Hodge claimed he was not aware of the urgent need to do so. This proved to be, as the Eighth Circuit Court was later to put it, "inconsistent with...several teletypes from FBI officials, agents requesting [Hodge] to compare submitted AR-15 rifle with .223 casing found at the scene, and [Hodge's] response to these teletypes."[55] Hodge also committed perjury by testifying that only he had handled the ballistics evidence, statements which proved to be false. When confronted with handwriting on the lab notes that was plainly not his own, he changed his testimony to admit that one lab assistant, Joseph Twardowski, had also been involved. Threatened with a handwriting analysis of the material, Hodge was forced to admit that he "misspoke" when he made even this "revised" assertion, and that the handwriting of at least one other person—the identity of whom Hodge professed not to know—appeared on the critical lab notes.[56]

Hodge's testimony created a host of problems for the government's case against Peltier. His claim that he failed to compare the Wichita AR-15 to the critical casing until late December or early January is literally incredible. Worse yet, if Hodge is to be believed, the FBI had numerous .223-caliber cartridges from the firefight scene fired by *AR-15s which have never been identified.* Either Hodge lied in his trial testimony that the .223-caliber cartridge had been matched to the Wichita AR-15 or the prosecutor lied when he asserted that only one AR-15 had been used in the firefight. Moreover, the fact that Hodge was willing to commit perjury to conceal the fact that persons other than himself and his assistant had possession of the crucial evidence cast doubt on the chain of custody of the .223-cartridge, and raised the possibility that the cartridge could have been inadvertently or deliberately switched in the lab. Faced with contradictions of this magnitude, the court deliberated for almost a year before holding oral arguments on October 15, 1985.

In a tacit admission that their circumstantial case based on the ballistics evidence was falling apart, the federal prosecutors now put forth the argument that Peltier had been convicted of aiding and abetting in the deaths of the agents, *not* of murdering them. "We can't prove who shot those agents,"[57] prosecutor Lynn Crooks admitted to the circuit court. When a confused judge asked Crooks whether he meant that Peltier had been aiding and abetting Butler and Robideau (who had been determined by a jury to have acted in self-defense), the flustered prosecutor replied:

Aiding and abetting whoever did the final shooting. Perhaps aiding and abetting himself. And hopefully the jury would believe that in effect he had done it all. But aiding and abetting, nevertheless.[58]

The appeals court, after deliberating for nearly another year, finally handed down their decision on September 22, 1986. They rejected the government's argument that Peltier had been convicted of aiding and abetting, noting that he had clearly been tried and committed to the jury as the principal. They also noted that the prosecution's assertion that a single AR-15 had been used in the firefight was untrue, citing evidence of several such weapons. Despite the contradictions exhibited by the prosecution's arguments, the court upheld Peltier's conviction. In defense of this dubious decision, the court argued:

> There are only two alternatives…to the government's contention that the .223 casing was ejected into the trunk of Coler's car when the Wichita AR-15 was fired at the agents. One alternative is that the .223 casing was planted in the trunk of Coler's car either before its discovery by the investigating agents or by the agents who reported its discovery. The other alternative is that a non-matching casing was originally found in the trunk and sent to the FBI laboratory, only to be replaced by a matching casing when the importance of a match to the Wichita AR-15 became evident…*We recognize that there is evidence in this record of improper conduct on the part of some FBI agents, but we are reluctant to impute even further improprieties to them* [emphasis added].[59]

It is clear, however, that what is at issue is not a matter of "improper conduct by some FBI agents" but of an illegal program of political repression coordinated at high levels within the Bureau. The probability of such a pattern of abuse resulting from the random actions of overenthusiastic individual agents is vanishingly small. In similar fashion, the court's other line of reasoning—that the suppressed evidence, had it been presented at trial, might "possibly" have led to Peltier's acquittal, while a distinct "probability" of this outcome was required before a retrial might be ordered—is thin to the point of nonexistence. Indeed, the Ninth Circuit Court of Appeals had already established the precedent of ordering a conviction overturned because new evidence might *possibly* have altered the original verdict, and it did so on the basis of exactly the same 1985 Supreme Court opinion that the Eighth Circuit claimed supported its denial of Peltier's appeal.[60]

The decision of the appeals court is the logical outcome of judicial collusion with the FBI's plan—enunciated in its July 20, 1976 report—to prevent Peltier from establishing the political environment of the firefight. Looked at in the narrow context prescribed by Judge Benson's rulings, it is possible to conclude that the new evidence would not have changed the jury's verdict. Viewed in the context of FBI counterinsurgency operations on Pine Ridge, however, it is not only probable, but—as the Cedar Rapids trial demonstrated—certain that the outcome of the trial would have been different. The Eighth Circuit Court rejected motions by the defense team for an *en banc* rehearing of the case. On October 5, 1987, the U.S. Supreme Court again refused without comment to hear the case.[61]

On December 3, 1990, Peltier began a new round of legal battles with the filing of a writ of *habeas corpus* in the U.S. Court for the Eastern District of Kansas.[62] The writ asserts that Peltier's constitutional rights to be informed of the charges on which he was tried and to defend himself against these charges were violated by the government. While the prosecution maintained at trial that Peltier was the "principal" in the killing of Coler and Williams—i.e., that he had actually fired the fatal shots at close range— it has since admitted that the government cannot prove this. The prosecution's "revised" claim is that Peltier was not tried as the principal but as an "aider and abettor," a charge he was never given the opportunity to defend himself against.

The prosecution claims this is an irrelevant distinction since the burden of proof is less stringent for aiding and abetting and the penalties are similar. However, the nature of the allowable arguments and evidence presented by the defense are different for aiding and abetting than for murder *per se*. It was the fact that Peltier was tried as the principal which left unchallenged Judge Benson's disallowal of the self-defense argument and the exclusion of evidence that FBI misconduct contributed to the firefight—evidence which led to the acquittal of his codefendants at Cedar Rapids. The *habeas* writ further claims that Peltier's constitutional right to a fair and impartial trial was violated by the atmosphere of intimidation created by the government's unwarranted "security arrangements" which pervaded the trial proceedings and other "enormous and continuing" federal misconduct.

The writ was remanded to the U.S. Court for the District of North Dakota (and Judge Benson) for consideration. As Benson was to be called as a witness on the issue of intimidation, the writ was reviewed by Federal Magistrate Karen Klein. She excluded the issues of intimidation and government misconduct by retroactively applying a recent egregious Supreme Court decision, *McClesky v. Zant,* which prevents a petitioner from raising an issue in a *habeas* writ which could theoretically have been raised in an earlier writ. A hearing on the remaining charge was conducted on October 2, 1991, and a determination is pending as we go to press.

On April 18, 1991, in an extraordinary action for someone in his position, Gerald Heaney—senior judge of the Eighth Circuit panel which heard Peltier's appeal—wrote a letter to Senator Daniel Inouye supporting his efforts to obtain executive clemency for Leonard Peltier. While continuing to defend the court's decision to reject Peltier's 1986 appeal, Heaney cites a number of "mitigating circumstances" which must be considered when reviewing the case. These include: 1) "[T]he United States government over-reacted at Wounded Knee. Instead of carefully considering legitimate grievances of the Native Americans, the response was essentially a military one which culminated in a deadly firefight on June 26, 1975 between the Native Americans and FBI agents." 2) "The United States government must share in the responsibility for the June 26 firefight," because of their role in "escalating the conflict." 3) "[M]ore than one person was involved in shooting the FBI agents." 4) "[T]he FBI used improper tactics in securing Peltier's extradition from Canada and in otherwise investigating and trying the Peltier case."[63] Judge Heaney had previously expressed his "discomfort" with the court's decision because, "It appeared...that the FBI was equally to blame for the shootout and that the entire responsibility can't be placed on Peltier."[64]

Conclusion

Today, the case of Leonard Peltier serves as a symbol—in both a positive and negative sense—to indigenous people everywhere who are struggling against illegal expropriation of their lands and destruction of their cultures. Peltier's uncompromising resistance fueled the growth of an international movement that had focused attention not only on his case, but on broader issues of indigenous land rights and political imprisonment in the United States. Literally millions of individuals worldwide have written letters and signed petitions demanding a new trial for Leonard Peltier. They have been joined by fifty members of the U.S. House of Representatives, fifty-one members of the Canadian Parliament (including the solicitor general at the time of Peltier's extradition), the Archbishop of Canterbury, Nobel Peace Prize winner Bishop Desmond Tutu, and many other political and religious leaders. In 1986, Peltier was awarded the International Human Rights Prize by the Human Rights Commission of Spain.[65]

In the negative sense, the U.S. government has made Leonard Peltier an example of how far it is willing to go to destroy a movement which is committed to defending the rights of indigenous peoples. The case provides a clear message that the alleged protections of civil and human rights under U.S. law are fictional where matters of "state security" are concerned. The systematic program of political repression of dissidents demonstrated in the Peltier case belies the U.S. government's publicly articulated advocacy of human rights. Until Leonard Peltier is freed, it is a fundamental disservice to political prisoners in other countries for the U.S. to advocate their cause. Their struggles are cheapened and potentially discredited by their cynical use as instruments of Cold-War propaganda.

Peltier continues his work as an activist from his prison cell. He has used the publicity surrounding his case to focus attention on wider issues such as the denial of religious rights to indigenous prisoners, denial of critical medical treatment to prisoners, and other violations of international human rights conventions. Meanwhile, his supporters are calling for a congressional investigation into the FBI criminal activity that led to his imprisonment. In light of recent revelations concerning similar FBI attacks on the Committee in Solidarity with the People of El Salvador (CISPES) and other such groups working in the U.S. for human rights, public sentiment may be favorable to such a proposal. Leonard Peltier may yet be proven innocent and returned to freedom. Until that time, his name remains a rallying cry for the struggle of all indigenous people and a condemnation of the U.S. government's blatant disregard for human rights within its own borders.

Notes

1. For the best account of Peltier's early history and involvement in AIM, see Matthiessen, Peter, *In the Spirit of Crazy Horse*, Viking Press, New York, 1983, pp. 33-58.
2. The Trail of Broken Treaties is the subject of two books: see Deloria, Vine Jr., *Behind the Trail of Broken Treaties: An Indian Declaration of Independence*, Delta Books, New York, 1974; and Editors, *BIA, I'm Not Your Indian Anymore, Akwesasne Notes*, Mohawk Nation via Rooseveltown, NY, 1974. For a description of Poltier's participation in the Trail, see Matthiessen, op. cit., pp. 51-6.
3. See Matthiessen, op. cit., pp. 56-8, for a description of the police attack on Peltier and the ultimate disposition of charges. As was later pointed out by Peltier's attorneys, Milwaukee "was the only trial Mr. Peltier has ever had where the government did not suppress material evidence and where he was able to present a full defense." See "Submission of Detailed Facts in Pre-Sentence Investigation Report," *U.S. v. Leonard Peltier*, CR 77-3003-1, U.S. Court for the District of North Dakota, November 1990, p. 12.
4. See Churchill, Ward, and Jim Vander Wall, *Agents of Repression: The FBI's Secret Wars Against the Black Panther Party and American Indian Movement*, South End Press, Boston, 1988, pp. 182-97, for an account of the creation of the GOONs and their connection to domestic counterintelligence operations. Concerning resources within the Lakota treaty area: the Black Hills alone contain what is estimated as being perhaps the most mineral-rich 100 square miles in the world.
5. The Wounded Knee siege and the events leading up to it are described in *Agents of Repression*, op. cit., pp. 59-83. Also see Editors, *Voices from Wounded Knee, 1973*, Akwesasne Notes, Mohawk Nation via Rooseveltown, NY, 1974.
6. Should there be any doubt about the purpose of such massive judicial harassment, Colonel Volney Warner (commander of the illegal 82nd Airborne Division presence at Wounded Knee) explained, "AIM's most militant leaders are under indictment, in jail or warrants are out for their arrest. But the government can win, even if no one goes to jail."
7. Quoted in *New York Times*, September 17, 1974. For more on the Wounded Knee Trials, see Matthiessen, op. cit., pp. 84-103; Churchill and Vander Wall, op. cit., pp. 287-94; and Weyler, Rex, *Blood of the Land: The Government and Corporate War Against the American Indian Movement*, Vintage Books, New York, 1984, pp. 111-21.
8. On the continuing pattern of judicial harassment of AIM activists and prosecutorial misconduct, see Churchill and Vander Wall, op. cit., pp. 329-42.
9. U.S. Commission on Civil Rights, *Report of Investigation: Oglala Sioux Tribe, General Election, 1974*, U.S. Commission on Civil Rights, Washington, D.C., October 1974.
10. See Johansen, Bruce, and Roberto Maestas, *Wasi'chu: The Continuing Indian Wars*, Monthly Review Press, New York, 1979, pp. 83-4.
11. U.S. Department of Justice, *Report of the Task Force on Indian Matters*, U.S. Government Printing Office, Washington, D.C., 1975, pp 42-3.
12. Matthiessen, op. cit., pp. 146-51. This interpretation is reinforced by discussions and interviews conducted by Jim Vander Wall and Ward Churchill with several camp residents, including Dino Butler, Bob Robideau, and Nilak Butler.
13. Memorandum, SAC Minneapolis (Joseph Trimbach) to Director, FBI, dated June 3, 1975 and titled, "Law Enforcement on the Pine Ridge Indian Reservation." The documentary film *Anna Mae: A Brave Hearted Woman*, Brown Bird Productions, Los Angeles, 1979, produced and directed by Lan Brookes Ritz, features this document and accompanies it with the maps issued to Bureau personnel on Pine Ridge, falsely reporting the locations of "AIM bunkers" and other alleged fortifications.
14. Churchill and Vander Wall, op. cit., pp. 236-8.
15. This account of the actions of the occupants of the red pickup regarding the initiation of the firefight and the eventual deaths of SAs Williams and Coler derives from an interview of the individual who actually fired the fatal shots (hereinafter referred to as "Interview"). The interview was conducted in Seattle by Peter Matthiessen and Bob Robideau in December 1989. Every precaution was taken to protect the identity of the person being interviewed. He wore a hood, gloves, and dark glasses, so that no part of his body was visible. His voice was electronically altered. The interview was undertaken, and the results made public, at the request of the interviewee. As to why he came forward, he stated, "My friend Leonard Peltier is in prison for the rest of his life for something he didn't do." He had heretofore hoped the appeals process would free Peltier. That having failed, he felt he had no alternative but to take the risk of going on record. However, he has no intention of

turning himself in. He points out that if Leonard Peltier has found no justice in U.S. courts, there is no reason to assume his own experience might be different. He also stated that, in thirteen years of imprisonment, Peltier has never pressured him to come forward and confess. Peltier's position has always been that it is irrelevant who fired the fatal shots; the AIM members were acting in self-defense, and no one should be imprisoned on this basis. It is rather the FBI which bears full responsibility for the deaths of Coler and Williams.

16. Churchill and Vander Wall, op. cit., pp. 238-43.
17. This account derives from a conversation between the author and Bob Robideau on September 28, 1990. A close variation also appears in Matthiessen, op. cit., pp. 560-1. As to the impact of discovering the identities of the attackers, Robideau commented, "We considered ourselves dead, from that moment on."
18. Interview, op. cit.
19. See Messerschmidt, Jim, *The Trial of Leonard Peltier,* South End Press, Boston, 1983, p. 101.
20. The AIM personnel were Leonard Peltier, Dino Butler, Bob Robideau, Joe Stuntz Killsright, Wilfred "Wish" Draper, Norman Brown, Mike "Baby AIM" Anderson, and Norman Charles. According to Robideau, at no time did the defending force exceed ten people: the aforementioned eight, plus the two people in the red pickup truck. The FBI would later claim that "at least 30" AIM members and supporters took part in the firefight.
21. Matthiessen, op. cit., pp. 190-1.
22. Churchill and Vander Wall, op. cit., pp. 244-5.
23. For a profile on Richard G. Held and his son, Richard W., see Churchill, Ward, "COINTELPRO as a Family Business: The Case of the Two Richard Helds," *Z Magazine,* March 1988.
24. Zigrossi publicly defined his role as being the heading up of a "colonial police force" overseeing a "conquered people." See Weir, David, and Lowell Bergman, "The Killing of Anna Mae Aquash," *Rolling Stone,* April 7, 1977, p. 55.
25. Letter from the Chairman of the U.S. Commission on Civil Rights, Arthur J. Flemming, to U.S. Attorney General Edward S. Levi dated July 22, 1975.
26. On James Brings Yellow, see Matthiessen, op. cit., p. 211.
27. Concerning LeDeaux, see ibid., p. 217.
28. On the Long Visitors, see Churchill and Vander Wall, op. cit., pp. 255-60.
29. The Bureau had imported a "public relations" (read: propaganda) specialist named Tom Coll to Pine Ridge, apparently for the express purpose of handling the dissemination of such disinformation during the days immediately following the firefight, when public impressions were of utmost importance. See Weisman, Joel D., "About that 'Ambush' at Wounded Knee," *Columbia Journalism Review,* September/October 1975, pp. 28-31.
30. The "aiding and abetting" charge is routinely added to federal indictments. Should the prosecutor have a weak case, the defendant can always be tried on such an "offense of general applicability," which carries the same penalty as the principle charge but carries a much lesser burden of proof.
31. See Matthiessen, op. cit., pp. 223-83 for the best account of the events leading up to the capture of the various fugitives.
32. A classic example of the government's use of bogus witnesses at Cedar Rapids is that of James Harper, who admitted under cross-examination that he habitually lied under oath in order to obtain favors from or gain advantage against the police. When he testified, he was awaiting sentencing on a burglary conviction. Clear indication that a false testimony deal had been struck lies in the fact that Harper later sued the government for "breach of contract" in having sent him to prison despite his having testified "as requested" against Butler and Robideau. See Churchill and Vander Wall, op. cit., pp. 301-2.
33. Quoted in Matthiessen, op. cit., p. 318.
34. Quoted in Churchill and Vander Wall, op. cit., p. 302.
35. FBI teletype from Gallegher to B.H. Cooke, dated August 20, 1976, titled "RESMURS—Contemplated Dismissal of Prosecution Against James Theodore Eagle; Continuing Prosecution of Leonard Peltier." The document is reproduced in Churchill, Ward, and Jim Vander Wall, *The COINTELPRO Papers: Documents from the FBI's Secret Wars Against Dissent in the United States,* South End Press, Boston, 1990, p. 287.
36. During an interview on the CBS news program *West 57th Street* aired September 14, 1989, federal prosecutor Lynn Crooks explained the use of the false Poor Bear affidavit to extradite Peltier:
> *Crooks:* I don't know why they shipped up [to Canada] what they did because I wasn't involved in it, but I can assure that if I would have been, I would have

shipped up her affidavits.

CBS: Even though you believed her not to be a credible witness?

Crooks: Yeah! During a probable cause stage, it wouldn't have bothered me at all. I'd have said, "Judge, here's what we've got..."

CBS: No matter how you cut it, you can't get away from the fact that it was her testimony that got Leonard Peltier extradited from Canada to stand trial...

Crooks: I guess I don't ultimately know, and ultimately I don't really care. Doesn't bother my conscience. If everything they say on that is right, it doesn't bother my conscience one bit.

37. The three Poor Bear affidavits are reproduced in *The COINTELPRO Papers,* op. cit., pp. 288-91. According to Poor Bear's subsequent testimony, one of the techniques of intimidation used by SAs Price and Wood was to show her morgue photos of the body of AIM member Anna Mae Aquash, reported to have been earlier threatened with death by Price, and found murdered on Pine Ridge on February 24, 1976. SA Wood seems to have explained to Poor Bear that he and Price could get away with such killings "because they were agents." Peltier trial transcript at 3790, quoted in *Agents of Repression,* op. cit., pp. 314-5. For additional information on the bizarre case of Aquash, see Brand, Johanna, *The Life and Death of Anna Mae Aquash,* James Lorimer Publishers, Toronto, Canada, 1978.

38. On the Marshall case, see *Agents of Repression,* op. cit., pp. 335-42.

39. Poor Bear's complete recantation was made before the Minnesota Review Commission to Investigate the FBI in Minneapolis during February 1977. The testimony was videotaped, but not transcribed. Videotape copies were reposited with the law office of Kenneth Tilsen in Minneapolis.

40. Teletype to Director, FBI, from ASAC, Rapid City, dated July 20, 1976, reproduced in *The COINTELPRO Papers,* op. cit., pp. 283-6.

41. See Messerschmidt, op. cit., pp. 40-1, for a point-by-point comparison between the FBI's analysis of the Cedar Rapids trial and Benson's evidentiary rulings in the Peltier case.

42. The prosecution went to great lengths to ensure that their carefully coached and coerced witnesses stuck to their story on this point. For instance, at one point in the testimony of Mike Anderson, the following exchange occurred:

Prosecutor *Evan Hultman:* And what, if anything happened?

Anderson: Well, I guess they [Coler and Williams] seen the orange pickup going down that way and they followed.

Hultman: Now, when you say "orange pickup," is that the red and white van to which...

Defense counsel objected, but Anderson quickly corrected his statements to reflect the story that the slain agents were following Peltier's van rather than a pickup. Further, agents such as J. Gary Adams, who had testified at Cedar Rapids that they'd heard radio transmissions suggesting that Coler and Williams had followed a red pickup onto the Jumping Bull property, changed their testimony against Peltier, swearing they'd heard their dead colleagues state they were following a red and white van. Judge Benson ruled any reference to these witnesses' Cedar Rapids testimony by the defense "inadmissable."

43. See *U.S. v. Leonard Peltier,* CR C77-3003, "Motion to Vacate Judgment and for a New Trial," pp. 40-5, for a summary of the pathologists' testimony and the inconsistencies therein.

44. Besides the Poor Bear affidavit, the government submitted, as part of the documentation supporting Peltier's extradition from Canada, an affidavit signed by SA Courtland Cunningham stating that he had personally found the cartridge casing in the trunk of Coler's car. At trial, Cunningham admitted under cross-examination that he himself hadn't "actually" found the casing. Instead, on the stand Cunningham contended that a fingerprint expert named Winthrop Lodge had found it on a completely different date from that previously sworn to in the affidavit, and that Lodge had then turned it over to him. Cunningham professed to be "unable to recall" to whom he'd given the cartridge casing. Nor could he (or anyone else) say where the cartridge casing went or who had handled it from that point until it turned up in the FBI ballistics lab halfway across the country. Consequently, no one could really attest to the fact that the item tested by Hodge was really even the same item supposedly found by Lodge or Cunningham, on one or another day, depending on which version you wish to accept, in Coler's trunk. In a normal trial, such hopelessly tainted "evidence" would simply have been disallowed. The trial of Leonard Peltier was, however, decidedly other than normal.

45. A witness testified at trial that he observed an AR-15 being placed in Robideau's car at Crow Dog's

Paradise which he "believed" had been used in the firefight. Peltier was not present at the time.

46. See "Motion to Vacate Judgment and for a New Trial," op. cit., pp. 6-12, for a summary of Hodge's testimony. Also see Messerschmidt, op. cit., pp. 89-93.

47. Ibid.

48. See Messerschmidt, op. cit., pp. 50-4, 66.

49. Peltier trial transcript at 5011, quoted in *Agents of Repression*, op. cit., p. 322.

50. See Dunne, Bill, "The U.S. Penitentiary at Marion, Illinois: An Instrument of Oppression," *New Studies on the Left*, Vol. 5, Nos. 1-2, 1989, pp. 20-8.

51. Transcript of the proceedings (oral arguments) in "Motion to Vacate Judgement and for a New Trial," at 7326-7.

52. It has never been explained how this classification, which applies to U.S. interests vis-à-vis foreign powers, is in any way applicable to what the government insists is a "purely domestic matter."

53. FBI teletype, Director to SAC, Rapid City (Norman Zigrossi), dated October 2, 1975 and captioned "RESMURS—PHYSICAL EVIDENCE—[deleted]." The teletype and associated lab notes concerning the firing-pin test at issue are reproduced in *The COINTELPRO Papers*, op. cit., pp. 296-7. When this withholding of plainly crucial exculpatory evidence became public knowledge, the government surfaced a ruse suggesting the defense had been in possession of the key document all along. As prosecutor Lynn Crooks asserted in his above-mentioned *West 57th Street* interview:

    Crooks: As we sat at trial, we're saying to ourselves, "When are they going to hit us with that October 31 [*sic*] teletype? We're waiting to get impeached. They don't do it! They never mentioned the stupid thing! They didn't use their best evidence!

    CBS: Well, they claim they never had it.

    Crooks: Aurgh! They're lying!

    Crooks' attempt was to confuse the October 2 teletype with another, dated October 31, which the defense did indeed have at trial. However, far from impeaching the government's position, the October 31 document simply states the key cartridge casing could not be matched to the Wichita AR-15, a finding consistent with trial testimony that firing-pin tests had been "inconclusive." The defense thus had no reason to make an issue of its contents. The conclusively negative results indicated in the October 2 document—which was in fact withheld from the defense—are a far different consideration. Crooks' unintended acknowledgment that the withheld information would have represented the "best evidence" of the the defense goes directly to the issue.

54. "Motion to Vacate Judgment and for a New Trial," op. cit.

55. U.S. Court of Appeals for the Eighth District, "Appeal from the U.S. District Court for the District of North Dakota," *U.S. v. Leonard Peltier* (written by Judge Gerald Heaney), September 11, 1986, p. 9.

56. As it turned out, the mysterious third party handwriting belonged to William Albrecht, an FBI laboratory trainee.

57. "Transcript of Oral Arguments" before the U.S. Court of appeals for the Eighth Circuit, in *U.S. v. Peltier*, October 22, 1985, p. 18.

58. Ibid.

59. "Appeal from the U.S. District Court for the District of North Dakota," op. cit., p. 16.

60. *U.S. v. Bagley*, U.S. 105 S. Ct. 3375 (1985).

61. The high court declined to review the case despite the fact that it had a compelling need to do so: the "probability" standard adopted by the Eighth Circuit was and is in direct conflict with the "possibility" standard already employed by the Ninth Circuit. Absent clarification of Supreme Court intent in *Bagley*, both standards remain in effect, an obvious contravention of the "equal justice" provision of the U.S. Constitution. The high court's refusal to hear Peltier's second appeal was therefore a glaring default on more than one level.

62. *Leonard Peltier v. G.L. Henman, Warden, U.S. Penitentiary, Leavenworth Kansas*, "Verified Petition for Writ of *Habeas Corpus* and Other Appropriate Relief," U.S. District Court for the Eastern District of Kansas, filed December 3, 1990.

63. Letter from Gerald W. Heaney, U.S. Senior Circuit Judge, to Senator Daniel K. Inouye, dated April 18, 1991.

64. Interview on the CBS news program *West 57th Street*, aired September 14, 1989.

65. On Canada, see *House of Commons Debate*, Vol. 128, No. 129, 1st Sess., 33rd Parliament, Official Report, April 17, 1986. Concerning the human rights award, see "Peltier back in Penitentiary, wins prize in Spain," *Rapid City Journal*, December 12, 1986.

Chapter XI

American Indian Women
At the Center of Indigenous Resistance
in Contemporary North America

M. Annette Jaimes with Theresa Halsey

A people is not defeated until the hearts of its women are on the ground.

Traditional Cheyenne Saying

The United States has not shown me the terms of my surrender.

Marie Lego
Pit River Nation, 1970

The two brief quotations forming the epigraph of this chapter were selected to represent a constant pattern of reality within Native North American life from the earliest times. This is that women have always formed the backbone of indigenous nations on this continent. Contrary to those images of meekness, docility, and subordination to males with which we women typically have been portrayed by the dominant culture's books and movies, anthropology, and political ideologues of both rightist and leftist persuasions, it is women who have formed the very core of indigenous resistance to genocide and colonization since the first moment of conflict between Indians and invaders. In contemporary terms, this heritage has informed and guided generations of native women such as the elder Marie Lego, who provided crucial leadership to the Pit River Nation's land claims struggle in northern California during the 1970s.[1]

In Washington state, women such as Janet McCloud (Tulalip) and Ramona Bennett (Puyallup) had already assumed leading roles in the fishing rights struggles of the '60s, efforts which, probably more than any other phenomena, set in motion the "hard-line" Indian liberation movements of the modern day. These were not political organizing campaigns of the ballot and petition sort. Rather, they were, and continue to be, conflicts involving the disappearance of entire peoples. As Bennett has explained the nature of the fishing rights confrontations:

At this time, our people were fighting to preserve their last treaty right—the right to fish. We lost our land base. There was no game in the area...We're dependent not just economically but culturally on the right to fish. Fishing is part of our art forms and religion and diet, and the entire culture is based around it. And so when we talk about [Euroamerica's] ripping off the right to fish, we're talking about cultural genocide.[2]

The fish-ins, discussed in Chapter Seven, were initially pursued within a framework of "civil disobedience" and "principled nonviolence," which went nowhere other than to incur massive official and quasi-official violence in response. "They [the police] came right on the reservation with a force of three hundred people," Bennett recounts. "They gassed us, they clubbed people around, they laid $125,000 bail on us. At that time I was a member of the Puyallup Tribal Council, and I was spokesman for the camp [of local fishing rights activists]. And I told them what our policy was: that we were there to protect our Indian fishermen. And because I used a voice-gun, I'm being charged with inciting a riot. I'm faced with an eight year sentence."[3] It was an elder Nisqually woman who pushed the fishing rights movement in western Washington to adopt the policy of armed self-defense which ultimately proved successful (the struggle in eastern Washington took a somewhat different course to the same position and results):

Finally, one of the boys went down to the river to fish, and his mother went up on the bank. And she said: "This boy is nineteen years old and we've been fighting on this river for as many years as he's been alive. And no one is going to pound my son around, no one is going to arrest him. No one is going to touch my son or I'm going to shoot them." And she had a rifle...Then we had an armed camp in the city of Tacoma.[4]

The same sort of dynamic was involved in South Dakota during the early 1970s, when elder Oglala Lakota women such as Ellen Moves Camp and Gladys Bissonette assumed the leadership in establishing what was called the Oglala Sioux Civil Rights Organization (OSCRO) on the Pine Ridge Reservation. According to Bissonette, "Every time us women gathered to protest or demonstrate, they [federal authorities] always aimed machine guns at us women and children."[5] In response, she became a major advocate of armed self-defense at the reservation hamlet of Wounded Knee in 1973, remained within the defensive perimeter for the entire 71 days the U.S. government besieged the Indians inside, and became a primary negotiator for what was called the "Independent Oglala Nation."[6] Both women remained quite visible in the Oglala resistance to U.S. domination despite a virtual counterinsurgency war waged by the government on Pine Ridge during the three years following Wounded Knee.[7]

At Big Mountain, in the former "Navajo-Hopi Joint Use Area" in Arizona, where the federal government is even now attempting to forcibly relocate more than 10,000 traditional Diné (Navajos) in order to open the way for corporate exploitation of the rich coal reserves underlying their land, it is again elder women who have stood at the forefront of resistance, refusing to leave the homes of their ancestors. One of them, Pauline Whitesinger, was the first to physically confront government personnel attempting to fence off her land. Another, Katherine Smith, was the first to do so with a rifle.[8] Such women have constituted a literal physical barrier blocking consummation of the government's relocation/mining effort for more than a decade.[9] Many similar stories, all of them accruing from the past quarter-century, might be told in order to demonstrate the extent to which women have galvanized and centered contemporary native resistance.

The costs of such uncompromising (and uncompromised) activism have often been high. To quote Ada Deer, who, along with Lucille Chapman, became an essential spokesperson for the Menominee restoration movement in Wisconsin during the late 1960s and early '70s: "I wanted to get involved. People said I was too young, too naïve—you can't fight the system. I dropped out of law school. That was the price I had to pay to be involved."[10] Gladys Bissonette lost a son, Pedro, and a daughter, Jeanette, murdered by federal surrogates on Pine Ridge in the aftermath of Wounded Knee.[11] Other native women, such as American Indian Movement (AIM) members Tina Trudell and Anna Mae Pictou Aquash, have paid with their own and sometimes their children's lives for their prominent defiance of their colonizers.[12] Yet, it stands as a testament to the strength of American Indian women that such grim sacrifices have served, not to deter them from standing up for the rights of native people, but as an inspiration to do so. Mohawk activist and scholar Shirley Hill Witt recalls the burial of Aquash after her execution-style murder on Pine Ridge:

> Some women had driven from Pine Ridge the night before—a very dangerous act—"to do what needed to be done." Young women dug the grave. A ceremonial tipi was set up...A woman seven months pregnant gathered sage and cedar to be burned in the tipi. Young AIM members were pallbearers: they laid her on pine boughs while spiritual leaders spoke the sacred words and performed the ancient duties. People brought presents for Anna Mae to take with her to the spirit world. They also brought presents for her two sisters to carry back to Nova Scotia with them to give to her orphaned daughters...The executioners of Anna Mae did not snuff out a meddlesome woman. They exalted a Brave Hearted Woman for all time.[13]

The motivations of indigenous women in undertaking such risks are unequivocal. As Maria Sanchez, a leading member of the Northern Cheyenne resistance to corporate "development" of their reservation puts it: "I am the mother of nine children. My concern is for their future, for their children, and for future generations. As a woman, I draw strength from the traditional spiritual people...from my nation. The oil and gas companies are building a huge gas chamber for the Northern Cheyennes."[14] Pauline Whitesinger has stated, "I think there is no way we can survive if we get moved to some other land away from ours. We are just going to waste away. People tell me to move, but I've got no place to go. I am not moving anywhere, that is certain."[15] Roberta Blackgoat, another leader of the Big Mountain resistance, concurs: "If this land dies, the people die with it. We are a nation. We will fight anyone who tries to push us off our land."[16] All across North America, the message from native women is the same.[17] The explicitly nationalist content of indigenous women's activism has been addressed by Lorelei DeCora Means, a Minneconjou Lakota AIM member and one of the founders of Women of All Red Nations (WARN):

> We are *American Indian* women, in that order. We are oppressed, first and foremost, as American Indians, as peoples colonized by the United States of America, *not* as women. As Indians, we can never forget that. Our survival, the survival of every one of us—man, woman and child—*as Indians* depends on it. Decolonization is the agenda, the whole agenda, and until it is accomplished, it is the *only* agenda that counts for American Indians. It will take every one of us—every single one of us—to get the job done. We haven't got the time, energy or resources for anything else while our lands are being destroyed and our children are dying of avoidable diseases and malnutrition. So we tend to view those who come to us wanting to form alliances on the basis of "new" and "different" or "broader" and "more important" issues to be a little less than friends, especially since most of them come from the Euroamerican population which benefits most directly from our ongoing colonization.[18]

As Janet McCloud sees it:

> Most of these 'progressive' non-Indian ideas like "class struggle" would at the present time divert us into participating as "equals" in our own colonization. Or, like "women's liberation," would divide us among ourselves in such a way as to leave us colonized in the name of "gender equity." Some of us can't help but think maybe a lot of these "better ideas" offered by non-Indians claiming to be our "allies" are intended to accomplish exactly these sorts of diversion and disunity within our movement. So, let me toss out a different sort of "progression" to all you marxists and socialists and feminists out there. *You* join *us* in liberating *our* land and lives. Lose the privilege *you* acquire at *our* expense by occupying *our* land. Make *that* your first priority for as long as it takes to make it happen. *Then* we'll join you in fixing up whatever's left of the class and gender problems in your society, and our own, if need be. *But*, if you're not willing to do that, then don't presume to tell *us* how we should go about our liberation, what priorities and values we should have. Since you're standing on our land, we've got to view you as just another oppressor trying to hang on to what's ours. And that doesn't leave us a whole lot to talk about, now does it?[19]

Myths of Male Dominance

A significant factor militating against fruitful alliances—or even dialogue—between Indians and non-Indians is the vast and complex set of myths imposed and stubbornly defended by the dominant culture as a means of "understanding" Native America both historically and topically. Aspects of the mythology are discussed throughout this volume, especially Chapters One, Twelve, Fourteen, and Fifteen. As concerns indigenous women in particular, this fantastical lexicon includes what anthropologist Eleanor Burke Leacock has termed the "myths of male dominance."[20]

Adherence to its main tenets of the stereotypes involved seems to be entirely trans-ideological within the "mainstream" of American life, a matter readily witnessed by recent offerings in the mass media by Paul Valentine, a remarkably reactionary critic for the *Washington Post,* and Barbara Ehrenreich, an ostensibly socialist-feminist columnist for *Time* Magazine and several more progressive publications.

In a hostile review of the film *Dances with Wolves* published in April 1991, Valentine denounces producer-director Kevin Costner for having "romanticized" American Indians.[21] He then sets forth a series of outlandish contentions designed to show how nasty things really were in North America before Europeans came along to set things right. An example of the sheer absurdity with which his polemic is laced is a passage in which he has "the Arapaho of eastern Colorado...igniting uncontrolled grass fires on the prairies" which remained barren of grass "for many years afterward," causing mass starvation among the buffalo (as any high school botany student might have pointed out, a fall burn-off actually *stimulates* spring growth of most grasses, prairie grasses included). He then proceeds to explain the lot of native women in precontact times as being the haulers of "the clumsy two stick travois used to transport a family's belongings on the nomadic seasonal treks" (there were virtually no precontact "nomads" in North America, and dogs were used to drag travois prior to the advent of horses).[22]

Ehrenreich, for her part, had earlier adopted a similar posture in a *Time* Magazine column arguing against the rampant militarism engulfing the United States during the fall of 1990. In her first paragraph, while taking a couple of gratuitous and utterly uninformed shots at the culture of the southeast African Masai and indigenous Solomon Islanders, she implies America's jingoist policies in the Persian Gulf had "descended" to the level of such "primitive"—and male dominated—"warrior cultures" as "the Plains Indian societies," where "the passage to manhood allowing young males to marry required the blooding of the spear, the taking of a scalp or head."[23] Ehrenreich's thoroughly arrogant use of indigenous cultures as a springboard upon which to launch into the imagined superiority of her own culture and views is no more factually supportable than Valentine's, and is every bit as degrading to native people of *both* genders. Worse, she extends her "analysis" as a self-proclaimed "friend of the oppressed" rather than as an unabashed apologist for the status quo.

The truth of things was, of course, rather different. Contra Ehrenreich's thesis, the Salish/Kootenai scholar D'Arcy McNickle long ago published the results of lengthy and painstaking research which showed that 70 percent or more of all precontact societies in North America practiced no form of warfare at all (for a description of the sort of "war" practiced by the remainder, see Chapter Twelve).[24] This may have been due in part to the fact that, as Laguna researcher Paula Gunn Allen has compellingly demonstrated in her recent book, *The Sacred Hoop,* traditional native societies were never "male dominated" and there were likely no "warrior cultures" worthy of the name before the European invasion.[25] There is no record of *any* American Indian society, even after the invasion, requiring a man to kill in war before he could marry. To the contrary, military activity—including being a literal warrior—was never an exclusively male sphere of endeavor.

Although it is true that women were typically accorded a greater social value in indigenous tradition—both because of their biological ability to bear children, and for reasons which will be discussed below—and therefore tended to be noncombatant to a much greater degree than men, female fighters were never uncommon once the necessity of real warfare was imposed by Euroamericans.[26] These included military commanders like Cousaponakeesa—Mary Matthews Musgrove Bosomworth, the "Creek Mary" of Dee Brown's 1981 novel—who led her people in a successful campaign against the British at Savannah during the 1750s.[27] Lakota women traditionally maintained at least four warrior societies of their own, entities which are presently being resurrected.[28] Among the Cherokees, there was Da'nawa-gasta, or "Sharp War," an especially tough warrior and head of a women's military society.[29] The Piegans maintained what has been mistranslated as "Manly-Hearted Women," more accurately understood as being "Strong-Hearted Women," a permanent warrior society.[30] The Cheyennes in particular fielded a number of strong women fighters, such as Buffalo Calf Road (who distinguished herself at both the Battle of the Rosebud in 1876 and during the 1878 "Cheyenne Breakout"), amidst the worst period of the wars of annihilation waged against them by the United States.[31] Many other native cultures produced comparable figures, a tradition into which the women of the preceding section fit well, and which serves to debunk the tidy (if grossly misleading and divisive) male/female, warlike/peaceful dichotomies deployed by such Euroamerican feminist thinkers as Ehrenreich and Robin Morgan.[32]

More important than their direct participation in military activities was native women's role in making key decisions, not only about matters of peace and war, but in all other aspects of socioeconomic existence. Although Gunn Allen's conclusion that traditional indigenous societies added up to "gynocracies" is undoubtedly overstated and misleading, this is not to say that Native American women were not politically powerful. Creek Mary was not a general *per se*, but essentially head of state within the Creek Confederacy. Her status was that of "Beloved Woman," a position better recorded with regard to the system of governance developed among the Cherokees slightly to the north of Creek domain:

> Cherokee women had the right to decide the fate of captives, decisions that were made by vote of the Women's Council and relayed to the district at large by the War Woman or Pretty Woman. The decisions had to be made by female clan heads because a captive who was to live would be adopted into one of the families whose affairs were directed by the clan-mothers. The clan-mothers also had the right to wage war, and as Henry Timberlake wrote, the stories about Amazon women warriors were not so farfetched considering how many Indian women were famous warriors and powerful voices in the councils...The war women carried the titled Beloved Women, and their power was great...The Women's Council, as distinguished from the District, village, or Confederacy councils, was powerful in a number of political and socio-spiritual ways, and may have had the deciding voice on which males would serve on the Coun-

cils...Certainly the Women's Council was influential in tribal decisions, and its spokeswomen served as War Women and Peace Women, presumably holding offices in the towns designated as red towns and white towns, respectively. Their other powers included the right to speak in the men's Council [although men lacked a reciprocal right, under most circumstances], the right to choose whom and whether to marry, the right to bear arms, and the right to choose their extramarital occupations.[33]

While Creek and Cherokee women "may" have held the right to select which males assumed positions of political responsibility, this was unquestionably the case within the Haudenosaunee (Six Nations Iroquois Confederacy) of New York state. Among the "Sixers," each of the fifty extended families (clans) was headed by a clan mother. These women formed a council within the confederacy which selected the males who would hold positions on a second council, composed of men, representing the confederacy's interests, both in formulation of internal policies and in conduct of external relations. If at any time, particular male council members adopted positions or undertook policies perceived by the women's council as being contrary to the people's interests, their respective clan mothers retained the right to replace them. Although much diminished after two centuries of U.S. colonial domination, this "Longhouse" form of government is ongoing today.[34]

The Haudenosaunee were hardly alone among northeastern peoples in according women such a measure of power. At the time of the European arrival in North America, the Narragansett of what is now Rhode Island were headed by a "sunksquaw," or female chief. The last of these, a woman named Magnus, was executed along with ninety other members of the Narragansett government after their defeat by English Major James Talcot in 1675.[35] During the same period, the Esopus Confederacy was led, at least in part, by a woman named Mamanuchqua (also known as Mamareoktwe, Mamaroch, and Mamaprocht).[36] The Delawares *generically* referred to themselves as "women," considering the term to be supremely complementary.[37] Among other Algonquin peoples of the Atlantic Coast region—e.g., the Wampanoag and Massachusetts Confederacies, and the Niaticks, Scaticooks, Niantics, Pictaways, Powhatans, and Caconnets—much the same pattern prevailed:

> From before 1620 until her death in 1677, a squaw-sachem known as the "Massachusetts Queen" by the Virginia colonizers governed the Massachusetts Confederacy. It was her fortune to preside over the Confederacy's destruction as the people were decimated by disease, war, and colonial manipulations...Others include the Pocasett sunksquaw Weetamoo, who was King Philip's ally and "served as a war chief commanding over 300 warriors" during his war with the British...Awashonks, another [woman head of state] of the Mid-Atlantic region, was squaw-sachem of the Sakonnet, a [nation] allied with the Wampanoag Confederacy. She [held her office] in the latter part of the seventeenth century. After fighting for a time against the British during King Philip's War, she was forced to surrender. Because she then convinced her warriors to fight with the British, she was able to save them from enslavement in the West Indies.[38]

Women's power within traditional Indian societies was also grounded in other ways. While patrilineal/patrilocal cultures did exist, most precontact North American civilizations functioned on the basis of matrilineage and matrilocality. Insofar as family structures centered upon the identities of wives rather than husbands—men joined women's families, not the other way around—and because men were usually expected to relocate to join the women they married, the context of native social life was radically different from that which prevailed (and prevails) in European and Euro-derived cultures.[39]

> Many of the largest and most important Indian peoples were matrilineal...Among these were: in the East, the Iroquois, the Siouan [nations] of the Piedmont and Atlantic coastal plain, the Mohegan, the Delaware, various other [nations] of southern New England, and the divisions of the Powhatan Confederacy in Virginia; in the South, the Creek, the Choctaw, the Chickasaw, the Seminole, and the [nations] of the Caddoan linguistic family; in the Great Plains, the Pawnee, the Hidatsa, the Mandan, the Oto, the Missouri, and the Crow and other Siouan [nations]; in the Southwest, the Navajo, and the numerous so-called Pueblo [nations], including the well known Hopi, Laguna, Acoma, and Zuñi.[40]

In many indigenous societies, the position of women was further strengthened economically, by virtue of their owning all or most property. Haudenosaunee women, for example, owned the fields which produced about two-thirds of their people's diet.[41] Among the Lakota, men owned nothing but their clothing, a horse for hunting, weapons and spiritual items; homes, furnishings, and the like were the property of their wives. All a Lakota woman needed to do in order to divorce her husband was to set his meager personal possessions outside the door of their lodge, an action against which he had no appeal under traditional law.[42] Much the same system prevailed among the Anishinabé and numerous other native cultures. As Mary Oshana, an Anishinabé activist, has explained it:

> Matrilineal [nations] provided the greatest opportunities for women: women in these [nations] owned houses, furnishings, fields, gardens, agricultural tools, art objects, livestock and horses. Furthermore, these items were passed down through female lines. Regardless of their marital status, women had the right to own and control property. The woman had control of the children and if marital problems developed the man would leave the home.[43]

Additional reinforcement of native women's status accrues from the spiritual traditions of most of North America's indigenous cultures. First, contrary to the Euroamerican myth that American Indian spiritual leaders are invariably something called "medicine men," women have always held important positions in this regard. Prime examples include Coocoochee of the Mohawks, Sanapia of the Comanches, and Pretty Shield of the Crows.[44] Among the Zuñi and other Puebloan cultures, women were members of the Rain Priesthood, the most important of that society's religious entities.[45] Women are also known to have played crucial leadership roles within Anishinabé, Blackfeet, Chilula, and Diné spiritual practices, as well as those of many other native societies.[46]

More important in some ways, virtually all indigenous religions on this continent exhibit an abundant presence of feminine elements within their cosmologies.[47] When contrasted to the hegemonic masculinity of the deities embraced by such "world religions" as Judaism, Christianity, and Islam—and the corresponding male supremacism marking those societies which adhere to them—the real significance of concepts like Mother Earth (universal), Spider Woman (Hopi and Diné), White Buffalo Calf Woman (Lakota), Grandmother Turtle (Iroquois), Sky Woman (Iroquois), Hard Beings Woman and Sand Altar Woman (Hopi), First Woman (Abanaki), Thought Woman (Laguna), Corn Woman (Cherokee), and Changing Woman (Diné) becomes rather obvious.[48] So too does the real rather than the mythical status of women in traditional Native American life. Indeed, as Diné artist Mary Morez has put it, "In [our] society, the woman is the dominant figure who becomes the wise one with old age. It's a [matrilineal/matrilocal] society, you know. But the Navajo woman never demands her status. She achieves, earns, accomplishes it through maturity. That maturing process is psychological. It has to do with one's feelings for the land and being part of the whole cycle of nature. It's difficult to describe to a non-Indian."[49]

Bea Medicine, a Hunkpapa Lakota scholar, concurs, noting that "Our power is obvious. [Women] are primary socializers of our children. Culture is transmitted primarily through the mother. The mother teaches languages, attitudes, beliefs, behavior patterns, etc."[50] Anishinabé writer and activist Winona LaDuke concludes, "Traditionally, American Indian women were never subordinate to men. Or vice versa, for that matter. What native societies have always been about is achieving balance in all things, gender relations no less than any other. Nobody needs to tell us how to do it. We've had that all worked out for thousands of years. And, left to our own devices, that's exactly how we'd be living right now."[51] Or, as Priscilla K. Buffalohead, another Anishinabé scholar, has put it, "[We] stem from egalitarian cultural traditions. These traditions are concerned less with equality of the sexes and more with the dignity of the individual and their inherent right—whether they be women, men or children—to make their own choices and decisions."[52]

Disempowerment

The reduction of the status held by women within indigenous nations was a first priority for European colonizers eager to weaken and destabilize target societies. With regard to the Montagnais and Naskapi of the St. Lawrence River Valley, for example, the French, who first entered the area in the 1550s, encountered a people among whom "women have great power...A man may promise you something and if he does not keep his promise, he thinks he is sufficiently excused when he tells you that his wife did not wish him to do it."[53] They responded, beginning in 1633, by sending Jesuit missionaries to show the natives a "better and more enlightened way" of comporting themselves, a matter well-chronicled by the priest, Paul Le Jeune:

Though some observers saw women as drudges, Le Jeune saw women as holding "great power" and having "in every instance...the choice of plans, of undertakings, of journeys, of winterings." Indeed, independence of women was considered a problem by the Jesuits, who lectured the men about "allowing" their wives sexual and other freedom and sought to introduce European principles of obedience.[54]

Most likely, the Jesuit program would have gone nowhere had the sharp end of colonization not undercut the Montagnais-Naskapi traditional economy, replacing it with a system far more reliant upon fur trapping and traders by the latter part of the 17th century.[55] As their dependence upon their colonizers increased, the Indians were compelled to accept more and more of the European brand of "morality." The Jesuits imposed a form of monogamy in which divorce was forbidden, implemented a system of compulsory Catholic education, and refused to deal with anyone other than selected male "representatives" of the Montagnais and Naskapi in political or economic affairs (thus deforming the Indian structure of governance beyond recognition).[56]

Positions of formal power such as political leadership, [spiritual leadership], and matrilocality, which placed the economic dependence of a woman with children in the hands of her mother's family...shifted. [Spiritual and political] leadership were male [by 1750], and matrilocality had become patrilocality. This is not so strange given the economics of the situation and the fact that over the years the Montagnais became entirely Catholicized.[57]

Among the Haudenosaunee, who were not militarily defeated until after the American Revolution, such changes took much longer. It was not until the early 19th century that, in an attempt to adjust to the new circumstances of subordination to the United States, the Seneca prophet Handsome Lake promulgated a new code of law and social organization which replaced their old "petticoat government" with a male-centered model more acceptable to the colonizers.[58] In attempting to shift power from "the meddling old women" of Iroquois society,

Handsome Lake advocated that young women cleave to their husbands rather than to their mothers and abandon the clan-mother controlled Longhouse in favor of a patriarchal, nuclear family arrangement...While the shift was never complete, it was sufficient. Under the Code of Handsome Lake, which was the tribal version of the white man's way, the Longhouse declined in importance, and eventually Iroquois women were firmly under the thumb of Christian patriarchy.[59]

To the south, "the British worked hard to lessen the power of women in Cherokee affairs. They took Cherokee men to England and educated them in European ways. These men returned to Cherokee country and exerted great influence on behalf of the British in the region."[60] Intermarriage was also encouraged, with markedly privileged treatment accorded mixed-blood offspring of such unions with English colonialists. In time, when combined with increasing Cherokee dependence on the British trade economy, these advantages resulted in a situation where "men with little Cherokee blood [and even less loyalty] wielded considerable power over the nation's policies."[61] Aping the English, this new male leadership set out to establish a plantation economy devoted to the growing of cotton and tobacco.

> The male leadership bought and sold not only black men and women but men and women from neighboring tribes, the women of the leadership retreated to Bible classes, sewing circles, and petticoats that rivaled those of their white sisters. Many of these upper-strata Cherokee women married white ministers and other opportunists, as the men of their class married white women, often the daughters of white ministers...Cherokee society became rigid and modeled on Christian white social organization of upper, middle, and impoverished classes usually composed of very traditional clans.[62]

This situation, of course, greatly weakened the Cherokee Nation, creating sharp divisions within it which have not completely healed even to the present day. Moreover, it caused Euroamericans in surrounding areas to covet not only Cherokee land *per se,* but the lucrative farming enterprises built up by the mixed-blood male caste. This was a powerful incentive for the U.S. to undertake the compulsory removal of the Cherokees and other indigenous nations from east of the Mississippi to points west during the first half of the 19th century.[63] The reaction of assimilated Cherokees was an attempt to show their "worth" by becoming even more ostentatiously Europeanized.

> In an effort to stave off removal, the Cherokee in the early 1800s, under the leadership of men such as Elias Boudinot, Major Ridge, and John Ross (later Principal Chief of the Cherokee in Oklahoma Territory), and others, drafted a constitution that disenfranchised women and blacks. Modeled after the Constitution of the United States, whose favor they were attempting to curry, and in conjunction with Christian sympathizers to the Cherokee cause, the new Cherokee constitution relegated women to the position of chattel...[Under such conditions], the last Beloved Woman, Nancy Ward, resigned her office in 1817, sending her cane and her vote on important questions to the Cherokee Council.[64]

Despite much groveling by the "sellouts," Andrew Jackson ordered removal of the Cherokees—as well as the Creeks, Choctaws, Chickasaws, and Seminoles—to begin in 1832.[65] By 1839, the "Trail of Tears" was complete, with catastrophic population loss for the indigenous nations involved.[66] By the latter stage, traditionalist Cherokees had overcome sanctions against killing other tribal members in a desperate attempt to restore some semblance of order within their nation: Major Ridge, his eldest son, John, and Elias Boudinot were assassinated on June 22, 1839.[67] Attempts were made to eliminate other members of the "Ridge Faction" such as Stand Watie, John A. Bell, James Starr, and George W. Adair, but these failed, and the assimilationist faction continued to do substantial damage to Cherokee sovereignty.[68] Although John Rollin Ridge, the Major's grandson, was forced to flee to California in 1850 and was unable to return to Cherokee Country until after the Civil War,[69] Stand Watie (Boudinot's younger brother) managed to lead a portion of the Cherokees into a disastrous alliance with the Confederacy from which the nation never recovered.[70]

Across the continent, the story was the same in every case. In *not one* of the more than 370 ratified and perhaps 300 unratified treaties negotiated by the United States with indigenous nations was the federal government willing to allow participation by native women. In *none* of the several thousand non-treaty agreements reached between the United States and these same nations were federal representatives prepared to discuss anything at all with women. In *no* instance was the United States open to recognizing a female as representing her people's interests when it came to administering the reservations onto which American Indians were ultimately forced; always, men were required to do what was necessary to secure delivery of rations, argue for water rights, and all the rest.[71] Meanwhile, as Rebecca Robbins points out in Chapter Three, the best and most patriotic of the indigenous male leadership—men like Tecumseh, Osceola, Crazy Horse, and Sitting Bull—were systematically assassinated or sent to far-away prisons for extended periods. The male leadership of the native resistance was then replaced with men selected on the basis of their willingness to cooperate with their oppressors. Exactly how native women coped with this vast alteration of their circumstances, and those of their people more generally, is a bit mysterious:

> If a generalization may be made, it is that female roles of mother, sister, and wife were ongoing because of the continued care they were supposed to provide for the family. But what of the role of women in relationship to agents, to soldiers guarding the "hostiles," and to their general physical deprivation in societies whose livelihood and way of life had been destroyed along with the bison? We are very nearly bereft of data and statements which could clarify the transitional status of women during this period. The strategies adopted for cultural survival and the means of transmitting these to daughters and nieces are valuable adaptive mechanisms which cannot be even partially reconstructed.[72]

These practical realities, imposed quite uniformly by the conquerors, were steadily reinforced by officially sponsored missionizing and mandatory education in boarding schools, processes designed to inculcate the notion that such disempowerment of Indian women and liquidation of "recalcitrant" males was "natural, right, and inevitable."[73] As Jorge Noriega notes in Chapter Thirteen, the purpose of the schools in particular was never to "educate" American Indian children, but rather to indoctrinate them into accepting the dissolution of their cultures, and the intrinsic "superiority" of the Euroamerican cultural values for which they were to abandon their own.[74] In certain instances, further instruction was provided to individuals selected to form a permanent "broker class" administering native societies on behalf of the United States.[75] "Manifest Destiny," which Euroamerica believed entitled it to undertake such culturally genocidal actions, was unequivocal. As George Ellis, a well-known Euroamerican clergyman and author, put it in 1882, at the very point the United States had completed its wars of conquest against Native America and was setting out to consolidate the manner of its colonial rule:

We [whites] have a full right, by our own best wisdom, and then even by compulsion, to dictate terms and conditions to them [Indians]; to use constraint and force; to say what we intend to do, and what we must and shall do...This rightful power of ours will relieve us from conforming to, or even consulting to any troublesome extent, the views and inclinations of the Indians whom we are to manage...The Indian must be made to feel he is in the grasp of a superior.[76]

Contemporary Conditions

The disempowerment of native women corresponded precisely with the extension of colonial domination of each indigenous nation. During the first half of the 20th century, federal authorities developed and perfected the mechanisms of control over Indian land, lives, and resources through such legislation as the General Allotment Act (passed in 1887, but very much ongoing through the 1920s), the 1924 Indian Citizenship Act, and the Indian Reorganization Act of 1934. All of this was done under the premises of the "Trust" and "Plenary Power" doctrines discussed at length elsewhere in this book, and all of it was done for profits taken at the direct expense of native people. As Cheyenne historian Roxanne Dunbar Ortiz has observed:

Throughout this century, the United States government has promoted the corporate exploitation of Indian lands and resources by making unequal agreements on behalf of Indian peoples and cooperating closely with transnational corporations in identifying strategic resources and land areas.[77]

Hence, indigenous nations were systematically denied use of and benefits from even those residual lands they nominally retained. Denied their traditional economies, they were compelled to become absolutely dependent upon government subsidies to survive or—where possible—to join the lowest paid sector of the U.S. workforce. Peoples which had been entirely self-sufficient for thousands of years—indeed, many of them had historically been quite wealthy—were reduced to abject poverty.[78] The capstone of this drive to utilize law as "the perfect instrument of empire" came during the 1950s, when the government set out to drive native people from the land altogether. Beginning in 1954, Congress effected statutes unilaterally "terminating" (dissolving, for purposes of federal recognition) entire indigenous peoples such as the Klamath and Menominee, and coercing thousands of others to relocate from their reservations to non-Indian urban centers (see Chapters One and Three). In this way, Indian reservations were systematically opened up for greater corporate utilization.[79] Once "urbanized," those Indians who had been able to find subsistence employment on farms or ranches and/or engage in gardening and limited livestock rearing of their own were forced into the most marginal occupations or left unemployed altogether.[80]

As concerns native women in the workforce, where 47.2 percent of them had been employed in agriculture in 1900, only 2.1 percent remained so by 1970. Meanwhile, whereas only 0.1 percent of them had been in low-paying clerical positions on high-cost urban economies at the turn of the century, 25.9 percent held

such jobs by 1970. For "service occupations" such as waiting tables, the figures were
12.1 percent in 1900, 25.9 percent in 1970.[81] The data for native men was even more
dismal, with nearly 65 percent being completely unemployed nationally.[82] By 1969,
even the most conservative statistics revealed that more than 40 percent of all
American Indians, as compared to 14 percent of the total population, lived below
the poverty line.[83] In an effort to compensate,

> Native American women's labor force participation rates rose sharply between
> 1970 and 1980, from 35 percent to 48 percent. Those who held full-time,
> year-round jobs earned nearly 89 percent as much as white women...Despite
> these gains, nearly three-quarters of American Indian women were employed
> in the secondary labor market in 1980, compared to two-thirds of European
> American women and one-third of European American men. Repressive,
> inaccessible, and inadequate education bears much of the blame for this low
> occupation status, along with discrimination by employers and fellow employ-
> ees and stagnation of the reservation economy. Almost one-quarter of all
> American Indian women had not completed high school in 1980, compared to
> 16 percent of white women.[84]

For Native American males, the situation was nearly as bad:

> Those men who managed to find full-time jobs earned...only three-fourths as
> much as white men. Moreover, American Indian men have suffered the highest
> rate of unemployment (17 percent in 1980), the highest rate of part-time work
> (58 percent), and a high rate of non-participation in the formal labor force (31
> percent)...A [heavily male-skewed] BIA study of the labor force status of the
> 635,000 American Indians living on and adjacent to reservations in January
> 1989 showed that one-third were unemployed and one-third earned less than
> $7,000. [85]

In 1976, the federal government itself officially acknowledged that American
Indians were by far the most impoverished ethnic group in North America, living
as a whole in conditions virtually identical to those prevailing in many Third World
locales.[86] In Canada, circumstances were much the same, with "unemployment,
suicide, school drop-out rates, health problems and housing shortages at epidemic
levels on most reserves."[87] With regard to native women in particular, as the
Canadian government admitted in 1979:

> Indian women likely rank among the most severely disadvantaged in Canadian
> society. They are worse off economically than both Indian men and Canadian
> women and although they live longer than Indian men, their life-expectancy
> does not approach that of Canadian women generally.[88]

Such poverty indeed breeds short life-spans—in 1980, a U.S. reservation-based
American Indian man could expect to live only slightly over forty-four years, a
woman barely two years longer on the average—as North America's highest rates of
death from malnutrition, exposure, diabetes, tuberculosis, typhoid, diphtheria,
measles, and even bubonic plague took their toll. Infant mortality among reservation-based Native Americans is also seven times the national average.[89] Under these

conditions, the despair experienced by American Indians of both genders has manifested itself in the most pronounced incidence of alcoholism of any ethnic group in the United States. In turn, the cycle of drunkenness results in vastly increased rates of death, not only from ailments like cirrhosis of the liver, but from accidents, often but not always involving automobiles.[90] Extreme social disruption is also caused by alcohol in other ways, such as children born with fetal alcohol syndrome, and child abuse and abandonment, unknown in traditional native societies.[91] The intensity of colonially induced despair also led Native North America as a whole to experience a wave of teen suicide during the 1980s which has run several times the national average.[92]

> In 1980, nearly one in four American Indian families was maintained by a woman (over twice the rate for whites and Asians), and 47 percent of these single-mother families were considered poor by federal guidelines. Among women with children under six, the poverty rate stood at a shocking 82 percent.[93]

On balance, the situation breeds frustration and rage of the most volatile sort, especially among native males, who have been at once heaped with a range of responsibilities utterly alien to their tradition—"head of the household," sole "breadwinner," and so forth—while being structurally denied any viable opportunity to act upon them.[94] In perfect Fanonesque fashion, this has led to a perpetual spiral of internalized violence in which Indian men engage in brutal (and all too often lethal) bar fights with one another, or turn their angry attentions on their wives and children.[95] Battering has become endemic on some reservations, as well as in the Indian ghettos which exist in most U.S. cities, with the result that at least a few Indian women have been forced to kill their spouses in self-defense.[96]

> A headline in the *Navajo Times* in the fall of 1979 reported that rape was the number one crime on the Navajo reservation. In a professional mental health journal of the Indian Health Services, Phyllis Old Dog Cross reported that incest and rape are common among the Indian women seeking services and that their incidence [was] increasing. "It is believed that at least 80 percent of the Native Women seen at the psychiatric service center (5 state area) have experienced some sort of sexual assault."[97]

As Paula Gunn Allen has observed,

> Often it is said [correctly] that the increase of violence against women is the result of various sociological factors such as oppression, racism, poverty, hopelessness, emasculation of men, and loss of male self-esteem as their place within traditional society has been systematically destroyed by increasing urbanization, industrialization, and institutionalization, but seldom do we notice that for the past forty to fifty years, American popular media have depicted American Indian men as bloodthirsty savages treating women cruelly. While traditional Indian men seldom did any such thing—and in fact amongst most [nations] abuse of women was simply unthinkable, as was abuse of children or the aged—the lie about "usual" male Indian behavior seems to have taken root and now bears its brutal and bitter fruit.[98]

Gunn Allen goes on to note,

> It is true that colonization destroyed roles that had given men their sense of
> self-esteem and identity, but the significant roles lost were not those of hunter
> and warrior. Rather, colonization took away the security of office men once
> derived from their ritual and political relationship to women.[99]

Throughout the 20th century, new federal policies have been formulated to
target the power of American Indian women specifically, usually within their
traditional capacity as familial anchors. One evidence of this has been the systematic and persistent forced transfer of Indian children into non-Indian custody, a
patent violation of the United Nations' 1948 Convention on Punishment and
Prevention of the Crime of Genocide.[100] As of 1974, the Association of American
Indian Affairs estimated that between 25 and 35 percent of all native youth were
either adopted by Euroamericans, placed in non-Indian foster homes, or permanently housed in institutional settings, while another 25 percent were "temporarily"
placed in government or church-run boarding schools each year.[101] Although strong
agitation, primarily by Indian women and their supporters, forced Congress to
partially correct the situation through passage of the Indian Child Welfare Act (P.L.
95-608; 25 U.S.C. 1901 *et seq.*) in 1978, the issue remains a very real one in 1991.

Even more grotesque was a policy of involuntary surgical sterilization—another
blatant breach of the Genocide Convention—imposed upon native women, usually
without their knowledge, by the Bureau of Indian Affairs' so-called Indian Health
Service (IHS) during the late 1960s and the first half of the '70s.[102] Existence of the
sterilization program was revealed through analysis of secret documents removed
by American Indian Movement members from the BIA's Washington, D.C. headquarters during its occupation by the Trail of Broken Treaties in November 1972
(see Chapter Three). A resulting 1974 study by WARN concluded that as many as
42 percent of all Indian women of childbearing age had by that point been sterilized
without their consent.[103] The WARN estimates were probably accurate, as is revealed in a subsequent General Accounting Office investigation, restricted to
examining only the years 1973-76 and a mere four of the many IHS facilities. The
GAO study showed that during the three-year sample period, 3,406 involuntary
sterilizations (the equivalent of over a half-million among the general population)
had been performed in just these four hospitals.[104] As a result of strong agitation by
native women and their supporters, the IHS was transferred to the Department of
Health and Human Services in 1978.

As Gunn Allen has aptly put it,

> Currently our struggles are on two fronts: physical survival and cultural
> survival. For women this means fighting alcoholism and drug abuse (our own
> and that of our husbands, lovers, parents, children); poverty...rape, incest,
> battering by Indian [and non-Indian] men; assaults on fertility and other health
> matters by the Indian Health Service and Public Health Service; high infant
> mortality due to substandard medical care, nutrition, and health information;
> poor educational opportunities or education that takes us away from our

traditions, language, and communities; suicide, homicide, or similar expressions of self-hatred; lack of economic opportunities; substandard housing; sometimes violent and often virulent racist attitudes and behaviors directed against us by an entertainment and educational system that wants only one thing from Indians: our silence, out invisibility, and our collective death...To survive culturally, American Indian women must often fight the United States government, the tribal [puppet] governments, women and men of their [nation] who are...threatened by attempts to change...the colonizers' revisions of our lives, values, and histories.[105]

Fighting Back

The patterns of resistance by which American Indians have fought back against the overwhelming oppression of their colonization are actually as old as the colonization itself, occurring in an uninterrupted flow from the early 1500s onward. As with any struggle, however, native resistance has been cyclical in terms of its intensity, and varied in its expression over time. The "modern era" in this regard was perhaps ushered in with the adoption by Indians of written articulation as a mode of political action. Women, beginning with the Northern Paiute writer and activist Sarah Winnemucca Hopkins, have played a decisive role in developing this new tool for indigenous utilization.[106] Winnemucca's autobiographical *Life Among the Piutes: Their Wrongs and Claims,* first published in 1883,[107] laid the groundwork for the subsequent efforts of the Santee Dakota writer Ohiyesa (Charles Eastman), whose early 20th-century books and articles yielded a significant effect in terms of altering the assimilationist policies of the federal government.[108]

Winnemucca was hardly alone in her endeavor. Contemporaneous to Ohiyesa—and carrying a much sharper edge in both her writing and her activism— was Zitkala-sa (Gertrude Bonnin), a Lakota who was the first to announce proudly and in print that she considered her own traditions not simply the equal of anything Euroamerica had to offer, but "superior to white ways and values."[109] She was followed by Ella Deloria, another Lakota author relatively unequivocal in her affirmation of "Indianness."[110] Together, these early Indian women writers set in motion a dynamic wherein native women reasserted their traditional role as "voice of the people," albeit through a much different medium than had historically prevailed. By the late 1970s, Native American literature had assumed a critical galvanizing role within indigenous liberation struggles in North America, and women such as Leslie Marmon Silko (Laguna), Wendy Rose (Hopi), Joy Harjo (Creek), Linda Hogan (Chickasaw), and Mary TallMountain (Athabascan) were providing the muscle and sinew of the effort.[111] The female presence in native literature has continued to increase in importance during the late 1980s and early 1990s, with the emergence of work by Louise Erdrich (Turtle Mountain Anishinabé), Chrystos (Menominee), and others.[112]

As noted earlier, translation of these literary sentiments into serious confrontations began to occur in noticeable fashion with the fish-in movement of the Pacific Northwest during the 1960s. This happened, in the words of Bobbi Lee, a Canadian

Métis active in the fishing rights struggle, "when the women just became fed up. They ran out of patience with what was going on and decided it was time to change things."[113] She describes her first demonstration at the Washington state capitol building:

> Most of the militants there at [the] demonstration in Olympia...were women and three of them did most of the speaking...They were traditionalists so there was nothing unusual about women acting as spokes[people] for the group. In fact, they told me they were having trouble getting the men involved. The only man who spoke was Hank Adams, who's been to a university and wasn't traditional.[114]

The same sort of thing happened with the American Indian Movement (AIM), an entity which received much of its early impetus from the fishing rights movement and the examples set by Marie Lego and others engaged in the Pit River land struggle. Mary Jane Wilson, an Anishinabé activist, was—along with Dennis Banks and George Mitchell—a founder of the organization in 1968.[115] As AIM began to grow, much of the grassroots membership which made it successful was comprised of women.[116] As was mentioned above, on the Pine Ridge Lakota Reservation, which became the focal point of the movement's pitched battles with federal forces during the mid-'70s, the staunchest and most active traditionalist support came from elder Oglala women.[117] Once again, those who established and maintained the AIM survival schools during the latter part of the decade were almost exclusively women.[118]

When it came to repression, however, males bore the brunt. Although female leadership had been readily apparent throughout the confrontation at Wounded Knee, the government simply repeated its historical pattern, targeting six Indian men—Russell Means (Oglala), Pedro Bissonette (Oglala), Leonard Crow Dog (Sicangu Lakota), Dennis Banks (Anishinabé), Carter Camp (Ponca), and Stan Holder (Wichita)—to face up to triple-life plus 88 years imprisonment in the so-called Wounded Knee Leadership Trials.[119] To be sure, AIM women *were* charged, brought to trial, and sometimes convicted—Kamook Nichols Banks (Oglala), Joanna LeDeaux (Oglala), and Nilak Butler (Inuit), to name but three examples, served appreciable sentences—but for every woman locked up, there were a dozen or more men.[120] Twenty-one women and two children were also among the minimum of 69 AIM members and supporters killed by government surrogates on Pine Ridge between mid-1973 and mid-1976, the peak period of the U.S. counterinsurgency warfare directed at the organization. The proportionate emphasis placed by federal authorities upon "neutralizing" AIM men is apparent in the fact that the remaining 46 fatalities were adult males.[121] As Madonna Thunderhawk, a Hunkpapa Lakota AIM member and a founder of WARN, described it in 1980:

> Indian women have *had* to be strong because of what this colonialist system has done to our men...alcohol, suicides, car wrecks, the whole thing. And after Wounded Knee, while all that persecution of the men was going on, we women had to keep things going.[122]

Carrying the weight in this fashion instilled in a whole generation of hard-line native women activists not only a strong sense of confidence in their own ability to get things done (as opposed to simply getting them started), but a deep sensitivity to the unequal degree of risk incurred by Indian men fighting to throw off the shackles—both physical and psychological—of colonization.[123] As veteran fishing rights activist Janet McCloud asserted after a 1980 meeting in which AIM was harshly criticized for its "male dominance" and the alleged "opportunism" of its more celebrated men:

> The tribal leaders and others who denounce AIM justify their actions by pointing out the human weaknesses of individual AIM people, with never a glance to their own...Indian people can disagree till doomsday about which defensive strategy is best, or whether we should even resist. If we continue to disagree on politics, policy, philosophy, and enter into destructive personality clashes, we will lose all...Few acknowledge that real change began to take place only after the tremendous sacrifices of the young [male] warriors of the American Indian Movement. The beneficiaries of the Movement [accept the gains] while the real warriors lie unrecognized in their graves or in prison cells...We need our warriors, and where are they? In prisons, in hiding, pursued relentlessly by the FBI...How many [of us] will take the time to send a card or a letter to the warriors rotting in prisons? It is time Indian people, those who have received most from the American Indian Movement, took some time to count their blessings, to give credit where credit is due. Don't forget the warriors, we may never see their like again.[124]

The AIM women's response to the sexism internalized by their male counterparts as part of the colonizing process was to resume the time-honored practice of establishing the political equivalent of traditional women's societies. WARN was first, initiated in 1974. It was followed by McCloud's Northwest Indian Women's Circle in 1981 and, more lately, the Indigenous Women's Network (IWN). Formed by Winona LaDuke and Ingrid Wasinawatok-El Issa (Oneida), a long-time AIM member and mainstay of the International Indian Treaty Council, IWN has lately begun to publish a journal entitled *Indigenous Woman*. The purpose of such organizations has been explained by WARN founder Phyllis Young (Hunkpapa Lakota):

> What we are about is drawing on our traditions, regaining our strength as women in the ways handed down to us by our grandmothers, and their grandmothers before them. Our creation of an Indian women's organization is not a criticism or division from our men. In fact, it's the exact opposite. Only in this way can we organize ourselves as Indian women to meet our responsibilities, to be fully supportive of the men, to work in tandem with them as partners in a common struggle for the liberation of our people and our land...The men understand this, and they support our effort. So, instead of dividing away from the men, what we are doing is building strength and unity in the traditional way.[125]

Correspondingly, the power and presence of women within the Indian liberation movement, already strong, has if anything increased since the 1960s and '70s.

During the 1980s, aside from the earlier-mentioned leadership of elder Diné women in the sustained resistance to forced relocation at Big Mountain, a comparable function has been assumed by the Western Shoshone sisters Mary and Carrie Dann in Nevada vis-à-vis a federal drive to take their people's homeland.[126] In northern California, it was Abby Abinanti, a Yurok attorney, who led the legal defense against a government/corporate plan to desecrate the "High Country", a locale sacred to her own and several other peoples in the area (see Chapter Nine). Anywhere confrontations over Indian rights are occurring in the United States, native women are playing crucial roles. Moreover, by the early '80s, women had (re)assumed the primary leadership position in sixty-seven of the 304 remaining reservation-based indigenous nations within the forty-eight contiguous states, and the number is growing steadily (see Chapter Three for examples).[127]

The struggle has also been sharp in Canada, where, under provision of Section (12) (1) (b) of the 1876 Indian Act (amended in 1951), a particularly virulent form of patrilineage was built into the definition of "Indian-ness." Under the act, a woman who married, not only a non-Indian but anyone outside her "tribe," was herself (along with her children), legally and automatically deprived of her "Indian Status."[128] Such reversal of traditional matrilineage principles—not to mention the overt racism and sexism involved—had been challenged from 1952 onward, notably by Mohawk leader Mary Two-Axe Early of the Caughnawaga Reserve in Québec.[129] After losing several cases on the issue in Canadian courts during the early '70s, a group of Maliseet women from the Tobique Reserve in New Brunswick decided to place the situation of one of their number, Sandra Lovelace Sappier, before the United Nations.

> The Tobique women's strategy of going to the United Nations did exert tremendous pressure on the [Ottawa] government to change the Indian Act. On December 29, 1977 the complaint of Sandra Lovelace against the Canadian government was communicated to the United Nations Human Rights Committee in Geneva, Switzerland. Because of delays by the Canadian government in responding to the Human Rights Committee's requests for information, the final verdict was not made until July 30, 1981. The decision found that Canada was in violation of the International Covenant on Civil and Political Rights. Canada was in breach of the Covenant because the Indian Act denied Sandra Lovelace the *legal* right to live in the community of her birth.[130]

As a result of the Lovelace case, the Canadian government was forced to make a further revision to the Indian Act in 1985 which eliminated discrimination against women, opening the way for resumption of traditional matrilineal/matrilocal expression among indigenous societies across the country. Along the way, the "Tobique Women's Political Action Group" was forced to confront the broker class of their own male population—placed in positions of "leadership" by the Canadian rather than their own governing system, and thus threatened by the women's actions—physically occupying tribal office buildings and effectively evicting the men, beginning in September 1977.[131] Their actions had considerable ramifications, as is witnessed by the fact that at the present time, native women in Canada often serve as chief spokespersons for their peoples. One example is that of Sharon Venne, a Cree attorney selected during the '80s to represent the Treaty Six nations of Alberta in international forums.[132] Another illustration is Norma Kassi, official spokesperson for the Swich'in Nation, elected member of the Yukon Legislative Assembly, and organizer of a broad coalition to oppose oil and gas development on the North Slope of Alaska.[133]

Thus, both north and south of the Euroamerican border separating the United States and Canada, intense struggles have been waged by indigenous people over the past three decades against the sorts of conditions depicted in the preceding section. While it is obvious that the problems confronted have not been solved, it is equally plain that substantial gains have been made in terms of positioning Native North America to change these circumstances through decolonization and reassertion of its self-determining, self-defining, and self-sufficient existence. In each instance, native women—as *Indians,* first, last, and always—have asserted their traditional right and assumed their traditional responsibility of standing at the very center of the fray.

Native American Women and Feminism

Given the reality that Native Americans today comprise only about 0.6 percent of the North American population, and the magnitude of the problems we face, it would seem imperative that we attract support from non-Indian groups, forming alliances and coalitions where possible on the basis of some mutually recognized common ground. Many efforts in this regard, some of them described elsewhere in this book, have been attempted by native activists with varying degrees of success. On the face of it, both the "matriarchal" aspects of indigenous traditions and the nature of many of the struggles engaged in by contemporary native women appear to lend themselves to such a union with what the broader population has come to describe as "feminism." Accordingly, a number of prominent native women activists such as Shirley Hill Witt, Rayna Green (Cherokee), Annie Wauneka (Diné), and Suzan Shown Harjo (Lakota/Creek) have, at least at times, adopted the feminist descriptor to define their own perspectives.[134] American Indian women's organizations of this persuasion, such as OHOYO, have also made appearances.[135] Paula Gunn Allen has gone further in her attempts to make the link, arguing that indigenous tradition represents the "red roots" of the feminist impulse among all people in North America, whether its various adherents and opponents realize it or not.[136]

It should be noted, however, that those who have most openly identified themselves in this fashion have tended to be among the more assimilated of Indian women activists, generally accepting of the colonialist ideology that indigenous nations are now legitimate sub-parts of the U.S. geopolitical corpus rather than separate nations, that Indian people are now a minority within the overall population rather than the citizenry of their own distinct nations. Such Indian women activists are therefore usually more devoted to "civil rights" than to liberation

per se. Native American women who are more genuinely sovereigntist in their
outlook have proven themselves far more dubious about the potentials offered by
feminist politics and alliances: "At the present time, American Indians in general
are not comfortable with feminist analysis or action within reservation or urban
Indian enclaves. Many Indian women are uncomfortable because they perceive it
(correctly) as white-dominated."[137] What this has meant in practice is, as Lorelei
Means has put it:

> White women, most of them very middle class and, for whatever they think
> their personal oppression is, as a group they're obviously the material benefi-
> ciaries of the colonial exploitation their society has imposed upon ours...they
> come and they look at the deformity of our societies produced by colonization,
> and then they criticize the deformity. They tell us we have to move "beyond"
> our culture in order to be "liberated" like them. It's just amazing...They
> virtually demand that we give up our own traditions in favor of what they
> imagine their own to be, just like the missionaries and the government and all
> the rest of the colonizers. It was being forced *away* from our own traditions that
> deformed us—that made the men sexists and things like that—in the first place.
> What we need to be is *more*, not less Indian. But every time we try to explain
> this to our self-proclaimed "white sisters," we either get told we're missing the
> point—we're just dumb Indians, after all—or we're accused of "self-hatred" as
> women. A few experiences with this sort of arrogance and you start to get the
> idea maybe all this feminism business is just another extension of the same old
> racist, colonialist mentality.[138]

Janet McCloud explains that, "Many Anglo women try, I expect in all sincerity,
to tell us that our most pressing problem is male supremacy. To this, I have to say,
with all due respect, *bullshit*. Our problems are what they've been for the past
several hundred years: white supremacism and colonialism. And that's a supremacism and a colonialism of which white feminists are still very much a part."[139] Pam
Colorado, an Oneida scholar working in Canada, observes:

> It seems to me the feminist agenda is basically one of rearranging social relations
> within the society which is occupying our land and utilizing our resources for
> its own benefit. Nothing I've encountered in feminist theory addresses the fact
> of our colonization, or the wrongness of white women's stake in it. To the
> contrary, there seems to be a presumption among feminist writers that the
> colonization of Native America will, even *should*, continue permanently. At
> least there's no indication any feminist theorist has actively advocated pulling
> out of Indian Country, should a "transformation of social relations" actually
> occur. Instead, feminists appear to share a presumption in common with the
> patriarchs they oppose, that they have some sort of inalienable right to simply
> go on occupying our land and exploiting our resources for as long as they like.
> Hence, I can only conclude that, like marxism, which arrives at the same
> outcome through class rather than gender theory, feminism is essentially a
> Euro-supremacist ideology and is therefore quite imperialist in its implica-
> tions.[140]

Evidence of the colonialist content of much Euroamerican feminist practice has been advanced, not just at the material level, but in terms of cultural imperialism. Andrea Smith, a Makah writing in *Indigenous Woman*, recently denounced feminism of the "New Age" persuasion for "ripping off" native ceremonies for their own purposes, putting them on notice that "as long as they take part in Indian spiritual abuse, either by being consumers of it, or by refusing to take a stand on [the matter], Indian women will consider white 'feminists' to be nothing more than agents in the genocide of [native] people."[141] Another increasingly volatile issue in this connection has been the appropriation and distortion of indigenous traditions concerning homosexuality by both "radical" or lesbian feminists and gay male activists.[142] Particularly offensive have been non-Indian efforts to convert the indigenous custom of treating homosexuals (often termed "berdache" by anthropologists) as persons endowed with special spiritual powers into a polemic for mass organizing within the dominant society.[143]

Although the special and deeply revered status accorded homosexuals by native societies derived precisely from their being relatively rare, the desire of non-Indian gays and lesbians to legitimate their preferences within the context of their own much more repressive society, and to do so in ways which reinforce an imagined superiority of these preferences, has led many of them to insist upon the reality of a traditional Native North America in which nearly *everyone* was homosexual. Unfortunately, Paula Gunn Allen, in pandering to the needs and tastes of non-Indian gay and lesbian organizers, has done much to reinforce their willful misimpressions of indigenous tradition:

> [L]esbianism and homosexuality were probably commonplace. Indeed, same-sex relationships may have been the norm for primary pair-bonding. There were clans and bands or villages, but the primary personal unit tended to include members of one's own sex rather than members of the opposite sex.[144]

Although Gunn Allen hurriedly goes on to note that it "is questionable whether these practices would be recognized as lesbian by the politically radical lesbian community of today,"[145] her sweeping exaggeration has been seized upon by those seeking to deploy their own version of "noble savage" mythology for political purposes. To paraphrase an Inuit lesbian poet who wishes not to be further identified, "I've always been very well accepted and supported within my community for who I am. But now comes this idea, brought in from the outside for reasons that really have nothing to do with us, that Indianness and homosexuality are somehow fused, that you can't 'really' be Indian unless you're gay or lesbian, or at least bisexual. The implication is that I'm assessed as being more traditional, and my heterosexual friends less traditional, on the basis of sexual preference. This is not an Indian idea. It's absurd, and it's deeply resented by all of us. But the danger is that it could eventually cause divisions among us Indians that never existed before, and right at the point when we're most in need of unity." Or, as Chrystos, also a lesbian, has put it:

> This is just another myth imposed by white people for their own purposes, at our expense. And while I may consider it to be more pleasant, it's really no

better than the myth of us being savage scalpers and torturers, stone age hunter-gatherers, and all the rest. We have all come to the point where we must pull ourselves together in our common humanity if we are to survive. That can only happen on the basis of *truth*, not the projection of still another white fantasy.[146]

For their efforts at lending a native voice to discussions of homosexuality in indigenous tradition, and leading things in a positive contemporary direction, both women have often been called "homophobic." Non-lesbian Indian women who have attempted to make the same points have often been labeled "heterosexist," a designation which prompted at least one of them to respond that "a very vocal part of the white women's movement seems to be afflicted with what you could call *homo* sexism."[147] Janet McCloud has concluded that, under such circumstances, there is little, if anything, to be gained by Indian women making a direct link-up with feminism.[148]

Other, less "radical," native women have arrived at essentially the same conclusion. Laura Waterman Wittstock, a Seneca leader, went on record early with the message that "tribalism, not feminism, is the correct route" for native women to follow.[149] Similarly, Blackfeet traditional Beverly Hungry Wolf, in her autobiography, is quite clear that only adherence to "the ways of [her] grandmothers" allowed her to remain unconfused in her cultural-sexual identity throughout her life.[150] They are joined by younger women like Anishinabé-Choctaw scholar Clara Sue Kidwell, who has explored the problems of communicating a coherent indigenous female cultural-sexual identity in the colonial context and determined that recovery of traditional forms is more than ever called for.[151] Even some Euroamerican feminist researchers who have applied analysis rather than "sisterhood is powerful"-style sloganeering to their understanding of Native North America concede that the "social and economic positions of Indian women make them more like Indian men" than like white women (conversely, of course, this makes Euroamerican women more like white men than like Indian women, a factor left conspicuously unremarked).[152]

The Road Ahead

Interestingly, women of other nonwhite sectors of the North American population have shared many native women's criticisms of the Euroamerican feminist phenomenon. African American women in particular have been outspoken in this regard. As Gloria Joseph argues:

> The White women's movement has had its own explicit forms of racism in the way it has given high priority to certain aspects of struggles and neglected others…because of the inherently racist assumptions and perspectives brought to bear in the first articulations by the White women's movement…The Black movement scorns feminism partially on the basis of misinformation, and partially due to a valid perception of the White middle class nature of the movement. An additional reason is due to the myopic ways that White feminists have generalized their sexual-political analysis and have confirmed their racism in the forms their feminism has assumed.[153]

The "self-righteous indignation" and defensiveness that Joseph discerns as experienced by most Euroamerican feminists when confronted with such critiques is elsewhere explained by bell hooks as a response resting in the vested interest of those who feel it:

> [F]eminist emphasis on "common oppression" in the United States was less a strategy for politicization than an appropriation by conservative and liberal women of a radical political vocabulary that masked the extent to which they shaped the movement so that it addressed and promoted their class interests...White women who dominate feminist discourse, who for the most part make and articulate feminist theory, have little or no understanding of white supremacy as a racial politic, of the psychological impact of class, of their [own] political status within a racist, sexist, capitalist state.[154]

"I was struck," hooks says in her book, *Ain't I A Woman*, "by the fact that the ideology of feminism, with its emphasis on transforming and changing the social structure of the U.S., in no way resembled the reality of American feminism. Largely because [white] feminists themselves, as they attempted to take feminism beyond the realm of radical rhetoric into the sphere of American life, revealed that they remained imprisoned in the very structures they hoped to change. Consequently, the sisterhood we all talked about has not become a reality."[155] It is time to "talk back" to white feminists, hooks argues, "spoiling their celebration, their 'sisterhood,' their 'togetherness.'"[156] This must be done because in adhering to feminism in its present form:

> We learn to look to those empowered by the very systems of domination that wound and hurt us for some understanding of who we are that will be liberating and we never find that. It is necessary for [women of color] to do the work ourselves if we want to know more about our experience, if we want to see that experience from perspectives not shaped by domination.[157]

Asian American women, Chicanas, and Latinas have agreed in substantial part with such assessments.[158] Women of color in general tend not to favor the notion of a "politics" which would divide and weaken their communities by defining "male energy" as "the enemy." It is not for nothing that no community of color in North America has ever produced a counterpart to white feminism's SCUM (Society for Cutting Up Men). Women's liberation, in the view of most "minority" women in the United States and Canada, cannot occur in any context other than the wider liberation, from Euroamerican colonial domination, of the peoples of which women of color are a part. Our sense of priorities is therefore radically—and irrevocably— different from those espoused by the "mainstream" women's movement.

Within this alienation from feminism lies the potential for the sorts of alliances which may in the end prove most truly beneficial to American Indian people. By forging links to organizations composed of other women of color, founded not merely to fight gender oppression, but also to struggle against racial and cultural oppression, native women can prove instrumental in creating an alternative movement of women in North America, one which is mutually respectful of the rights, needs, cultural particularities, and historical divergences of each sector of its membership, and which is therefore free of the adherence to white supremacist hegemony previously marring feminist thinking and practice. Any such movement of women—including those Euroamerican women who see its thrust as corresponding to their own values and interests as human beings—cannot help but be of crucial importance within the liberation struggles waged by peoples of color to dismantle the apparatus of Eurocentric power in every area of the continent. The greater the extent to which these struggles succeed, the closer the core agenda of Native North America—recovery of land and resources, reassertion of self-determining forms of government, and reconstitution of traditional social relations within our nations— will come to realization.

Notes

1. For further information on Marie Lego and the context of her struggle, see Jaimes, M. Annette, "The Pit River Indian Land Claims Dispute in Northern California," *Journal of Ethnic Studies,* Vol. 4, No. 4, Winter 1987.
2. Quoted in Katz, Jane B., *I Am the Fire of Time: The Voices of Native American Women,* E.P. Dutton Publisher, New York, 1977, p. 146.
3. Quoted in ibid., p. 147. Bennett was eventually acquitted after being shot, while seven months pregnant, and wounded by white vigilantes.
4. Ibid.
5. Quoted in ibid., p. 141.
6. The best account of the roles of Gladys Bissonette and Ellen Moves Camp during the siege may be found in Editors, *Voices from Wounded Knee, 1973, Akwesasne Notes,* Mohawk Nation via Rooseveltown, NY, 1974.
7. Churchill, Ward, and Jim Vander Wall, *The COINTELPRO Papers: Documents on the FBI's Secret Wars Against Dissent in the United States,* South End Press, Boston, 1990, pp. 231-302. Also see Matthiessen, Peter, *In the Spirit of Crazy Horse,* Viking Press, New York, (2nd edition) 1991.
8. Kammer, Jerry, *The Second Long Walk: The Navajo-Hopi Land Dispute,* University of New Mexico Press, Albuqerque, 1980, pp. 1-2, 209.
9. For further information on Big Mountain, see Parlow, Anita, *Cry, Sacred Land: Big Mountain, USA,* Christic Institute, Washington, D.C., 1988.
10. Quoted in Katz, op. cit., p. 151. For further background on Ada Deer, see her autobiography (Deer, Ada, with R.E. Simon, Jr., *Speaking Out,* Children's Press, Chicago, 1970).
11. On the murders of Pedro and Jeanette Bissonette, see Churchill, Ward, and Jim Vander Wall, *Agents of Repression: The FBI's Secret Wars Against the Black Panther Party and the American Indian Movement,* South End Press, Boston, 1988, pp. 187, 200-3.
12. Concerning the murders of Tina Manning Trudell, her three children (Ricarda Star, age five; Sunshine Karma, three; and Eli Changing Sun, one), and her mother, Leah Hicks Manning, see ibid., pp. 361-4. On Aquash, see Brand, Johanna, *The Life and Death of Anna Mae Aquash,* James Lorimar Publishers, Toronto, 1978.
13. Hill Witt, Shirley, "The Brave-Hearted Women: The Struggle at Wounded Knee," *Akwesasne Notes,* Vol. 8, No. 2, 1976, p. 16.
14. Quoted in Katz, op. cit., pp. 145-6.
15. Quoted in Kammer, op. cit., p. 18.
16. From a talk delivered during International Women's Week, the University of Colorado at Boulder, April 1984 (tape on file).
17. Such sentiments are hardly unique to the United States. For articulations by Canadian Indian women, see Silman, Janet, *Enough is Enough: Aboriginal Women Speak Out,* The Women's Press, Toronto, 1987.
18. From a talk delivered during International Women's Week, the University of Colorado at Boulder, April 1985 (tape on file).

19. From a talk delivered during International Women's Week, University of Colorado at Boulder, April 1984 (tape on file).

20. Burke Leacock, Eleanor, *Myths of Male Dominance: Collected Articles on Women Cross-Culturally,* Monthly Review Press, New York, 1981.

21. Valentine, Paul, "Dances with Myths," *Washington Post;* reprinted in the *Boulder* [Colorado] *Daily Camera,* April 7, 1991.

22. Valentine also informs us that these "nomadic hunters and gatherers moved from spot to spot, strewing refuse in their wake" (What sort of "refuse?" Plastic? Aluminum cans? Polyvinyl Chlorides?) before running down the usual litany of imagined native defects: "[Indians] were totalitarian, warlike and extremely brutal. Some practiced slavery, torture, human sacrifice and cannibalism, and imposed rigid social dictatorships." That there is not one shred of solid evidence supporting *any* of this is no bother. Valentine and his ilk simply condemn anyone bothering with the facts as a "politically correct...revisionist." Left unexplained is why anyone might deliberately seek to be politically *in*correct, or why blatant inaccuracies or lies—such as those in which they trade—shouldn't be revised and corrected.

23. Ehrenreich, Barbara, "The Warrior Culture," *Time,* October 15, 1990. It should be noted that the practice of scalping, derived from the taking of heads, was introduced to North America by the British, who had earlier developed the technique during the conquest and colonization of Ireland (see Canny, Nicholas P., "The Ideology of English Colonization: From Ireland to America," *William and Mary Quarterly,* 3rd Ser., No. 30, 1973, pp. 575-98). For a more detailed response, see Ward Churchill's letter on the article (frozen out of *Time*) in *Z Magazine,* November 1990.

24. McNickle, D'Arcy, *The Surrounded,* University of New Mexico Press, Albuquerque, (2nd edition) 1978.

25. Gunn Allen, Paula, *The Sacred Hoop: Recovering the Feminine in American Indian Traditions,* Beacon Press, Boston, 1986, p. 266.

26. Indication of the relatively higher valuation placed upon women may be found in the fact that among the Iroquois, Susquehannahs, and Abenakis ("Hurons"), for example, the penalty for killing a woman was double that for killing a man (see Thomas Foreman, Caroline, *American Indian Women Chiefs,* Hoffman Printing Co., Muskogee, OK, 1954, p. 9). On the diversity of native women's social functions and activities, see Shirer Mathes, Valerie, "A New Look at the Role of Women in Indian Societies," *American Indian Quarterly,* Vol. 2, No. 2, 1975, pp. 131-9.

27. See Thomas Foreman, op. cit., pp. 85-7. Also see Coulter, E. Merton, "Mary Musgrove, Queen of the Creeks: A Chapter of the Early Georgia Troubles," *Georgia Historical Quarterly,* Vol. 11, No. 1, 1927, pp. 1-30, and Corry, John Pitts, "Some New Light on the Bosworth Claims," *Georgia Historical Quarterly,* No. 25, 1941, pp. 195-224. The novel in question is Brown, Dee, *Creek Mary's Blood,* Simon and Schuster Publishers, New York, 1981.

28. Discussion with Madonna Thunderhawk (Hunkpapa Lakota), April 1985; discussion with Robert Grey Eagle (Oglala Lakota), July 1991.

29. Thomas Foreman, op. cit., p. 85.

30. See Lewis, Oscar, "Manly-Hearted Women Among the Northern Piegan," *American Anthropologist,* No. 43, 1941, pp. 173-87.

31. On Buffalo Calf Road, see Agonito, Rosemary, and Joseph Agonito, "Resurrecting History's Forgotten Women: A Case Study from the Cheyenne Indians," *Frontiers: A Journal of Women's Studies,* No. 6, Fall 1981, pp. 8-9; and Sandoz, Mari, *Cheyenne Autumn,* Avon Books, New York, 1964). Information on four other 19th-century warrior women may be found in Ewers, John C., "Deadlier than the Male," *American Heritage,* No. 16, 1965, pp. 10-13. More generally, see Medicine, Bea, "'Warrior Women': Sex Role Alternatives for Plains Indian Women," in Patricia Albers and Beatrice Medicine, eds., *The Hidden Half: Studies of Plains Indian Women,* University Press of America, Lanham, MD, 1983, pp. 267-80.

32. Robin Morgan's *The Demon Lover: On the Sexuality of Terrorism* (W.W. Norton Publishers, New York, 1989), in which any female engaged in physical combat is found to be the mere pawn of some man (or at least "male energy") is the most extraordinarily insulting and demeaning treatise possible, not only for Native American women, but for African Americans like Assata Shakur, Latinas like Lolita Labrón and Alejandrina Torres, Europeans like Ingrid Barabass and Monica Helbing, Euroamericans like Susan Rosenberg and Linda Evans, and perhaps a quarter of the female populations of Africa, Asia, and Palestine.

33. Gunn Allen, op. cit., pp. 36-7. She is drawing on Timberlake, Lt. Henry, *Lieutenant Henry*

Timberlake's Memoirs, Marietta, GA, 1948, p. 94.

34. Concerning the ongoing nature of the Longhouse government, and women's role in it, see Anonymous, "A Woman's Ways: An Interview with Judy Swamp," *Parabola,* Vol. 5, No. 4, 1980, pp. 52-61. Also see Cook, Katsi, "The Women's Dance: Reclaiming Our Powers on the Women's Side of Life," *Native Self-Sufficiency,* No. 6, 1981, pp. 17-19.

35. See Grumet, Robert Steven, "Sunksquaws, Shamans, and Tradeswomen: Middle-Atlantic Coastal Algonkian Women During the 17th and 18th Centuries," in Mona Etienne and Eleanor Burke Leacock, eds., *Women and Colonization: Anthropological Perspectives,* Praeger Publishers, New York, 1980.

36. Ibid., pp. 51-2.

37. See Wallace, Anthony F.C., "Women, Land, and Society: Three Aspects of Aboriginal Delaware Life," *Pennsylvania Archaeologist,* No. 17, 1947, pp. 1-35; and Weslager, C.S., "The Delaware Indians as Women," *Journal of the Washington Academy of Science,* No. 37, September 15, 1947, pp. 298-304.

38. Gunn Allen, op. cit., p. 35. She relies heavily on Grumet, op. cit.

39. For further information on these customs, see Niethammer, Carolyn, *Daughters of the Earth: The Lives and Legends of Native American Women,* Macmillan Publishers, New York, 1977. Also see Kidwell, Clara Sue, "The Power of Women in Three American Indian Societies," *Journal of Ethnic Studies,* Vol. 6, No. 3, 1979, pp. 113-21. An overview of the extent to which matrilineal/matrilocal societies predominated in precontact Native North America, see Lowie, Robert H., "The Matrilineal Complex," *University of California Publications in Archaeology and Ethnology,* No. 16, 1919-1920, pp. 29-45.

40. Terrell, John Upton, and Donna M. Terrell, *Indian Women of the Western Morning: Their Life in Early America,* Anchor Books, New York, 1974, p. 24.

41. See Brown, Judith K., "Economic Organization and the Position of Women Among the Iroquois," *Ethnohistory,* Vol. 17, Nos. 3-4, Summer-Fall 1970, pp. 151-67. Also see Trigger, Bruce G., "Iroquoian Matriliny," *Pennsylvania Archaeologist,* No. 48, 1978, pp. 55-65.

42. See Powers, Marla N., *Oglala Women: Myth, Ritual and Reality,* University of Chicago Press, Chicago, 1986, p. 89.

43. Oshana, Mary, "Native American Women in Westerns: Reality and Myth," *Frontiers: A Journal of Women's Studies,* No. 6, Fall 1981, p. 46.

44. See Hornbeck Tanner, Helen, "Coocoochee: Mohawk Medicine Woman," *American Indian Culture and Research Journal,* Vol. 3, No. 3, 1979, pp. 23-42; Jones, David, *Sanapia: A Comanche Medicine Woman,* Holt, Rinehart and Winston Publishers, New York, 1968; and Linderman, Frank, *Pretty Shield: Medicine Woman of the Crows,* John Day Publishers, New York, 1932; reprinted 1974.

45. Terrell and Terrell, op. cit., p. 25.

46. See Landes, Ruth, *The Ojibwa Religion and the Midewiwin,* University of Wisconsin Press, Madison, 1968; Kent, Susan, "Hogans, Sacred Circles and Symbols: The Navajo Use of Space," in David Brugge and Charlotte J. Frisbie, eds., *Essays in Honor of Leland Wyman,* Museum of New Mexico Press, Santa Fé, 1982; Lake, Robert G., "Chilula Religion and Ideology: A Discussion of Native American Humanistic Concepts and Processes," *Humbolt Journal of Social Relations,* Vol. 7, No. 2, 1980, pp. 113-34; and Kehoe, Alice, "Old Woman Had Great Power," *Western Canadian Journal of Anthropology,* Vol. 6, No. 3, 1976, pp. 68-76. Also see Thrift Nelson, Ann, "Native American Women's Ritual Sodalities in Native North America," *Western Canadian Journal of Anthropology,* Vol. 6, No. 3, 1976, pp. 29-67.

47. For a thorough analysis of the metatheological precepts embodied in indigenous American spirituality, see Deloria, Vine Jr., *God Is Red,* Grossett and Dunlap Publishers, New York, 1973; reprinted by Dell Books, New York, 1983. Further elaboration is provided in his *Metaphysics of Modern Existence,* Harper and Row Publishers, New York, 1979.

48. Contrary to the contentions of University of Colorado Professor of Religious Studies Sam Gill, the idea of Mother Earth—which is quite universal among Native North Americans—was not imported from Europe (Gill, Sam D., *Mother Earth: An American Story,* University of Chicago Press, Chicago, 1987). For detailed refutation, see the special section of *Bloomsbury Review* (Vol. 8, No. 5, September-October 1988) edited by M. Annette Jaimes and devoted to critique of Gill's thesis and methods.

49. Quoted in Katz, op. cit., p. 126. For further background on the status of Diné women, see Stewart, Irene, *A Voice in Her Tribe: A Navajo Woman's Own Story,* Ballena Press, Socorro, NM, 1980;

and Roessel, Ruth, *Women in Navajo Society,* Navajo Resource Center, Rough Rock, AZ, 1981.
50. Quoted in Katz, op. cit., p. 123.
51. From a talk delivered during International Women's Week, University of Colorado at Boulder, April 1985 (tape on file).
52. Buffalohead, Priscilla K., "Farmers, Warriors, Traders: A Fresh Look at Ojibway Women," *Minnesota History,* No. 48, Summer 1983, p. 236.
53. Thwaites, Rubin Gold, ed., *The Jesuit Relations and Allied Documents,* Vol. 5 (of 71 Volumes), Burrow Brothers Publishers, Cleveland, 1906, p. 179.
54. Leacock, op. cit., p. 35.
55. For a broader examination of the impact of the fur trade upon the internal structures of indigenous societies, see Van Kirk, Sylvia, *Many Tender Ties: Women in Fur-Trade Society, 1670-1870,* University of Oklahoma Press, Norman, 1980
56. Leacock, "Montagnais Women and the Jesuit Program for Colonization," in ibid., pp. 43-62.
57. Gunn Allen, op. cit., p. 40.
58. The expression "petticoat government" comes from the British colonialist John Adair in regard to the Cherokee Nation. See Brown, John P., *Old Frontiers,* State Historical Society of Wisconsin, Madison, 1938, p. 20.
59. Gunn Allen, op. cit., p. 33. She relies upon Brandon, William, *The Last Americans: The Indian in American Culture,* McGraw-Hill Publishers, New York, 1974, p. 214.
60. Gunn Allen, op. cit., p. 37.
61. Ibid. It should be noted that this calculated and vicious colonialist use of mixed-bloods as a means to undercut traditional societies, a tactic which is ongoing in the present day, is a primary cause of the sort of racially-oriented infighting among Indians which continues to confuse the questions of Indian identity addressed in Chapter Four.
62. Ibid.
63. For a solid sample of the avaricious sentiments involved in this federal policy, see U.S. Congress, *Speeches on the Passage of the Bill for Removal of the Indians, Delivered in the Congress of the United States, April and May, 1830,* Perkins and Marvin Publishers, Boston, 1830; Kraus Reprint Co., Millwood, NY, 1973.
64. Gunn Allen, op. cit., pp. 37-8. It should be noted that the three men named did not share the same position on Cherokee removal. John Ross, "despite his large degree of white blood," was an ardent Cherokee patriot and fought mightily against U.S. policy (see Eaton, Rachel E., *John Ross and the Cherokee People,* Cherokee National Museum, Muskogee, OK, 1921). Boudinot and Major Ridge (or "The Ridge"), were devout assimilationists who worked—for a fee—to further U.S. interests by engineering an appearance of acceptance of removal among their own people (see Wilkins, Thurman, *Cherokee Tragedy: The Ridge Family and the Decimation of a People,* University of Oklahoma Press, Norman, [2nd edition, revised] 1986). On Nancy Ward, see Tucker, Norma, "Nancy Ward: Gighau of the Cherokees," *Georgia Historical Quarterly,* No. 53, June 1969, pp. 192-200.
65. On the forced relocation, see Pirtle, Caleb III, *The Trail of Broken Promises: Removal of the Five Civilized Tribes to Oklahoma,* Eakin Press, Austin, TX, 1987.
66. Cherokee demographer Russell Thornton estimates that about 10,000 Cherokees—approximately half the nation's population—perished as a result of the Trail of Tears. See Thornton, Russell, *The Cherokees: A Population History,* University of Nebraska Press, Lincoln, 1990, pp. 73-7.
67. Starr, Emmet McDonald, *Starr's History of the Cherokee Indians,* Indian Heritage Association, Fayetteville, AK, 1922; reprinted 1967, p. 113.
68. Wardell, Morris L., *A Political History of the Cherokee Nation, 1838-1907,* University of Oklahoma Press, Norman, 1938; reprinted 1977, p. 17.
69. See Parins, James W., *John Rollin Ridge: His Life and Works,* University of Nebraska Press, Lincoln, 1991.
70. See Franks, Kenny A., *Stand Watie and the Agony of the Cherokee Nation,* Memphis State University Press, Memphis, TN, 1979.
71. The author has been through hundreds of the relevant documents—all of them engineered in Washington, D.C.—without ever coming across a single reference to federal negotiators dealing with a native woman responsibly. Instead, they appear to have been quite uniformly barred from meetings and other proceedings, these being "men's work" in the Euroamerican view. Early reservation records are replete with the same attitude.

72. Medicine, Bea, "The Interaction of Culture and Sex Roles in Schools," in U.S. Department of Education, Office of Educational Research and Development, National Institute of Education, *Conference on Educational and Occupational Needs of American Indian Women,* October 1976, U.S. Government Printing Office, Washington, D.C., 1980, p. 149.

73. For an excellent first-hand recounting of the process, see Lindsey, Lilah Denton, "Memories of the Indian Territory Mission Field," *Chronicles of Oklahoma,* No. 36, Summer 1958, pp. 181-98.

74. The extent to which Indians were provided just enough "education" to disorient them in their traditional ways, and condition them to accept subordination to Euroamerica, is revealed in the federal government's own data from the third quarter of the 20th century. In an official study, it was shown that—despite a century of governmentally imposed "schooling"—Native Americans still exhibited the lowest level of educational attainment of any U.S. population group. See U.S. Department of Health, Education and Welfare, *A Statistical Portrait of the American Indian,* U.S. Government Printing Office, Washington, D.C., 1976.

75. The term "broker class" comes from Acuña, Rodolfo, *Occupied America: A History of Chicanos,* Harper and Row Publishers, New York, (3rd edition) 1988.

76. Quoted in Debo, Angie, *A History of the Indians of the United States,* University of Oklahoma Press, Norman, 1970, p. 238.

77. Dunbar Ortiz, Roxanne, "Land and Nationhood: The American Indian Struggle for Self-Determination and Survival," *Socialist Review,* Nos. 63-64, May-August 1982, p. 107.

78. A good survey of the extent of indigenous wealth may be found in Weatherford, Jack, *Indian Givers: How the Indians of the Americas Transformed the World,* Crown Publishers, New York, 1989.

79. For a detailed examination of the surge in corporate activity in the West which accompanied termination and relocation in the 1950s, and which has continued thereafter, see Wiley, Peter, and Robert Gottlieb, *Empires in the Sun: The Rise of the American West,* G.P. Putnam's Sons, Publishers, New York, 1982.

80. A useful reading on the effects of relocation upon native women is Hanson, Wynne, "The Urban Indian Woman and Her Family," *Social Casework: The Journal of Contemporary Social Work,* October 1980, pp. 476-83.

81. These data come from a table provided in Amott, Teresa L., and Julie A. Matthaei, *Race, Gender and Work: A Multicultural Economic History of United States,* South End Press, Boston, 1991, p. 48.

82. U.S. Bureau of the Census, *1970 Census of the Population, Vol. I: Characteristics, of the Population, Part I, United States Summary,* U.S. Government Printing Office, Washington, D.C., 1971, Section I, Table 90, p. 390.

83. *Conference on the Educational and Occupational Needs of American Indian Women,* op. cit., p. 304.

84. Amott and Matthaei, op. cit., pp. 58-9.

85. Ibid., pp. 57, 59-60.

86. See *A Statistical Portrait of the American Indian,* op. cit. A good reading to accompany these data is Hart, LaDonna, "Enlarging the American Dream: American Indian Women," *American Education,* Vol. 13, No. 4, 1977.

87. Silman, op. cit., p. 11.

88. Research Branch, P.R.E., *Indian and Inuit Affairs Program: A Demographic Profile of Registered Indian Women,* Ottawa, Canada, October 1979, p. 31.

89. U.S. Department of Health and Human Services, *Chart Series Book,* Public Health Service, Washington, D.C., 1988 (HE20.9409.988). For perspectives on how these data apply to native women specifically, see Wood, Rosemary, "Health Problems Facing American Indian Women," in *Conference on Educational and Occupational Needs of American Indian Women,* op. cit.

90. On the Pine Ridge Reservation in South Dakota, for example, a stretch of road—about one mile long—between the off-reservation hamlet of White Clay (Nebraska) and the village of Pine Ridge is marked by a billboard displaying a skull wearing a war bonnet and captioned with a warning not to drink and drive. Over the past twenty years, more than a hundred Indians have died on this tiny strip of asphalt, having gotten drunk in White Clay and then attempted to drive home.

91. See Asetoyer, Charon, "Fetal Alcohol Syndrome—'Chemical Genocide,'" in *Indigenous Women on the Move,* IWGIA Document 66, International Work Group on Indigenous Affairs, Copenhagen, 1990, pp. 87-92.

92. The worst case seems to have occurred on the Wind River Reservation in Wyoming, where

fourteen Shoshone and Arapaho youths between fourteen and eighteen years of age took their own lives in 1985.

93. Amott and Matthaei, op. cit., p. 59.

94. For an analysis of at least some of the causative factors in one major indigenous society, see Medicine, Bea, "The Dakota Family and the Stresses Thereon," *Pine Ridge Research Bulletin*, No. 9, 1969, pp. 1-20.

95. For a survey on current conditions in both the United States and Canada, see LaDuke, Winona, "Domestic Violence in a Native Community: The Ontario Native Women's Association Report and Response," *Indigenous Woman*, Vol. 1, No. 1, Spring 1991, pp. 38-41. For the most lucid articulation of why the colonized tend to turn such rage upon one another rather than upon the colonizers who generate it, see Fanon, Frantz, *The Wretched of the Earth*, Grove Press, New York, 1966.

96. A celebrated case is that of Rita Silk Nauni, a Lakota woman who killed her abusive husband, only to be arrested and brutalized by police in Oklahoma, tried, convicted of murder, and sentenced to life imprisonment. See Lee, Pelican, and Jane Wing, "Rita Silk Nauni vs. the State," *Off Our Backs*, No. 11, February 1981.

97. Gunn Allen, op. cit., p. 191. She is quoting from Old Dog Cross, Phyllis, "Sexual Abuse, a New Threat to Native American Women: An Overview," *Listening Post: A Periodical of the Mental Health Programs of the Indian Health Services*. Vol. 6, No. 2, April 1982, p. 18.

98. Gunn Allen, op. cit., p. 192.

99. Ibid., p. 202.

100. See Blackbear Walker, Tillie, "American Indian Children: Foster Care and Adoptions," in *Conference on the Educational and Occupational Needs of American Indian Women*, op. cit., pp. 185-210.

101. Marks-Jarvis, Gail, "The Fate of the Indian," *National Catholic Reporter*, May 27, 1977, p. 4. Another means undertaken to undermine women's familial role may be found in the 1978 Supreme Court ruling in *Santa Clara Pueblo v. Martinez* (436 U.S. 49), in which it was concluded that an all male tribal council had the prerogative of excluding the children of a woman who married a non-tribal member from membership in the tribe while including the children of men who married non-tribal members. While the action of the Santa Clara tribal council and the Supreme Court's ruling were consistent with a supposedly traditional Santa Clara system of patrilineage, both groups left unaddressed the fact that the father of the children in question is a member of the matrilineal society. Hence, the children were left with no recognition or rights as Indians at all. Further, there are strong indications that Santa Clara is a traditionally matrilineal rather than patrilineal culture (Hill, W. W., *An Ethnography of the Santa Clara Pueblo*, University of New Mexico Press, Albuquerque, 1982). Regardless of the correct interpretation of Santa Clara tradition, the outcome of this case obviously holds broad potential ramifications for all of Indian Country.

102. See Dillingham, Brint, "Indian Women and IHS Sterilization Practices," *American Indian Journal*, Vol. 3, No. 1, January 1977, pp. 27-8. During this same and earlier periods, similar involuntary sterilization programs were being performed on other women of color, as with Chicanas of the Los Angeles area (see Acuña, op. cit., p. 395). It is estimated that by 1966, one-third of the women of childbearing age on the U.S.-controlled island of Puerto Rico had been sterilized without their informed consent (see Ostalaza, Margarita, *Politica Sexual y Socialización Política de la Mujer Puertorriqueña la Consolidación del Bloque Histórico Colonial de Puerto Rico*, Ediciones Huracán, Río Piedras, Puerto Rico, 1989). On the mainland, the Puerto Rican women's organization MULANEH discovered that, by 1979, 44 percent of Puertorriqueñas in New Haven, Connecticut had been sterilized. In Hartford, Connecticut, the figure stood at 51 percent (see Committee for Abortion Rights and Against Sterilization Abuse," in *Women Under Attack: Abortion, Sterilization Abuse, and Reproductive Freedom*, CARASA, New York, 1979).

103. An extract of the WARN study may be found in Women of All Red Nations, *Native American Women*, International Indian Treaty Council, New York, 1975. A summary is also contained in WARN, *Women of All Red Nations*, We Will Remember Group, Porcupine, SD, 1978.

104. Cited in Larson, Janet, "And Then There Were None: IHS Sterilization Practice," *Christian Century*, No. 94, January 26, 1976. Also see Wagner, Bill, "Lo, the Poor and Sterilized Indian," *America*, No. 136, January 29, 1977.

105. Gunn Allen, op. cit., pp. 191, 193.

106. For the most comprehensive biography, see Whitney Canfield, Gae, *Sarah Winnemucca of the Northern Paiutes*, University of Oklahoma Press, Norman, 1983.

107. Winnemucca Hopkins, Sarah, *Life Among the Piutes: Their Wrongs and Claims*, privately printed, Boston, 1883; reprinted by Chalfant Press, Bishop, CA, 1969.

108. See Wilson, Raymond, *Ohiyesa: Charles Eastman, Santee Sioux*, University of Illinois Press, Urbana, 1983.

109. See particularly, Bonnin, Gertrude (Zitkala-sa), "Why I Am A Pagan," *Atlantic Monthly*, No. 90, 1902, pp. 801-3. Bonnin's major works were *Old Indian Legends* (Ginn and Co., Publishers, Boston, 1901; reprinted by the University of Nebraska Press, Lincoln, 1985) and *American Indian Stories* (Hayward Press, Washington, D.C., 1921; reprinted by the University of Nebraska Press, Lincoln, 1979). For biographical and critical analysis, see Stout, Mary, "Zitkala-sa: The Literature of Politics," in Bo Schöler, ed., *Coyote Was Here: Essays on Contemporary Native American Literary and Political Mobilization*, SEKLOS, University of Aarhus, Aarhus, Denmark, 1984, pp. 70-8.

110. Ella Cara Deloria's most important book in terms of political content was probably *Speaking of Indians*, Friendship Press, New York, 1944; reprinted by Dakota Press, Vermillion, SD, 1979. For biographical and critical analysis, see Medicine, Bea, "Ella C. Deloria: The Emic Voice," *Melus*, Vol. 7, No. 4, Winter 1980, pp. 23-30.

111. Interesting insights into the position of women within the American Indian literary movement of the 1970s and '80s may be found in Swann, Brian, and Arnold Krupat, eds., *Recovering the World: Essays on Native American Literature*, University of California Press, Berkeley, 1987. For a broad sample of the writing involved, see Gunn Allen, Paula, *Spider Woman's Granddaughters: Traditional Tales and Contemporary Writing by American Indian Women*, Beacon Press, Boston, 1989.

112. See, for example, Erdrich, Louise, *Love Medicine* (Holt, Rinehart and Winston Publisher, New York, 1984) and *Tracks* (Holt, Rinehart and Winston Publishers, New York, 1989); Chrystos, *Not Vanishing* (Press Gang Publishers, Vancouver, B.C., 1988) and *Dream On* (Press Gang Publishers, Vancouver, B.C., 1991).

113. Lee, Bobbi, *Bobbi Lee: Indian Rebel*, LSM Information Center, Richmond, B.C., Canada, 1975, p. 89.

114. Ibid., pp. 91-2.

115. Conversation with Dennis J. Banks, March 1988 (notes on file).

116. Probably the best account to date of rank-and-file female participation in AIM may be found in Crow Dog, Mary, with Richard Erdoes, *Lakota Woman*, Grove, Weidenfeld Publishers, New York, 1990.

117. See *Voices From Wounded Knee*, op. cit.

118. On AIM's educational efforts, see Braudy, Susan, "We Will Remember Survival School: The Women and Children of the American Indian Movement," *Ms. Magazine*, No. 5, July 1976, pp. 94-120.

119. On the gender disparity in targeting, and the "Leadership Trials" themselves, see *Agents of Repression*, South End Press, Boston, 1988. The maximal jeopardy mentioned was faced by Russell Means, who walked out of Wounded Knee charged with forty-seven felonies and three misdemeanors.

120. On the three women mentioned, see ibid. Traditional Oglala women who were AIM supporters were also sometimes targeted for politically motivated prosecution. See Giese, Paula, "Free Sarah Bad Heart Bull," *North Country Anvil*, No. 13, October-November 1974, pp. 64-71.

121. The women and children were Priscilla White Plume (7/14/73), Lorinda Red Paint (2/27/74), Roxeine Roark (4/19/74), Delphine Crow Dog (11/9/74), Elaine Wagner (11/30/74), Yvette Lorraine Lone Hill (12/28/74), Edith Eagle Hawk and her two children (3/21/75), Jeanette Bissonette (3/27/75), Hilda R. Good Buffalo (4/4/75), Jancita Eagle Deer (4/4/75), Leah Spotted Eagle (6/15/75), Olivia Binias (10/26/75), Janice Black Bear (10/26/75), Michelle Tobacco (10/27/75), Lydia Cut Grass (1/5/76), Lena R. Slow Bear (2/6/76), Anna Mae Pictou Aquash (approximately 2/14/76), Betty Jo Dubray (4/28/76), Julia Pretty Hips (5/9/76), Betty Means (7/3/76), and Sandra Wounded Foot (7/19/76). For a complete list of AIM casualties on Pine Ridge during this period, see *The COINTELPRO Papers*, op. cit., pp. 393-4.

122. Quoted in Matthiessen, Peter, *In the Spirit of Crazy Horse*, op. cit., p. 417.

123. For additional information on this period, see LaDuke, Winona, "In Honor of Women Warriors," *Off Our Backs*, No. 11, February 1981.

124. McCloud, Janet, "Open Letter," *Oyate Wicaho,* January 1981.
125. Statement at Manderson, SD, November 1978 (tape on file).
126. See Thorpe, Dagmar, "Native Political Organizing in Nevada: A Woman's Perspective," *Native Self-Sufficiency,* No. 6, 1981.
127. *The Sacred Hoop,* op. cit., p. 31. It should be noted that the federal government currently recognizes the formal existence of 482 "tribes," but not all have reservation land bases.
128. This is referred to as the "Status Question" in Canada. See Jamiesson, Kathleen, *Indian Women and the Law in Canada: Citizens Minus,* Advisory Council on the Status of Women/Indian Rights for Indian Women, Ottawa, 1978.
129. Ibid.
130. Silman, op. cit., p. 176.
131. Ibid. Aside from Sandra Lovelace Sappier, other members of the Action Group are Glenna Perley, Caroline Ennis, Lilly Harris, Ida Paul, Eva Saulis, Juanita Perley, Shirley Bear, Karen Perley, Mavis Goerers, Joyce Sappier, Bet-te Paul, and Cheryl Bear.
132. For a sample of Sharon Venne's work in this regard, see her "Treaty and Constitution in Canada: A View from Treaty Six," in Ward Churchill, ed., *Critical Issues in Native North America,* IWGIA Document 62, International Work Group on Indigenous Affairs, Copenhagen, 1989, pp. 96-115.
133. On Norma Kassi, see Wright, Ismaelilllo, and Robin Wright, eds., *Native Peoples in Struggle: Cases from the Fourth Russell Tribunal and Other International Forums,* Anthropology Resource Center and ERIN Publications, Bombay, NY, 1982.
134. See, for example, Green, Rayna, "Diary of a Native American Feminist," *Ms. Magazine,* No. 10, July 1982. Also see Hill Witt, Shirley, "Native Women Today: Sexism and the Indian Woman," *Civil Rights Digest,* No. 6, Spring 1974, pp. 29-35; and Wauneka, Annie D., "The Dilemma for Indian Women," *Wassaja,* No. 4, September 1976.
135. OHOYO was established on the basis of a federal grant under the Women's Educational Equity Act (WEEA) in 1974. It was to create "an Indian brand of feminism," according to the director of the WEEA, a non-Indian woman. There was always a serious tension between its Washington, D.C.-based "leadership," with its preoccupation with gender issues, and the priorities of the grassroots membership, which sought to focus on matters such as land and treaty rights. The national office of OHOYO was strongly criticized by WARN in 1981 for "dividing the Indian community, and diverting attention away from the real struggles of Indian people." The organization was defunded and dissolved in 1985.
136. See "Who Is Your Mother? Red Roots of White Feminism," in *The Sacred Hoop,* op. cit., pp. 209-21.
137. Ibid., p. 224.
138. Lorelei Means talk, op. cit.
139. Janet McCloud talk, op. cit.
140. Letter to Ward Churchill, October 1985 (copy provided to author).
141. Smith, Andrea, "The New Age Movement and Native Spirituality," *Indigenous Woman,* Vol. 1, No. 1, Spring 1991, pp. 18-19.
142. One of the more glaring example of this phenomenon within the gay male community has been Walter Williams' book, *The Spirit and the Flesh: Sexual Diversity in American Indian Culture,* Beacon Press, Boston, 1986.
143. "Berdache" is an utterly inappropriate term by which to describe American Indian homosexuality insofar as it refers to the practice of certain sectors of the Arab male population of keeping slave boys for sexual purposes.
144. *The Sacred Hoop,* op. cit., p. 256.
145. Ibid.
146. Talk given during International Women's Week, University of Colorado at Boulder, April 1991 (tape on file).
147. Conversation with Vivian Locust (Oglala Lakota), June 1990 (notes on file).
148. Bomberry, Dan, ed., "Sage Advice From a Long Time Activist: Janet McCloud," *Native Self-Sufficiency,* No. 6, 1981.
149. See Waterman Wittstock, Laura, "Native American Women in the Feminist Milieu," in John Maestas, ed., *Contemporary Native American Address,* Brigham Young University Press, Salt Lake City, 1976.
150. Hungry Wolf, Beverly, *The Ways of My Grandmothers,* William Morrow Publishers, New York, 1980.

151. See Kidwell, Clara Sue, "American Indian Women: Problems of Communicating a Cultural/Sexual Identity," *The Creative Woman*, Vol. 2, No. 3, 1979, pp. 33-8.
152. See, for example, Jamieson, Kathleen, "Sisters Under the Skin: An Exploration of the Implications of Feminist Materialist Perspective Research," *Canadian Ethnic Studies*, Vol. 13, No. 1, 1981, pp. 130-43.
153. Joseph, Gloria I., and Jill Lewis, *Common Differences: Conflicts in Black and White Feminist Perspectives*, South End Press, Boston, 1981, pp. 4-6.
154. hooks, bell, *Feminist Theory: From Margin to Center*, South End Press, Boston, 1984, pp. 4-6.
155. hooks, bell, *Ain't I A Woman: Black Women and Feminism*, South End Press, Boston, 1981, p. 190.
156. hooks, bell, *Talking Back: Thinking Feminist, Thinking Black*, South End Press, Boston, 1989, p. 149.
157. Ibid., pp. 150-1.
158. For a sample of these perspectives, see Moraga, Cherríe, and Gloria Anzadúa, eds., *This Bridge Called My Back: Writings by Radical Women of Color*, Kitchen Table Press, New York, 1983.

Chapter XII

Patriots and Pawns
State Use of American Indians in the Military and the Process of Nativization in the United States

Tom Holm

> I went to Vietnam, was wounded twice and won the Silver Star, not because I
> have any particular loyalty to the United States, but because I have loyalty to
> my own people, my own tradition. We are pledged by a treaty to provide
> military assistance to the U.S. in times of war. I know that the U.S. has broken
> its part of the bargain with us, but we are more honorable than that. If we
> respond in kind, we are no better than they are. The point is, we are better than
> they; we honor our commitments, always have and always will. Even the ones
> which are inconvenient or unpleasant. So, it was my obligation to do what I
> did, even though I didn't really want to.
>
> American Indian Special Forces Veteran, 1985

Since 1917 American Indians, mainly males, have served in the United States
military in numbers far exceeding their proportion of the population. In World
War I approximately 10,000 Indians served in the armed forces and during World
War II over 25,000 Indians, not counting those in the officer corps, saw duty.[1] A
large percentage of those who served in World War II joined others freshly recruited
for service in Korea. It has been estimated that over 42,000 Indian military personnel
were stationed in Southeast Asia during the Vietnam War. According to Veterans'
Administration and census figures there are around 160,000 living veterans who
are American Indians.[2] These figures indicate that fully 10 percent of all living
Native Americans in the United States are military veterans. Compared to the
general population, nearly three times as many Indians have served in the armed
forces as non-Indians during the 20th century.

The most obvious reasons underlying this very high incidence of military
service is that Indians have been recruited heavily, especially and rigidly con-

scripted, or have volunteered in greater proportion than their non-Indian peers. Historically, the Bureau of Indian Affairs (BIA) has aided both recruitment and conscription. The Indian schools and reservation agencies served as recruitment stations and draft boards during both world wars. Several Indian veterans, as a matter of fact, recall being directly recruited for duty by their boarding school teachers.[3] Additionally, and unlike the situation experienced by non-Indians, the agencies and local draft boards have been in a position to compare the tribal rolls against draft registrations, making it highly unlikely that eligible Indian males would be overlooked for conscription.[4]

American Indian volunteerism, in any case, appears to have been extremely high over the past several generations. During World War I, the Onondaga and several other traditional native governments declared war on Germany independently of the United States, and viewed service in the military as part of their own treaty obligations to the United States. A number of native leaders of the period made attempts to raise all-volunteer Indian regiments for service in France.[5] During World War II several national magazines reported that Indians were showing up at the agencies, rifles in hand, ready to fight. Although certainly used as propaganda by the War Department, these stories were based on the fact that the numbers of Indian volunteers for military service more than doubled in the first six months of the war.[6] In our study of 170 Indian veterans of the Vietnam War, Harold Barse, Steve Silver, Robin LaDue, and I found that over 80 percent volunteered for duty, many of them in "elite" or particularly hazardous units.

Ethnic Soldiers and State Elites

Before turning to American Indian motives for joining the military service, it would be beneficial to examine why the United States has recruited or conscripted Indians in such high proportional numbers. In general, militaries not only protect the nation from foreign invasion, but promote the causes of and provide security for the hierarchical apparatuses of the state. In plural societies or imperial systems, state elites, both in uniform and out, have to judge which national or ethnic groups can serve in the military without turning the guns around and posing a threat to the state. Elites have to look at the political as well as the combat reliability of the groups in question.[7] Ideally, they want troops who are both loyal to the state and have special propensities toward soldiering.[8] Even in modern militaries, ethnicity or nationality cannot be ignored. In the same light, modern militaries do not seek to ensure a proportional balance of ethnic group members in the armed forces. Rather, they utilize interethnic relationships to the state's advantage. In this way, modern state militaries resemble older imperial military systems.[9] Modern militaries, however, tend not to maintain separate ethnic or national military units as did the old empires. Great Britain is one of the few states left on earth that still maintains distinct national or ethnic regiments, but the Scottish Black Watch and other Highlands units, as well as the Gurkha Rifles, are at this point probably maintained more because of tradition than for the sake of capitalizing militarily or politically on interethnic or national rivalries.[10]

Recruiting ethnic minorities for military service can become a double-edged sword. Although it saves the elite from having to expend its own sons in a conflict, there is always the risk that minority troops will turn on the state. The classic example is probably that of the 1857 "India Mutiny" against the British Empire, but there are many other noteworthy instances in which this has happened.[11] No state can afford to have a substantial portion of its own trained and equipped military force turn on it. The employment of ethnic troops also tends to put the elite under a moral obligation to a minority group which has suffered for it on the battlefield, at least in theory. In some cases the state recognizes its obligation, in others it does not.[12] Most militaries now incorporate members of various ethnic groups into "mainstream" units, but use them in logistics and other noncombat roles if their loyalty is questionable. Members of ethnic groups of doubtful political reliability are left relatively unarmed within their support roles and are either dispersed or their numbers are limited to manageable levels.[13]

A group's political reliability, from the standpoint of state elites, should be relatively easy to determine. A group is usually viewed as reliable if its members largely possess essentially the same values as those of the state hierarchy. The group is then "allowed" to demonstrate its loyalty to the "legitimate authority" of the central government. It does so because its members stand, at least ostensibly, to benefit from and participate in the dominant politico-economic system as a result of services rendered on the battlefield. The subordinated group's values, in other words, have been made to match the ideological underpinnings of the state which has colonized it. Groups striving for legitimacy as members of a particular body politic, even if they have no traditional values or customs in common with state elites, can also become reliable. They can be undergoing change or at least making the attempt to alter their value systems or, for some, demonstrating loyalty to gain greater benefits from the state. A perfect illustration of this may be found in volunteers from various "Nordic peoples"—such as the Belgians, Dutch, Danes, and Norwegians—and others, like the French, who signed up for service in Germany's Waffen SS during World War II. [14]

Alternatively, a group dependent on the state for even a marginal economic existence or some degree of social and cultural autonomy might also be considered safe because it is understood by all concerned that demonstrations of disloyalty could do harm to the group as a whole. Members of subordinated ethnicities may also join the militaries of their colonizers piecemeal, often because they have assigned martial endeavor a positive meaning within their own cultural/social/philosophical tradition and perceive no other means of pursuing it. The Highland Scots and, perhaps to a lesser extent, the Welsh afford instructive examples on both counts, as do the Gurkhas.[15]

Occasionally ethnic soldiers are used even though the group or nation to which they belong is not seeking legitimacy and cannot therefore be considered truly reliable. In certain instances, the group as a whole may be in open resistance to some or even all impositions posed by the central government. Such a group may nonetheless be considered "safe" from a military point of view because it lacks the population size or political cohesion to constitute a viable threat in its own right. The history of British imperialism is replete with relevant examples.[16] More recently, the use by the United States of the H'Mong in Laos, and the so-called Montagnards of South Vietnam (particularly the Rhadé, Jarai and Bahnar peoples), against North Vietnam comes to mind.[17] Indeed, the phenomenon has by this point become so widespread that it forms a cornerstone of the "low-intensity warfare" strategy currently taught at the U.S. Army's War College.[18]

Combat reliability is a much more complex attribute to analyze. No one can know beforehand how an individual will act in combat. Courage or the ability to take orders simply are not measurable on a group basis. On the one hand, Germany learned a bitter lesson concerning the lack of motivation among such essentially coerced "ethnic allies" as Bulgaria and Romania on the Eastern Front during the early 1940s.[19] On the other, history reveals no shortage of instances in which supposedly "cowardly" peoples have stood and fought ferociously at a given moment, while those customarily seen as being endowed with a true "warrior spirit" have broken and run.[20] For the most part, state elites seem to judge a group's propensity for soldiering according to stereotypes. The mythology built around any particular people means at least as much as the group's actual military track record.[21]

One feature of warfare, or perhaps of the psychology of conquerors, is that the victors often endow their enemies with unusual military strengths. The enemy has to be crafty, vigorous, determined, and tenacious, as well as brave and brutal. If the enemy were otherwise, the "valiant actions" of the victorious army would be rendered meaningless. In a colonial context, economics might dictate why a given nation embarks on conquest, but colonizers normally justify their actions in terms of bringing progress and civilization to a "savage" indigenous population.[22] A militarily conquered group is given a bit more status. Savage but courageous natives are somehow more "worthy" of being "civilized." The mythic "martial race" has been invented and reinvented throughout history.[23] It certainly follows that militaries would seek aid from a martial race, especially if the group had become loyal to the state. There is, of course, a vast amount of historical evidence to show that state elites regularly enlist the help of conquered groups imbued with such characteristics. The Romans, for instance, utilized German and French auxiliaries; Great Britain maintained Scottish, Gurkha, and Sikh units; even New Zealand formed an all-Maori combat battalion during World War II.[24]

Indians in U.S. Military History

The United States has a long history of racism and Indian-hating. The stereotypical Indian is really an invention of Europeans and their descendents in the New World. In conventional Euroamerican mythology, the "Savage Indian" brutalized and mutilated peaceful colonists, raped their women, kidnapped their children, and pillaged their towns. The Indian was and is seen as a primitive barrier to progress and civilization, an evil and remorseless enemy to be vanquished through any means and at all costs. Ironically, the Indian was and is simultaneously perceived as a symbol of the pristine wilderness, a child-like guardian of nature, at times a brave and noble foe.[25] Eventually, whites would come to look upon at least some Indian leaders as they did Robert E. Lee, as valiant leaders of lost crusades.[26]

The idea of Indians as members of a "martial race," although not among the initial perceptions of native people articulated by European colonists, is older than the United States itself. For example, Colonel James Smith, who claimed to have been the captive of an unnamed Indian people between 1755 and 1759, and who later served in the Revolutionary Army against the British, wrote in 1799 a short but very appreciative treatise on American Indian modes of warfare. Smith's account was accurate enough and his observations bolstered the idea that Indians were uniquely adept warriors. As a product of "black powder" warfare, in which armies armed with muskets marched to within forty yards of an enemy in order to pour relatively inaccurate lead balls into the foe's closely packed ranks, Smith was especially interested in the psychology of courage. In Smith's view, American Indians were courageous beyond reason:

> If they are surrounded they will fight while there is a man of them alive, rather than surrender. When Colonel John Armstrong surrounded the Cattanyan town, on the Allegheny river, Captain Jacobs, a Delaware chief, with some warriors, took possession of a house, defended themselves for some time, and killed a number of our men. As Jacobs could speak English, our people called on him to surrender. He said, that he and his men were warriors, and they would all fight while life remained. He was again told that they should be well used if they would only surrender; and if not, the house should be burned down over their heads. Jacobs replied, he could eat fire, and when the house was in a flame, he, and they that were with him, came out in a fighting position, and were all killed. As they are a sharp, active kind of people, and war is their principal study, in this they have arrived at considerable perfection.[27]

Smith reviewed several incidents like Chief Jacob's stand, told of how the British armies had suffered tactically at the hands of Indian warriors during the French and Indian Wars and anticipated some of the ideas of Carl von Clauswitz, whose book, *On War,* first published in 1832, became the most widely taught theoretical study of warfare.[28] According to Smith, Indians "endeavor to annoy their enemy, and save their own men" and "never bring on an attack without considerable advantage." Indian tactics, in other words, employed the Prussian general's concepts of mobility and economy of force and mass (i.e., the concentration of force at the critical time and place). Smith's praise of individual Indian warriors and the tactics they used was unmitigated:

> The business of the private warriors is to be under command, or punctually to obey orders; to learn to march abreast in scattered order, so as to be in readiness to surround the enemy, or to prevent being surrounded; to be good marksmen, and active in the use of arms; to practise running; to learn to endure hunger or hardship with patience and fortitude; to tell the truth at all times to their officers, but more especially when sent out to spy the enemy.[29]

During the American Revolution, utilization of these methods—actually precursors of what has come to be taught as "irregular" or "guerrilla" warfare at the U.S. Army War College—by indigenous nations allied with the British (especially the Mohawks) greatly complicated the rebels' efforts to gain their independence.[30] On the other hand, Smith indicated that adoption of these same tactics by rebel units like Ethan Allen's "Green Mountain Boys" and by commanders such as Francis "The Swamp Fox" Marion had helped the Americans attain final victory:

> May we not conclude, that the progress we had made in their [the Indians'] art of war, contributed considerably towards our success, in various respects, when contending with Great Britain for liberty?[31]

During the period leading up to and following the War of 1812, formative U.S. international and military policies were shaped to a considerable extent by the threats posed, by Tecumseh's native alliance in the Ohio River Valley, and by the Creek Confederacy's "Redstick War" further south, in the Georgia-Alabama-Tennessee area. Certainly, General William Henry Harrison's victories over Tecumseh, first at the Battle of Tippecanoe in 1812 and then at the Thames River ("Fallen Timbers") on September 10, 1813, did much to propel him into the presidency.[32] It is equally fair to say that, in some respects, Andrew Jackson owed the reputation that carried him into the White House more to the success of his 1814 campaign against the Redsticks than to his 1813 defeat of the British at New Orleans.[33]

Since that time, whites have added mystical and almost superhuman qualities to their imagery of Indian warriors. In combining the idea of Indians as a martial race with the notion of Indians as the ultimate practitioners of "woodcraft" outlined in the works of James Fenimore Cooper and other early 19th-century novelists, whites were infected with the "Indian scout syndrome."[34] Indians, in the dominant mythology, could detect the presence of an enemy from a bent blade of grass or could conceal themselves from their opponents in an open field. Whites apparently believed that these mystical traits, to the extent they existed at all, were genetically inherited rather than learned.[35] Because of such ideas, native peoples were eagerly recruited by both the Union and the Confederacy, each with some degree of success, during the Civil War. For the North, the Creeks—by that point long-since forcibly relocated to the "Permanent Indian Territory" of Oklahoma—formed an independent "Home Guards" regiment of about 3,350 that acquitted itself well during the course of Grant's campaign in the West. For the South, Cherokee leaders John Ross and Stand Watie formed a regiment of their own, shortly followed by a mixed Choctaw/Chickasaw regiment, both of which fought in battles such as Wilson's Creek and Bird Creek (1861), Pea Ridge (1862), and Honey Springs (1864).[36]

The performance of Indian regiments fighting more or less conventionally during the Civil War—real guerrilla tactics were practiced exclusively by Euroamerican units such as Confederate General J.E.B. Stuart's cavalry and the notorious Quantrill's Raiders of the Kansas frontier—should have served finally to belie the Cooperesque mythos concerning Native America's unique fighting characteristics. This was not the case, however, and the myth—along with more practical motivations like securing the services of individuals who truly knew the terrain on which the Army would fight, and the practices of the foes it would face—prompted the military to continue its devotion to retaining native scouts for deployment in its various "Indian Wars." By the period of the wars in the Great Plains and Sonora Desert regions during the second half of the 19th century, permanent scout or "auxiliary" companies were integral to all U.S. frontier regiments.[37]

During World War I, Indians were for the first time integrated directly into white regiments. This, however, did not mean they were necessarily treated like other soldiers. The *Indian's Friend*, the newsletter of a mostly non-Indian organization dubbed "Friends of the Indian" and dedicated to Indian assimilation, proudly reported that "Indians in the regiments are being used for scouting and patrol duty because of the *natural instinct* which fits them for this kind of work (emphasis added)."[38] Almost immediately after America's entrance into World War II, the media began to exploit stereotypical imagery built around the scout syndrome for propaganda purposes. Stanley Vestal, a Euroamerican ethnologist of high repute, wrote that the Indian was "a realistic soldier" who "never gave quarter or expected it."[39] Harold Ickes, the Secretary of the Interior, stated in an article in a national magazine that "the Indian" was "uniquely valuable" to America's war effort because:

> [He has] endurance, rhythm, a feeling for timing, co-ordination, sense percep-
> tion, an uncanny ability to get over any sort of terrain at night, and better than
> all else, an enthusiasm for fighting. He takes a rough job and makes a game of
> it. Rigors of combat hold no terrors for him; severe discipline and hard duties
> do not deter him.[40]

The media attention given to the Indian war effort served as perhaps some of the most useful U.S. propaganda during World War II. Popular magazines like the *Saturday Evening Post, Collier's, New Republic,* and *Reader's Digest* reported that Indians were fully committed to ridding the world of fascism. The motion picture industry, that most powerful of image-making media, began subtly to change its depiction of American Indians. Hollywood horse operas tended to glorify the American expansionist past. Screen Indians were normally portrayed as barriers to progress, raping and pillaging without conscience or higher civilized values, but during World War II westerns began to portray, more and more, the "Indian companion" character who, just as he had done in the war, aided whites in the crusade against injustice and tyranny.[41] War movies exploited this new image of Indians even further.

Although the services of a special Navajos-only Marine unit of "Code-Talkers" in the Pacific Theater—they communicated battlefield messages by radio in a highly colloquial form of Navajo, a "code" the Japanese were never able to break—were probably Native America's most singular contribution to World War II, Hollywood kept right on with its recasting of Indian scouts in modern garb.[42] Soon, the steely-eyed, stoic Indian member of the All-American platoon became an American cinematic cliché.[43] Such imagery of the Indian warrior seems rooted in the American psyche in a manner which is transideological and timeless as well. During the

Vietnam War, even Euroamerican historian Wilbur Jacobs, an individual who has done much to debunk other aspects of the mythology surrounding native people, succumbed to the stereotype. Indians were conquered by Europeans, he observed:

> ...not because they were beaten by better warriors or strategists, but because they could not fight off the overwhelming number of the enemy and his two horned devil: disease and liquor. Even today we imitate him. There is no higher calling in the military service than that of the ["Indian-style"] commando-ranger who gallantly fights our battles the world over.[44]

The scout syndrome was very evident among commanders in the field during the Korean and Vietnam wars. Indian soldiers and marines were often assigned perilous duties according to the stereotypes of their immediate superiors. Jack Miles, a Sac and Fox-Creek infantry veteran of the Korean War, once related to the author that:

> In Korea, my platoon commander *always* sent me out on our reconnaissance patrols. He called me "Chief" like every other Indian, and probably thought that I could see and hear better than the white guys. Maybe he thought I could track down the enemy. I don't know for sure, but I guess he figured that Indians were warriors and hunters by nature.[45]

In our survey of American Indian veterans of the Vietnam War, one of the most common respondent complaints was that their commanders on the company and platoon levels habitually assigned them to walk point on patrols more frequently than non-Indians. Troops in Vietnam considered walking point dangerous because the point man acted as a scout and walked ahead of a unit's main body. Generally, the danger in walking point had to do with the topography or the flora in an area of operations. If a unit was moving through tall elephant grass, for example, the point man could literally walk into a concealed enemy position. He would also be in the position most likely to trip mines and booby traps. In ambush situations, the point man would often be allowed to pass by in order for the ambushers to attack a unit's middle in the hope of taking out the command structure of machine guns. The point would then be cut off from support, and could be killed at leisure.[46]

Infantrymen who took part in our survey frequently expressed the opinion that they were ordered to walk point for no other reason than because they were Indians. A Menominee from Wisconsin related that his platoon commander though that since Indians "grew up in the woods" they should know how to track and generally "feel" when something in the immediate area was disturbed or out of place. Apparently, the platoon commander thought that Indians were "racially endowed" with the ability to "read" their environments.[47] Another veteran, a Navajo from Arizona, concurred with the judgment that Indians had been stereotyped by their platoon commanders' scout syndrome and stated that it had made the war some-what more dangerous for him personally.

> I was stereotyped by the cowboy and Indian movies. Nicknamed "Chief" right away. Non-Indians claimed Indians could see through trees and hear the unhearable. Bullshit, they believed Indians could walk on water.[48]

In several instances, disproportionately high in relation to the size of our sample, Indians who participated in the survey indicated the situation was such in Vietnam that they ended up committed exclusively, not just to walking point, but to scouting activities *per se*. Usually, this came through their volunteering (or "being volunteered") for service in Long Range Reconnaissance Patrol (LRRP; pronounced "lurp") platoons formed within each infantry battalion deployed in Southeast Asia. This was especially hazardous duty involving the sending of very small teams (usually six men) into remote locales thought—and in many cases known—to be occupied by significant numbers of enemy soldiers. The LRRP team would explore its assigned area and report back what it found by radio. In the event it was discovered by the enemy during its scouting mission, the team would frequently be wiped out.[49] One Indian veteran of the LRRPs, a Creek/Cherokee, explained his motivations in joining the program:

> They kept running me on point during the day, and putting me out on listening posts at night. The company I was with, 4th Division, you know, it was all draftees who didn't have a clue what to do if we got hit. So, I knew I was going to die the minute we made serious contact [with enemy forces]. I'd be out there all by myself, and there'd be nobody to back me up. So I volunteered to run LRRP missions. At least then I knew the people around me knew what they were doin'. Besides, in the LRRPs our objective was to avoid contact, not seek it out. It was scary business, but all things considered I figured my best shot at living through Vietnam was to be a LRRP. Crazy, ain't it?[50]

After 1968, the various LRRP units were consolidated as the 75th Ranger Group, a tacit admission by the Pentagon that an extraordinarily high percentage of Native American service personnel had been channeled into Ranger duty all along, even when they'd expressly avoided signing up and training for it.[51] Those who had actively sought out such an occupational profile all too frequently landed in the even more esoteric reconnaissance or "hunter-killer" units formed with the Special Operations Group created by the Military Assistance Command, Vietnam (MAC-V-SOG). This secret unit—it is still highly classified and euphemistically referred to as the "Studies and Observations Group"—consistently undertook suicidally high risk operations with casualty rates sometime exceeding 1000 percent per year.[52] So prevalent was Indian participation in these operations that it has been enshrined in the public consciousness in the character of "Billy" in the recent Arnold Schwartzenegger movie *Predator*.

Given the stereotypes and their proven high level of professionalism, both in combat and out (a very high proportion of Vietnam era Indian veterans are airborne [paratrooper] qualified, for example), it is easy to understand why U.S. military elites would want to utilize American Indian troops. But, from the standpoint of these same elites, Native Americans would not necessarily be politically reliable. After all, the United States made war for a century and a half on the indigenous nations of North America, dispossessed them of their lands, stripped away numerous native institutions, laid waste to many indigenous cultures, and left Indians as a whole among the poorest of North America's poor. A nazi propagandist asked the obvious question during World War II: "How could American Indians think of bearing arms for their exploiters?"[53] Conversely, the query would be how the United States could be so stupid as to allow them into its armed forces.

The answer lies, from the federal perspective, most directly in a matter of scale. Because of the tiny size of the native population relative to that of non-Indians in the United States, and because of the compartmentalization of the native population into hundreds of distinct and widely dispersed nationalities, U.S. elites have been more and more willing to view Indians—no matter what proportion of them are well trained and experienced militarily—as being a "safe" minority rather than a tangible threat to the Euroamerican status quo. In fact, there is considerable evidence suggesting that federal policymakers have seen an ever greater incorporation of native people into the U.S. military apparatus as a key mechanism through which the sorts of socialization by which an "assimilation of the Indian race" into the cultural complex of its colonizers might ultimately be accomplished.[54]

This trend has continued into the 1990s, as young Indian males—and, increasingly, young females as well—have been driven into the military by reason of reservation conditions fostered by a decade of "Reaganomics," by misdirected understandings of their own cultural traditions, or both. There are, of course, consequences to such circumstances. Although data are as yet unavailable concerning what proportion of the U.S. force sent into combat in the 1991 Gulf War was American Indian, or in what military specializations they served, indications are that their participation may be proportionately higher than that of any other racial or ethnic group, and higher than their own rate of involvement in Vietnam. All one need have done to acquire a sense of this was drive through any reservation in the country during the period when Operation Desert Storm was in progress and observe the sheer saturation of yellow ribbons—symbolizing the desire that militarily absent sons and daughters return safely—tied to trees, lamp posts, and virtually every other vertical object.

Traditional Indian "Militarism"

Much has been made by the dominant society of the fact that most indigenous cultures located north of the Río Grande have warrior traditions which predate contact with Europeans. In some cases, non-Indian anthropologists and "ethnohistorians" have gone so far as to formally describe selected native cultures as "Warrior Societies."[55] Such analyses have given rise to a general conception—held in both academic and popular non-Indian circles—that precontact Native North America was a bloodthirsty place, engaged mainly in a perpetual slaughter of one people by another.[56] Politically, such mythology has served colonial interests by allowing for the postulation that, had Europeans not come along to accomplish the job, American Indians would eventually have butchered each other off anyway. This "we're no worse than they were" syndrome is intended to "prove" that, at least in a relativistic sense, Euroamericans have done nothing for which they need now apologize or atone.

The fact is, however, that while traditional Native Americans (of both genders, as Jaimes and Halsey point out in Chapter Eleven) avidly pursued "war" as an honorable activity, it was of a form so radically different from that developed in Europe as to be of an entirely different genus. Not only were there no wars of annihilation fought in North America prior to the coming of Europeans—a matter lately recognized by Kirkpatrick Sale and other non-Indian historians—but the purpose of indigenous warfare seems to have been (with rare exceptions) something altogether different from killing. Honor accrued in cultures solely on the basis of exhibitions of personal bravery. The best-known example is the practice of "counting coup" developed among the various societies of the Great Plains. The object of this exercise was to get close enough to an armed opponent—an individual capable of inflicting great physical harm or even death—touch him with your hand or a stick specially designed for this purpose, and then get away.[57]

For this act, a warrior would be awarded an eagle feather, notched or decorated in certain ways to reflect the amount of risk entailed and consequent degree of honor. Obviously, a dead opponent offered no danger, and so no award at all was bestowed for killing. The more eagle feathers one garnered, the greater one's status.[58] In a way, the whole thing was rigged to keep enemies alive in order that the contest might continue perpetually. Virtually all native societies practiced some variation on this theme, with theft of horses assuming an increasingly greater importance in such status rituals, particularly in areas west of the Mississippi, after they were introduced to this continent by the Spanish somewhere around 1530.[59] As Sale has put it:

> [A]s to pre-Columbian warfare we know almost nothing, and what little we do know suggests that where wars took place, they were infrequent, short, and mild; in fact "war"...seems a misnomer for the kinds of engagements we imagine might have taken place, in which some act of bravery or retribution rather than death, say, or territory, would have been the object, and two "war parties" might skirmish without effect on either one and none at all on home villages. Early European settlers often made a mockery of Indian warfare...John Underhill wrote of the Pequots that their wars were "more for pastime than to conquer and subdue enemies," and Henry Spelman, who lived among the Powhatans, said that "they might fight seven yeares and not kill seven men"...Organized violence, in short, was not an attribute of traditional Indian societies, certainly not as compared with their European contemporaries, and on the basis of this imperfect record what is most remarkable about them is their apparent lack of conflict and discord.[60]

By way of analogy, traditional Indian warfare had much more in common with Euroamerican contact sports like football, boxing, and hockey than with wars fought in the European manner. This, of course, is not to say that nobody was ever killed or maimed in native warfare. They were—just as they are in modern contact sports—but the point of the exercise was *not* as a rule purposefully lethal. Still, there were times when someone would die in the encounters, often at the hands of an opponent desperate to avoid the humiliation of having coup counted upon him. There are also instances on record of peoples who determined that things had become cost-prohibitive and therefore suspended raiding and other warlike activities for a year or more after the death of even *one* of their young men under such circumstances.[61] Such deaths did frequently bring about a desire for vengeance on the part of the families and associates of victims, a matter which sometimes resulted in reciprocal killing. More often, it resulted in the taking of a captive—usually a young male, but females as well—from among the killer's people.[62]

To replace the loss experienced by the dead warrior's group, a process of naturalization, compulsory to be sure, was instituted through which those captured were made part of the capturing people. What the captives were not was "slaves." There is no evidence of the dehumanizing and commercialized chattel slavery developed by Europe anywhere in the Americas—including the much maligned Aztec and Inca empires—prior to the Spanish arrival. Indeed, it appears that the resident Tainos were truly bewildered by the whole notion of slavery when Columbus first introduced the *encomienda* system on the island of Española in 1493.[63] In the southeastern portion of what is now the United States, indigenous nations such as the Creeks and Seminoles made it a standing practice, until their forced removals during the 1830s, to take in and adopt as their own the steady stream of African slaves escaping from Euroamerican plantations.[64]

All of this changed, to be sure, upon arrival of the first Europeans. When the British began offering a bounty on the heads, and then, for convenience, the scalps of Indians, native people—believing such mutilation to have religious significance to the Europeans—responded in kind.[65] At first, it seems to have been generally felt that exhibition of these "trophies" might frighten Europeans into ceasing such practices against Indians. It didn't work. Instead, colonial propagandists, representing the very governments that had invented the practice, shrilled loudly about how horrified they were that any people could be so savage as to scalp and otherwise disfigure the dead.[66] When Indians took white captives to replace losses experienced at the hands of European soldiers and settlers, the propagandists escalated, churning out lurid tales of "fates worse than death" suffered by the "unfortunate victims."[67]

After a couple of massacres on the scale of that occurring at the Pequot village of Mystic in 1637, many of the indigenous nations of New England aligned themselves with the French in an effort to push the English (whom they considered homicidal maniacs) out of their territory.[68] The British, confronted by this alliance, responded by negotiating a military pact with the powerful Haudenosaunee (Iroquois) Confederacy. The resulting series of "French and Indian Wars" saw native peoples set at odds with one another in ways that had never before pertained. Placed in the position of fighting for survival for the first time, increasingly equipped with the lethal technology of their "allies," and faced with a serious erosion of their historic territories because of expanding European "settlement," Indians began to kill both the European interlopers and each other in ever increasing numbers.[69] Across the continent, the pattern was repeated.

Despite the steady imposition of European concepts and technologies of warfare, particularly during the 19th century, there is compelling evidence suggesting that native peoples were never able really to accept the concept of unrestrained killing. Indians, it seems, killed when—and to the extent—they felt they had to in order to accomplish limited objectives, invariably defensive.[70] The historical record is studded with instances when groups of warriors, in a position to complete the wholesale annihilation of an opposing Euroamerican force, broke off engagements as soon as the foe showed an inclination to retreat. A noteworthy example occurred on June 17, 1876, when allied Lakotas and Cheyennes defeated an army command under General George Crook, augmented by Crow and Shoshone auxiliaries, at the Rosebud Creek in southern Montana. When Crook began a general withdrawal on June 18, the "hostiles" simply let him go.[71] Their capacity to have done otherwise was amply demonstrated a few days later, on June 25, against Custer's troops in the nearby valley of the Little Big Horn.[72]

Serious dislocations in traditional indigenous territorial and economic relationships occurred as the result of rapid Euroamerican expansion, and various smaller native peoples increasingly aligned with the United States—in efforts to preserve themselves—against larger ones.[73] Modes of "intertribal" warfare became consequently more bitter.[74] Still, even an Anglocentric historian like Anthony McGinnis, who recently wrote an entire book attempting to prove the thesis that such fighting was "the primary cause of violence on the western frontier" (and that the U.S. role was benevolently focused upon getting the savages to stop "murdering" one another), is forced to admit that, even during the worst period of combat in the West, Indians were still clinging wherever possible to their "old ways" of non-lethal warfare. For instance, he recounts, in a chapter titled "The Climax of Warfare," a clash between Crows and Yanktonai Nakotas occurring in 1869 along Montana's Musselshell River:

> The Crows quickly crossed the water and charged the enemy, then the Sioux turned and charged the Crows. The fighting lasted all afternoon...[O]ne set of warriors would make a flashy attack, swooping down on their opponents, glorious in their paint and feathers and filling the air with arrows and bullets. When the enemy got sufficiently reorganized, the warriors whirled their mounts and attempted their own attack. The Indians wasted a lot of ammunition, but the only casualty was one unfortunate Sioux horse.[75]

Even at the very end of the period of conquest, raiding was focused mainly on the theft of horses rather than killing. McGinnis notes that the major effort on the northern plains for 1888 involved nine Yanktonais stealing thirty horses from the Crows, with casualties occurring on neither side. The most significant affair in 1889 concerned a small party of Bloods stealing as many as forty-five horses from the Crows. Again, there were no casualties. And, in the last recorded foray by a bona fide war party, conducted in June 1889, five Yanktonais from the Fort Peck Reservation attempted unsuccessfully to steal Crow horses.[76] After that, "[a]s late as 1892, the Court of Indian Offenses for the Blackfoot Agency tried the famous Piegan warrior White Quiver for the theft of four Crow horses. However, the court released him for lack of evidence."[77]

Attempts to Maintain Native Balance

It does not necessarily follow that because a group accepts a new technology, institution, or religion it also accepts a completely new system of values. American Indians have a long history of altering ("syncretizing") alien cultural impositions in ways which serve their own sense of cultural integrity and continuity.[78] This has been true of, among other things, the horse and steel-bladed knives, rifles and glass trade beads, iron pots and calico cloth.[79] The Cherokee Baptists, to name but one example, have adopted a Euroamerican religion, but have given it a distinctly Cherokee meaning. In a Cherokee Baptist church there are seven deacons/medicine men representing the seven clans, the Cherokee language is liturgical, baptism serves more as a confirmation right than as a ritual washing of sins, and emphasis is placed much more heavily upon community ceremony than on individual salvation.[80] For want of a better term, the process could be labeled "nativization."[81]

It can be said with a good deal of certainty that some native peoples in the United States have attempted to nativize service in the American armed forces as a way of adapting to a changed environment in ways that preserve their own traditions. For this reason, many indigenous nations have maintained into the present day certain of the forms, such as warrior societies, by which they historically accommodated and reconciled the disruptions caused by physical conflicts with other peoples. Among the Oklahoma Creeks, for example, the practice of dividing familial identifications along lines of "white" (peace) and "red" (war) clans still persists.[82] The Kiowas maintain their traditional Gourd and Black Leggings warrior societies, the Cheyennes their Crazy Dogs (or "Dog Soldiers," as they are more often known), the Lakotas their Tokalas and other societies, and the Navajos have means of their own.[83] Even the Pueblos, whose ancient traditions strongly oppose violence in any form, have specially selected war priests and warrior sodalities.[84]

Despite numerous complaints and government prohibitions against their performance throughout the 19th and early 20th centuries, many Indian cultures maintained a wide variety of ceremonies related to warfare. In 1919, assimilationist Commissioner of Indian Affairs Cato Sells expressed his irritation at the fact that dances and honoring ceremonies were being conducted among a number of native peoples for the Indian soldiers who had just returned from the trenches in France.[85] Honoring and purification ceremonies for Indian veterans followed World War II despite the widespread idea in the United States that Indian soldiers would refuse to take part in their "yesterday's culture."[86] The Lakotas held victory ceremonies; Kiowas took part in soldier dances; Cherokees were ritually cleansed of the taint of battle by medicine men; and Navajos went through complex "Enemy Way" ceremonies in order to restore them to a harmonious place in the Navajo world.[87]

At this point, it would be well to emphasize the significance of ceremonies to the maintenance of Indian identity and the individual's sense of peoplehood. Indigenous nations are holistic societies. That is to say religion, land, language, ceremony, and kinship structures are all part of an organic whole on which rests the continued well-being of the particular society. Ernest L. Schusky, an anthropologist, ably described the interrelationship of land, people, and religion in traditional societies in his preface to *Political Organization of Native North Americans:*

> The Sioux or Lakota…often spoke of the disappearance of their people. When I answered that census figures showed their population was increasing, they countered that parts of their reservations were continually being lost. They concluded there could be no more Indians when there was no more Indian land. Several older men told me that the original sacred Pipe given the Lakota in the Beginning was getting smaller. The Pipe shrank with the loss of land. When the land and Pipe disappeared, the Lakota would be gone…I have heard similar tales among the Iroquois, in the Southwest, and in Alaska when land was an issue. For many Native Americans, an Indian identity is intertwined with rights to [the] land.[88]

Like land, traditional ceremonies are inextricably linked with identity. To the Lakota the Pipe and its attending rituals are one and the same as religion. If central ceremonies are lost, then the power and thus the Lakota identity are equally in peril.[89] Variations on the same theme apply to every indigenous culture in North America.

The warrior societies have always maintained rigid distinctions between war and peace and seek to regulate the psychologies and behaviors of their members accordingly. They play important roles in specialized ceremonies designed to aid individuals as well as whole peoples in making the transition from peace to war and back again. Warriors were and are ritually prepared for war and offered protective medicine to ensure their safe return, often through ceremonies and use of symbologies unique to their specific groups. More importantly, many of these societies devised purification ceremonies in order to bring the individual warrior and the rest of the community back into a harmonious state upon completion of hostilities. The purpose is to purge returning warriors of the trauma of battle lest they bring back memories of conflict and seek to perpetuate patterns of behavior which would be unacceptable to the community in its ordinary functioning.

Examples of preserved and/or revived traditional war-related ceremonies are numerous and range from the relatively simple to the highly elaborate. For instance, a Navajo veteran who participated in our survey was given a "Blessing Way" ceremony prior to his overseas tour of duty. This ceremony, which lasts over a period of several days, is a highly formalized narrative of the Navajo creation legend and a curing ritual intended to make sure an individual is in harmony with his or her surroundings. It was utilized in the case of this particular veteran as protective medicine. Other veterans mentioned carrying protective charms given to them by elders and close relatives. Cleansing ceremonies are equally important among several native groups. The above-mentioned Navajo veteran was given an "Enemy Way" upon his arrival home from Vietnam. The Enemy Way is a four-day ritual in which the healer narrates the story of the Hero Twins who killed the monsters of the world in order to make it a safe place for human beings. As the story goes:

> The Twins were successful in their attempts to kill all the Monsters. However, in the process of destroying the Monsters the Twins abused their special powers

and weapons and disrupted the harmony in nature by killing some people. As a consequence, the Twins became ill and misfortunes set in upon them. Another Holy Being recognized that the Twins had put themselves out of harmony with nature by killing, and thus needed a special ceremony to restore them to harmony. Thus was born the first "Enemy Way."[90]

In effect, the ritual removes the stigma of death and the disharmony caused by war. Other Indian Vietnam veterans were greeted with special honoring dances, peyote ceremonies, and prayer meetings. Several veterans who took part in our survey and who no longer lived within their home communities were honored or purified by ceremony in one way or another. One Cherokee veteran living in Oklahoma City traveled at the insistence of his wife to visit a Cherokee doctor over 100 miles away. He had to be purified or he would not have been rightfully allowed on the Cherokee ceremonial grounds again. His "bloody hands" would have tainted other Cherokee ceremonies. A Menominee veteran in Wisconsin told of how he made the presentation of an eagle feather to another veteran at an intertribal pow-wow. The recipient, a Lakota from South Dakota, was paid one of the highest honors a Menominee can bestow on a person. According to Menominee custom, eagle feathers are only given away by spiritual leaders and warriors.

In addition to being honored and perhaps purged of the taint of war, some Indian veterans are aided by what can only be called a social absorption of combat-related trauma. A brief look at the way traditional Cherokee communities function could best explain this process. In these communities mature men and women, those forty and over, are usually the breadwinners and political leaders. Younger men, especially those under twenty-five, have little if anything to do with the economy or the running of the community. As Albert L. Wahrhaftig writes:

> Looking at Cherokee men in terms of different role expectations appropriate to different age groups of men, two things about the young are readily apparent. There is no niche for them within the institutional structure of a Cherokee settlement; and furthermore, the processes of Cherokee socialization operate to pull Cherokee men out of the settlement even as the absence of structural niche and social reward conspire to push them out.[91]

Younger men are expected to leave the community for a time, and most often they either find jobs in urban areas, do migrant labor, or enter the military. When they eventually return (some never do), they are resocialized into the Cherokee pattern of behavior, bringing with them information and experience of use to the people as a whole. The elders listen to the newly returned younger man's adventures and relate them "to the ancient matrix of Cherokee knowledge conveyed through myth and Indian medicine."[92] Many Cherokee veterans have reported that they were in fact resocialized in the way described above. Their relatives asked them about their service in the military and their participation in combat. For the most part, their experiences were related to and tended to confirm the Cherokee belief that war was the ultimate evil. By the time of their complete reentry into the community, the veterans' experiences were shared on an intellectual level by the entire settlement. Such circumstances are, in their way, typical of the whole of contemporary Native North America.

Reaffirming "Indian-ness"

All things considered, such nativizing processes have probably engendered a better rate of psychological healing among Native American combat veterans than has proven possible among non-Indian veterans, especially those of the Vietnam era.[93] Attempts to traditionalize contemporary military experiences, however, have often proven insufficient in and of themselves to accomplish what they are designed and intended to do. Again, this appears to be particularly the case among Vietnam era combat veterans. What the outcome will be with more recent participants in U.S. imperial exercises such as Operation Just Cause in Panama and the Gulf War, of course remains to be seen. Although it is in some ways likely that the mass slaughter of retreating Iraqis which attended the final days of Operation Desert Storm might produce Vietnam-style effects among at least some American Indian veterans, it also may be that the video game quality of the means by which much (or most) of the killing was carried out could serve to blunt or even negate such effects. The very short duration of the actual fighting in Kuwait and southern Iraq may also prove to be a significant factor affecting the feelings of Indian participants regarding what happened.

In this sense, the effects of the Gulf War upon Native America may in some ways parallel those of World War I, another conflict in which U.S. involvement was brief, decisive, and somewhat "remote" from the bulk of the killing that went on. In effect, wartime experience served more than anything else to confirm native participants in the staunch traditionalist belief that "white people really *are* crazy," after all. This allowed the World War I experience to be somewhat marginalized and treated as an unfortunate anomaly in native life, a mistake not to be repeated (this was, in any event, supposedly "the war to end all wars"). By and large, World War I veterans seem to have sublimated the worst of their wartime experiences in postwar struggles to end allotment of reservation lands and the like.[94] Psychological reconciliation under such circumstances was a relatively easy matter for most Indian veterans.

World War II saw a significant portion of an entire generation of Indians carrying a very different sensibility into combat. This was the notion that exemplary service in the army of one's colonizer could lead to rewards for one's entire people by colonial elites. Such sentiments carried on through the Korean War despite clear signs that the United States had no intention whatsoever of making the promised pay-offs—increased dignity accorded native people in American life, increased material well-being of Native America, and so forth—that most Indian veterans of this period had fought, at least in some part, to attain.[95] Instead, the country entered the period of termination and relocation policies discussed in Chapters One and Three. Further, as Churchill and LaDuke explain in Chapter Eight, on "Radioactive Colonialism," rather than some greater degree of autonomy being granted to those indigenous nations that retained their reservation land bases, ever greater federal and corporate control has been exerted over their resources.[96] Correspondingly, by the government's own admission, American Indians have been kept in a perpetual state of powerlessness and destitution.[97]

Each year that has passed since the ends of World War II and the Korean War has led to a greater sense of betrayal by American Indian veterans of those wars. The result was a sort of "lost generation" of Indians who felt sold out by, and that they had unintentionally sold *themselves* out to, the government they sought to serve.[98] The consequent confusion afflicting this group, placed as it has been in the position of "representing" Indians while forever seeking to reconcile the unreconcilable in its relationship to the United States, has increasingly beset Native North America through the present day. It seems that the only psychological recourse open to Indians is not only to deny the magnitude of the extent to which they were misled by Washington, but to assert with increasing stubbornness the exact opposite.[99] Hence, a perverse equation has emerged throughout Indian Country: the greater the degree to which the government may be abusing a given people at a given moment, the greater the degree of "patriotism"—the uttering of jingoistic speeches, heading of pow-wow grand entries with American flags, etc.—exhibited by the more visible sectors of its "responsible leadership" and their adherents.[100]

By the time Vietnam came around, conditions were ripe for a very different outcome. As the Creek/Cherokee veteran quoted earlier put it:

> I went into the army and to Vietnam because I'd seen the same John Wayne movies as everyone else and thought I was doing an honorable thing, that war was the "Indian Way." And, of course, the government was saying at the time that we had this treaty—the SEATO Treaty—to uphold. So I went...But when I got to Vietnam, I found that my job was to run missions into what everybody called "Indian Country." That's what they called enemy territory...I woke up one morning fairly early in my tour and realized that instead of being a warrior like Crazy Horse, I was a scout used by the army to track him down. I was on the wrong side of everything I wanted to believe I was about...And then I found out the SEATO Treaty never even required the United States to do what it was doing in Southeast Asia. It was all a total lie. Besides, by then I'd figured out that even if it did, it didn't matter. Why was I fighting to uphold a U.S. treaty commitment half-way around the world when the United States was violating its treaty commitments to my own people and about 300 other Indian nations?...I was fighting the wrong people, pure and simple, and I've never gotten over it.

This veteran and many others were experiencing what the sociologist C. Wright Mills once termed "cognitive dissonance," and of the most extreme sort. This is when the sets of values and philosophical beliefs one holds turn out to be dramatically at odds with the operant realities one encounters. Among many Indian Vietnam era combat veterans, this manifested itself not only in the political dimension described above, but in more directly personal expectations as well, as expressed by one of them:

I was raised in the belief that what is most honorable in being a warrior is the demonstration of personal bravery while acting in defense of the people. I went to Vietnam looking for that sort of honor. But there was no one to defend. I found myself in the position of fighting and killing the very people, the villagers, whose way of life the government said I was there to protect and preserve. And the premium wasn't on bravery. Not at all. It was on body counts, success was measured by the number of "enemy" dead. You got rewarded for killing, the more the merrier, by remote control: artillery, napalm, white phosphorus, cluster bombs, you name it...There was no honor in it. It had nothing to do with Indian traditions of warfare. It was just insanity, the white man's blood lust, the same kind of thing that was done at Sand Creek, over and over and over. Only instead of fighting back against it, I found myself a part of doing it. That's why I threw all my medals away. That's why I won't participate in honoring ceremonies or pow-wows. And that's why I came back to this country permanently at war with the United States.

Psychological disjuncture of this depth and intensity could not be reconciled by resort to traditional native ceremonial methods of social and spiritual reintegration, and the experience of the World War II-Korea generation had used up whatever currency might have been found in embracing a false sort of patriotism in order to "adjust." One major result was the rise of a "new Indian militancy" during the late 1960s and early '70s, through which Vietnam veterans and those most closely associated with them joined with the most traditional native elders to attempt to reconstitute the actuality (rather than simply the ritual forms) of indigenous warrior societies.[101] Such entities were, and where they still exist still are, often physically aggressive in their pursuit of Indian *national* rights vis-à-vis the United States, yet—in the manner customary to North America's indigenous cultures—entirely defensive in their resort to actual violence. Many of them have also consciously sought to link their efforts to (re)assert Indian sovereignty to the decolonization struggles of other peoples, especially other indigenous peoples, around the world. For instance, by the mid-'70s members of several warrior societies embraced, both figuratively and tangibly, the Vietnamese war of national liberation that they had been fighting against shortly before.[102]

Most notable among these efforts was the American Indian Movement (AIM), the leadership of which included John Trudell (Santee Dakota), Carter Camp (Ponca), Stan Holder (Wichita), Bill Means (Oglala Lakota), John Arbuckle (Omaha), and a number of other Vietnam combat veterans. AIM's spectacular reaffirmation of Indian-ness during actions such as the occupations of Alcatraz Island (1969), Mt. Rushmore (1970), the Mayflower Replica (1971) and the Bureau of Indian Affairs Building in Washington (1972) undoubtedly did much to reconcile the wartime experiences of its participants, and pointed to a direction by which non-veteran Indian youth (of both genders) might acquire a far more bona fide and legitimate warrior status than through service in the military apparatus of their colonizers.[103] During the seventy-one-day siege of Wounded Knee in 1973, however, and in the three years of unremitting violence that occurred on the surrounding Pine Ridge

Reservation, it was demonstrated that the government was still quite prepared to engage in literal Indian wars to maintain the colonial status quo.[104]

As AIM casualties spiraled, and federal propagandists unleashed all the tools of their trade in efforts to discredit the movement's motives and intentions, the viability and appropriateness of its tactics came under increasing question by other Indians.[105] Hence, AIM—at least in a direct organizational sense—lost much of its early potential to serve as a much-needed galvanizing force in contemporary Indian life. The relative demise of the movement during the 1980s created a considerable disorientation among native young people. Within this vacuum of alternatives, the impact of Reaganomics and related factors during the past decade has served to propel a much greater proportion of young Indians into the military—and consequently into various U.S. military adventures in Central America, the Caribbean, the Middle East and elsewhere—than would in all probability otherwise have been the case.[106]

Probably, the trend toward an increased militarization of Native America in the '90s can be favorably altered only through a new resurgence of reaffirmed native traditionalism, whether within a revitalized AIM or some replacement organization or movement. As was noted above, the recent experiences of Indians in the military are unlikely to yield this result, at least in the ways and to the extent Vietnam did. Thus, it remains incumbent upon the now aging generation of Vietnam veterans to draw the necessary lessons from what we have attempted heretofore, regroup ourselves, and try it again. We must discover a model which can work and set the necessary example. Sustainable and truly *Indian* alternatives to U.S. military service must be found. Otherwise, the next century will find us continuing in the mode developed for us during this one, not as free and self-determining peoples, but as patriots and pawns of the North American colonial order. We owe it to our future generations—indeed, to all humanity—to do better than that.

Notes

1. Hale, Duane, "Forgotten Heroes: American Indians in World War I," *Four Winds*, No. 3, 1982, pp. 39-41. Also see Office of Indian Affairs, *Indians in the War*, Haskell Indian School, Lawrence, KS, 1945, and Bernstein, Alison R., *American Indians and World War II*, University of Oklahoma Press, Norman, 1991.
2. U.S. Department of Defense, Veterans Administration, "Table of the Estimated Number of American Indian Veterans by State of Residence," *Talking Leaf*, No. 2, 1973, p. 3, and U.S. Bureau of the Census, *1980 Census of the Population, Vol. 1, Characteristics of the Population*, U.S. Government Printing Office, Washington, D.C., 1983, Chapter C., "General Social and Economic Characteristics." Also see Stanley, Sam, and Robert K. Thomas, "Current Demographic and Social Trends Among North American Indians," *Annals of the American Academy of Political and Social Science*, No. 436, 1978, pp. 111-20.
3. McCartney, James, *A Papago Traveler*, University of Arizona Press, Tucson, 1985, pp. 68-70. Also see Johnson, Broderick R., ed., *Navajos and World War II*, Navajo Community College Press, Tsaile, AZ, 1977, pp. 11-12.
4. *Indians in the War*, op. cit.
5. U.S. Department of Interior, Bureau of Indian Affairs, *Annual Report of the Commissioner of Indian Affairs*, 60th Cong., 1st Sess., U.S. Government Printing Office, Washington, D.C., 1918.
6. Collier, John, "The Indian in a Wartime Nation," *Annals of the American Academy of Political and Social Science*, No. 223, 1942, p. 29. For context, see Philp, Kenneth, *John Collier's Crusade*

for Indian Reform, University of Arizona Press, Tucson, 1980.

7. For analysis from the imperialist perspective itself, see Cromer, Earl of, *Ancient and Modern Imperialism*, Murray Publishers, London, 1910. Also see MacRory, Patrick, *The Fierce Pawns*, J.B. Lippencott Publishers, Philadelphia, 1966.

8. An excellent study of this phenomenon may be found in Barat, Amiya, *The Bengal Native Infantry*, Firma K.L. Mukmopadhyay, Calcutta, 1962. Also see Gopal, Ram, *How the British Occupied Bengal*, Asia Publishing House, London, 1963.

9. See Enloe, Cynthia, *Ethnic Soldiers: State Security in a Divided Society*, Penguin Press, Baltimore, 1980.

10. On the transformation of the significance attached to units such as the Black Watch and the Gurkha Rifles during the modern period, see Barnett, Correlli, *Britain and Her Army, 1509-1970*, Penguin Press, London, 1970. Also see Howard, Philip, *The Black Watch*, Hamish Hamilton Publishers, London, 1968, and Bolt, David, *Gurkhas*, Weidenfeld and Nicolson Publishers, London, 1967.

11. See Hilton, Major General Richard, *The Indian Mutiny*, Hollis and Carter Publishers, London, 1957. Also see Pollack, Sam, *Mutiny for the Cause*, Leo Cooper Publishers, London, 1969.

12. On the "lessons learned" by the British military in this regard, see Luvass, Jay, *The Education of an Army, 1815-1940*, University of Chicago Press, Chicago, 1964.

13. Enloe, op.cit., p. 21. A prime example of how "unreliable" groups are handled within imperial systems is that of the Irish at the hands of the British. For analysis and description of the consequences, see Hennessy, Maurice N., *The Wild Geese: The Irish Soldier in Exile*, Devin-Adair Co., Publishers, Old Greenwich, CT., 1973.

14. On these "legions" and their motivations, see Höhne, Heinze, *The Order of the Death's Head: The Story of Hitler's SS*, Coward-McCann Publishers, New York, 1969, esp. pp. 436-82. Also see Stein, George H., *The Waffen SS: Hitler's Elite Guard at War, 1939-1945*, Cornell University Press, Ithaca, NY, 1966.

15. See Sinclair-Stevenson, Christopher, *The Gordon Highlanders*, Hamish Hamilton Publishers, London, 1968, Sutherland, Douglas, *The Argyll and Sutherland Highlanders*, Leo Cooper Publishers, London, 1969, and Oatts, L.B., *The Highland Light Infantry*, Leo Cooper Publishers, London, 1969. On the Gurkhas, see Bolt, op. cit.

16. For accounts of instances during the 19th century, see Bond, Brian, *Victorian Military Campaigns*, Praeger Publishers, New York, 1967, and Farwell, Byron, *Queen Victoria's Little Wars*, W.W. Norton Publishers, New York, 1972. For more recent fare, see Geraghty, Tom, *Inside the SAS*, Ballantine Books, New York, 1980.

17. By far the best overall account of these programs may be found in Stanton, Shelby L., *Green Berets at War: U.S. Army Special Forces in Southeast Asia, 1956-1975*, Presidio Press, San Francisco, 1985. Also see U.S. Department of the Army, Col. Francis J. Kelly, *U.S. Army Special Forces, 1961-1971*, U.S. Government Printing Office, Washington, D.C., 1973.

18. See Klare, Michael T., and Peter Kornbluh, eds., *Low Intensity Warfare: Counterinsurgency, Proinsurgency, and Antiterrorism in the Eighties*, Pantheon Press, New York, 1988.

19. On the performance of the Bulgarians and Romanians in the USSR, see Clark Alan, *Barbarossa: The Russian-German Conflict, 1941-45*, Macmillan Publishers, London, 1965.

20. For an interesting survey, see Dupuy, R. Ernest, and Trevor Dupuy, *The Encyclopedia of Military History*, Harper and Row Publishers, New York, 1970.

21. This rule would seem to apply as much to the colonizers' self-assessment as to assessments of the colonized. See Caryle, Thomas, *On Heroes, Hero-Worship and the Heroic in History*, Chapman and Hall Publishers, London, 1840.

22. An excellent elaboration of this theme may be found in Harvey Pearce, Roy, *The Savages of America: A Study of the Indian and the Idea of Civilization*, Johns Hopkins University Press, Baltimore, (revised edition) 1965.

23. Young, Warren L., *Minorities in the Military*, Greenwood Press, Westport, CT, 1982, pp. 5-10.

24. Ibid., p. 21. The example of the Maoris is especially interesting, given that the British had shortly before considered them "true savages," worthy of being on the receiving end of outright exterminationist warfare. See Harrop, A.J., *England and the Maori Wars*, Whitcombe and Tombs Publishers, Australia and New Zealand, 1937.

25. See Berkhofer, Robert F. Jr., *The White Man's Indian: Images of the American Indian from Columbus to the Present*, Alfred A. Knopf Publishers, New York, 1978. Also see Drinnon, Richard, *Facing West: The Metaphysics of Indian Hating and Empire Building*, University of

Minnesota Press, Minneapolis, 1980.

26. In this vein, see Sandoz, Mari, *Crazy Horse: Strange Man of the Oglalas*, University of Nebraska, Lincoln, 1961.

27. Quoted in Washburn, Wilcomb E., ed., *The Indian and the White Man*, Anchor Books, New York, 1964, p. 268.

28. See Dyer, Gwynne, *War*, Dorsey Press, New York, 1985, p. 76. Also see Rapaport, Anatole, ed., *Clauswitz on War*, Penguin Books, Baltimore, 1968.

29. Quoted in Washburn, op. cit., p. 266.

30. On the Mohawk campaign in upstate New York, see Graymont, Barbara, *The Iroquois in the American Revolution*, Syracuse University Press, Syracuse, NY, 1972. For analysis of influences upon modern military doctrine, see Paddock, Alfred H. Jr., *U.S. Army Special Warfare: Its Origins*, National Defense University Press, Washington, D.C., 1982.

31. Quoted in ibid., p. 265. For a detailed analysis of native influences on the tactics of the rebel units mentioned, see Asprey, Robert B., *War in the Shadows: The Guerrilla in History* (2 Vols.), Doubleday Publishers, Garden City, NJ, 1975.

32. See Edmunds, R. David, *Tecumseh and the Quest for American Indian Leadership*, Little Publishers, Boston, 1984.

33. On the Redsticks, see Martin, Joel W., *Sacred Revolt: The Muskogees' Struggle for a New World*, Beacon Press, Boston, 1991. Also see Owsley, Frank Lawrence Jr., *The Struggle for the Gulf Borderlands: The Creek War and the Battle of New Orleans, 1812-1815*, University Presses of Florida, Gainesville, 1981.

34. For an insightful handling of these literary developments, see Churchill, Ward, "Literature in the Colonization of American Indians: An Historical Study," *Journal of Ethnic Studies*, Vol. 10, No. 3, Fall 1982.

35. An accurate depiction of the sort of intensive real-life training, beginning at a very early age, which went into the make-up of a 19th-century Indian male may be found in Ambrose, Steven E., *Crazy Horse and Custer: The Parallel Lives of Two American Warriors*, Doubleday Publishers, Garden City, NJ, 1975.

36. On the Civil War Indian regiments, see Debo, Angie, *A History of the Indians of the United States*, University of Oklahoma Press, Norman, 1970, pp. 172-80.

37. See Dunlay, Thomas, *Wolves for the Blue Soldiers: Indian Scouts and Auxiliaries with the U.S. Army, 1860-90*, University of Nebraska Press, Lincoln, 1982. Also see Grinnell, George Bird, *Two Great Scouts and Their Pawnee Battalion*, University of Nebraska Press, Lincoln, 1973.

38. *The Indian's Friend*, January 1918.

39. Vestal, Stanley, "The Plains Indian and the War," *Saturday Review of Literature*, No. 25, 1942, p. 9.

40. Ickes, Harold, "Indians Have a Name for Hitler," *Collier's Magazine*, No. 113, 1944, p. 58. Also see "Indian Soldiers Vow to Dance in Berlin," *Parade Magazine*, September 1942, pp. 17-19.

41. See Fryar, Ralph, and Natasha Fryar, *The Only Good Indian...The Hollywood Gospel*, Drama Book Specialists/Publishers, New York, 1972. Also see Stedman, William Raymond, *Shadows of the Indian: Stereotypes in American Culture*, University of Oklahoma Press, Norman, 1982.

42. On the Navajo Code-Talkers, see Paul, Doris, *They Spoke Navajo*, Dorrance Publisher, Philadelphia, 1974 and *They Talked Navajo: The United States Marine Corps Navajo Code Talkers of World War II*, Navajo Tribal Museum, Window Rock, AZ, 1972. Also see Johnson, Philip, "The Marine Corps Hymn in Navajo," *The Master Key*, September 1945, p. 153 and Simmons, Isabel, "The Unbreakable Code," *Marine Corps Gazette*, November 1971, pp. 4-6.

43. See Holm, Tom, "Fighting the White Man's War: The Extent and Legacy of American Indian Participation in World War II," *Journal of Ethnic Studies*, No. 9, 1981, pp. 69-81.

44. Jacobs, Wilbur, *Dispossessing the American Indian: Indians and Whites on the Colonial Frontier*, University of Chicago Press, Chicago, 1972, p. 166.

45. Miles, Jack I., interview with author, 1981 (tape on file).

46. Useful sketches of the tactics involved will be found in West, Capt. Francis J. Jr. (USMC Ret.), *Small Unit Action in Vietnam, Summer 1966*, Arno Press, New York, 1981 and Garland, Lt. Col. Albert N., *Infantry in Vietnam: Small Unit Actions in the Early Days, 1965-1966*, The Battery Press, Nashville, TN, 1982. The hazards of walking point in the Marine Corps are graphically depicted in a novel by Gustav Hasford, *The Short Timers*, Bantam Books, New York, 1979.

47. Anonymous (by request), interview with author, 1983 (tape on file).

48. Anonymous (by request), interview with author, 1982 (tape on file).

49. For more on the operational realities of these units, see Lanning, Michael Lee, *Inside the LRRPs: Rangers in Vietnam*, Ivy Books, New York, 1988.

50. Anonymous (by request), interview with author, 1983 (tape on file).

51. For details of the transition to Ranger status, see Lanning, op. cit., pp. 50-74. Accurate descriptions of the sort of duty experienced during this period may be found in two novels and a recent book of nonfiction. See Miller, Ken, *Tiger the LRRP Dog*, Ballantine Books, New York, 1983; Scott, Leonard B., *Charlie Mike*, Ballantine Books, New York, 1985; and Ericson, Don, and John L. Rotondo, *Charlie Rangers*, Ivy Books, New York, 1989.

52. On MAC-V-SOG, see Stanton, op. cit., pp. 218-29.

53. Quoted in Neuberger, Richard L., "The American Indian Enlists," *Asia and the Americas*, No. 42, November 1942, p. 628.

54. For analysis, see Prucha, Francis Paul, *Americanizing the American Indian: Writings by the "Friends of the Indian," 1800-1900*, University of Nebraska Press, Lincoln, 1973, and *American Indian Policy in Crisis: Christian Reformers and the Indian, 1865-1900*, University of Oklahoma Press, Norman, 1976. An exceedingly illuminating articulation of the entire dynamic may be found in Austin, Mary, "Why Americanize the Indian?" *Forum*, September 1929, p. 169.

55. For use of the term, see, for example, Hassrick, Royal B., *The Sioux: Life and Customs of a Warrior Society*, University of Oklahoma Press, Norman, 1964. A more "conceptual" interpretation—couched as if the whole fallacy were real—may be found in Smith, Marian, "The War Complex of the Plains Indians," *Proceedings of the American Philosophical Society*, LXXVIII, 1936, pp. 425-64.

56. See Turney-High, Harry Holbert, *Primitive War: Its Practices and Concepts*, University of South Carolina Press, Columbia, (2nd edition) 1934.

57. A good description of the practice among one people is given in Wagner, Glendolin Damon, and William A. Allen, *Blankets and Moccasins: Plenty Coups and His People, the Crows*, Claxton Publishers, Caldwell, ID, 1936. For a sample of how the tradition has been distorted in non-Indian scholarship, see Grinnell, George Bird, "Coup and Scalp Among the Plains Indians," *American Anthropologist*, No. 12, 1910, pp. 296-310.

58. See Miskin, Bernard, *Rank and Warfare Among the Plains Indians*, Monographs on American Ethnology, Vol. III, J.J. Augustin Publishers, New York, 1940.

59. See Roe, Frank Gilbert, *The Indian and His Horse*, University of Oklahoma Press, Norman, 1955. Also see Ewers, John C., *The Horse in Blackfoot Indian Culture, with Comparative Material from Other Western Tribes*, Smithsonian Institution, Bureau of Ethnology, Bulletin 59, U.S. Government Printing Office, Washington, D.C., 1955.

60. Sale, Kirkpatrick, *The Conquest of Paradise: Columbus and the Columbian Legacy*, Alfred A. Knopf Publishers, New York, 1990.

61. Accounts of such may be found in the journals of many early European travelers in Indian Country. See, for instance, Catlin, George, *North American Indians: Being Letters and Notes on Their Manners, Customs, and Conditions, Written During Eight Years' Travel Amongst the Wildest Tribes of Indians in North America, 1832-1839* (2 Vols.), Leary, Stuart and Company, Philadelphia, 1913. Sometimes this was cast as "cowardice" on the Indians' part. See Dodge, Col. Richard Irving, *Our Wild Indians: Thirty-Three Years' Personal Experience Among the Red Men of the Great West. A Popular Account of Their Social Life, Religion, Habits, Traits, Customs, Exploits, etc., With Thrilling Adventures and Experience on the Great Plains and in the Mountains of the Wide Frontier*, Archer House Publishers, New York, 1882.

62. This is covered in part in Bieder, Robert R., "Scientific Attitudes Toward Indian Mixed-Bloods in Early Nineteenth Century America," *Journal of Ethnic Studies*, No. 8, 1980, pp. 17-30.

63. On the *encomiendo*, see Sale, op. cit. Also see Konig, Hans, *Columbus: His Enterprise*, Monthly Review Press, New York, 1976, and Paiewonsky, Michael, *Conquest of Eden, 1493-1515*, Mapes Monde Editore, St. Thomas, Virgin Islands, 1991.

64. See Jacobs, Paul, et al., *To Serve the Devil*, Vol. 1: *Natives and Slaves*, Random House Publishers, New York, 1971. Also see Perdue, Theda, *Slavery and the Evolution of Cherokee Society, 1540-1866*, University of Tennessee Press, Knoxville, 1979. Another good reading is Forbes, Jack D., "Mustees, Half-Breeds and Zambos in Anglo North America: Aspects of Black-Indian Relations," *American Indian Quarterly*, No. 7, 1983, pp. 57-83.

65. The origins of scalping seem to lie in 16th-century British policies directed against the dissident Irish. See Canny, Nicholis P., "The Ideology of English Colonization: From Ireland to America,"

William and Mary Quarterly, 3rd Ser., XXX, 1973, pp. 575-98.

66. See Harvey Pearce, Roy, "Significance of the Captivity Narrative," *American Literature,* No. 19, March 1947, pp. 1-20. Also see Quinn, David Beers, "Anti-Indian Sentiment in Early Colonial Literature," *The Indian Historian,* Vol. 2, No. 1, Spring 1969.

67. For a modern summation of this early mythology, see Knowles, Nathaniel, "The Torture of Captives by the Indians of Eastern North America," *Proceedings of the American Philosophical Society,* LXXXII, 1940, pp. 151-225. For critical analysis, see Harvey Pearce, Roy, "The Metaphysics of Indian Hating," *Ethnohistory,* IV, 1957, pp. 27-40.

68. See Leach, Douglas Edward, *Flintlock and Tomahawk: New England in King Philip's War,* W.W. Norton Publishers, New York, 1958 and Bourne, Russell, *The Red King's Rebellion: Racial Politics in New England, 1675-1678,* Atheneum Books, New York, 1990. Also see Vaughan, Alden T., "Pequots and Puritans: The Causes of the War of 1637," *William and Mary Quarterly,* 3rd Ser., XXI, 1964, pp. 256-69.

69. See Otterbein, Keith F., "Why the Iroquois Won: An Analysis of Iroquois Military Tactics," *Ethnohistory,* XI, 1964, pp. 56-63. Also see Malone, Patrick M., "Changing Military Technology Among the Indians of Southern New England, 1600-1677," *American Quarterly,* No. 25, 1973, pp. 48-63, and Trigger, Bruce G., "The Mohawk-Mahican War 1624-28: The Establishment of a Pattern," *Canadian Historical Review,* LII, 1971, pp. 276-86.

70. This, to be sure, includes attacks upon "peaceful" settlers (and wagon trains, etc.), who were, after all, engaged in nothing less than armed physical invasions of native homelands. Even at that, outright attacks were usually not initiated until the invaders had been warned in various ways to leave. A few exemplary raids would then be conducted to drive home the point. When this failed, serious attacks would begin.

71. On the June 17 battle, see Vaughn, J.W., *With Crook at the Rosebud,* University of Nebraska Press, Lincoln, 1956.

72. There are many books on the Custer fight. See, for example, Sandoz, Mari, *The Battle of the Little Big Horn,* Curtis Books, New York, 1966.

73. Newcomb, W.W. Jr., "A Re-examination of the Causes of Plains Warfare," *American Anthropologist,* N.S., LII, 1950, pp. 317-50. Also see Calloway, Colin G., "The Inter-Tribal Balance of Power on the Great Plains, 1760-1800," *Journal of American Studies,* No. 16, April 1982, pp. 25-47.

74. Detailed examination of this trend is provided in Secoy, Frank Raymond, *Changing Military Patterns on the Great Plains, 17th Century-Early 19th Century,* J.J. Augustin Publishers, New York, 1953. Also see Vestal, Stanley, *New Sources of Indian History, 1850-1891,* University of Oklahoma Press, Norman, 1934.

75. McGinnis, Anthony, *Counting Coup and Cutting Horses: Intertribal Warfare on the Northern Plains, 1738-1889,* Cordillera Press, Evergreen, CO, 1990, p. 144.

76. Ibid., p. 191. Also see Goebel, Paul, and Dorothy Goebel, *Lone Bull's Horse Raid,* Bradbury Press, New York, 1973.

77. McGinnis, op. cit., p. 191. Also see Ewers, John C., *The Blackfeet: Raiders of the Northern Plains,* University of Oklahoma Press, Norman, 1958.

78. Probably the best collection of studies concerning such phenomena may be found in Walker, Deward E. Jr., ed., *The Emergent Native Americans: A Reader in Cultural Contact,* Little, Brown Publishers, New York, 1977. Also see McNickle, D'Arcy, *Native American Tribalism: Indian Survivals and Renewals,* Oxford University Press, London/New York, 1973.

79. For good area studies of these factors, see Jacobs, Wilbur, *Diplomacy and Indian Gifts: Anglo-French Rivalry Along the Ohio and Northwest Frontiers,* Stanford University Press, Palo Alto, CA, 1950, and Wood, W. Raymond, and Thomas D. Thiesson, eds., *Early Fur Trade on the Northern Plains: Canadian Traders Among the Mandan and Hidatsa Indians, 1738-1818,* University of Oklahoma Press, Norman, 1985.

80. See King, Duane H., *The Cherokee Nation: A Troubled History,* University of Tennessee Press, Knoxville, 1979. Secondarily, see Kleber, L.C., "Religion Among the American Indians," *History Today,* No. 28, February 1978, pp. 81-7.

81. See usage in Walker, op. cit.

82. Green, Donald E., *The Creek People,* Indian Tribal Series Books, Phoenix, 1973.

83. The Plains warrior societies are mentioned in Hertzberg, Hazel W., *The Search for an American Indian Identity: Modern Pan-Indian Movements,* Syracuse University Press, Syracuse, NY, 1971. On the Navajos, see Young, Robert, *A Political History of the Navajo Nation,* Navajo Community College Press, Tsaile, AZ, 1978.

84. Sando, Joe, *The Pueblo Indians,* Indian Historian Press, San Francisco, 1976. Also see Jones, Oakah L. Jr., *Pueblo Warriors and the Spanish Conquest,* University of Oklahoma Press, Norman, 1966.
85. U.S. Department of Interior, Bureau of Indian Affairs, *Annual Report of the Commissioner of Indian Affairs,* 65th Cong., 2d Sess., U.S. Government Printing Office, Washington, D.C., 1919, p. 16.
86. Villard, Oswald G., "Wardship and the Indian," *Christian Century,* No. 61, 1944, p. 397.
87. Howard, James H., "The Lakota Victory Dance, World War II," *North Dakota History,* No. 18, 1951, pp. 31-40. Also see Johnson, op. cit.
88. Schusky, Ernest L., ed., *Political Organization of Native North Americans,* University Press of America, Washington, D.C., 1981, pp. vii-viii.
89. See DeMallie, Raymond, and Elaine Jahner, eds., *Lakota Belief and Ritual,* University of Nebraska Press, Lincoln, 1980.
90. Holm, op. cit., p. 75.
91. Wahrhaftig, Albert L., "More than Mere Work: The Subsistence System of Oklahoma's Cherokee Indians," unpublished presentation made at the Southwest Anthropological Association Annual Conference, San Francisco, 1973, p. 4.
92. Ibid., p. 7.
93. See Wilson, John P., "Conflict, Stress, and Growth: Effects of War on Psychological Development Among Vietnam Veterans," in Charles R. Figley and Seymour Leventman, eds., *Strangers at Home: Vietnam Veterans Since the War,* New York, 1980, pp. 123-65. Also see Bonior, David E., Steven M. Champlin, and Timothy S. Kolly, *The Vietnam Veteran: A History of Neglect,* Praeger Publishers, New York, 1984.
94. This dynamic is considered in the early chapters of Taylor, Graham D., *The New Deal and American Indian Tribalism,* University of Nebraska Press, Lincoln, 1980. Also see Philp, Kenneth L., *John Collier's Crusade for Indian Reform, 1920-1954,* University of Arizona Press, Tucson, 1980.
95. There are numerous studies leading to this general conclusion. For a sample, see Stevens, Alden, "Whither the American Indian?" *Survey Graphic,* March 1940, pp. 168-78; Ritzenthaler, Robert, and Mary Sellers, "The Impact of War on an Indian Community," *American Anthropologist,* No. 45, 1943, pp. 326-9; Useem, John, et al., "Wartime Cultural and Employment Adjustments of the Rosebud Sioux," *Applied Anthropology,* No. 2, 1943, pp. 1-9; Badt, Milton B., "I Cut His Throat," *Nevada State Bar Journal,* No. 11, 1946, pp. 23-6; Adair, John, and Evon Voght, "The Returning Navajo and Zuñi Veteran," *American Anthropologist,* No. 46, 1947, pp. 10-39; LaFarge, Oliver, "They Were Good Enough for the Army, *Harper's,* November 1947, pp. 22-27; Adair, John, and Evon Voght, "Navajo and Zuni Veterans" *American Anthropologist,* No. 51, 1949, pp. 547-68; Voght, Evon, "Navajo Veterans: A Study in Changing Values," *Papers of the Peabody Museum of American Archeology and Ethnology,* Harvard University, No. 41, 1951; and Provinse, John, "The American Indian in Transition," *American Anthropologist,* No. 56, 1968, pp. 168-77.
96. See Nash, Gerald D., *The American West Transformed: The Impact of the Second World War,* Indiana University Press, Bloomington/Indianapolis, 1988.
97. On federal control and native powerlessness, see U.S. Commission on Civil Rights, *The Navajo Nation: An American Colony,* U.S. Government Printing Office, Washington, D.C., 1976. On the extent of destitution in Native America, see U.S. Department of Health and Human Services, *Chart Series Book,* Public Health Service, Washington, D.C., 1988 (HE20.9409.988).
98. There is no comprehensive study of this phenomenon. In general, see Bernstein, op. cit. Partial views may be obtained in Johnson, op. cit.; LaFarge, Oliver, ed., *The Changing Indian,* University of Oklahoma Press, Norman, 1942; and Hauptman, Lawrence M., *The Iroquois Struggle for Survival: World War II to Red Power,* Syracuse University Press, Syracuse, NY, 1986.
99. An interesting early examination of such trends may be found in Mead, Margaret, *The Changing Culture of the Indian Tribe,* G.P. Putnam's Sons, Publishers, New York, 1966. Also see the relevant sections of Swaggerty, W.R., ed., *Scholars and the Indian Experience: Recent Writing in the Social Sciences,* Indiana University Press, Bloomington/Indianapolis, 1984.
100. Examination of such garish displays may be found in Levine, Stuart, and Nancy O. Lurie, *The American Indian Today,* Penguin Books, Baltimore, 1972.
101. On the rise of Indian militancy during the Vietnam era, see Steiner, Stan, *The New Indians,* Harper and Row Publishers, New York, 1968; and Josephy, Alvin M. Jr., *Red Power: The*

American Indians' Fight for Freedom, McGraw-Hill Publishers, New York, 1971. Another good reading in this regard is Cornell, Stephen, *Return of the Native: American Indian Political Resurgence*, Oxford University Press, London/New York, 1988.

102. See Deloria, Vine Jr., *Behind the Trail of Broken Treaties: An American Indian Declaration of Independence*, University of Texas Press, Austin, (2nd edition) 1984; and Burnette, Robert, with John Koster, *The Road to Wounded Knee*, Bantam Books, New York, 1974.

103. Probably the best book on the early days of AIM to date is Matthiessen, Peter, *In the Spirit of Crazy Horse*, Viking Press, New York, (2nd edition) 1991. Also see Josephy, Alvin M. Jr., *Now That the Buffalo's Gone: A Study of Today's American Indians*, University of Oklahoma Press, Norman, (2nd edition) 1984.

104. On the counterinsurgency war fought against AIM on Pine Ridge, see Johansen, Bruce, and Roberto Maestas, *Wasi'chu: The Continuing Indian Wars*, Monthly Review Press, New York, 1979, and Weyler, Rex, *Blood of the Land: The U.S. Government and Corporate War Against the American Indian Movement*, Everest House Publishers, New York, 1983.

105. On casualties and disinformation, see Churchill, Ward, and Jim Vander Wall, *Agents of Repression: The FBI's Secret Wars Against the Black Panther Party and the American Indian Movement*, South End Press, Boston 1988, and *The COINTELPRO Papers: Documents from the FBI's Secret Wars Against Dissent in the United States*, South End Press, Boston, 1990.

106. See Hertzberg, Hazel W., "Reaganomics on the Reservation," *The New Republic*, November 22, 1982.

Chapter XIII

American Indian Education in the United States
Indoctrination for Subordination to Colonialism

by Jorge Noriega

With only minor exceptions the history of Indian education has been primarily the transmission of white American education, little altered, to the Indian child as a one-way process. The institution of the school is one that was imposed and controlled by non-Indian society...its goals primarily aimed at removing the child from his aboriginal culture and assimilating him into the dominant white culture.

Estelle Fuchs and Robert J. Havighurst
To Live on this Earth

The "formal education" of the indigenous peoples of North America began at virtually the moment in which the European drive to colonize the continent began in earnest. At least as early as 1611, French Jesuit missionaries opened schools along the St. Lawrence River in which they actively pursued Louis XIV's edict, issued a year earlier, that where possible, long-term native resistance to French rule should be neutralized by implementation of a program to "educate the children of the Indians in the French manner."[1] The priests, in some cases directly supported by troops, complied with vigor, removing native youngsters from their families for extended periods, often forcibly. Trapped in prototypical boarding schools, usually situated a considerable distance from their communities, the children were drilled extensively in such subjects as French language and customs, Catholicism, basic academics (the famous "three Rs," plus French history), singing, animal husbandry, carpentry, and handicrafts. Meanwhile, their traditional languages and cultures, religions and world views were systematically denigrated and suppressed.[2]

The Spanish Jesuits, who had pioneered a system of some thirty mission schools in Paraguay and Uruguay from 1609 onward—these were termed "Reductions," an entirely appropriate description given their intended role in diminishing indigenous cultural integrity to the point of nonexistence—passed along the benefits of their experience to the Dominicans and Franciscans, who were quick to attempt to duplicate such feats in North America.[3] As Evelyn C. Adams put it in his 1946 book, *American Indian Education,* a quasi-official rationalization of the whole thrust of colonialist pedagogy in what is now the United States:

> Religious orders worked valiantly in the [16th] century to set up missions in Florida where they were confronted by many obstacles. The failure of the program was due largely to the unsettled state of the Indians, the absence of mineral wealth, and the resistance of the English [immediately to the north]. Success came early in New Mexico where many tribes were found living in communities. The natives were taught in a number to read, write, sing, and play musical instruments. Crafts and trades were also taught, and in these many of the Indians were skillful and clever, and became tailors, shoemakers, carpenters, and blacksmiths. The Christian doctrine and Spanish customs were taught to all Indians.[4]

Such efforts by the Spanish were continued well into the 19th century in California, where the San Diego Mission, established in 1769, had been expanded into a complex of twenty facilities extending as far northward as San Francisco.[5] These, according to Adams, were as "successful" as those in Paraguay. Augmentation of the clerics by troops allowed for imposition of a strict regimen:

> The religious instruction given to Indians over eleven years old, twice daily, and to children over five, once each day, was oral and did not require literacy. The government wanted the friars to teach the Indians in Spanish as an aid to controlling remote outposts…and it prevailed wherever the government was in control. The Indians marched to church, to work, and to their meals under a precisely regimented routine. A sunrise bell called all over nine years of age to religious services.[6]

British Protestants followed much the same course as the Catholics. Both charters issued to the Virginia Company (1606 and 1609) to establish the first English colony in North America contained clauses requiring "conversion" of Indians by what were called educational means. Consequently, in 1617 a fund of 500£ which was collected from the colonists, and enhanced by a further 500£ contributed by the Anglican Bishops in England, was established for purposes of founding what was to be called the East India School for Indians at Charles City and an Indian college near Henrico.[7] Land had been set aside for these institutions by 1621, but the plan was aborted the following year when the native nations of the area—thoroughly offended by colonialist duplicity and pretensions to cultural superiority—launched a war which destroyed both towns in which the schools were to be located. There followed an extended period in which a series of wars and diplomatic initiatives were undertaken by the British Crown to sufficiently pacify the indigenous nations of the Piedmont Plain to allow educational efforts to be resumed.[8]

Further to the north, things were moving along a bit more smoothly from the colonialist point of view. Military conquest of the native nations of coastal New

England had occurred more rapidly than in the southerly colonies, and the "Reverend John Eliot, a brilliant young graduate of Cambridge University who looked upon Christianity, civilization, and learning as inseparable...established nine self-sustaining Indian communities which were known as villages of praying Indians" that served as the embryo of what was intended to become a full-fledged "educational system" devoted to the task of Europeanizing the native intellect.[9] As a result, in 1654, the first Indian "higher educational institution" in North America was established at Harvard College, in Massachusetts.[10] This was the focal point of a steadily growing apparatus for "training Indian minds" in the region for nearly a century. Thereafter, a new and more comprehensive effort was undertaken:

> A second systematized program of Indian education was developed in New England during the middle of the eighteenth century. The Reverend Eleazer Wheelock, a graduate of Yale University and a Congregational minister, founded Moor's Charity School for Indians in 1755, in Lebanon, Connecticut; and Dartmouth College in 1769, in Dresden, now Hanover, New Hampshire...Wheelock's policy of Indian education was in sharp contrast to that of Eliot, who organized Indian settlements. [His model imposed] missionary training [upon] Indian students in boarding schools far removed from tribal environment.[11]

By 1693, things had also "progressed" in Virginia and other more southerly colonies to the point that a number of boarding schools had been set up—only one facility, at Fort Reservation, was actually proximate to native communities—and the first Indian students were being enrolled at the College of William and Mary, in Williamsburg. In 1723, the native student population at the latter institution had become sufficient to cause a separate domicile, Brafferton House, to be erected as a means of segregating them from Euroamerican students.[12] In New York, New Jersey, and Pennsylvania, the process moved apace as Sir William Johnson and the Reverends Samuel Kirkland, John Brainord and David Draineid made inroads among the powerful Haudenosaunee (Iroquois)[13] and Delaware Confederacies.[14] By the point at which the American Revolution occurred at the end of the 18th century, schooling was a firmly entrenched principle of the colonialist relationship to Native North American nations.

The Form and Function of Colonial Education

As even Adams was prepared to admit, all of this had everything to do with the furtherance of colonial settlement, almost nothing to do with the betterment of indigenous intellectual existence.[15] Martin Carnoy has framed the matter much more sharply: "Since schooling was brought to non-Europeans as a part of empire...it was all along integrated into an effort to bring indigenous peoples into imperialist/capitalist structures."[16] In effect, the system by which Native Americans are purportedly "educated" by Euroamerica has from the onset been little more than a means by which to supplant indigenous cultures. This has had, or at least has been intended to have, the predictable effect of demolishing the internal cohesion of native societies, thereby destroying the ability of these societies to resist conquest and colonization. Further, "Western schools were used to develop indigenous elites which served as intermediaries between [colonizer and colonized]; they were used to incorporate indigenous peoples into...roles defined by the dominant capitalist class [of the colonizing powers]."[17] Proof of this may be found in the fact that in "decolonized" settings the world over:

> The vast majority of the tiny portion of highly educated non-Europeans in colonized countries chose to emulate Europeans and leave their own people behind. The success story of colonial schooling is the small number of Third World "independence" leaders who chose to break the economic and political ties by which industrial countries control them...Therefore, old-style imperialism and colonialism have all but disappeared and the great empires of [previous centuries] have been dismantled, but education systems in ex-colonies remain largely intact after independence. Curriculum, language, and, in some cases, even the nationality of the teachers themselves, are carried over from the colonial period. In many ways, the relationship between ex-colony and ex-colonizer is stronger economically and culturally than during the colonial administration.[18]

In other words, education has been the mechanism by which colonialism has sought to render itself effectively permanent, creating the conditions by which the colonized could be made essentially *self*-colonizing, eternally subjugated in psychic and intellectual terms and thus eternally self-subordinating in economic and political terms: "Rather than building independence and self-reliance among the [oppressed], schools are used to ensure, as much as possible and apparently with some success, that those in the worst economic positions do not rebel against the system which represses them and identify with leaders who would work within the framework of action set by the dominating ruling class...The purpose of Western schooling as it was instituted around the world was to make people useful in the new hierarchy [of perpetual Eurocentric domination]."[19] As the noted Tunisian psychologist Albert Memmi has explained:

> In order for the colonizer to be a complete master, it is not enough for him to be so in actual fact, but he must believe in its [colonialism's] legitimacy. In order for that legitimacy to be complete, it is not enough for the colonized to be a slave, he must accept his role. The bond between colonizer and colonized is thus destructive and creative. It destroys and recreates the two partners of colonization into colonizer and colonized. One is disfigured into an oppressor, a partial, unpatriotic and treacherous being, worrying only about his privileges and their defense; the other into an oppressed creature, whose development is broken and who compromises by his defeat.[20]

In order for this to occur, reality must be replaced by mythic constructions intended to anchor impressions of the "natural superiority" of the colonizer among oppressed and oppressor alike. "The history which is taught [the colonized] is not his own." Memmi goes on, "Everything seems to have taken place out of [her] country...The books talk to him of a world which in no way reminds him of his own."[21] Or, as Remi Clignet has put it, "'Assimilation' [of the oppressed into the conceptual paradigm of the oppressing culture] becomes the ideological framework within which the colonizer stresses the universality of his own culture, and reduces the aspirations...experienced by the colonized into individual rather than collective terms."[22] It is a classic divide-and-rule strategy, immeasurably enhanced by the fact that the ruled are typically divided not only among but literally *within* themselves.

The lingering of such circumstances once formal decolonization has occurred, can be apprehended within the conventional rubric of "dependency theory" or "theories of neocolonialism" designed to explain the ongoing material effects of direct imperial domination.[23] Just as it can be argued that the net effect of the colonialist expropriation of resources has been the "underdevelopment" of the economies of the colonized, leaving indigenous peoples in the post-colonial context in far worse physical circumstances than before they were "discovered" and invaded—and therefore in abject need of material assistance from those who became hyperdeveloped at their expense—so too can the concept be applied to the psychological and intellectual situation of the colonized.[24] The net result has been an inculcation of beliefs among the oppressed that their collective impoverishment results, not from the ravages attending colonial rule, but from innate deficiencies within their *own* characters and cultures.[25] The obvious resolution to their malady—when viewed from this carefully engendered perspective— *must* lie in an ever closer embrace of the very entity which placed them in such dire straits in the first place. Thus are what Eduardo Galeano has termed the "open veins" of the colonized and formerly colonized kept flowing, even after the "Age of Imperialism" has officially passed.[26]

Development of the U.S. Model

At the time that England's Atlantic Seaboard colonies consummated their struggle to break away from the Crown, establishing the United States, relatively little had been accomplished by way of subverting indigenous societies inland from the coastal plain.

> Despite two and a half centuries of colonial endeavor to modify Indian culture the majority of the natives remained untutored in the European sense and their basic economy was unchanged. Indian political and religious concepts had not been fundamentally altered. Communal land ownership and tribal organization continued and the native gods...still met the spiritual needs. This was true because there were extensive land areas still unsettled and also undiscovered by the Europeans, on which [indigenous nations] could pursue unmolested what to them was a normal mode of life.[27]

Actually, as Ward Churchill points out in Chapter Five, the British King George II had issued a proclamation in 1763 forbidding settlement west of a line running roughly along the crest of the Appalachian Mountains. This had effectively precluded the need for the extension of the English colonial school system further into the North American interior, but had also served as a major catalyzing factor in the colonialist revolt against Crown rule. Now, after successful creation of a separate nation of their own, the newly independent colonists were avid to resume territorial expansion. They were, however, at something of a (temporary) military disadvantage vis-à-vis the native peoples whom they intended to subordinate, and whose land they planned to expropriate. Hence, a high premium was initially placed upon the arts of diplomacy and subversion for purposes of attaining U.S. goals and objectives. Particularly in the latter regard, the preexisting colonialist model for educating natives was admirably suited. It was therefore quickly adapted to its new context. Actually, the process had begun along with the revolution:

> Indian education received government aid immediately after the colonists revolted. The concentration of military strength against Great Britain was the paramount issue and it was up to the government to win the support [or at least the neutrality] of as many [indigenous nations] as possible. Ministers and teachers maintained by congressional funds were stationed among the Indians to serve as diplomatic agents...The Continental Congress authorized the Indian Commissioners in 1776 to engage a minister and a blacksmith for the Delaware Indians, and also to ascertain the terms under which Jacob Fowler and Joseph Johnson would serve as teachers among the New York Indians.[28]

Additionally:

> Funds were appropriated in the interest of peace by the Continental Congress for the maintenance of Indian students at Dartmouth College and the College of New Jersey which is now Princeton University. Eleazer Wheelock received five hundred dollars in 1775 for the support of Dartmouth College...In 1778 the Board of War directed that other requests by Wheelock be complied with, and in 1780 it recommended a grant of five thousand dollars. The College of New Jersey received congressional aid in 1781 for three Delaware Indians.[29]

Those native nations which had not been militarily subdued were less than enthusiastic about the alleged benefits accruing to them through such federal largess. In 1792, Benjamin Franklin recorded the reply of Cornplanter, a Seneca leader, to an overture initiated by Thomas Jefferson to provide free higher education for selected Iroquois youth:

> [Y]ou, who are wise, must know that different Nations have different Conceptions of things; and you will therefore not take it amiss, if our ideas of this kind of Education happens not to be the same as yours. We have had some experience of it; Several of our young people were formerly brought up at the Colleges of the Northern Provinces; they were instructed in all your Sciences; but, when they came back to us, they were bad Runners, ignorant of every means of living in the Woods, unable to bear either Cold or Hunger, knew neither how to build a Cabin, take a Deer, or kill an Enemy, spoke our Language imperfectly, were therefore neither fit for Hunters, Warriors, nor Counsellors; they were totally good for nothing. We are however not the less oblig'd by your kind Offer, tho' we decline in accepting it; and, to show our grateful Sense of it, if the Gentlemen of Virginia will send us a Dozen of their Sons, we will take great Care of their Education, instruct them in all we know, and make *Men* of them. [30]

The United States, of course, did not avail itself of the opportunity to have even a few of its young people trained to view the world as Indians. Instead, the government geared up the vehicle by which it sought to obtain the opposite result, appropriating the whopping sum (for its day) of $20,000 per year to this purpose in 1793.[31] Educational "services" were a prominent part of a "reward" for the Indians' politico-military alliance with the rebels during the revolution, extended under a treaty made the following year with the Oneida, Tuscarora, and Stockbridge nations in New York state.[32] Similarly, provision of instruction, usually in the "arts of civilization," was a "bonus" incorporated into treaties with the Creek Confederacy of the Southeast (1801), the Kaskaskias of present-day Illinois (1803), and the Delawares (1804), a nation which had by then been pushed westward into the Ohio River valley.[33] As more and more native nations east of the Mississippi River were subordinated to the rapidly expanding Euroamerican population, emphasis upon destruction of their cultural integrity was increased.[34]

In 1819, Congress established the "Civilization Fund," an annual appropriation of $10,000—in addition to those monies already allocated for the purpose—for "education of the frontier tribes." This was followed, in 1820, by acceptance of a proposal by Secretary of War John C. Calhoun that future treaties with indigenous nations be required to directly incorporate provision of additional cash annuities for instruction so that Indians might "be initiated in the habits of industry, and a portion taught the mechanical arts."[35] For delivery of the intended program, the government relied primarily on missionaries supplied by the American Board of Commissioners for Foreign Missions, established collectively by the Congregational, Presbyterian, and Dutch Reform churches in 1810.[36] It was in this context that the real contours of what might be described as the "U.S. model" of colonialist education began to emerge.

> The first [comprehensive] system of boarding and day schools to be proposed was submitted to the government in 1820 by the Reverend Cyrus Kingsbury of the American Board. A total of seventeen thousand dollars was set aside for the construction and equipment of schools among the Choctaws, and six thousand dollars were made available annually for their maintenance. The plan called for four boarding schools and thirty-two day schools. Each of the former was to accommodate from eighty to a hundred students and each of the latter from twenty to forty students...[Additionally,] missions for Indians were established in 1820 and 1821 west of the Mississippi River by the American Board at Dwight, Arkansas, among the Cherokees [who were already being relocated to that area from their more easterly homeland in the Georgia-Tennessee region]; and by the Presbyterian Church at Harmony, Missouri, and at Union, in the Indian Territory [Oklahoma] among the Osage.[37]

By 1825, a report of the newly created Indian Office of the Department of War indicated that 216 teachers had been deployed to handle 916 students in thirty-two schools.[38] The program continued to expand over the next decade, and was shortly supplemented by the advent of what were called "Manual Labor Schools." The first such entity, the Choctaw Academy, was established in 1834 in Scott County, Kentucky.

Run by the Reverend Thomas Henderson, a Baptist minister, the school was designed to instruct its students in "letters, labor and mechanical arts, and morals and Christianity."[39] The Academy began auspiciously enough (from the government's perspective)—"training many Indian leaders," as Adams put it—but general forced removal of the Choctaws and other indigenous nations from east of the Mississippi to the "permanent Indian territory" of Oklahoma during the late 1830s complicated the logistics of the institution's administration rather severely, causing a sharp increase in the cost of running it. It was therefore forced to shut down in 1842.[40]

The Methodist Episcopal Society had already stepped into the breach, however, having open a comparable facility at Leavenworth, Kansas in 1839. The new academy concentrated largely on relocated Shawnees and imposed a rigid military-style work regimen upon its students as a means, not only of inculcating a dramatically non-Indian sense of order among them, but of generating the revenues necessary to support itself. Endowed with 400 acres of agricultural land, school officials compelled the students to—among other things—split 37,000 rails to fence in fields. The children were then required to plow, maintain, and harvest the same fields in order to eat. Given that no labor costs were associated with this enterprise, surplus crops could be marketed at a decisive profit, the proceeds going to underwrite other aspects of the academy's overhead (this is essentially the infamous "chain gang" concept utilized in the prison systems of Southern states).[41]

> The school offered religious, academic, and practical instruction. Six hours were spent daily in the classroom, and six at work on practical projects. The boys worked on the farm and in two shops, and the girls attended to domestic affairs and studied under the direction of expert teachers of spinning and weaving. The manual labor that was a part of the daily schedule was suspended on Saturdays and Sundays. The students arose at four o'clock in the morning and retired at eight at night.[42]

The experiment in modified slavery undertaken at Leavenworth proved so successful in the estimation of both the church and the government that the Methodists were authorized to open a similar facility at Fort Coffee, Oklahoma in 1844. It included the innovation of completely segregating male students from females—girls attended what was called New Hope Academy, the boys Fort Coffee Academy, located some five miles away—a practice which attenuated the sense of social and cultural isolation of those enrolled there, making them more susceptible to "transformation." The Presbyterians, convinced by these Methodist "breakthroughs" (and by federal offers to subsidize such a venture), soon developed a manual labor school of their own; opened at Long Prairie, Minnesota, in 1848, it focused mainly on Winnebagos.[43] Such institutions devoted to indigenous youth were complemented at about the same time by establishment of "Pattern Farms" on which Indian adults were drilled in the same subjects and work ethic as their children.[44]

> The agency farm, sometimes called a Pattern Farm, was under the direction of farmer teachers appointed by the local Indian agent [who was, in turn, appointed by the Indian Office in the Department of War]. The government tried to develop

an apprenticeship type of training for the Indians but crop production usually eclipsed the instructional phase of the program...For example, [there was] Agent John Beach's Pattern Farm of more than one hundred acres in a fertile Iowa valley among the Sac and Fox tribes...In 1840 Agent Beach reported that the Indians were skilled workmen in the blacksmith shop [and] in half a dozen annual reports that followed reference was made to excellent harvest of corn, wheat, beans, potatoes, pumpkins, and other crops sufficient for subsistence of the Indians and their flocks.[45]

The notion of forced labor as part of Indian education—both as a means of "developing" the native "character," and as a way of financing further expansion of the system itself—had by then taken hold at every level of the process.

In 1848 there were sixteen manual labor schools in operation and seven additional ones were under construction. There were eighty-seven other schools [boarding schools, day schools, and seminaries], and the total enroll-ment exceeded thirty-five hundred. *All students performed some kind of labor either within or outside of school hours. Adults, too, were being taught to work like the white man* [emphasis added].[46]

By 1868, the numbers had increased to 109 schools with an enrollment of more than 4,600 students.[47] These, for obvious reasons, were concentrated among indigenous nations which had already been militarily pacified. The Choctaws, for example, were on the receiving end of seven community day schools, an adult education program, and a range of boarding schools and higher educational edifices including the Chuahla Female Seminary, Wheelock School for Girls, Norwalk School for Boys, Armstrong Academy, Igunobi Female Seminary, Koonshu Female Seminary, and the Spenser Academy, as well as the two-part Fort Coffee complex. The Choctaws were also afforded access to the Cherokee Female Seminary and the Male Cherokee Academy, both located in Tahlequah, Oklahoma. Comparable "educational infrastructures" were being created within the Chickasaw, Creek, and Seminole nations as well.[48] By the end of the century, when the federal government assumed direct control over their school systems, it was discovered that "several hundred...day and boarding schools" had become operational with regard to these five nations alone.[49]

In part, graduates from these institutions were groomed to comprise a "responsible leadership" among their respective peoples, offsetting and in many cases negating the authority and effectiveness of traditional national leaders who were far less compliant in regard to serving U.S. interests. More frequently, they were themselves deployed as teachers under the premise that Indians would be more credible than non-Indians in such capacities, not only among their own specific peoples, but eventually among such still "hostile" nations as the Cheyenne and Lakota, Kiowa and Comanche, Arapaho and Apache. In this way, Indian students targeted for training in the early stages of U.S. colonialist education were used essentially as a virus, a medium through which to hurry along a calculated process of sociocultural decay "from within," thus speeding the day in which Native America might be predicted to become fully integrated into the Euroamerican state structure.

Maturation of the Model

During the 1870s and '80s, as the last effective military resistance by indigenous nations wound down, the process by which alien educational forms were imposed upon their children, always one-sided and coercive, became dramatically more so. In 1870, Congress authorized an annual appropriation of $100,000 "for the support of industrial and other schools among tribes not otherwise provided for," an estimated population of 50,000 overseen by seventeen different agencies strung out across the southwestern desert region, as well as the Great Basin and plains areas.[50] The facilities involved were run directly by various churches and missionary societies which, in 1869, had been provided with overall authority by President Ulysses S. Grant to act in behalf of the government, appointing all Indian agents and hiring all personnel employed on the reservations.[51] Attendance at these mission schools was made mandatory by regulation on many reservations for all native children aged six through sixteen. The practice of indigenous religions by students was prohibited across the board as students were compelled to undergo daily instruction in Christianity. Similarly, the speaking of native languages was proscribed in favor of English.[52] As the matter was put by Commissioner of Indian Affairs E.A. Hayt:

> I [have] expressed very decidedly the idea that Indians should be taught in the English language *only*...There is not an Indian pupil whose tuition is paid by the United States Government who is permitted to study *any* other language than our own vernacular—the language of the greatest, most powerful, and enterprising nationalities under the sun. The English language as taught in America is good enough for all her people of all races [emphasis added].[53]

By the mid-'70s, it had become apparent that reliance upon day schools afforded students far too much proximity to their families and communities—and thus a continuing interaction with their own cultures—for the degree of general deculturation desired by federal planners to occur.

> The greatest difficulty is experienced in freeing the children attending day schools from the language and habits of their untutored and often savage parents. When they return to their homes at night, and on Saturdays and Sundays, and are among their own surroundings, *they relapse more or less into their former moral and mental stupor* [emphasis added].[54]

Hence, by the end of the decade an increasing emphasis was placed upon the more costly but far more efficient boarding school model wherein Indian children could be isolated from the "contaminating" influences of their own societies for years on in end. The idea behind this shift, successfully advocated by U.S. Commissioner of Education John Eaton, Jr., undoubtedly evolved to some extent from earlier boarding school experiments such as Dartmouth and the Choctaw Academy.[55] More importantly, however, in its new manifestation the concept drew heavily from the example of penal procedures developed to break the wills of some of the most "recalcitrant" of the indigenous resistance leaders. Indeed, when the first institution of this new phase—the Carlisle Indian School, in Carlisle, Pennsylvania—was opened on November 1, 1879, it was headed by Captain (later General) Richard H. Pratt, former commandant of the infamous Fort Marion Prison, near St. Augustine, at which the Seminole leader Osceola had been assassinated in 1838, at which the hard core of Cheyenne Dog Soldiers were even then incarcerated, and to which Geronimo and other prominent members of the Chiricahua Apache resistance would be sent a few years later.[56]

Following the lead established by the manual labor schools, half of each student's day at Carlisle was consumed in classroom and chapel activities, the other half working a farm which comprised a portion of the institutional property and was intended to defray the expense of maintaining it (girls' needlework, etc., was also marketed for this purpose); in fact, "students performed all institutional work" from the outset.[57] Reveille and lights out were strictly enforced, silence was required during meals, haircuts and formal dress codes (ties for boys, petticoats for girls) were rigidly imposed.[58] At Carlisle, which remained open until the end of the 1917-18 school year, family visits were severely restricted and students were not allowed to return home, even in the summers; instead, mandatory "vacation work" was secured for them by school authorities, the wages used to "relieve the financial burden" entailed in boarding them during the academic year. Additionally, there was the "Outing System:"

> When the student completed his school training he was placed with a white family for three years. The government paid fifty dollars a year for his medical care and clothing, and his labor was to compensate for the benefits derived from the home situation.[59]

It was not unusual, under these conditions, for a child to be taken at age six or seven and to never see his or her home and family again until age seventeen or eighteen. At this point, they were often *sent* back, but in a condition largely devoid of conceptions of both their own cultures and their intended roles within them. Already functional outcasts within their own societies, the circumstances of boarding school returnees were typically exacerbated by local Indian agents who sought them out for preferential treatment in exchange for their participation in the building of "alternative" social and governmental structures intended to undermine and eventually replace the traditional forms possessed by their peoples.[60] Altogether, the whole procedure conforms to one of the criteria—the forced transfer of children from a targeted racial, ethnic, national, or religious group to be reared and absorbed by a physically dominating group—specified as a Crime Against Humanity under the United Nations 1948 Convention on Punishment and Prevention of the Crime of Genocide.[61]

Pratt's pilot program was so well suited to federal ambitions to completely assimilate native peoples that it rapidly spawned a host of imitations. For instance, the American Missionary Society's Hampton Institute, run by General Samuel C. Anderson near Old Point Comfort, Virginia, was used for this purpose from 1880 until 1912.[62] In 1883, Congress also authorized the conversion of former frontier army posts into Carlisle-type boarding schools. Within two years, this had been accomplished at Fort Stevenson (Dakota Territory), Fort Hall (Idaho), Fort Ripley (Minnesota), and the Cantonment (Indian Territory). In 1879, Pratt could report only 158 initial student participants—of a total estimated Indian student population of slightly under 20,000—in his undertaking; by 1889, 10,500 of an estimated 36,000 were in facilities patterned on his model.[63] The entire apparatus was administered under a newly created (in 1885) Education Division of the Bureau of Indian Affairs (BIA) headed by John H. Oberly; the boarding school portion of the effort fell under an Education Division department entitled the "Civilization Division."[64]

Native people, to be sure, resisted what was being done as best they could. Among the Hopi, for example, families hid their children from roving Mormon missionaries bent upon gathering up the youngsters and shipping them off to what became the Intermountain School in Utah. In 1883, the local Indian agent, J.H. Fleming, requested a detachment of troops from nearby Fort Defiance to assist in the roundup. Despite their reputation as staunch pacifists, the Hopis met the soldiers by bombarding them with rocks from atop their mesas, forcing the army into temporary retreat.[65] It was all for naught, however, as the missionaries were eventually able to procure approximately 15 percent of all Hopi youth, sending them hundreds of miles north from their Arizona homeland for years on end before returning them imbued with attitudes and mindsets as far removed from the Hopi worldview as is possible to conceive. The result, of course, was a deep and deliberate fracturing—into "Mormon Hopi" and "Traditional Hopi" camps—of what had theretofore been an extremely cohesive society. The effects have lasted into the present day.[66]

During this same period, new weapons of the U.S. assimilationist arsenal, such as the 1887 General Allotment Act, were deployed as a means of "pulverizing...the tribal mass" of Indians wherever they might be found.[67] The system of Indian education sponsored by the government was coupled directly to this emerging body of policy, a matter which became patently obvious with the appointment of Daniel Dorcester as Superintendent of Indian Schools during the tenure of Indian Commissioner Thomas J. Morgan (1889-1893):

> Attendance was made compulsory [for all native children, aged five to eighteen] and the agent was made responsible for keeping the schools filled, by persuasion if possible, by withholding rations or annuities from the parents, and by other means if necessary...[I]n 1893 the Secretary of Interior, instead of the agent, was empowered to withhold rations and annuities. Disciplinary measures were severe. Pupils...who were guilty of misbehavior might either receive corporal punishment or be imprisoned in the guardhouse [a special "reform school" was also established to handle "incorrigible" students who clung to their traditions]. "Unusual, cruel, or degrading punishment" was prohibited. However, school jails were not abolished until 1927...The food was not sufficiently nourishing, huge dormitories were overcrowded, and health supervision was generally neglected. The age range of the students from five to twenty-one included many young children...*A sincere effort was made to develop the type of school that would destroy tribal ways.* (emphasis added)[68]

Between 1870 and the end of fiscal year 1882, the government expended a little over $800,000 training Indians to think and conduct themselves as non-Indians. In 1883, the annual appropriation for this purpose was increased by 262 percent and, by the end of Commissioner Morgan's incumbency a decade later, the yearly allocation of federal funds had swelled to some $2,350,000.[69] Despite such relatively heavy investment in consolidating a viable model of colonialist education, however, and its statutory requirement that *all* American Indian children be subjected to indoctrination within that model's facilities, Congress proved itself unwilling to commit the financial resources necessary to truly universalize the system in Indian Country.[70] Consequently, although the regimentation with which participating students were put through their paces increased steadily, by 1901 the Commissioner of Indian Affairs was forced to acknowledge that the number of Indians enrolled in BIA schools had shrunk to barely over 16,000. Among Navajos, for example, a mere 300 of the estimated 5,000 school-aged children were actually enrolled and attending classes. On the White Mountain (Chiricahua) Apache Reservation the figures were eighty of 488. Of 2,280 Anishinabé youth in Minnesota, only 600 were in school.[71]

This situation created conditions which prevented the outright obliteration of many indigenous cultures intended by most federal education planners. Despite the best efforts of BIA officials, missionaries, and teachers to stamp them out, indigenous languages, spiritual practices, and sociopolitical forms were not only continued by tribal elders, but transmitted from generation to generation, more or less in accordance with the time-honored educational customs of native peoples.[72] Federal desires (and rhetoric) notwithstanding, considerably more Indians were educated, however covertly, through traditionalist rather than colonial institutions until a point well into the 1940s. The upshot was that, while the government's goal of creating a genuine comprador strata of its own "federally educated Indians" within native societies was advancing apace, the wider objective of fostering an outright disintegration of indigenous cultures fell far short of expectations.[73]

This not only left an extensive and continuously regenerating base of native traditionalism available with which indigenous cultures sustained themselves throughout the first half of the 20th century, it also allowed a certain degree of breathing room utilized by the traditionals to gradually devise strategies for defending their societies against many of the worst effects of the colonialist indoctrination process.[74] By the 1960s, extension of this "culture of resistance" had led to a resurgence of overt indigenous nationalism and, in some instances, the beginnings of a calculated appropriation of aspects of the Euroamerican educational structure for native purposes.[75] Had the government been willing to expend the funds necessary to enforce universal compulsory education upon all or even the bulk of American Indian youth during the late 19th and early 20th centuries, the outcome might very well have been quite different.

Into the Modern Era

By 1906, the need for a broadening of the pedagogical base through which native children could be processed for assimilative purposes had become so apparent—and Congress so reluctant to approve the massive funding increases needed for a large-scale expansion of the boarding school system—that Indian Commissioner Frances E. Leupp approved a plan to begin a wholesale diversion of certain categories of Indian students directly into public schools.[76] Here, he reasoned, being subsumed within an overwhelming number of non-Indian "peers" might serve to propel such unfortunates away from their own traditions and even more rapidly into the realm of Euroamerican tastes, values, and sensibilities. The idea held the appeal of eliminating most of the federal costs associated with an across-the-board indoctrination of young Indians to "the ways of civilization" and, in Leupp's opinion, held the prospect of proving so successful as to make the whole of the government's "Indian education business" superfluous "after only a few generations."[77] This shift in emphasis was begun somewhat tentatively.

> From 1917 to 1923 two hundred thousand dollars were provided annually [to place Indian children in public schools], and in 1924, fifty thousand dollars were added. From 1925 to 1929 three hundred and fifty thousand dollars were made available annually, and in 1929 the amount was increased by fifty thousand dollars. A law was passed in 1929 requiring Indian children who were not under government supervision to attend public schools in accordance with state laws; and state officials were authorized to enter Indian-occupied lands to enforce the measure.[78]

In 1924, the so-called Committee of One Hundred, prominent non-Indians appointed by the House of Representatives to study and make recommendations concerning "final resolution" of the U.S. "Indian Problem," concluded that Leupp had been correct in his assessment that far greater emphasis needed to be placed upon training grassroots Indians to "think white."[79] This was followed, in 1928, by an even stronger reinforcement of the idea by a Senate-appointed commission headed by University of Chicago professor Lewis Meriam: "[Our] belief is that it is a sound policy of national economy to make generous expenditure in the next few decades with the object of winding up the national administration of Indian affairs."[80]

> The fundamental requirement is that the task of the Indian Service be recognized as *primarily educational,* in the broadest sense of the word, and that it be made an efficient educational agency, devoting its main energies to the social and economic advancement of Indians, *so that they may be absorbed into the prevailing civilization or fitted to live in the presence of that civilization* [emphasis added].[81]

Cumulatively, a result of such pronouncements was, in 1934, passage of the Indian Reorganization Act (IRA), a law which in part required a greater BIA emphasis upon the mass education of indigenous children. The Johnson-O'Malley (JOM) Act (48 *Stat.* 596)—a bill providing for payment of federal funds into state accounts in exchange for state assumption of responsibility in delivering Indian educational services through the public schools—was passed the same year. Substantial appropriations were provided with which to underwrite both prongs of the new educational initiative.[82] The impact of the two statutes was immediate, reversing within a decade the previous proportions of native youngsters in school and out.

In 1943, there were 265 government schools with an enrollment of thirty-four thousand. Indian public school enrollment exceeded that figure, and more than twelve thousand eligible Indian children were not in any school. There were eighteen non-reservation boarding schools, thirty-one reservation boarding schools, and 216 day schools. Elementary grades were offered in 258 schools and partial or full high school in sixty-three. From 1933 to 1943 there was a loss of sixteen boarding schools and a gain of eighty-four [much less expensive] day schools, making a total of sixty-eight schools; enrollment had shifted from three-fourths in boarding schools in 1933 to two-thirds in day schools by 1943.[83]

The trend toward phasing out boarding schools in favor of the much more broadly focused day school/public school combination did incur a substantial degree of opposition, beginning in the mid-1940s, from a body of reactionary legislators who preferred the bludgeon rather than subversion as a means of eradicating indigenous cultures. They were quite outspoken in their demands that the "coddling" of native children be ended.

> The Indian Bureau is tending to place too much emphasis on the day school located on the Indian reservation as compared with the opportunities afforded Indian children in the off-reservation boarding schools where they can acquire an education in healthful and cultural surroundings without the handicap of having to spend their out-of-school hours in tepees, shacks with dirt floors, and no windows, in tents, in wickiups, in hogans, or in surroundings where English is never spoken, where there is a complete lack of furniture, and where there is sometimes active antagonism or an abysmal indifference to the virtues of an education.[84]

Although those holding this attitude were unable to bring about a scrapping or even curtailment of day school initiatives, they were able to keep the remaining boarding schools open for decades and actually increase the number of such facilities during the 1950s and '60s. Correspondingly, the numbers of native children consigned to such institutions *rose* substantially between 1950 and 1975. Of the 52,000 Indian children over whose education the BIA maintained direct responsibility in 1973, more than 35,000 were in boarding schools.[85] At that point, "schools like Theodore Roosevelt Boarding School at Fort Apache, New Mexico, [were] still housed in old army forts." Many, such as those at Chilocco (Oklahoma), Anadarko (Oklahoma), Oglala (South Dakota), Flandreau (South Dakota), and Phoenix (Arizona), were completely dilapidated and functioned more as holding pens than schools. Others, such as the Toyei, Shonto, and Rock Point Boarding Schools, on the Navajo Reservation, the Intermountain Indian Boarding School in Utah, and the Institute for American Indian Arts (IAIA; opened in 1962, in the facilities of the old

Santa Fé Indian Boarding School) in New Mexico, were quite modern, having been recently constructed or refurbished.[86] It was not until the very end of the 1970s that another round of closures finally finished some of the very worst institutions, such as Chilocco and Anadarko. Intermountain was not closed until the mid-'80s and others, such as IAIA, Rock Point, and Toyei, remain fully operational at the present time.

Ironically, it was precisely the same senators and representatives who most vociferously championed the harsh boarding school environment who also pushed through the termination and relocation legislation of the 1950s (see Chapters Three, Four, and Five), thus dumping many thousands of additional Indian students into the *public* school system.[87] By the late '60s, in the context of widespread social agitation by various "minority groups," notably African Americans, this had the unintended effect of precipitating a marked reinforcement of the very legislative and educational postures the reactionaries had so staunchly opposed. In 1966, President Lyndon Johnson appointed a White House Task Force headed by Walsh McDermott, a professor at Cornell University, which suggested that incipient unrest among Native Americans might be alleviated if an impression of greater Indian "input" into educational and other sorts of federal programming was fostered. In March 1968, Johnson followed up by sending a "Message on Indian Affairs" to Congress in which he reiterated the main points advanced by the task force.[88] Johnson's replacement, Richard M. Nixon, weighed in on July 8, 1970 with a "Message on Indian Policy" which articulated essentially the same principles, but placed them within a lofty-sounding rubric of "self-determination" for native people (see Chapter Three).[89]

The outcome of all this was the passage, in 1972, of the Indian Education Act (86 *Stat.* 344), which purportedly widened the extent of "Native American participation in and control over the education of their children."[90] In actuality, the bill coopted genuine Indian demands, serving only to formalize "procedures and programs that had previously existed at the discretion of funding agencies...increasing bureaucratic involvement, [and] serving...to debilitate rather than facilitate progress in Indian education."[91] After several years of escalating confrontation by organizations such as the American Indian Movement (AIM), Congress enacted a second statute—the Indian Self-Determination and Educational Assistance Act of 1975 (25 U.S.C.A. 450a-450n)—which was claimed by its sponsors to finally return such things as schooling to direct Indian control. However, as has been noted elsewhere, the 1975 act was more than anything simply a slightly revised regurgitation of the Indian Reorganization Act of 1934, and was thus "merely a rehash of a policy nearly half a century old."[92] The Indian-specific programming entailed in the 1972 and 1975 acts was coupled to "multicultural" initiatives in which Native Americans were included, with the result that the channels of indigenous "access" to both reservation and mainstream educational systems was rapidly expanded. By 1982, Lumbee educator Dean Chavers was to observe:

> Unique to the present era are a great variety of specially-funded projects in Indian education, from federal, state, and foundation sources. There are some

2,000 Indian education projects now in operation across the country at the elementary and secondary levels, most of them funded by the Office of Indian Education in the Department of Education, and the BIA Johnson-O'Malley program. Others are funded through the Gifted and Talented program, the Office of Bilingual Education and Minority Language Affairs in the Department of Education, Head Start, Follow Through, Right to Read, and others.[93]

The question, however, remained as always not whether Indian youth was to be afforded a greater degree of "educational opportunity," but what *sort* of instruction they received once placed in school. Indian radicals quickly analyzed the significance of the "new" federal posture as being a consummation of the colonial apparatus of domination. As Phyllis Young, an AIM member involved during the '70s with that organization's attempts to establish autonomous alternative schools—called "Survival Schools"—on reservations, later put it:

> The government had spent several generations "educating" a sector of the Indian population to identify its interests with those of the colonial status quo. These people had been trained to see themselves and their nations through the eyes of the colonizer, conditioned to think about everyone and everything in ways approved by the colonizer. These were what the government called, still calls, "responsible" Indians...which means, of course, they were and are people who see themselves as being responsible to the government which has colonized them. Now, these, without exception, were the people placed in charge of Indian education by the Education and Self-Determination Act of 1975...So, nothing really changed...Aside from some cosmetic alterations like the inclusion of beadwork, traditional dance, basket weaving and some language classes, the curriculum taught in Indian schools remained exactly the same, reaching exactly the same conclusions, indoctrinating children with exactly the same values as when the schools were staffed entirely by white people. Only now it was supposedly more credible to grassroots people, because people who were visibly Indian were doing the teaching and administering...You've got to hand it to them in a way. It's really a perfect system of colonization, convincing the colonized to colonize *each other* in the name of "self-determination" and "liberation."[94]

Madonna Thunderhawk, another AIM member involved with the Survival School effort, has assessed the means by which parameters of content and approach have been enforced against "Indian controlled" education under the 1975 act:

> Just in case some of these colonized Indian teachers and administrators might start to break loose from the brainwashing they'd undergone during their own schooling and attempt to do something useful by way of actually *educating* the kids in their classrooms about, say, the *real* history of Indian-white relations in this country, or the *real* nature of the present Indian-federal relationship, or the *real* meanings of our treaties, or *anything* like that, the feds always retained their ways of putting things back in line...Of course, the government controlled the purse strings all along. Step out of line, and you lose your funding. Then you have to shut down your school, eh? Then there's the matter of accreditation. Even if you somehow manage to make your school self-supporting financially,

which is no mean feat given the poverty imposed upon Indian country, they can always pull your accreditation. And that means the diplomas you issue to students who graduate are basically worthless, at least in terms of getting a job or applying to college. If you are an administrator, they can revoke your administrator's certification. If you're a teacher, they can revoke your teaching certificate. In both cases, that makes you unemployable in your field...And when all else fails—as it did with the Survival Schools because we made a matter of pride and a matter of policy to do what we did without a penny of federal money, and we didn't care about accreditation and certification and all those other things—then they use more direct measures like audits and vandalism and police harassment to put you out of business.[95]

Jimmie Durham, a Cherokee who served as the founding director of AIM's International Indian Treaty Council during the late '70s, sums up:

None of this has anything at all to do with education. The stated purpose of Indian education at the elementary and secondary levels has, since the very first moment, always been "vocational." Right? They were going to teach Indians, who were already agriculturalists, how to farm. Or they were going to teach them how to be carpenters, or blacksmiths, or cobblers, or seamstresses, or whatever...more lately, it's been nurses and electricians, and accountants, and computer technicians, and *teachers*. And always there was this secondary, more "academic" emphasis; reading skills and English language, history and civics, just enough to allegedly make Indians "good citizens" of the U.S....Well it's all bullshit. All of it...Indians never needed anybody to teach them a vocation until somebody came along and took away the resources upon which their vocations were based...So the whole thing, Indian education, has never been anything other than a way of rationalizing the process of expropriation by the expropriators, and confusing the same process for those being expropriated...If Indian education really had *anything* at all to do with the imparting of vocational skills, Indian unemployment wouldn't still be running above sixty percent, would it? You see what I mean...The same with "academics." They never teach you anything you can do anything with. They just pound enough bogus information into you to get you seriously confused about who you are, who your friends are, how the world really works, and what you can or should do about it. As long as you're confused in those ways, you can never pose a threat to those who wield power over you, your people, your land, your future generations...*That's* the purpose of the Indian education system in this country, and it always has been. Hell, those who run it have never cared whether Indians even finish the process, just as long as they're sufficiently confused about everything that's fundamental—and are therefore effectively useless to themselves and everybody else—before they leave.[96]

Much of Durham's view is borne out by the federal government's own statistics. The 1980 census, the last from which comprehensive data has been extrapolated, reveals that, nearly fifty years after passage of the JOM and IRA, barely 83 percent of Native Americans complete a grade school education, and only 56 percent complete high school. About 16 percent complete a two-year college program of study. Less than 4 percent graduate from a four-year college, and about 3 percent hold a graduate degree of some sort.[97] On the other hand, virtually every American Indian in the country has been mandatorily exposed to several years of indoctrination through a curricular body which remains virulently Eurocentric in both its overall thrust and most of its particulars.[98] Tellingly, of those Indians completing a college education, well over half have been tracked into programs leading them to pursue "educational vocations" through which they will usually dispense more of the same to younger Indians.[99]

"Higher" Education

Leaving aside a few anomalous situations such as the experiments at Dartmouth and Cambridge Colleges beginning in the 18th century, the model of education created for American Indians in the United States lacked a university-level component until the mid-1930s. Before that point, the few indigenous college graduates generally conformed to the examples set by Arthur Parker, a Seneca Indian, and Charles Curtis, a mixed-blood and thoroughly assimilated Kaw who became a career senator from Kansas and, for a while, vice president of the United States. The former, while employed as official Indian representative within the New York state government, refused to endorse the 1921 Everett Report spelling out his own people's land entitlements vis-à-vis the state (see Chapter Five). The latter used the combination of his "Indian-ness" and high position to push through a 1898 bill (the "Curtis Act," 30 *Stat.* 354) which brought about total dissolution of the land base of many native nations in Oklahoma, and continued to work to divest Indians of their property until well into the 1930s.[100]

By 1934, the decision to make the internal colonies of Native North America more self-administering through the IRA and related measures indicated a concomitant need for cultivation of many additional Parkers and Curtises. The idea was to create a much broader and more technically proficient indigenous elite to act as surrogates for U.S. interests in Indian Country.

> Prior to the passage of the Indian Reorganization Act, Federal provision for the higher education of Indians had been negligible. A small Federal appropriation and limited tribal funds had been available since 1931 for courses in technical and industrial training, and in 1932 an appropriation not to exceed ten thousand dollars was designated for vocational and higher education. In contrast, an amount not in excess of two hundred and fifty thousand dollars was authorized in 1934 for the higher and technical education of those Indians organized under the [IRA]; and the following year, a hundred and seventy-five thousand dollars were appropriated for additional [higher educational] assistance. An Act was passed in 1936 [49 *Stat.* 1458; an amendment of JOM] authorizing contracts between the government and the states for the education of Indians in such secondary schools, universities, and special schools as are open to all residents of the state.[101]

At about the same time, Bacone College (Muscogee, Oklahoma)—until that point the only exclusively Indian-focused higher educational facility in the country—was joined by the Haskell Institute (Lawrence, Kansas), a former secondary-level boarding school which was converted into a two-year technical college for selected Indians. This was coupled to the development of scholarship programs at the Colorado State College of Agricultural and Technical Arts (now Fort Lewis College) at Durango, Mills College in Oakland, California, and the University of Michigan, in addition to those already existing at Harvard University and Dartmouth College. Euroamerican patriotic and civic organizations such as the Daughters of the American Revolution, Society of Colonial Dames, Illinois Federation of Women's Clubs, and the Massachusetts Indian Society (an outgrowth of the assimilationist "Friends of the Indian" society of the 19th century) committed additional private resources to supplement the governmental-institutional undertakings.[102]

Things remained relatively constant through the 1940s and '50s, with the result that there were a total of only 1,400 American Indian university students in the United States in 1963. By 1968, however, this number had more than doubled, to slightly over 3,000. Then, with the outburst of "Red Power" politics which began to sweep the country in the latter year, the figure suddenly leapt to about 23,000 by 1972, and continued to grow to an estimated 30,000 in 1978.[103] Since then, the native student population first plateaued and, during the second half of the '80s, began to decline noticeably.[104] The rapid influx of native students to academia during the late 1960s and early- to mid-'70s also corresponded rather directly to the appearance of significant gains in transforming the university environment into a laboratory for positive social change posted by the Black liberation and student power movements, as well as other "militant" sectors of the population, during the same period.[105] For a time, there seemed to be a genuine belief among many Indian young people—fostered to a considerable extent by radical activists in organizations such as AIM and the National Indian Youth Council—that it might be possible to carve out "liberated zones" for themselves on college campuses and to use these as a basis from which to undertake the decolonization of Native North America itself.[106] By 1979, researchers of the phenomenon discovered that more than three dozen American Indian Studies programs had been created at various colleges and universities in barely five years.[107]

The earlier-noted federal Indian education programming at the elementary and secondary levels was complemented during the late '60s and early '70s by "several dozen specially-funded projects at the college level, funded by the Office of Indian Education, the Office of Bilingual Education, the Education Professions Development Act, and the National Science Foundation, among others."[108] Multicultural programming extended through the Department of Education's "TRIO" effort—encompassing Upward Bound, Talent Search, and Special Services components—had an additional effect in terms of tracking selected Indian high-schoolers toward college degree programs in technical fields,[109] as did private organizations such as the American Indian Science and Engineering Society (AISES) and the Council of Energy Resource Tribes (CERT) Education Fund, both highly interlocked with and financially dependent upon non-Indian corporate entities extracting super-profits from reservation resources.[110]

Beginning in 1969, with the establishment of Navajo Community College (Tsaile, AZ), the government also began to underwrite the creation of reservation-based community colleges, mainly devoted to the teaching of advanced vocational skills. By the early '80s, there were twenty-five such institutions scattered across Indian Country, all of them firmly under control of federal accreditation agencies.[111] By the latter point, even some of the more devoted advocates of such "Indian-controlled higher educational institutions" had begun to see that their imagined "alternative" was merely a sophisticated continuation of business as usual. As the rather establishmentarian Lumbee educator Dean Chavers observed at the time:

> Since the bureaucracy which operates the federal Indian system is not account-able to the persons it serves, the operation of the system is the U.S. equivalent of domestic colonialism. As a colonized people, natives are in a no-win position, holding few positions of power, with little authority or control over their own lives, and living a largely anomic existence. The bureaucrats act as very efficient gatekeepers, allowing only information which they want dissem-inated to pass through the channels of communication...The controllers of education in the United States define the product which is to be considered for development by faculty members, and this product for higher education has been defined as scientific research. This concentration on scientific research has tended to denigrate knowledge that is arrived at in other ways, or other ways of seeking truth [thus serving to reinforce the Eurocentric status quo at every step along the way to a degree].[112]

During the period of intense societal ferment in which the upsurge in Indian college enrollment occurred, the response of the status quo was one of containment. Ground was given by educational administrators and policymakers in which ostensibly autonomous programs were initiated, not only by Native Americans, but by African Americans, Chicanos and Puertorriqueños, Asian Americans, and women.[113] Once the social movements which had given rise to these circumstances had spent themselves (or had been physically repressed by the state), however, the institutional hierarchy once again asserted itself. By and large, the hard-won "minority" programs were not dismantled. Rather, they were converted into a form of "glorified vo-tech" and made "accountable," in the name of "academic stan-dards," "quality" and the like, to the very edifices of intellectual Eurocentrism and male supremacism that they had been established to counteract.[114] By the end of the 1970s, it had become a normative reality in academia that those who taught in Ethnic and Women's Studies programs were required to be "credentialed" by the very white male academic power structure they were allegedly hired to offset.[115] In short order, of course, such programs were largely staffed by individuals willing to engage exclusively in "responsible" scholarship, professing knowledge entirely acceptable to the status quo.[116] As AIM leader Russell Means has put it:

> You go to any major airport in the country and you're guaranteed to see at least three "Indians" all decked out in their institutional three-piece blue suits, their hair all freshly razor-cut and blow-dried, carrying their perfectly professional-looking little briefcases, rushing around to catch their planes to Washington,

D.C. That's the image of the modern Indian sell-out, and it's a rapidly growing phenomenon...True, a lot of them work for corporations or directly for the government, as they've been trained to do almost since birth. But most of them are the so-called "Indian educators" who are completely sold out, and whose business it is to see that the next generation of Indian children grow up to be just like them. What they're forever rushing off to do is to wag their tails like good dogs and report to their federal masters how well they're doing at brainwashing our kids to think and act like little white people. That way they get the old pat on the head from the feds: more money, more "status," another silly award for "education excellence." In the alternative, they've been ordered to D.C. to attend "workshops" where the feds give them the next set of instructions as to how they're to proceed...It's disgusting, demeaning and degrading just to have to *look* at these people, who the government says are the only "legitimate Indian representatives." The educational system in this country—*especially* the "higher" education system—is one of the worst enemies presently confronting our nations, at least as it's presently structured.[117]

Under such conditions, the best, brightest, and most socially committed Indian students have tended to drop out in droves, while those most inclined by their earlier conditioning to pursue vocational tracks fitting well within the colonial paradigm tend to excel (or at least get by).[118] Recent data indicates that fewer than 5 percent of all Native American students at the university level are pursuing a course of study which might be expected to result in anything other than a further consolidation of the self-colonizing dynamic in which they and their people have become increasingly mired since 1934.[119] By the same token, only a handful of Indian Studies programs—there are now more than 100—offer a curriculum or possess a faculty with the competence to offer any other outcome.[120] Indeed, at this point, Euro-indoctrinated Indian faculty often provide the first line of defense for Eurocentric institutions seeking to keep out (or at bay) those more liberation-minded native scholars who would inevitably tend to "rock the boat" (and thus show the sell-outs up for what they are). Altogether, the higher educational dimension of American Indian education serves at present as little more than the capstone to the whole colonialist system of indoctrinating and thus dominating indigenous peoples of North America perfected by Euroamerica over the past three centuries.[121]

Alternatives

Bright spots in the dismal panorama which comprises contemporary American Indian education are exceedingly hard to find. Nonetheless, they *are* there. As with any system which has grown as rapidly and extensively as that pertaining to the indoctrination of Indians over the past quarter-century, certain entities and individuals have inevitably "fallen through the cracks" of the control network effected by the status quo. In an important essay published in 1987, Juaneño/Yaqui scholar M. Annette Jaimes pointed to a selection of these—all of them at the university level—and elaborated the conceptual basis upon which they might be amplified and expanded into a viable alternative to the colonialist model, using certain aspects of its existing structure for the purpose.[122] In this, she followed leads articulated by others, such as Vine Deloria, Jr., and Ward Churchill, somewhat earlier. As Deloria put it in 1986, American Indian Studies efforts must adopt a consciously anti-colonialist stance if they are to be bona fide academic endeavors:

> Indian Studies programs must...define their goals as encompassing all relevant knowledge and information concerning the relationship between American Indians and the rest of the world, be it the federal government, other religions, the world of arts and music, or international and domestic economies.[123]

Churchill had by then already called for development of conscious alliances between Indian Studies practitioners and other sectors of academe—other Ethnic Studies and Women's Studies components, and certain elements of the left-oriented intellectual community—opposed to what he described as the "White Studies" model of U.S. education.[124] His call was for an explicitly politicized variety of multicultural education as a means of avoiding the sorts of fragmentation and isolation he felt accounted for the preceding failures of virtually all potential alternatives to educational orthodoxy in the United States.[125] Such views were increasingly endorsed by a scattering of other indigenous educators as the '80s moved along, and in some instances attempts to pilot unabashedly anti-imperialist variants of American Indian Studies curricula were attempted.[126]

In perhaps the most noteworthy example, Jaimes (as director) and Churchill (as Indian Studies instructor) collaborated during the latter part of the 1980s to deliver what was called the "TRIBES Institute" to a selected group of incoming freshman students through the University Learning Center at the University of Colorado at Boulder (UCB).[127] Underwritten by the CERT Education Fund (based in Denver), the project was designed to deliver a full semester's college-level instruction in just eight weeks during the summer. The curriculum consisted of computer-assisted mathematics and physical sciences courses, as well as an "English" component (reading comprehension and expository writing), all keyed to—indeed, integrated with—a central Indian Studies course focusing on policy studies, law, and economic development alternatives. The final project of the UCB TRIBES program was for groups of students to advance a comprehensive plan applying newly gained knowledge to achieving genuine self-determination for the residents of a hypothetical Indian reservation.[128]

The project was resoundingly successful in terms of attracting and retaining students: in its final year at UCB, it brought a record thirty-six students to campus, "graduating" 33 of them with an average of twelve credit hours apiece, and at an unprecedented overall grade point average (ascertained by standardized tests).[129] At the end of that year, however, CERT Fund Director Lucille Echohawk, citing vaguely defined "problems" with the project's delivery, withdrew her organization's support to the UCB endeavor.[130] In 1990, she committed CERT funds to an undertaking at Colorado State University at Fort Collins which was devoid of the explicit anti-colonialist theme evident in the UCB effort. The result was graduation of only fourteen students (the rest having withdrawn from the program, with prejudice, by week five), with an average of fewer than nine credit hours and a substantially lower average GPA.[131] Serious accusations of financial impropriety (not the spectacular collapse in academic performance) caused CERT to relocate the TRIBES Program to the Colorado School of Mines in Golden for 1991. There, the project graduated only six students, again with deficiencies in credit hours earned and a deteriorating aggregate GPA.[132] Echohawk continues to insist that the "problems"—read, *politics*—attending the record-breaking and successful 1989 UCB project cycle "justified" her subsequent squandering of the program's patently obvious benefit to participating students, a matter which says all that needs saying about CERT's real "educational" agenda and the principles of those Russell Means described above as "sell-outs."

Although the TRIBES experience at UCB speaks eloquently to the extent of the hurdles which must be cleared if modern American Indian education is ever to be torn free from the imperial grip of the Euroamerican governmental/corporate elite and those Indians who willingly serve its interests, it *did* register solid proof that liberated forms of pedagogy still strike a responsive cord—despite the layers of indoctrination which have been imposed upon them in grade and high school— among a wide spectrum of indigenous students. Having amply demonstrated that the approach *can* work, Churchill and Jaimes set about devising a comparable curricular structure for application within the newly formed American Indian Studies Program within the Center for Studies of Ethnicity and Race in America (CSERA) at UCB.[133] At present, in cooperation with Vine Deloria, who joined the CSERA Indian Studies faculty in 1990, they are in the process of implementing it as a model for possible replication in other institutions. Similar efforts have recently been undertaken in the American Indian Studies Program at Cornell University, in the American Studies Program at SUNY Buffalo, and elsewhere.

Such bright spots represent but a tiny point of departure in any attempt to staunch the flow of what amounts to a veritable sea of negativity and false consciousness presently engulfing American Indian education as a whole. However, to follow a formulation advanced by Herbert Marcuse, they may ultimately prove to be the "Archimedean point" from which false consciousness can be breached, setting in motion the process leading to "a more comprehensive emancipation" from colonialism and oppression, not only for Native Americans, but for everyone else as well.[134] The alternative, should attempts by CSERA's, Cornell's, and other Indian Studies programs to achieve a genuinely liberatory structure fail, we will all be consigned—as Deloria so aptly phrased it—to an "education" in which we collectively "recite certain facts and give football cheers, [because] we really have little else to cheer about." We are at a crossroads. The matter could go either way.[135]

Notes

1. Quoted in Fuchs, Estelle, and Robert J. Havighurst, *To Live on this Earth: American Indian Education*, Anchor Books, Garden City, NY, 1973, p. 2. Further information on Jesuit education in the process of French colonization in North America may be found in Mulvey, Sister Mary Doris, *French Catholic Missionaries in the Present United States, 1604-1791*, Catholic University of America Press, Washington, D.C., 1936. Most comprehensively, see Thwaites, Rubin G.

(ed.), *The Jesuit Relations and Allied Documents* (73 Vols.), Burrows Brothers Publishers, Cleveland, OH, 1919.

2. A good discussion of mission school pedagogy in "New France" may be found in Orata, Pedro T., *Democracy and Indian Education*, U.S. Department of Interior, Office of Indian Affairs, Washington, D.C., 1938. Also see Wrong, George M., *The Rise and Fall of New France* (2 Vols.), Macmillan Publishers, New York, 1928.

3. See Hanke, Lewis, *The First Social Experiments in America: A Study of the Development of Spanish Indian Policy in the Sixteenth Century*, Harvard University Press, Cambridge, MA, 1934. Considerable data may also be obtained from Charlevoix, Pierre F.X. de, S.J., *The History of Paraguay* (2 Vols.), Printer to the Royal Society, London, 1769.

4. Adams, Evelyn C., *American Indian Education: Government Schools and Economic Progress*, King's Crown Press, Morningside Heights, New York, 1946, p. 9. Also see O'Daniel, Victor F., *Dominicans in Early Florida*, United States Catholic Historical Society, New York, 1930; Lanning, John T., *The Spanish Missions of Georgia*, University of North Carolina Press, Chapel Hill, 1935; and O'Rourke, Theodore P., *Franciscan Missions in Texas* Catholic University of America Press, Washington, D.C., 1927.

5. See Englehart, Charles A. (Fr. Zephyrin), *The Missions and Missionaries of California* (4 Vols.), James H. Barry Publishers, San Francisco, 1908-1916.

6. Adams, op. cit., p. 11. Also see Bishop, Herbert E., "The Mission as a Frontier Institution in the Spanish-American Colonies," *American Historical Review*, Vol. XXIII, October 1917, pp. 42-61.

7. See Stith, William, *The History of the First Discovery and Settlement of Virginia*, William Parks Publisher, Williamsburg, VA, 1747. Another very informative primary tract is Humphreys, David, *An Historical Account of the Incorporated Society for Propagation of the Gospel in Foreign Parts*, Joseph Downing Publishers, London, 1730. Also see Andrews, Charles M., *Our Earliest Colonial Settlements*, New York University Press, New York, 1933; and Land, Robert H., "Henrico and Its College," *William and Mary Quarterly*, Vol. XVIII, 1938.

8. On this period of warfare and diplomacy, see Wissler, Clark, *Indians of the United States: Four Centuries of their History and Culture*, Doubleday, Dornan and Co., Publishers, New York, 1940. Also see Osgood, Herbert L., *The American Colonies in the Seventeenth Century* (3 Vols.), Macmillan Publishers, New York, 1904.

9. Adams, op. cit., p. 17. Also see Eliot, John, *New England's First Fruits*, Joseph Sabin Publishers, New York, 1865.

10. A very interesting account may be found in Pierce, Benjamin, *A History of Harvard University from its Founding in the Year 1636 to the Period of the American Revolution*, Brown, Shattuck and Co., Publishers, Cambridge, MA, 1833. Of related interest, see Davis, Andrew M., "The Indian College at Cambridge," *Magazine of American History*, Vol. XXIV, July 1890.

11. Adams, op. cit., p. 18. For Wheeler's own view of what he was seeking, see his "Narrative, 1762, of the Original Design, Progress, and Present State of the Indian Charity School in Lebanon, Connecticut," *Old South Leaflets*, Vol. I, No. 22, n.d. An indispensable insight into the impact of the Dartmouth experience upon its students during the formative period may be found in McCallum, James D., ed., *The Letters of Eleazer Wheelock's Indians*, Dartmouth College Publications, Hanover, NH, 1932. Also see Richardson, Leon B., *The History of Dartmouth College* (2 Vols.), Dartmouth College Publications, Hanover, NH, 1932.

12. Randolph, J.W., *The History of William and Mary, 1660-1874*, Randolph and English Publishers, Richmond, VA, 1874.

13. William Johnson was essentially Britain's ambassador to the Haudenosaunee from 1756 until his death in 1774. Using Kirkland's mission schools as a medium, he relied upon the "education" of selected Iroquois leaders to assist in forging a military alliance with the confederacy against the French. See Stone, William L. Jr., *The Life and Times of Sir William Johnson* (2 Vols.), J. Munsell Publisher, Albany, NY, 1865; and Lothrop, Samuel K., "The Life of Samuel Kirkland," *The Library of American Biography*, 2d Series, Vol. XV. Also see Hunt, George T., *The Wars of the Iroquois*, University of Wisconsin Press, Madison, 1940.

14. On the Brainerd brothers' work among the Delaware, see Brainerd, Thomas, *The Life of John Brainerd, 1720-1781*, Presbyterian Publication Co., Philadelphia, PA, 1865; and Edwards, Jonathan, ed., *The Memoirs of David Brainerd*, Converse Publishers, New Haven, CT, 1822. Also see Hecheweider, John G.E., *A Narrative of the Mission of the United Brethren among the Delaware and Mohegan Indians from its Commencement in 1740 to the Close of the Year 1808*, McCartney and Davis Publishers, Philadelphia, PA, 1820.

15. Adams, op. cit., p. 23.
16. Carnoy, Martin, *Education as Cultural Imperialism*, David McKay Publishers, New York, 1974, p. 16.
17. Ibid. This concept is handled well in Kemp, Tom, *Theories of Imperialism*, Dobson Books, London, 1967. For a more pedantic view, see Symanski, Albert, *The Logic of Imperialism*, Praeger Publishers, New York, 1981.
18. Ibid., p. 17. For further elaboration on this theme, see Brown, Michael Barrett, *After Imperialism*, Humanities Press, New York, 1970.
19. Ibid., p. 18. On the concept of Eurocentric domination, see Amin, Samir, *Eurocentrism*, Monthly Review Press, New York, 1989.
20. Memmi, Albert, *The Colonizer and the Colonized*, Beacon Press, Boston, p. 89.
21. Ibid., p. 105.
22. Clinget, Remi, "Damned If You Do, Damned If You Don't: The Dilemmas of Colonizer-Colonized Relations," *Comparative Education Review*, Vol. 15, No. 3, October 1971, p. 301.
23. For a succinct articulation of these ideas, see Galtung, Johan, "A Structural Theory of Imperialism," *Journal of Peace Research*, Vol. 8, No. 2, Summer 1971.
24. The term underdevelopment was popularized by Andre Gunder Frank; see his *Capitalism and Underdevelopment in Latin America*, Monthly Review Press, New York, 1969.
25. Considerable development of this theme may be found in Memmi, Albert, *Dominated Men*, Orion Press, New York, 1968.
26. Galeano, Eduardo, *The Open Veins of Latin America: Five Centuries of the Pillage of a Continent*, Monthly Review Press, New York, 1973.
27. Adams, op. cit., p. 26.
28. Ibid., pp. 27-8. Also see Schaaf, Gregory, *Wampum Belts and Peace Trees: George Morgan, Native Americans and Revolutionary Diplomacy*, Fulcrum Publishers, Golden, CO, 1990.
29. Adams, op. cit., p. 28. Also see Cox, Isaac J., "The Indian as Diplomatic Factor in the Old Northwest," *Chicago Historical Society Proceedings*, Vol. V, 1910, pp. 265-303.
30. Franklin, Benjamin, *Two Tracts, Information to Those Who Would Remove to America and Remarks Concerning the Savages of North America*, London, (3rd Edition) 1794, pp. 28-9; excerpted in Labaree, Leonard W., *et al.*, eds., *The Papers of Benjamin Franklin*, Yale University Press, New Haven, CT, 1961, pp. 481-3.
31. The sum was reduced to $15,000 per year in 1803, but then supplemented from other quarters. Details of the various sources and appropriations throughout the entire period may be found in U.S. Congress, *Journals of the Continental Congress* (34 Vols.), U.S. Government Printing Office, Washington, D.C., 1905-1909.
32. This and all other treaty texts referred to in the present essay may be found in Kappler, Charles J., ed., *Indian Treaties, 1778-1883*, Interland Publishing Co., New York, (second printing) 1973.
33. See generally, Downes, Randolph C., *Council Fires on the Upper Ohio*, University of Pittsburgh Press, Pittsburgh, 1940. The arrangement with the Kaskaskia is particularly interesting insofar as the Indians had a long-standing relationship with French Jesuits. Consequently, the rabidly anti-Catholic Continental Congress was placed in the position of funding the missionary work of priests in the area as an expedient to subverting the ability of the Illinois Indians to resist conquest and colonization. See Schuyler, Robert L., *The Transition in Illinois from British to American Government*, Columbia University Press, New York, 1909. Also see Palm, Sister Mary Borgias, *The Jesuit Missions of the Illinois Country*, unpublished doctoral dissertation, St. Louis University, St. Louis, 1930. Of related interest, see Phelps Kellogg, Louise, *The French Régime in Wisconsin and the Northwest*, State Historical Society of Wisconsin (Vol. XV), Madison, 1925.
34. The period immediately following the military defeat in 1813 of Tecumseh's confederacy and the "Redstick Rebellion" of the Creek Confederacy the following year—the last coherent military resistance of indigenous people east of the Mississippi—witnessed a dramatic surge in federal initiatives to foster "education of the savages." See Edmunds, R. David, *Tecumseh and the Quest for American Indian Leadership*, Little Publishers, Boston, 1984; and Martin, Joel W., *Sacred Revolt: The Muskogees' Struggle for a New World*, Beacon Press, Boston, 1991.
35. These moves are covered in McLeod, William C., *The American Indian Frontier*, Alfred A. Knopf Publishers, New York, 1928. Another interesting handling may be found in Williams, Francis F., *The Blending of Cultures*, Walter Alfred Bock, Government Printer, Port Moresby, NY, 1935. Also see Morse, Jedidiah, *A Report to the Secretary of War of the United States on Indian Affairs*, S. Converse Publishers, New Haven, CT, 1822.

36. See Nichols, Claude A., *Moral Education among the North American Indians*, Columbia University Teachers College Bureau of Publications, New York, 1930.
37. Adams, op. cit., pp. 32-3. Also see Abel, Annie H., "The History of Events Resulting in Indian Consolidation West of the Mississippi River," *The American Historical Association Annual Report*, Vol. I, 1906, pp. 235-454.
38. U.S. Commissioner of Indian Affairs, *Annual Report*, U.S. Government Printing Office, Washington, D.C., 1825.
39. A summary of the Academy may be found in Brod, Rodney L., *Choctaw Education*, LPS and Associates, Box Elder, MT, 1979. For the general context in which this was occurring, see Foreman, Grant, *Advancing the Frontier, 1830-1860*, University of Oklahoma Press, Norman, 1933.
40. Adams, op. cit., p. 36. Also see Foreman, Grant, *Indian Removal: The Immigration of the Five Civilized Tribes to Oklahoma*, University of Oklahoma Press, Norman, 1953.
41. American Indian Policy Review Commission Report on Indian Education, *Final Report of Task Force Five*, U.S. Government Printing Office, Washington, D.C., 1976.
42. Adams, op. cit., p. 37. Also see Reisner, Edward H., *The Evolution of the Common School*, Macmillan Publishers, New York, 1930.
43. Hoopes, Alban W., *Indian Affairs and their Administration with Special Preference to the Far West, 1849-1860*, University of Pennsylvania Press, Philadelphia, 1932.
44. U.S. Commissioner of Indian Affairs, *Annual Report*, U.S. Government Printing Office, Washington, D.C., 1848. Also see Hoopes, op. cit.
45. Adams, op. cit., p. 40.
46. Ibid., p. 41. The author is relying on the annual report of the Secretary of War for 1848.
47. U.S. Commissioner of Indian Affairs, *Annual Report*, U.S. Government Printing Office, Washington, D.C., 1868.
48. Considerable additional information may be obtained in Berkhofer, Robert F. Jr., *Salvation and the Savage: An Analysis of Protestant Missions and American Indian Response, 1787-1862*, University of Kentucky Press, Knoxville, 1965.
49. Adams, op. cit., pp. 39-40.
50. Ibid., p. 50.
51. This is well covered in Rushmore, Elsie M., *The Indian Policy during Grant's Administration*, Marion Press, New York, 1914.
52. U.S. Senate, Committee on Labor and Public Welfare, Subcommittee on Indian Education, *Indian Education: A National Tragedy—A National Challenge* (Report No. 95-501), 91st Cong., 1st Sess., U.S. Government Printing Office, Washington, D.C., 1969.
53. U.S. Commissioner of Indian Affairs, *Annual Report*, U.S. Government Printing Office, Washington, D.C., 1880, p. xxiii. Quoted in James, M. Annette, and Ward Churchill, "Behind the Rhetoric: 'English Only' as Counterinsurgency Warfare," *Issues in Radical Therapy/New Studies on the Left*, Vol. XIII, Nos. 1-2, Winter-Spring 1988, pp. 42-50.
54. U.S. Commissioner of Indian Affairs, *Annual Report, 1886*, op. cit., p. xxiv.
55. This theme, and several quotations from Eaton, are contained in Willard W. Beatty's quasi-official apologia for the boarding school system, *Education for Culture Change*, U.S. Department of Interior, Bureau of Indian Affairs (Chilocco Indian School), Chilocco, OK, 1953.
56. For Pratt's own view, see his *Battlefield and Classroom: Four Decades with the American Indian*, Yale University Press, New Haven, CT, 1964. A more official perspective is contained in Pratt, Richard H., *et al.*, "Circular No. 4," attached to U.S. Commissioner of Indian Affairs, *Annual Report*, U.S. Government Printing Office, Washington, D.C., 1884. On the imprisonment and subsequent murder of Osceola on January 27, 1838, see Boyd, Mark F., "Asi-Yahola or Osceola," *Florida Historical Quarterly*, Vol. XXXIII, Nos. 1-2, January/April 1955. On the Cheyennes, see Rushmore, op. cit. On Geronimo's incarceration at Fort Marion, see Barrett, S.M., ed., *Geronimo: His Own Story*, E.P. Dutton Co., New York, 1971.
57. Adams, op. cit., p. 52.
58. Superb photos of this enforced physical transformation appear in Roessel, Robert A. Jr., *Pictorial History of the Navajo from 1860 to 1910*, Navajo Curriculum Center, Rough Rock Demonstration School, Rough Rock, AZ, 1980, pp. 121-4.
59. Adams, op. cit.
60. The process is delineated very well with regard to one indigenous nation in Thompson, Laura, *A Culture in Crisis: A Study of the Hopi Indians*, Harper and Brothers Publishers, New York,

1950. More broadly, see Galleher, Ruth A., "The Indian Agent in the United States since 1850," *Iowa Journal of History and Politics*, Vol. XIV, April 1916, pp. 173-238. The position of Indian agent was eliminated from the federal bureaucracy in 1908.

61. For the text of the 1948 Genocide Convention, see Brownlie, Ian, ed., *Basic Documents on Human Rights*, Oxford University Press, London/New York, 1971.

62. Hampton, of course, is primarily known during this period as having been an industrial school devoted to training former slaves to "earn a living" in their newly emancipated state. The first Indian students were a group of recalcitrant warriors (adults) transferred there by Pratt from Fort Marion Prison. See "Circular No. 4," op. cit.

63. Adams, op. cit., pp. 53-4.

64. Jackson, Curtis E., and Marcia J. Galli, *A History of the Bureau of Indian Affairs and Its Activities Among Indians*, R&E Research Associates, San Francisco, 1977. Also see McKinley, Francis, Stephen Bayne and Glen Nimnicht, *Who Should Control Indian Education?* Far West Laboratory for Educational Research and Development, Berkeley, 1970.

65. Lummis, Charles, *Bullying the Hopi*, Prescott College Press, Prescott, AZ, 1968, pp. 20-1. Also see James, Harry, ed., *Pages from Hopi History*, University of Arizona Press, Tucson, 1976.

66. One example is the division of the village of Oraibi, the oldest continuously occupied site in North America, into two villages—Old Oraibi (inhabited by followers of the traditional Kikmongwe ways) and New Oraibi (built for Mormonized Hopis)—once those who had been taken to boarding schools began to return and "assert themselves." See Titiev, Misha, *Old Oraibi, Papers of the Peabody Museum of American Archaeology and Ethnology*, Vol. 22, No. 1, Harvard University Press, Cambridge, MA, 1944. More generally, see Thompson, Laura, and Alice Joseph, *The Hopi Way*, University of Michigan Press, Ann Arbor, 1944.

67. The quote comes from Indian Commissioner Frances E. Leupp in his book *The Indian and His Problem*, Charles Scribner's Sons, New York, 1910 (reprinted by Arno Press, New York, 1971), p. 93.

68. Adams, op. cit., pp. 55-6, 70. Such aspects of the boarding school experience were restricted neither to the turn-of-the-century time period, nor to the United States. As late as the end of the 1970s, students continued to report being "deloused" with DDT upon arrival, and routine beatings for "infractions" such as speaking to one another in their native tongues. The same procedures have pertained in Canada; see Johnson, Basil H., *Indian School Days*, Key Porter Books, Ltd., Toronto, 1988.

69. Jackson and Galli, op. cit., p. 31.

70. Funding levels hardly kept pace with escalating per capita costs as boarding school pedagogy became ever more regimented. According to Interior Department annual summaries, the federal boarding school expenditures, once adjusted for inflation, did not increase appreciably from 1897 to 1930.

71. U.S. Department of Interior, *Annual Report: Indian Affairs*, U.S. Government Printing Office, Washington, D.C., 1901, pp. 1-2, 26.

72. A wonderful example of how this worked may be found in the perpetuation of the Potlatch cultures of the Pacific Northwest despite their being officially criminalized by both the U.S. and Canadian governments during the 1890s. For a succinct analysis of the means used to this end in one native society (essentially representative of all which participated), see Cole, Douglas, "Underground Potlatch: How the Kwakiutl kept the Faith," *Natural History*, October 1991, pp. 50-3.

73. According to an official government study undertaken during the late 1920s, well under a quarter of all Indian youth were being "formally educated" by 1925. Of those, more than half were receiving only a "partial" indoctrination. See Meriam, Lewis, et al., *The Problem of Indian Administration*, Johns Hopkins University Press, Baltimore, 1928.

74. Many aspects of this are well covered, albeit from a rather paternalistic viewpoint, in Spindler, George D., ed., *Education and Culture: Anthropological Perspectives*, Holt, Rinehart and Winston Publishers, New York, 1963.

75. This roughly corresponds to the issuance of the dissident "Declaration of Indian Purpose" at the Chicago Indian Conference in 1961, the founding of the National Indian Youth Council (NIYC) by Clyde Warrior the same year, and commencement of "fish-in" activities in the Pacific Northwest in 1963. The declaration appears in Josephy, Alvin M. Jr., *Red Power: The American Indian's Fight For Freedom*, McGraw-Hill Publishers, New York, 1971, pp. 37-40. Warrior and the founding of NIYC are covered in Steiner, Stan, *The New Indians*, Harper and Row

Publishers, New York, 1968. On the fish-in movement, see American Friends Service Committee, *Uncommon Controversy: Fishing Rights of the Muckleshoot, Puyallup, and Nisqually Indians*, University of Washington Press, Seattle, 1970.

76. Leupp's regulations, effected in 1906, were not codified in law for more than a decade, under the Act of May 25, 1918 (40 *Stat. L.* 564): "[H]ereafter no appropriation, except appropriations made pursuant to treaties, shall be used to educate children of less than one-fourth Indian blood whose parents are citizens of the United States and the State wherein they live and where there are adequate free-school facilities provided." For all practical intents and purposes, this meant that children of less than one quarter "blood quantum" would no longer be considered as Indians by federal and state governments. For further discussion of the application of eugenics coding against American Indians in the United States, see Chapter Four.

77. Leupp, op. cit. The government had also experimented with "contract" schools, run as private business or religious enterprises by non-Indians, beginning with a pilot program launched on the Tulalip Reservation in Washington state in September 1869. Although the idea was simply an extension of the mission school concept which had formed the backbone of the federal Indian education effort until about 1870, it was described by the Justice Department as being a possible conflict with the constitutional prohibition against state-funded religious activity. Congress finally abolished the federal contract system in 1897. However, Commissioner Leupp managed to circumvent the law through deceptive accounting practices, beginning in 1905. His method was to simply allocate the necessary "education funds" to "tribal governments" composed of carefully selected individuals who had completed their boarding school training and who functioned under direct control of BIA authorities on their reservations. These entities, upon instruction from the commissioner, let and paid the contracts each year with the federal funds provided for this purpose. As of late 1991, the illegal subterfuge continues, usually in the name of "Indian self-determination."

78. Adams, op. cit., pp. 66-7. The law referred to is the Act of February 15, 1929 (45 *Stat.* 1185).

79. U.S. House of Representatives, Committee of One Hundred, *The Indian Problem: Resolution of the Committee of One Hundred Appointed by the Secretary of Interior and Review of the Indian Problem*, H. Doc. 149 (Serial 8392), 68th Cong., 1st Sess., U.S. Government Printing Office, Washington, D.C., 1928.

80. Meriam, op. cit., p. 16.

81. Ibid., p. 21.

82. For context on the IRA and JOM educational initiatives, see Deloria, Vine Jr., and Clifford M. Lytle, *The Nations Within: The Past and Future of American Indian Sovereignty*, Pantheon Press, New York, 1984.

83. Adams, op. cit., p. 80.

84. U.S. Congress, Joint Committee on Indian Affairs (1944), quoted in *Indian Education: A National Tragedy—A National Challenge*, op. cit., p. 157.

85. Fuchs and Havighurst, op. cit., p. 228.

86. Ibid., pp. 222-45.

87. On the relocation influx and its effects, see Guillemin, Jeanne, *Urban Renegades: The Cultural Strategy of American Indians*, Columbia University Press, New York, 1975.

88. Striner, Herbert E., *Towards a Fundamental Program for the Training, Employment and Economic Opportunity of the American Indian*, W.E. Upjohn Institute for Employment Research, Washington, D.C., 1968.

89. Office of the President of the United States, *Recommendations for Indian Policy* (Doc. No. 91-363), 91st Cong., 2d Sess., U.S. Government Printing Office, Washington, D.C., July 8, 1970.

90. Kennedy, Senator Edward M., Statement on CBS News, August 14, 1972.

91. Deloria, Vine Jr., and Clifford M. Lytle, *American Indians, American Justice*, University of Texas Press, Austin, 1983, pp. 22-3.

92. Ibid., p. 23.

93. Chavers, Dean, "False Promises: Barriers in Indian Education," *Integrateducation*, Vol. XIX, Nos. 1-2, January 1982, p. 14.

94. Young, Phyllis, telephone interview, June 19, 1986 (tape on file).

95. Thunderhawk, Madonna, conversation with Ward Churchill, April 1985; tape provided by Churchill. On the AIM Survival Schools, see Braudy, Susan, "We Will Remember Survival School: The Women and Children of the American Indian Movement," *Ms. Magazine*, No. 5, July 1976, pp. 94-120.

96. Durham, Jimmie, talk at Alfred University, March 1990 (tape on file).
97. These data are extracted from U.S. Bureau of the Census, *1980 Census of the Population: General Social and Economic Characteristics (PC 80-1-C1)*, U.S. Government Printing Office, Washington, D.C., December 1983.
98. Ogbu, J.U., "Cultural Discontinuities and Schooling," *Anthropology and Education Quarterly*, Vol. 12, No. 4, 1982, pp. 1-10.
99. The figures are 17.8 percent in elementary/preschool education, 14 percent in educationally related counseling, 8.4 percent in educational administration, 7.5 percent in art education, 3.7 percent in music education, for a total of 51.4 percent of all Indian college graduates. An additional 6.5 percent move into college-level teaching. It is also probable that a hefty proportion of the 4.7 percent who take degrees in sociology, 2.8 percent in economics, 2.8 percent in psychology, 1.9 percent in chemistry, 1.9 percent in mathematics, and 1.9 percent in biology pursue teaching as a vocation during all or part of their careers. These data derive from a chart compiled by Charlotte Heth and Susan Guyette in *Issues for the Future of American Indian Studies*, American Indian Studies Center, UCLA, 1985, p. 12. For analysis of implications, see Jaimes, M. Annette, "The Myth of Indian Education in the American Educational System," *Action in Teacher Education*, Vol. 5, No. 3, 1985.
100. For an assessment of the "example" set by Curtis, and the impact of his political activities, albeit from a reverse angle, see Burke, Charles H., "Indians Making Progress Learning the White Man's Way," *School Life*, No. 9, 1924. Also see Philp, Kenneth R., *John Collier's Crusade for Indian Reform, 1920-1954*, University of Arizona Press, Tucson, 1977.
101. Adams, op. cit., p. 83.
102. Ibid., pp. 82-3. Also see Collier, John, "United States Indian Administration as a Laboratory in Ethnic Relations," *Social Research*, No. 12, September 1945, pp. 265-303.
103. This was still only about half of parity in college-level participation by American Indians. See U.S. Commission on Civil Rights, *Social Indicators of Inequality for Minorities and Women*, U.S. Government Printing Office, Washington, D.C., 1978.
104. Heth and Guyette, op. cit.
105. On the inroads made by Black liberationists into the academy during the second half of the '60s, see Brown, Roscoe, "The White University Must Respond to Black Students' Needs," *Negro Digest*, Vol. 18, No. 5, 1969. For a recap of the impact and thinking of the primarily Euroamerican student power movement during the same period, see Davidson, Carl, *The New Radicals in the Multiversity and Other Writings on Student Syndicalism*, Charles Kerr Publishers, Chicago, 1990.
106. For a prominent illustration, see the chapter entitled "The Academic Aborigine" in Steiner, op. cit.
107. Churchill, Ward, and Norbert S. Hill, Jr., "Indian Education at the University Level: An Historical Survey," *Journal of Ethnic Studies*, Vol. 7, No. 3, 1979, pp. 44-58. Also see Churchill, Ward, "National Patterns in Contemporary Indian Studies Programs," in James R. Young, ed., *Multicultural Education and the American Indian*, American Indian Studies Center, UCLA, 1979, pp. 55-68.
108. Chavers, op. cit.
109. On TRIO and other federal programs affecting Indians, see Thompson, Thomas, ed., *The Schooling of Native America*, American Association of Colleges for Teacher Education, Washington, D.C., 1978.
110. On AISES, see the organization's annual reports for fiscal information, and its publication, *Winds of Change*, for insight into its corporately oriented educational philosophy. On the Council of Energy Resource Tribes, see LaDuke, Winona, "CERT; An Outsider's View In," in Joseph Jorgenson, ed., *Native Americans and Energy Resource Development II*, Anthropological Resource Center/Seventh Generation Fund, Cambridge, MA, 1984.
111. On the community colleges, see Duchene, Maryls, "A Profile of Indian Community Colleges," *Integrateducation*, Vol. XIX, Nos. 1-2, January 1982, pp. 23-7. They are also covered in Native American Information Center, *Indian College Programs*, Bacone College, Muscogee, OK, 1980.
112. Chavers, op. cit., pp. 15-6.
113. On this theme, see Reed, David, *Education for Building a People's Movement*, South End Press, Boston, 1981.
114. A good analysis of this trend may be found in Shore, Ira, *Culture Wars: School and Society in the Conservative Restoration, 1969-1984*, Routledge and Kegan Paul, Boston, 1986. For use of

the of the term "glorified vo-tech," see the highly critical essay on American Indian Studies programs by Cherokee scholar Russell Thornton, entitled "American Indian Studies: A Revisit," in James R. Young, ed., *American Indian Issues in Higher Education*, American Indian Studies Center, UCLA, 1981, pp. 3-10. The disillusionment expressed in the latter article should be contrasted in Thornton's "American Indian Studies as an Academic Discipline," *American Indian Culture and Research Journal*, Vol. 2, Nos. 3-4, 1978.

115. One measure of how this has worked may be found in the relatively large number of MAs, and even BAs, who held professorial positions in the United States in 1970, when the professorate was still all but exclusively white and male. By 1980, after non-whites and women had begun to enter university faculties in some significant numbers, a Ph.D. was suddenly considered to be an "absolute minimum requirement" for such employment. This meant, of course, that every woman or minority who entered the faculty was required to undergo a grueling, multi-year "dissertation" process overseen almost exclusively, and with virtually arbitrary power, by the very white male academics whose canonical deficiencies the people of color and women were allegedly intended to address. Moreover, "out group" doctoral candidates were (and are) required to produce an "intellectual product" acceptable in its form and content to the committee, which is to say to the very people they were, of necessity, critiquing. It was and is, obviously and intentionally, an impossible scenario from any perspective other than that of the Eurocentrist male status quo.

116. A classic case is that of Webster Two Hawk, former president of the Rosebud Sioux Tribe in South Dakota and head of the National Tribal Chairman's Association, who traveled to Washington, D.C. at federal expense in 1972 to publicly take the side of the Nixon administration against AIM and other "irresponsible" Indians involved in the Trail of Broken Treaties occupation of the BIA building. For his trouble, he was promptly voted out of office on his home reservation and replaced by Robert Burnette, a primary Trail organizer. He was then quickly hired to head the American Indian Studies program at the University of South Dakota at Vermillion, undoubtedly because of the deep insights into his people's beliefs and sensibilities he had so recently displayed. Needless to say, no one affiliated with AIM has ever been hired onto the faculty at USD/Vermillion, while a number of Two Hawks' friends and associates have. The matter eloquently bespeaks the sorts of views on Indians, Indian-ness and Indian Affairs transmitted through the South Dakota Indian Studies program, reflective as it is of many others.

117. Means, Russell, lecture to students of the TRIBES program, University of Colorado at Boulder, July 1988 (tape on file).

118. McDonald, Andrew, "Why do Indian Students Drop Out of College?" in *The Schooling of Native America*, op. cit. Also see Jaimes, M. Annette, "Higher Educational Needs of American Indian Students," *Integrateducation*, Vol. XIX, Nos. 1-2, January 1982, pp. 7-12. Of related interest, see Wilkinson, Gerald, "Educational Problems in the Indian Community: A Comment on Learning as Colonialism," in the same publication, same issue, pp. 42-50.

119. Heth and Guyette (op. cit.) provide an array of charts demonstrating this.

120. See ibid., pp. 113-17, for a complete list.

121. See Deloria, Vine Jr., "Education and Imperialism," *Integrateducation*, Vol. XIX, Nos. 1-2, January 1982, pp. 58-63.

122. Jaimes, M. Annette, "American Indian Studies: Toward an Indigenous Model," *American Indian Culture and Research Journal*, Vol. 11, No. 3, Fall 1987, pp. 1-16.

123. Deloria, Vine Jr., "Indian Studies—The Orphan of Academia," *Wicazo Sa Review*, Vol. 2, No. 2, 1986.

124. Churchill, Ward, "White Studies: The Intellectual Imperialism of Contemporary U.S. Education," *Integrateducation*, Vol. XIX, Nos. 1-2, 1982, pp. 51-7.

125. Churchill, Ward, "White Studies or Isolation: An Alternative Model for Native American Studies Programs," in *American Indian Issues in Higher Education*, op. cit., pp. 19-34.

126. See, for example, Barriero, José, "The Dilemma of American Indian Education," *Indian Studies Quarterly*, Vol. 1, No. 1, 1984, pp. 4-5.

127. The TRIBES—Tribal Resource Institute in Business, Engineering and Science—effort had been run for several years, under direction of Lucille Echohawk (Pawnee), at Colorado College, in Colorado Springs, Colorado. There, abysmal academic performance and complaints of chronic drunkenness among unmotivated students resulted in the project's potential effectiveness diminishing to near zero. Things had in fact become so bad that the program was notorious in Indian Country, and native parents widely refused to allow their children to participate, even at no cost. TRIBES was moved to UCB's Learning Center, directed overall by Ward Churchill, in 1987 as a last ditch to

salvage the effort and inject some degree of academic integrity. The project was considerably restored during its first two years of operational existence at UCB under the handling of Richard B. Williams, a Cheyenne-Oglala. Jaimes assumed the institute's directorship for 1989.

128. See Churchill, Ward, "The Buffalo Tribe Curriculum Model," University Learning Center, University of Colorado at Boulder, March 1987. Churchill has noted in correspondence to the author that he followed the thinking of Paulo Freire, among others, in developing the curriculum. See especially, Freire's *Pedagogy of the Oppressed*, Continuum Books, New York, 1981; and *Education for Critical Consciousness*, Continuum Books, New York, 1982.

129. Jaimes, M. Annette, *TRIBES, 1989: Final Report and Evaluation*, University Learning Center, University of Colorado at Boulder, September 1989.

130. Letter from David Lester, Executive Director, Council of Energy Resource Tribes, to Ward Churchill, Director, University Learning Center, University of Colorado at Boulder, October, 1989.

131. Vicente, Francis, *TRIBES, 1990: Final Report and Evaluation*, Colorado State University, Fort Collins, September 1990.

132. Anonymous, *TRIBES, 1991: Preliminary Report and Evaluation*, Colorado School of Mines, Golden, August 1991.

133. Jaimes, M. Annette, and Ward Churchill, "American Indian Studies: A Positive Alternative," *The Bloomsbury Review*, Vol. 8, No. 5, September/October 1988.

134. Marcuse, Herbert, "Repressive Tolerance," in Robert Paul Wolff, Barrington Moore, Jr., and Herbert Marcuse, *A Critique of Pure Tolerance*, Beacon Press, Boston, 1969.

135. Deloria, "Education and Imperialism," op. cit., p. 63.

Chapter XIV

The Great Pretenders
Further Reflections on Whiteshamanism

by Wendy Rose

They came for our land, for what grew or could be grown on it, for the resources in it, and for our clean air and pure water. They stole these things from us, and in the taking they also stole our free ways and the best of our leaders, killed in battle or assassinated. And now, after all that, they've come for the very last of our possessions; now they want our pride, our history, our spiritual traditions. They want to rewrite and remake these things, to claim them for themselves. The lies and thefts just never end.

Margo Thunderbird, 1988

I am that most schizophrenic of creatures, an American Indian who is both poet and anthropologist. I have, in fact, a little row of buttons up and down my ribs that I can press for the appropriate response: *click,* I'm an Indian; *click,* I'm an anthropologist; *click,* I'll just forget the whole thing and write a poem. I have also been a critic of the "whiteshaman movement," to use an expression coined by Geary Hobson, Cherokee critic. The term "whiteshaman," he says, rightly belongs to "the apparently growing number of small-press poets of generally white, Euro-Christian American background, who in their poems assume the persona of the shaman, usually in the guise of an American Indian medicine man. To be a poet is simply not enough; they must claim a power from higher sources."[1] Actually, the presses involved are not always small, as is witnessed by the persona adopted by Gary Snyder in his Pulitzer Prize-winning book of verse, *Turtle Island.*[2] In any event, Hobson is referring to a group of writers, including Louis Simpson, Charles Olson, Jim Cody, John Brandi, Gene Fowler, Norman Moser, Michael McClure, Barry Gifford, Paul Steinmetz, and David Cloutier, all of whom subscribe to—and go decisively beyond the original intent of—Jerome Rothenburg's 1976 assertion that:

> The poet, like the shaman, withdraws to solitude to find his poem or vision, then returns to sound it, give it life. He performs alone—because his presence is

considered crucial and no one else has arisen to act in his place. He is also like the shaman in being at once an outsider, and yet a person needed for the validation of a certain type of experience important to the group...like the shaman, he will not only be allowed to act mad in public, but he will often be expected to do so. The act of the poet—& his poetry—is like a public act of madness. It is like what the Senecas, in their great dream ceremony, now obsolete, called "turning the mind upside down"...It is the primal exercise of human freedom against/& for the tribe.[3]

I would expand upon Hobson's definition by observing that not all whiteshamans are Americans, poets, nor even white. A perfect example is that of Carlos Castaneda, author of the best-selling series of "Don Juan" epics purporting to accurately reveal the "innermost secrets" of a purely invented "Yaqui sorcerer."[4] I would further add that whiteshamans pretending to higher sources may or may not refer to themselves as shamanic. Some of those within the movement have professed more secular intimacies with Native American cultures and traditions. This is well illustrated by Ruth Beebe Hill, who pretended in her book *Hanta Yo* to have utilized her association with a single American Indian man—"Chunksa Yuha," otherwise known as Alonzo Blacksmith—to uncover not only 19th-century social, sexual, and spiritual forms, but an "archaic dialect" of the Lakota language unknown to the Lakota themselves.[5]

Such claims, whether sacred or secular, are uniformly made with none of the community acknowledgment and training essential to the positions in question. Would it not be absurd to aver to be a Rabbi if one were neither Jewish nor even possessed an elementary knowledge of Judaism? Or that one were a jet aircraft pilot without having been inside an airplane? Yet, preposterous as whiteshaman assertions may be on the face of it, there seems to be an unending desire on the part of the American public to absorb such "knowledge" as the charlatans care to produce. Further, the proliferation of such "information" typically occurs to the exclusion of far more accurate and/or genuinely native material, a matter solidly reinforcing the profound ignorance of things Indian afflicting most of society. As the Lakota scholar Vine Deloria, Jr. has put it:

> The realities of Indian belief and existence have become so misunderstood and distorted at this point that when a real Indian stands up and speaks the truth at any given moment, he or she is not only unlikely to be believed, but will probably be contradicted and "corrected" by the citation of some non-Indian and totally inaccurate "expert." More, young Indians in universities are now being trained to see themselves and their cultures in terms prescribed by such experts rather than in the traditional terms of the tribal elders . . . In this way, the experts are perfecting a system of self-validation in which all semblance of honesty and accuracy is lost. This is not only a travesty of scholarship, but it is absolutely devastating to Indian societies.[6]

Hobson and others have suggested that the assumption of shaman status or its secular counterparts by non-native writers is part of a process of "cultural imperialism" directly related to other claims on Native American land and lives.[7] By appropriating indigenous cultures and distorting them for its own purposes, their reasoning goes, the dominant society can neatly eclipse every aspect of contemporary native reality, from land rights to issues of religious freedom. Pam Colorado, an Oneida scholar working at the University of Calgary in Canada, frames the matter:

The process is ultimately intended to supplant Indians, even in areas of their own customs and spirituality. In the end, non-Indians will have complete power to define what is and is not Indian, even for Indians. We are talking here about an absolute ideological/conceptual subordination of Indian people in addition to the total physical subordination [we] already experience. When this happens, the last vestiges of real Indian society and Indian rights will disappear. Non-Indians will then "own" our heritage and ideas as thoroughly as they now claim to own our land and resources."[8]

Whiteshamans and their defenders, assuming a rather amazing gullibility on the part of American Indians, usually contend they are "totally apolitical." Some have pointed out that the word "shaman" is itself of Tungus (Siberian) origin[9] and insist that their use of it thus implies nothing specifically Native American, either in literal content or by impression.[10] They often add the insulting caveat that American Indian writers know less of their ancestral traditions and culture than non-native anthropologists.[11] Finally, most argue that "artistic license" or "freedom of speech" inherently empowers them to do what they do, no matter whether Indians like it (and, ultimately, no matter the cost to native societies).[12] Native American scholars, writers, and activists have heard these polemics over and over again. It is time to separate fact from fantasy in this regard.

Anatomy of Whiteshamanism

First, it must be noted that the term "shaman" is merely one of convenience, as are the terms "Indian," "American Indian," "Native American," and so on. The Siberian origin of the word is in this sense irrelevant at best and, more often, polemically obfuscatory. Moreover, whiteshamans do not construct their writings or antics after the Siberian model, even when they use the term "shaman" to describe themselves and the processes of their craft. Their works, whether poetic, novelistic, or theoretical, are uniformly designed and intended to convey conceptions of "Indian-ness" to their readers. This remains true regardless of the literal content of the material at issue, as is readily evident in "Blackfoot/Cherokee" author Jamake Highwater's (aka: Jay Marks, a non-Indian) extended repackaging of Greek mythology and pop psychology in the garb of supposed "primal Native American legends."[13]

Further, during performances, whiteshamans typically don a bastardized composite of psuedo-Indian "style" buckskins, beadwork, headbands, moccasins, and sometimes paper masks intended to portray native spiritual beings such as Coyote or Raven. They often appear carrying gourd rattles, eagle feathers, "peace pipes," medicine bags, and other items reflective of native ceremonial life. Their readings are frequently accompanied by the burning of sage, "pipe ceremonies," the conducting of chants and beating of drums of vaguely native type, and the like. One may be hard-pressed to identify a particular indigenous culture being portrayed, but the obviously intended effect is American Indian. The point is that the whiteshaman reader/performer aspires to "embody the Indian," in effect "becoming" the "real" Indian even when actual native people are present. Native reality is thereby subsumed and negated by imposition of a "greater" or "more universal" contrivance.

This leads to a second major point. Whiteshamanism functions as a subset of a much broader assumption within the matrix of contemporary Eurocentric domination holding that non-Indians always (inherently) know more about Indians than do Indians themselves. It is from this larger whole that whiteshamanism draws its emotional and theoretical sustenance and finds the sense of empowerment from which it presumes to extend itself as "spokesperson" for Indians, and ultimately to substitute itself for Indians altogether. Illustrations of this abound, especially within anthropology, linguistics, and the various social sciences. Allow me to recall, by way of example, a few of my own experiences as an employee of a large, university-connected anthropology museum during the mid-to-late 1970s.

- One famous anthropologist whose specialty is northern California insisted that northwestern California Indians were no longer familiar with their ancient form of money, long shells called "dentalia" or tooth-shells. The comment was stimulated by the fact that I was wearing some of these very same shells—which had been given to me by a Yurok woman as payment for a painting—around my neck.
- A basket specialist assured me that basket-hats are no longer worn by California Indian women. Yet, nearly every weekend such women attended the same social functions as I, wearing basket-hats that had been passed down through their families and, more importantly, were still being made.
- A woman who was both an anthropologist and an art collector told me that pottery was no longer produced at Laguna Pueblo. She continued to insist on this, even after I told her the names of the women who produce it there.
- A famous ethnohistorian informed me that I'd never see a California Indian woman with chin tattoos. I have in fact seen them, albeit rarely.
- A very well-known linguist asked me to escort a group of Yuki elders around the museum, and then confided to me that it was a shame no one spoke Yuki anymore. The elders spoke to one another in Yuki the entire time they were there.
- The "expert" on Laguna Pueblo pottery said to me, face to face, that Indians only *think* they know more about themselves than anthropologists. She wanted to impress upon me how "pathetic" my own people really were, and how much more enlightened and superior were her own.

Taken singly, these episodes are not important. But taken together, and added to the enormous pile of similar events and conversations Indians might collectively recount, it is apparent that a pattern exists: taken as a group, Euroamericans consider themselves to be uniquely qualified to explain the rest of humanity, not only to Euroamerica, but to everyone else as well. Coupled to this bizarre notion, whiteshamanism is simply the acting out of a much greater dynamic of cultural usurpation, employing a peculiarly "ritualistic" format.

The "Pioneer Spirit"

What are the implications of this? Consider that a working (if often sublimated) definition of "universality" is very much involved. It is reflected perfectly in the presumed structure of knowledge and in the real structure of "universities" through which this knowledge is imparted in contemporary society. The "core" of information constituting the essential canon of every discipline in academe—from philosophy to literature, from history to physical science, from art to mathematics—is explicitly derived from thought embodied in the European tradition. This is construed as encapsulating all that is fundamentally meaningful within the "universal attainment of human intellect." The achievements and contributions of all other cultures are considered, when they are considered at all, only in terms of appendage (filtered through the lense of Eurocentric interpretation), adornment (to prove the superiority of the Euro-derived tradition), esoteric specialization (to prove that other traditions, unlike those derived from Europe, are narrow and provincial rather than broad and universal).[14]

Always and everywhere, the inclusion of non-European intellectual content in the academy is absolutely predicated upon its conformity to sets of "standards" conceived and administered by those adhering to the basic precepts of Euro-derivation. The basic "qualification" demanded by academe of those who would teach non-European content is that they first receive "advanced training" and "socialization" in doctoral programs steeped in the supposed universality of Euro-derivation. Non-European subject matters are thus intrinsically subordinated to the demands of Eurocentrism at every level within U.S. institutions of higher learning. There are no exceptions: the intended function of such inclusion is to fit non-European traditions into positions assigned them by those of the Eurocentric persuasion. The purpose is to occupy and consume other cultures just as surely as their land and resources have been occupied and consumed.[15]

Such circumstances are quite informative in terms of the more generalized socio-cultural situation. In the construction at hand, those who embrace the Euro-derivation of "universal knowledge" are considered by definition to be the normative expression of intellectual advancement among all humanity. They are "citizens of the world," holders of "the big picture," having inherent rights to impose themselves and their "insights" everywhere and at all times, with military force if need be. The rest of us are consigned by the same definition to our "parochialism" and "provinciality," perceived as "barriers to progress" in many instances, "helped" by our intellectual "betters" to overcome our "conceptual deficiencies" in others.[16] The phenomenon is integral to Euroamerican culture, transcending all ideological boundaries demarcating conservatism and progressivism; a poster popular among science fiction readers of both political persuasions shows a 15th-century European ship sailing a star-map and asks: "What would have happened if Ferdinand and Isabella had said no?"

If, as the academics would have it, Indians "no longer really know" or at least lack access to their traditions and spirituality (not to mention land tenure), then it follows that they are no longer "truly" Indian. If culture, tradition, spirituality, oral literature, and land are not theirs to protect, then such things are free for the taking.

An anthropologist or folklorist hears a story or a song and electronically reproduces it, eventually catalogues it and perhaps publishes it. According to the culture of the scholar, it is then *owned* by "science" in exactly the same fashion as native land, once "settled" by colonizers, is said to be owned by them.[17] Stories, songs, ceremonies, and other cultural ingredients can be—and often are—stolen as surely as if they were tangible objects removed by force. There is a stereotype about the "savage" who is afraid a camera will steal his soul. It will indeed, and much more, as will the tape recorder, the typewriter, and the video cassette. The process is as capable, and as purposeful, in first displacing and then replacing native people within their own cultural contexts as were earlier processes of "discovery" and "settlement" in displacing us from and replacing us upon our land. What is at issue is the extension across intellectual terrain of the more physically oriented 19th-century premise of "Manifest Destiny."

Anthropologists often contend they do not have any appreciable effect upon their own societies, but the fact is that the public does swallow and regurgitate anthropological concepts, usually after about twenty years. At that point, one generally finds efforts undertaken to put to popular use the cultural territory that anthropology has discovered, claimed, and tentatively expropriated in behalf of the dominant society. The subsequent popular endeavors serve to settle and "put to good use" this new cultural territory. This is the role of the whiteshamans. Theirs is a fully sanctioned, even socially mandated activity within the overall imperial process of Eurocentrism. It should thus come as no surprise to serious students of American culture that editors, publishers, reviewers, and most readers greatly prefer the nonsense of whiteshamanism to the genuine literature of American Indians. The situation is simply a continuation of the "Pioneer Spirit" in American life.

Appropriation and Denial

The anthropologist of me is always a little embarrassed. When I am called upon to speak anthropologically, I find myself apologizing or stammering that I'm not *that* kind of anthropologist. I feel like the housewife-prostitute who must go home to clean house for her unknowing husband. She must lie or she must admit her guilt. Native Americans expect me to reflect the behavior they have come to anticipate from non-native anthropologists. If I live in *their* camp, the native reasoning goes, it follows that I must have joined ranks with them; it is therefore expected that I will attempt to insinuate myself into tribal politics where I have no business. Non-native anthropologists expect me either to be what Delmos Jones has called a "superinformant" or a spy for the American Indian Movement, watching their every action with the intent of "causing trouble."[18]

The irony of all this is that I'm really NOT that kind of anthropologist. My dissertation involves a cultural-historical perspective on published literature by American Indians. Such a degree should be, perhaps, granted by the English or literature departments, but such is not the case. At the university where I worked toward my doctorate in anthropology, the English department refused to acknowledge two qualified American Indian applicants for a position during the '80s, with the statement—made to the Coordinator of Native American Studies—that "Native American literature is not part of American Literature." In the same English department, a non-Indian graduate student was also awarded a degree on the basis of a dissertation on "Native American Literature." The student focused upon the work of four authors, *none* of whom was an Indian. The four writers are all known whiteshamans.

Native American literature is considered (by Euroamericans) to be "owned" by anthropology, as American Indians themselves are seen as "owned" by anthropologists. Our literature is merely ethnographic, along with our material culture and kinship systems. This is not, of course, restricted to Native American societies; Fourth World peoples everywhere are considered copyrightable in the same way. Maori, Native Hawaiian, Papuan, Cuna, Thai, and other people around the globe have been literarily colonized just as they have been economically, politically, and militarily colonized.[19] Not so the literature of the Euro-derived (with certain exceptions, such as homosexuals, prisoners, etc.—all groups not "normal"). My position is that all literature must be viewed ethnographically. All literatures provide information about the culture of both writer and subject. All literatures are potential tools for the anthropologist—but not one "type" of literature more than any other. What literature is not ethnic? What person has no ethnicity? American Indians are not "more ethnic" than Polish-Americans or Anglo-Americans; they are simply called upon more frequently and intensively to deal with their ethnicity.

I do not believe the work of N. Scott Momaday, Leslie Marmon Silko, and Simon J. Ortiz is "ethnic" more so than the work of Robert Creeley, Studs Terkel, or Charles Bukowski. But you will not usually find Momaday, Silko, and Ortiz in bookstores or libraries according to their genre (fiction or poetry). Their work will most often be shelved as "anthropology," "Native Americana," "Indians," "Western," or even "Juvenile" (Indians being "kid stuff"). One plays Indian, one dresses up and pretends. Bookstore managers have told me that neither Leslie Silko's novel *Ceremony* nor her later volume of prose and poems, *Storyteller,* could be classified or sold as "regular fiction" because no one would buy them unless they were specifically interested in Indians. Hence, the work is shelved under "Indian." Period. A book by Silko thereby becomes a mere artifact, a curio. It is presumed to be unimportant that hers also happens to be some of the finest prose and poetry available from any author, of either gender or any ethnic background. The same can be said of the writing of others—Maurice Kenny, Joy Harjo, James Welch, Linda Hogan, Barnie Bush, and Mary TallMountain among them—forced into the same "quaint" pigeonhole of classification.

But, if a Native American writer happens to gain international prominence, as in the case of Scott Momaday—his novel *A House Made of Dawn* won the 1969 Pulitzer Prize for Literature—the critics and ethnographers exclaim that the author and his or her work is "not really Indian."[20] Rather, it suddenly falls within the "mainstream of American letters."[21] On the other hand, the stereotypical and grossly distortive work of Hyemeyohsts Storm, a man only marginally Indian, and whose material earned him the wrath of the Northern Cheyenne people with whom he claimed affiliation,[22] was considered by a specialist in "minority American literature" to be more "genuinely Indian" than the writing of Momaday, whose genetic and cultural heritage cannot be questioned (his father is a well-known Kiowa artist, his mother an equally well-known Cherokee educator).23 A great many comparable examples of this phenomenon might be cited.

Freedom (with Reservations)

While the Indian of me is continually bent double from the force of being hit by the literary-colonial canon, the anthropologist of me is always looking for cultural explanations for whiteshamanism and its emotional impact. Feelings run deep on both sides and people tend to take sides on the issue, even if they are not otherwise interested in literary matters. I have found that much of the controversy over whiteshamanism involves fundamental, cherished concepts held by Europeans and Euroamericans involving art, freedom, and what it means to be an artist. These ideas do not, as is often claimed by their advocates, deviate from—much less transcend—the more directly and overtly imperialist manifestations discussed above. To the contrary, they dovetail quite nicely with the rest of the Pioneer Spirit.

All of us, native and non-native, are ethnocentric at our deepest levels. No amount of anthropological training or insight can abolish ethnocentrism, although we can become aware of it and learn to take it into consideration on a day-to-day basis. The problem is that the notion of intrinsic universalism lodged within Euro-derived tradition usually precludes those of that tradition from acknowledging either the fact or the meaning of their own ethnicity. I've encountered literally scores of white students over the years who have professed in various ways to have "no culture." Sometimes they bemoan this circumstance, sometimes they appear to take a certain pleasure in it. Either way, they purport to inhabit "reality," while culture is a habitat reserved exclusively for those whose heritage deviates from their own. Ethnicity, for the mainstream, is thus specifically the domain of Others. The attitude is absolutely pervasive: A short time ago, I even saw a section in a variety store advertising its products for "ethnic hair."

Rather than taking pride in their own deeply rooted ethnicity, most Euroamericans feel duty-bound to sublimate it. Instead of being proud of who they are, they run about making liberal statements about "loving everybody," believing everyone to be "the same under the skin" and so on. The fact is that even the most avowedly progressive Euroamericans seem to want a Disney-ish world in which everyone is a different shade of the same thing, everyone a member of the same cultural "reality" except for things which are "safely" different: food, dress, dancing, and crafts; sometimes language. Beyond these distinctions, they hold that we should *all* be "entitled" to "share equally" in what they hold to be the loftiest and "most natural" aspiration of humanity: Freedom, the more total the better. In noting this to be the case, Edmund Carpenter observed, "The message is clear: we should love them because they are like us. But the statement has its questioning brother: what if they *aren't* like us?"[24]

What Euroamerican, other than those of fascistic persuasion, can be comfortable with the notion that total freedom is a pathological concept? Yet my father's Hopi people see it that way. In the Hopi view, no one would want to be that completely alone and uncontrolled unless there was something seriously wrong with them. In the Hopi Way, and in most other native traditions, to want to be away from people is seen as a form of madness. The very worst punishment indigenous societies can inflict, much worse than death or imprisonment, is exile or to be stigmatized by your people. Conversely, to be allowed to participate in society represents the essence of fulfillment: To be assigned responsibility and acknowledged by the group as having made a useful contribution is the highest accolade. Acceptance by and inclusion among the people are the highest principles governing native life.

By contrast, the typical Euro-derived pattern, in an ideal state, would be for people to live absolutely "free" or "unbound." Euroamericans define freedom in a certain way, primarily politically, and no longer think to question whether it's bad or good. The pursuit of freedom is supposedly why their ancestors left Europe. Freedom is why their ancestors fought for independence from Europe. Freedom is why they continuously penetrated "the frontier." Freedom is why they came in the California and Yukon gold rushes; if you have enough money, you can "live free." Freedom is why they save up (or compulsively spend) that money today. Freedom is why they went to college, send their kids to college. Freedom is why they retire at a certain age. And yet "freedom" as they envision it is an extremely culture-specific value.

Likewise, "art" and being "an artist" are culture-specific ideas that relate to freedom; the "freest" individuals in society are supposed to be artists. Artists can be eccentric, they act however they wish, only to be forgiven because they are artists and therefore free. It is freedom and not creativity that arouses jealousy among Euroamerican non-artists. When a Euroamerican hears that I give poetry readings all over the country, she or he invariably turns wistful and remarks, "You're so lucky. You have all that freedom to travel. I sure wish I could." (Could what? Write poetry? No, freely travel). Native people, on the other hand, often extend genuine condolences that my work forces me to spend so much time so far from home, away from the obligations and responsibilities which lend a central meaning to life. The dichotomy in values couldn't be clearer. These ideas about art and freedom are at the center of the conflict about whiteshamanism.

In Euro-derived society, art is separated from everyday life. For instance, an artist typically works at night rather than when other people work. Art is special, elite (much of it requiring specialized training in "appreciation"), non-utilitarian, self-expressive, solitary, ego-identified, self-validating, innovative (to make it perpetually "new"), unique, and—in its "highest" forms—"without rules." It is a hallmark of the greatest artists, those who "change history," that they break rules, discarding everything "old." Scholars and critics refer to favored artists as "breaking the mold" or "flying in the face of tradition." The whiteshaman says to the American Indian critic, "You can't tell me what to write. I have the right to do whatever I want. This is art; there are no rules." Within the context of whiteshaman culture, truth and freedom are at stake. He or she honestly views the Indian critic as abusing artistic freedom (or "poetic license"), as trying to restrict the unrestrictable, as *trespassing.* The pioneer cannot allow the native to say "go home."[25]

Native American views are different regarding freedom and art. We are not a uniform people, of course, from arctic to tropic and coast to coast, and so my statements must be generalizations, more or less true for most American Indian societies. In life and art, there are rules, and this is good. These rules were given to us, they belong to us, and we must not only follow them, but guard them. Rules exist governing form, content, context, and personnel. Of these, context may be the most important, and yet for the Euro-derived artist it seems to be of negligible significance. A white male art teacher once said to me, "Art is everywhere." Even the many movements which call themselves "countercultural" or "revolutionary" have bought into the European system enough to revolt against it and use its structure to fuel the revolt. Their "alternatives" are merely extensions of the European tradition. They are not, and have never been, "a whole new thing."

American Indian views on art tend to be trans-tribal, especially now when so many diverse native cultures are united by a single colonial language and electronic media. Art must be community-oriented (it may be sacred, but not supernatural; *nothing* is supernatural), it must be useful, it must be beautiful and functional at the same time (the ideas are inseparable, for functioning is part of beauty, and vice versa), it is good if more than one person has a hand in its production, and its completion is always an excellent excuse for a party. There are occasions when the party (or feast, or ceremony) is part of the art form. The artist is not above or otherwise separated from the rest of society; she or he feels no particular desire to be recognized alone or considered different from other people. The artist contributes a particular skill to the welfare and survival, not to mention happiness, of the community.

Native American art is fitted into a continuum where it may or may not change, but certainly will not be pressured to be innovative. Innovation is a consideration that is more often than not rejected by the group, but successful, acceptable, useful innovation is always welcome. The point is that the artist does not innovate just for the sake of innovating; by itself, innovation is not part of the criteria for "good art." The artist is not expected to be eccentric or any way noticeably different from anyone else. Quite the contrary. These ideas—the Euroamerican and American Indian—are obviously in fundamental conflict. It is equally obvious that people on both sides will not normally think about them as I have presented them; people just don't sit down and analyze their behavior in a cultural context. So the conflicts go unrecognized, the whiteshaman and the Native American writer occupying the same turf, but running according to different sets of rules.

Displacement

Aside from the psychological and spiritual impact of whiteshamans on American Indian writers, there are practical effects as well. Indian writers are struggling like others in an age of budget cuts and lack of respect for literature. Most Indians write in English and use literary forms that are European and Asian in origin. These forms are generally combined with images, subject matter, and philosophy drawn from the native heritage. Few of us consciously think about what part of a particular poem came from what heritage, but the combinations are there to be studied. Not only have we adopted aspects of form and style that are non-native, but many of us have adopted the concept of what it *means* to be a writer. Even while this concept is in conflict with native sensibilities, we understand that, as professional writers, we are entitled to earn a living if we work hard enough and well enough, that we may profit from earning degrees in college, that if we give a reading and do a good job we will receive applause and people will say nice things about us in public.

Still, behind all this is the native idea that, if we succeed as writers, we are making a valuable contribution to our communities. We become role models for younger people, we speak at community gatherings (and may be asked to do so by those who respect our special skills with words), and the like.When we are in our communities, we are artists, or storytellers, or historians, in the native tradition. We are accepted, found worthy and useful. We fit in, and are thereby fulfilled. And yet, being of peoples who are now physically colonized, we must also sustain ourselves in other ways. So, when we go out to the lecture halls of fancy universities, we must become artists in a much more Euro-derived sense (though not all the way, because we never actually believe in it). To do this, we want and need our work to be read by both natives and non-natives, to be respected, to be reviewed, and to sell. Ours is always the balancing act between selling and selling out; the market for sell-outs is invariably a good one.

As a poet, I am continually frustrated by the restrictions placed on my work by the same people who insist that poets should not be restricted. It is expected—indeed, *demanded*—that I do a little "Indian-dance," a shuffle and scrape to please the tourists (as well as the anthropologists). Organizers of readings continually ask me to wear beadwork and turquois, to dress in buckskin (my people don't wear much buckskin; we've cultivated cotton for thousands of years), and to read poems conveying pastoral or "natural" images. I am often asked to "tell a story" and "place things in a spiritual framework." Simply *being* Indian—a real, live, breathing, up-to-date Indian person—is not enough. In fact, other than my genetics, this is the precise opposite of what is desired. The expectation is that I adopt, and thereby validate, the "persona" of some mythic "Indian being" who never was. The requirement is that I act to negate the reality of my—and my people's—existence in favor of a script developed within the fantasies of our oppressors.

I can and do refuse. Sometimes, I am invited to read anyway. More often, I am told that there are other poets "out there" who will prove to be more compliant with the needs of the organizers and, frequently, of their audiences. Invariably, by this it is meant that there are non-Indian poets ready and willing to assume the role of what "real Indians" are "supposed" to be like. As an Indian, I am rendered "unreal." By the same token, the non-Indians displace me as "Indian reality." On more than one occasion when I ended up sharing a podium with whiteshamans, I have been told pointblank that I am only a prop to make them look more "authentic." Even in the best of settings, when I read poetry about a political issue or anything else that is not a part of native culture (as perceived by non-natives), people frequently express disappointment, even outrage. Every other American Indian poet I know has undergone exactly the same sorts of experiences.

A logical consequence of these circumstances is that when "Indian content" is sought in a literary event, non-Indians are far more likely than Indians to be solicited to participate in the representation of "Indian-ness." Whiteshamans attract far more invitations to read their "Indian poetry" than do actual Indian poets. Correspondingly, because of their relative celebrity, they tend to accrue larger fees and honoraria for readings than do Indian poets, even when appearing in the same programs. A further consequence is that they are placed in positions from which to publish their "Indian" material, in larger press runs, often at higher prices and at higher royalty rates, than are most Indian writers. The "Indian biz" has proven quite lucrative for a number of whiteshamans. Not so the careers of all but a scant handful of Native American writers. The result has been a marked stilling of the genuine voice of Native America and its replacement by the utterances of an assortment of hucksters and carnival barkers.

Cults of the Culture Vultures

One thing Indians are spectacularly ill-equipped to do that whiteshamans appear to do quite effortlessly is build a cult around themselves. The whiteshamans become self-proclaimed "gurus," dispensing not only poetry but "healing" and "medicine," "blessing" people. In this area, they have no competition at all. I do not know of a single Native American poet who would make such a claim, although you will find a scattering of non-poets, such as the notorious "Sun Bear" (Vincent LaDuke) involved in these goings on.[26] You will find whiteshamans at bogus "medicine wheel" gatherings, ersatz sweat-lodge ceremonies, and other fad events using vaguely Indian motifs. You will not usually find them around Indians at genuine Indian events. Even Sun Bear, who is a Chippewa by "blood," admitted to members of Colorado AIM that he never participated in or attended bona fide native activities.[27] Given the nature of his own transgressions against the cultural integrity of his people, he felt—undoubtedly accurately—that he'd be "unwelcome."

When you deal with cultists, you are in deep waters. A while ago, in Alaska, I spoke to a university audience and made some mention that I believed the information in books by Carlos Castaneda to be fabricated. A non-Indian woman stood up and angrily shouted that I was anti-semitic and probably didn't believe in the Holocaust either.[28] At a more recent event at a small university in upstate New York, I was confronted by a non-native man who took it upon himself to "explain" to me how Jamake Highwater's transparently bogus ramblings had "done more for Indians than the work of any other writer." When I and several Indian colleagues sharply disagreed, the man informed us we were "hopelessly deluded."[29] I know of no legitimate Indian writer with such a fanatical following, for Indians are taught, above all, to value truth. The sanctity of language must not, within our traditions, be used to abuse this value. The last thing a Don Juan cultist wants is to meet a *real* Yaqui holy person.

This is standard fare in whiteshaman circles, and it knows no ideological boundaries. A truly amazing example involves a sector of Euroamerican feminism devoted to "rediscovering the lost power of women through the ages." Not unnaturally, native women—who have traditionally experienced a full measure of social, economic, political, and spiritual empowerment within their own cultures—have become the focus of considerable attention from this quarter. But, given their interest in Indian women, have these feminists turned to their native sisters for insight, inspiration, and guidance? No. Instead, they flock to the books and lectures of Lynn Andrews, a white woman from Beverly Hills who has grown rich claiming to have been taught by two traditional Cree women (with Lakota names) in Canada about the eternal struggle between the righteousness of native women's "spirit power" against malignantly evil male spirits.[30]

Andrews, of course, maintains she has been "sent back as a spiritual messenger" by her invented teachers to spread the word of these utterly un-Indian "revelations." And, inevitably, any time a native woman—even a Cree such as Sharon Venne—attempts to refute the author's false assertions, she is shouted down by her white "sisters," often for not knowing the "inner meaning" of native culture as well as Andrews, and usually for having internalized the "sexism" by which "Indian men prevent the truth from being known" by women.[31] Typically, subscribers to the Andrews cult describe the *Indian* women who confront their guru as being "arrogant and insensitive," a truly incredible projection of their own psychological and behavioral characteristics upon the primary victims of their actions. Small wonder, under the circumstances, that Native American women have always been conspicuously absent from "the women's movement."

When I discussed my view of Andrews' *Medicine Woman* with a well-known white male scholar of Indian literature, I was startled when he stated his belief that such ludicrous fiction could be true—as it was and is promoted to be true—because if a person *were* to serve as a "bridge" between Indians and whites, it would *have* to be a white person. He could never really articulate why he thought this to be so necessarily true. Such unidirectional presumption lies at the very core of all Eurocentric cultural imperialism and offers lucid illustration as to the crux of what has served to impair intercultural understanding and communication in this society for so long. In the end, he is as much a part of the Andrews cult as any of the near-giggling groupies lining up to obtain autographed copies of her "literary works."

Fear and Loathing Among the Literati

Before closing, I would like to talk about certain misunderstandings regarding criticism by Native Americans of the whiteshamans and their followers. The fear exists among non-native writers that we are somehow trying to bar them from writing about Indians at all, that Indian people might be "staking a claim" as the sole interpreters of Indian cultures, most especially of that which is sacred, and asserting that only Indians can make valid observations on themselves. Such fears are not based in fact; I know of no Indian who has ever said this. Nor do I know of any who secretly think it. We accept as given that whites have as much prerogative to write and speak about us and our cultures as we have to write and speak about them and theirs. The question is how this is done and, to some extent, why it is done.

The problem with whiteshamans is one of integrity and intent, not topic, style, interest, or experimentation. Many non-Indian people have—from the stated perspective of the non-native viewing things native—written honestly and eloquently about any number of Indian topics, including those we hold sacred. We readily acknowledge the beauty of some poetry by non-natives dealing with Indian people, values, legends, or the relationship between human beings and the American environment. A non-native poet is obviously as capable of writing about Coyote and Hawk as an Indian poet. The difference is in the promotion, so to speak. A non-native poet cannot produce an *Indian* perspective on Coyote or Hawk, cannot see Coyote or Hawk in an Indian way, and cannot produce a poem expressing Indian spirituality. What can be produced is another perspective, another view, another spiritual expression. The issue, as I said, is one of integrity and intent.

The principle works in both directions. As an Indian person who was deeply impressed with the oral literature of the Catholic Church during my childhood, I might compose verse based in this poetic form. I might go on to publish the poems. I might also perform them, with proper intonation, as in Mass. All of this is appropriate and permissible. But I would not and *could* not claim to be a priest. I could not tell the audience they were actually experiencing the transmutation that occurs during Mass. At the point I did endeavor to do such things, a discernable line of integrity—both personal and artistic—would have been crossed. Artistic freedom and emotional identification would not make me a priest, nor would the "uplifting" of my audience—no matter how gratifying to them, and to me—make them participants in Mass. To evoke my impression of the feel of the Mass and its liturgy does not necessitate my lying about it.

There is a world of difference between a non-Indian man like Frank Waters writing about Indians and a non-Indian man like Jamake Highwater claiming through his writing that he has in fact *become* "an Indian." Similar differences exist between a non-Indian woman like Marla N. Powers who expresses her feelings about native spirituality honestly, stating that they are her perceptions, and white women like Lynn Andrews and "Mary Summer Rain" perpetrating the fraud of having been appointed "mediums" of Indian culture.[32] And, of course, the differences between non-Indians like John Neihardt who rely for their information upon actual native sources, and those like Andrews and Castaneda who simply invent them, should speak for themselves. As an Indian, as a poet, and as an anthropologist, I can wholeheartedly and without inconsistency accept the prerogatives claimed by the former in each case while rejecting the latter without hesitancy or equivocation. And I know of no American Indian aligned with his or her own heritage and traditions who would react otherwise.

Conclusion

So what is to be done about all this? For starters, readers of this essay should take the point that whiteshamanism is neither "okay," "harmless," nor "irrelevant," no more than any other form of racist, colonialist behavior. Correspondingly, they must understand that there is nothing "unreasonable" or "unfair" about the Indian position on the matter. As concerns the literary arena, we demand only informational and artistic integrity and mutual respect. It is incumbent upon Euroamerica, first and foremost, to make the whiteshamans and their followers understand that their "right" to use material from other cultures stems from those cultures, not from themselves. It must be impressed on them in no uncertain terms that there is nothing innately superior separating them from the rest of humanity, entitling them to trample upon the rights of others, or enabling them to absorb and "perfect" unfamiliar material better than the originators of that material. The only *right* they have when dealing with native-derived subject matters is to present them honestly, accurately, and—if the material is sensitive or belongs to another group or specific person—with permission. If their response to what they've seen, heard, or otherwise experienced is subjective and interpretive, we insist only that they make this known from the outset, so as not to confuse their impressions with the real article.

Application of a bit of common sense by the public would prove helpful. Those who have a genuine desire to learn about American Indians should go out of their way to avoid being *misled* into thinking they are reading, seeing, or hearing a native work. Most whiteshamans have demonstrated a profound ignorance of the very traditions they are trying to imitate or subsume, and so they have mostly imitated each other. Many of them claim to deploy an authentically Native American model, but speak rhetoric about "inventing their own myths," a literal impossibility within *real* indigenous traditions. Any mythology stemming from experiences in a university or along city streets is unlikely to include any recognizable coyotes, and confusion in this area precludes genuine intercultural communication faster and more thoroughly than any other single factor. Until such communication is realized, we are all going to remain very much mired in the same mess in which we now collectively find ourselves, interculturally speaking.

Adoption of a pro-active attitude in this regard on the part of avowed progressives would likely prove effective. If they are truly progressive, they will demand— loudly and clearly—that not only authors, but publishers and organizers of events make it plain when "the facts" are being interpreted by a representative of a non-native culture. The extension of misinformation along these lines should be treated as seriously as any other sort of propaganda, and transgressors discredited— branded as liars, or perhaps sued for fraud—when revealed. It follows that book-stores—especially alleged "alternative" outlets—need to hear, with emphasis, that their progressive clientele objects to both their stocking of whiteshaman trash *and* to the absence of real Native American material on their shelves. Those who queue up to participate in, defend, or apologize for whiteshamanism must at last be viewed and treated as what they are. An unequivocally negative response to this sort of cultural imperialism on the part of large numbers of non-Indians would undoubtedly go far toward ending at least the worst of the practices at issue.

Native people, on the other hand, must come to understand that whiteshamans did not just pop up out of the blue and decide to offend Indians. They are responding, at least to some extent, to a genuinely felt emotional need within the dominant society. The fact that they are concomitantly exploiting other people for profit according to the sanctions and procedures of their own culture does not alter this circumstance. In spite of itself, whiteshamanism has touched upon something very real. An entire population is crying out for help, for alternatives to the spiritual barrenness they experience, for a way out of the painful trap in which their own worldview and way of life have ensnared them. They know, perhaps intuitively, that the answers—or part of the answers—to the questions producing their agony may be found within the codes of knowledge belonging to the native peoples of this land. Despite what they have done to us during the past 500 years, it would be far less than Indian of us were we not to endeavor to help them. Such are our Ways, and have always been our Ways.

Perhaps we can treaty now. Perhaps we can regain a balance that once was here, but now seems lost. If poets and artists are the prophets and expressers of history— as thinkers of both the American Indian and Euro-derived traditions have suggested in different ways—then it may well be that our task is simply to take back our heritage from the whiteshamans, shake it clean and bring it home. In doing so, we not only save ourselves from much that is happening to us, but empower ourselves to aid those who have stolen and would continue to steal so much from us, to help them locate their *own* power, their *own* traditions as human beings among human beings, as relatives among relatives not only of the human kind. Perhaps then they can come into themselves as they might be, rather than as they have been, or as they are. Perhaps then we can at last clasp hands, not as people on this land, but of this land, and go forward together. As Seattle, leader of the Suquamish people, once put it, "Perhaps we will be brothers after all...We shall see."

Notes

1. Hobson, Geary, "The Rise of the White Shaman as a New Version of Cultural Imperialism," in Geary Hobson, ed., *The Remembered Earth*, Red Earth Press, Albuquerque, NM, 1978, pp. 100-8. An interesting, if unintended, history of the evolution of whiteshamanism in American letters may be found in Castro, Michael, *Interpreting the Indian: Twentieth Century Poets and the Native American*, University of New Mexico Press, Albuquerque, 1983.
2. Snyder, Gary, *Turtle Island*, New Directions Publishers, New York, 1974. It should be noted that Snyder may have set the entire whiteshaman phenomenon in motion with his "shaman songs" included in his *Myths and Texts*, Totem Press, New York, 1960.
3. Rothenberg, Jerome, "Pre-Face to a Symposium on Ethnopoetics," *Alcheringa: Ethnopoetics*, n.s. 2, No. 4, p. 4. Rothenberg is, like Gary Snyder, in some ways the prototype of the contemporary whiteshaman: see his *Poems, 1964-67*, Black Sparrow Press, Los Angeles, 1968; *A Book of Testimony*, Tree Books, San Francisco, 1971; *Poems for the Game of Silence, 1960-1970*, Dial Press, New York, 1971; *The Notebooks*, Membrane Press, Milwaukee, 1976; and *A Seneca Journal*, New Directions Publishers, New York, 1978. His essays are also of interest: see "Total Translation," in Abraham Chapman, ed., *Literature of the American Indians: Views and Interpretations*, New American Library, New York, 1978, pp. 292-307; and "Changing

the Present, Changing the Past: A New Poetics," in *Talking Poetics from Naropa Institute*, Vol. 2, Shambala Publications, Boulder, CO, 1978. His "expertise" on shamanism is also "confirmed" in certain of the collections he's edited: see *Technicians of the Sacred: A Range of Poetries from Africa, America, Asia and Oceania*, Doubleday Publishers, Garden City, NY, 1969; *Shaking the Pumpkin: Traditional Poetry of the Indian North Americas*, Doubleday Publishers, Garden City, NY, 1972; and, with George Quasha, *America, a Prophecy: A New Reading of American Poetry from Pre-Columbian Times to the Present*, Random House Publishers, New York, 1974.

4. The Castaneda books in question are *The Teachings of Don Juan: A Yaqui Way of Knowledge*, University of California Press, Los Angeles, 1968; *A Separate Reality: Further Conversations with Don Juan*, Simon and Schuster, New York, 1971; *Journey to Ixtlan: The Lessons of Don Juan*, Simon and Schuster, New York, 1972; *Tales of Power*, Simon and Schuster, New York, 1974; and *The Second Ring of Power*, Simon and Schuster, New York, 1977. All of Castaneda's assertions were "academically validated" through his publication of a "scholarly paper" entitled "The didactic uses of hallucinogenic plants: An examination of a system of teaching," in *Abstracts of the 67th Annual Meeting of the American Anthropological Association* in 1968 and UCLA's 1973 award of a Ph.D. in anthropology to Castaneda on the basis of a dissertation entitled *Sorcery: A Description of the World* (actually a retitled manuscript of *Journey to Ixtlan*).

5. Hill, Ruth Beebe, *Hanta Yo: An American Saga*, Doubleday Publishers, Garden City, NY, 1977. For detailed American Indian criticism, see Deloria, Vine Jr., "Hanta Yo: Super Hype" *Co-Evolution Quarterly*, Fall 1979 and "The Twisted World of Hanta Yo," *Minority Notes*, Vol. 1, No. 1, Spring 1979. Also see Medicine, Beatrice, "Hanta Yo: A New Phenomenon," *The Indian Historian*, Vol. 12, No. 2, Spring 1979 and Taylor, Allan R., "The Literary Offenses of Ruth Beebe Hill," *American Indian Culture and Research Journal*, Vol. 4, No. 3, Summer 1980.

6. Deloria, Vine Jr., lecture presented during American Indian Awareness Week, University of Colorado at Boulder, as quoted by Ward Churchill in "A Little Matter of Genocide: Native American Spirituality and New Age Hucksterism," *Bloomsbury Review*, Vol. 8, No. 5, September/October 1988, pp. 23-4.

7. Marmon Silko, Leslie, "An Old-time Indian Attack Conducted in Two Parts: Part One, Imitation 'Indian' Poems; Part Two, Gary Snyder's *Turtle Island*," in Hobson, ed., op. cit., pp. 211-6; Young Bear, Ray, "in disgust and in response to indian-type poetry written by whites published in a mag which keeps rejectin' me," in *Winter of the Salamander: The Keeper of Importance*, Harper and Row Publishers, New York, 1979, pp. 118-20; Rose, Wendy, "For the White Poets Who Would be Indian" and "The Anthropology Convention," in *Lost Copper*, Malki Museum Press, Morongo Indian Reservation, Banning, CA, 1980; Sainte-Marie, Buffy, "This Country 'Tis of Thy People Your Dying," in *The Buffy Sainte-Marie Songbook*, Grosset and Dunlap Publishers, New York, 1971, pp. 164-6.

8. Pam Colorado, as quoted in Churchill, op. cit.

9. As Hobson (op. cit., p. 100) puts it: "[I]n *Webster's New Collegiate Dictionary* (1968) Shaman is shown to have evolved from Russian, and from Tungusic *saman*, and perhaps, even ultimately from the Sanskrit s'ramana—meaning beggar monk. Its current meaning seems to be 'a priest or conjurer of shamanism; loosely, a medicine man.' Shamanism, in the same dictionary, is defined as 'primarily, the primitive religion of the Ural-Altic peoples of northern Asia and Europe, in which the unseen world of gods, demons, and ancestral spirits is conceived as being responsive only to the shamans.' Funk & Wagnall's *Standard College Dictionary* (1963) confirms these definitions, adding only the word 'wizard' in regard to the shaman."

10. This is not always the case, however. See Mary Douglas, "The Authenticity of Castaneda"—a rabid defense of a his whiteshamanism and its validity in terms of "understanding" Native Americans ("a great advance in anthropology")—in Richard B. de Mille, ed., *The Don Juan Papers: Further Castaneda Controversies*, Ross-Erikson Publishers, Santa Barbara, CA, 1980, pp. 25-31.

11. For an exemplary display of this sort of argument and attitude, see Clifton, James E., *The Invented Indian: Cultural Fictions and Government Policies*, Transaction Books, New York, 1990.

12. A near-perfect example of this argument appears in a letter by Judith Abel of McKlouth, Kansas appearing in the February 1991 issue of *Z Magazine*. Abel's letter addresses Ward Churchill's article, "Advent of the Plastic Medicine Men"—in which he contends "spiritual hucksters" are complicit in the cultural genocide of American Indians—appearing in the December 1990 issue of the same magazine. Churchill's analysis appears correct, Able holds, but is marred by his missing the "fact" that such activities are legitimate insofar as they fall under "free speech."

13. The books in question are Highwater's *Ritual of the Wind*, Viking Press, New York, 1977; *Anpao:*

An American Indian Odyssey, J.J. Lippincott Publishers, Philadelphia, 1977; *The Sweetgrass Lives On: Fifty Contemporary Indian Artists,* Lippincott and Crowell Publishers, New York, 1980; *The Sun, He Dies: The End of the Aztec World,* Harper and Row Publishers, New York, 1980; and especially *The Primal Mind: Vision and Reality in Indian America,* Harper and Row Publishers, New York, 1981. The Grecian content of Highwater's "interpretations" of American Indian mythos has been exhaustively demonstrated by Assiniboin-Sioux scholar Hank Adams in a manuscript entitled *Cannibal Green.* Adams' material has, of course, gone unpublished, other than an extract printed in the native rights journal *Akwesasne Notes* in early 1985. All the better to allow promoters such as David Jackson to pen pieces such as "Jamake Highwater's Native Intelligence," *Village Voice,* May 3, 1983, pp. 37-9.

14. For an in-depth examination of these assumptions, see Carnoy, Martin, *Education as Cultural Imperialism,* David McKay Publishers, New York, 1974.
15. Analysis of these problems is offered in Jaimes, M. Annette, "American Indian Studies: Toward an Indigenous Model," *American Indian Culture and Research Journal,* Vol. 11, No. 3, 1987, pp. 1-16. Also see Deloria, Vine Jr., "Education and Imperialism," *Integrateducation,* Vol. 19, Nos. 1-2, 1982.
16. This way of thinking is discussed brilliantly in Amin, Samir, *Eurocentrism,* Monthly Review Press, New York, 1989.
17. This is precisely the tradition whiteshamans have picked up on. Its literary origins may probably be found in Mary Hunter Austin's appropriative *Path of the Rainbow: An Anthology of Songs and Chants from the Indians of North America,* Liveright Publishers, New York, 1918 and *The American Rhythm: Studies and Re-Expressions of Amerindian Songs,* Houghton-Mifflin Co., Boston, 1923. Oliver LaFarge pioneered contemporary Euroamerica's ethnographic appropriation of "Indian-ness" in literature, writing as a Navajo in his Pulitzer Prize-winning 1927 novel, *Laughing Boy,* Pocket Books Edition, New York, 1969. Vachel Lindsay was perhaps the first modern Euroamerican poet to cash in, adopting an Indian "persona" in "Our Mother Pocahontas" (see his *Collected Poems,* Macmillan Publishers, New York, 1946.
18. Jones, Delmos J., "Towards a Native Anthropology," *Human Organization,* Vol. 29, No. 4, 1970, pp. 251-9.
19. For an exposition on this topic, see Graburn, Nelson H.H., ed., *Ethnic and Tourist Arts: Cultural Expressions from the Fourth World,* University of California Press, Berkeley, 1976, pp. 1-2 of the introduction.
20. Momaday, N. Scott, *A House Made of Dawn,* Harper and Row Publishers, New York, 1968.
21. This argument is advanced most formally in Sollors, Werner, *Beyond Ethnicity: Descent and Consent in American Culture,* Oxford University Publishers, New York/London, 1986.
22. Storm, Hyemeyohsts, *Seven Arrows,* Ballantine Books, New York, 1972. For the Northern Cheyenne response, see *Wassaja,* Vol. 2, No. 7, April-May, 1974 and Vol. 2, No. 7, August 1974. Also see Costo, Rupert, "Seven Arrows Desecrates Cheyennes," *The Indian Historian,* Vol. 4, No. 2, Summer 1972, p. 41. Despite such protests from the people allegedly depicted, Storm's subsequent book, *Song of the Heyoehkah,* Harper and Row Publishers, San Francisco, 1981, is in precisely the same vein...and produced with equal lavishness by the publisher.
23. Larson, Charles R., *American Indian Fiction,* University of New Mexico Press, Albuquerque, 1978, pp. 1-2.
24. Carpenter, Edmund, *Oh, What a Blow that Phantom Gave Me!* Holt, Rinehart, and Winston Publishers, New York, 1972, p. 97.
25. All of this is epitomized in the vernacular of the poetic trade. See Sutton, Walter, *American Free Verse: The Modern Revolution in Poetry,* New Directions Press, New York, 1973.
26. Sun Bear's books, many of them written in collaboration with a bona fide whiteshaman "Wabun" (Marlise James), include *At Home in the Wilderness,* Naturegraph Publications, 1973; *Buffalo Hearts,* Bear Tribe Publications, Spokane, WA, 1976; *The Bear Tribe's Self-Reliance Book,* Bear Tribe Publications, Spokane, WA, 1977 (reprinted by Prentice-Hall Press, New York, 1988); *Sun Bear: The Path of Power,* Bear Tribe Publications, Spokane, WA, 1983 (reprinted by Prentice-Hall Press, New York, 1987); *The Roaring of the Sacred River,* Prentice-Hall Press, New York, 1986; *The Book of the Vision Quest,* Prentice-Hall Press, New York, 1987; *Walk in Balance: The Path to Healthy, Happy, Harmonious Living,* Prentice-Hall Press, New York, 1989; and *Black Dawn/Bright Day,* Bear Tribe Publications, Spokane, WA, 1990. Other "Indians" involved in this sort of thing include Doug Boyd, a supposed Cherokee who has authored *Rolling Thunder,* Dell Books, New York, 1976 and Tony Shearer, allegedly of non-specific "tribal" heritage, whose *The Lord of the Dawn: Quetzalcoatl,* Naturegraph Publications, 1971 and *The Praying Flute,* Naturegraph Publications, 1988, are rather

worse than Castaneda's.

27. Churchill, "Plastic Medicine Men," op. cit.
28. Such a reaction is hardly extraordinary. For published versions of the same thing, see Staniford, Philip, "I Come to Praise Carlos, Not to Bury Don Juan," in de Mille, op. cit., pp. 151-3. This behavior is quite in line with the sort of validation Castaneda has received from "scholarly" sources (e.g.: Littleton, C. Scott, "An emic account of sorcery: Carlos Castaneda and the rise of a new anthropology," *Journal of Latin American Lore*, Vol. 2, No. 2, 1976; McDermott, Richard, "Reason, Rules and the Ring of Experience: Reading our World into Carlos Castaneda's Works," *Human Studies*, Vol. 2, No. 1, 1979, pp. 31-46) even after the dimensions of the hoax he'd perpetrated were becoming apparent to anyone who cared to look.
29. This exchange occurred during the "Voices from Native North America" conference series at Alfred University, Alfred, New York, February 9, 1991.
30. The book at issue here is Andrews, Lynn, *Medicine Woman*, Harper and Row Publishers, New York, 1982. Andrews' other volumes, all of them in kind, include *Flight of the Seventh Moon: The Teaching of the Shields*, Harper and Row Publishers, New York, 1985; *Jaguar Woman*, Harper and Row Publishers, New York, 1986; *Star Woman*, Harper and Row Publishers, New York, 1987; *Teachings Around the Sacred Wheel*, Harper and Row Publishers, New York, 1989; and *Crystal Woman*, Warner Books, New York, 1990. In 1988, Harper and Row also packaged *Medicine Woman*, *Jaguar Woman*, and *Star Woman* as a boxed set under the title *Medicine Woman Trilogy*.
31. Venne brought this up during her presentation at the "Voices from Native North America" conference series at Alfred University, Alfred, NY, November 10, 1990.
32. The Mary Summer Rain books include *Spirit Song* (1986), *Phoenix Rising: No-Eyes Vision of Things to Come* (1987), *Dreamwalker: The Path of Sacred Power* (1988), and *Phantoms Afoot: Journies Into the Night* (1989), all published by Whitford Press, West Chester, PA.

Chapter XV

Cowboys and...
Notes on Art, Literature, and American Indians in the Modern American Mind

by Jimmie Durham

...the exploring party returned to England with such good accounts of the new country that Queen Elizabeth named it Virginia in honor of herself.

Wilbur F. Gordy, *Elementary History of the United States*

I recollected seeing a boy who was shot down near the house. His arm and thigh were broken, and he was so near the burning house that the grease was stewing out of him. In this situation he was still trying to crawl along; but not a murmur escaped him, though he was only about twelve years old. So sullen is the Indian, when his dander is up, that he had sooner die than make a noise, or ask quarter. The number that we took prisoner, being added to the number we killed amounted to a hundred and eighty-six.

Davey Crockett, *Diary*

For the Other remains to be discovered. The fact is worthy of astonishment.

Tzvetan Todorov, *The Conquest of America*

In an installation in California's Museum of Man, Luiseño Indian artist James Luna put himself in a display case. Viewing "the body," a Euroamerican woman said to her husband, "Dear, I think he is alive." The husband replied, "Don't be silly; they don't put live ones in museums."

Luna makes other installations wherein American Indian people are represented by only a few articles of clothing, sometimes by cowboy boots and hats which are typical "Indian" dress today. In New York, much of my own work has dealt with what Jean Fisher has called "the necrophilous codes of the museum,"[1] and with misrepresentation and misidentification of "Native Americans" by our colonizers. Luna and I did not know of each other's work. At opposite ends of the United States we addressed similar problems, because, I believe, the problems are so intolerably before us.

This chapter is concerned with the invisibility of American Indians in the Americas—not to plead the case for more visibility but to attempt a tentative investigation into the ramifications of the "presence of the absence/absented Indian body" in American discourse.[2] This solid vacuum is a special case. I feel, therefore, that I must tell anecdotes to convince readers that the situation actually exists. Certainly for readers from the Americas, it is necessary (at least from my experiences) to approach the subject obliquely. The following few "bullets," then, are related only by the invisible theme of invisible American Indians.

- The great Shawnee resistance leader Tecumseh was killed around 1810 in Ohio Territory. One of the most famous generals in the U.S. Civil War, William Tecumseh Sherman, was born in Ohio surely not much more than ten years later. How is it that Sherman was named after the most hated and feared man of the time, while the Indian wars were still—further west and south—in full bloom?

- Naomi Bliven, reviewing Nirad Chaudhuri's autobiography in the *New Yorker* magazine, compares England's colonization of India not to its colonization of American Indians, but of American whites. She, feeling herself and her country as "fellow" colonized persons, has a sympathy with Chauduri and India.[3]

- In V.S. Naipaul's book about the American South, Anne Siddons, a white novelist from Georgia, states, "We [Southern whites] were a conquered and occupied people, the only people in the United States to be like that."[4]

- At a recent convention of the College Art Association (CAA) in New York, a Brazilian woman showed slides of Brazilian paintings. The paintings were traditional-looking in form, done on stretched canvas or linen in oils or acrylics. Her thesis was to show, by the styles of the paintings that, as she put it, "the Brazilian people are truly a new people." If Europeans are then the "Old People," who are the Indians of Brazil? Obviously, they are considered either as a special type of property of the "new people," or not at all.

- In the United States, people phrase their questions about Indians in the past tense, not only to me and other "natives," but also to groups. It is not unusual for us to answer in the past tense. Once, in South Dakota, a white man asked, "What did the Indians eat?" One of our elders replied without irony, "We ate corn, beans, and squash." (That is the standard answer in U.S. school books).

- There is in the United States—and to a lesser extent in Chile and Argentina—a curious phenomenon that is seldom given intellectual consideration: whites claiming to be "part Indian," and even more, whites who claim to be Indian. Surely there is not another part of the world wherein members of a racist oppressor society claim to be members of the oppressed group. (These Euroamericans do not, of course, claim any of the concomitant disadvantages of being an Indian.)

It also seems necessary to state that the indigenous people of the Americas are colonized and that the colonization is not simply the language of some political rhetoric from past decades. Europe may be passing through a post-colonial time, but we in the Americas still live in a colonial period. Our countries were invaded, genocide was and is committed against us, and our land and lives are taken over for the profit of the colonizer.[5] Although I do not want to express moral outrage, since this investigation is about American discourse and not about an "Indian problem," I ask you to imagine my state of mind when once more I say we are *colonized* peoples. We are not "primitives" who suffer under culture shock by contact with "more developed societies." Yet in my experience, if I were addressing a live audience, someone would question the simple facts: "But didn't you at first welcome the settlers?" or "Weren't relationships friendly at first?"

For the peoples of Europe, the "Other" may be a foreigner, a person from another place. For those Europeans who have established permanent colonies, such as the United States and Canada, Australia, South Africa, or the Latin American countries, it cannot follow that the Other is the colonized person "here at home" because that would call into question the legitimacy of the colonial state. In these states, the Other must be denied one way or another. Golda Meir said that there were no Palestinians, and South Africa has always claimed there were no Africans in the area until the arrival of the settlers. "Aboriginals" have only recently been included in Australia's census, and of course the North American pioneers "tamed a wilderness."[6]

The Myth of the United States

There is something unique about the U.S. It was the first settler colony to establish itself *against* and through denial of its original inhabitants. It developed thereby a narrative that was more complete, more satisfying, than similar narratives in Canada and Latin America. That narrative has generated new cultural and political behavior that has been a main influence in the modern world. When, as a political activist in the 1070s, I attempted to present a case to the United Nations, I was more than intimidated by the tenacity with which other countries upheld the American narrative.[7] And that was in the most obvious and unsubtle political discourses. The economic power of the United States does not seem reason enough for the propagation of its central myth, because the myth was expanding its influence long before the United States obtained its majority. The narrative in question has its origins in Europe, of course. But the U.S. refined—that is, coarsened—the European premise of "the primitive" so that it became more than operable for industrial expansionism.

America's narrative about itself centers upon, has its operational center in, a hidden text concerning its relationship with American Indians. That central text *must* be hidden, sublimated, and acted out. Native American artists, as artists and as persons responsible to our peoples, have traditionally attempted intervention, but even our attempts are seen as quite minor entertainment. As we approach the fifth centennial anniversary of Columbus, many people throughout the Americas renew certain superficial discourses about their history. That seems to be for purposes of repeating reassuring known propositions. In the United States, we Indians are now called upon to speak within this framework. The difficulty is not so much that we are expected to say known things as that our speaking at such a time is a known thing. Coming just at the moment when institutions in the United States are already reinforcing racism by celebrating "multiculturalism," I suspect this new development in fact makes intervention on our part more difficult.

The United States, because of its actual guilt—as opposed to some thought-out or not thought-out perception of guilt—has had a nostalgia for itself since its beginnings. Even now, one may read editorials almost daily about America's "loss of innocence" at some point or another, and about some time in the past when America was truly good. The self-righteousness and insistence upon innocence began as the United States began, with invasion and mass murder. The master narrative of the United States has not (cannot be) changed. It has been broadened. It has been broadcast. This narrative is only superficially concerned with taming the wilderness and "crossing new frontiers." The U.S. has developed a concept and a reality of the state, I might say of "statism," because U.S. culture is by definition so completely ideological.

The profound operative concept has to do with a specifically American premise about the Other. Any poll taken in the United States would show, I think, that Americans imagine that the Ohio Valley region mentioned earlier has always in some way belonged to their country, that in fact what is now its continent-wide national expanse of territory has always been somehow the rightful property of the U.S. state. It is a country that may continually expand (and as a state, not as a "commonwealth" or "empire") but that cannot give up any territory even if, as in the case of Puerto Rico, the territory has been proven to be held illegally. There is an unbroken line between the first American Thanksgiving Day, celebrating the slaughter of an entire native village, and the overwhelming popularity of George Bush's slaughter of thousands in the 1991 invasion of the Persian Gulf. Whether from the Right or the Left, whether the topic is the Persian Gulf or Robert Mapplethorpe, criticism in the United States must ultimately depend on the "American-ness" or "Un-American-ness" of the project being criticized. It must rely on ideology and statism.[8]

Can we assume from this that there is no United States other than in its ideological and expansionist statism? The question is not meant spitefully. I once explained "American Indian" legal rights and the consequent demands of the American Indian Movement to a member of the Institute for Policy Studies. His response was, "That would mean the breakup of the United States." And he was undoubtedly correct. Suppose Germany had *begun* with the Holocaust and its denial. The intellectual or political admission of the situation might have caused a breaking up of the state. But the comparison is a little silly. Unlike the Third Reich, the U.S. is a continual and movable holocaust. The matter is simply not acknowledged.

In 1914, the U.S. Marines were slaughtering Yaqui Indians in the center of Mexico for the "protection" of European settlers. (After Mexico consolidated its revolution in the 1920s, it too commenced the killing of Yaquis and Apaches, the last recorded military engagement having occurred in 1938). The last battle between U.S. troops and my own Cherokee people was in 1923. For the Lakota, the last such "incident" happened in 1975. Who knows when or where the next will occur, because surely the process has not ended. The United States has been continuously at war, continuously invading and killing the indigenous peoples of this continent since the advent of the Jamestown and Plymouth Colonies.[9] Yet, according to conventional histories, its "age of expansion" *began* in 1898 with the invasions of the Philippines, Puerto Rico, and Cuba, just after the "last" of its "Indian Wars" (!).[10]

The United States is, and has always been, an aggressive, wantonly expansionist power, first and foremost on its "home turf," every square inch of which was torn from the original inhabitants. This is sometimes stated, but never given real consideration in terms of its actual implications. Let me pose the question clearly: *If Indians are not to be considered victims of colonial aggression, how are we to be considered?* I am tempted to write the question twice, for emphasis. It implies a second question, however: Why are we not considered as colonized by anyone other than ourselves? For any Indian, the questions are subjective and quotidian: *How might I exist?*

The master narrative of the U.S. proclaims there were no Indians in this country, only wilderness, "vacant land." Then, that the Indians were *in need* of the U.S. and its "gifts of civilization and enlightenment." Then, that the Indians all died, unfortunately. Then, that the Indians of today are 1) basically happy with their situation, and 2) in any event, no longer "real" Indians. Then, most importantly, it is held that this is the "complete" story. Nothing contrary can be heard. Europeans might at last search for "authenticity" among the primitives, but Americans already know the complete story. The narrative is finished and known and of no contemporary importance. The settlers claim the discourse on Indians as their own special expertise, yet the expertise is of such a familial, at-home nature that it is not worthy of exploration. Husbands know their wives very well, of course, but the wives, as known property, cannot be subjects of serious discussions among husbands; less can they speak on their own behalf to the husbands. Euroamericans have invented themselves as being cowboys (frontiersmen, pioneers). So, they believe that if, in fact, there might be "Indians," those Indians would be silent partners in wilderness-taming activities—that is, like the wives of paternalist culture.[11]

This is the American state's idea and central scheme. It is a scheme necessary for the state's very existence. How might *it* otherwise exist? The United States has always been, necessarily, both "biggest" and "best." Because of its atrocities, it *must* be innocent and the *most* just, and it must expand, "progressing," "moving on." How else to escape what it is, what it has done?[12] If America's notion of itself has seemed to fit so well the times we call modern, isn't it because that notion itself created these times? What I am calling an American notion is a European project, except the European states cannot themselves carry it out efficiently. They are too intertwined with their own sense of place. The state called "France" is connected to a place also called "France," from which, in the beginning, it arose. At the end of its empire, Great Britain can still return to its meager island off the coast of Europe. It too has a place of origin.

The state called "America," on the other hand, is connected only to an independent settler colony. It has no place of its own, nor did it ever. The economic power of the United States is losing its grip in much of the world, but in the end, to where might this state return? It is *only* a state, *only* a political entity, so its ideological base and its narrative must be absolute. If someone imagines otherwise, at the end of America's external empire it would follow that there be an actual place that is America. Would *my* country become free of the U.S. during this dissolution of empire? If so, where then is America? If not, how can it be that the empire has dissolved? Do I myself really come from any place? Is the country of my people really only a sub-theme, an artifact within the Great American Story?

Reality Eclipsed

The denial of American Indians in American discourse requires a lengthy investigation, and what I've presented is merely the roughest of outlines. We may, however, consider some curiosities as brief evidence. First, there is little intellectual interest in the situation. The existing discourse on Native Americans is always sentimentally moral. Edmund Wilson's least-known book, *Apology to the Iroquois*, for example, is properly seen as no more than an apology.[13] It contains no analysis of the conditions of U.S. society that make his apology seem necessary to him. Aside from Roy Harvey Pearce's *Savagism and Civilization*, ahead of its time and academically sequestered, and Leslie Fiedler's *The Return of the Vanishing American*, more literary reportage than anything else, there has been no serious Euroamerican literary treatment of the United States' relation to its indigenous populations.[14] Instead, there has been a stunning silence.

The settlers must consume us. There is no one to challenge their ownership of us except ourselves. And any autonomous action on our part, of course, cannot be allowed. In American literature, "the Indian" is always a passive witness to the cowboy's action. Neither Queequeg in *Moby Dick* nor Tonto in *The Lone Ranger* nor Chief Broom in Ken Kesey's *One Flew Over the Cuckoo's Nest* have speaking parts.[15] The same may be rightly said of every other Indian character inhabiting the pages of Euroamerican fiction, a situation very different from that pertaining to other colonial contexts. There is a vast difference between Tonto and Gunga Din. Gunga Din, as the Good Indian fighting the Bad Indian on behalf of the Empire, is capable of heroic deeds. In the United States, the Good Indian is necessarily passive; like Cochise in the film *Broken Arrow* (1950), his role is simply to allow the settlers in.

It is in cinema that we can most easily see that the myth of the United States is not intellectually challenged. The Lone Ranger is always alone in a wilderness he does not quite call home. (His home might be named "traveling the earth to protect the settlers.") It is amazing that he can be so alone; I mean, without any of us at all. At first, John Wayne as the Lone Ranger in films such as *The Searchers* (1956) saved innocents from the savages.[16] In the last great wave of Hollywood westerns—*High Noon* (1952), *Shane* (1953), *et al.*—the hero and the settlers are all by themselves on the endless prairies. They cannot remember when they last "had" to have killed Indians (it has been at least several months, a long while in the typical American memory). At some point late at night, by the campfire, presumably, the Lone Ranger ate Tonto. By the time Alan Ladd becomes the Lone Ranger in *Shane*, his Indian companion has been consumed. Now, the Lone Ranger himself becomes stoic, silent, the Noble Savage, but so much neater and more satisfactory at the job than the squalid Red Man whose characteristics he has swallowed.

In the 1970s, films such as *Soldier Blue* (1970) and *Little Big Man* (1971) used Indians as the backdrop for America's coming to terms with its war in Vietnam. Nothing has had, though, the impact of the earlier movies. At any rate, film critics from James Agee to Pauline Kael have seen nothing noteworthy about America's image of itself as seen through the camera's not looking at the real situation with Indians. Every other part of the American myth may now be critically examined. The central, operational part, the part involving conquest and genocide, remains sacred and consequently obscured. Americans retain the right to be pioneers. It follows that American Indians cannot have a Sidney Poitier, Cicely Tyson or Harry Belafonte, much less a Richard Pryor, Whoopie Goldberg or Eddie Murphy. The indigenous populations must be always and essentially unreal, a figment of the national imagination. No more or less.[17]

This manifests itself plainly in the blatant racism of comic strip characters with exaggerated facial features and "Indian" names such as "Leapin' Lizard," sports teams named the "Cleveland Indians" and "Washington Redskins." The use of real Indian names to sell every sort of product from "Navajo" and "Cheyenne" vehicles to "AIM" toothpaste passes unmentioned by the American public. I once thought of making an installation using the more obviously viciously racist images of Indians, juxtaposing them with the Noble Savage type depictions associated with "Cherokee" clothing and "Big Chief" writing tablets. The title would have been "Which is the Correct Way to Portray Indians?" But I didn't, because it seemed to me that even the most sensitive and perceptive American viewers would be able to smile and remove themselves from any involvement in the situation. This is no different from their collective ability to psychically remove themselves from our actual, ongoing physical suffering.[18]

This leads to a second curiosity, conceptually bound to the first, revealing itself in the political arena. The civil rights movement of the early 1960s, and even the debates as far back as the pre-Civil War period, created a situation wherein the struggles of African Americans are seen as an agenda item for the entire country (in both positive and negative senses), not exclusively the concern of Black people. The Black liberation struggle of the late '60s and early '70s intensified this circumstance. Something of the sort, albeit to a noticeably lesser extent, has also happened regarding Chicanos and Japanese Americans. But no such perception or preoccupation has evolved in relation to American Indians. Native peoples in America remain invisible on their own land, precisely because it *is* our land.

The African, Asian and Latin American peoples are seen as having legitimate political struggles, as part of an important concept called "human rights." American Indians obviously cannot be called "Americans." We cannot, therefore, be considered politically. We must be spoken of mythically, as American Indians, or anthropologically, as "Amerinds." We are thereby effectively removed from the arena of political discourse in exactly the same way we are removed from artistic, literary, and cinematic discourse. Instead of fundamental human rights, we have more specialized and esoteric "Rights of Indigenous Populations."[19] This is a set of rights, even now being formulated and articulated, which precludes intellectual consideration and substitutes sentimental feeling. European colonization of Africa and even the U.S. exploitation of Latin America are generally seen as being outrageous and intolerable. Our circumstance, on the other hand, is usually viewed as something of an "inevitable historical tragedy."[20]

The United States takes great pride in describing its government as one "of laws, not men." According to the American Civil Liberties Union and similar institutions, any breach of the provisions of the U.S. Constitution is a breach of that valuable "rule of law" by which "the people" are protected against despotic tyranny. Yet we native people are consistently denied our legal rights.This denial causes alienation and poverty in extreme forms. Congress and the courts persistently pretend our rights are somehow too mysterious to decipher, while the public presses no demands that their representatives' comportment in this regard be changed in any constructive way. To the contrary, public sentiment often congeals upon the theme that governmental entities too often "coddle"—merely by acknowledging their existence—the thin residue of native survivors of the settlers' earlier butchery and cannibalism.[21]

América Latina

The Master said, "What is necessary is to rectify names—If names be not correct, language is not in accordance with the truth of things. If language is not in accordance with the truth of things, affairs cannot be carried on to success."

Confucian Analects,
Book XIII

We divide the world into North and South. It is understood that the concept "Third World" is in large part concerned with the Southern hemisphere versus the Northern. In that simplistic scenario, American Indians in the United States and Canada are once more negated, and Indians in Latin America are negated by being made part of the Latino project. Intellectuals of the Third World, perhaps even more than those of the First World, have often accepted a monolithic idea of "Third Worldism" of which they are proudly a part, or which they must overcome en route to "progress" and "development."

I have written that the United States is unique, yet its narrative as a colonial power differs from those of Latin American countries only by its degree of completeness. In a way, Latin American culture remains closely tied to Europe. It remains colonial in a more traditionally European sense. For that reason, the U.S. narrative has "won" over those of Latin America. The mythical Plains Indian of the United States has become the archetype for "Indian-ness," has become the "Red Indian" even for the indigenous peoples of Latin America.[22] Once again it may be useful to relate some anecdotal curiosities:

- Latin Americans do not know what "an Indian" looks like. Even in countries such as Bolivia and Peru, where native populations are huge, a person with typically Indian size and facial features is characterized as *Chino/a:* "Chinese." By contrast, someone who is large, robust, and with the features typical of southern Spain will be called *El Indio:* "the Indian."[23]

- In Latin America, one knows an Indian by his "Indian suit." Quite often, a person who is quite obviously racially Indian, but culturally alienated from her or his society, will be "passed" as "Spanish." Conversely, one finds those of obvious European ancestry dressing in native garb and boasting of their "Indian-ness," even the "Indian-ness" of *Latin* America as a whole. Paul Gauguin, for instance, a pure-bred and cultured Frenchman, learned to adopt this attitude as his own.[24]

- The literature of Latin America, as in the North, chronicles very well the alienation of settlers sans Indians. Colombian novelist Gabriel García Márquez lived part of his childhood in the countryside, where the bulk of Colombia's indigenous population resides. At that time, and at the time he was writing his novels, and at the time his novels are set, rural Indians became politically organized and were consequently hunted down and slaughtered by the state.[25] No hint of this has ever entered into García Márquez' writing; his pages simply contain no Indians at all.

- Juan Rulfo, the Mexican writer who is cited as an inspiration by so many other Latin American authors, could never produce so much as the ghost of an Indian inhabiting the Mexican village in which he set his work.

- "Latin American literary giant" Miguel Asturias' "sympathetic" novel, *Men of Maize,* so mythologized Guatemala's Mayans that they seem more like exotic animals than human beings.[26] Asturias subsequently became an official in the government which systematically razed real Indian villages, often butchering the residents.

- In Isabelle Allende's recent novel of the Allende years in Chile, *The House of the Spirits,* which attempts to provide some overview of the conditions in her country at the time, the only Indians present are so placidly evil and so inscrutable that the author cannot maintain an interest in them herself. One is described as having "tiny oriental eyes." Later in the same book, "mongoloid" (Down's Syndrome) children are also described as having "tiny oriental eyes." Allende's Indians, like virtually all Latin American Indians, do not speak languages. Instead, they speak "dialects."[27] (Throughout Latin America, *lengua,* language, is reserved for Europeans. Indians speak *dialectos.)*

- While the United States advertises itself as a "nation of immigrants," Mexico claims the battle between Cortez and the Aztecs "was neither a victory nor a defeat, but the birth pains of a new race and a new nation," thus nullifying the existence of hundreds of indigenous "tribes" who today still fight for enough land to stand on.[28]

- In Brazil, Indians are still "wards of the state," neither adult human beings nor children within the legal system.[29]

- Uruguay makes a weirdly contradictory boast. It says it captured and killed the last Indian within its borders in 1926. Simultaneously, Uruguayans are prone to considering themselves *gauchos,* Indian-European *mestizo* cowboys. The country claims to be the "Switzerland of South America," just as Costa Rica—reputedly another "Indian-free zone"—has called itself the "Switzerland of Central America." Here, one may see the American insanity in its most basic form. Even discounting those Indians from other countries imported to wait tables, and the confused identities of their own citizenries, neither Uruguay nor Costa Rica could be—and indeed are not—"Indian-less" in their own right. Noticeable native populations continue to exist in both places.[30]

The great bulk of the Europeans who make up the countries of the Americas have never left Europe. They brought it along with them. They are always and obviously never at home here. Their true feelings about the actual land are fear and contempt. In their minds, they still live on a frontier, always ready to pull up stakes and move somewhere else. After 500 years they still know very little of the local flora and fauna (many Latin Americans still believe that armadillos, like vultures, eat carrion), and seem to believe that indigenous knowledge of such things is either occult or some sort of animal cunning.[31] The difference between the look and feel of the cities and developed countrysides of Europe and those of the Americas is striking. Europeans appear to feel at home in Europe. Euroamericans have never felt at home.

The *patria* that springs from their exaggerated patriotism—"The American Way," "Our Mexican Heritage," etc.—is a combination of the political state and defensive bravado. It is not based in or on the land. In no other countries have both the people and the governments had such a will to despoil the natural habitat. It is the despoliation done by colonizers pretending to be native, without need for the most simple concern for native peoples. The settlers feel they must consume us. They insist they have a historic right to us, and often that they *are* us.

In the American countries where we are no longer a significant percentage of the population, we have a great fear of populism. The "populace," whether composed of picturesque peasants or radical students, is always a ready lynch mob against Indians, either by direct action or programmatically. In Latin America as in the United States, schemes for progress are *always* against Indians, the various nationalisms *always* anti-Indian. Both Peru and Brazil are well known examples of that, but Panama might be a more instructive example. The United States invented Panama from a piece of Colombia. The U.S. interest, and consequently the interest of the Panamanian government, was the canal zone. Indians in Panama's southern forests were thereby protected by disinterest. The same "tribe" in northern Colombia was and is hunted down for extermination. When the canal is returned to Panama, there could well be a development of interest in the entirety of "its" territory by the Panama's Latino population. Indians within Panama will then face the same fate as their relatives in northern Colombia.[32]

The governments of Latin America often develop a sense of selfhood and unity for their countries and regions by appearing to oppose U.S. imperialism. The United States may thus be seen as a benefactor to Latin American nationalist sentiment. In any case, it is clear that countries such as Argentina, Brazil, and Chile would be quite willing to fill any imperialist vacuum created by a disappearance of U.S. influence in their locales. The settler colonies most often tied their desire for independence from European "fatherlands" (or "mother countries") to a perceived "softness" toward "savages" on the part of the parent states. The progressive intelligentsia of Latin America has adopted the pose, "we are all the same people." They take our land, our music, our clothes and our history. In turn, they insist we take up their struggles. Gothlay (Geronimo), the Chiricahua Apache leader, said in his surrender speech to the U.S. Army: "So, you have captured me. The Mexicans would have killed me."[33] Nothing has changed today.

I have tried to present the outrageous idea that the profound division in the Americas is not between North and South, but between Indians and settlers. As the hidden operant for all American narratives, its discourse is not a product of U.S. imperialism, but its instructor. The concealment and its methods have served to take away from Indians a reality in the world, and therefore our voices in the world. I began this section with a quotation from Confucius about names. The false terminology used against us is so pervasive that any of its words call up the (false) idea of "Indian-ness." The word "tribe" comes from the three peoples who originally founded Rome ("Tribunal," based on the number three, comes from the same root.) It is not a descriptive word, nor a scientific one. Its use in anthropology has been completely discredited, and came from the European concept of human progress at the pinnacle of which were the capitals of Europe. "Tribe," "chief," and similar words do not describe a part of reality for any people. They are descriptive only within the discourse of enclosure and concealment, for purposes of fabricating impressions of relative primitiveness.

In the U.S., Indian reservations are governed by "tribal councils," created and controlled by the federal Bureau of Indian Affairs. Those opposed to the councils usually are said to have organized themselves under a system of "traditional chiefs." We cannot insist that the world learn the terms for leaders in our own languages (almost 300 languages within the U.S. alone), nor can we realistically insist that the terminology of modern states be applied, such as "president" or "prime minister." At best, one ends up with "tribal president," "tribal chair," or in the case of my own people, "president of the Cherokee Nation of Indians." In that example, the use of the word "nation" has been rendered synonymous with the word "tribe." (One does not, after all, refer to the "president of the Nation of France" or "president of the French Nation.")

It is not understood that we are colonized, but it is well understood that we are *not* to be considered as nations in the sense of modern, independent nation-states. Therefore, any demand on our part for a different terminology is perceived as mere sensitivity to racism, as in African American's insistence against the term "Negro." The world knows very well who we are, how we look, what we do, and what we say—from the narrative of the oppressor. The knowledge is false, but it is known. We, then, are left somewhere else (no-where else). By the very act of speaking, we contribute to the silence, the nullification laid upon us. It is not as though we ourselves are speaking from some pristine state of savage grace. Colonization is not external to the colonized, and it makes for neither wisdom nor charity among the colonized. Made to feel unreal, inauthentic, we often participate in our own oppression by assuming identities or attitudes within the colonial structure.

Eating Indian Artists

This century began with Indian people attempting more individual efforts (as opposed to communal efforts) at intervention in the cultural and political narratives of the American state. Among artists, those efforts still today are usually made with constant reinforcement of the individual's identity and authenticity by employing parts of the stereotype. One's Indian community cannot authenticate or designate a position in the world of art because that world is of the colonizer. One must approach the colonizer for the space and license to make art. The colonizer, of course, will not grant such license, but will pretend to under certain circumstances.

In different ways, Guayasamin in Ecuador; Tamayo in Mexico; Alan Houser, Oscar Howe, and C.N. Gorman in the United States produced what Blaise Tobias has called "Indian-flavored art." Tobias means art within the European tradition, but with recognizable signs of "Indian-ness." No matter how foolishly (or wisely) or cynically those efforts have been conducted, they were attempts to intervene in the Americas' master narrative. Conversely, no matter how successful the individual artist became, the attempts cancelled themselves because of the nature of the narrative.[34]

In the 1960s and '70s, there was a veritable explosion of "American Indian" art in the United States and Canada. The sociological reasons for it, I believe, are connected with the American settlers' anxiety about themselves at the time. With the civil rights and Black liberation movements, the New Left and feminist movements, the counterculture, "The War," and assassinations culminating in the Watergate scandal, the U.S. needed to adjust its self-image without admitting any new images. The hippies had already adopted their ideals of our ways and dress to suit their self-image (a variation of the cowboy-as-Indian theme), so the idea had only to be expanded and cleaned up a bit.

I do not believe we necessarily produced more, or more talented, artists during that time, although it may be true simply because a larger market suddenly existed. What seems more pertinent is the fact that the market arrived at all. But the market has never been an "art market." It has always been a sub-outlet, the "Indian art market." It did not come about because of our demands, but because of America's needs. Hence, the subject matter of "Indian" art was the "Indian" face, the "Indian" body romanticized, not by us, but by "their" image of us.

The three most successful Indian artists of the period were Fritz Scholder, R.C. Gorman, and T.C. Cannon. Scholder painted post-expressionist "Indian Chiefs" in full regalia, using brilliant magentas, greens, and oranges. The facial features and bodily forms were blurred, indistinct, as though part of the painterly landscape. Gorman painted and drew Indian women sentimentally, wrapped in blankets and placed like stones in decorative Southwest desert landscapes. Cannon gave his neo-realist chiefs a little Oklahoma powwow glitz: metallic paints and contemporary trappings in settings which were always clearly in the past. Other artists, such as Earl Biss and Kevin Red Star, each borrowing some "advanced style" from the lexicon of Eurocentrism, shortly joined the queue of those allegedly depicting Indians in terms which were "real, not red." Theirs, it was proclaimed, was a "consciously angry and political" representation.[35]

We had begun our "new" political activism in New York state and Oklahoma during the 1950s. Our resistance became nationally visible in 1969-70 with the takeover of Alcatraz Island. The trend increased over the next two years with the seizure of the Mayflower Replica at Plymouth, Massachusetts on Thanksgiving Day 1971 and the occupation of the Bureau of Indian Affairs headquarters in Washington, D.C. on the eve of the 1972 presidential election. After the massive resistance at the hamlet of Wounded Knee in 1973, I became a full-time activist in the American Indian Movement (AIM).[36] I was continuously incredulous at the way the American public seemed to welcome our struggle, although I was never surprised at their ignorance of what it was we were struggling *for*. Completely passive, even complacent, people felt that the "Indian struggle" was one they knew. It was one they had sympathy with, *as if it were their own*, and they *knew* we did not threaten them. We would not ask for a seat anywhere.

In public addresses, no matter what the situation or atrocity we described, we received the same audience responses: standing ovations, and then the questions, "What did Indians eat?"—"How can I find out about my Cherokee grandmother?"— "Where can I learn about Indian rituals and healing herbs?"—"Would you like to see my collection of Indian etchings?" As our situation worsened, America loved us all the more. By 1980, Euroamericans were teaching our "shamanism" in universities. White students were participating in Sun Dances and peyote ceremonies. Every shopping mall in the country had a store which sold Cherokee magic quartz crystals, and every airport had a boutique selling "Indian" dress and artifacts along with cowboy gear. As Ralph Lauren's television commercial has it, "the spirit of the West is everywhere today."

Our lives, and our rights, continue to deteriorate. The Indian art market continues to expand, but it has never been ours. It has served only to isolate Indian artists through commercial success in a specialized area not unlike the beacon offered by basketball to Blacks. James Luna has said, "What should be the foremost intent of American Indian artists is opportunity to say, not to be spoken for or about...it is truly unfortunate that there are so few Indian artists who address current issues of Indian communities or those of contemporary American art."[37] Those of us who have considered ourselves militant or traditional—in the real Indian sense of that term—have often relied upon some strategy or another for presenting the "plight of the Indian," that is, using art to attempt to show our situation to people in the United States or to show our view of the United States to itself. It is natural, probably, or at least understandable, given the situation, that we make that error. But it is an error because such attempts are expected and accepted within the narrative. "Indian suffering" is part of the entertainment. Finally, though, to accept any idea of ourselves as the subject matter for our art is potentially a trap.

Artists Eating Indians

Today, we have non-Indian artists using us as subject matter once more. It is a phenomenon that seems exactly connected to the special American discourse about primitives and primitivism. Witness the success of the neo-surrealism offered by the Polish-American painter Paul Pletka, or the varied but equally ersatz imagery of Veloy Vigil and Frank Howell. Observe the Euroamerican woman who has assumed the name Kaylynn Sullivan Two Trees in order to "authenticate" her appropriation of Pueblo Indian pottery designs and use of "ritual" objects such as deer antlers in her work. Brazilian photographer Claudia Andujar has taken the Yanomami people in the Amazon as her exclusive property. Her photos of abstracted parts of Indian bodies, arranged with exotic flora, have made her reputation. She has therefore founded a committee to create a "park" for the Yanomami.

The German artist Lother Baumgarten has also made a reputation using Indians as subject matter, but in a more sophisticated way. According to a mutual friend, Baumgarten's intention is in part to address a new, more committed, concept of anthropology, yet the anthropology remains a science of the Other. (If anthropology were truly the "study of mankind," why are Europeans not studied equally with everyone else?) Although I sometimes use the Cherokee writing system in my own work, when I saw that Baumgarten had used it as a principle element in an installation in Pittsburg, I felt appropriated and sort of cancelled.

Mexico has a history of portraying "its" Indians in art at least since Diego Rivera, so much so that Mexican art is often perceived as consisting mainly of such portrayals. The sculptor Zuñiga makes large bronzes of groups of Indian women in a style that recalls Henry Moore. How are we expected to look at those placid and elemental giant bodies? Were the models friends with Zuñiga? Did they appreciate the likeness he achieved? Did they cook beans and tortillas for him? How else might he have approached them, discerning the "inner essence" he supposedly depicts?

Francisco Toledo is probably Mexico's most important contemporary artist. He comes from the Zapotec city of Juchitan in southern Mexico and has remained close to the community and committed to the people's struggles. In the early '80s, Toledo, along with Gloria and Victor de la Cruz, published a magazine, *Guchachi Reza,* in Juchitan. It had poems in Spanish and Zapotec, with illustrations by well-known artists such as Cuevas, Gallegos, and Ruís, and included letters about the area from D.H. Lawrence, Edward Weston, and others. Besides presenting explanations of Zapotec language by anthropologists, the magazine chronicled the history of their struggles. But to present such a collection to the very Spanish art world of Mexico City, a bastion of settler "Indianitude," without challenging that system, is to invite appropriation.

"Indianicity" is an actual employed term in Latin America. In Colombia, Antonio Caro has been doing installations using the signature of Quintin Lamé, an Indian leader in the early part of this century. (Lamé's signature has a sort of calligraphic design.) Caro is not an Indian, but he is committed to producing work that is socially oriented. In an interview in *Arte en Colombia,* he stated that his work about Lamé "combines art, sociology and ethnology," and that he allied himself with "indigenism" (indigenismo).[38]

Quintin Lamé's kinsman Justiano Lamé was assassinated in the late 1970s by
Colombian troops. I expect I would not really like to see documents of Justiano's
life hanging in an art gallery, but Caro's selection of a figure from a safer and more
distant past, who happened to have an artistic signature, seems insulting.

As America becomes more comfortable in redeploying its Indian myths, the
more invisible we become as people. This is true even if—or, more likely, *especially
if*—we are allowed to participate. One wants, of course, to develop ideas for effective
strategies for intervention in the American narrative. It is not a narrative about us.
It is absolutely *not* about us. There is nothing to correct, no footnotes for us to add.
The negation of Indians informs every aspect of American culture. It is most obvious
in the language: U.S. businessmen speak of "shooting their way out of the thicket,"
"circling the wagons," "sending out scouts," and "scalping" the unwary. The most
destitute section of the Bronx is called "Fort Apache," and unruly American
children act like "wild Indians." That is just the surface.

Americans have a reputation for "moving on," not only physically, but intellectually as well. Culturally, in art, literature, daily life, not simply in academic
circles, knowledge is reduced to facts that are to be assimilated so that one may
move on. The public is rightly called "consumers." The energy and vitality for
which the New World is famous come from vampirical activities. Americans must
always be at the height of their empire. It is a nice empire, and democratic. Much
of Europe has been forced to accommodate a token of receptivity to interventions
in its myths. As America pretends to copy that model, it becomes more closed, but
"kinder and gentler." I continue to think that this "soft" tightness itself might show
us a potential weakness in the system, so I continue to experiment.

Notes

1. Fisher, Jean, "Jimmie Durham," in *Matoaka Ale Attakulakula Anel Guledisgo Hnihi*, exhibition catalogue, Matt's Gallery, London, 1900.
2. Fisher, Jean, private letter.
3. Chaudhiri, Nirad, *Autobiography of an Unknown Indian*, Addison-Wesley Publishers, New York, 1989. Bliven's review appeared in the *New Yorker*, November 21, 1988.
4. Naipaul, V.S., *A Turn in the South*, Vintage International Books, New York, 1988.
5. For a succinct exploration of this topic, see Churchill, Ward, "Indigenous Peoples in the U.S.: A Struggle Against Internal Colonialism," *Black Scholar*, Vol. 16, No. 1, February 1985.
6. An excellent elaboration on this theme may be found in Todorov, Tzetan, *The Conquest of America*, Harper and Row Publishers, New York, 1984.
7. The term is used in the same general sense as in Bhabha, Homi K., ed., *Narration and Nation*, Routledge Publishers, New York, 1990. Its immediate application is explored further in Durham, Jimmie, *Columbus Day*, West End Press, Minneapolis, 1983.
8. An exposition in depth of this idea will be found in Drinnon, Richard, *Facing West: The Metaphysics of Indian Hating and Empire Building*, Schoken Books, New York (second edition) 1990.
9. For a well-rounded portrait of the early genocide, see Jennings, Francis, *The Invasion of America: Indians, Colonialism, and the Cant of Conquest*, University of North Carolina Press, Chapel Hill, 1975.
10. Prior to this rush beyond the confines of the North American continent, expansion was known, not as expansion, but simply as "settlement" or "wilderness-taming." For an overview, see Turner, Frederick, *Beyond Geography: The Western Spirit Against the Wilderness*, Rutgers University Press, New Brunswick, NJ, 1983.
11. Interestingly, a similar relationship seems to exist between Euroamerican women and women of

color. See hooks, bell, *Ain't I a Woman? Black Women and Feminism,* South End Press, 1981.

12. Investigations of much the same phenomenon in related contexts may be found in Chomsky, Noam, *Necessary Illusions: Thought Control in Democratic Societies,* South End Press, Boston, 1989.

13. Wilson, Edmund, *Apology to the Iroquois,* Farrar, Strauss, and Cudahy Publishers, New York, 1960.

14. Harvey, Pearce Roy, *Savagism and Civilization: A Study of the American Indian in the American Mind,* Johns Hopkins University Press, Baltimore, 1953; Fiedler, Leslie A., *The Return of the Vanishing American,* Stein and Day Publishers, New York, 1968.

15. Melville, Herman, *Moby Dick,* Modern Library, New York, 1950; Kesey, Ken, *One Flew Over the Cuckoo's Nest,* Viking Press, New York, 1973.

16. For a comprehensive listing of films of this type, see Friar, Ralph and Natasha Friar, *The Only Good Indian...The Hollywood Gospel,* Drama Book Specialists/Publishers, New York, 1972.

17. Further analysis can be found in Bataille, Gretchen, and Charles L.P. Silet, eds., *The Pretend Indians: Images of Native Americans in the Movies,* Iowa State University Press, Ames, 1980. Also see Stedman, William Raymond, *Shadows of the Indian: Stereotypes in American Culture,* University of Oklahoma, Norman, 1982.

18. See Berkhofer, Robert F. Jr., *The White Man's Indian: Images of the American Indian from Columbus to the Present,* Alfred A. Knopf Publishers, New York, 1978.

19. This is the actual vernacular. See Martinez Cobo, José R., "Study of the Problem of Discrimination Against Indigenous Populations," Subcommission on Prevention of Discrimination and Protection of Minorities, Commission on Human Rights, United Nations Economic and Social Council, 36th Session, September 1983 (UN/ID# E/CN.4/Sub .2/1983/21/Add. 8).

20. The archetype for this way of thinking is Rodman Wannamaker's *The Vanishing Race,* first published in 1913, rereleased in 1972 by Eagle Books, New York.

21. An ugly selection of such sentiments is accommodated in Clifton, James E., ed., *The Invented Indian: Cultural Fictions and Government Policies,* Transaction Books, New Brunswick, NJ, 1990.

22. See, for instance, Díaz-Polanco, Héctor, "Indigenismo, Populism, and Marxism," *Latin American Perspectives,* Vol. 9, Issue 33, Spring 1982, pp. 42-61.

23. For practical applications, see Flores, Caballero L., *El Integracionismo Latinamericano Mito o Realidad,* Universidad Nacional Federico Villareal Facultad de Educación y Ciencias Humanas, Lima, Peru, 1965.

24. Letter from Gauguin to Theo Van Gogh, "On Painting," circa November 20, 1889, cited in Marla Prather and Charles F. Stuchey, eds., *Gauguin: A Retrospective,* Park Lane, New York, 1989, p. 109.

25. On decimation of the indigenous population inside Colombia, see Dostal, Walter, ed., *The Situation of the Indian in South America,* World Council of Churches and the Ethnological Institute of the University of Bern, Geneva, Switzerland, 1972.

26. Asturias, Miguel, *Men of Maize,* Delacorte Press, New York, 1975.

27. Allende, Isabel, *The House of the Spirits,* Bantam Books, New York, 1985.

28. This is an inscription over the entrance to Mexico City's Museum of Anthropology, but it is also so widely quoted in Mexico as to serve as something of a national motto.

29. An examination of Brazil's native peoples may be found in Hemming, John, *Red Gold: The Conquest of Brazilian Indians,* Macmillan Publishers, London, 1978. Also see Bodard, Lucien, *Green Hell: Massacre of the Brazilian Indians,* Outerbridge and Dienstfrey Publishers, New York, 1969.

30. CSUCA, *Estructura Demografia y Migracions Internas en Centroamerica,* San José, Costa Rica, 1978.

31. Examples of such thinking abound. For prime fare, see Dane, Christopher, *The American Indian and the Occult,* Popular Library, New York, 1973.

32. For close examination of the emergence and early evolution of Panama, see Kepner, Charles O. Jr., and Jay H. Soothill, *The Panama Empire,* Vanguard Press, New York, 1935.

33. Gothlay is quoted to this effect in Faulk, Obie B., *The Geronimo Campaign,* Oxford University Press, New York, 1969, p. 135.

34. See Brody, J.J., *Indian Painters and White Patrons,* University of New Mexico, Albuquerque, 1971.

35. It is interesting that the only real breakthrough achieved by any of this group came via another medium altogether. At about the time he quit painting Indians, Scholder published a little-known book of bad-quality Polaroid photos of the way "Indian-ness" is popularly depicted in contemporary United States society. See Scholder, Fritz, *Indian Kitsch,* Northland Press, Flagstaff, AZ, 1979.

36. The period is chronicled in Burnette, Robert, and John Koster, *The Road to Wounded Knee,* Bantam, New York, 1974.

37. Luna, James, *Catalogue,* Cultural de la Raza, San Diego, 1985.

38. *Arte en Colombia,* No. 12, 1988.

Epilogue

Looking for Columbus
Thoughts on the Past, Present and Future of Humanity

John Mohawk

Your time of decay may be distant, but it will surely come, for even the white man, whose God walked and talked with him as friend to friend, could not escape our common destiny...

Seattle
Suquamish Leader, circa 1853

In the 1940s, an anthropologist named Ruth Benedict wrote a book called *Race, Science, and Politics*, not much remembered today.[1] In this book she makes the following proposition: that most societies begin with the claim that they are in some way or other a chosen people, and that this claim is the starting point for the development of ethnocentrism in the world. Chosen peoples are disconnected from other peoples because the others are *not* chosen. We can take these kinds of thoughts and assumptions to quite distant points; we can build a great deal of ideology around being the chosen and being in contradiction to the chosen.

The West shares a common story about its origins: God spoke to Abraham and demanded of him absolute and unquestioned obedience to His authority. From that story spring three major world religious traditions. The Christian tradition tells the story this way: that the first revelation was given to certain tribes of the Middle East, then the mantle of that tradition was handed over to people who were organizing a peasant religion in Rome, and then the peasant religion in Rome became the state religion in Rome and of the Byzantine Empire. So, as we roll toward 1492, we see an interesting discussion going on in Europe about Europeans' shared ethnicity.[2]

Physically, Europe is not a continent. Where is the water separating Europe from Asia? It is culture that separates Europe from Asia. Western Europe roughly comprises the countries that in the Middle Ages were Latin Christendom, and Eastern Europe consists of those countries that in the Middle Ages were Eastern Orthodox Christendom. It was about 1257 A.D. when the Pope claimed hegemony over

439

the secular emperors in Western Europe and formulated the ideology that Europeans, that Christians, were a unified ethnicity even though they spoke many different languages.[3] So, by 1492 we have a well-established tradition of Christian/European religious/ethnic exclusivity, and it is with this tradition that we open the latest chapter in the human experience, the history of the last 500 years.

Theological Racism

The first Spanish in the Americas did not distinguish themselves from Indians as Spaniards; they distinguished themselves from Indians as Christians.[4] Only later, after they had christianized many Indians, did they have to change that. The "Indian," like the European, is an idea. The notion of "Indians" was invented to distinguish the indigenous peoples of the New World from Europeans. The "Indian" is the person on shore, outside of the boat. The "Indian" is emphatically non-European in the ethnic sense.[5] Aside from that, the Americas were filled with peoples as radically different from one another as they are from Swedes or Chinese. There are hundreds of cultures, languages, ways of living in Native America. The place was a model of diversity at the time of Columbus' arrival. Yet Europeans did not see this diversity. They created the concept of "the Indian" to give what they did see some kind of unification, to make it a single entity they could deal with, because they could not cope with the reality of 400 different cultures. And, from that time to this, the white man has in fact created Indians in the image he wanted to see.[6] In the earliest reports of his voyages to reach Europe, Columbus said he had met all these nice people. They never lie, they never cheat, they never steal, they always live in nice places, and they always have plenty to eat. There had been a medieval story which said that somewhere in the world there still existed a Garden of Eden. In the beginning, the people who heard Columbus' accounts said: "Aha, these Indians are the people who inhabit the Garden of Eden." The message was that there existed a people who did not live under the oppressive order that Europe lived under: the human being who lives under this order of nature grows into a "noble man," a pure human being.[7] The first round of arguments, then, was to glorify nature, to glorify Indians as they appeared in the European imagination.

This first round of discussion was followed almost immediately by a second round, most carefully articulated in 1550 by the Spanish scholar Juan Ginés de Sepúlveda, who argued that Indians were not human beings, that they could not have souls, and that they should be ruthlessly exploited by the conquistadors as beasts of burden. This second round of dialogue, which held that Indians were dirty and vile and lived "brutish and short" lives, also held that nature itself was dirty and brutish.[8] It vilified nature and viewed it as an enemy of humanity.

Now, which of these two models—the idea of anarchy and human solidarity, of naked people living on the beach and eating all they wanted to, living without taxes, without an army; or the idea of an ordered society with prisons and armies and taxes—which of these two models do you think the monarchs, ruling by "divine right," and other authorities of Europe were going to embrace? Let us ask ourselves what the governmental tradition of Europe was prior to 1492. There was a little castle and a little clearing and people living around that. Then there was a man who lived in the castle who had a horse and armor, and he made all the decisions. In modern parlance, we call this a military dictatorship. There was one man, and he decided what was going to happen, and if you didn't like that, he got out his sword, chopped off your head, and asked if there was anyone else who disagreed with him. That was European government: one man, one sword, one vote![9]

No area of the globe has a bloodier history than Europe. And the reason for this is the outrageous intolerance of people claiming for centuries and centuries to be the chosen ones of God, to be a special people, a "superior race of men." The wealthy and powerful elite carefully selected those thoughts and ideas that fundamentally supported the structured European society they themselves ran.[10]

Scientific Racism

In the 19th century, when religion was by and large being gradually put aside, Europeans and their descendants in other parts of the world found themselves no longer willing to listen to charismatic leaders who claimed to have direct access to God's word.[11] They started to move toward the idea that everything can be known through science. Here, we enter upon a period in which science becomes a religion, a secular religion. In this, we encounter a very interesting phenomenon: somehow, all the attitudes that existed under the previous theological order find their way into the new scientific order, not only unchanged, but with a renewed and revitalized life. Beginning about 1830, you find Europeans suddenly starting to believe that the reasons things are as they are, the reason Europeans are everywhere successful in conquest, is not just because they are spiritually and militarily superior to those they encounter, but because they are *biologically* superior as well. We begin to see books that talk about an evolutionary development of humankind as though societies are to be qualified and quantified. Europeans begin to look about and see "primitive" societies as less than "civilization."[12] Hence, as they looked about the world, Europeans quickly came to observe all the other peoples of the world as if they were looking down at them from the top of the Empire State Building.

On this side of the ocean, the 19th century saw the West's Eurocentrism aimed squarely and practically at Indians. On the other side, the classical theoretical racists—the "scientific racists," as they are usually called— claimed that Western civilization had experienced no significant influences from Semitic people, or the Black people of Egypt, or any other non-European tradition. Europe was, they argued, a purely "Aryan" construction.[13] It is this aspect of scientism that laid the groundwork for the ideology—continually being focused, refined and sharpened over ensuing decades—which became a madness in Europe, a madness singling out Semites and their contemporary representatives, the Jews, for "special treatment." It created the fever which gave rise to nazism and the Holocaust.[14]

This way of thinking began with the religious intolerance of the Christian order and its assertions of European ascendancy. It survived the challenges to the Bible, its spirit dressed in scientific clothing, and found its way into the 20th century, creating the conditions for the World War II (which was in some ways really just another religious war). There was never any tangible evidence that Aryans were biologically superior to anybody. But it became an article of faith, and people believed it.

Ecological Racism

The huge ecological changes brought by the industrial revolution came about as a result of decisions made, not by the American electorate, but by small interest groups in board rooms during the 19th and 20th centuries.[15] So today we are not being visited by God, but by our own stupidity and the stupidity of the people who went before us. We often help create that condition of stupidity by finding ourselves unable to resist the assumptions of hierarchy and class privilege which created the environment in which those decisions were made in the past, the present, and— unless we do something about it—in the future. People who live in the hierarchical societies accruing from the matrices of Christianity and scientism do not work in the interest of future generations, they work in the interest of the bottom line. And the interests of the bottom line have nothing to do with the survival of our species on this planet.[16]

It is essential that we understand that the intolerance arising out of Eurocentrism is what has caused the crisis of our times. Eurocentrism not only creates anthropocentrism—which comes directly from the tradition calling upon "man" to go out and assert "dominion" over nature—but ordains that people are not open to any other thinking. I was at a discussion at the Harvard Divinity School not long ago when a speaker got up and said, "Humans are obviously superior to all other life forms on Earth." I wanted to ask him to define "superior." Without trees to create oxygen, humans can't breath, so they are a *dead* life form. If we don't understand ourselves in relation to the very big picture of the planet, as a biological living thing, then we don't understand the world we are living in. We can make abysmally ignorant statements such as "mankind is superior to all other life forms on earth," but, *however* you define "superior," it is immaterial to nature. Nature doesn't care what your ideologies are.

Toward a Viable Future

For 500 years we have seen both a clashing and an intermixing of cultures. Over all but the last decade or so, America has espoused the ideology of "the melting pot," and yet that approach has failed to enrich this culture. So, we're beginning to arrive at the realization that we might have to adopt a more pluralistic approach; instead of requiring everybody to be the same, maybe we should learn to live with one another, and allow for a genuine multiplicity of cultures. We are living in a world in which difference is just a simple fact of life, but our collective thinking has yet to truly come to grips with this reality. This *has* to change.

A workable world mentality means that we are going to have to make peace with those who are different from us. We must also come together in the realization that social initiatives, social justice, and ecology have to go hand in hand. As long as people don't have enough to eat, as long as people are driven off their lands, as long as investment banks in the industrialized world finance dams that displace people in the Third and Fourth Worlds, there will be people scrambling down hillsides cutting down the forests in order to find a place to live and a way to make a living.[17]

I offer you the suggestion that we need to reevaluate our thinking. We need to look at the old philosophies and ask ourselves whether that is where we want to put our energies. Or should we look at other peoples' ways of thinking about the world and its societies, and decide anew how human priorities and human societies ought to be constructed? We need to give ourselves permission to trust our own thinking and not allow bureaucrats and crazed guys at the pulpit to do our thinking for us. And we need to take *this* kind of ideology and make it work for us on *the land*.[18]

We are going to have to ask ourselves what our resources are. Our first resource is human compassion, gained through the clear use of our minds, which will allow us to make the best use of the human family. And another of our best resources emerges when we think clearly about the peoples who have alternative answers to the questions that are not being answered by the society we live in. For the first time in human history it is possible to talk to the jungle-dwelling Indians of South America in a European language at a North American conference and find out what they think about the world they live in and the world we live in. It is possible for the first time to take all the knowledge of the whole family of humanity and start plotting a course toward a viable future. It is possible at last to look at the modern period, not as a process of crisis and decline, but as a wonderful opportunity to amalgamate and pull things together, and to make the world our library. It at last is possible, in other words, not only to finally find the real meaning of Columbus, but to bury it.

Notes

1. Benedict, Ruth, *Race, Science, and Politics*, Viking Press, New York, 1945.
2. See Wolf, Philippe, *The Awakening of Europe: The Growth of European Culture from the Ninth Century to the Twelfth*, Cox and Wyman, Ltd., London, 1968.
3. A very interesting reading in this regard, albeit one which focuses on a much later period, is Anderson, Benedict, *Imagined Communities: Reflections on the Origin and Spread of Nationalism*. Thetford Press, Ltd., London, 1983.
4. For a succinct exposition on this theme, see Hanke, Lewis, *Aristotle and the American Indians: A Study in Race Prejudice in the Modern World*, Indiana University Press, Bloomington/Indianapolis, 1959.
5. An in-depth study of the thinking involved may be found in Hanke, Lewis, *All Mankind is One: A Study in the Disputation Between Bartolomé de Las Casas and Juan Ginés de Sepúlveda in 1550 on the Intellectual and Religious Capacity of American Indians*, Northern Illinois University Press, DeKalb, 1974.

6. For delineation of the process by which this has occurred, see Berkhofer, Robert F. Jr., *The White Man's Indian: Images of the American Indian from Columbus to the Present*, Alfred A. Knopf Publishers, New York, 1978.

7. See Morison, Samuel Eliot, ed. and trans., *Journals and Other Documents on the Life and Voyages of Christopher Columbus*, Heritage Publishers, New York, 1963. Also see Sargent, Daniel, *Christopher Columbus*, Bruce Publishing, Milwaukee, 1941.

8. A good treatment of Sepúlveda's thought may be found in Williams, Robert A. Jr., *The American Indian in Western Legal Thought: The Discourses of Conquest*, Oxford University Press, London/New York, 1990. Also see *Aristotle and the American Indians*, op. cit, and *All Mankind is One*, op. cit.

9. For an excellent assessment of medieval European law and governance, see Berman, Harold J., *Law and Revolution: The Formation of the Western Legal Tradition*, Cambridge University Press, Cambridge, 1983.

10. This is traced quite well in O'Connell, Robert L., *Of Arms and Men: A History of War, Weapons and Aggression*, Oxford University Press, London/New York, 1989. Also see McNeill, William H., ed., *The Pursuit of Power: Technology, Armed Force and Society Since A.D. 1000*, University of Chicago Press, Chicago, 1982.

11. This transition is covered rather neatly in Drinnon, Richard, *Facing West: The Metaphysics of Indian Hating and Empire Building*, Schocken Books, New York, (second edition) 1990.

12. An illuminating discussion of this trend may be found in Jordan, Winthrop D., *The White Man's Burden*, Oxford University Press, London/New York, 1974. Also see Gould, Steven Jay, *The Mismeasure of Man*, W.W. Norton Publishers, New York, 1981.

13. The development of the "Aryan" theory of racial scientism is covered quite well in the early chapters of Bernal, Martin, *Black Athena: The Afroasiatic Roots of Classical Civilization*, Vol. 1, Princeton University Press, Princeton, NJ, 1987.

14. See Cecil, Robert, *The Myth of the Master Race: Alfred Rosenberg and Nazi Ideology*, Dodd and Mead Co., Publishers, New York, 1972.

15. Actually, the process began much earlier. See Crosby, Alfred W., *Ecological Imperialism: The Biological Expansion of Europe, 900-1900*, Cambridge University Press, Cambridge, 1986.

16. An interesting European cognition of all this is contained in Gorz, Andre, *Ecology as Politics*, South End Press, Boston, 1981. Also see Chase, Steve, ed., *Defending the Earth: A Dialogue Between Murray Bookchin and Dave Foreman*, South End Press, Boston, 1991; Barho, Rudolph, *From Red to Green*, Verso Publishers, London, 1984; and Devall, Bill, and George Sessions, *Deep Ecology: Living as if Nature Mattered*, Peregrine Smith Books, Salt Lake City, 1985.

17. The fundamental inequalities involved are being played out in "brush-fire wars" around the globe as nation-states continue their attempts to subdue and dominate indigenous peoples. See Nietschmann, Bernard, "The Third World War," *Cultural Survival Quarterly*, Vol. 11, No. 3, Fall 1987, pp.1-16.

18. For more in this vein, see Editors, "A Basic Call to Consciousness," *Akwesasne Notes*, Mohawk Nation via Rooseveltown, NY, 1976.

About the Contributors

Ward Churchill (Creek/Cherokee Métis) is Associate Professor of Communications and Coordinator of American Indian Studies with the Center for Studies of Ethnicity and Race in America (CSERA) at the University of Colorado at Boulder. He is, with Glenn T. Morris, Co-Director of the Colorado chapter of the American Indian Movement. A prolific writer on Indian affairs, he is a regular columnist with *Z Magazine* and editor of the journal *New Studies on the Left*. His books include *Marxism and Native Americans* (1983), *Culture versus Economism* (1984), *Critical Issues in Native North America* (1989), *Critical Issues in Native North America, Volume II* (1991), and *Fantasies of the Master Race* (1992). He is presently completing a socio-political history of AIM, and a popular history of Native America since 1492.

Vine Deloria, Jr. (Standing Rock Sioux) is Professor of American Indian Studies (with CSERA), Law, and Political Science at the University of Colorado at Boulder. Long considered the Dean of American Indian intellectuals, his books include *Custer Died for Your Sins* (1969), *We Talk, You Listen* (1970), *Of Utmost Good Faith* (1971), *God Is Red* (1973), *Behind the Trail of Broken Treaties* (1974), *The Indian Affair* (1974), *Indians of the Pacific Northwest* (1975), *The Metaphysics of Modern Existence* (1978), *The Nations Within* (1983), *American Indians, American Justice* (1984), and *American Indian Policy in the Twentieth Century* (1985). He is currently pursuing a comprehensive study of treaties and agreements between American Indian nations and other powers.

Jimmie Durham (Cherokee) is a former AIM member and national organizational liaison to the Native American Support Committees. He was founding Director of the International Indian Treaty Council, the world's first United Nations consultative Non-Governmental Organization. An accomplished essayist and poet, Durham is author of *Columbus Day* (1983). Founder of the Society for a Community of Artists in New York City, he now resides in Cuernavaca, Mexico, from whence he engages in the creation of sculpture and performance art. He exhibits internationally and features prominently in Lucy Lippard's *Mixed Blessings* (1990).

Marianna Guerrero (Mestiza Apache) is the pseudonym of an indigenous human rights activist who, for reasons of security related to her work, wishes not to be further identified at the present time.

Theresa Halsey (Standing Rock Sioux) is a long-time community activist, mostly focusing on educational issues. She is currently Director of the Title V American Indian Education Program with the Boulder Valley (Colorado) School District.

Tom Holm (Creek) is Associate Professor of American Indian Studies and Political Science at the University of Arizona. He is prominent in American Indian veterans' affairs, and his essays on this and other topics have appeared in the *Journal of Ethnic Studies* and various professional publications nationally. His first book is forthcoming from the University of Oklahoma Press in 1992.

Evelyn Hu-DeHart is Professor of History and Director of CSERA at the University of Colorado at Boulder. Her books include *Yaqui Resistance and Survival* (1985).

Institute for Natural Progress is a collective research organization founded by Ward Churchill and Winona LaDuke in 1982. It produces occasional studies of issues and policies important to the well-being of Native North America. Churchill assumed the lead role in preparing the INP contribution to this volume.

M. Annette Jaimes (Juaneño/Yaqui) is a Lecturer in American Indian Studies with CSERA. She has served as a delegate of the International Indian Treaty Council to the United Nations Working Group on Indigenous Human Rights (1985, 1986). An Associate Editor of the journal *New Studies on the Left,* Jaimes was also co-editor of *Hispanic Access to Higher Education* (1984). Her essays have appeared frequently in journals such as *Akwesasne Notes, Wicazo Sa Review, American Indian Culture and Research Journal, Policy Review* and *Journal of Ethnic Studies.* She is currently engaged in a post-doctoral fellowship with the Society for the Humanities at Cornell University. She is also editing the forthcoming *Fantasies of the Master Race* (1992), a collection of critical literary essays by Ward Churchill.

Winona LaDuke (Anishinabé) is a well-known American Indian rights and environmental activist. She was a founder of both the North American Native Women's Network and Anishinabé Akeeng (People's Land Organization) on her native White Earth Reservation in northern Minnesota. Her writings have been published widely in journals such as *Akwesasne Notes, Insurgent Sociologist, Co-Evolution Quarterly, New Studies on the Left, Z Magazine, Socialist Review, New Age, URPE* and *Radical America,* and she was a recipient of the 1988 Reebok International Human Rights Award. LaDuke presently resides with her husband and two children in the town of Moose Factory, on James Bay, where she is heavily involved in the struggle to block hydroelectric development in northern Ontario.

Phil Lane, Jr. (Yankton Sioux/Chickasaw) is a recognized Indian leader in community development and substance abuse treatment and prevention. He is an Associate Professor and Co-Coordinator, with Lenore Stiffarm, of the Four Worlds Development Project at the University of Lethbridge in Alberta, Canada. Lane has worked extensively with indigenous peoples in both North and South America, has authored numerous articles on related topics, and is an award-winning film producer (*Images of Indians* and *Walking with Grandfather*).

John Mohawk (Seneca) is a Lecturer in Social Philosophy and American Studies at SUNY Buffalo. A long-time native rights activist and former editor of *Akwesasne Notes,* he also served as an editor of *BIA, I'm Not Your Indian Anymore* (1973) and *Voices From Wounded Knee, 1973* (1974). His other books include *A Basic Call to Consciousness* (1976). Mohawk is a frequent contributor to journals such as *The Northeast Indian Quarterly* and *Native Nations.*

Glenn T. Morris (Shawnee) is Associate Professor of Political Science and Director of the Fourth World Center for Study of Indigenous Law and Politics at the University of Colorado at Denver. He is also Co-Director of Colorado AIM and a founder of the American Indian Anti-Defamation League. Long active in native rights and international affairs, Morris is editor of *The Fourth World Bulletin*, a contributing editor for *New Studies on the Left*, and was a co-editor of *Indian Self-Governance: Perspectives on the Political Status of Indigenous Nations in the United States of America* (1989).

Jorge Noriega (Mestizo) is a former counselor with the American Indian Educational Opportunity Program at California State University/Northridge. He is currently a Lecturer in American Indian Studies at the University of Lethbridge.

Rebecca Robbins (Standing Rock Sioux) is editor of the journal *Thought and Action* for the American Education Association. Her essays have appeared in *New Studies on the Left, Wicazo Sa Review* and other journals. She is a former Assistant Professor of Education at Arizona State University.

Wendy Rose (Hopi) is Associate Professor of Anthropology at Fresno City College. A widely recognized poet and essayist, she has published verse in a number of literary journals, including *Contact II*. Her books include *Hopi Roadrunner Dancing* (1973), *Long Division: A Tribal History* (1976), *Academic Squaw: Reports from the World of the Ivory Tower* (1977), *Builder Kachina: A Going Home Cycle* (1979), *Lost Copper* (1980), *What Happened When the Hopi Hit New York* (1982) and *Half-Breed Chronicles* (1987).

Lenore Stiffarm (Gros Ventre) is Associate Professor and Coordinator of the Four Worlds Development Project at the University of Lethbridge, Alberta, where she specializes in indigenous American demography and development strategies. While working with the American Indian Studies Center at UCLA, she was co-author of *Ethnic Groups in Los Angeles: Quality of Life Indicators* (1987).

Jim Vander Wall is a long-time activist and supporter of indigenous rights in North America. Since 1978, he has served as Co-Director of the Leonard Peltier Support Group in the Denver metropolitan area. An Associate Editor of *New Studies on the Left*, he is co-author, with Ward Churchill, of *Agents of Repression: The FBI's Secret Wars Against the Black Panther Party and the American Indian Movement* (1988) and *The COINTELPRO Papers: Documents from the FBI's Secret Wars Against Dissent in the United States* (1990).

DeLinda Wunder is a graduate student in English and employee of the Center for Conflict Resolution at the University of Colorado at Boulder. Raised near the Wind River Shoshone-Arapaho Reservation in Wyoming, she has participated as a staff member in several American Indian and multicultural education efforts since 1980.

Index

Index of Indian Nations

Mohawk, 318. *See also*
Haudenosaunee
Mohegans, 150
Montagnais-Naskapi, 320
Muckleshoot Nation, 218
Muscogee (Creek) Confederacy, 88

Naragansetts, 150
Nez Percé, 91, 97, 98
Nisqually, 220

Oglala Lakotas, 97, 108, 134, 312
Oglalas, 89, 164, 167, 292. *See also*
Lakota
Oklahoma Cherokees, 45-46
Oneida, 19, 96, 191 (map), 377. *See
also* Haudenosaunee
Onondaga. *See* Haudenosaunee
O'Odham. *See* Ak Chin O'Odham and
Tohono O'Odham
Oohinunpa (Two Kettles), 89, 164
Osages, 33, 98
Osceola, 91
Ottawas, 32, 38

Paintes, 202
Papagos, 242. *See also* Tohono
O'Odham
Passamaquoddy, 148-49
Pawnees, 33
Penobscots, 148-49
Peorias, 38
Piegans, 33
Pima, 40, 45, 195, 205. *See also* Ak
Chin O'Odham
Pima-Maricopas, 205-06
Potawatomi, 98
Pueblos, 89
Puyallups, 218, 223, 224

Quinalts, 219, 228
Salish, 98
Schaghticokes, 150

Seminoles, 14, 91, 151, 203
Seneca. *See* Haudenosaunee
Shawnee, 91
Sicangu (Brûlé), 89, 164
Sihasapa (Blackfeet), 89, 164
Sioux, 198. *See also* Lakotas
Six Nations Confederacy, 98
Southern Cheyennes, 1
Southern Utes, 1
Squamish, 218

Tlingit Nation, 19
Tohono O'Odhams (Papagos), 151,
204, 244
Tolowas, 275
Tonkawas, 38
Turtle Mountain Anishinabé (Chip-
pewa), 98
Tuscarora, 377
Two Kettles. *See* Oohinunpa

Umatilla Confederated Tribes, 203
Utes, 1, 205, 206

Walapai, 45
Walla Wallas, 38
Wampanoags, 150
Warm Springs Confederation, 222
Western Shoshones (Newe), 34, 169
Winnebagos, 33
Wyandotte, 38

Yakimas, 20-21, 89, 95-96, 194-95,
222, 226, 227, 230, 261
Yana, 38
Yanktonai Dakotas, 33, 205
Yaqui Confederation, 89, 426
Yavapai, 206
Yokuts, 40
Yuroks, 275

Zuñiga, 436

About South End Press

South End Press is a nonprofit, collectively-run book publisher with over 175 titles in print. Since our founding in 1977, we have tried to meet the needs of readers who are exploring, or are already committed to, the politics of radical social change.

Our goal is to publish books that encourage critical thinking and constructive action on the key political, cultural, social, economic, and ecological issues shaping life in the United States and in the world. In this way, we hope to give expression to a wide diversity of democratic social movements and to provide an alternative to corporate publishing.

Through the Institute for Social and Cultural Change, South End Press works with other political media projects—*Z Magazine;* Speak Out!, a speakers bureau; the Publishers Support Project; and the New Liberation News Service—to expand access to information and critical analysis. If you would like a free catalog of South End Press books or information about our membership program—which offers two free books and a 40% discount on all titles—please write to us at South End Press, 116 Saint Botolph Street, Boston, MA 02115.

Other titles of interest from South End Press:

COINTELPRO PAPERS: Documents from the FBI's Secret Wars Against Dissent in the United States
Ward Churchill and Jim Vanderwall

AGENTS OF REPRESSION: The FBI's Secret War Against the American Indian Movement and the Black Panther Party
Ward Churchill and Jim Vanderwall

MARXISM AND NATIVE AMERICANS
edited by Ward Churchill

THE TRIAL OF LEONARD PELTIER
Jim Messerschmidt